The Greeks believed that the *Iliad* and the *Odyssey* were composed by a single poet whom they named Homer. Nothing is known of his life. While seven Greek cities claim the honor of being his birthplace, ancient tradition places him in Ionia, located in the eastern Aegean. His birthdate is undocumented as well, though most modern scholars now place the composition of the *Iliad* and the *Odyssey* in the late eighth or early seventh century B.C.

ROBERT FAGLES is Arthur W. Marks '19 Professor of Comparative Literature, Emeritus, at Princeton University. He is the recipient of the 1997 PEN/Ralph Manheim Medal for Translation and a 1996 Academy Award in Literature from the American Academy of Arts and Letters. Fagles has been elected to the Academy, the American Academy of Arts and Sciences, and the American Philosophical Society. He has translated the poems of Bacchylides. His translations of Sophocles' *Three Theban Plays*, Aeschylus' *Oresteia* (nominated for a National Book Award) and Homer's *Iliad* (winner of the 1991 Harold Morton Landon Translation Award by The Academy of American Poets, an award from The Translation Center of Columbia University, and the New Jersey Humanities Book Award) are published in Penguin Classics. His original poetry and his translations have appeared in many journals and reviews, as well as in his book of poems, *I, Vincent: Poems from the Pictures of Van Gogh*. Mr. Fagles was one of the associate editors of Maynard Mack's Twickenham Edition of Alexander Pope's *Iliad* and *Odyssey*, and, with George Steiner, edited *Homer: A Collection of Critical Essays*. Mr. Fagles' most recent work is a translation of Homer's *Odyssey*, available from Penguin.

BERNARD KNOX is Director Emeritus of Harvard's Center for Hellenic Studies in Washington, D.C. His essays and reviews have appeared in numerous publications and in 1978 he won the George Jean Nathan Award for Dramatic Criticism. His works include *Oedipus at Thebes: Sophocles' Tragic Hero and His Time*; *The Heroic Temper: Studies in Sophoclean Tragedy*; *Word and Action: Essays on the Ancient Theatre*; *Essays Ancient and Modern* (awarded the 1989 PEN/Spielvogel-Diamonstein Award); *The Oldest Dead White European Males and Other Reflections on the Classics*; and *Backing into the Future: The Classical Tradition and its Renewal*. Mr. Knox is the editor of *The Norton Book of Classical Literature*, and has also collaborated with Robert Fagles on the *Odyssey* and *The Three Theban Plays*.

PENGUIN BOOKS

HOMER

The
Iliad

TRANSLATED BY
Robert Fagles

INTRODUCTION AND
NOTES BY
BERNARD KNOX

PENGUIN BOOKS

Published by the Penguin Group

Penguin Group (USA) Inc., 375 Hudson Street, New York, New York 10014, U.S.A.

Penguin Group (Canada), 90 Eglinton Avenue East, Suite 700, Toronto,
    Ontario, Canada M4P 2Y3 (a division of Pearson Penguin Canada Inc.)

Penguin Books Ltd, 80 Strand, London WC2R 0RL, England

Penguin Ireland, 25 St Stephen's Green, Dublin 2, Ireland (a division of Penguin Books Ltd)

Penguin Group (Australia), 250 Camberwell Road, Camberwell,
    Victoria 3124, Australia (a division of Pearson Australia Group Pty Ltd)

Penguin Books India Pvt Ltd, 11 Community Centre, Panchsheel Park,
New Delhi – 110 017, India

Penguin Books (NZ), 67 Apollo Drive, Mairangi Bay, Auckland 1311, New Zealand
    (a division of Pearson New Zealand Ltd)

Penguin Books (South Africa) (Pty) Ltd, 24 Sturdee Avenue,
    Rosebank, Johannesburg 2196, South Africa

Penguin Books Ltd, Registered Offices: 80 Strand, London WC2R 0RL, England

First published in the United States of America by
Penguin Books USA Inc., 1990
Published in Penguin Books 1991

50 49 48 47 46 45 44 43

Books 3, 18 and 22 of this version of the *Iliad* appeared originally in *Grand Street*, Book 6 in *TriQuarterly*. Part of Bernard Knox's Introduction appeared in *Grand Street*.

The illustrations on display pages are traditional Greek motifs, redrawn by Ann Gold.

THE LIBRARY OF CONGRESS HAS CATALOGUED THE HARDCOVER AS FOLLOWS:
Homer.
[Iliad. English]
The Iliad / Homer ; translated by Robert Fagles ;
introduction and notes by Bernard Knox.
p.   cm.
Includes bibliographical references.
1. Achilles (Greek mythology)—Poetry.   2. Trojan War—Poetry.
I. Fagles, Robert.   II. Knox, Bernard MacGregor Walker.   III. Title.
ISBN: 0-670-83510-2 (hc.)
ISBN 978-0-14-044592-3 (pbk.)
PA4025.A2F33   1990
883'.01—dc20   89-70695

Printed in the United States of America

To the memory of my father and my mother
and for Lynne, Katya and Nina—

humeis gar theai este, pareste te, iste te panta,
hêmeis de kleos oion akouomen oude ti idmen—

"*Homer* makes us Hearers," Pope has said, "and *Virgil* leaves us Readers." So the great translator of Homer, no doubt unknowingly, set at odds the claims of an oral tradition and those of a literary one, as we would call the two traditions now. Homer's work is a performance, even in part a musical event. Perhaps that is the source of his speed, directness and simplicity that Matthew Arnold heard—and his nobility too, elusive yet undeniable, that Arnold chased but never really caught. Surely it is a major source of Homer's energy, the loft and carry of his imagination that sweeps along the listener together with the performer. For there is something powerful in his song, "that unequal'd Fire and Rapture"— Pope again—"which is so forcible in *Homer*, that no Man of a true Poetical Spirit is Master of himself" while he experiences the *Iliad*. "In *Homer*, and in him only, it burns every where clearly, and every where irresistibly." But it also brings to light the Homeric Question facing all translators: How to convey the power of his performance in the medium of writing? "*Homer* makes us Hearers, and *Virgil* leaves us Readers."

Yet the contrast may be too extreme. Virgil the writer was certainly no stranger to recitation. Homer the performer, as the Introduction speculates, may have known a rudimentary form of writing. And writing may have lent his work some qualities we associate with texts in general—idiosyncrasies at times, and pungency and wit—and with the *Iliad* in particular, its architectonics, its magnificent scale, and the figure of Achilles. But even if Homer never used an alphabet himself, he now seems less the creature of an oral tradition whom Milman Parry discovered, and more and more its master, as envisioned by Parry's son, Adam. Homer the brilliant improviser deployed its stock, inherited features with all the individual talent he could muster. Never more so, in fact, than in his use of the fixed and formulaic, frequently repeated phrase. Not only is Homer often less formulaic, but the formulas themselves are often more resonant, more apt and telling in their contexts than the hard Parryites had argued for at first. So the original form of Homer's work, while a far cry from a work of literature as we know it now, is not exactly a song either, pure and simple. It may be more the record of a song, building over the poet's lifetime perhaps, or what Marianne Moore would call "a simulacrum of spontaneity."

Obviously at a far remove from Homer, in this translation I have tried to find a middle ground (and not a no man's land, if I can help it) between the features of his performance and the expectations of a contemporary reader. Not a line-for-line translation, my version of the *Iliad* is, I hope, neither so literal in rendering Homer's language as to cramp and distort my own—though I want to convey as much of what he says as possible—nor so literary as to brake his energy, his forward drive—though I want my work to be literate, with any luck. For the more literal approach would seem to be too little English, and the more literary seems too little Greek. I have tried to find a cross between the two, a modern English Homer.

Of course it is a risky business, stating what one has tried to do or, worse, the principles one has used (petards that will probably hoist the writer later). But a word or two of explanation seems in order, and the first refers to the more fixed and formulaic parts of Homer. I have treated them in a flexible, discretionary way, not incompatible with Homer's way, I think—especially when his formulas are functional as well as fixed—while also answering to the ways we read today. It is a matter of "riding easy in the harness," as Robert Frost once said of democracy, and my practice ranges from the pliant to the strict. With one of the most frequently repeated phrases, for example—the line that introduces individual speeches—I have been the freest, trying to anticipate the speaker's nuance of the moment yet retaining, at least, the ritual of introductory words for every speech. When Homer introduces a speech of "winged words," however, I rarely if ever omit that well-known phrase, though I like the flight of the words to vary, with a quick burst at times and a longer drift at others, according to what a character has to say. And so with Hector's flashing helmet, in the epithet that clings to Hector's name: I like to ally its gleaming with his actions, now nodding his head in conversation, now rushing headlong into the front lines. But a flashing helmet it is, again and again, and not only to make his own career appear more meteoric and abruptly snuffed out but also to support a chain of tragic ironies throughout the poem. For the flashing helmet—Hector's own at first—is soon replaced by the one he strips from Patroclus when he kills him: the helmet of Achilles. So as prophecy would have it, when Achilles destroys Hector in revenge he must destroy himself as well, his flashing mirror-image embodied in his victim, and the helmet he will wear, fire-new and forged by Hephaestus, flashes like the helmet of Ares when Achilles closes for the kill (Book 20.45,

22.158).[1] The more the epithet recurs, in short, the more its power can recoil. And the inevitability of its recoil for Hector is further stressed by a repeated passage in the Greek repeated verbatim in the English version. The words that describe the death of Patroclus are exactly those that describe the death of Hector six books later (16.1001–5, 22.425–29): the first death, both in the mind of Achilles the avenger and in the style of his maker, will have served as warrant for the second. All in all, then, I have tried for repetition with a difference when variation seems useful, repetition with a grim insistence when the scales of Zeus, the Homeric moral balance, is at issue.

Turning briefly to Homer's metrics: though my way is more remote, it is also meant to occupy a flexible middle ground, here between his hexameter line—his "ear, ear for the sea-surge," as Pound describes it— and a tighter, native English line. If, as the Introduction claims, the strongest weapon in Homer's poetic arsenal is variety within a metrical norm, the translation opts for a freer give-and-take between the two, and one that offers a good deal more variety than uniformity. Working from a loose five- or six-beat line but inclining more to six, I expand at times to seven beats—to imply the big reach of a simile or some vehement outburst in discourse or the pitched fury of combat on the field— or contract at times to three, to give a point in speech or action sharper stress. Such interplay between variety and norm results, I suppose, from a kind of tug-of-war peculiar to translation, between trying to encapsulate the meaning of the Greek on the one hand and trying to find a cadence for one's English on the other, yet joining hands, if possible, to make a line of verse. I hope it results, at any rate, not only in giving my own language a slight stretching it may need and sometimes gets these days, but also in lending Homer the sort of range in rhythm, pace and tone that may make an *Iliad* engaging to a modern reader. It may be a way as well, again at a far remove, of trying to suggest the tension in Homer's metrics, his blend of mass and movement both—so much *ongkos* yet so much grace and speed.

In aiming for these and other objectives in a version of the *Iliad*, I have had many kinds of help. The greatest has come from my collaborator, Bernard Knox, whom I would rather call a comrade. Not only has he written the Introduction and Notes to the translation but he has commented on my drafts for several years. And when I leaf through

[1] Here and throughout the volume, except for the list of textual variants on p. 619, line numbers refer to the translation, where the line numbers of the Greek text will be found at the top of every page.

those pages now, his commentary seems to ring my typescript so completely that I might be looking at a worse-for-wear, dog-eared manuscript encircled by a scholiast's remarks. Or is it something of a battle-map as well? The vulnerable lines at the center are shored up by a combat-tested ally, whose squads reinforce the weakest sectors and who deciphers Homer's order of the day and tells a raw recruit what war—the movements of armies and the sentiments of soldiers—is all about. And more, what tragedy—in this, the first tragedy—really means. In Book 9 of the *Iliad* old Phoenix calls for a man of words and a man of action too. My good fortune has been to work with such a man.

Several modern scholars and critics, cited in the bibliography, have helped as well, and so have several modern translators of the *Iliad*, in whole or part. Each has introduced me to a new aspect of the poem, another potential for the present. "For if it is true," as Maynard Mack proposes, "that what we translate from a given work is what, wearing the spectacles of our time, we see in it, it is also true that we see in it what we have the power to translate." So my debts to others are considerable, and here I say my thanks to William Arrowsmith, Robert Graves, Martin Hammond, Richmond Lattimore, Christopher Logue, Paul Mazon, Ennis Reese and E. V. Rieu. A few I have known in person, most I have never met. Yet I suspect we all have known each other in a way, having trekked across the same territory, perhaps having all encountered the nightmare that haunted Pope—"that he was engaged in a long journey," as Joseph Spence reports, "puzzled which way to take, and full of fears" that it would never end. And if you reach the end, the fears may start in earnest. In any event, the translator I have known the best is the one to whom I owe the most, Robert Fitzgerald, both for the power of his example and because, at a sensitive moment, he heartened me to "fit on your greaves and swordbelt and face the moil or the melee."

Many other friends have come to my side, some by reading, some by listening to me read the work-in-progress, and responding in close detail with criticism or encouragement or a healthy combination of the two. Most encouraging of all, none has asked me, "Why another *Iliad*?" For each understood, it seems, that if Homer was a performer, then his translator might aim to be one as well, and that no two performances of the same work—surely not of a musical composition, so probably not of a work of language either—will ever be the same. The timbre and tempo of each will be distinct, let alone its deeper resonance, build and thrust. My thanks, then, to Marilyn Arthur, Paul Auster, Sandra Bermann, Charles Beye, Claudia Brodsky, Beth Brombert, Victor Brombert, Clarence Brown, Rebecca Bushnell, Robert Connor, Robert F. Goheen, Rachel Hadas, Robert Hollander, Samuel Hynes, Edmund Keeley, Nita Krevans, Janet Lembke, David Lenson, William Levitan, Herbert Marks, J. D. McClatchy, Earl Miner, William Mullen, Georgia Nugent, Joyce Carol Oates, Joanna Prins, Michael Putnam, David Quint, Richard Reid, James Richardson, Charles Segal, Steven Shankman, Michael Simpson, Raymond Smith, Paolo Vivante and Theodore Weiss.

And several classicists have lent a steady hand: William A. Childs, George Dunkel, Elaine Fantham, Andrew Ford, John Keaney, Richard Martin, Glenn Most and Froma Zeitlin. The published commentaries of other scholars, cited among the further readings, and even some unpublished have helped us on our way, thanks to the kindness and alacrity of their authors. Our book was in its later stages when M. M. Willcock sent the galleys of his second volume, Books 13 through 24. And the remaining parts of the commentary-in-progress under G. S. Kirk's editorship— his own work on Books 5 through 8, J. B. Hainsworth's on 9 through 12, Richard Janko's on 13 through 16, Mark W. Edwards' on 17 through 20 and Nicholas Richardson's on 21 through 24—luckily arrived while each was still in proof or typescript. The first impulse for the translation, however, came from the late W. B. Stanford, who, one afternoon in County Wicklow many years ago, sketched out my route for returning to the source.

The roofs of some great houses have extended welcome shelter to the translator and his work. Theodore and Mary Cross have turned Nantucket into Ithaca West with their Homeric hospitality. The Rockefeller Foundation provided a resident fellowship at the Villa Serbelloni in Bellagio during May 1985. Princeton University gave me leaves of absence in the spring semesters of 1982, 1985 and 1989, and, more important, the chance to study Homer with many students who have been an education to me. The Program in Hellenic Studies at the university twice appointed me to a Stanley J. Seeger Fellowship, first to begin the translation on Greek terrain, then to complete it there years later. The secretariat of Comparative Literature, from its leader, Carol Szymanski, to Gary Fuchs, to the Quietwriter and lately, the LaserJet, have been invaluable in helping to prepare the final manuscript. And close to the zero hour Deborah Fryer shared the task of placing the Greek line numbers throughout the text.

To produce the book at hand, my editor, Kathryn Court, assisted by Caroline White, has treated the writing and the writer, too, with energy, affection and address. Beena Kamlani's efforts to copy-edit a fairly large and unruly manuscript have been heroic. Ann Gold, with all her artistry joined by Amy Hill's, has designed a volume to companion the two that came before it. Anita Karl and James Kemp have drawn up the fine maps to guide the reader through the wilds of Homer's world. Mary Sunden has labored long and hard with Joe Marcey and Peter Smith to find this version of the *Iliad* some readers. And the good people at Viking Penguin—Michael Jacobs, Christine Pevitt, Leigh Butler, Paul Slovak, Marcia Burch, Faye Darnall, Maureen Donnelly, Daniel Lundy, Cynthia Achar, Roni Axelrod—all have been loyal allies in New York. In London Peter Carson and Paul Keegan have been generous hosts to the latest Homer in the house. Before he left the publisher my former editor, Alan Williams, who saw me through the troubles of Aeschylus and Sophocles, gave my plans a happy push toward Troy. Prior to the present volume, Ben Sonnenberg graciously opened the pages of *Grand Street* and ran three books of the translation. Reginald Gibbons gave another book a timely berth in *TriQuarterly*. And through it all, without the unfailing stay and strategies of my friend and agent Georges Borchardt, assisted by Cindy Klein, this *Iliad* might never have been published.

"The Classics, it is the Classics!" Blake exclaimed, with pointed reference to Homer, "that Desolate Europe with Wars!" The violence of the *Iliad* can be overpowering, as it was for Simone Weil and many others, yet, as the Introduction observes, Homer makes that violence coexist with humanity and compassion, as close together as the city at war and the city at peace emblazoned on Achilles' shield. If the translation offers any sense of this, it is because the translator has often consulted the familiar spirits of Adam and Anne Parry, and always relied on the Muses summoned in the dedication, chief among them Lynne.

R.F.

Princeton, New Jersey
June 17, 1990

A NOTE ON THIS PRINTING:

This printing contains minor revisions of the text.

R.F. and B.K.

June 2001

CONTENTS

NOTES

INTRODUCTION

THE ILIAD

"Iliad" is a word that means "a poem about Ilium" (i.e., Troy), and Homer's great epic poem has been known as "The *Iliad*" ever since the Greek historian Herodotus so referred to it in the fifth century B.C. But the title is not an adequate description of the contents of the poem, which are best summed up in its opening line: "the rage of Peleus' son Achilles." The incident that provoked Achilles' rage took place in the tenth and final year of the Achaean attack on Troy, and though Homer does work into his narrative scenes that recall earlier stages of the war (the muster of the Achaean forces in Book 2, for example, and Priam's first sight of Agamemnon and the other Achaean chieftains in Book 3), the rage of Achilles—its cause, its course and its disastrous consequences—is the theme of the poem, the mainspring of the plot.

Chryses, a priest of Apollo, whose daughter has been carried off by the Achaeans in one of their raids, comes to the camp to ransom her. But she has been assigned, in the division of the booty, to the king who commands the Achaean army, Agamemnon, and he refuses to give her up. Her father prays for help to Apollo, who sends a plague that devastates the Achaean camp. Achilles, leader of the Myrmidons, one of the largest contingents of the Achaean army, summons the chieftains to an assembly. There they are told by the prophet Calchas that the girl must be returned to her father. Agamemnon has to give her up, but demands compensation for his loss. Achilles objects: let Agamemnon wait until more booty is taken. A violent quarrel breaks out between the two men, and Agamemnon finally announces that he will take recompense for his loss from Achilles, in the form of the girl Briseis, Achilles' share of the booty. Achilles represses an urge to kill Agamemnon and withdraws from the assembly, threatening to leave for home, with all his troops, the next day. The priest's daughter is restored to him, Apollo puts an end to the plague, and Briseis is taken away from Achilles' tent by Agamemnon's heralds.

Achilles turns to his goddess mother Thetis, asking her to prevail on Zeus, father of gods and men, to inflict loss and defeat on the Achaeans, so that they will realize how much they need him. Zeus is won over by

Thetis (to whom he is indebted for help on a previous occasion), and in spite of the vehement objections of his wife Hera (who, like his daughter Athena, hates the Trojans and works for their destruction), he turns the tide of battle against the Achaeans. The Trojan leader Hector, son of Troy's old King Priam, drives the Achaeans back on their beached ships, round which they are forced to build a wall and ditch. At the urging of his chieftains, Agamemnon sends ambassadors to Achilles, offering him rich prizes and the hand of his daughter in marriage if he will return to the fighting line. The offer is refused, but the pleas of one of the ambassadors, Phoenix, an older man who belongs to Achilles' household, do have some effect: Achilles withdraws his threat to leave the next day; he will stay until Hector and the Trojans reach his own ships.

The battle resumes and now the Trojan onslaught breaches the wall and threatens the ships. The Achaean chieftains—Agamemnon, his brother Menelaus, Diomedes and Odysseus—are wounded one by one. Achilles' closest friend, Patroclus, sent by Achilles to find out how things stand in the Achaean camp, brings back the news and also pleads with Achilles to relent. He does so only partly; he agrees to let Patroclus go into battle with Achilles' troops, wearing Achilles' armor. This is enough: the Trojans in their turn are thrown back. But Patroclus is killed by the god Apollo, Troy's protector, and by Hector, who strips off Achilles' armor and puts it on himself.

Achilles' rage is now directed against Hector, the killer of his dearest friend. He is reconciled with Agamemnon, and as soon as his mother brings him a splendid suit of armor, made by the smith-god Hephaestus, he returns to the battle, and after slaughtering many Trojans, meets and kills Hector. He lashes Hector's corpse to his chariot and drags it to his own tent; he intends to throw it to the dogs and birds of prey. For Patroclus he holds a magnificent funeral, complete with athletic contests and human sacrifice. Whenever renewed grief for the loss of his friend overcomes him, he drags Hector's body around Patroclus' grave. But the body has been preserved from corruption by divine intervention, and the gods now decide (not unanimously, for Hera and Athena object) to send a message to Achilles through his mother: he is to release Hector's body for ransom paid by King Priam of Troy. Achilles agrees, but what he does not anticipate is the arrival in his tent of Priam himself, alone, in the middle of the night. Instead of sending a herald, he has brought the ransom himself and begs for the body of his son. Achilles is reminded of his own father, also an old man who will never see his son again; Achilles knows, for his mother has told him, that his death is to come soon after Hector's. He sends Priam safely back with Hector's body to Troy and so, runs the last line of the poem, "the Trojans buried Hector breaker of horses" (24.944 in the translation). We know already that the death of Troy's main defender seals the fate of the city and that, as Thetis told Achilles: "hard on the heels of Hector's death your death / must come at once" (18.112–13).

This summary is the bare bones of an epic poem that consists in the original Greek of 15,693 lines of hexameter verse, composed—probably in the late eighth or early seventh century B.C.—by a poet known to later ages as Homer, for whose life and activity no trustworthy information has come down to us. The poem, in other words, is some 2,700 years old. How, the reader may well ask, did it survive through such an expanse of time? By whom, for whom, and how and in what circumstances was it composed? Perhaps the best way to proceed to an exploration of these questions (no one can promise a complete and certain answer) is backward—from the text of this book.

It is a translation, by Robert Fagles, of the Greek text edited by David Monro and Thomas Allen, first published in 1902 by the Oxford University Press. This two-volume edition is printed in a Greek type, complete with lower- and uppercase letters, breathings and accents, which is based on the elegant handwriting of Richard Porson, an early-nineteenth-century scholar of great brilliance, who was also an incurable alcoholic as well as a great wit. This was of course not the first font of Greek type; in fact, the first printed edition of Homer, issued in Florence in 1488, was composed in type that imitated contemporary Greek handwriting, with all its complicated ligatures and abbreviations. Early printers tried to make their books look like handwritten manuscripts because in scholarly circles printed books were regarded as vulgar and inferior products—cheap paperbacks, so to speak.

Back to 1488, then, there is a continuous history of the printed text of Homer, differing a little from one editor to another but essentially fixed. Before that Homer existed only as a handwritten book. Such handwritten copies had been in circulation in Italy for a hundred years or so before the first printed edition. Petrarch had tried to learn Greek but gave up; Boccaccio succeeded and also in 1360 had a chair of Greek founded in Florence. But before Petrarch, Dante, though he put Homer in his limbo of non-Christian poets, had never read him, and could not have read him even if he had seen a text. For the best part of a thousand years, since the end of the Roman Empire, the knowledge of Greek had been lost in Western Europe. In the fourteenth century it was reintroduced into Italy from Byzantium, where a Greek-speaking Christian empire had maintained itself ever since Constantine made the city the capital of the eastern half of the Roman Empire. The knowledge of Greek and the manuscripts of the Greek classics, Homer included, came to Italy just in time; in May 1453 Byzantium fell to the Ottoman Turks, and the Greek empire of the East came to the end of its thousand-year career. During its long life it had carefully preserved, copied and recopied a select number of the Greek masterpieces of pre-Christian times, Homer prominent among them. The immediate predecessors of the printed edition of Florence were bound manuscript books written on vellum or on paper in a cursive minuscule script complete with accents and breathings. These books were the final phase of the process of copying by hand that went all the way back to the ancient world. In the ninth century the new minuscule handwriting had been adopted; since it separated words, it was easier to read than its predecessor, a hand consisting of freestanding capital letters without word division—the standard writing of the ancient world. In the second to fifth centuries A.D., the form and material of the books had changed: parchment with its longer life had replaced papyrus, and the codex form, our book form—folded quires of paper sewn at the back—had replaced the roll. In the ancient world the *Iliad* consisted of a number of papyrus rolls, the text written in columns on the inside surface. The rolls could not be too big (or they would break when opened for reading); a long poem like the *Iliad* might require as many as twenty-four—in fact it is possible the so-called books of our text represent an original division into papyrus rolls.

In this form the poem was known to the scholars who edited it and wrote commentaries on it in Alexandria, the city founded by Alexander before he set out on his epic march to India in the late fourth century B.C. And it was in this form (though, before the Alexandrian scholars made a standard edition, with many variations from one text to another) that copies were to be found all over the Greek world of the fourth and fifth centuries B.C. There must have been texts in circulation in the sixth century too, for we hear of official recitations at Athens and find echoes of Homer in sixth-century poets. In the seventh century B.C., we are moving back into the dark. In the poets of this century (whose work survives only in fragments) there are epithets, phrases and even half-lines that are also common in Homer. Though these poets—Tyrtaeus, Callinus, Alcman and Archilochus—may be using tags common to a general epic tradition, it seems more likely that these echoes betray acquaintance with the work we know as Homer's. There is also a vase, discovered on the island of Ischia, off the coast of Naples, and dated to before 700 B.C., which has an inscription that seems to refer to the famous cup of Nestor described in our *Iliad* (11.745–53). And echoes in art are also found in the early seventh century—illustrations of scenes from the *Odyssey*, for example, on vases dated in the 670s.

But back beyond about 700 B.C. we cannot go. Evidence for this period is rare; in fact we know very little about Greece in the eighth century, still less, if possible, about Greece in the ninth. All we have is the archaeological record—geometric pots, graves, some weapons. It is the era of Greek history known, because of our almost total ignorance about it, as the Dark Age.

All we have is the tradition, what the Greeks of historical times believed they knew about Homer. Herodotus believed that he lived four hundred years, not more, before his own time; that would put him in the ninth century. The great Homeric scholar Aristarchus of Alexandria believed that he lived about 140 years after the Trojan War; since the Trojan War was generally dated (in our terms) around 1200 B.C., Aristarchus' Homer was much earlier than the Homer of Herodotus. Men might disagree about his date, but everyone believed that he was blind, and though some thought he came from Chios (a so-called Homeric hymn mentions a blind singer from Chios), others traced his origin to Smyrna. It was also generally assumed that Homer, though he speaks of singing and probably did sing in performance, was a poet using the same means of composition as his fifth-century successors—that is, writing. Even those who thought that his poems were not combined into their present shape until long after his death (that, for example, the last part of the *Odyssey* is a later addition), even those who believed that different poets wrote the *Iliad* and the *Odyssey*, the so-called Separatists— everyone assumed that Homer was a poet composing as all poets since have done: with the aid of writing. And so did all succeeding centuries down to the eighteenth. Pope, whose translation of the *Iliad* is the finest ever made, speaks of Homer as if he were a poet like Milton or Shakespeare or himself. "HOMER," so begins his Preface, "is universally allow'd to have had the greatest Invention of any Writer whatever . . ." Homer, it is taken for granted, *wrote*.

There had been one skeptic in the ancient world who thought differently. He was not a Greek but a Jew, Joseph ben Matthias. He wrote in Greek (for which, as he admits, he had a little help) a history of the Jewish rebellion against Roman rule in the first century A.D. and its savage repression by the emperor Titus—events in which he had played a prominent role. But he also wrote a pamphlet, countering the claim of a Greek writer, Apion, that the Jews had no history to speak of, since they were hardly mentioned in the works of Greek historians. Besides defending the historicity of the Old Testament chronicles, Josephus (to give him his Greek name) counterattacked by pointing out that the Greeks did not learn to write until very late in their history. The heroes of the Trojan War were "ignorant of the present-day mode of writing," he said, and even Homer "did not leave his poems in writing"; his separate songs were "transmitted by memory" and "not unified until much later."

It is true that (with one remarkable exception, which is discussed later) no one in the *Iliad*—or, for that matter, the *Odyssey*—knows how to read or write. The Mycenaean scribes had used the complicated Linear B syllabary—eighty-seven signs for different combinations of consonant and vowel. It was a system only professional scribes could handle; in any case, all memory of it was lost with the destruction of the Mycenaean centers in the twelfth century B.C. The Greeks did not learn to write again until much later. This time, they took over an alphabet of fewer than twenty-five letters from the Phoenicians, a Semitic people whose merchant ships, sailing from their cities Tyre and Sidon on the Palestinian coast, reached every island and harbor of the Mediterranean Sea. The Phoenician alphabet consisted of signs for consonants only. The Greeks appropriated their symbols (Alpha and Beta are meaningless words in Greek, but their Phoenician equivalents, Aleph and Beth, mean "ox" and "house"), but by assigning some of the letters to the vowels, they created the first efficient alphabet, a letter system that provided one, and only one, sign for each sound in the language.

Just when this creative adaptation took place is a subject of scholarly disagreement. Some of the letter shapes of the earliest Greek inscriptions look as if they had been copied from Phoenician scripts that date from as far back as the twelfth century. On the other hand, the earliest examples of Greek alphabetic writing, scratched or painted on broken pottery and found all over the Greek world from Rhodes in the east to Ischia off the coast of Naples in the west, are dated, by their archaeological contexts, to the last half of the eighth century B.C.

But it was not until the eighteenth century that the possibility of Homeric illiteracy was once again proposed. The English traveler Robert Wood, in his *Essay on the Original Genius of Homer* (1769), suggested that Homer had been as illiterate as his own Achilles and Odysseus. The German scholar F. A. Wolf elaborated the theory in a learned discourse entitled *Prolegomena ad Homerum*, and the Homeric Question was launched on its long and complicated career. For if Homer was illiterate, Wolf declared, he could not possibly have composed poems as long as the *Iliad* and *Odyssey*; he must have left behind him shorter, ballad-like poems which, preserved by memory, were later (much later, in Wolf's opinion) put together in something like the form we now possess. Wolf's thesis was almost universally accepted as soon as published. It came at the right time. Almost a century before this, the Neapolitan philosopher Giambattista Vico had claimed that the Homeric poems were not the creation of one man but of the whole Greek people. The spirit of the age now sought to find works of untutored genius, songs and ballads, the expression of a people's communal imagination—a contrast to the artificial culture and literature of the Age of Reason. The Romantic rebellion was at hand. Everywhere in Europe scholars began to collect, record and edit popular song, ballad, epic—the German *Nibelungenlied*, the Finnish *Kalevala*, Percy's *Reliques of Ancient English Poetry*. And this was the age that saw the popularity, especially in Germany and France, of a forged collective bardic epic: the story of Ossian, a Gaelic hero, translated from the original Gaelic and collected in the Highlands by James Macpherson. In spite of the fact that Macpherson was never able to produce the originals, "Ossian" was admired by Goethe and Schiller; it was the favorite book of Napoleon Bonaparte. They should have listened to Samuel Johnson, who called the book "as gross an imposition as ever the world was troubled with."

In such an atmosphere of enthusiasm for folk poetry the discovery of a primitive Homer was more than welcome. And scholars, convinced that the *Iliad* and *Odyssey* consisted of ancient shorter poems which had been sewn together by later compilers and editors, now addressed with enthusiasm the task of deconstruction, of picking out the stitches and isolating the original "lays" or "ballads" in their primitive, pure beauty. The exercise continued throughout the whole of the nineteenth and into the twentieth century.

It continued because of course no two scholars could agree about how to take the poems apart. This was understandable, since the criteria they were using—inconsistency of character, imbalance of structure, irrelevance of theme or incident, clumsiness of transition—are notoriously subjective. At first the affair was a free-for-all; it seemed almost as if there were a competition to see who could find the greatest number of separate ballads. Karl Lachmann, in the mid-nineteenth century, after claiming that the newly discovered *Nibelungenlied* was a mosaic of short ballads (a theory now believed by no one), went on to divide the *Iliad* into eighteen original heroic songs. A similar theory of the origin of the *Chanson de Roland* was popular at about the same time. The idea was not as impossible as it now sounds; in fact, a contemporary of Lachmann, the Finnish scholar and poet Lönnrot, collected Finnish ballads on his travels as a country doctor in the most backward parts of the country and put them together to form the great Finnish epic, the *Kalevala*, a poem that has ever since been the foundation of the Finnish national consciousness. But Lachmann's analytical methods produced no agreement, only scholarly squabbles, conducted with the customary venom, about how long the pieces should be and exactly where to use the knife.

A different approach to the problem was to claim that there was one original, fairly long poem, *The Wrath of Achilles*, not too long to have been composed orally and transmitted by memory, and that over the centuries additions were made—a theory of accretion. The most convincing champion of this theory was the English Liberal banker and historian George Grote, whose great *History of Greece* is still a classic in the field. He announced firmly that no history in the modern sense of the word could be written for Greece before the middle of the eighth century—there was no evidence. But since what the Greeks *believed* about those dark ages was all-important for their later ideas and actions, he devoted the first twenty-one chapters of his ten-volume work (published in 1846) to what he calls "Legendary Greece." And he there proposed that the original core of the *Iliad* was a short "Wrath of Achilles" containing what we now know as Books 1, 8 and 11 to 22 of the poem. In this short *Iliad*, he claimed, "the series of events is more rapid, more unbroken and more intimately knit together in the way of cause and effect than in the other books." Grote's original *Iliad*—*Ur-Ilias* as the Germans soon began to call it—is very different from ours. It contains the quarrel between the chieftains (Book 1), the rout of the Greeks and Zeus's warning to the gods not to interfere (Book 8), the Trojan attack on the ships, the death of Patroclus, the reentry of Achilles into the fighting, the death of Hector. And there it stops. No meeting of Hector and Andromache at the Scaean Gates (Book 6), no embassy to Achilles (Book 9), no journey of Priam to ransom Hector's body (Book 24). A harsher, more savage poem; the humane touches, said Grote, belong to a later, more civilized age. This theory too could not be summarily dismissed; it seems likely that this is precisely how the great French medieval epic, the *Chanson de Roland*, had grown to its present size—from an original song commemorating the death of impetuous Roland and wise Oliver in a rearguard engagement at Roncevalles, fighting the Mohammedan infidels, to a vast epic which, reaching its final form at the end of the twelfth century, reflected the spirit of the Crusades.

The nineteenth century was the age that saw the birth of the scientific historical spirit. And also of the history of language—the discipline of linguistics. All this had a bearing on the problem. If in fact some sections of the *Iliad* were older than others, they should contain linguistic features characteristic of an earlier stage of the language than that to be found in the more recent additions. Similarly, the later parts of the poem should contain allusions to customs, laws, objects and ideas belonging to the later historical period and vice-versa. Toward the end of the century a fresh criterion emerged for gauging the antiquity of different sections of the poem—the archaeological criterion. For with Heinrich Schliemann's excavations at Troy and Mycenae, and those of Sir Arthur Evans at Cnossos, a previously unknown civilization was revealed. If there was any historicity to Homer's account of the Achaean world which organized the attack on Troy, it must be a reference to *this* world—a world of gold masks, bronze weapons, palaces and fortifications—not to the archaeologically poverty-stricken Greece of the Dark Age. Now, by finding in Homer descriptions of objects that corresponded to something excavated from a Bronze Age site, the scholar could date a passage, because it was clear that with the destruction of the Mycenaean and Minoan palaces, all memory of that age had disappeared in Greece. Schliemann and Evans had discovered things Herodotus and Thucydides had no idea of.

Of these three approaches, the linguistic seemed the most promising, the most likely to yield objective criteria. Studies of the origins of Greek in the Indo-European family of languages had progressed along generally agreed and scientific lines: the history of the Greek language and the Greek dialects had become an exact discipline. Surely the linguistic analysis of the text would confirm or refute theories of earlier and later strata in the poems.

The language of Homer is of course a problem in itself. One thing is certain: it is not a language that anyone ever spoke. It is an artificial, poetic language—as the German scholar Witte puts it: "The language of the Homeric poems is a creation of epic verse." It was also a difficult language. For the Greeks of the great age, that fifth century we inevitably think of when we say "the Greeks," the idiom of Homer was far from limpid (they had to learn the meaning of long lists of obscure words at school), and it was brimful of archaisms—of vocabulary, syntax and grammar—and of incongruities: words and forms drawn from different dialects and different stages of the growth of the language. In fact, the language of Homer was one nobody, except epic bards, oracular priests or literary parodists would dream of using.

This does not mean that Homer was a poet known only to scholars and schoolboys; on the contrary the Homeric epics were familiar as household words in the mouths of ordinary Greeks. They maintained their hold on the tongues and imaginations of the Greeks by their superb literary quality—the simplicity, speed and directness of the narrative technique, the brilliance and excitement of the action, the greatness and imposing humanity of the characters—and by the fact that they presented the Greek people, in memorable form, with the images of their gods and the ethical, political and practical wisdom of their cultural tradition. Homer was thus at once contemporary in content and antique in form. The texture of Homeric epic was for the classic age of Greece like that of the Elgin Marbles for us—weathered by time but speaking to us directly: august, authoritative, inimitable, a vision of life fixed forever in forms that seem to have been molded by gods rather than men.

The language of Homer is the "creation of epic verse" in a strict sense too: it is created, adapted and shaped to fit the epic meter, the hexameter. This is a line, as its name indicates, of six metrical units, which may, to put it crudely, be either dactyls (a long plus two shorts) or spondees (two longs) in the first four places but must be dactyl and spondee in that order in the last two (rarely spondee and spondee, never spondee followed by dactyl). The syllables are literally long and short; the meter is based on pronunciation time, not, as in our language, on stress. But unlike most English verse, the meter does not allow departures from the basic norms—such phenomena as the Shakespearean variations on the basic blank verse line, still less the subtleties of Eliot's prosody in *The Waste Land*.

Yet though it is always metrically regular, it never becomes monotonous; its internal variety guarantees that. This regularity imposed on variety is Homer's great metrical secret, the strongest weapon in his poetic arsenal. The long line, which no matter how it varies in the opening and middle always ends in the same way, builds up its hypnotic effect in book after book, imposing on things and men and gods the same pattern, presenting in a rhythmic microcosm the wandering course to a fixed end which is the pattern of the rage of Achilles and the travels of Odysseus, of all natural phenomena and all human destinies.

The meter itself demands a special vocabulary, for many combinations of long and short syllables that are common in the spoken language cannot be admitted to the line—any word with three consecutive short syllables, for example, any word with one short syllable between two longs. This difficulty was met by choosing freely among the many variations of pronunciation and prosody afforded by Greek dialectal differences; the epic language is a mixture of dialects. Under a light patina of Attic forms (easily removable and clearly due to the preeminence of Athens as a literary center and then of the book trade) there is an indissoluble mixture of two different dialects, Aeolic and Ionic. But the attempts of the linguists to use this criterion for early (Aeolic) and late (Ionic) ran into the dilemma that Aeolic and Ionic forms sometimes appear inextricably tangled in the same line or half-line. Much was hoped from the use of the digamma as a criterion. This was a letter, representing the sound we represent by *w*, that disappeared from the Greek alphabet early on, as the consonant ceased to be sounded in the spoken language. Unfortunately, in many cases the relative dates assigned to passages on this basis conflicted with the data suggested by other criteria. In a passage in Book 23, for example, the meter shows that the word ergon was pronounced in its older form, *(w)ergon* (it means "work" and in fact is from the same Indo-European root as our word). This would indicate that the account of the funeral games of Patroclus in Book 23 is one of the oldest parts of the poem. In Book 14 there is a passage that contains the same word, but this time the presence of the digamma would disrupt the meter: Book 14 then must be late. But this runs counter to Grote's theory; for him, Book 23 is part of the late addition and Book 14 is very old, part of the "original" *Iliad*. This example is one among many; Homer uses or discards the digamma at will. There is no way of isolating different strata on this basis.

The attempts to dissect the *Iliad* along historical lines were no more satisfactory (except of course to their authors). There are indeed passages which seem to imply different historical backgrounds, but they are not passages that are identifiable as early or late by the criteria of linguistic difference or structural analysis. All through the poems, for example, the weapons and arms of the heroes are bronze; this was the Bronze Age. Iron *is* mentioned but as a precious metal (as one would expect during the early years of its appearance on the scene); in Book 23 a piece of iron is offered by Achilles as a prize for the weight-throwing contest. Yet in the fourth book the Trojan archer Pandarus has an iron arrowhead, mentioned quite casually as if that were normal. Arrowheads are not things you expect to get back once you have shot them— they are, to use a military cliché, expendable. In this passage iron is obviously cheap. Book 4 also presents us with a simile in which a man fells a poplar tree with an iron ax; elsewhere we meet proverbial phrases like "heart hard as iron," which indicate complete familiarity with the metal. It certainly looks as if these are different historical layers, but once again, there is no way to extract them. Book 23 for example, which contains the reference to iron as a valuable rarity, is considered a late addition by the believers in an *Ur-Ilias*. And so with many other historical discrepancies—horseback riding only in Book 10 and in similes; twin-horse chariots in every battle except those of Books 8 and 11, where we find four-horse chariots; trumpets mentioned in similes but never employed in the action; fishing mentioned in similes, but none of the heroes ever eats fish (though they are encamped on the shore). Most of the shields are round but Ajax has a huge one like a tower. This sounds like the strange body-shield seen on some of the Mycenaean frescoes. Can Ajax be an older, Mycenaean component of the epic? Hardly, for Hector is described as having the same shield.

Historical analysis, then, fails to account for the amalgam, and the high hopes aroused by archaeology soon faded too. There are not many objects in Homer that resemble anything discovered by the spade of the excavator. Two stand out. One is the cup of Nestor described in Book 11 (745–53), which has some resemblance to (and some differences from) a cup found at Mycenae by Schliemann. The other is a remarkable helmet: "a helmet made of leather / . . . outside the gleaming teeth of a white-tusked boar / ran round and round in rows stitched neat and tight" (10.305–8). Such helmets, and artistic representations of them, have been found at Mycenaean sites, on Crete, at Mycenae, on Delos, but never in late archaeological contexts. Here there seems to be a genuine memory of the Bronze Age. But it is found in Book 10, the one book every so-called Analyst agrees must be a late addition to the original poem.

It is not surprising, in view of such frustrating results, that by the beginning of the twentieth century, opinion had begun to swing away from analysis and to concentrate on the qualities of the poem itself, to stress the unity of the main action rather than the digressions and in-consistencies, above all to explore the elaborate correspondences of structure that often link scene to scene. The architecture of the poem is magnificent, and it strongly suggests the hand of one composer, but it is true that there is a certain roughness in the details of the execution. The poem does contain, in an indissoluble amalgam, material that seems linguistically and historically to span many centuries. And it does contain long digressions, and some disconcerting inconsistencies, some weak-nesses of construction. What sort of poet composed it, and how did he work?

The answer was supplied by an American scholar, whose name was Milman Parry. Parry, who came from California and was an assistant professor at Harvard when he was killed in a gun accident at an early age, did his most significant work in Paris; in fact, he wrote it in French.

It has only recently been translated, by his son, Adam, who met an equally tragic end, also at an early age. Milman Parry's work was not appreciated or even fully understood until after his death; but once understood, it radically altered the terms of the problem.

Parry's achievement was to prove that Homer was a master of and heir to a tradition of oral epic poetry that reached back over many generations, perhaps even centuries. He drew attention to the so-called ornamental epithets, those long high-sounding labels that accompany every appearance of a hero, a god, or even a familiar object. Agamemnon, for example, is "lord of men" or "wide-ruling," Achilles is "brilliant," "godlike" or "swift-footed," Apollo is "one who shoots from afar," the Achaeans are "strong-greaved" or "bronze-cloaked," Hera is "white-armed" and ships are "black," "round," "hollow" or "swift." These recurring epithets had of course been noticed before Parry, and their usefulness understood. They offer, for each god, hero or object, a choice of epithets, each one with a different metrical shape. In other words, the particular epithet chosen by the poet may have nothing to do with, for example, whether Achilles is "brilliant" or "swift-footed" at this particular point in the poem—the choice depends on which epithet fits the meter.

Parry pursued this insight of the German analytical scholars to its logical end and demonstrated that in fact there was an intricate system of metrical alternatives for the recurring names of heroes, gods and objects. It was a system that was economical—hardly any unnecessary alternatives—but had great scope—there was a way to fit the names into the line in any of the usual grammatical forms they would assume. Parry demonstrated that the system was more extensive and highly organized than anyone had dreamed, and he also realized what it meant. It meant that this system had been developed by and for the use of oral poets who *improvised*. In Paris he met scholars who had studied such improvising illiterate bards still performing in Yugoslavia. He went there to study their operations himself.

The Homeric epithets were created to meet the demands of the meter of Greek heroic poetry, the dactylic hexameter. They offer the improvising bard different ways of fitting the name of his god, hero or object into whatever section of the line is left after he has, so to speak, filled up the first half (that too, quite possibly, with another formulaic phrase). The Achaeans, for example—one of the names used for the Greeks, *Achaioi*—are often "strong-greaved": *ěǔknēmīděs Ăchāiōi*, a line ending. "Stay your ground, all of you strong-greaved Achaeans," says the prophet Calchas, encouraging the troops: *āll' ǎgě, mīmnětě pāntěs, ěǔ-*

knēmīdĕs Áchāiōi. A few lines earlier, however, he has asked them, "Why have you fallen silent?": *tīpt' ănĕō ĕgĕnĕsthĕ . . .* How will the bard finish *this* line? *Ĕūknēmīdĕs Áchāiōi* will fit the meter, for the two opening phrases are of the same metrical length. But it will produce a junction of two short open vowels: *ĕgĕnĕsthĕ ĕūknēmīdĕs Áchāiōi*, and this usually results in elision, the suppression of one of the two short vowels— *ĕgĕnĕsth' ĕūknēmīdĕs*—an unacceptable metrical combination. The solution is simple. The Achaeans cease to be "strong-greaved" and become "long-haired"—a formula starting with a consonant, which avoids the hiatus: *tīpt' ănĕō ĕgĕnĕsthĕ, kărē kŏmŏōntĕs Áchāiōi*. The bard may also need to fit the Achaeans into a different part of the line and in a different grammatical case. In Book 7, for example, the gods watch the Greeks toil and suffer in the battle. "So they toiled . . ."—*hōs hŏi mĕn pŏnĕŏntŏ*— "the long-haired Achaeans"—*kărē kŏmŏōntĕs Áchāiōi* (not "strong-greaved"—that would have produced elision: *pŏnĕŏnt' ĕūknēmīdĕs*). Two lines later, however, "the gods, seated by Zeus of the lightning bolt, watched the great labor"—*mĕgă ērgŏn*—"of the Achaeans": *Áchāiōn*— genitive case. To fill the rest of this line the bard needs an epithet of the form – ᴗ ᴗ – –. The Achaeans can't be "strong-greaved" or "long-haired," then; they have to be "bronze-cloaked": *chălkŏchĭtōnōn*. The choice of the epithet is dictated by the meter. Agamemnon is "shepherd of the people," "lord of men," "son of Atreus," "wide-ruling" or "brilliant" according to his grammatical case and his position in the line. So for Achilles and Zeus, Hera and Hector. As for ships, their position in the line and case determines whether they are "black," "round," "seagoing" or "well-benched."

This system, obviously the product of invention, refinement and elimination of superfluities over generations, could only be the work of oral bards, and in fact similar phenomena, though infinitely less sophisticated, are found in oral poetry, living and dead, in other languages. There was more to it, of course, than handy epithets. Whole lines, once honed to perfection by the bards of the tradition, became part of the repertoire; they are especially noticeable in recurring passages like descriptions of sacrifice, of communal eating and drinking. Such passages give the oral singer time to concentrate on what is coming next, and if he is a creative oral poet, to elaborate his own phrases mentally as he recites the formulas that he can sing without effort. He is helped, too, by the formulaic nature of whole themes, great type-scenes—the arming of the warrior for battle, the duels of the champions, the assembly of the warriors. These are traditional patterns which the audience expects and the bard may vary but not radically change.

There is one aspect of Parry's discovery, however, that changed the whole problem of the nature of our Homeric text. The oral bard who uses such formulaic language is not, as scholars in the nineteenth century who struggled with the problem of illiterate bards all assumed, a poet reciting from memory a fixed text. He is improvising, along known lines, relying on a huge stock of formulaic phrases, lines and even whole scenes; but he is improvising. And every time he sings the poem, he does it differently. The outline remains the same but the text, the oral text, is flexible. The poem is new every time it is performed.

If Homer's poetry is the culmination of a long tradition of such oral composition, many of the problems that bedeviled the Analysts are solved. Over the course of generations of trial and error, formulas are introduced and rejected or retained for their usefulness in improvisation, without regard to linguistic consistency or historical accuracy. The language of the poets becomes a repository of all the combinations that have proved useful. Small wonder that Aeolic and Ionic forms appear in the same line, that a Mycenaean boar-tusk helmet can turn up in a passage full of very late linguistic forms, that people sometimes give dowries and sometimes demand payment for their daughter's hand, that cremation and inhumation are practiced side by side. As each new generation of singers recreates the song, new formulas may be created, ew themes and scenes introduced; reflections of contemporary reality creep into descriptions of the fighting, especially into the similes. But the dedication of epic poetry to the past and the continuing usefulness of so much traditional phraseology will slow the process of modernization and produce the unhistorical amalgam of customs, objects and linguistic forms that we find in our Homeric text.

It is the fate of most new and valuable insights to be enthusiastically developed beyond the limits of certainty, or even of probability, and Parry's demonstration that Homeric poetry had an oral base has not escaped that fate. Phrases, even whole lines, that are repeated often enough to qualify as formulaic are indeed characteristic of the poet's diction, but they do not account for more than a part of it—about one third of the whole. In an attempt to raise the formulaic element to a higher level, Parry counted as formulas expressions whose metrical pattern and position in the line were identical and which contained one word in common: for example, *tĕuchĕ ĕthēkĕ; álgĕ' ĕthēkĕ; kŭdŏs ĕthēkĕ*— he "put" the arms, the sorrows, the glory on. Not content with this, Parry went on to suggest, hesitantly, the inclusion in the system of similar expressions which, however, did *not* contain one word in common: *dōkĕn hĕtāirŏ*, for example, and *tĕuchĕ kŭnēssĭn*—"he gave to his comrade," "he made [him prey] for the dogs." Some of Parry's followers have been less hesitant, and by this and other extensions of the meaning of "formula" have boosted the inherited content of Homer's verse to ninety percent. This of course leaves very little room for Homer as an individual creative poet. It seems in fact to be a return to the idea of Giambattista Vico: the poems are the creation of a people, of a tradition, of generations of nameless bards.

But the argument for full formularity has feet of clay. A poet composing in a strict, demanding meter is bound to repeat syntactical combinations in identical positions and the stricter the meter, the higher the incidence of such repeated patterns. English has no meters as precisely demanding as Homer's, but Alexander Pope, to take an example, is rich in lines that by strict Parryite standards would qualify him as an illiterate bard. For example:

> The Smiles of Harlots, and the Tears of Heirs
> The Fate of Louis and the Fall of Rome
>
> Proclaim their Motions, and provoke the War
> Maintain thy Honours, and enlarge thy Fame
>
> The shining Helmet, and the pointed Spears
> The silver Token, and the circled Green
>
> Weak was his Pace, but dauntless was his Heart
> Lame are their Feet, and wrinkled is their Face

Samuel Johnson, in fact, wrote a description of Pope's technique that has more than a little resemblance to Parry's conception of the oral poet. "By perpetual practice, language had in his mind a systematical arrangement; having always the same use for words, he had words so selected and combined as to be ready at his call."

Extravagant claims for the predominance of formula in Homeric poetry have now been generally discounted, and even Parry's basic theses have been shown to need modification in the light of later examination. There are many cases, for example, where a truly formulaic epithet does in fact seem to be poetically functional in its context. There are cases where verbal repetition is so poetically effective that it must be the result of poetic design rather than the working of a quasi-mechanical system. Careful investigation of the type-scenes—the ceremony of sacrifice, the arming of the warrior, and so on—has revealed that although sometimes whole verses are repeated from one scene to another, no two scenes are exactly similar. "Each occurrence," to quote a recent evaluation (Edwards, p. 72), "is unique, and often specifically adapted to its context." Even the basic concept of economy, the strict limitation of the epithets for one god or hero to those needed in different cases and positions, has been questioned: a recent study shows that in his analysis of the epithets for Achilles, Parry considered only the phrases containing the hero's name, ignoring other ways of identifying Achilles, such as "Peleus' son" (Shive, passim). All this, together with the monumental scale and the magnificent architecture of the *Iliad*, makes the image of Homer as an illiterate bard, totally dependent on ready-made formulas and stock scenes for improvised performance, hard to accept.

There is nevertheless fairly general agreement that Parry was right in one thing: Homer's unique style does show clearly that he was heir to a long tradition of oral poetry. But there is one problem that Parry raised but did not solve: Homer may or may not have been as illiterate as his forerunners, but at some time the *Iliad* and *Odyssey* were written down. When, by whom, for what purpose and in what circumstances was this done?

The most likely date for the composition of the *Iliad* is the fifty years running from 725 to 675 B.C. That is also the time to which the earliest examples of Greek alphabetic writing can be dated. Did Homer take advantage of the new technique to record for future singers the huge poem he had composed without the aid of writing? Did writing perhaps play a role in its composition? To both these questions Parry's collaborator and successor, Albert Lord, gave an emphatically negative answer. "The two techniques are . . . mutually exclusive . . . It is conceivable that a man might be an oral poet in his younger years and a written poet later in life, but it is not possible that he be *both* an oral and a written poet at any given time in his career" (p. 129). Lord based this assertion on his experience with Yugoslav oral poets who, when they came into contact with literate urban societies, lost their gift for improvised recitation. He envisaged a Homer, an oral bard at the height of his powers, who dictated his poem to a scribe, one who had mastered the new art of writing. This was of course how the songs of the illiterate Yugoslav bards had been written down (sometimes with the aid of recording equipment sophisticated for its time) by Parry and Lord.

This scenario did not satisfy everyone. The analogy with modern Yugoslavia, for example, was flawed. When the bards there learned to read and write, they were immediately exposed to the corrupting influence of newspapers, magazines and cheap fiction, but if Homer learned to write in the late eighth century, there was little or nothing for him

to read. Lord's generalization about the incompatibility of the two tech-
niques has been questioned by students of oral poetry; in other parts of
the world (particularly in Africa), they find no such dichotomy. "The
basic point . . . is the continuity of oral and written literature. There is
no deep gulf between the two: they shade into each other both in the
present and over many centuries of historical development, and there
are innumerable cases of poetry which has both 'oral' and 'written'
elements" (Finnegan, p. 24). Furthermore, the extant specimens of al-
phabetic writing of the eighth and early seventh centuries B.C. make it
hard to believe in a scribe of the period who could take dictation at or,
for that matter, anywhere near performance speed: the letters are free-
standing capitals, crudely and laboriously formed, written from right to
left or from right to left and left to right on alternate lines. One critic,
in fact, irreverently conjured up a picture of Homer dictating the first
line (or rather the first half-line) of the *Iliad*: "*Mênin aeide thea* . . . You
got that?"

A different scenario for the transition from oral performance to writ-
ten text was developed by Geoffrey Kirk. The epics were the work of
an oral "monumental composer," whose version imposed itself on bards
and audiences as the definitive version. They "then passed through at
least a couple of generations of transmission by decadent and quasi-
literate singers and rhapsodes" (Kirk, *Commentary*, I, 1985, p. xxv)—
that is, performers who were not themselves poets. Lord's objection to
this, that memorization plays no part in the living oral tradition, was
based on Yugoslav experience, but elsewhere—in Somalia, for exam-
ple—very long poems are recited from memory by professional reciters
who are themselves, in many cases, poets.

What neither of these theories explains, however, is the immense
length of the poem. Why should an oral, illiterate poet, whose poetry
exists only in its performance before an audience, create a poem so long
that it would take several days to perform? For that matter, if his poetry
existed only in performance, how *could* he create a poem of such length?
If, on the other hand, he delivered different sections of it at different
times and places, how could he have elaborated the variations on theme
and formula and the inner structural correspondences that distinguish
the Homeric epics so sharply from the Yugoslav texts collected by Parry
and Lord?

It is not surprising that many recent scholars in the field have come
to the conclusion that writing did indeed play a role in the creation of
these extraordinary poems, that the phenomena characteristic of oral
epic demonstrated by Parry and Lord are balanced by qualities peculiar

to literary composition. They envisage a highly creative oral poet, master of the repertoire of inherited material and technique, who used the new instrument of writing to build, probably over the course of a lifetime, an epic poem on a scale beyond the imagination of his predecessors.

The last half of the eighth century was the time in which writing was coming into use all over the Greek world. Homer must have known of its existence, but the traditional nature of his material naturally forbade its appearance in the relentlessly archaic world of his heroes, who belonged to the time when men were stronger, braver and greater than men are now, a world in which men and gods spoke face-to-face. Even so, Homer does show, in one particular instance, that he was conscious of the new technique. In Book 6 Glaucus tells the story of his grandfather Bellerophon. Proetus, king of Argos, sent him off with a message to the king of Lycia, Proetus' father-in-law; it instructed the king to kill the bearer. "[He] gave him tokens, / murderous signs, scratched in a folded tablet . . . " (6.198–99). There has been much discussion about the nature of these signs but the word Homer uses—*grapsas*, literally "scratching"—is later the normal word used for "writing," and *pinax* —"tablet"—is the word used by later Greeks to describe the wooden boards coated with wax that were used for short notes.

If Homer could write, what did he write on? Obviously "tablets" would not be adequate. We do not know when papyrus, the paper of the ancient world, was first available in Greece, though we do know that it came at first not from its almost exclusive source, Egypt—which was not opened to Greek merchants until the sixth century B.C.—but from the Phoenician port the Greeks called Byblos (the Greek word for book was *biblion*—our "Bible"). Archaeological evidence for Phoenician imports into Greece dates from the ninth century B.C. and Phoenician traders are mentioned in the *Iliad* (23.828) and their operations described with a wealth of detail in the *Odyssey*. But even if papyrus was not available in quantity, there were other materials, such as animal skins. Herodotus, writing in the fifth century B.C., says that in his time the Ionian Greeks still used the word *diphthera*—"skin"—when they meant "book."

The crudity of the script in the eighth century meant that writing was a laborious business. If Homer did use writing in the composition of the poem, it is likely that the process extended over many years. Episodes from the tale of Achilles' rage and its consequences would be brought to near perfection in oral performance and then written down; gradually a complete text would be assembled, to be refined in detail and extended by insertions. The text contains in fact one example of such second thoughts, the inclusion of Phoenix in the embassy to Achilles in Book 9.

Nestor chooses three ambassadors to go to Achilles' tent and urge him to rejoin the Achaean ranks: they are Phoenix, Ajax and Odysseus. Phoenix, we learn later in the poem, was not only commander of one of Achilles' five regiments of Myrmidons but also the older man who brought him up from boyhood. What is he doing in the Achaean camp? Why is he not with Achilles and the Myrmidons, preparing to leave Troy? No explanation is offered and as the ambassadors leave on their mission more puzzles emerge. For the whole extent of the passage describing their journey and Achilles' greeting when they reach his tent, the verbal and adjectival forms applied to them are not, as we would expect, plural; they are dual, a special Greek termination system that indicates firmly that two and no more than two people are concerned. It looks as if an original version had only two ambassadors and that Phoenix was added later—to make the longest, most affecting and most effective of the three appeals to Achilles. Homer added Phoenix to an original version but forgot not only to explain his presence in Agamemnon's council but also to amend the dual forms.

The surprising thing is that they stayed in the text. If Homer, as in Lord's model, had dictated his poem to a scribe, he could hardly have failed to notice the discrepancy and correct it. In fact Lord records such corrections in the course of dictation in Yugoslavia. In this case correction would have been easy; any oral bard could rework the lines to substitute plural forms for dual (so, for that matter, can any modern scholar familiar with Homeric diction). And it seems hard to imagine the lines going uncorrected in Kirk's scenario of a monumental poem preserved by recitation for a generation or two before being written down. Any rhapsode (and in the earlier generation they would have been oral poets themselves) could have corrected the lines without effort and would have seen no reason not to do so. There seems to be only one possible explanation of the survival of these dual forms in the text: that the text was regarded as authentic, the exact words of Homer himself. And that can only mean that there was a written copy.

This is of course pure speculation, but so are all other attempts to explain the origin of the text that has come down to us. We shall never be able to answer the questions it raises with any certainty and must rest content with the fact that a great poet marshaled the resources of an age-old traditional art to create something new—the epic of Achilles' rage and Hector's death, which has been a model for epic poetry ever since.

THE TROJAN WAR

The background of the rage of Achilles is a war between the assembled armies of the Achaean cities and Troy, a rich, fortified city on the coast of Asia Minor near the Hellespont, the narrow western outlet of the long passage from the Black Sea to the Aegean. For the Greeks of later ages, the *Iliad* was history. Even Thucydides, who cast a critical eye on accounts of past ages, accepted the Pan-Achaean expedition against Troy, though he thought that Homer exaggerated its size and importance. It was not until the nineteenth century that the historicity of Homer's war was seriously questioned; Grote, for one, dismissed any "history" of events before 776 B.C. (the foundation date of the Olympic Games and of the calendar based on its recurrence every fourth year) as mere legend. But Schliemann's excavations at Troy and Mycenae, as well as other sites mentioned in Homer, revealed a previously unsuspected Bronze Age civilization; its bronze armor, its weapons and many particular objects—a cup like Nestor's, for example—seemed to correspond to Homer's descriptions, and its approximate date (determined by archaeological evidence) seemed to coincide with the date assigned by ancient Greek scholars to the Trojan War. When in the 1950s the inscriptions on clay tablets found on the Mycenaean site at Pylos, as well as on the Minoan site of Cnossos in Crete, were deciphered as Greek, a very archaic stage of the language that had some close correspondences with Homeric Greek, the historicity of Homer's *Iliad* seemed to be something only a hard-line skeptic could deny.

But skeptics there were (the late Sir Moses Finley among them) and their doubts soon proved to be well grounded. The tablets were for the most part inventory lists: quantities of olives, spices, wheat, records of land leases, registers of personnel, reserves of chariots, some of them recorded as broken. They are the day-to-day ledger entries of a bureaucratic monarchy that has its counterparts in the kingdoms of the Near East but has little to do with the world of piratical chieftains on the beachhead of Troy. There are Homeric names on the tablets, but though some of them are Achaean (Orestes, Adrastus), others are Trojan (Tros, Hector), and Hector, far from being a warrior prince, is a "servant of the god" and "holds a lease." As for the fire-blackened seventh layer of Schliemann's excavations at Hissarlik (the archaeologists' candidate for Homer's Troy), it can tell us nothing about its destruction—which may have been the result of earthquake rather than siege and sack. It is only one of many cities all over the Near East that went down to destruction in the late Bronze Age. The only evidence that its destroyers were an Achaean army led by the lords of Mycenae and all the cities listed in the Achaean catalogue in Book 2 of the *Iliad* is the poem itself, a poem that is supposed to have preserved the memory of these events over the course of some five illiterate centuries.

The epic muse, however, is not the muse of history; her vision of past events is always suspect. The twelfth-century manuscript of the *Chanson de Roland*, a poem that almost certainly has oral origins, tells the heroic tale of the great invasion of Moslem Spain led by Charlemagne, and of the deaths of Roland and his friend Oliver in the pass of Roncesvalles, where the Frankish rear guard was attacked by Moslem hordes led by beys and pashas. The invasion took place in A.D. 778. Forty years later, Einhard wrote his famous *Life of Charlemagne*, from which we learn that the rear guard was attacked not by Moslems but by the Basques, who were Christians like the Franks. This substitution does not inspire confidence in oral poetic tradition as a historical source; it would suggest by analogy that the historic core of the *Iliad* may have been a battle between Trojans and Hittites or a war between Mycenae and Thebes.

But though we may have our doubts, the Greeks of historic times who knew and loved Homer's poem had none. For them history began with a splendid Panhellenic expedition against an Eastern foe, led by kings and including contingents from all the more than one hundred and fifty places listed in the catalogue in Book 2. History began with a war. That was an appropriate beginning, for the Greek city-states, from their first appearance as organized communities until the loss of their political independence, were almost uninterruptedly at war with one another. The Greek *polis*, the city-state, was a community surrounded by potential enemies, who could turn into actual belligerents at the first sign of aggression or weakness. The permanence of war is a theme echoed in Greek literature from Homer to Plato. We Achaeans, says Odysseus in the *Iliad*, are

> "the men whom Zeus decrees, from youth to old age,
> must wind down our brutal wars to the bitter end
> until we drop and die, down to the last man."   (14.105–7)

And in Plato's *Laws* the Cretan participant in the discussion says: "Peace is just a name. The truth is that every city-state is, by natural law, engaged in a perpetual undeclared war with every other city-state." There was no lack of declared wars, either. The citizens of Athens in the great century of Greek civilization, the fifth B.C., were at war, on land and sea, for more years than they were at peace. In the Louvre in Paris there is an inscription, dating from the early 450s, that lists the names of 171 men of one of the ten Athenian tribes, who died "in war, on Cyprus, in Egypt, in Phoenicia, at Halieis, Aegina, Megara in the same year." Athens at this time was fighting not only the Persian Empire but also her former ally against Persia, Sparta and its Peloponnesian League. She had been fighting the Persians continually since 480 and Sparta since 460. In 448 she made peace with Persia and in 446 with Sparta and the League. But the peace lasted only fifteen years. In 431 the Peloponnesian War began, to end in 404 with the surrender of Athens and the loss of her naval empire.

The fighting Homer describes—duels between chieftains who ride up to the battle line in chariots, dismount, and exchange speeches, sometimes quite long ones, before engaging man-to-man with spear and shield—is clearly a creation of the epic muse rather than a representation of actual battle conditions. The Mycenaeans had chariots in quantity, as Linear B inventories show (over two hundred chariots at Cnossos, for example), but such expensive equipment would have been put to better use, and although hand-to-hand combatants may shout at each other, they do not make speeches. Yet for Homer's later audiences and readers, the combats of heroes in the *Iliad* did not seem unfamiliar, since Greek battles, for centuries after his time, were fought by armored infantry at close quarters; archers were rare and cavalry was used only in pursuit, after the enemy infantry line had been broken and turned to flight. Though the citizen-soldier of the *polis* did not fight individual duels but faced the enemy as part of a disciplined line of overlapping shields, he still exchanged spear-thrusts with his opposite number in the opposing phalanx, and he could recognize as the real thing Homer's account of what metal can do to human flesh:

> *Achilles lunged [at Demoleon] . . .*
> *he stabbed his temple and cleft his helmet's cheekpiece.*
> *None of the bronze plate could hold it—boring through*
> *the metal and skull the bronze spearpoint pounded,*
> *Demoleon's brains splattered all inside his casque . . .*   (20.449–54)

A few lines later Achilles kills another Trojan:

> *speared him square in the back where his war-belt clasped,*
> *golden buckles clinching both halves of his breastplate—*
> *straight on through went the point and out the navel,*

> *down on his knees he dropped—*
> *screaming shrill as the world went black before him—*
> *clutched his bowels to his body, hunched and sank.*   (20.470–75)

There is no attempt to gloss over the harsh realities of the work of killing ("work," *ergon*, is one of Homer's words for what men do in battle) and no attempt, either, to sentimentalize the pain and degradation of violent death.

> *But Meriones caught him in full retreat, he let fly*
> *with a bronze-tipped arrow, hitting his right buttock*
> *up under the pelvic bone so the lance pierced the bladder.*
> *He sank on the spot, hunched in his dear companion's arms,*
> *gasping out his life as he writhed along the ground*
> *like an earthworm stretched out in death, blood pooling,*
> *soaking the earth dark red . . .*   (13.749–55)

Men die in the *Iliad* in agony; they drop, screaming, to their knees, reaching out to beloved companions, gasping their life out, clawing the ground with their hands; they die roaring, like Asius, raging, like the great Sarpedon, bellowing, like Hippodamas, moaning, like Polydorus.

And death is the end: Homer offers no comforting vision of life beyond the grave. In the *Chanson de Roland* Archbishop Turpin promises the heroes of Charlemagne's army a place among the blessed, a promise fulfilled in the poem, for when Roland dies an angel and two saints carry his soul to Paradise. For Homer's heroes no such rewarding prospect presents itself. For most of those whose life is violently suppressed in the poem, the formulas used concern themselves simply with the physical destruction of the body, followed by the extinction of life in it: "and hateful darkness seized him," "darkness engulfed his eyes." Where, very rarely, a phrase suggests the departure of the life for some other destination, it is not Paradise but the House of Hades, lord of the dead. Only one soul in the poem comes back from that house: it is Patroclus, who haunts Achilles' dreams, calling for his burial so that he can rest at last. "Even in Death's strong house," says Achilles, "there is something left, / a ghost, a phantom—true, but no real breath of life"(23.122–23). Patroclus is concerned for proper disposal of his body and indeed it is for the body, not the soul, that the Homeric heroes feel concern: many of the champions who fall mortally wounded have been fighting to gain control of the corpse of a prominent foe or to save the corpse of a comrade from the enemy. Archbishop Turpin finally prevails on Roland to blow his horn and summon Charlemagne by pointing out that though it is now too late for the king to save them, he may be able to bury their bodies in a church and save them from wolves, pigs and dogs. But as is clear from their prayers and from the visitation of the angels who come to take the soul of Roland to Paradise, it is the soul, not the body, that is their real concern. The contrast between the two attitudes is clear to see in the Homeric parallel to the angelic escort that comes for Roland. Zeus sends Apollo to rescue the corpse of his son Sarpedon, almost unrecognizable now since it is "covered over head to toe, / buried under a mass of weapons, blood and dust" (16.743–44). Apollo lifts the body out of the melee, washes the blood off it in a running river, and gives it to the brothers Sleep and Death, who are to transport it to Sarpedon's home in Lycia for due burial with tomb and gravestone. "These," says Zeus, "are the solemn honors owed the dead" (16.789). But the poet does not encourage illusions about the fate of the body once the life has gone out of it; if not rescued for burning and burial, it may shrivel in the heat of the sun, it may become food for the birds of the air, the dogs of the earth, the eels and fish of the waters. And if not protected by divine interference, its wounds will be host to flies, which will breed worms.

Nevertheless the *Iliad* is a poem that celebrates the heroic values war imposes on its votaries. War has its deadly fascination for those who have grown up in its service. "It is well that it is so terrible," said Lee, as he watched Hooker's doomed columns start across the river at Fredericksburg, "or we should grow too fond of it." And though the warriors of the *Iliad* often rail against their condition, they can also enjoy to the full war's intoxicating excitements. They revel in the exultation of victory as they taunt a fallen adversary with threats of exposure of his corpse, or with a bitter sarcasm, as when Patroclus mocks one of his victims, who, his face crushed by a stone, dives from his chariot: "Look what a springy man, a nimble, flashy tumbler!" (16.868). Even Hector, by far the most civilized of all the warriors at Troy, can list with pride and a kind of joy his credentials as a seasoned fighter.

> "War—I know it well, and the butchery of men.
> Well I know, shift to the left, shift to the right
> my tough tanned shield. That's what the real drill,
> defensive fighting means to me. I know it all,
> how to charge in the rush of plunging horses—
> I know how to stand and fight to the finish,
> twist and lunge in the War-god's deadly dance."   (7.275–81)

And though, in a series of recurrent formulas, war is characterized as "dreadful," "man-killing," "hateful," to list only a few of the epithets, it can also appear, again in a recurrent formula, as "bringing glory to man." Warriors are described as "eager" or even "yearning" for battle, and one of the common words for combat, *charmê*, comes from the same root as the word *chairô*—"rejoice." In one passage, in fact, this etymology is emphasized as two warriors, holding the line in a desperate situation, are described as *charmêi gêthosunoi*—"rejoicing in (the joy of) battle."

In some of Homer's descriptions of killing, the victor's joy of battle and the hideous suffering of the victim are evenly balanced. As in the account of the death of an obscure Trojan charioteer, Thestor, who, terrified by the approach of Patroclus,

> *cowering, crouched in his fine polished chariot,*
> *crazed with fear, and the reins flew from his grip—*
> *Patroclus rising beside him stabbed his right jawbone,*
> *ramming the spearhead square between his teeth so hard*
> *he hooked him by that spearhead over the chariot-rail,*
> *hoisted, dragged the Trojan out as an angler perched*
> *on a jutting rock ledge drags some fish from the sea,*
> *some noble catch, with line and glittering bronze hook.*
> *So with the spear Patroclus gaffed him off his car,*
> *his mouth gaping round the glittering point*
> *and flipped him down facefirst,*
> *dead as he fell, his life breath blown away.*   (16.478–89)

The hallucinatory power of this passage stems partly from the deliberate, craftsmanlike way Patroclus delivers his blow, partly from the hypnotized, terror-struck passivity of the victim. Its realism has been questioned: could one man really pull another out of a chariot in this way? Perhaps he could—if the spearhead were triangular and the blunt rear angles of the blade became wedged in the flesh and if, as seems likely, the wounded man would follow the motion of the spear in withdrawal, rather than resisting it. But clearly Homer is walking the borderline of credibility here. He does it for a reason: that simile. It emphasizes the grotesque appearance of violent death by a comparison with a familiar fact of everyday life: Thestor is gaping like a fish on the hook. The spear-thrust destroys his dignity as a human being even before it takes his life. But the simile does something more: it shows us the action from the point of view of the killer—the excitement of the hunter dispatching his prey, the joy of the fisherman hauling in his catch. The lines combine two contrary emotions: man's instinctive revulsion from bloodshed and his susceptibility to the excitements of violence. And they are typical of the poem as a whole. Everywhere in Homer's saga of the rage of Achilles and the battles before Troy we are made conscious at one and the same time of war's ugly brutality and what Yeats called its "terrible beauty." The *Iliad* accepts violence as a permanent factor in human life and accepts it without sentimentality, for it is just as sentimental to pretend that war does not have its monstrous ugliness as it is to deny that it has its own strange and fatal beauty, a power, which can call out in men resources of endurance, courage and self-sacrifice that peacetime, to our sorrow and loss, can rarely command. Three thousand years have not changed the human condition in this respect; we are still lovers and victims of the will to violence, and so long as we are, Homer will be read as its truest interpreter.

This was recognized by Simone Weil in an essay written long before she left her native France for wartime London, where she filled her brilliant notebooks with reflections on Greek literature and philosophy in the short time left to her to live. This classic (and prophetic) statement—*L'Iliade ou le Poème de la Force*—presented her vision of Homer's poem as an image of the modern world.

The true hero, the true subject, the center of the *Iliad*, is force. Force as man's instrument, force as man's master, force before which human flesh shrinks back. The human soul, in this poem, is shown always in its relation to force: swept away, blinded by the force it thinks it can direct, bent under the pressure of the force to which it is subjected. Those who had dreamed that force, thanks to progress, now belonged to the past, have seen the poem as a historic document; those who can see that force, today as in the past, is at the center of all human history, find in the *Iliad* its most beautiful, its purest mirror.

She goes on to define what she means by force: "force is what makes the person subjected to it into a thing." She wrote these words in 1939: the article was scheduled for publication in the *Nouvelle Revue Française*, but before it could be printed Paris was in the hands of the Nazis and her compatriots, like all Europe, were subjected to force and turned into things—corpses or slaves.

"Its most beautiful, its purest mirror . . ." The most marvelous lines
in the *Iliad* owe their unearthly, poignant beauty to the presence of
violence, held momentarily in reserve but brooding over the landscape.
They are the lines that end Book 8 and describe the Trojans camped on
the plain, awaiting the next dawn, which will launch them on their
attack on the Greek fortification.

> *And so their spirits soared*
> *as they took positions down the passageways of battle*
> *all night long, and the watchfires blazed among them.*
> *Hundreds strong, as stars in the night sky glittering*
> *round the moon's brilliance blaze in all their glory*
> *when the air falls to a sudden, windless calm . . .*
> *all the lookout peaks stand out and the jutting cliffs*
> *and the steep ravines and down from the high heavens bursts*
> *the boundless bright air and all the stars shine clear*
> *and the shepherd's heart exults—so many fires burned*
> *between the ships and the Xanthus' whirling rapids*
> *set by the men of Troy, bright against their walls.*   (8.638–49)

These are surely the clearest hills, the most brilliant stars and the brightest
fires in all poetry, and everyone who has waited to go into battle knows
how true the lines are, how clear and memorable and lovely is every
detail of the landscape the soldier fears he may be seeing for the last
time.

THE TROJANS

The city, the *polis*, as the Greeks called it, was for them the matrix of
civilization, the only form of ordered social life they could understand;
it is the exclusive form assumed by ancient Greek culture from its be-
ginning to its end. The city was small enough so that the citizens knew
one another, participated in a communal life, shared the common joy
of festivals, the sorrow of public bereavement, the keen excitement of
competition, the common heritage of ancestral tombs and age-old sanc-
tified places. The destruction of a city is a calamity all the more deeply
felt because of the close cohesion of its inhabitants and their attachment,
reinforced over generations from a mythical past, to its landmarks and
buildings.

The first city we hear of in Greek literature is Troy. It is characteristic
of the *Iliad*'s tragic viewpoint that this city, the literary prototype of all

Greek cities, is to be destroyed. The poem ends before Troy falls, but we are left in no doubt about its fate. One of the deep sources of the tragic force of the *Iliad* is that the city of Troy is doomed, doomed to go down in fire and slaughter under the assault of the Achaeans, whose cities are far away and half-forgotten in the long siege, whose home for ten years has been the raw world of tent shelters and beached ships.

Homer's Troy has been assigned a few traits that sound Oriental (or at any rate non-Greek)—Priam's fifty sons, for example—but it is still recognizably a Greek *polis*. It is a site chosen with an eye to defensive capabilities, with a high eminence that serves as a citadel, a sacred area for the temples and palaces. It is near the junction of two rivers, and it depends on the produce of the surrounding plain, which is rich plowland and grows wheat. It is fortified against attackers: it is well-walled and well-built, it has steep ramparts and gates. These fortifications enclose a vision of civilized life, the splendors of wealth and peace. The city contains, for example, "Priam's palace, that magnificent structure / built wide with porches and colonnades of polished stone" (6.289–90). It is at the gates of this palace that the Trojans hold their assemblies. The city has its hallowed landmarks: the Scaean and Dardanian Gates, the tombs of the royal ancestor Ilus in the plain, of old Aesyetes, and of Myrine; the oak tree by the Scaean Gates (6.283), the fig tree near the tomb of Ilus, and the hot and cold springs . . .

> where the wives of Troy and all their lovely daughters
> would wash their glistening robes in the old days,
> the days of peace before the sons of Achaea came . . .   (22.185–87)

And in the city are those riches the Achaeans dream of, of which they promise each other shares when the city falls, those riches which, even though the nine years' war has reduced them to a level that Hector regards with dismay (18.334–38), are still enormous. We are given a glimpse of them in Book 6 when Hecuba goes into the royal storeroom to select an offering for Athena, and again in Book 24 when Priam assembles the ransom for Hector's body.

But the wealth of Troy is apparent also from the fact that time after time Trojan warriors, menaced with death as they lose a fight, offer a rich ransom:

> "Take us alive, Atrides, take a ransom worth our lives!
> Vast treasures are piled up in Antimachus' house,
> bronze and gold and plenty of well-wrought iron—

father would give you anything, gladly, priceless ransom
if only he learns we're still alive in Argive ships!''   (11.153–57)

So the sons of Antimachus to Agamemnon, and in similar terms Adrestus begs Menelaus for his life and Dolon supplicates Odysseus. In all three cases the ransom is refused—the war has turned savage in its final phase. But in time gone by, Trojan ransom money has been a steady source of wealth for the Achaeans; it is clear from Thersites' sarcastic questions addressed to Agamemnon, in Book 2, that this was a regular traffic. "Still more gold you're wanting? More ransom a son / of the stallion-breaking Trojans might just fetch from Troy?" (2.267–68). The repeated appeals to accept ransom are not only indicative of Troy's immense wealth, they are also a reminder of Trojan attitudes: the belief, typical of rich, civilized cities, that wealth can always buy a solution, and the illusion that civilized ways of warfare—quarter for disarmed men or men who surrender, ransom and exchange of prisoners—are laws as valid and universal as the laws under which their own civilization lives. Inside Troy the manners of civilized life are preserved; there are restraints on anger, there is courtesy to opponents, kindness to the weak—things that have no place in the armed camp on the shore. In the city, those who have most cause to blame, even to hate, Helen, the old men of Troy, members of the council, murmur to each other praise for her beauty as they express their wish that she would go back to the Achaeans; and old Priam, who has lost sons because of her presence in Troy and will lose more—Hector above all, and all Troy with him—Priam too treats her with kindness and generous understanding.

Unfortunately for Troy, the Trojans have the defects of their qualities: they are not so much at home in the grim business of war as their opponents. In Book 3 Priam comes to the battlefield to seal the oaths that fix the terms of the duel between Paris and Menelaus, but he cannot bear to stay and watch the fight: he fears for his son. And Paris, the loser in the duel, is rescued by the goddess Aphrodite and returned to the arms of Helen. He is more at home in his splendid palace than on the battlefield. But he knows his strengths as well as his limitations; he answers Helen's bitter mockery with equanimity, and accepts his brother's harsh but just reproaches calmly, with a claim that war is not the whole of life and that preeminence in other spheres has its importance:

''. . . don't fling in my face the lovely gifts
of golden Aphrodite. Not to be tossed aside,
the gifts of the gods, those glories . . .
whatever the gods give of their own free will—''   (3.77–80)

But Troy is not at peace: it is under siege, and by men who mean to raze it from the face of the earth. The arts of peace are useless now. Troy will not be saved by the magnanimity and tender-heartedness of Priam nor by Paris' brilliance in the courts of love. If it is to survive it will do so because of the devotion, courage and incessant efforts of one man, Priam's son Hector. On him falls the whole burden of the war. He is a formidable warrior, formidable enough so that in Book 7 no Achaean volunteers to face him in single combat until they are tongue-lashed by Menelaus and then by Nestor. But war is not his native element. Unlike Achilles, he is clearly a man made for peace, for those relationships between man and man, and man and woman, which demand sympathy, persuasion, kindness and, where firmness is necessary, a firmness expressed in forms of law and resting on granted authority. He is a man who appears most himself in his relationships with others. It is significant that our first view of him in action is not in combat but in an attempt to stop it. Announcing Paris' offer to fight Menelaus and so settle the war, he moves ahead of the Trojan ranks and forces them to a seated position with his spear; meanwhile he is the target of Achaean arrows and stones, until Agamemnon calls a halt. It was a dangerous initiative and one that demanded immense authority, a force of personality recognized by both sides.

But his true quality is seen in his relationship with his fellow countrymen and his family. In Book 6 the seer Helenus sends him back to Troy to organize a sacrifice and procession to Athena. He no sooner appears than the wives and daughters of the Trojans come running, to ask for news of their "brothers, friends and husbands" (6.285); he is their stay and support, the man to whom they turn for comfort. In the palace of Paris, Helen tells him to sit and rest, but he will not: he must visit his own wife and child before he goes back to the fight. He finds Andromache on the wall, with their son. She weeps and begs him to be careful, as wives have begged their husbands all through history.

> "Reckless one,
> my Hector—your own fiery courage will destroy you!
> Have you no pity for him, our helpless son? Or me,
> and the destiny that weighs me down, your widow . . .   (6.482–85)

And she begs him to cease fighting in the forefront of the hand-to-hand battle on the plain, to adopt a defensive strategy and command from the walls. Hector's sad reply reveals his tragic dilemma. His feeling for her prompts him to accept her suggestion but he cannot do it. He is the leader, the commander, as his name suggests: Hector means "Holder." He is the one who holds the Trojan defense steady by his example and he must fight in the front ranks. In any case, the standards of martial valor by which he has always lived will not permit it:

> *"All this weighs on my mind too, dear woman.*
> *But I would die of shame to face the men of Troy*
> *and the Trojan women trailing their long robes*
> *if I would shrink from battle now, a coward."*   (6.522–25)

But deep in his heart he knows that the effort is futile, that Troy is doomed. He realizes what that will mean for her and hopes that he will not live to hear her cries as she is led off to slavery. He is distracted from this dark vision of the future by the terrified cries of his own baby son, who recoils screaming from the bronze-clad man who moves to embrace him. Forebodings of the future, no matter how well-founded, have to be brushed aside if life is to go on, and Hector now speaks in more hopeful terms as he prays that his son will grow up to be a greater man than his father and then comforts his sorrowing wife. This scene reveals the greatness of Hector as a complete man; we see not only the devotion of the warrior who does his duty and fights for his people, even though he knows that they are doomed, but also his greatness as a husband and father—a striking contrast with the atmosphere of the armed camp on the shore.

It is Hector's misfortune that Troy is not at peace but at war. He must return to the battle, which now, in accordance with the will of Zeus, turns against the Achaeans. Hector fights courageously, stubbornly, at times exultantly in the near madness of victorious slaughter. But even this berserk fury is still the fighting spirit of the man of the *polis*, the protector of the community, not the individual rage for glory and booty of a Diomedes or an Achilles. When, at the flood-tide of success, with the Achaeans pinned against their ships, an omen is read by the seer Polydamas as a warning to retreat, Hector will have none of it, will not put his trust in birds and the interpreters of their movements. "Fight for your country—" he says, "that is the best, the only omen!" (12.281). It is one of the most famous lines in the poem, respected and admired by the Greeks of later centuries as the epitome of patriotic courage, of the mood that inspired men to defend their own city, great or small, in the face of overwhelming odds, hostile portents and omens of disaster. It is for his country that he is fighting, and he fights well enough so that

the will of Zeus is fulfilled: the Achaeans are penned up in their forti-
fications, the first Achaean ship is fired. Hector is lord of the battlefield;
indeed, from what we have seen of champions in combat in the poem
so far, he can claim to be the best man, Greek or Trojan. But that is
because we have not yet seen Achilles in battle. And when we do, and
Homer recreates for us the irresistible violence of the man born and
shaped for battle, who values life, his own included, as nothing, the
killer in his own domain—lion in the bush, shark in the water—we
realize that Hector's defeat and death are inevitable.

The *Iliad* is a poem that lives and moves and has its being in war, in
that world of organized violence in which a man justifies his existence
most clearly by killing others. This violence is Achilles' native element:
only in violence are his full powers exerted, his talents fully employed.
And he has deliberately chosen this sphere of activity, in which he is
invincible, though he knows it will end in his early death.

> "Mother tells me,
> *the immortal goddess Thetis with her glistening feet,*
> *that two fates bear me on to the day of death.*
> *If I hold out here and I lay siege to Troy,*
> *my journey home is gone, but my glory never dies.*
> *If I voyage back to the fatherland I love,*
> *my pride, my glory dies . . .*
> *true, but the life that's left me will be long . . ."*
>
> (9.497–504)

And he has chosen glory and death at Troy. The natural consequence
of that choice is a fierce devotion to the glory which he has preferred
to a long life; any diminution of that glory, any hint that he is not the
center of the world of violence, is an intolerable insult. And Agamem-
non, in the quarrel that opens the poem, strikes at the roots of his pride,
at that self-esteem which he prizes above life itself.

> "*You* are *nothing to me—you and your overweening anger!*
> *. . . I will be there in person at your tents*
> *to take Briseis in all her beauty, your own prize—*
> *so you can learn just how much greater I am than you . . ."*
>
> (1.213–19)

This is an unforgivable insult; it denies Achilles any claim to honor at
all, it treats him as a man of no worth, in fact as a subject, an inferior.

Achilles starts to draw his sword. For him there can be only one answer to such words: "so you can learn just how much greater I am than you" amounts to a denial of his right to exist. For the honor of Achilles is more important than that of other men; he has already chosen an early death for honor's sake. His intention was to "thrust through the ranks and kill Agamemnon now" (1.225), and he would have done so if Athena had not intervened. Instead he withdraws to his tents and, through his mother Thetis and her supplication of Zeus, brings about the Trojan resurgence, which will send so many valiant souls of heroes down to Hades. For more than three quarters of the poem Achilles takes no part in the fighting; when at last, with Patroclus dead and the fight raging over his corpse, Achilles is ready to fight, he has no armor—he cannot even help rescue the body of his friend. He goes to the edge of the ditch to show himself to the Trojans and shout an announcement that he will return to the battle. And later, in the new panoply made by Hephaestus and brought by Thetis, he advances for the first time in the poem against the Trojan ranks. We have seen many men fight in the *Iliad* so far, but not Achilles. We have heard of his fighting in the past, from himself and others, but now Homer must show it to us, give us a picture of the supreme violence, goaded to fury and at the highest pitch of its relentless skill and strength. He does not fail us. The violence of Books 20 and 21 makes what has gone before seem child's play.

Death is the lot of the Trojans who stand in the way of Achilles as he seeks out Hector, the new object of his rage. One after another he cuts them down and the death blows are hideously, unnecessarily strong. Others he drives into the river Xanthus and plunges in after them, killing in the water. Later he meets one who escaped from the river and, weary and sweating, has thrown his weapons on the ground. It is one of Priam's sons, Lycaon, who had been Achilles' prisoner once, had been ransomed and returned to Troy, only to meet his death now. As Achilles raises his spear, Lycaon runs under it, clasps Achilles' knees and pleads for life. But Achilles will take no prisoners now. Once he did, but now, for the Trojans who killed his friend Patroclus, there is no pity in his heart, none, above all, for the sons of Priam, the brothers of Hector. In a famous and terrifying passage, he formulates the creed of the warrior devoted to death:

"Come, friend, you too must die. Why moan about it so?
Even Patroclus died, a far, far better man than you.
And look, you see how handsome and powerful I am?
The son of a great man, the mother who gave me life

> *a deathless goddess. But even for me, I tell you,*
> *death and the strong force of fate are waiting.*
> *There will come a dawn or sunset or high noon*
> *when a man will take my life in battle too—*
> *flinging a spear perhaps*
> *or whipping a deadly arrow off his bow.''*   (21.119–28)

"Friend, you too must die . . . " That macabre word "friend" is sincerely
meant; it is a recognition of equality, the equality of men of war, all of
whom must face violent death. And Lycaon recognizes his death sen-
tence. He lets go of Achilles' spear and sinks "back down . . . / spreading
both arms wide" (21.130–31) in a resigned gesture of relaxation to take
the blow of Achilles' sword. And Achilles turns back to the slaughter.
"Die, Trojans die— / till I butcher all the way to sacred Troy" (21.146–
47). And die they do, all those who cannot get back inside the walls,
through the gate where Hector takes his stand to meet, at last, his mighty
opposite.

The whole poem has been moving toward this duel between the two
champions, but there has never been any doubt about the outcome. The
husband and father, the beloved protector of his people, the man who
stands for the civilized values of the rich city, its social and religious
institutions, will go down to defeat at the hands of this man who has
no family, who in a private quarrel has caused the death of many of
his own fellow soldiers, who now in a private quarrel thinks only of
revenge, though that revenge, as he well knows, is the immediate prel-
ude to his own death. And the death of Hector seals the fate of Troy;
it will fall to the Achaeans, to become the pattern for all time of the
death of a city. The images of that night assault—the blazing palaces,
the blood running in the streets, old Priam butchered at the altar, Cas-
sandra raped in the temple, Hector's baby son thrown from the battle-
ments, his wife Andromache dragged off to slavery—all this,
foreshadowed in the *Iliad*, will be stamped indelibly on the consciousness
of the Greeks throughout their history, immortalized in lyric poetry, in
tragedy, on temple pediments and painted vases, to reinforce the stern
lesson of Homer's presentation of the war: that no civilization, no matter
how rich, no matter how refined, can long survive once it loses the
power to meet force with equal or superior force.

But Homer's view of the war is more somber still. From the point of
view of the powers that rule his universe, the gods, all the human
struggles, the death of heroes, the fall of cities, are only of passing
interest, to be forgotten as they are replaced by similar events played

out by different actors. Troy will fall now, but so someday will the cities of its conquerors. And the great wars that brought glory and death to the heroes will not even be allowed to leave a mark on the landscape. When Hector was threatening the Greek ships, the Achaeans built a great protective wall around them, with a ditch in front. After the fighting was over Apollo and Poseidon destroyed the wall . . .

> *flinging into it all the rivers' fury.*
> *All that flow from the crests of Ida down to breaking surf . . .*
> *The channels of all those rivers—Apollo swung them round*
> *into one mouth and nine days hurled their flood against the wall*
> *and Zeus came raining down, cloudburst powering cloudburst,*
> *the faster to wash that rampart out to open sea.*
> *The Earth-shaker himself, trident locked in his grip,*
> *led the way, rocking loose, sweeping up in his breakers*
> *all the bastions' strong supports of logs and stones . . .*
> *He made all smooth along the rip of the Hellespont*
> *and piled the endless beaches deep in sand again*
> *and once he had leveled the Argives' mighty wall*
> *he turned the rivers flowing back in their beds again*
> *where their fresh clear tides had run since time began.*
>
> *So in the years to come Poseidon and god Apollo*
> *would set all things to rights once more.*   (12.21–42)

Man's highest efforts, his struggles on the face of the earth are, from the heavenly point of view, insignificant, his huge military constructions merely a surface disturbance to be readjusted. As even now, on the beaches of the 1944 Normandy landing—Sword, Juno, Gold, and Utah and Omaha, where once the great artificial harbors, the Mulberries, floated, loaded with vehicles and munitions—now the waves and the sand show hardly a trace of the gigantic enterprise . . . at most an occasional rusted grenade pin or the worn rubber heel of a GI boot. As at Troy, things have been set to rights.

THE GODS

The subject of the poem is the rage of Achilles against Agamemnon, a human passion, but the prologue speaks also of gods. "What god drove them to fight with such a fury? / Apollo the son of Zeus and Leto" (1.9–10). A few lines earlier we have been told that as heroes fell in battle, "the will of Zeus was moving toward its end" (1.6). Are the events of the poem the creation of the will of Zeus and Apollo, or of the will of Achilles? To what extent is Achilles a free and responsible agent? It is a question raised by many other passages in the poem, as gods inspire, restrain, terrify or rescue individual heroes. How far can men whose actions so often seem to be the product of direct divine intervention be held responsible? Is there, in fact, in Homer any fully formed concept of free and responsible human action? It would seem at first as if the answer were No. In the quarrel in Book 1 Achilles refrains from killing Agamemnon on the spot because Athena grasps him by the hair and forbids it. But a closer look at this and similar passages where human action is prompted by divine suggestion reveals that the Homeric conception of divine interference is an extremely subtle one. Athena seizes Achilles by the hair just as he draws his sword, but we have been told that before he drew it, he had considered the alternative.

> Should he draw the long sharp sword slung at his hip,
> thrust through the ranks and kill Agamemnon now?—
> or check his rage and beat his fury down?
> As his racing spirit veered back and forth,
> just as he drew his huge blade from its sheath,
> down from the vaulting heavens swept Athena . . .   (1.224–29)

She comes, as it were, as the representation of that more cautious course he had considered, to urge its claims. And it is remarkable that she uses language not of command but of persuasion. "Down from the skies I come to check your rage / if only you will yield" (1.242–43). The Greek word here translated "yield"—*pithêai*—is actually a form of the verb *peithô*, "to persuade." There is a correlation here between divine intervention and independent human action; they seem to work together, or rather they seem to be the same thing viewed from two different angles. And there are of course passages in the *Iliad* where a man comes to a decision, choosing between alternatives, with no divine suggestion or intervention at all. We see Odysseus in the thick of battle, his flanks threatened, debate with himself whether to run for it or fight on; he comes to the conclusion that he must stay and fight. His impulse to run is countered by his fear of being thought a coward; the warrior code asserts its authority even in the face of almost certain death (11.477–86). But this is still a free decision, as Homer makes clear when later he puts Menelaus in the same situation, gives him many of the same formulas of debate, for and against retreat, and has him come to the opposite conclusion—he withdraws from the battle (17.101–21). Usually, however, important human decisions involve the participation of a god; divine intervention and human responsibility coexist.

This is not the only pair of philosophical irreconcilables that Homer rides in tandem: he presents us also with Destiny and its voice Prophecy on the one hand, together with the will of Achilles and Zeus on the other. Events are determined, we are expressly told at the beginning of the poem and elsewhere, by the will of Zeus, who is presented to us in the poem as a figure more stable, more majestic, than the other gods. And yet on more than one occasion the will of Zeus is thwarted by fate, as in the case of Sarpedon, his beloved son. As he sees him closing in combat with Patroclus, Zeus laments: "Sarpedon, the man I love the most, my own son— / doomed to die at the hands of Menoetius' son Patroclus" (16.515–16).

Many attempts have been made to reconcile these two ideas, to assert the overriding power of Zeus's will on the one hand, or that of a nameless destiny on the other, but in fact the coexistence of these irreconcilables is not a phenomenon confined to Homer's imagined world. In any civilization which makes a place in its thought for free will (and therefore individual responsibility) and pattern (and therefore overall meaning), the two concepts—fixed and free—exist uneasily cheek by jowl. The only escape from this logical contradiction is the prison of rigid determinism, a pattern fixed from the beginning and not subject to change, or on the other hand, the complete freedom and meaningless anarchy of an unpredictable universe. And Greek thought, like ours (or those of us at least who still live in the humane traditions of the West), tries to embrace the logical contradiction of freedom and order combined.

In Homer the combination is a subtle one; the idea of destiny, of what is fixed, is flexible. Zeus can predict the future—the deaths of Patroclus, of Achilles, the fall of Troy—and in all these cases it is impossible to say whether the result is destiny or his will or both. But sometimes the possibility is raised that what is fated will actually be annulled by divine will—or even by human. So when Achilles in his rage storms against the routed Trojans and comes right up to the walls, Zeus stirs the gods to go into battle to delay the swift advance of Achilles. "Now," he says, "with his rage inflamed for his friend's death, / I fear he'll raze the walls against the will of fate" (20.35–36).

"Against the will of fate. . . . " These lines so upset some ancient editors, men schooled in philosophy and especially the Stoic and Epicurean quarrels about fate and freedom that, in the interests of logical consistency, they tried to suppress the offending lines and substitute the following passage: "But it is not fated that the well-built city of Troy should be sacked in Achilles' lifetime. It will be taken by the wooden horse. . . ."

It is thought possible, then, in Homer's vision, that Achilles can somehow break the pattern; in fact he must be prevented. And Zeus can break it too. He laments the fate of Sarpedon—and is tempted to save him. But his consort Hera recalls him to a sense of duty.

> *"Do as you please, Zeus . . .*
> *but none of the deathless gods will ever praise you.*
> *And I tell you this—take it to heart, I urge you—*
> *if you send Sarpedon home, living still, beware!*
> *Then surely some other god will want to sweep*
> *his own son clear of the heavy fighting too.*
> *Look down. Many who battle round King Priam's*
> *mighty walls are sons of the deathless gods—*
> *you will inspire lethal anger in them all."*   (16.526–34)

And her argument prevails. Destiny could, theoretically, be defied, but only at the risk of chaos. Zeus lets Sarpedon go down to death.

The Olympian gods are a family like many a family on earth. It has an all-powerful, philandering father, who cannot be defied but may be deceived, a watchful, jealous and intriguing wife, and sons and daughters who vie for their parents' favor as they pursue their individual aims. These gods play their part in the poem, in close contact with the human beings. And gods and men, for Homer, are very much alike—in shape, in speech, even in motive, in passion, in forms of action. The most passionate of the gods involved in the struggle are Hera, the wife of Zeus, and Athena, his daughter; they hate Troy and the Trojans with a bitter, merciless hatred. We are not told why they nurse this savage hatred for the Trojans until Book 24, where the famous Judgment of Paris is mentioned (24.31–36 and note ad loc). It is typical of a certain school of thought about Homer that these lines, the only explicit mention of the Judgment of Paris in the *Iliad*, have been suspected as a later addition; the beauty contest of the goddesses is too frivolous a motif for the high tragedy of the poem. But this leaves the unsuccessful goddesses' raw hatred for Troy unexplained. It seems clear from the casual, almost cryptic, way Homer refers to the story that it was perfectly familiar to his audience, and Hera's motive for hating Troy, the insult to her beauty, is perfectly consonant with the picture of Hera as the jealous divine wife

Homer presents elsewhere in the *Iliad*—in her plot against Heracles, Zeus's child by a mortal woman (14.300–8), and her brutal assault on Artemis, Zeus's child by another goddess (21.557–66). Hell hath no fury like a goddess scorned. And this personal motive has its opposite side: the unfailing support given to the Trojans by the winner of the beauty contest, Aphrodite, and her intervention to save Paris from his fate at the hands of Menelaus (3.439–41).

The reasons for divine intervention are trivial, human, all too human. Yet these gods, imagined in the likeness of man in all his strength and weakness, but magnified in scale, are figures symbolic of those aspects of our lives that seem incomprehensible and uncontrollable. Athena prompts the archer Pandarus to shoot Menelaus (not that he did not want to) and so destroys what for a moment seemed a chance to end the war (4.99–159). Both sides, now Achilles is absent, want peace, but the war goes on. We too have seen and may see again similar situations, and when the catastrophe comes on us in spite of the universal desire to avoid it, we fall back on explanations that are perhaps more sophisticated but no more satisfactory: the irrationality of human nature, the will of history (Croce's phrase), the will of God or even pure accident—and in the last analysis these explanations are just as metaphysical as Homer's gods.

The gods intervene also in a more direct fashion: they sometimes take part in the fighting. They do so to protect human favorites or, on a grander scale, to instill courage and combat-fury into individual heroes and even whole armies, as Poseidon does (14.422–610) in defiance of Zeus's nonintervention order. This is not a modern way of looking at battle, but it is a striking way of expressing one of the mysteries of combat—the unpredictable currents of aggressive courage or faltering panic which sweep through armies, the mysterious factor known as morale. It is not a factor that can be fed into the computer (though that expert on the subject, Napoleon, said it was three times as important as matériel), and everyone who has been in battle knows how intangible and unpredictable it is, how hard-pressed, outgunned men can suddenly take the offensive and turn the tables, how victorious advancing units can develop an uneasiness about their flanks that can turn into panic. And in fact battle is always unpredictable. In the early years of the fifteenth century, as the English armies, masters of southern and central France in a hundred years' war, found themselves besieged and threatened by French troops they had beaten scores of times, who were now led by a peasant girl from Domrémy, men fell back on explanations no less unworldly than Homer's gods. Joan herself claimed that the

Archangel Michael had appeared and told her to kick the English out of France, *"bouter les Anglais hors de la France,"* and the English firmly believed that she was sent not by an angel but by the Devil, and burned her as a witch at Rouen. And historians still find it impossible to explain, in purely rational terms, how she could have accomplished what she did.

Sometimes, however, the Homeric gods do more than protect and encourage; they actually join in the fighting, usually against one another, though in Book 5 Ares kills a Greek warrior and is in his turn wounded by Diomedes, who has already wounded Aphrodite. When Zeus encourages them to join in the fighting, as Achilles comes out to attack the Trojans, gods fight against gods: Athena against Ares and Aphrodite, Hephaestus against the river-god Xanthus, Hera against Artemis. The only one of these contests that is treated with epic dignity is that between Hephaestus and Xanthus, fire against water, against the immense strength of the river that came close to drowning Achilles. But when Athena downs Ares with a stone and then punches Aphrodite in, of all places, the breasts, when Hera smiles as she boxes the ears of Artemis with her bow, no reaction other than laughter seems possible. These wounds heal quickly, and even if they did not, the gods are exempt from the ultimate consequence of action: they cannot lose their lives— no matter what they do; they will survive. And given this crucial difference between gods and men, only men can have true dignity on the battlefield; the presence of gods there is an impertinence. The immunity of the gods, who fight their mock battles while men stand and die, casts into higher relief the tragic situation of the men who risk and suffer not only pain and mutilation but the prospect, inevitable if the war goes on long enough, of death, of the total extinction of the individual personality.

The gods are immortal; they are not subject to time. They have all the time in the world. And so they are not subject to change, to the change brought by age, to the change brought by learning from suffering and a realization of limitations. They will always be what they are now and have always been; they are all the same at the end of the *Iliad* as at the beginning. They do not change, do not learn. How could they? They are the personification of those mysterious forces which through their often violent interaction produce the harsh patterns of human life— the rise and fall of nations, the destructiveness of the earthquake, the terror of the flood, the horrors of the plague, but also the sweetness of passionate love, the intoxication of wine, the extra strength that surges through a warrior's limbs at the moment of danger.

As personalities (and that is how Homer and the Greeks always saw them), they are very different from one another, but they have, besides immortality, one other thing in common—a furious self-absorption. Each one is a separate force which, never questioning or examining the nature of its own existence, moves blindly, ferociously, to the affirmation of its will in action. The Homeric god recognizes no authority outside itself—except superior force. How are arguments settled in heaven? Like this: "Obey my orders," says Zeus to Hera,

> "for fear the gods, however many Olympus holds,
> are powerless to protect you when I come
> to throttle you with my irresistible hands."   (1.681–83)

The other gods do not argue with Zeus, though they may try to trick him, as Hera does successfully (14.187–421), and he does not explain his will to them, he threatens and enforces. There are no moral questions involved, only the clash of wills, intent on manifesting their existence—whether by bringing Troy to destruction or by driving Helen back into bed with Paris, as in the strange scene where Aphrodite, in the shape of an old woman, acts the procuress. "Quickly—Paris is calling for you, come back home! / There he is in the bedroom, the bed with inlaid rings . . . " (3.450–51). Helen recognizes the goddess and resists her temptation: "Maddening one, my Goddess, oh what now? / Lusting to lure me to my ruin yet again?" (3.460–61). "Lusting" is not too strong a word; the mating of male and female is Aphrodite's very existence; that is why she is so stubborn to procure it. And she flares up in anger:

> "Don't provoke me—wretched, headstrong girl!
> Or in my immortal rage I may just toss you over,
> hate you as I adore you now—with a vengeance . . . "
>
>   So she threatened
> and Helen the daughter of mighty Zeus was terrified.   (3.480–86)

And well she might be. Helen has nothing but her beauty and the charm it casts on all men; without Aphrodite she would be nothing. And Aphrodite plays the same role on Olympus as on earth. She gives Hera, who wants to divert Zeus's attention from the battle so Poseidon can help the Achaeans,

> *the breastband,*
> *pierced and alluring, with every kind of enchantment*
> *woven through it . . . There is the heat of Love,*
> *the pulsing rush of Longing, the lover's whisper,*
> *irresistible—madness to make the sanest man go mad.*   (14.257–61)

Zeus in his sphere of power, Aphrodite in hers, are irresistible. To be a god is to be totally absorbed in the exercise of one's own power, the fulfillment of one's own nature, unchecked by any thought of others except as obstacles to be overcome; it is to be incapable of self-questioning or self-criticism. But there are human beings who are like this. Preeminent in their particular sphere of power, they impose their will on others with the confidence, the unquestioning certainty of their own right and worth that is characteristic of gods. Such people the Greeks called "heroes"; they recognized the fact that they transcended the norms of humanity by according them worship at their tombs after death. Heroes might be, usually were, violent, antisocial, destructive, but they offered an assurance that in some chosen vessels humanity is capable of superhuman greatness, that there are some human beings who can deny the imperatives which others obey in order to live.

The heroes are godlike in their passionate self-esteem. But they are not gods, not immortal. They are subject, like the rest of us, to failure, above all to the irremediable failure of death. And sooner or later, in suffering, in disaster, they come to realize their limits, accept mortality and establish (or reestablish) a human relationship with their fellowmen. This pattern, recurrent in the myths of the Greeks and later to be the model for some of the greatest Athenian tragedies, is first given artistic form in the *Iliad*.

ACHILLES

There are in the poem two human beings who are godlike, Achilles and Helen. One of them, Helen, the cause of the war, is so preeminent in her sphere, so far beyond competition in her beauty, her power to enchant men, that she is a sort of human Aphrodite. In her own element she is irresistible. Every king in Greece was ready to fight for her hand in marriage, but she chose Menelaus, king of Sparta. When Paris, the prince of Troy, came to visit, she ran off with him, leaving husband and daughter, without a thought of the consequences for others. Her willful action is the cause of all the deaths at Troy, those past and those to come. When she left with Paris she acted like a god, with no thought of anything but the fulfillment of her own desire, the exercise of her own nature. But when the *Iliad* opens she has already come to realize the meaning for others of her actions, to recognize that she is a human being. She criticizes herself harshly as she speaks to Priam:

> *"if only death had pleased me then, grim death,*
> *that day I followed your son to Troy, forsaking*
> *my marriage bed, my kinsmen and my child . . . "*   (3.209–11)

She feels responsible for the human misery she sees all around her, something the gods never do. When Zeus and Hera settle their quarrel about the fate of Troy (4.28–79), Zeus gives way but claims her acquiescence whenever he in his turn may wish to destroy a city. Not only does she accept, she actually offers him three cities, those she loves best: Argos, Sparta and Mycenae. That is how the fate of nations is decided. Human suffering counts for nothing in the settlement of divine differences. The gods feel no responsibility for the human victims of their private wars. But Helen has come at last to a full realization of the suffering she has caused; too late to undo it, but at least she can see herself in the context of humankind and shudder at her own responsibility. "My dear brother," she says to Hector,

> *"dear to me, bitch that I am, vicious, scheming—*
> *horror to freeze the heart! Oh how I wish*
> *that first day my mother brought me into the light*
> *some black whirlwind had rushed me out to the mountains*
> *or into the surf where the roaring breakers crash and drag*
> *and the waves had swept me off before all this had happened!"* (6.408–13)

This acceptance of responsibility accounts for her resistance when the goddess Aphrodite urged her to go to bed with Paris; in that scene she fell below the level of divine indifference—as from the human point of view she rose above it. She has ceased to be a mere existence, an unchanging blind self. She has become human and can feel the sorrow, the regret, that no human being escapes.

At the beginning of the *Iliad* Helen has already broken out of the prison of self-absorption, but this is the point at which Achilles enters it. The *Iliad* shows us the origin, course and consequences of his rage, his imprisonment in a godlike, lonely, heroic fury from which all the rest of the world is excluded, and also his return to human stature. The road to this final release is long and grim, strewn with the corpses of many a Greek and Trojan, and it leads finally to his own death.

There are, of course, objections that may be made to such a view of Achilles as a tragic hero, a fully created character whose motives and action form an intelligible unity. Prominent among them are the contradictions and inconsistencies in Achilles' reactions to events that many critics claim to detect in the text of the poem. These are telltale signs, according to one school, of oral improvisation under the pressure of performance; the result, according to another, of later editorial activity. It may be, however, that the critics have underestimated the elegance and sophistication of Homer's narrative technique (a constant danger for those who persist in thinking of him purely in terms of oral composition). In his creation of character Homer spares us the rich, sometimes superfluous, detail we have come to associate with that word in modern fiction; he gives us only what is necessary to his purpose. Similarly, in his presentation of motivation, he is economical in the extreme. In those sections of the poem where personal relationships and motives are important—the debate in Book 1, the embassy in Book 9, the meeting of Achilles and Priam in Book 24—Homer's method is dramatic rather than epic. The proportion of direct speech to narrative is such that these scenes, the embassy in particular, could be performed by actors, and as is clear from Plato's dialogue *Ion*, the later rhapsodes who gave Homeric recitations exploited the dramatic potential of Homer's text to the full. Like a dramatist, Homer shows us character and motivation not by editorial explanation but through speech and action. And he also invokes the response of an audience familiar with heroic poetry and formulaic diction, counting on their capacity to recognize significant omissions, contrasts, variations and juxtapositions. We are not told what is going on in the mind of his characters; we are shown. Homer, like the god Apollo at Delphi in Heraclitus' famous phrase, does not say, nor does he conceal—he indicates.

Achilles plays no part in the events described in Books 2 through 8; he sits by his ships on the shore, waiting for the fulfillment of his mother's promise. And by the end of Book 8, the supplication of Thetis and the will of Zeus have begun to produce results. The Greeks are in retreat, penned up in their hastily fortified camp at nightfall, awaiting the Trojan assault, which will come with daybreak. And Agamemnon yields to Nestor's advice to send an embassy to Achilles, urging him to return to the battle line. He admits that he was wrong and proposes to make amends:

> *"Mad, blind I was!*
> *Not even I would deny it . . .*
> *But since I was blinded, lost in my own inhuman rage,*
> *now, at last, I am bent on setting things to rights:*
> *I'll give a priceless ransom paid for friendship."*   (9.138–45)

In a bravura passage, he details the priceless ransom. Not only will he return Briseis and swear an oath that he has never touched her, he will give Achilles lavish gifts—gold, horses and women among them. He will also offer him the hand of one of his three daughters, with seven cities as her dowry.

It is a magnificent offer, but there is one thing missing: Agamemnon offers no apology to Achilles, no admission that he was in the wrong. Quite the contrary. His initial confession that he was mad is effectively canceled out by the way he ends:

> *"Let him submit to me! . . .*
> *Let him bow down to me! I am the greater king,*
> *I am the elder-born, I claim—the greater man."*   (9.189–93)

This is a harsh summons to obedience. The word translated "submit" is a passive form, *dmêthêto*, of the verb *damadzô*, which means "tame," "subdue." It is a word the Homeric poems use of the taming of wild asses, the taming of a bride by a man, of the subjection of a people to a ruler, of a beaten warrior to the victor. Agamemnon will still not recognize Achilles' claim to honor as predominant in battle; in fact these words reveal that the splendid gifts reflect honor on Agamemnon rather than Achilles. They are the enormous bounty a ruler can, if he wishes, bestow on a subject, and will do so only if the subject recognizes his place.

Once the ambassadors arrive, Odysseus describes the plight of the Achaeans, begs Achilles to relent and then launches into the recital of the magnificent gifts Agamemnon offers in recompense. The whole of the long recital, rich in detail and rising in intensity throughout, is repeated almost verbatim from Agamemnon's speech; the audience relished a repeat of such a virtuoso passage—this is one of the pleasures of oral poetry in performance. But this is no mere oral poet repeating mechanically, no mere servant of the tradition. We are suddenly reminded that Odysseus' speech is not just a welcome reprise of Agamemnon's brilliant catalogue of gifts—it is a speech of a wily ambassador in a delicate situation. Odysseus cuts short the repetition of Agamemnon's speech with the line "All this— / I would extend to him if he will end his anger" (9.187–88). And we remember what came next, what Odysseus has suppressed: "Let him submit to me!" (189).

Achilles' reply is a long, passionate outburst; he pours out all the resentment stored up so long in his heart. He rejects out of hand this embassy and any other that may be sent; he wants to hear no more speeches. Not for Agamemnon nor for the Achaeans either will he fight again. He is going home, with all his men and ships. As for Agamemnon's gifts,

> "I loathe his gifts . . .
> I wouldn't give you a splinter for that man!
> Not if he gave me ten times as much, twenty times over, all
> he possesses now, and all that could pour in from the world's end—
> not all the wealth that's freighted into Orchomenos, even into Thebes,
> Egyptian Thebes where the houses overflow with the greatest troves
>   of treasure . . .
> no, not if his gifts outnumbered all the grains of sand
> and dust in the earth—no, not even then could Agamemnon
> bring my fighting spirit round until he pays me back,
> pays full measure for all his heartbreaking outrage!"   (9.462–73)

"Pays full measure for all his heartbreaking outrage"—this is the point. Achilles is a killer, the personification of martial violence, but there is one area in which his sensibilities are more finely tuned than the antennae of a radar scanner—that of honor among men. And he senses the truth. Odysseus did not report Agamemnon's insulting demand for submission, but Achilles is not deceived. In all Odysseus did say there was no hint that Agamemnon regretted his action, no semblance of an apology, nothing that "pays full measure for all his heartbreaking outrage." Seen in this context, the gifts are no gifts, they are an insult. Gold, horses, women—he has no need of such bribes. And the offer of Agamemnon's daughter is that of an overlord to a subject; without an apology, an admission of equal status, it is one more symbol of subordination. His father will find him a bride at home; he will live there in peace, live out his life, choose the other destiny his goddess mother told him he carried toward the day of his death:

> "If I voyage back to the fatherland I love,
> my pride, my glory dies . . .
> true, but the life that's left me will be long . . . "   (9.502–4)

This speech of Achilles is sometimes seen as a repudiation of the heroic ideal, a realization that the life and death dedicated to glory is a game not worth the candle.

> *"Cattle and fat sheep can all be had for the raiding,*
> *tripods all for the trading, and tawny-headed stallions.*
> *But a man's life breath cannot come back again—*
> *no raiders in force, no trading brings it back,*
> *once it slips through a man's clenched teeth."*   (9.493–97)

These are indeed strange words for Achilles, but in the context of the speech as a whole they are not inconsistent with his devotion to honor. It is the loss of that honor, of recognition as the supreme arbiter of the war, which has driven him to these formulations and reflections. He would still be ready to choose the other destiny, a short life with glory, if that glory had not been taken away from him by Agamemnon, and were not even now, in the absence of an apology, withheld.

In the face of this passionate rejection there is nothing Odysseus can say. It is Phoenix, Achilles' tutor and guardian from the days of his boyhood, who now takes up the burden. In the name of that relationship he asks Achilles to relent. Even the gods, he says, can be moved, by prayer and supplication. He goes on to describe the spirits of Prayer, "daughters of mighty Zeus." *Litai* is the Greek word, and "prayer" is not an exact translation, for the English word has lost some of its original sense of "supplication"—the root sense of the Greek. These "Prayers for forgiveness" are humble and embarrassed—"they limp and halt,/ . . . can't look you in the eyes" (9.609–12). Their attitude represents the embarrassment of the man who must apologize for his former insolence: it is hard for him to humble himself; it affects even his outward semblance. But he makes the effort, and the Prayers, the entreaties, come to repair the damage done by *Atê*, the madness of self-delusion and the ruin it produces—they must not be refused.

But this appeal, too, will fall on deaf ears. And with some justice. Apollo relented in Book 1, but only after full restitution was made and a handsome apology—"Prayers for forgiveness." And where are the prayers, the embarrassed pleas of Agamemnon? The madness of Agamemnon is all too plain, but Achilles has seen no prayers from him— only from Odysseus, and then from Phoenix. Who now tries again, with an example of another hero, Meleager, who relented, but too late: a prophetic paradigm in the framework of the poem. He, too, withdrew from the fighting in anger, endangered his city, refused entreaties of his fellow citizens and even of his father, refused the gifts they offered him, and finally, when the enemy had set fire to the city, yielded to the entreaties of his wife and returned to the battle. But the gifts he had spurned were not offered again. You in your turn, Phoenix is saying, will someday relent, if Hector drives the Achaeans back on their ships, but if so, you will fight without the gifts that are the visible symbols of honor, the concrete expression of the army's appreciation of valor. Phoenix is talking Achilles' language now, and it has its effect: Achilles admits that he finds Phoenix' appeal disturbing—"Stop confusing / my fixed resolve with this, this weeping and wailing" (9.745–46). And he speaks now not of leaving the next day but of remaining by the ships and ends by announcing that the decision, to stay or to leave, will be taken on the morrow.

Ajax, the last to speak, does not mention Agamemnon but dwells on the army's respect and affection for Achilles. It is the plea of a great, if simple, man and again Achilles is moved. Though he still feels nothing but hate for Agamemnon, he now decides that he will stay at Troy. But he will not fight until

> " . . . the son of wise King Priam, dazzling Hector
> batters all the way to the Myrmidon ships and shelters,
> slaughtering Argives, gutting the hulls with fire."
> (9.796–98)

Since his ships, as we have been told, are drawn up on the far flank of the beachhead, this is small comfort for Agamemnon; the embassy is a failure.

The battle resumes, and Zeus fulfills his promise to Thetis: Hector and the Trojans drive the Achaeans back on their ships. The main Achaean fighters—Agamemnon, Diomedes and Odysseus—are wounded and retire from the melee. Achilles, watching all this from his tent, sends Patroclus off to inquire about another wounded man who has been brought back to the ships, Machaon, the physician of the Greek army. And he revels in the setbacks of the Achaeans. "Now," he says, "I think they will grovel at my knees, / our Achaean comrades begging for their lives" (11.719–20). This passage is of course one of the mainstays of those who wish to attribute Book 9 to a later poet: it seems to them to show ignorance of the embassy to Achilles. But this is because they take it that Agamemnon's offer of gifts was a fully adequate satisfaction; Grote (the most eloquent champion of this view) even speaks

of "the outpouring of profound humiliation" by the Greeks and from
Agamemnon especially. But as we have seen, Odysseus' speech to
Achilles contained not the slightest hint of apology on Agamemnon's
part, and certainly nothing like what Achilles demands—that Agamem-
non pay "full measure for all his heartbreaking outrage." There was no
supplication made on behalf of Agamemnon; Phoenix' mention of the
Litai that come humbly and embarrassed to beg favor only underscored
the point. Now, says Achilles, now they are beginning to feel the pinch,
they will fall at my knees, in the suppliant position of abject prostration,
a confession of utter weakness and dependence.

Patroclus comes back from the tents of the Achaeans with news of
Machaon's wound and with a purpose: Nestor has primed him to ask
Achilles, if he will not fight himself, to send Patroclus out in his armor.
What Achilles now hears from Patroclus is the kind of balm for his
wounded pride that he had hardly dared to hope for. Not only is Hector
at the ships but:

> *"There's powerful Diomedes brought down by an archer,*
> *Odysseus wounded, and Agamemnon too, the famous spearman,*
> *and Eurypylus took an arrow-shot in the thigh . . . "*   (16.28–30)

This should be enough to satisfy even Achilles: no more dramatic proof
of his superiority in battle could be imagined. And he begins to relent.
Though he is still resentful of Agamemnon's treatment of him, "Let
bygones be bygones now. Done is done. / How on earth can a man rage
on forever?" (16.69–70). He is willing to save the Achaeans, now that
they are suitably punished for the wrong they did him. Why, then, does
he not go into battle himself? He tells us:

> *"Still, by god, I said I would not relax my anger,*
> *not till the cries and carnage reached my own ships.*
> *So you, you strap my splendid armor on your back,*
> *you lead our battle-hungry Myrmidons into action!—"*   (16.71–74)

But Patroclus is not to go too far. He is to drive the Trojans back from
the ships, no more: above all, he is not to assault Troy. He is to win
glory for Achilles by beating off the Trojan attack, and then "they'll
send her back, my lithe and lovely girl, / and top it off with troves of
glittering gifts" (16.99–100). Unlike the Meleager in Phoenix' caution-
ary tale, he will receive the gifts once offered and refused, even though
he does not join the fighting himself.

All through this speech confused emotions are at war within him. What does he really want? He talks of the restitution of Briseis and gifts, the compensation offered and refused before. He talks of "the beloved day of our return" (16.95). Perhaps he does not know himself at this moment. But at the end of the speech there comes out of him the true expression of the godlike self-absorption in which he is still imprisoned.

> "Oh would to god—Father Zeus, Athena and lord Apollo—
> not one of all these Trojans could flee his death, not one,
> no Argive either, but we could stride from the slaughter
> so we could bring Troy's hallowed crown of towers
> toppling down around us—you and I alone!"   (16.115–19)

Clearly what he really wishes for is a world containing nothing but himself and his own glory, for Patroclus, whom he now sends out in his own armor, he regards as a part of himself. This solipsistic dream of glory—"everybody dead but us two," as a scandalized ancient commentator summarized it—so offended the great Alexandrian scholar Zenodotus that he condemned the lines as the work of an interpolator who wished to inject into the *Iliad* the later Greek idea (for which the text gives no warrant) that Achilles and Patroclus were lovers.

All too soon the news comes from the battlefield: Patroclus is dead and the armies are fighting over his corpse. Achilles will return to the battle now, to avenge his friend; he sees the death of Patroclus as the fatal consequence of his quarrel with Agamemnon and wishes that "strife could die from the lives of gods and men" (18.126). He will make peace with Agamemnon. "Enough. / Let bygones be bygones. Done is done" (18.131–32). But this is not regret or self-criticism: he is still angry. "Despite my anguish I will beat it down, / the fury mounting inside me, down by force" (18.133–34). But he is angrier still with Hector. "Now I'll go and meet that murderer head-on, / that Hector who destroyed the dearest life I know" (18.135–36). His mother has just told him that his death is fated to come soon after Hector's, and though deeply disturbed by this news, he accepts his fate. Not to avenge Patroclus by killing Hector would be a renunciation of all that he stands for and has lived by, the attainment of glory, of the universal recognition that there is "no man my equal among the bronze-armed Achaeans" (18.124).

He cannot go into battle at once, for he has no armor; his father's panoply has been stripped from the corpse of Patroclus. Hector wears it now. Thetis goes off to have the god Hephaestus make new armor for her son, and when she brings it he summons an assembly of the

Achaeans, as he had done at the very beginning of the poem. The wounded kings, Odysseus, Diomedes, Agamemnon, their wounds testimony to Achilles' supremacy in combat, come to hear him. His address is short. He regrets the quarrel with Agamemnon and its results. He is still angry—that emerges clearly from his words—but he will curb his anger: he has a greater cause for anger now. He calls for an immediate general attack on the Trojan ranks, which are still marshaled outside the city walls, on the level ground.

Agamemnon's reply to Achilles' short, impatient speech is long and elaborate. It is, in fact, an excuse. Achilles has come as close as he ever could to saying that he was wrong, but Agamemnon, even now, tries to justify himself as he addresses not only Achilles but also the army as a whole, which, as he is fully aware, blames him for the Achaean losses. His opening lines are an extraordinary appeal to the assembly for an orderly reception of his speech: "when a man stands up to speak, it's well to listen. / Not to interrupt him, the only courteous thing" (19.91–92). He disclaims responsibility for his action.

> ". . . I am not to blame!
> *Zeus and Fate and the Fury stalking through the night,*
> they *are the ones who drove that savage madness in my heart . . ."*
> (19.100–2)

He is the victim, he claims, of *Atê*, the madness of self-delusion and the ruin it produces. "I *was* blinded," he says, "and Zeus stole my wits . . . " (19.163). He is talking now to a full assembly of the Achaeans, which includes

> *Even those who'd kept to the beached ships till now,*
> *the helmsmen who handled the heavy steering-oars*
> *and stewards left on board to deal out rations—* (19.48–50)

At the council of the kings, when the embassy to Achilles was decided on, he had spoken more frankly: "Mad, blind I was! / Not even *I* would deny it" (9.138–39). He does not make so honest an admission of responsibility here. And now he promises to deliver the gifts that were offered and refused, and to restore Briseis and swear a great oath that he has not touched her.

To all this, Achilles is utterly indifferent. He shows no interest in Agamemnon's excuses or in the gifts: clearly he feels that this is all a waste of time. He has only one thing on his mind: Hector. And he urges immediate resumption of the fighting. He is talking of sending back into combat men who are many of them wounded, all of them tired, hungry, thirsty. Odysseus reminds him of the facts of life. "No fighter can battle all day long, cut-and-thrust / till the sun goes down, if he is starved for food" (19.193–94). Odysseus suggests not only time for the army to rest and feed, but also a public ceremony of reconciliation: the acceptance of Agamemnon's gifts, the swearing of the oath about Briseis. Agamemnon approves the advice and gives orders to prepare a feast. But Achilles' reply is brusque and uncompromising. He is not interested in ceremonies of reconciliation which will serve to restore Agamemnon's prestige; he is not interested in Agamemnon's excuses, still less in food; he thinks of one thing and one thing only: Hector. He is for battle now, and food at sunset, after the day's work. The corpse of Patroclus makes it impossible for him to eat or drink before Hector's death avenges Patroclus and reestablishes Achilles' identity as the unchallengeable, unconquerable violence of war personified:

> "You talk of food?
> I have no taste for food—what I really crave
> is slaughter and blood and the choking groans of men!"   (19.253–55)

Achilles' outburst is inhuman—godlike, in fact. But the others are men, and Odysseus reminds him what it is to be human.

> ". . . We must steel our hearts. Bury our dead,
> with tears for the day they die, not one day more.
> And all those left alive, after the hateful carnage,
> remember food and drink—"
>   (19.271–74)

Human beings must put limits to their sorrow, their passions; they must recognize the animal need for food and drink. But not Achilles. He will not eat while Hector still lives. And as if to point up the godlike nature of his passionate intensity, Homer has Athena sustain him, without his knowledge, on nectar and ambrosia, the food of the gods.

When he does go into battle, the Trojans turn and run for the gates; only Hector remains outside. And the two champions come face-to-face at last. Hector offers a pact to Achilles, the same pact he has made before the formal duel with Ajax in Book 7—the winner to take his opponent's armor but give his body to his fellow soldiers for burial. The offer is harshly refused. This is no formal duel, and Achilles is no Ajax; he is hardly even human: he is godlike, both greater and lesser than a man.

The contrast between the raw, self-absorbed fury of Achilles and the civilized responsibility and restraint of Hector is maintained to the end. It is of his people, the Trojans, that Hector is thinking as he throws his spear at Achilles: "How much lighter the war would be for Trojans then / if you, their greatest scourge, were dead and gone!" (22.339–40). But it is Hector who dies, and as Achilles exults over his fallen enemy, his words bring home again the fact that he is fighting for himself alone; this is the satisfaction of a personal hatred. The reconciliation with Agamemnon and the Greeks was a mere formality to him, and he is still cut off from humanity, a prisoner of his self-esteem, his obsession with honor—the imposition of his identity on all men and all things.

> *"Hector—surely you thought when you stripped Patroclus' armor*
> *that you, you would be safe! Never a fear of me,*
> *far from the fighting as I was—you fool!*
> *Left behind there, down by the beaked ships*
> *his great avenger waited, a greater man by far—*
> *that man was I . . . "*   (22.390–95)

He taunts Hector with the fate of his body. "The dogs and birds will maul you, shame your corpse / while Achaeans bury my dear friend in glory!" (22.397–98). And in answer to Hector's plea and offer of ransom for his corpse, he reveals the extreme of inhuman hatred and fury he has reached:

> *"Beg no more, you fawning dog—begging me by my parents!*
> *Would to god my rage, my fury would drive me now*
> *to hack your flesh away and eat you raw—"*   (22.407–9)

This is how the gods hate. His words recall those of Zeus to Hera in Book 4:

> *"Only if you could breach*
> *their gates and their long walls and devour Priam*
> *and Priam's sons and the Trojan armies raw—*
> *then you just might cure your rage at last."*   (4.39–42)

And as Achilles goes on we recognize the tone, the words, the phrases:

> *"No man alive could keep the dog-packs off you,*
> *not if they haul in ten, twenty times that ransom*

and pile it here before me and promise fortunes more—
no, not even if Dardan Priam should offer to weigh out
your bulk in gold! Not even then . . . ''

(22.411–15)

We have heard this before, when he refused the gifts of Agamemnon:

''Not if he gave me ten times as much, twenty times over, all
he possesses now, and all that could pour in from the world's end—. . .
no, not if his gifts outnumbered all the grains of sand
and dust in the earth—no, not even then . . . ''

(9.464–71)

It is the same rage now as then, implacable, unappeasable, like the rage of Hera and Athena—only its object has changed.

Achilles lashes Hector's body to his chariot and, in full view of the Trojans on the walls, drags it to his tent, where he organizes a magnificent funeral for Patroclus. After the burning of the pyre, the hero's memory is celebrated with funeral games—contests, simulated combat, in honor of a fallen warrior. Such was the origin, the Greeks believed, of all the great games—the Olympian, the Pythian, the Isthmian, the Nemean Games, and in Homer himself we hear of funeral games for Amarynceus of Elis and for Oedipus of Thebes. The honor paid to the dead man is marked by the richness of the prizes and the efforts of the contestants. Here the prizes are offered by Achilles, so he himself does not compete. There are to be many contests: a chariot race (which earns the longest and most elaborate description), a boxing match, wrestling, a foot race; after that a fight in full armor, weight throwing and an archery contest. As the events are described we see all the great Achaean heroes, familiar to us from battle-scenes, locked now not in combat but in the fierce effort of peaceful contest. Homer takes our minds away from the grim work of war and the horror of Achilles' degradation of Hector's corpse to show us a series of brilliant characterizations of his heroes in new situations. But the most striking feature of this account of the games is the behavior of Achilles. This seems to be a different man. It is the great Achilles of the later aristocratic tradition, the man of princely courtesy and innate nobility visible in every aspect of his bearing and conduct, the Achilles who was raised by the centaur Chiron. It is a vision of what Achilles might have been in peace, if peace had been a possibility in the heroic world, or, for that matter, in Homer's world. "The man," says Aristotle in the *Politics*, "who is incapable of working in common, or who in his self-sufficiency has no need of others, is no part of the community, like a beast, or a god." As far as his fellow Achaeans are concerned, Achilles has broken out of the self-imposed prison of godlike unrelenting fury, reintegrated himself in society, returned to something like human feeling; he is part of the community again.

All through the games he acts with a tact, diplomacy and generosity that seem to signal the end of his desperate isolation, his godlike self-absorption; we almost forget that Hector's corpse is still lying in the dust, tied to his chariot. But if we had forgotten we are soon reminded. Once the games are over, Achilles, weeping whenever he remembers Patroclus—"his gallant heart— / What rough campaigns they'd fought to an end together" (24.8-9)—drags Hector's corpse three times around Patroclus' tomb. But Apollo wards off corruption from the body, and on Olympus the gods are filled with compassion for Hector: all the gods, that is, except Hera, Athena and Poseidon—a formidable combination. Apollo (the champion of Troy as the other three are its enemies) speaks up for action to rescue Hector's body. For him, Achilles is the lower extreme of Aristotle's alternatives—a beast:

> "—like some lion
> going his own barbaric way, giving in to his power,
> his brute force and wild pride . . . "   (24.48-50)

Hera, on the other hand, sees him as closer to the other alternative—a god: "Achilles sprang from a goddess—one I reared myself" (24.71). So Zeus makes a decision designed to satisfy both sides: Thetis is to tell Achilles to surrender Hector's body to Priam, but Priam is to come as suppliant to Achilles' tents, bringing a sign of honor, a rich ransom.

When Thetis conveys to Achilles the will of Zeus, his attitude is exactly the same as his reaction to Agamemnon's renewed offer of gifts after the death of Patroclus—cold indifference. He agrees to accept the ransom, but his speech shows no relenting; his heart is still of iron. What is needed to break the walls down, to restore him to full humanity, is the arrival in his tent not of the herald, whom he evidently expected to bring the ransom, but of Priam himself, alone, a suppliant in the night. And that unforeseen confrontation is what Zeus now moves to bring about.

The god Hermes guides Priam safely through the Achaean sentries and through the gate that bars the entrance to Achilles' courtyard; Priam takes Achilles by surprise as he sits at table, his meal just finished. His appearance, unannounced, is a mystery, a thing unprecedented, and Achilles is astonished. Homer expresses that astonishment by means of a simile, one of the most disconcerting of the whole poem:

> *as when the grip of madness seizes one*
> *who murders a man in his own fatherland and flees*
> *abroad to foreign shores, to a wealthy, noble host,*
> *and a sense of marvel runs through all who see him . . .*　　(24.563–66)

It seems to reverse the situation, as if Priam, not Achilles, were the killer. And yet it is carefully chosen. For Achilles, a child of the quarrelsome, violent society of the Achaeans we know so well from the bitter feuds of the camp, from old Nestor's tales of cattle raids, ambush and border war, from the tales of Achaean suppliants fleeing their homeland with blood on their hands—for Achilles, the appearance of a distinguished stranger and his gesture of supplication evoke the familiar context of the man of violence seeking shelter. Achilles cannot imagine the truth. And now Priam tells him who he is—but not at once. First he invokes the memory of Achilles' father—pining at home for a son he may never see again. And then he reveals his identity and makes his plea. It ends with the tragic and famous lines: "I have endured what no one on earth has ever done before— / I put to my lips the hands of the man who killed my son" (24.590–91).

And Achilles begins to break out at last from the prison of self-absorbed, godlike passion; "like the gods," Priam called him, but that is the last time this line-end formula (exclusive to Achilles) appears. He will move now to man's central position between beast and god. But the change is not sudden. The stages in his return to human feelings are presented with masterly psychological insight. Achilles took the old man's hands and pushed him "gently," says Homer, away, and wept. Not for Priam but for his own aged father, to whose memory Priam had appealed and who will soon, like Priam, lose a son. He raises Priam to his feet and sits him in a chair, and speaks to him in awed admiration: "What daring," he asks, "brought you down to the ships, all alone . . . ?" (24.606). It was indeed an action calling for the kind of extraordinary courage that is Achilles' own preeminent quality. He comforts the old man, with what small comfort mortals can take for their lot. From his two urns of good and evil, Zeus dispenses now evil, now evil mixed with good. So it was with Peleus, Achilles' own father, who had great honor and possessions. But then:

"only a single son he fathered, doomed at birth,
cut off in the spring of life—
and I, I give the man no care as he grows old
since here I sit in Troy, far from my fatherland,
a grief to you, a grief to all your children."   (24.630–34)

That last phrase is a new view of the war; he sees it now from Priam's point of view. And moves on from pity for his own father to pity for the bereaved king of Troy. "And you too, old man, we hear you prospered once . . . / But then the gods of heaven brought this agony on you—" (24.635–40). This is a new way of thinking for Achilles; he sees himself as another man must see him—as he must appear to the father of his enemy, Hector.

He tells Priam to bear up and endure, but the old man, his moment of danger past, his end accomplished, grows impatient and asks for Hector's body at once. Suddenly we are shown that the newfound emotions have only a precarious existence in Achilles' heart; at any moment they may be overwhelmed by a return of his anger, his self-centered rage. He knows this himself and warns Priam not to go too fast; he knows how tenuous a hold his new mood has:

"No more, old man, don't tempt my wrath, not now!
. . . Don't stir my raging heart still more.
Or under my own roof I may not spare your life, old man—
suppliant that you are . . ."   (24.656–69)

Achilles goes to collect the ransom, and when he orders Hector's body to be washed and anointed, he gives orders to have it done out of Priam's sight:

He feared that, overwhelmed by the sight of Hector,
wild with grief, Priam might let his anger flare
and Achilles might fly into fresh rage himself,
cut the old man down . . .   (24.684–87)

He knows himself. This is a new Achilles, who can feel pity for others, see deep into their hearts and into his own. For the first time he shows self-knowledge and acts to prevent the calamity his violent temper might bring about. It is as near to self-criticism as he ever gets, but it marks the point at which he ceases to be godlike Achilles and becomes a human being in the full sense of the word.

He tells Priam Hector's body is ready. And offers him food. It will be Priam's first meal since his son's death. And he speaks to Priam as Odysseus had spoken to Achilles before the battle: there must be a limit to mourning for the dead; men must eat and go on with their lives.

> "Now, at last, let us turn our thoughts to supper.
> Even Niobe with her lustrous hair remembered food,
> though she saw a dozen children killed in her own halls . . .
> Nine days they lay in their blood . . .
> then on the tenth . . .
> . . . Niobe, gaunt, worn to the bone with weeping,
> turned her thoughts to food."
>
> (24.707–22)

It is an admission of mortality, of limitations, of the bond that unites him to Priam, and all men.

He has a bed made for Priam outside the tent, for any Achaean coming into the tent and seeing Priam would tell Agamemnon. Achilles assumes the role of the old king's protector; even in his newfound humanity he is still a man alone—his sense of honor will not allow him to let Priam fall into the Achaeans' hands. And he promises to hold off the fighting for the twelve days Priam needs for the funeral of Hector. He has come at last to the level of humanity, and humanity at its best; he has forgotten himself and his wrongs in his sympathy for another man. It is late; only just in time, for when the fighting resumes, he will fall in turn, as his mother told him and as Hector prophesied with his dying breath. The poem ends with the funeral of Hector. But this is the signal for the resumption of the fighting. The first line of the poem gave us the name of Achilles, and its last line reminds us of him, for his death will come soon, as the fighting resumes. The poem ends, as it began, on the eve of battle.

The tragic course of Achilles' rage, his final recognition of human values—this is the guiding theme of the poem, and it is developed against a background of violence and death. But the grim progress of the war is interrupted by scenes which remind us that the brutality of war, though an integral part of human life, is not the whole of it. Except for Achilles, whose worship of violence falters only in the final moment of pity for Priam, the yearning for peace and its creative possibilities is never far below the surface of the warriors' minds. This is most poignantly expressed by the scenes that take place in Troy, especially the farewell scene between Hector and Andromache, but the warriors' dream of peace is projected over and over again in the elaborate similes, those comparisons with which Homer varies the grim details of the bloodletting, and which achieve the paradoxical effect of making the particulars of destructive violence familiar by drawing for illustration on the peaceful, ordinary activities of everyday life. Dead men and armor are trampled under the wheels of Achilles' chariot as white barley is crushed under the hoofs of oxen on a threshing floor (20.559–67); hostile forces advancing against each other are like two lines of reapers in the wheat or barley field of a rich man, cutting their way forward (11.76–82); the two fronts in tense deadlock at the Achaean wall hold even like the scales held by a widow, working for a pitiful wage, as she weighs out her wool (12.502–5); the combatants fighting for possession of Sarpedon's corpse swarm over it like flies over the brimming milk buckets in spring (16.745–47); Menelaus bestrides the body of Patroclus as a lowing cow stands protectively over its first-born calf (17.3–6); Ajax is forced back step by step like a stubborn donkey driven out of a cornfield by boys who beat him with sticks (11.653–62). These vivid pictures of normal life, drawn with consummate skill and inserted in a relentless series of gruesome killings, have a special poignancy; they are one of the features of Homer's evocation of battle which make it unique: an exquisite balance between the celebration of war's tragic, heroic values and those creative values of civilized life that war destroys.

These two poles of the human condition, war and peace, with their corresponding aspects of human nature, the destructive and creative, are implicit in every situation and statement of the poem, and they are put before us, in something approaching abstract form, on the shield which the god Hephaestus has made for Achilles. Its emblem is an image of human life as a whole. Here are two cities, one at peace and one at war. In one a marriage is celebrated and a quarrel settled by process of law; the other is besieged by a hostile army and fights for its existence. Scenes of violence—peaceful shepherds slaughtered in an ambush, Death dragging away a corpse by its foot—are balanced by scenes of plowing, harvesting, work in the vineyard and on the pasture, a green on which youths and maidens dance. War has its place on the shield, but it is the lesser one; most of the surface is covered with scenes of peaceful life—the pride of the tilled land, wide and triple-plowed, the laborers reaping with sharp sickles in their hands, a great vineyard heavy with grape clusters, young girls and young men carrying the sweet fruit away in baskets, a large meadow in a lovely valley for the sheep flocks, and, above all, the dance, that formal symbol of the precise and ordered relations of people in peaceful society.

Here young boys and girls, beauties courted
with costly gifts of oxen, danced and danced,
linking their arms, gripping each other's wrists.
And the girls wore robes of linen light and flowing,
the boys wore finespun tunics rubbed with a gloss of oil,
the girls were crowned with a bloom of fresh garlands,
the boys swung golden daggers hung on silver belts.
And now they would run in rings on their skilled feet,
nimbly, quick as a crouching potter spins his wheel,
palming it smoothly, giving it practice twirls
to see it run, and now they would run in rows,
in rows crisscrossing rows—rapturous dancing.
A breathless crowd stood round them struck with joy
and through them a pair of tumblers dashed and sprang,
whirling in leaping handsprings, leading out the dance.   (18.693–707)

And all around the outermost rim of the shield the god who made it set the great stream of the Ocean River, the river that is at once the frontier of the known and imagined worlds and the barrier between the quick and the dead.

The imbalance of these scenes on the shield of Achilles shows us the total background of the carnage of the war; it provides a frame which gives the rage of Achilles and the death of Hector a true perspective. But it is not enough. The *Iliad* remains a terrifying poem. Achilles, just before his death, is redeemed as a human being, but there is no consolation for the death of Hector. We are left with a sense of waste, which is not adequately balanced even by the greatness of the heroic figures and the action; the scale descends toward loss. The *Iliad* remains not only the greatest epic poem in literature but also the most tragic.

Homer's Achilles is clearly the model for the tragic hero of the Sophoclean stage; his stubborn, passionate devotion to an ideal image of self is the same force that drives Antigone, Oedipus, Ajax and Philoctetes to the fulfillment of their destinies. Homer's Achilles is also, for archaic Greek society, the essence of the aristocratic ideal, the paragon of male beauty, courage and patrician manners—"the splendor running in the blood," says Pindar, in a passage describing Achilles' education in the cave of the centaur Chiron. And this, too, strikes a tragic note, for Pindar sang his praise of aristocratic values in the century which saw them go down to extinction, replaced by the new spirit of Athenian democracy. But it seems at first surprising that one of the most famous citizens of that democracy, a man whose life and thought would seem to place him at the extreme opposite pole from the Homeric hero, who was so far removed from Achilles' blind instinctive reactions that he could declare the unexamined life unlivable, that Socrates, on trial for his life, should invoke the name of Achilles. Explaining to his judges why he feels no shame or regret for a course of action that has brought him face-to-face with a death sentence, and rejecting all thought of a compromise that might save his life (and which his fellow citizens would have been glad to offer), he cites as his example Achilles, the Achilles who, told by his mother that his own death would come soon after Hector's, replied: "Then let me die at once—" rather than "sit by the ships . . . / a useless, dead weight on the good green earth" (18.113–23).

And yet, on consideration, it is not so surprising. Like Achilles, he was defying the community, hewing to a solitary line, in loyalty to a private ideal of conduct, of honor. In the last analysis, the bloodstained warrior and the gentle philosopher live and die in the same heroic, and tragic, pattern.

Though the English spelling of ancient Greek names faces modern poet-translators with some difficult problems, it was not a problem at all for Shakespeare, Milton, Pope and Tennyson. Except in the case of names that had through constant use been fully Anglicized—Helen, Priam, Hector, Troy, Trojans—the poets used the Latin equivalents of the Greek names that they found in the texts of Virgil and Ovid, whose poems they read in school. These are the forms we too are familiar with, from our reading of English poets through the centuries: Hecuba, Achilles, Ajax, Achaeans, Patroclus.

Recent poet-translators have tried to get closer to the original Greek and have transliterated the Greek names directly, not through the medium of their Latin adaptations. One translator, for example, presents his readers with Hékabê, Akhilleus, Hektor, Aías, Akhaians and Patróklos. Another shares most of these spellings but, perhaps finding the combination *kh* unsuited to English, strikes a compromise—Achilleus, Achaians. All translators compromise when it comes to such fully naturalized forms as Helen, Trojans and Argives (*Helenê*, *Trôes* and *Argeioi* in the Greek), and they also retreat from strict transliteration in cases like Rhodes (*Rhodos*) and Thrace (*Thrêikê*).

This is an area in which no one can claim perfect consistency: we too offer a compromise. Its basis, however, is a return to the traditional practice of generations of English poets—the use of Latinate spellings except for those names that have become, in their purely English forms, familiar in our mouths as household words.

Rigid adherence to this rule would of course make unacceptable demands: it would impose, for example, Minerva instead of Athena, Ulysses for Odysseus, and Jupiter or Jove for Zeus. We have preferred the Greek names, but transliterated them on Latin principles: *Hêrê*, for example, is Hera in this translation; *Athênê* is Athena. Elsewhere we have replaced the letter *k* with *c* and substituted the ending *us* for the Greek *os* in the names of persons (*Patroklos* becomes Patroclus). When, however, a personal name ends in *ros* preceded by a consonant, we have used the Latin ending *er*: Meleager for *Meleagros*, Teucer for *Teukros*.

The Greek diphthongs *oi* and *ai* are represented by the Latin diphthongs *oe* and *ae* (Boeotia for *Boiotia*, Achaean for *Akhaian*) and the Greek diphthong *ou* by the Latin *u* (Lycurgus for *Lykourgos*).

This conventional Latinate spelling of the names has a traditional pronunciation system, one that corresponds with neither the Greek nor the Latin sounds. Perhaps "system" is not the best word for it, since it is full of inconsistencies. But it is the pronunciation English poets have used for centuries, the sounds they heard mentally as they composed and that they confidently expected their readers to hear in their turn. Since there seems to be no similar convention for the English pronunciation of modern transliterated Greek—is the *h* sounded in *Akhilleus*? is Diomedes pronounced *dee-oh-may'-days* or *dee-oh-mee'-deez*?—we have thought it best to work with pronunciation that Keats and Shelley would have recognized.

As in Achilles (*a-kil'-eez*), *ch* is pronounced like *k* throughout. The consonants *c* and *g* are hard (as in *cake* and *gun*) before *a*—Lycaon (*leye-kay'-on*), Agamemnon (*a-ga-mem'-non*); before *o*—Corinth (*kor'-inth*), Gorgon (*gor'-gon*); before *u*—Curetes (*koo-ree'-teez*), Guneus (*goon'-yoos*); and before other consonants—Patroclus (*pa-tro'-klus*), Glaucus (*glaw'-kus*). They are soft (as in *cinder* and *George*) before *e*—Celadon (*se'-la-don*), Agenor (*a-jee'-nor*); before *i*—Cicones (*si-koh'-neez*), Phrygia (*fri'-ja*); and before *y*—Cythera (*si-thee'-ra*), Gyrtone (*jur-toh'-nee*). The final combinations *cia* and *gia* produce *sha*—Lycia (*li'-sha*)—and *ja*—Phrygia (*fri'-ja*)—respectively.

There are however cases in which the pronunciation of the consonants does not conform to these rules. One of the names of the Greeks, for example—Argives—is pronounced with a hard *g* (*ar'-geyevz* not *ar'-jeyevz*), by analogy with the town of Argos. And the combination *cae* is pronounced with a soft *c*, since the diphthong *ae* is sounded as *ee*—Caesar (*see'-zar*) is a familiar example.

The vowels vary in pronunciation, sometimes but not always according to the length of the Latin (or Greek) syllable, and the reader will have to find guidance in the rhythm of the English line or consult the Pronouncing Glossary at the back of the volume. Final *e* is always sounded long: Hebe (*hee'-bee*); final *es* is pronounced *eez*, as in Achilles. In other positions, the letter *e* may represent the sound heard in *sneeze* or that heard in *pet*. The letter *i* may sound as in *bit* or *bite*: Achilles (*a-kil'-eez*) or Atrides (*a-treye'-deez*). The two sounds are also found for *y*—Cythera (*si-thee'-ra*) or Lycaon (*leye-kay'-on*)—while *o* is pronounced as in Olympus (*o-lim'-pus*) or Dodona (*doh-doh'-na*). In this spelling system, *u* except in the ending *us* and in combination with other vowels (see below) is always long, since it represents the Greek diphthong *ou*. But it may be pronounced either *you* as in *dew*—Bucolion (*bew-kol'-i-on*)—or *oo* as in *glue*—Guneus (*goon'-yoos*).

The diphthongs *oe* and *ae* are both pronounced *ee*—Achaeans (*a-kee'-unz*), Phoebus (*fee'-bus*). The combination *aer* does not produce a diphthong: Laertes (*lay-ur'-teez*); in other cases where these letters are sounded separately, a dieresis is used: Danaë (*da'-nay-ee*). The diphthong *au* is pronounced *aw*—Glaucus (*glaw'-kus*)—but in name endings, Menelaus, for example, it is not a diphthong, and the vowels are pronounced separately (*me-ne-lay'-us*). Since his name is familiar to the English reader, we have thought it unnecessary to use the dieresis in similar cases. The ending in *ous* is similar: Pirithous (*peye-ri'-tho-us*). The ending in *eus* is sounded like *yoos*—Odysseus (*o-dis'-yoos*), except in the case of the name of three rivers—Alpheus (*al-fee'-us*), Peneus (*pee-nee'-us*) and Spercheus (*spur-kee'-us*)—and that of the builder of the Trojan horse, Epeus (*e-pee'-us*) and the king of Lemnos, Euneus (*yoo-nee'-us*).

All other vowel combinations are pronounced not as diphthongs but as separate vowels. The sequence *ei* is pronounced *ee'-i*: Briseis (*breye-see'-is*); double *o* as *oh-o*: Deicoon (*dee-i'-koh-on*). Similarly, *oi* is treated not as a diphthong but as two separate sounds—Oileus (*oh-eel'-yoos*), except in the case of Troilus, a name that has been fixed in this Latin spelling since Chaucer and is pronounced *troy'-lus*.

Obviously we cannot claim complete consistency even within the limits we have imposed on the system. We have occasionally retreated in dismay before some cases where a Latinate form seemed grotesque. Ajax, for example, is a form familiar in English, but there are two men with his name, and when Homer speaks of them in the plural we have used the (Latinized) Greek plural form *Aeantes* in preference to *Ajaxes* or the Latin *Aiaces*. Where no Latin form exists, as in the case of Poseidon, we have used the transliterated Greek, and here again English usage escapes the trammels of our rules, for Poseidon is traditionally pronounced *po-seye'-don* (not *po-see'-i-don*), and the same applies to the Pleiades (*pleye'-a-deez*). But we can claim to have reduced the unsightly dieresis to a minor factor and to have given the reader who comes to Homer for the first time a guide to pronunciation that will stand him or her in good stead when reading other poets who mention Greek names. We have also provided a Pronouncing Glossary of all the proper names in the text, which indicates stress and English vowel length.

HOMERIC
GEOGRAPHY:
Mainland Greece

Location uncertain: ○ △ ?

Labels within parentheses
indicate modern-day
place names

Oloosson

Peneus River

Acheloüs River

Tricca

Oechalia

Dodona

○ Ithome

THESPROTIA

Acheron
River

Ephyra

MYRM

(IONIAN

Sperche

SEA)

DULICHION ?

AETOLIANS

Olenus

○ Pylene

ECHINADES

Mt.
Neriton

Pleuron

• Calydon

ITHACA

Chalcis

CEPHALLENIANS

SAME

Aegion •

Helice

Myrsinus

Kms.
0   60
0   60
Miles

PELOPONNESE

SAME

ZACYNTHUS

(IONIAN

SEA)

Myrsinus

BUPRASION

ELIS

EPEANS

Hyrmine

Elis

Phia

Thryon

Arene

PARRHASIA

Alpheus River

Aegion
Helice

Aegae
Hyperesia

Mt. Erymanthus

Pellene

Mt. Cyllene

Gonoëssa

Pheneos

Stymphalus

Araethyrea

Orchomenos

Orniae

ARCADIANS

Mantinea

Tegea

Dorion

Cyparisseis

MESSENIA

PYLIANS

Anthea

Pedasus

Phera

Pylos

Hire

Aepea

Enope

Cardamyle

Sparta

Amyclae

Pharis

Brysiae

MT. TAYGETUS

Laas

Oetylus

Messe

HOMERIC
GEOGRAPHY:
The Peloponnese

Location uncertain: o ?

Labels within parentheses
indicate modern-day place names

HOMERIC
GEOGRAPHY:
The Aegean and
Asia Minor

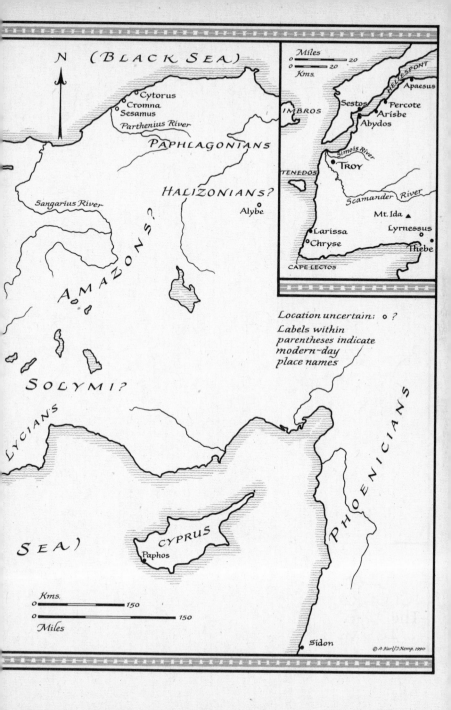

N (BLACK SEA)

Cytorus
Cromna
Sesamus
Parthenius River

PAPHLAGONIANS

HALIZONIANS?

Sangarius River

Alybe

A M A Z O N S ?

S O L Y M I ?

LYCIANS

Location uncertain: ○ ?
Labels within
parentheses indicate
modern~day
place names

PHOENICIANS

S E A)

CYPRUS

Paphos

Sidon

© A.Karl/J.Kemp, 1990

Kms.
0   150
0   150
Miles

Miles
0   20
0   20
Kms.

IMBROS

HELLESPONT

Apaesus

Sestos   Percote
            Arisbe
        Abydos

TENEDOS

Simois River

TROY

Scamander River

Mt. Ida ▲

Larissa   Lyrnessus
Chryse   Thebe

CAPE LECTOS

HOMER:
THE ILIAD

BOOK ONE

The Rage of Achilles

Rage—Goddess, sing the rage of Peleus' son Achilles,
murderous, doomed, that cost the Achaeans countless losses,
hurling down to the House of Death so many sturdy souls,
great fighters' souls, but made their bodies carrion,
feasts for the dogs and birds,
and the will of Zeus was moving toward its end.
Begin, Muse, when the two first broke and clashed,
Agamemnon lord of men and brilliant Achilles.

    What god drove them to fight with such a fury?
Apollo the son of Zeus and Leto. Incensed at the king   10
he swept a fatal plague through the army—men were dying
and all because Agamemnon spurned Apollo's priest.
Yes, Chryses approached the Achaeans' fast ships
to win his daughter back, bringing a priceless ransom

and bearing high in hand, wound on a golden staff,
the wreaths of the god, the distant deadly Archer.
He begged the whole Achaean army but most of all
the two supreme commanders, Atreus' two sons,
"Agamemnon, Menelaus—all Argives geared for war!
May the gods who hold the halls of Olympus give you   20
Priam's city to plunder, then safe passage home.
Just set my daughter free, my dear one . . . here,
accept these gifts, this ransom. Honor the·god
who strikes from worlds away—the son of Zeus, Apollo!"

    And all ranks of Achaeans cried out their assent:
"Respect the priest, accept the shining ransom!"
But it brought no joy to the heart of Agamemnon.
The king dismissed the priest with a brutal order
ringing in his ears: "Never again, old man,
let me catch sight of you by the hollow ships!   30
Not loitering now, not slinking back tomorrow.
The staff and the wreaths of god will never save you then.
The girl—I won't give up the girl. Long before that,
old age will overtake her in *my* house, in Argos,
far from her fatherland, slaving back and forth
at the loom, forced to share my bed!
                                    Now go,
don't tempt my wrath—and you may depart alive."

    The old man was terrified. He obeyed the order,
turning, trailing away in silence down the shore
where the battle lines of breakers crash and drag.   40
And moving off to a safe distance, over and over
the old priest prayed to the son of sleek-haired Leto,
lord Apollo, "Hear me, Apollo! God of the silver bow
who strides the walls of Chryse and Cilla sacrosanct—
lord in power of Tenedos—Smintheus, god of the plague!
If I ever roofed a shrine to please your heart,
ever burned the long rich bones of bulls and goats
on your holy altar, now, now bring my prayer to pass.
Pay the Danaans back—your arrows for my tears!"

His prayer went up and Phoebus Apollo heard him.   50
Down he strode from Olympus' peaks, storming at heart
with his bow and hooded quiver slung across his shoulders.
The arrows clanged at his back as the god quaked with rage,
the god himself on the march and down he came like night.
Over against the ships he dropped to a knee, let fly a shaft
and a terrifying clash rang out from the great silver bow.
First he went for the mules and circling dogs but then,
launching a piercing shaft at the men themselves,
he cut them down in droves—
and the corpse-fires burned on, night and day, no end in sight.   60

Nine days the arrows of god swept through the army.
On the tenth Achilles called all ranks to muster—
the impulse seized him, sent by white-armed Hera
grieving to see Achaean fighters drop and die.
Once they'd gathered, crowding the meeting grounds,
the swift runner Achilles rose and spoke among them:
"Son of Atreus, now we are beaten back, I fear,
the long campaign is lost. So home we sail . . .
if we can escape our death—if war and plague
are joining forces now to crush the Argives.   70
But wait: let us question a holy man,
a prophet, even a man skilled with dreams—
dreams as well can come our way from Zeus—
come, someone to tell us why Apollo rages so,
whether he blames us for a vow we failed, or sacrifice.
If only the god would share the smoky savor of lambs
and full-grown goats, Apollo might be willing, still,
somehow, to save us from this plague."

So he proposed
and down he sat again as Calchas rose among them,
Thestor's son, the clearest by far of all the seers   80
who scan the flight of birds. He knew all things that are,
all things that are past and all that are to come,
the seer who had led the Argive ships to Troy
with the second sight that god Apollo gave him.
For the armies' good the seer began to speak:

"Achilles, dear to Zeus . . .
you order me to explain Apollo's anger,
the distant deadly Archer? I will tell it all.
But strike a pact with me, swear you will defend me
with all your heart, with words and strength of hand.   90
For there is a man I will enrage—I see it now—
a powerful man who lords it over all the Argives,
one the Achaeans must obey . . . A mighty king,
raging against an inferior, is too strong.
Even if he can swallow down his wrath today,
still he will nurse the burning in his chest
until, sooner or later, he sends it bursting forth.
Consider it closely, Achilles. Will you save me?"

    And the matchless runner reassured him: "Courage!
Out with it now, Calchas. Reveal the will of god,   100
whatever you may know. And I swear by Apollo
dear to Zeus, the power you pray to, Calchas,
when you reveal god's will to the Argives—no one,
not while I am alive and see the light on earth, no one
will lay his heavy hands on you by the hollow ships.
None among all the armies. Not even if you mean
Agamemnon here who now claims to be, by far,
the best of the Achaeans."
                            The seer took heart
and this time he spoke out, bravely: "Beware—
he casts no blame for a vow we failed, a sacrifice.   110
The god's enraged because Agamemnon spurned his priest,
he refused to free his daughter, he refused the ransom.
That's why the Archer sends us pains and he will send us more
and never drive this shameful destruction from the Argives,
not till we give back the girl with sparkling eyes
to her loving father—no price, no ransom paid—
and carry a sacred hundred bulls to Chryse town.
Then we can calm the god, and only then appease him."

    So he declared and sat down. But among them rose
the fighting son of Atreus, lord of the far-flung kingdoms,   120

Agamemnon—furious, his dark heart filled to the brim,
blazing with anger now, his eyes like searing fire.
With a sudden, killing look he wheeled on Calchas first:
"Seer of misery! Never a word that works to my advantage!
Always misery warms your heart, your prophecies—
never a word of profit said or brought to pass.
Now, again, you divine god's will for the armies,
bruit it about, as fact, why the deadly Archer
multiplies our pains: because I, I refused
that glittering price for the young girl Chryseis.   130
Indeed, I prefer *her* by far, the girl herself,
I want her mine in my own house! I rank her higher
than Clytemnestra, my wedded wife—she's nothing less
in build or breeding, in mind or works of hand.
But I am willing to give her back, even so,
if that is best for all. What I really want
is to keep my people safe, not see them dying.
But fetch me another prize, and straight off too,
else I alone of the Argives go without my honor.
That would be a disgrace. You are all witness,   140
look—*my* prize is snatched away!"

                                        But the swift runner
Achilles answered him at once, "Just how, Agamemnon,
great field marshal . . . most grasping man alive,
how can the generous Argives give you prizes now?
I know of no troves of treasure, piled, lying idle,
anywhere. Whatever we dragged from towns we plundered,
all's been portioned out. But collect it, call it back
from the rank and file? *That* would be the disgrace.
So return the girl to the god, at least for now.
We Achaeans will pay you back, three, four times over,   150
if Zeus will grant us the gift, somehow, someday,
to raze Troy's massive ramparts to the ground."

    But King Agamemnon countered, "Not so quickly,
brave as you are, godlike Achilles—trying to cheat *me*.
Oh no, you won't get past me, take me in that way!
What do you want? To cling to your own prize

while I sit calmly by—empty-handed here?
Is that why you order me to give her back?
No—if our generous Argives *will* give me a prize,
a match for my desires, equal to what I've lost,   160
well and good. But if they give me nothing
I will take a prize myself—your own, or Ajax'
or Odysseus' prize—I'll commandeer her myself
and let that man I go to visit choke with rage!
Enough. We'll deal with all this later, in due time.
Now come, we haul a black ship down to the bright sea,
gather a decent number of oarsmen along her locks
and put aboard a sacrifice, and Chryseis herself,
in all her beauty . . . we embark her too.
Let one of the leading captains take command.   170
Ajax, Idomeneus, trusty Odysseus or you, Achilles,
you—the most violent man alive—so you can perform
the rites for us and calm the god yourself."

                                    A dark glance
and the headstrong runner answered him in kind: "Shameless—
armored in shamelessness—always shrewd with greed!
How could any Argive soldier obey your orders,
freely and gladly do your sailing for you
or fight your enemies, full force? Not I, no.
It wasn't Trojan spearmen who brought me here to fight.
The Trojans never did *me* damage, not in the least,   180
they never stole my cattle or my horses, never
in Phthia where the rich soil breeds strong men
did they lay waste my crops. How could they?
Look at the endless miles that lie between us . . .
shadowy mountain ranges, seas that surge and thunder.
No, you colossal, shameless—we all followed you,
to please you, to fight for you, to win your honor
back from the Trojans—Menelaus and you, you dog-face!
What do *you* care? Nothing. You don't look right or left.
And now you threaten to strip me of my prize in person—   190
the one I fought for long and hard, and sons of Achaea
handed her to me.

My honors never equal yours,
whenever we sack some wealthy Trojan stronghold—
my arms bear the brunt of the raw, savage fighting,
true, but when it comes to dividing up the plunder
the lion's share is yours, and back I go to my ships,
clutching some scrap, some pittance that I love,
when I have fought to exhaustion.

                                    No more now—
back I go to Phthia. Better that way by far,
to journey home in the beaked ships of war.   200
I have no mind to linger here disgraced,
brimming your cup and piling up your plunder."

   But the lord of men Agamemnon shot back,
"*Desert*, by all means—if the spirit drives you home!
I will never beg you to stay, not on *my* account.
Never—others will take my side and do me honor,
Zeus above all, whose wisdom rules the world.
You—I hate you most of all the warlords
loved by the gods. Always dear to your heart,
strife, yes, and battles, the bloody grind of war.   210
What if you are a great soldier? That's just a gift of god.
Go home with your ships and comrades, lord it over
        your Myrmidons!
You *are* nothing to me—you and your overweening anger!
But let this be my warning on your way:
since Apollo insists on taking my Chryseis,
I'll send her back in my own ships with *my* crew.
But I, I will be there in person at your tents
to take Briseis in all her beauty, your own prize—
so you can learn just how much greater I am than you
and the next man up may shrink from matching words with me,   220
from hoping to rival Agamemnon strength for strength!"

   He broke off and anguish gripped Achilles.
The heart in his rugged chest was pounding, torn . . .
Should he draw the long sharp sword slung at his hip,

thrust through the ranks and kill Agamemnon now?—
or check his rage and beat his fury down?
As his racing spirit veered back and forth,
just as he drew his huge blade from its sheath,
down from the vaulting heavens swept Athena,
the white-armed goddess Hera sped her down: 230
Hera loved both men and cared for both alike.
Rearing behind him Pallas seized his fiery hair—
only Achilles saw her, none of the other fighters—
struck with wonder he spun around, he knew her at once,
Pallas Athena! the terrible blazing of those eyes,
and his winged words went flying: "Why, why now?
Child of Zeus with the shield of thunder, why come now?
To witness the outrage Agamemnon just committed?
I tell you this, and so help me it's the truth—
he'll soon pay for his arrogance with his life!"   240

Her gray eyes clear, the goddess Athena answered,
"Down from the skies I come to check your rage
if only you will yield.
The white-armed goddess Hera sped me down:
she loves you both, she cares for you both alike.
Stop this fighting, now. Don't lay hand to sword.
Lash him with threats of the price that he will face.
And I tell you this—and I *know* it is the truth—
one day glittering gifts will lie before you,
three times over to pay for all his outrage.   250
Hold back now. Obey us both."

> So she urged
and the swift runner complied at once: "I must—
when the two of you hand down commands, Goddess,
a man submits though his heart breaks with fury.
Better for him by far. If a man obeys the gods
they're quick to hear his prayers."

> And with that
Achilles stayed his burly hand on the silver hilt
and slid the huge blade back in its sheath.
He would not fight the orders of Athena.

Soaring home to Olympus, she rejoined the gods   260
aloft in the halls of Zeus whose shield is thunder.

    But Achilles rounded on Agamemnon once again,
lashing out at him, not relaxing his anger for a moment:
"Staggering drunk, with your dog's eyes, your fawn's heart!
Never once did you arm with the troops and go to battle
or risk an ambush packed with Achaea's picked men—
you lack the courage, you can see death coming.
Safer by far, you find, to foray all through camp,
commandeering the prize of any man who speaks against you.
King who devours his people! Worthless husks, the men you rule—   270
if not, Atrides, this outrage would have been your last.
I tell you this, and I swear a mighty oath upon it . . .
by this, this scepter, look,
that never again will put forth crown and branches,
now it's left its stump on the mountain ridge forever,
nor will it sprout new green again, now the brazen ax
has stripped its bark and leaves, and now the sons of Achaea
pass it back and forth as they hand their judgments down,
upholding the honored customs whenever Zeus commands—
This scepter will be the mighty force behind my oath: 280
someday, I swear, a yearning for Achilles will strike
Achaea's sons and all your armies! But then, Atrides,
harrowed as you will be, *nothing* you do can save you—
not when your hordes of fighters drop and die,
cut down by the hands of man-killing Hector! Then—
then you will tear your heart out, desperate, raging
that you disgraced the best of the Achaeans!"

                                            Down on the ground
he dashed the scepter studded bright with golden nails,
then took his seat again. The son of Atreus smoldered,
glaring across at him, but Nestor rose between them,   290
the man of winning words, the clear speaker of Pylos . . .
Sweeter than honey from his tongue the voice flowed on and on.
Two generations of mortal men he had seen go down by now,
those who were born and bred with him in the old days,
in Pylos' holy realm, and now he ruled the third.

He pleaded with both kings, with clear good will,
"No more—or enormous sorrow comes to all Achaea!
How they would exult, Priam and Priam's sons
and all the Trojans. Oh they'd leap for joy
to hear the two of you battling on this way,   300
you who excel us all, first in Achaean councils,
first in the ways of war.

                      Stop. Please.
Listen to Nestor. You are both younger than I,
and in my time I struck up with better men than you,
even you, but never once did they make light of me.
I've never seen such men, I never will again . . .
men like Pirithous, Dryas, that fine captain,
Caeneus and Exadius, and Polyphemus, royal prince,
and Theseus, Aegeus' boy, a match for the immortals.
They were the strongest mortals ever bred on earth,   310
the strongest, and they fought against the strongest too,
shaggy Centaurs, wild brutes of the mountains—
they hacked them down, terrible, deadly work.
And I was in their ranks, fresh out of Pylos,
far away from home—they enlisted me themselves
and I fought on my own, a free lance, single-handed.
And none of the men who walk the earth these days
could battle with those fighters, none, but they,
they took to heart my counsels, marked my words.
So now you listen too. Yielding is far better . . .   320
Don't seize the girl, Agamemnon, powerful as you are—
leave her, just as the sons of Achaea gave her,
his prize from the very first.
And you, Achilles, never hope to fight it out
with your king, pitting force against his force:
no one can match the honors dealt a king, you know,
a sceptered king to whom great Zeus gives glory.
Strong as you are—a goddess was your mother—
he has more power because he rules more men.
Atrides, end your anger—look, it's Nestor!   330
I beg you, cool your fury against Achilles.

Here the man stands over all Achaea's armies,
our rugged bulwark braced for shocks of war."

  But King Agamemnon answered him in haste,
"True, old man—all you say is fit and proper—
but this soldier wants to tower over the armies,
he wants to rule over all, to lord it over all,
give out orders to every man in sight. Well,
there's one, I trust, who will never yield to *him*!
What if the everlasting gods have made a spearman of him?   340
Have they entitled him to hurl abuse at *me*?"

    "Yes!"—blazing Achilles broke in quickly—
"What a worthless, burnt-out coward I'd be called
if I would submit to you and all your orders,
whatever you blurt out. Fling them at others,
don't give me commands!
Never again, *I* trust, will Achilles yield to *you*.
And I tell you this—take it to heart, I warn you—
my hands will never do battle for that girl,
neither with you, King, nor any man alive.   350
You Achaeans gave her, now you've snatched her back.
But all the rest I possess beside my fast black ship—
not one bit of it can you seize against my will, Atrides.
Come, try it! So the men can see, that instant,
your black blood gush and spurt around my spear!"

    Once the two had fought it out with words,
battling face-to-face, both sprang to their feet
and broke up the muster beside the Argive squadrons.
Achilles strode off to his trim ships and shelters,
back to his friend Patroclus and their comrades.   360
Agamemnon had a vessel hauled down to the sea,
he picked out twenty oarsmen to man her locks,
put aboard the cattle for sacrifice to the god
and led Chryseis in all her beauty amidships.

Versatile Odysseus took the helm as captain.

All embarked,

the party launched out on the sea's foaming lanes
while the son of Atreus told his troops to wash,
to purify themselves from the filth of plague.
They scoured it off, threw scourings in the surf
and sacrificed to Apollo full-grown bulls and goats   370
along the beaten shore of the fallow barren sea
and savory smoke went swirling up the skies.

So the men were engaged throughout the camp.
But King Agamemnon would not stop the quarrel,
the first threat he hurled against Achilles.
He called Talthybius and Eurybates briskly,
his two heralds, ready, willing aides:
"Go to Achilles' lodge. Take Briseis at once,
his beauty Briseis by the hand and bring her here.
But if he will not surrender her, I'll go myself,   380
I'll seize her myself, with an army at my back—
and all the worse for him!"

He sent them off
with the strict order ringing in their ears.
Against their will the two men made their way
along the breaking surf of the barren salt sea
and reached the Myrmidon shelters and their ships.
They found him beside his lodge and black hull,
seated grimly—and Achilles took no joy
when he saw the two approaching.
They were afraid, they held the king in awe   390
and stood there, silent. Not a word to Achilles,
not a question. But he sensed it all in his heart,
their fear, their charge, and broke the silence for them:
"Welcome, couriers! Good heralds of Zeus and men,
here, come closer. You have done nothing to me.
You are not to blame. No one but Agamemnon—
he is the one who sent you for Briseis.
Go, Patroclus, Prince, bring out the girl
and hand her to them so they can take her back.

But let them both bear witness to my loss . . .   400
in the face of blissful gods and mortal men,
in the face of that unbending, ruthless king—
if the day should come when the armies need *me*
to save their ranks from ignominious, stark defeat.
The man is raving—with all the murderous fury in his heart.
He lacks the sense to see a day behind, a day ahead,
and safeguard the Achaeans battling by the ships."

    Patroclus obeyed his great friend's command.
He led Briseis in all her beauty from the lodge
and handed her over to the men to take away.   410
And the two walked back along the Argive ships
while she trailed on behind, reluctant, every step.
But Achilles wept, and slipping away from his companions,
far apart, sat down on the beach of the heaving gray sea
and scanned the endless ocean. Reaching out his arms,
again and again he prayed to his dear mother: "Mother!
You gave me life, short as that life will be,
so at least Olympian Zeus, thundering up on high,
should give me honor—but now he gives me nothing.
Atreus' son Agamemnon, for all his far-flung kingdoms—   420
the man disgraces me, seizes and keeps my prize,
he tears her away himself!"

                    So he wept and prayed
and his noble mother heard him, seated near her father,
the Old Man of the Sea in the salt green depths.
Suddenly up she rose from the churning surf
like mist and settling down beside him as he wept,
stroked Achilles gently, whispering his name, "My child—
why in tears? What sorrow has touched your heart?
Tell me, please. Don't harbor it deep inside you.
We must share it all."

                 And now from his depths   430
the proud runner groaned: "You know, you know,
why labor through it all? You know it all so well . . .
We raided Thebe once, Eetion's sacred citadel,
we ravaged the place, hauled all the plunder here

and the armies passed it round, share and share alike,
and they chose the beauty Chryseis for Agamemnon.
But soon her father, the holy priest of Apollo
the distant deadly Archer, Chryses approached
the fast trim ships of the Argives armed in bronze
to win his daughter back, bringing a priceless ransom   440
and bearing high in hand, wound on a golden staff,
the wreaths of the god who strikes from worlds away.
He begged the whole Achaean army but most of all
the two supreme commanders, Atreus' two sons,
and all ranks of Achaeans cried out their assent,
'Respect the priest, accept the shining ransom!'
But it brought no joy to the heart of Agamemnon,
our high and mighty king dismissed the priest
with a brutal order ringing in his ears.
And shattered with anger, the old man withdrew   450
but Apollo heard his prayer—he loved him, deeply—
he loosed his shaft at the Argives, withering plague,
and now the troops began to drop and die in droves,
the arrows of god went showering left and right,
whipping through the Achaeans' vast encampment.
But the old seer who knew the cause full well
revealed the will of the archer god Apollo.
And I was the first, mother, I urged them all,
'Appease the god at once!' That's when the fury
gripped the son of Atreus. Agamemnon leapt to his feet   460
and hurled his threat—his threat's been driven home.
One girl, Chryseis, the fiery-eyed Achaeans
ferry out in a fast trim ship to Chryse Island,
laden with presents for the god. The other girl,
just now the heralds came and led her away from camp,
Briseus' daughter, the prize the armies gave me.
But you, mother, if you have any power at all,
protect your son! Go to Olympus, plead with Zeus,
if you ever warmed his heart with a word or any action . . .

    Time and again I heard your claims in father's halls,   470
boasting how you and you alone of all the immortals

rescued Zeus, the lord of the dark storm cloud,
from ignominious, stark defeat . . .
That day the Olympians tried to chain him down,
Hera, Poseidon lord of the sea, and Pallas Athena—
you rushed to Zeus, dear Goddess, broke those chains,
quickly ordered the hundred-hander to steep Olympus,
that monster whom the immortals call Briareus
but every mortal calls the Sea-god's son, Aegaeon,
though he's stronger than his father. Down he sat,   480
flanking Cronus' son, gargantuan in the glory of it all,
and the blessed gods were struck with terror then,
they stopped shackling Zeus.
                              Remind him of that,
now, go and sit beside him, grasp his knees . . .
persuade him, somehow, to help the Trojan cause,
to pin the Achaeans back against their ships,
trap them round the bay and mow them down.
So all can reap the benefits of their king—
so even mighty Atrides can see how mad he was
to disgrace Achilles, the best of the Achaeans!"   490

     And Thetis answered, bursting into tears,
"O my son, my sorrow, why did I ever bear you?
All I bore was doom . . .
Would to god you could linger by your ships
without a grief in the world, without a torment!
Doomed to a short life, you have so little time.
And not only short, now, but filled with heartbreak too,
more than all other men alive—doomed twice over.
Ah to a cruel fate I bore you in our halls!
Still, I shall go to Olympus crowned with snow   500
and repeat your prayer to Zeus who loves the lightning.
Perhaps he will be persuaded.
                              But you, my child,
stay here by the fast ships, rage on at the Achaeans,
just keep clear of every foray in the fighting.
Only yesterday Zeus went off to the Ocean River
to feast with the Aethiopians, loyal, lordly men,

and all the gods went with him. But in twelve days
the Father returns to Olympus. Then, for your sake,
up I go to the bronze floor, the royal house of Zeus—
I'll grasp his knees, I think I'll win him over."

                                        With that vow   510
his mother went away and left him there, alone,
his heart inflamed for the sashed and lovely girl
they'd wrenched away from him against his will.
Meanwhile Odysseus drew in close to Chryse Island,
bearing the splendid sacrifice in the vessel's hold.
And once they had entered the harbor deep in bays
they furled and stowed the sail in the black ship,
they lowered the mast by the forestays, smoothly,
quickly let it down on the forked mast-crutch
and rowed her into a mooring under oars.   520
Out went the bow-stones—cables fast astern—
and the crew themselves swung out in the breaking surf,
leading out the sacrifice for the archer god Apollo,
and out of the deep-sea ship Chryseis stepped too.
Then tactful Odysseus led her up to the altar,
placing her in her loving father's arms, and said,
"Chryses, the lord of men Agamemnon sent me here
to bring your daughter back and perform a sacrifice,
a grand sacrifice to Apollo—for all Achaea's sake—
so we can appease the god   530
who's loosed such grief and torment on the Argives."

     With those words he left her in Chryses' arms
and the priest embraced the child he loved, exultant.
At once the men arranged the sacrifice for Apollo,
making the cattle ring his well-built altar,
then they rinsed their hands and took up barley.
Rising among them Chryses stretched his arms to the sky
and prayed in a high resounding voice, "Hear me, Apollo!
God of the silver bow who strides the walls of Chryse
and Cilla sacrosanct—lord in power of Tenedos!   540
If you honored me last time and heard my prayer
and rained destruction down on all Achaea's ranks,

now bring my prayer to pass once more. Now, at last,
drive this killing plague from the armies of Achaea!"

His prayer went up and Phoebus Apollo heard him.
And soon as the men had prayed and flung the barley,
first they lifted back the heads of the victims,
slit their throats, skinned them and carved away
the meat from the thighbones and wrapped them in fat,
a double fold sliced clean and topped with strips of flesh.   550
And the old man burned these over dried split wood
and over the quarters poured out glistening wine
while young men at his side held five-pronged forks.
Once they had burned the bones and tasted the organs
they cut the rest into pieces, pierced them with spits,
roasted them to a turn and pulled them off the fire.
The work done, the feast laid out, they ate well
and no man's hunger lacked a share of the banquet.
When they had put aside desire for food and drink,
the young men brimmed the mixing bowls with wine   560
and tipping first drops for the god in every cup
they poured full rounds for all. And all day long
they appeased the god with song, raising a ringing hymn
to the distant archer god who drives away the plague,
those young Achaean warriors singing out his power,
and Apollo listened, his great heart warm with joy.

Then when the sun went down and night came on
they made their beds and slept by the stern-cables . . .
When young Dawn with her rose-red fingers shone once more,
they set sail for the main encampment of Achaea.   570
The Archer sent them a bracing following wind,
they stepped the mast, spread white sails wide,
the wind hit full and the canvas bellied out
and a dark blue wave, foaming up at the bow,
sang out loud and strong as the ship made way,
skimming the whitecaps, cutting toward her goal.
And once offshore of Achaea's vast encampment
they eased her in and hauled the black ship high,

far up on the sand, and shored her up with timbers.
Then they scattered, each to his own ship and shelter.   580

But *he* raged on, grimly camped by his fast fleet,
the royal son of Peleus, the swift runner Achilles.
Now he no longer haunted the meeting grounds
where men win glory, now he no longer went to war
but day after day he ground his heart out, waiting there,
yearning, always yearning for battle cries and combat.

But now as the twelfth dawn after this shone clear
the gods who live forever marched home to Olympus,
all in a long cortege, and Zeus led them on.
And Thetis did not forget her son's appeals.   590
She broke from a cresting wave at first light
and soaring up to the broad sky and Mount Olympus,
found the son of Cronus gazing down on the world,
peaks apart from the other gods and seated high
on the topmost crown of rugged ridged Olympus.
And crouching down at his feet,
quickly grasping his knees with her left hand,
her right hand holding him underneath the chin,
she prayed to the lord god Zeus, the son of Cronus:
"Zeus, Father Zeus! If I ever served you well   600
among the deathless gods with a word or action,
bring this prayer to pass: honor my son Achilles!—
doomed to the shortest life of any man on earth.
And now the lord of men Agamemnon has disgraced him,
seizes and keeps his prize, tears her away himself. But you—
exalt him, Olympian Zeus: your urgings rule the world!
Come, grant the Trojans victory after victory
till the Achaean armies pay my dear son back,
building higher the honor he deserves!"
                                        She paused
but Zeus who commands the storm clouds answered nothing.   610
The Father sat there, silent. It seemed an eternity . . .
But Thetis, clasping his knees, held on, clinging,
pressing her question once again: "Grant my prayer,

once and for all, Father, bow your head in assent!
Or deny me outright. What have *you* to fear?
So I may know, too well, just how cruelly
I am the most dishonored goddess of them all."

                                        Filled with anger
Zeus who marshals the storm clouds answered her at last:
"Disaster. You will drive me into war with Hera.
She will provoke me, she with her shrill abuse.   620
Even now in the face of all the immortal gods
she harries me perpetually, Hera charges *me*
that I always go to battle for the Trojans.
Away with you now. Hera might catch us here.
I will see to this. I will bring it all to pass.
Look, I will bow my head if that will satisfy you.
That, I remind you, that among the immortal gods
is the strongest, truest sign that I can give.
No word or work of mine—nothing can be revoked,
there is no treachery, nothing left unfinished   630
once I bow my head to say it shall be done."

     So he decreed. And Zeus the son of Cronus bowed
his craggy dark brows and the deathless locks came pouring
down from the thunderhead of the great immortal king
and giant shock waves spread through all Olympus.

     So the two of them made their pact and parted.
Deep in the sea she dove from radiant Mount Olympus.
Zeus went back to his own halls, and all the gods
in full assembly rose from their seats at once
to meet the Father striding toward them now.   640
None dared remain at rest as Zeus advanced,
they all sprang up to greet him face-to-face
as he took his place before them on his throne.
But Hera knew it all. She had seen how Thetis,
the Old Man of the Sea's daughter, Thetis quick
on her glistening feet was hatching plans with Zeus.
And suddenly Hera taunted the Father, son of Cronus:
"So, who of the gods this time, my treacherous one,

was hatching plans with you?
Always your pleasure, whenever my back is turned,   650
to settle things in your grand clandestine way.
You never deign, do you, freely and frankly,
to share your plots with me—never, not a word!"

     The father of men and gods replied sharply,
"Hera—stop hoping to fathom all my thoughts.
You will find them a trial, though you are my wife.
Whatever is right for you to hear, no one, trust me,
will know of it before you, neither god nor man.
Whatever I choose to plan apart from all the gods—
no more of your everlasting questions, probe and pry no more."   660

     And Hera the Queen, her dark eyes wide, exclaimed,
"Dread majesty, son of Cronus, what are you saying?
Now surely I've never probed or pried in the past.
Why, you can scheme to your heart's content
without a qualm in the world for me. But now
I have a terrible fear that she has won you over,
Thetis, the Old Man of the Sea's daughter, Thetis
with her glistening feet. I know it. Just at dawn
she knelt down beside you and grasped your knees
and I suspect you bowed your head in assent to her—   670
you granted once and for all to exalt Achilles now
and slaughter hordes of Achaeans pinned against their ships."

     And Zeus who marshals the thunderheads returned,
"Maddening one . . . you and your eternal suspicions—
I can never escape you. Ah but tell me, Hera,
just what can you *do* about all this? Nothing.
Only estrange yourself from me a little more—
and all the worse for you.
If what you say is true, that must be my pleasure.
Now go sit down. Be quiet now. Obey my orders,   680
for fear the gods, however many Olympus holds,

are powerless to protect you when I come
to throttle you with my irresistible hands."

                                        He subsided
but Hera the Queen, her eyes wider, was terrified.
She sat in silence. She wrenched her will to his.
And throughout the halls of Zeus the gods of heaven
quaked with fear. Hephaestus the Master Craftsman
rose up first to harangue them all, trying now
to bring his loving mother a little comfort,
the white-armed goddess Hera: "Oh disaster . . .   690
that's what it is, and it will be unbearable
if the two of you must come to blows this way,
flinging the gods in chaos just for mortal men.
No more joy for us in the sumptuous feast
when riot rules the day.
I urge you, mother—you know that I am right—
work back into his good graces, so the Father,
our beloved Father will never wheel on us again,
send our banquets crashing! The Olympian lord of lightning—
what if he would like to blast us from our seats?   700
He is far too strong. Go back to him, mother,
stroke the Father with soft, winning words—
at once the Olympian will turn kind to us again."

    Pleading, springing up with a two-handled cup,
he reached it toward his loving mother's hands
with his own winning words: "Patience, mother!
Grieved as you are, bear up, or dear as you are,
I have to see you beaten right before my eyes.
I would be shattered—what could I do to save you?
It's hard to fight the Olympian strength for strength.   710
You remember the last time I rushed to your defense?
He seized my foot, he hurled me off the tremendous threshold
and all day long I dropped, I was dead weight and then,
when the sun went down, down I plunged on Lemnos,
little breath left in me. But the mortals there
soon nursed a fallen immortal back to life."

    At that the white-armed goddess Hera smiled
and smiling, took the cup from her child's hands.
Then dipping sweet nectar up from the mixing bowl
he poured it round to all the immortals, left to right.   720
And uncontrollable laughter broke from the happy gods
as they watched the god of fire breathing hard
and bustling through the halls.

                                That hour then
and all day long till the sun went down they feasted
and no god's hunger lacked a share of the handsome banquet
or the gorgeous lyre Apollo struck or the Muses singing
voice to voice in choirs, their vibrant music rising.

    At last, when the sun's fiery light had set,
each immortal went to rest in his own house,
the splendid high halls Hephaestus built for each   730
with all his craft and cunning, the famous crippled Smith.
And Olympian Zeus the lord of lightning went to his own bed
where he had always lain when welcome sleep came on him.
There he climbed and there he slept and by his side
lay Hera the Queen, the goddess of the golden throne.

BOOK TWO

The Great Gathering of Armies

Now the great array of gods and chariot-driving men
slept all night long, but the peaceful grip of sleep
could not hold Zeus, turning it over in his mind . . .
how to exalt Achilles?—how to slaughter
hordes of Achaeans pinned against their ships?
As his spirit churned, at last one plan seemed best:
he would send a murderous dream to Agamemnon.
Calling out to the vision, Zeus winged it on:
"Go, murderous Dream, to the fast Achaean ships
and once you reach Agamemnon's shelter rouse him,   10
order him, word-for-word, exactly as I command.
Tell Atrides to arm his long-haired Achaeans,
to attack at once, full force—
now he can take the broad streets of Troy.
The immortal gods who hold Olympus clash no more,

Hera's appeals have brought them round and all agree:
griefs are about to crush the men of Troy."

At that command

the dream went winging off, and passing quickly
along the fast trim ships, made for the king
and found him soon, sound asleep in his tent   20
with refreshing godsent slumber drifted round him.
Hovering at his head the vision rose like Nestor,
Neleus' son, the chief Agamemnon honored most.
Inspired with Nestor's voice and sent by Zeus,
the dream cried out, "Still asleep, Agamemnon?
The son of Atreus, that skilled breaker of horses?
How can you sleep all night, a man weighed down with duties?
Your armies turning over their lives to your command—
responsibilities so heavy. Listen to me, quickly!
I bring you a message sent by Zeus, a world away   30
but he has you in his heart, he pities you now . . .
Zeus commands you to arm your long-haired Achaeans,
to attack at once, full force—
now you can take the broad streets of Troy!
The immortal gods who hold Olympus clash no more,
Hera's appeals have brought them round and all agree:
griefs from Zeus are about to crush the men of Troy!
But keep this message firmly in your mind.
Remember—let no loss of memory overcome you
when the sweet grip of slumber sets you free."   40

With that the dream departed, leaving him there,
his heart racing with hopes that would not come to pass.
He thought he would take the city of Priam then,
that very day, the fool. How could he know
what work the Father had in mind? The Father,
still bent on plaguing the Argives and Trojans both
with wounds and groans in the bloody press of battle.
But rousing himself from sleep, the divine voice
swirling round him, Atrides sat up, bolt awake,
pulled on a soft tunic, linen never worn,   50
and over it threw his flaring battle-cape,

under his smooth feet he fastened supple sandals,
across his shoulder slung his silver-studded sword.
Then he seized the royal scepter of his fathers—
its power can never die—and grasping it tightly
off he strode to the ships of Argives armed in bronze.

Now the goddess Dawn climbed up to Olympus heights,
declaring the light of day to Zeus and the deathless gods
as the king commanded heralds to cry out loud and clear
and muster the long-haired Achaeans to full assembly.   60
Their cries rang out. Battalions gathered quickly.

But first he called his ranking chiefs to council
beside the ship of Nestor, the warlord born in Pylos.
Summoning them together there Atrides set forth
his cunning, foolproof plan: "Hear me, friends—
a dream sent by the gods has come to me in sleep.
Down through the bracing godsent night it came
like good Nestor in features, height and build,
the old king himself, and hovering at my head
the dream called me on: 'Still asleep, Agamemnon?   70
The son of Atreus, that skilled breaker of horses?
How can you sleep all night, a man weighed down with duties?
Your armies turning over their lives to your command—
responsibilities so heavy. Listen to me, quickly!
I bring you a message sent by Zeus, a world away
but he has you in his heart, he pities you now . . .
Zeus commands you to arm your long-haired Achaeans,
to attack at once, full force—
now you can take the broad streets of Troy!
The immortal gods who hold Olympus clash no more,   80
Hera's appeals have brought them round and all agree:
griefs from Zeus are about to crush the men of Troy!
But keep this message firmly in your mind.'

                                                  With that
the dream went winging off and soothing sleep released me.
Come—see if we can arm the Achaeans for assault.

But first, according to time-honored custom,
I will test the men with a challenge, tell them all
to crowd the oarlocks, cut and run in their ships.
But you take up your battle-stations at every point,
command them, hold them back.''

                              So much for his plan.   90
Agamemnon took his seat and Nestor rose among them.
Noble Nestor the king of Pylos' sandy harbor
spoke and urged them on with all good will:
"Friends, lords of the Argives, O my captains!
If any other Achaean had told us of this dream
we'd call it false and turn our backs upon it.
But look, the man who saw it has every claim
to be the best, the bravest Achaean we can field.
Come—see if we can arm the Achaeans for assault.''

    And out he marched, leading the way from council.   100
The rest sprang to their feet, the sceptered kings
obeyed the great field marshal. Rank and file
streamed behind and rushed like swarms of bees
pouring out of a rocky hollow, burst on endless burst,
bunched in clusters seething over the first spring blooms,
dark hordes swirling into the air, this way, that way—
so the many armed platoons from the ships and tents
came marching on, close-file, along the deep wide beach
to crowd the meeting grounds, and Rumor, Zeus's crier,
like wildfire blazing among them, whipped them on.   110
The troops assembled. The meeting grounds shook.
The earth groaned and rumbled under the huge weight
as soldiers took positions—the whole place in uproar.
Nine heralds shouted out, trying to keep some order,
"Quiet, battalions, silence! Hear your royal kings!''
The men were forced to their seats, marshaled into ranks,
the shouting died away . . . silence.
                              King Agamemnon
rose to his feet, raising high in hand the scepter
Hephaestus made with all his strength and skill.
Hephaestus gave it to Cronus' son, Father Zeus,   120

and Zeus gave it to Hermes, the giant-killing Guide
and Hermes gave it to Pelops, that fine charioteer,
Pelops gave it to Atreus, marshal of fighting men,
who died and passed it on to Thyestes rich in flocks
and he in turn bestowed it on Agamemnon, to bear on high
as he ruled his many islands and lorded mainland Argos.
Now, leaning his weight upon that kingly scepter,
Atrides declared his will to all Achaea's armies:
"Friends—fighting Danaans, aides-in-arms of Ares!
Cronus' son has trapped me in madness, blinding ruin—   130
Zeus is a harsh, cruel god. He vowed to me long ago,
he bowed his head that I should never embark for home
till I had brought the walls of Ilium crashing down.
But now, I see, he only plotted brutal treachery:
now he commands me back to Argos in disgrace,
whole regiments of my men destroyed in battle.
So it must please his overweening heart, who knows?
Father Zeus has lopped the crowns of a thousand cities,
true, and Zeus will lop still more—his power is too great.
What humiliation! Even for generations still to come,   140
to learn that Achaean armies so strong, so vast,
fought a futile war . . . We are still fighting it,
no end in sight, and battling forces we outnumber—
by far. Say that Trojans and Argives both agreed
to swear a truce, to seal their oaths in blood,
and opposing sides were tallied out in full:
count one by one the Trojans who live in Troy
but count our Achaeans out by ten-man squads
and each squad pick a Trojan to pour its wine—
many Achaean tens would lack their steward then!   150
That's how far we outnumber them, I'd say—Achaeans
to Trojans—the men who hail from Troy at least.
But they have allies called from countless cities,
fighters brandishing spears who block my way,
who throw me far off course,
thwarting my will to plunder Ilium's rugged walls.
And now nine years of almighty Zeus have marched by,
our ship timbers rot and the cables snap and fray

and across the sea our wives and helpless children
wait in the halls, wait for our return . . . And we?   160
Our work drags on, unfinished as always, hopeless—
the labor of war that brought us here to Troy.
So come, follow my orders. All obey me now.
Cut and run! Sail home to the fatherland we love!
We'll never take the broad streets of Troy."

                                        Testing his men
but he only made the spirit race inside their chests,
all the rank and file who'd never heard his plan.
And the whole assembly surged like big waves at sea,
the Icarian Sea when East and South Winds drive it on,
blasting down in force from the clouds of Father Zeus,   170
or when the West Wind shakes the deep standing grain
with hurricane gusts that flatten down the stalks—
so the massed assembly of troops was shaken now.
They cried in alarm and charged toward the ships
and the dust went whirling up from under rushing feet
as the men jostled back and forth, shouting orders—
"Grapple the ships! Drag them down to the bright sea!
Clean out the launching-channels!" Shrill shouts
hitting the heavens, fighters racing for home,
knocking the blocks out underneath the hulls.   180

    And now they might have won their journey home,
the men of Argos fighting the will of fate, yes,
if Hera had not alerted Athena: "Inconceivable!
Child of Zeus whose battle-shield is thunder,
tireless one, Athena—what, is *this* the way?
All the Argives flying home to their fatherland,
sailing over the sea's broad back? Leaving Priam
and all the men of Troy a trophy to glory over,
Helen of Argos, Helen for whom so many Argives
lost their lives in Troy, far from native land.   190
Go, range the ranks of Achaeans armed in bronze.
With your winning words hold back each man you find—
don't let them haul their rolling ships to sea!"

The bright-eyed goddess Pallas lost no time.
Down she flashed from the peaks of Mount Olympus,
quickly reached the ships and found Odysseus first,
a mastermind like Zeus, still standing fast.
He had not laid a hand on his black benched hull,
such anguish racked his heart and fighting spirit.
Now close beside him the bright-eyed goddess stood   200
and urged him on: "Royal son of Laertes, Odysseus,
great tactician—what, is *this* the way?
All you Argives flying home to your fatherland,
tumbling into your oar-swept ships? Leaving Priam
and all the men of Troy a trophy to glory over,
Helen of Argos, Helen for whom so many Argives
lost their lives in Troy, far from native land!
No, don't give up now. Range the Achaean ranks,
with your winning words hold back each man you find—
don't let them haul their rolling ships to sea!"   210

He knew the goddess' voice—he went on the run,
flinging off his cape as Eurybates picked it up,
the herald of Ithaca always at his side.
Coming face-to-face with Atrides Agamemnon,
he relieved him of his fathers' royal scepter—
its power can never die—and grasping it tightly
off he strode to the ships of Argives armed in bronze.

Whenever Odysseus met some man of rank, a king,
he'd halt and hold him back with winning words:
"My *friend*—it's wrong to threaten you like a coward,   220
but you stand fast, you keep your men in check!
It's too soon to see Agamemnon's purpose clearly.
Now he's only testing us, soon he'll bear down hard.
Didn't we all hear his plan in secret council?
God forbid his anger destroy the army he commands.
The rage of kings is strong, they're nursed by the gods,
their honor comes from Zeus—
they're dear to Zeus, the god who rules the world."

When he caught some common soldier shouting out,
he'd beat him with the scepter, dress him down: 230
"You *fool*—sit still! Obey the commands of others,
your superiors—you, you deserter, rank coward,
you count for nothing, neither in war nor council.
How can all Achaeans be masters here in Troy?
Too many kings can ruin an army—mob rule!
Let there be one commander, one master only,
endowed by the son of crooked-minded Cronus
with kingly scepter and royal rights of custom:
whatever one man needs to lead his people well."

So he ranged the ranks, commanding men to order—   240
and back again they surged from ships and shelters,
back to the meeting grounds with a deep pounding din,
thundering out as battle lines of breakers crash and drag
along some endless beach, and the rough sea roars.

The armies took their seats, marshaled into ranks.
But one man, Thersites, still railed on, nonstop.
His head was full of obscenities, teeming with rant,
all for no good reason, insubordinate, baiting the kings—
anything to provoke some laughter from the troops.
Here was the ugliest man who ever came to Troy.   250
Bandy-legged he was, with one foot clubbed,
both shoulders humped together, curving over
his caved-in chest, and bobbing above them
his skull warped to a point,
sprouting clumps of scraggly, woolly hair.
Achilles despised him most, Odysseus too—
he was always abusing both chiefs, but now
he went for majestic Agamemnon, hollering out,
taunting the king with strings of cutting insults.
The Achaeans were furious with him, deeply offended.   260
But he kept shouting at Agamemnon, spewing his abuse:
"Still moaning and groaning, mighty Atrides—why now?
What are you panting after now? Your shelters packed
with the lion's share of bronze, plenty of women too,

crowding your lodges. Best of the lot, the beauties
we hand you first, whenever we take some stronghold.
Or still more gold you're wanting? More ransom a son
of the stallion-breaking Trojans might just fetch from Troy?—
though I or another hero drags him back in chains . . .
Or a young woman, is it?—to spread and couple,   270
to bed down for yourself apart from all the troops?
How shameful for you, the high and mighty commander,
to lead the sons of Achaea into bloody slaughter!
Sons? No, my soft friends, wretched excuses—
women, not men of Achaea! Home we go in our ships!
Abandon him here in Troy to wallow in all his prizes—
he'll see if the likes of us have propped him up or not.
Look—now it's Achilles, a greater man he disgraces,
seizes and keeps his prize, tears her away himself.
But no gall in Achilles. Achilles lets it go.   280
If not, Atrides, that outrage would have been your last!"

So Thersites taunted the famous field marshal.
But Odysseus stepped in quickly, faced him down
with a dark glance and threats to break his nerve:
"What a flood of abuse, Thersites! Even for you,
fluent and flowing as you are. Keep quiet.
Who are *you* to wrangle with kings, you alone?
No one, I say—no one alive less soldierly than you,
none in the ranks that came to Troy with Agamemnon.
So stop your babbling, mouthing the names of kings,   290
flinging indecencies in their teeth, your eyes
peeled for a chance to cut and run for home.
We can have no idea, no clear idea at all
how the long campaign will end . . .
whether Achaea's sons will make it home unharmed
or slink back in disgrace.
                        But there you sit,
hurling abuse at the son of Atreus, Agamemnon,
marshal of armies, simply because our fighters
give Atrides the lion's share of all our plunder.
You and your ranting slander—*you*'re the outrage.   300

I tell you this, so help me it's the truth:
if I catch you again, blithering on this way,
let Odysseus' head be wrenched off his shoulders,
never again call me the father of Telemachus
if I don't grab you, strip the clothing off you,
cloak, tunic and rags that wrap your private parts,
and whip you howling naked back to the fast ships,
out of the armies' muster—whip you like a cur!"

And he cracked the scepter across his back and shoulders.
The rascal doubled over, tears streaking his face   310
and a bloody welt bulged up between his blades,
under the stroke of the golden scepter's studs.
He squatted low, cringing, stunned with pain,
blinking like some idiot . . .
rubbing his tears off dumbly with a fist.
Their morale was low but the men laughed now,
good hearty laughter breaking over Thersites' head—
glancing at neighbors they would shout, "A terrific stroke!
A thousand terrific strokes he's carried off—Odysseus,
taking the lead in tactics, mapping battle-plans.   320
But here's the best thing yet he's done for the men—
he's put a stop to this babbling, foulmouthed fool!
Never again, I'd say, will our gallant comrade
risk his skin to attack the kings with insults."

So the soldiers bantered but not Odysseus.
The raider of cities stood there, scepter in hand,
and close beside him the great gray-eyed Athena
rose like a herald, ordering men to silence. All,
from the first to lowest ranks of Achaea's troops,
should hear his words and mark his counsel well.   330
For the good of all he urged them: "Agamemnon!
Now, my king, the Achaeans are bent on making you
a disgrace in the eyes of every man alive. Yes,
they fail to fulfill their promise sworn that day
they sailed here from the stallion-land of Argos:
that not until you had razed the rugged walls of Troy

would they sail home again. But look at them now,
like green, defenseless boys or widowed women
whimpering to each other, wailing to journey back.
True, they've labored long—they're desperate for home.   340
Any fighter, cut off from his wife for one month,
would chafe at the benches, moaning in his ship,
pinned down by gales and heavy, raging seas.
A month—but look at us.
This is the ninth year come round, the ninth
we've hung on here. Who could blame the Achaeans
for chafing, bridling beside the beaked ships?
Ah but still—what a humiliation it would be
to hold out so long, then sail home empty-handed.
Courage, my friends, hold out a little longer.   350
Till we see if Calchas divined the truth or not.
We all recall that moment—who could forget it?
We were all witnesses then. All, at least,
the deadly spirits have not dragged away . . .

                                             Why,
it seems like only yesterday or the day before
when our vast armada gathered, moored at Aulis,
freighted with slaughter bound for Priam's Troy.
We were all busy then, milling round a spring
and offering victims up on the holy altars,
full sacrifice to the gods to guarantee success,   360
under a spreading plane tree where the water splashed,
glittering in the sun—when a great omen appeared.
A snake, and his back streaked red with blood,
a thing of terror! Olympian Zeus himself
had launched him into the clean light of day . . .
He slid from under the altar, glided up the tree
and there the brood of a sparrow, helpless young ones,
teetered high on the topmost branch-tips, cowering
under the leaves there, eight they were all told
and the mother made the ninth, she'd borne them all—   370
chirping to break the heart but the snake gulped them down
and the mother cried out for her babies, fluttering over him . . .
he coiled, struck, fanging her wing—a high thin shriek!

But once he'd swallowed down the sparrow with her brood,
the son of crooked Cronus who sent the serpent forth
turned him into a sign, a monument clear to see—
Zeus struck him to stone! And we stood by,
amazed that such a marvel came to light.
                                        So then,
when those terrible, monstrous omens burst in
on the victims we were offering to the gods,   380
Calchas swiftly revealed the will of Zeus:
'Why struck dumb now, my long-haired Achaeans?
Zeus who rules the world has shown us an awesome sign,
an event long in the future, late to come to birth
but the fame of that great work will never die.
As the snake devoured the sparrow with her brood,
eight and the mother made the ninth, she'd borne them all,
so *we* will fight in Troy that many years and then,
then in the tenth we'll take her broad streets.'
So that day the prophet revealed the future—   390
and now, look, by god, it all comes to pass!
Up with you, all you Argives geared for combat,
stand your ground, right here,
until we take the mighty walls of Priam!"
                                        He fired them so
the armies roared and the ships resounded round them,
shattering echoes ringing from their shouts
as Argives cried assent to King Odysseus' words.
And Nestor the noble horseman spurred them more:
"What disgrace! Look at you, carrying on
in the armies' muster just like boys—fools!   400
Not a thought in your heads for works of battle.
What becomes of them now, the pacts and oaths we swore?
Into the flames with councils, all the plans of men,
the vows sealed with the strong, unmixed wine,
the firm clasp of the right hand we trusted!
We battle on in words, as always, mere words,
and what's the cure? We cannot find a thing.
No matter how many years we wrangle here.
                                        Agamemnon—

never swerve, hold to your first plan of action,
lead your armies headlong into war!   410
The rest of them? Let them rot, the one or two
who hatch their plans apart from all the troops—
what good can they win from that? Nothing at all.
Why, they'd scuttle home before they can even learn
if the vows of Zeus with his dark cloudy shield
are false or not. Zeus the son of almighty Cronus,
I remind you, bowed his head that day we boarded ship,
all the Argives laden with blood and death for Troy—
his lightning bolts on the right, good omens blazing forth.
So now let no man hurry to sail for home, not yet . . .   420
not till he beds down with a faithful Trojan wife,
payment in full for the groans and shocks of war
we have all borne for Helen.

                              But any soldier
wild with desire to reach his home at once—
just let him lay a hand on his black benched ship
and right in front of the rest he'll reach his death!
But you, my King, be on your guard yourself. Come,
listen well to another man. Here's some advice,
not to be tossed aside, and I will tell it clearly.
Range your men by tribes, even by clans, Agamemnon,   430
so clan fights by the side of clan, tribe by tribe.
Fight this way, if the Argives still obey you,
then you can see which captain is a coward,
which contingent too, and which is loyal, brave,
since they will fight in separate formations of their own.
Then, what's more, if you fail to sack the city,
you will know if the will of god's to blame
or the cowardice of your men—inept in battle."

    And King Agamemnon took his lead, saluting:
"Again, old man, you outfight the Argives in debate!   440
Father Zeus, Athena, Apollo, if only I had ten men
like Nestor to plan with me among Achaea's armies—
then we could topple Priam's citadel in a day,
throttle it in our hands and gut Troy to nothing.

But Cronus' son, Zeus with his shield of storm
insists on embroiling me in painful struggles,
futile wars of words . . .
Imagine—I and Achilles, wrangling over a girl,
battling man-to-man. And I, I was the first
to let my anger flare. Ah if the two of us   450
could ever think as one, Troy could delay
her day of death no longer, not one moment.
Go now, take your meal—the sooner to bring on war.
Quickly—let each fighter sharpen his spear well,
balance his shield well, feed his horses well
with plenty of grain to build their racing speed—
each man look well to his chariot's running order,
nerve himself for combat now, so all day long
we can last out the grueling duels of Ares!
No breathing space, no letup, not a moment, not   460
till the night comes on to part the fighters' fury!
Now sweat will soak the shield-strap round your chest,
your fist gripping the spear will ache with tensing,
now the lather will drench your war-team's flanks,
hauling your sturdy chariot.
                                    But any man I catch,
trying to skulk behind his long beaked ships,
hanging back from battle—he is finished.
No way for *him* to escape the dogs and birds!"
                                    So he commanded
and the armies gave a deep resounding roar like waves
crashing against a cliff when the South Wind whips it,   470
bearing down, some craggy headland jutting out to sea—
the waves will never leave it in peace, thrashed by gales
that hit from every quarter, breakers left and right.
The troops sprang up, scattered back to the ships,
lit fires beside their tents and took their meal.
Each sacrificed to one or another deathless god,
each man praying to flee death and the grind of war.
But the lord of men Agamemnon sacrificed a fat rich ox,
five years old, to the son of mighty Cronus, Zeus,
and called the chiefs of all the Argive forces: 480

Nestor first and foremost, then King Idomeneus,
the Great and Little Ajax, Tydeus' son Diomedes
and Odysseus sixth, a mastermind like Zeus.
The lord of the war cry Menelaus came uncalled,
he knew at heart what weighed his brother down.
They stood in a ring around the ox, took up barley
and then, rising among them, King Agamemnon
raised his voice in prayer: "Zeus, Zeus,
god of greatness, god of glory, lord god
of the dark clouds who lives in the bright sky,   490
don't let the sun go down or the night descend on us!
Not till I hurl the smoke-black halls of Priam headlong—
torch his gates to blazing rubble—rip the tunic of Hector
and slash his heroic chest to ribbons with my bronze—
and a ruck of comrades round him, groveling facedown,
gnaw their own earth!"
                                        And so Agamemnon prayed
but the son of Cronus would not bring his prayer to pass,
not yet . . . the Father accepted the sacrifices, true,
but doubled the weight of thankless, ruthless war.
Once the men had prayed and flung the barley,   500
first they lifted back the heads of the victims,
slit their throats, skinned them and carved away
the meat from the thighbones and wrapped them in fat,
a double fold sliced clean and topped with strips of flesh.
And they burned these on a cleft stick, peeled and dry,
spitted the vitals, held them over Hephaestus' flames
and once they'd charred the thighs and tasted the organs
they cut the rest into pieces, pierced them with spits,
roasted them to a turn and pulled them off the fire.
The work done, the feast laid out, they ate well   510
and no man's hunger lacked a share of the banquet.
When they had put aside desire for food and drink,
Nestor the noble old horseman spoke out first:
"Marshal Atrides, lord of men Agamemnon,
no more trading speeches now. No more delay,
putting off the work the god puts in our hands.
Come, let the heralds cry out to all contingents,

full battle-armor, muster the men along the ships.
Now down we go, united—review them as we pass.
Down through the vast encampment of Achaea,   520
the faster to rouse the slashing god of war!"

Agamemnon the lord of men did not resist.
He commanded heralds to cry out loud and clear
and summon the long-haired Achaean troops to battle.
Their cries rang out. The battalions gathered quickly.
The warlords dear to the gods and flanking Agamemnon
strode on ahead, marshaling men-at-arms in files,
and down their ranks the fiery-eyed Athena bore
her awesome shield of storm, ageless, deathless—
a hundred golden tassels, all of them braided tight   530
and each worth a hundred oxen, float along the front.
Her shield of lightning dazzling, swirling around her,
headlong on Athena swept through the Argive armies,
driving soldiers harder, lashing the fighting-fury
in each Achaean's heart—no stopping them now,
mad for war and struggle. Now, suddenly,
battle thrilled them more than the journey home,
than sailing hollow ships to their dear native land.

As ravening fire rips through big stands of timber
high on a mountain ridge and the blaze flares miles away,   540
so from the marching troops the blaze of bronze armor,
splendid and superhuman, flared across the earth,
flashing into the air to hit the skies.

                              Armies gathering now
as the huge flocks on flocks of winging birds, geese or cranes
or swans with their long lancing necks—circling Asian marshes
round the Cayster outflow, wheeling in all directions,
glorying in their wings—keep on landing, advancing,
wave on shrieking wave and the tidal flats resound.
So tribe on tribe, pouring out of the ships and shelters,
marched across the Scamander plain and the earth shook,   550
tremendous thunder from under trampling men and horses
drawing into position down the Scamander meadow flats

breaking into flower—men by the thousands, numberless
as the leaves and spears that flower forth in spring.

The armies massing . . . crowding thick-and-fast
as the swarms of flies seething over the shepherds' stalls
in the first spring days when the buckets flood with milk—
so many long-haired Achaeans swarmed across the plain
to confront the Trojans, fired to smash their lines.

The armies grouping now—as seasoned goatherds   560
split their wide-ranging flocks into packs with ease
when herds have mixed together down the pasture:
so the captains formed their tight platoons,
detaching right and left, moving up for action—
and there in the midst strode powerful Agamemnon,
eyes and head like Zeus who loves the lightning,
great in the girth like Ares, god of battles,
broad through the chest like sea lord Poseidon.
Like a bull rising head and shoulders over the herds,
a royal bull rearing over his flocks of driven cattle—   570
so imposing was Atreus' son, so Zeus made him that day,
towering over fighters, looming over armies.

Sing to me now, you Muses who hold the halls of Olympus!
You are goddesses, you are everywhere, you know all things—
all we hear is the distant ring of glory, we know nothing—
who were the captains of Achaea? Who were the kings?
The mass of troops I could never tally, never name,
not even if I had ten tongues and ten mouths,
a tireless voice and the heart inside me bronze,
never unless you Muses of Olympus, daughters of Zeus   580
whose shield is rolling thunder, sing, sing in memory
all who gathered under Troy. Now I can only tell
the lords of the ships, the ships in all their numbers!

First came the Boeotian units led by Leitus and Peneleos:
Arcesilaus and Prothoënor and Clonius shared command
of the armed men who lived in Hyria, rocky Aulis,

Schoenus, Scolus and Eteonus spurred with hills,
Thespia and Graea, the dancing rings of Mycalessus,
men who lived round Harma, Ilesion and Erythrae
and those who settled Eleon, Hyle and Peteon,   590
Ocalea, Medeon's fortress walled and strong,
Copae, Eutresis and Thisbe thronged with doves,
fighters from Coronea, Haliartus deep in meadows,
and the men who held Plataea and lived in Glisas,
men who held the rough-hewn gates of Lower Thebes,
Onchestus the holy, Poseidon's sun-filled grove,
men from the town of Arne green with vineyards,
Midea and sacred Nisa, Anthedon-on-the-marches.
Fifty ships came freighted with these contingents,
one hundred and twenty young Boeotians manning each.   600

Then men who lived in Aspledon, Orchomenos of the Minyans,
fighters led by Ascalaphus and Ialmenus, sons of Ares
whom Astyoche bore in Actor son of Azeus' halls
when the shy young girl, climbing into the upper rooms,
made love with the god of war in secret, shared his strength.
In her two sons' command sailed thirty long curved ships.

Then Schedius and Epistrophus led the men of Phocis—
two sons of Iphitus, that great heart, Naubolus' son—
the men who held Cyparissus and Pytho's high crags,
the hallowed earth of Crisa, Daulis and Panopeus,   610
men who dwelled round Anemoria, round Hyampolis,
men who lived along the Cephisus' glinting waters,
men who held Lilaea close to the river's wellsprings.
Laden with all their ranks came forty long black ships
and Phocian captains ranged them column by column,
manning stations along the Boeotians' left flank.

Next the Locrians led by racing Ajax, son of Oileus,
Little Ajax—a far cry from the size of Telamonian Ajax—
a smaller man but trim in his skintight linen corslet,
he outthrew all Hellenes, all Achaeans with his spear.   620
He led the men who lived in Opois, Cynus, Calliarus,

Bessa and Scarphe, the delightful town of Augeae,
Tarphe and Thronion down the Boagrius River.
In Oilean Ajax' charge came forty long black ships,
Locrians living across the straits from sacrosanct Euboea.

And the men who held Euboea, Abantes breathing fury,
Chalcis and Eretria, Histiaea covered with vineyards,
Cerinthus along the shore and Dion's hilltop streets,
the men who held Carystus and men who settled Styra.
Elephenor, comrade of Ares, led the whole contingent,   630
Chalcodon's son, a lord of the fierce Abantes.
The sprinting Abantes followed hard at his heels,
their forelocks cropped, hair grown long at the back,
troops nerved to lunge with their tough ashen spears
and slash the enemies' breastplates round their chests.
In Elephenor's command sailed forty long black ships.

Next the men who held the strong-built city of Athens,
realm of high-hearted Erechtheus. Zeus's daughter Athena
tended him once the grain-giving fields had borne him,
long ago, and then she settled the king in Athens,   640
in her own rich shrine, where sons of Athens worship him
with bulls and goats as the years wheel round in season.
Athenians all, and Peteos' son Menestheus led them on,
and no one born on the earth could match that man
in arraying teams of horse and shielded fighters—
Nestor his only rival, thanks to Nestor's age.
And in his command sailed fifty long black ships.

Out of Salamis Great Telamonian Ajax led twelve ships
drawn up where Athenian forces formed their line of battle.

Then men of Argos and Tiryns with her tremendous walls   650
and Hermione and Asine commanding the deep wide gulf,
Troezen, Eionae and Epidaurus green with vines
and Achaea's warrior sons who held Aegina and Mases—
Diomedes lord of the war cry led their crack contingents
flanked by Sthenelus, far-famed Capaneus' favorite son.

Third in the vanguard marched Euryalus strong as a god,
son of King Mecisteus son of Talaus, but over them all,
with cries to marshal men Diomedes led the whole force
and his Argives sailed in eighty long black ships.

Next the men who held Mycenae's huge walled citadel,   660
Corinth in all her wealth and sturdy, strong Cleonae,
men of Orniae, lovely Araethyrea and Sicyon,
Adrastus' domain before he ruled Mycenae,
men of Hyperesia, Gonoëssa perched on hills,
men who held Pellene and those who circled Aegion,
men of the coastal strip and Helice's broad headland.
They came in a hundred ships and Agamemnon led them on,
Atreus' royal son, and marching in his companies
came the most and bravest fighting men by far.
And there in the midst, armed in gleaming bronze,   670
in all his glory, he towered high over all his fighters—
he was the greatest warlord, he led by far the largest army.

Next those who held Lacedaemon's hollows deep with gorges,
Pharis, Sparta and Messe, crowded haunt of the wild doves,
men who lived in Brysiae and Augeae's gracious country,
men who held Amyclae, Helos the seaboard fortress,
men who settled Laas and lived near Oetylus:
Agamemnon's brother, Menelaus lord of the war cry
led their sixty ships, armed them apart, downshore,
and amidst their ranks he marched, ablaze with valor,   680
priming men for attack. And his own heart blazed the most
to avenge the groans and shocks of war they'd borne for Helen.

Next the men who lived in Pylos and handsome Arene,
Thryon, the Alpheus ford and finely-masoned Aepy,
men who lived in Cyparisseis and Amphigenia,
Pteleos, Helos and Dorion where the Muses met
the Thracian Thamyris, stopped the minstrel's song.
From Oechalia he came, from Oechalia's King Eurytus,
boasting to high heaven that he could outsing the very Muses,

the daughters of Zeus whose shield resounds with thunder.   690
They were enraged, they maimed him, they ripped away
his voice, the rousing immortal wonder of his song
and wiped all arts of harping from his mind.
Nestor the noble old horseman led those troops
in ninety sweeping ships lined up along the shore.

    And those who held Arcadia under Cyllene's peak,
near Aepytus' ancient tomb where men fight hand-to-hand,
men who lived in Pheneos and Orchomenos rife with sheep,
Stratia, Rhipe and Enispe whipped by the sudden winds,
men who settled Tegea, Mantinea's inviting country,   700
men who held Stymphalus, men who ruled Parrhasia—
the son of Ancaeus led them, powerful Agapenor
with sixty ships in all, and aboard each vessel
crowded full Arcadian companies skilled in war.
Agamemnon himself, the lord of men had given them
those well-benched ships to plow the wine-dark sea,
since works of the sea meant nothing to those landsmen.

    Then the men who lived in Buprasion, brilliant Elis,
all the realm as far as Hyrmine and Myrsinus, frontier towns
and Olenian Rock and Alesion bound within their borders.   710
Four warlords led their ranks, ten-ship flotillas each,
and filling the decks came bands of Epean fighters,
two companies under Thalpius and Amphimachus, sons
of the line of Actor, one of Eurytus, one of Cteatus.
Strong Diores the son of Amarynceus led the third
and the princely Polyxinus led the fourth,
the son of King Agasthenes, Augeas' noble stock.

    Then ocean men from Dulichion and the Holy Islands,
the Echinades rising over the sea across from Elis—
Meges a match for Ares led their troops to war,   720
a son of the rider Phyleus dear to Zeus who once,
enraged at his father, fled and settled Dulichion.
In his son's command sailed forty long black ships.

Next Odysseus led his Cephallenian companies,
gallant-hearted fighters, the island men of Ithaca,
of Mount Neriton's leafy ridges shimmering in the wind,
and men who lived in Crocylia and rugged Aegilips,
men who held Zacynthus and men who dwelled near Samos
and mainland men who grazed their flocks across the channel.
That mastermind like Zeus, Odysseus led those fighters on.   730
In his command sailed twelve ships, prows flashing crimson.

And Thoas son of Andraemon led Aetolia's units,
soldiers who lived in Pleuron, Pylene and Olenus,
Chalcis along the shore and Calydon's rocky heights
where the sons of wellborn Oeneus were no more
and the king himself was dead
and Meleager with his golden hair was gone.
So the rule of all Aetolian men had passed to Thoas.
In Thoas' command sailed forty long black ships.

And the great spearman Idomeneus led his Cretans,   740
the men who held Cnossos and Gortyn ringed in walls,
Lyctos, Miletus, Lycastus' bright chalk bluffs,
Phaestos and Rhytion, cities a joy to live in—
the men who peopled Crete, a hundred cities strong.
The renowned spearman Idomeneus led them all in force
with Meriones who butchered men like the god of war himself.
And in their command sailed eighty long black ships.

And Heracles' son Tlepolemus tall and staunch
led nine ships of the proud Rhodians out of Rhodes,
the men who lived on Rhodes in three island divisions,   750
Lindos and Ialysus and Camirus' white escarpment,
armies led by the famous spearman Tlepolemus
whom Astyochea borè to Heracles filled with power.
He swept her up from Ephyra, from the Selleis River
after he'd ravaged many towns of brave young warlords
bred by the gods. But soon as his son Tlepolemus
came of age in Heracles' well-built palace walls

the youngster abruptly killed his father's uncle—
the good soldier Licymnius, already up in years—
and quickly fitting ships, gathering partisans,   760
he fled across the sea with threats of the sons
and the sons' sons of Heracles breaking at his back.
But he reached Rhodes at last, a wanderer rocked by storms,
and there they settled in three divisions, all by tribes,
loved by Zeus himself the king of gods and mortals
showering wondrous gold on all their heads.

Nireus led his three trim ships from Syme,
Nireus the son of Aglaea and King Charopus,
Nireus the handsomest man who ever came to Troy,
of all the Achaeans after Peleus' fearless son.   770
But he was a lightweight, trailed by a tiny band.

And men who held Nisyrus, Casus and Crapathus,
Cos, Eurypylus' town, and the islands called Calydnae—
combat troops, and Antiphus and Phidippus led them on,
the two sons of the warlord Thessalus, Heracles' son.
In their command sailed thirty long curved ships.

And now, Muse,
sing all those fighting men who lived in Pelasgian Argos,
the big contingents out of Alus and Alope and Trachis,
men of Phthia and Hellas where the women are a wonder,
all the fighters called Achaeans, Hellenes and Myrmidons   780
ranked in fifty ships, and Achilles was their leader.
But they had no lust for the grind of battle now—
where was the man who marched their lines to war?
The brilliant runner Achilles lay among his ships,
raging over Briseis, the girl with lustrous hair,
the prize he seized from Lyrnessus—
after he had fought to exhaustion at Lyrnessus,
storming the heights, and breached the walls of Thebes
and toppled the vaunting spearmen Epistrophus and Mynes,
sons of King Euenus, Selepius' son. All for Briseis   790
his heart was breaking now . . . Achilles lay there now
but he would soon rise up in all his power.

Then men of Phylace, Pyrasus banked in flowers,
Demeter's closed and holy grove and Iton mother of flocks,
Antron along the shore and Pteleos deep in meadows.
The veteran Protesilaus had led those troops
while he still lived, but now for many years
the arms of the black earth had held him fast
and his wife was left behind, alone in Phylace,
both cheeks torn in grief, their house half-built.   800
Just as he vaulted off his ship a Dardan killed him,
first by far of the Argives slaughtered on the beaches.
But not even then were his men without a captain,
yearn as they did for their lost leader. No,
Podarces a fresh campaigner ranged their units—
a son of Iphiclus son of Phylacus rich in flocks—
Podarces, gallant Protesilaus' blood brother,
younger-born, but the older man proved braver too,
an iron man of war. Yet not for a moment did his army
lack a leader, yearn as they did for the braver dead.   810
Under Podarces sailed their forty long black ships.

And the men who lived in Pherae fronting Lake Boebeis,
in Boebe and Glaphyrae and Iolcos' sturdy ramparts:
their eleven ships were led by Admetus' favored son,
Eumelus, born to Admetus by Alcestis, queen of women,
the most radiant daughter Pelias ever fathered.

Then men who lived in Methone and Thaumacia,
men who held Meliboea and rugged ridged Olizon:
Philoctetes the master archer had led them on
in seven ships with fifty oarsmen aboard each,   820
superbly skilled with the bow in lethal combat.
But their captain lay on an island, racked with pain,
on Lemnos' holy shores where the armies had marooned him,
agonized by his wound, the bite of a deadly water-viper.
There he writhed in pain but soon, encamped by the ships,
the Argives would recall Philoctetes, their great king.
But not even then were his men without a captain,
yearn as they did for their lost leader. No,

Medon formed them up, Oileus' bastard son
whom Rhene bore to Oileus, grim raider of cities.   830

    And men who settled Tricca, rocky Ithome terraced high
and men who held Oechalia, Oechalian Eurytus' city:
the two sons of Asclepius led their units now,
both skilled healers, Podalirius and Machaon.
In their command sailed forty curved black ships.

    And men who held Ormenion and the Hyperian Spring,
men who held Asterion, Titanos' chalk-white cliffs:
Eurypylus marched them on, Euaemon's shining son.
In his command sailed forty long black ships.

    And the men who settled Argissa and Gyrtone,   840
Orthe, Elone, the gleaming citadel Oloosson:
Polypoetes braced for battle led them on,
the son of Pirithous, son of deathless Zeus.
Famous Hippodamia bore the warrior to Pirithous
that day he wreaked revenge on the shaggy Centaurs,
routed them out of Pelion, drove them to the Aethices.
Polypoetes was not alone, Leonteus shared the helm,
companion of Ares, Caeneus' grandson, proud Coronus' son.
And in his command sailed forty long black ships.

    And Guneus out of Cyphus led on two and twenty ships   850
and in his platoons came Enienes and battle-tried Peraebians
who pitched homes in the teeth of Dodona's bitter winters,
who held the tilled acres along the lovely Titaressus
that runs her pure crystal currents into Peneus—
never mixed with Peneus' eddies glistening silt
but gliding over the surface smooth as olive oil,
branching, breaking away from the river Styx,
the dark and terrible oath-stream of the gods.

    And Prothous son of Tenthredon led the Magnesians,
men who lived around the Peneus, up along Mount Pelion   860

sloped in wind-whipped leaves. Racing Prothous led them on
and in his command sailed forty long black ships.

These, these were the captains of Achaea and the kings.
Now tell me, Muse, who were the bravest of them all,
of the men and chariot-teams that came with Atreus' sons?

The best by far of the teams were Eumelus' mares
and Pheres' grandson drove them—swift as birds,
matched in age and their glossy coats and matched
to a builder's level flat across their backs.
Phoebus Apollo lord of the silver bow   870
had bred them both in Perea, a brace of mares
that raced the War-god's panic through the lines.
But best by far of the men was Telamonian Ajax
while Achilles raged apart. The famed Achilles
towered over them all, he and the battle-team
that bore the peerless son of Peleus into war.
But off in his beaked seagoing ships he lay,
raging away at Atrides Agamemnon, king of armies,
while his men sported along the surf, marking time,
hurling the discus, throwing spears and testing bows.   880
And the horses, each beside its chariot, champing clover
and parsley from the marshes, waited, pawing idly.
Their masters' chariots stood under blankets now,
stored away in the tents while the rank and file,
yearning for their leader, the great man of war,
drifting here and there throughout the encampment,
hung back from the fighting.
                              But on the armies came
as if the whole earth were devoured by wildfire, yes,
and the ground thundered under them, deep as it does
for Zeus who loves the lightning, Zeus in all his rage   890
when he lashes the ground around Typhoeus in Arima,
there where they say the monster makes his bed of pain—
so the earth thundered under their feet, armies trampling,
sweeping through the plain at blazing speed.
                                      Now the Trojans.

Iris the wind-quick messenger hurried down to Ilium,
bearing her painful message, sent by storming Zeus.
The Trojans assembled hard by Priam's gates,
gathered together there, young men and old,
and rushing closer, racing Iris addressed them,
keying her voice to that of Priam's son Polites.   900
He had kept a watch for the Trojans, posted atop
old Aesyetes' tomb and poised to sprint for home
at the first sign of Argives charging from the ships.
Like him to the life, the racing Iris urged, "Old Priam,
words, endless words—that is your passion, always,
as once in the days of peace. But ceaseless war's upon us!
Time and again I've gone to battle, fought with men .
but I've never seen an army great as this. Too much—
like piling leaves or sand, and on and on they come,
advancing across the plain to fight before our gates.   910
Hector, I urge you first of all—do as I tell you.
Armies of allies crowd the mighty city of Priam,
true, but they speak a thousand different tongues,
fighters gathered here from all ends of the realm.
Let each chief give commands to the tribe he leads,
move them out, marshal his own contingents—now!"

Hector missed nothing—that was a goddess' call.
He broke up the assembly at once. They rushed to arms
and all the gates flung wide and the Trojan mass surged out,
horses, chariots, men on foot—a tremendous roar went up.   920

Now a sharp ridge rises out in front of Troy,
all on its own and far across the plain
with running-room around it, all sides clear.
Men call it Thicket Ridge, the immortals call it
the leaping Amazon Myrine's mounded tomb, and there
the Trojans and allies ranged their troops for battle.

First, tall Hector with helmet flashing led the Trojans—
Priam's son and in his command by far the greatest, bravest army,
divisions harnessed in armor, veterans bristling spears.

And the noble son of Anchises led the Dardanians—   930
Aeneas whom the radiant Aphrodite bore Anchises
down the folds of Ida, a goddess bedded with a man.
Not Aeneas alone but flanked by Antenor's two sons,
Acamas and Archelochus, trained for every foray.

And men who lived in Zelea under the foot of Ida,
a wealthy clan that drank the Aesepus' dark waters—
Trojans all, and the shining son of Lycaon led them on,
Pandarus, with the bow that came from Apollo's own hands.

And the men who held the land of Apaesus and Adrestia,
men who held Pityea, Terea's steep peaks—the units led   940
by Adrestus joined by Amphius trim in linen corslet,
the two good sons of Merops out of Percote harbor,
Merops adept beyond all men in the mantic arts.
He refused to let his two boys march to war,
this man-killing war, but the young ones fought him
all the way—the forces of black death drove them on.

And the men who lived around Percote and Practios,
men who settled Sestos, Abydos and gleaming Arisbe:
Asius son of Hyrtacus led them on, captain of armies,
Hyrtacus' offspring Asius—hulking, fiery stallions   950
bore him in from Arisbe, from the Selleis River.

Hippothous led the Pelasgian tribes of spearmen,
fighters who worked Larissa's dark rich plowland.
Hippothous and Pylaeus, tested soldier, led them on,
both sons of Pelasgian Lethus, Teutamus' scion.

Acamas and the old hero Pirous led the Thracians,
all the Hellespont bounds within her riptide straits.

Euphemus led the Cicones, fighters armed with spears,
son of Troezenus, Ceas' son, a warlord bred by the gods.

Pyraechmes led the Paeonians, reflex bows in hand,   960
hailing from Amydon far west and the broad river Axius,
Axius, clearest stream that flows across the earth.

That burly heart Pylaemenes led his Paphlagonians
out of Enetian country, land where the wild mules breed:
the men who held Cytorus and lived in range of Sesamus,
building their storied halls along the Parthenius River,
at Cromna, Aegialus and the highland fortress Erythini.

Odius and Epistrophus led the Halizonians out of Alybe
miles east where the mother lode of silver came to birth.

Chromis led the Mysian men with Ennomus seer of birds—   970
but none of his winged signs could beat off black death.
Down he went, crushed by racing Achilles' hands, destroyed
in the river where he slaughtered other Trojans too.

Ascanius strong as a god and Phorcys led the Phrygians
in from Ascania due east, primed for the clash of combat.

Mesthles and Antiphus led Maeonia's proud contingent,
Talaemenes' two sons sprung from the nymph of Gyge Lake
led on Maeonian units born and bred under Mount Tmolus.

Nastes led the Carians wild with barbarous tongues,
men who held Miletus, Phthires' ridges thick with timber,   980
Maeander's currents and Mount Mycale's craggy peaks.
Amphimachus and Nastes led their formations on,
Nastes and Amphimachus, Nomion's flamboyant sons.
Nastes strolled to battle decked in gold like a girl,
the fool! None of his trappings kept off grisly death—
down he went, crushed by racing Achilles' hands, destroyed
at the ford where battle-hard Achilles stripped his gold away.

And last, Sarpedon and valiant Glaucus marched the Lycians on
from Lycia far south, from the Xanthus' swirling rapids.

BOOK THREE

Helen Reviews
the Champions

Now with the squadrons marshaled, captains leading each,
the Trojans came with cries and the din of war like wildfowl
when the long hoarse cries of cranes sweep on against the sky
and the great formations flee from winter's grim ungodly storms,
flying in force, shrieking south to the Ocean gulfs, speeding
blood and death to the Pygmy warriors, launching at daybreak
savage battle down upon their heads. But Achaea's armies
came on strong in silence, breathing combat-fury,
hearts ablaze to defend each other to the death.

When the South Wind showers mist on the mountaintops,   10
no friend to shepherds, better than night to thieves—
you can see no farther than you can fling a stone—
so dust came clouding, swirling up from the feet of armies
marching at top speed, trampling through the plain.

Now closer, closing, front to front in the onset
till Paris sprang from the Trojan forward ranks,
a challenger, lithe, magnificent as a god,
the skin of a leopard slung across his shoulders,
a reflex bow at his back and battle-sword at hip
and brandishing two sharp spears tipped in bronze   20
he strode forth, challenging all the Argive best
to fight him face-to-face in mortal combat.

Soon as the warrior Menelaus marked him,
Paris parading there with his big loping strides,
flaunting before the troops, Atrides thrilled
like a lion lighting on some handsome carcass,
lucky to find an antlered stag or wild goat
just as hunger strikes—he rips it, bolts it down,
even with running dogs and lusty hunters rushing *him*.
So Menelaus thrilled at heart—princely Paris there,   30
right before his eyes. The outlaw, the adulterer . . .
"Now for revenge!" he thought, and down he leapt
from his chariot fully armed and hit the ground.

But soon as magnificent Paris marked Atrides
shining among the champions, Paris' spirit shook.
Backing into his friendly ranks, he cringed from death
as one who trips on a snake in a hilltop hollow
recoils, suddenly, trembling grips his knees
and pallor takes his cheeks and back he shrinks.
So he dissolved again in the proud Trojan lines,   40
dreading Atrides—magnificent, brave Paris.

                                        At one glance
Hector raked his brother with insults, stinging taunts:
"Paris, appalling Paris! Our prince of beauty—
mad for women, you lure them all to ruin!
Would to god you'd never been born, died unwed.
That's all I'd ask. Better that way by far
than to have you strutting here, an outrage—
a mockery in the eyes of all our enemies. Why,
the long-haired Achaeans must be roaring with laughter!

They thought *you* the bravest champion we could field,   50
and just because of the handsome luster on your limbs,
but you have no pith, no fighting strength inside you.
What?—is *this* the man who mustered the oarsmen once,
who braved the seas in his racing deep-sea ships,
trafficked with outlanders, carried off a woman
far from her distant shores, a great beauty
wed to a land of rugged spearmen?
                              You . . .
curse to your father, your city and all your people,
a joy to our enemies, rank disgrace to yourself!
So, you can't stand up to the battling Menelaus?   60
You'd soon feel his force, that man you robbed
of his sumptuous, warm wife. No use to you then,
the fine lyre and these, these gifts of Aphrodite,
your long flowing locks and your striking looks,
not when you roll and couple with the dust.
What cowards, the men of Troy—or years ago
they'd have decked you out in a suit of rocky armor,
stoned you to death for all the wrongs you've done!"

And Paris, magnificent as a god, replied,
"Ah Hector, you criticize me fairly, yes,   70
nothing unfair, beyond what I deserve.
The heart inside you is always tempered hard,
like an ax that goes through wood when a shipwright
cuts out ship timbers with every ounce of skill
and the blade's weight drives the man's stroke.
So the heart inside your chest is never daunted.
Still, don't fling in my face the lovely gifts
of golden Aphrodite. Not to be tossed aside,
the gifts of the gods, those glories . . .
whatever the gods give of their own free will—   80
how could we ever choose them for ourselves?
                              Now, though,
if you really want me to fight to the finish here,
have all Trojans and Argives take their seats
and pit me against Menelaus dear to Ares—

right between the lines—
we'll fight it out for Helen and all her wealth.
And the one who proves the better man and wins,
he'll take those treasures fairly, lead the woman home.
The rest will seal in blood their binding pacts of friendship.
Our people will live in peace on the rich soil of Troy,   90
our enemies sail home to the stallion-land of Argos,
the land of Achaea where the women are a wonder . . ."

When Hector heard that challenge he rejoiced
and right in the no man's land along his lines he strode,
gripping his spear mid-haft, staving men to a standstill.
But the long-haired Argive archers aimed at Hector,
trying to cut him down with arrows, hurling rocks
till King Agamemnon cried out in a ringing voice,
"Hold back, Argives! Sons of Achaea, stop your salvos!
Look, Hector with that flashing helmet of his—   100
the man is trying to tell us something now."

They held their attack. Quickly men fell silent
and Hector pleaded, appealing to both armed camps:
"Hear me—Trojans, Achaeans geared for combat!
Hear the challenge of Paris,
the man who caused our long hard campaign.
He urges all the Trojans, all the Argives too,
to lay their fine armor down on the fertile earth
while Paris himself and the warrior Menelaus
take the field between you and fight it out   110
for Helen and all her wealth in single combat.
And the one who proves the better man and wins,
he'll take those treasures fairly, lead the woman home.
The rest will seal in blood their binding pacts of friendship."

He stopped. A hushed silence held the ranks.
And Menelaus whose cry could marshal armies
urged both sides, "Now hear me out as well!
Such limited vengeance hurts me most of all—
but I intend that we will part in peace, at last,

Trojans and Achaeans. Look what heavy casualties   120
you have suffered just for me, my violent quarrel,
and Paris who brought it on you all. Now we'll fight—
and death to the one marked out for doom and death!
But the rest will part in peace, and soon, soon.
Bring two lambs—a white male and a black ewe
for the Sun and Earth—and we'll bring a third for Zeus.
And lead on Priam too, Priam in all his power,
so the king himself can seal our truce in blood—
his royal sons are reckless, not to be trusted:
no one must trample on the oath we swear to Zeus.   130
The minds of the younger men are always flighty,
but let an old man stand his ground among them,
one who can see the days behind, the days ahead—
that is the best hope for peace, for both our armies."

The Achaean and Trojan forces both exulted,
hoping *this* would end the agonies of war.
They hauled their chariots up in ranks, at rest,
the troops dismounted and stripped away their arms
and laid them down on the earth, crowded together—
hardly a foot of plowland showed between them.   140
Back to the city Hector sent two heralds now
to bring the lambs at once and summon Priam
while King Agamemnon sent Talthybius off,
heading down to the ships for one more lamb.
The herald obeyed his captain's orders quickly.

And now a messenger went to white-armed Helen too,
Iris, looking for all the world like Hector's sister
wed to Antenor's son, Helicaon's bride Laodice,
the loveliest daughter Priam ever bred.
And Iris came on Helen in her rooms . . .   150
weaving a growing web, a dark red folding robe,
working into the weft the endless bloody struggles
stallion-breaking Trojans and Argives armed in bronze
had suffered all for her at the god of battle's hands.

Iris, racing the wind, brushed close and whispered,
"Come, dear girl, come quickly—
so you can see what wondrous things they're doing,
stallion-breaking Trojans and Argives armed in bronze!
A moment ago they longed to kill each other, longed
for heartbreaking, inhuman warfare on the plain.   160
Now those very warriors stand at ease, in silence—
the fighting's stopped, they lean against their shields,
their long lances stuck in the ground beside them.
Think of it: Paris and Menelaus loved by Ares
go to fight it out with their rugged spears—
all for you—and the man who wins that duel,
you'll be called his wife!"
      And with those words
the goddess filled her heart with yearning warm and deep
for her husband long ago, her city and her parents.
Quickly cloaking herself in shimmering linen,   170
out of her rooms she rushed, live tears welling,
and not alone—two of her women followed close behind,
Aethra, Pittheus' daughter, and Clymene, eyes wide,
and they soon reached the looming Scaean Gates.

  And there they were, gathered around Priam,
Panthous and Thymoetes, Lampus and Clytius,
Hicetaon the gray aide of Ares, then those two
with unfailing good sense, Ucalegon and Antenor.
The old men of the realm held seats above the gates.
Long years had brought their fighting days to a halt   180
but they were eloquent speakers still, clear as cicadas
settled on treetops, lifting their voices through the forest,
rising softly, falling, dying away . . . So they waited,
the old chiefs of Troy, as they sat aloft the tower.
And catching sight of Helen moving along the ramparts,
they murmured one to another, gentle, winged words:
"Who on earth could blame them? Ah, no wonder
the men of Troy and Argives under arms have suffered
years of agony all for her, for such a woman.
Beauty, terrible beauty!   190

A deathless goddess—so she strikes our eyes!

But still,

ravishing as she is, let her go home in the long ships
and not be left behind . . . for us and our children
down the years an irresistible sorrow."

They murmured low
but Priam, raising his voice, called across to Helen,
"Come over here, dear child. Sit in front of me,
so you can see your husband of long ago,
your kinsmen and your people.
I don't blame you. I hold the gods to blame.
They are the ones who brought this war upon me,   200
devastating war against the Achaeans—

Here, come closer,
tell me the name of that tremendous fighter. Look,
who's that Achaean there, so stark and grand?
Many others afield are much taller, true,
but I have never yet set eyes on one so regal,
so majestic . . . That man must be a king!"

And Helen the radiance of women answered Priam,
"I revere you so, dear father, dread you too—
if only death had pleased me then, grim death,
that day I followed your son to Troy, forsaking   210
my marriage bed, my kinsmen and my child,
my favorite, now full-grown,
and the lovely comradeship of women my own age.
Death never came, so now I can only waste away in tears.
But about your question—yes, I have the answer.
That man is Atreus' son Agamemnon, lord of empires,
both a mighty king and a strong spearman too,
and he used to be my kinsman, whore that I am!
There was a world . . . or was it all a dream?"

Her voice broke but the old king, lost in wonder,   220
cried out, "How lucky you are, son of Atreus,
child of fortune, your destiny so blessed!
Look at the vast Achaean armies you command!

Years ago I visited Phrygia rife with vineyards,
saw the Phrygian men with their swarming horses there—
multitudes—the armies of Otreus, Mygdon like a god,
encamped that time along the Sangarius River banks.
And I took my stand among them, comrade-in-arms
the day the Amazons struck, a match for men in war.
But not even those hordes could match these hordes of yours,   230
your fiery-eyed Achaeans!"

                          And sighting Odysseus next
the old king questioned Helen, "Come, dear child,
tell me of that one too—now who is he?
Shorter than Atreus' son Agamemnon, clearly,
but broader across the shoulders, through the chest.
There, you see? His armor's heaped on the green field
but the man keeps ranging the ranks of fighters like a ram—
yes, he looks to me like a thick-fleeced bellwether ram
making his way through a big mass of sheep-flocks,
shining silver-gray."

                          Helen the child of Zeus replied,   240
"That's Laertes' son, the great tactician Odysseus.
He was bred in the land of Ithaca. Rocky ground
and he's quick at every treachery under the sun—
the man of twists and turns."

                          Helen paused
and the shrewd Antenor carried on her story:
"Straight to the point, my lady, very true.
Once in the past he came our way, King Odysseus
heading the embassy they sent for your release,
together with Menelaus dear to Ares.
I hosted them, treated them warmly in my halls   250
and learned the ways of both, their strategies, their traits.
Now, when they mingled with our Trojans in assembly,
standing side-by-side, Menelaus' shoulders
mounted over his friend's in height and spread,
when both were seated Odysseus looked more lordly.
But when they spun their appeals before us all,
Menelaus spoke out quickly—his words racing,
few but clear as a bell, nothing long-winded

or off the mark, though in fact the man was younger.
But when Odysseus sprang up, the famed tactician   260
would just stand there, staring down, hard,
his eyes fixed on the ground,
never shifting his scepter back and forth,
clutching it stiff and still like a mindless man.
You'd think him a sullen fellow or just plain fool.
But when *he* let loose that great voice from his chest
and the words came piling on like a driving winter blizzard—
then no man alive could rival Odysseus! Odysseus . . .
we no longer gazed in wonder at his looks.''

                                        Catching sight
of a third fighter, Ajax, the old king asked her next,   270
"Who's that other Achaean, so powerful, so well-built?
He towers over the Argives, his head, his massive shoulders!''

    And Helen in all her radiance, her long robes, replied,
"Why, that's the giant Ajax, bulwark of the Achaeans.
And Idomeneus over there—standing with his Cretans—
like a god, you see? And the Cretan captains
form a ring around him. How often Menelaus,
my good soldier, would host him in our halls,
in the old days, when he'd sail across from Crete.
And now I see them all, the fiery-eyed Achaeans,   280
I know them all by heart, and I could tell their names . . .
but two I cannot find, and they're captains of the armies,
Castor breaker of horses and the hardy boxer Polydeuces.
My blood brothers. Mother bore them both. Perhaps
they never crossed over from Lacedaemon's lovely hills
or come they did, sailing here in the deep-sea ships,
but now they refuse to join the men in battle,
dreading the scorn, the curses hurled at me . . .''

    So she wavered, but the earth already held them fast,
long dead in the life-giving earth of Lacedaemon,   290
the dear land of their fathers.

                        Now through Troy
the heralds brought the offerings for the gods,

sacred victims to bind and seal the oaths:
two lambs and the wine that warms the heart,
the yield of the vine, filling a goatskin sack,
and the herald Idaeus carried a gleaming bowl
and golden winecups. Reaching the old king's side
the crier roused him sharply: "Son of Laomedon, rise up!
They are calling for you now, commanders of both armies,
stallion-breaking Trojans and Argives armed in bronze—   300
come down to the plain so you can seal our oaths.
Now Paris and Menelaus, Atrides loved by Ares,
will fight it out with their rugged spears for Helen,
and Helen and all her treasures go to the man who wins.
The rest will seal in blood their binding pacts of friendship.
Our people will live in peace on the rich soil of Troy.
Our enemies sail home to the stallion-land of Argos,
the land of Achaea where the women are a wonder."

A shudder went shooting through the old man
but he told his men to yoke the team at once.   310
They promptly obeyed and Priam climbed aboard,
pulling the reins back taut. Antenor flanked him,
mounting the gleaming car, and both men drove the team
through the Scaean Gates, heading toward the plain.

Reaching the front, they climbed down from the chariot,
onto the earth that feeds us all, and into the space
between Achaean and Trojan lines they marched.
Lord Agamemnon rose at once to greet them both
with the great tactician Odysseus by his side.
The noble heralds brought on the victims   320
marked for the gods to seal and bind the oaths.
They mixed the contenders' wine in a large bowl
and rinsed the warlords' waiting hands with water.
Atreus' son drew forth the dagger always slung
at his battle-sword's big sheath, cut some tufts
from the lambs' heads, and heralds passed them round
to Achaean and Trojan captains. Then Atreus' son

Agamemnon stood in behalf of all, lifted his arms
and prayed in his deep resounding voice, "Father Zeus!
Ruling over us all from Ida, god of greatness, god of glory!   330
Helios, Sun above us, you who see all, hear all things!
Rivers! And Earth! And you beneath the ground
who punish the dead—whoever broke his oath—
be witness here, protect our binding pacts.
If Paris brings Menelaus down in blood,
he keeps Helen himself and all her wealth
and we sail home in our racing deep-sea ships.
But if red-haired Menelaus brings down Paris,
the Trojans surrender Helen and all her treasures.
And they pay us reparations fair and fitting,   340
a price to inspire generations still to come.
But if Priam and Priam's sons refuse to pay,
refuse me, Agamemnon—with Paris beaten down—
then I myself will fight it out for the ransom,
I'll battle here to the end of our long war."

                                                    On those terms
he dragged his ruthless dagger across the lambs' throats
and let them fall to the ground, dying, gasping away
their life breath, cut short by the sharp bronze.
Then dipping up the wine from the mixing bowls,
brimming their cups, pouring them on the earth,   350
men said their prayers to the gods who never die.
You could hear some Trojan or Achaean calling, "Zeus—
god of greatness, god of glory, all you immortals!
Whichever contenders trample on this treaty first,
spill their brains on the ground as this wine spills—
theirs, their children's too—their enemies rape their wives!"

    But Zeus would not fulfill their prayers, not yet . . .
Now Priam rose in their midst and took his leave:
"Hear me, Trojans, Achaeans geared for combat—
home I go to windy Ilium, straight home now.   360
This is more than I can bear, I tell you—
to watch my son do battle with Menelaus

loved by the War-god, right before my eyes.
Zeus knows, no doubt, and every immortal too,
which fighter is doomed to end all this in death."

      And laying the victims in the chariot, noble Priam
climbed aboard, pulling the reins back taut.
Antenor flanked him, mounting the gleaming car,
and back they drove again, heading home to Troy.
But Priam's son Prince Hector and royal Odysseus   370
measured off the ground for single combat first,
then dropped two stones in a helmet, lots for casting—
who would be first to hurl his bronze-tipped spear?
The armies prayed and stretched their hands to the gods.
You could hear some Trojan or Achaean pleading, "Father Zeus!
Ruling over us all from Ida, god of greatness, glory!
Whoever brought this war on both our countries,
let him rot and sink to the House of Death—
but let our pacts of friendship all hold fast!"

                                           So they prayed
as tall Hector, eyes averted under his flashing helmet,   380
shook the two lots hard and Paris' lot leapt out.
The troops sat down by rank, each beside his horses
pawing the ground where blazoned war-gear lay. And now—
one warrior harnessed burnished armor on his back,
magnificent Paris, fair-haired Helen's consort.
First he wrapped his legs with well-made greaves,
fastened behind the heels with silver ankle-clasps,
next he strapped a breastplate round his chest,
his brother Lycaon's that fitted him so well.
Then over his shoulder Paris slung his sword,   390
the fine bronze blade with its silver-studded hilt,
and then the shield-strap and his sturdy, massive shield
and over his powerful head he set a well-forged helmet,
the horsehair crest atop it tossing, bristling terror,
and last he grasped a spear that matched his grip.
Following step by step
the fighting Menelaus strapped on armor too.

Both men armed at opposing sides of the forces,
into the no man's land between the lines they strode,
glances menacing, wild excitement seizing all who watched,   400
the stallion-breaking Trojans and Argive men-at-arms.
Striking a stand in the dueling-ground just cleared
they brandished spears at each other, tense with fury.
Suddenly Paris hurled—his spear's long shadow flew
and the shaft hit Menelaus' round shield, full center—
not pounding through, the brazen point bent back
in the tough armor.
                    But his turn next—Menelaus
reared with a bronze lance and a prayer to Father Zeus:
"Zeus, King, give me revenge, he wronged me first!
Illustrious Paris—crush him under my hand!   410
So even among the men to come a man may shrink
from wounding the host who showers him with kindness."

Shaking his spear, he hurled and its long shadow flew
and the shaft hit Paris' round shield, hit full center—
straight through the gleaming hide the heavy weapon drove,
ripping down and in through the breastplate finely worked,
tearing the war-shirt, close by Paris' flank it jabbed
but the Trojan swerved aside and dodged black death.
So now Menelaus drew his sword with silver studs
and hoisting the weapon high, brought it crashing down   420
on the helmet ridge but the blade smashed where it struck—
jagged shatters flying—it dropped from Atrides' hand
and the hero cried out, scanning the blank skies,
"Father Zeus—no god's more deadly than you!
Here I thought I'd punish Paris for all his outrage—
now my sword is shattered, right in my hands, look,
my spear flew from my grip for nothing—I never hit him!"

Lunging at Paris, he grabbed his horsehair crest,
swung him round, started to drag him into Argive lines
and now the braided chin-strap holding his helmet tight   430
was gouging his soft throat—Paris was choking, strangling.
Now he'd have hauled him off and won undying glory

but Aphrodite, Zeus's daughter quick to the mark,
snapped the rawhide strap, cut from a bludgeoned ox,
and the helmet came off empty in Menelaus' fist.
Whirling it round the fighter sent it flying
into his Argives scrambling fast to retrieve it—
back at his man he sprang, enraged with brazen spear,
mad for the kill but Aphrodite snatched Paris away,
easy work for a god, wrapped him in swirls of mist   440
and set him down in his bedroom filled with scent.
Then off she went herself to summon Helen
and found her there on the steep, jutting tower
with a troop of Trojan women clustered round her.
The goddess reached and tugged at her fragrant robe,
whispering low, for all the world like an old crone,
the old weaver who, when they lived in Lacedaemon,
wove her fine woolens and Helen held her dear.
Like her to the life, immortal Love invited,
"Quickly—Paris is calling for you, come back home!   450
There he is in the bedroom, the bed with inlaid rings—
he's glistening in all his beauty and his robes!
You'd never dream he's come from fighting a man,
you'd think he's off to a dance or slipped away
from the dancing, stretching out at ease."

                                              Enticing so
that the heart in Helen's breast began to race.
She knew the goddess at once, the long lithe neck,
the smooth full breasts and the fire in those eyes—
and she was amazed, she burst out with her name:
"Maddening one, my Goddess, oh what now?   460
Lusting to lure me to my ruin yet again?
Where will you drive me next?
Off and away to other grand, luxurious cities,
out to Phrygia, out to Maeonia's tempting country?
Have you a favorite mortal man there too?

                                        But why now?—
because Menelaus has beaten your handsome Paris
and hateful as I am, he longs to take me home?
Is that why you beckon here beside me now

with all the immortal cunning in your heart?
Well, go to him yourself—*you* hover beside him!   470
Abandon the gods' high road and be a mortal!
Never set foot again on Mount Olympus, never!—
suffer for Paris, protect Paris, for eternity . . .
until he makes you his wedded wife—that or his slave.
Not I, I'll never go back again. It would be wrong,
disgraceful to share that coward's bed once more.
The women of Troy would scorn me down the years.
Oh the torment—never-ending heartbreak!"

    But Aphrodite rounded on her in fury:
"Don't provoke me—wretched, headstrong girl!   480
Or in my immortal rage I may just toss you over,
hate you as I adore you now—with a vengeance.
I might make you the butt of hard, withering hate
from both sides at once, Trojans and Achaeans—
then your fate can tread you down to dust!"
                                              So she threatened
and Helen the daughter of mighty Zeus was terrified.
Shrouding herself in her glinting silver robes
she went along, in silence. None of her women
saw her go . . . The goddess led the way.

    And once they arrived at Paris' sumptuous halls   490
the attendants briskly turned to their own work
as Helen in all her radiance climbed the steps
to the bedroom under the high, vaulting roof.
There Aphrodite quickly brought her a chair,
the goddess herself with her everlasting smile,
and set it down, face-to-face with Paris.
And there Helen sat, Helen the child of Zeus
whose shield is storm and lightning, glancing away,
lashing out at her husband: "So, home from the wars!
Oh would to god you'd died there, brought down   500
by that great soldier, my husband long ago.
And how you used to boast, year in, year out,
that you were the better man than fighting Menelaus

in power, arm and spear! So why not go back now,
hurl your challenge at Menelaus dear to Ares,
fight it out together, man-to-man again?

                                     Wait,
take my advice and call a halt right here:
no more battling with fiery-haired Menelaus,
pitting strength against strength in single combat—
madness. *He* just might impale you on his spear!"   510

But Paris replied at once to Helen's challenge:
"No more, dear one—don't rake me with your taunts,
myself and all my courage. This time, true,
Menelaus has won the day, thanks to Athena.
I'll bring him down tomorrow.
Even we have gods who battle on our side.

                            But come—
let's go to bed, let's lose ourselves in love!
Never has longing for you overwhelmed me so,
no, not even then, I tell you, that first time
when I swept you up from the lovely hills of Lacedaemon,   520
sailed you off and away in the racing deep-sea ships
and we went and locked in love on Rocky Island . . .
That was nothing to how I hunger for you now—
irresistible longing lays me low!"

He led the way to bed. His wife went with him.
And now, while the two made love in the large carved bed,
Menelaus stalked like a wild beast, up and down the lines—
where could he catch a glimpse of magnificent Paris?
Not a single Trojan, none of their famous allies
could point out Paris to battle-hungry Menelaus.   530
Not that they would hide him out of friendship,
even if someone saw him—
all of them hated him like death, black death.
But marshal Agamemnon called out to the armies,
"Hear me now, you Trojans, Dardans, Trojan allies!
Clearly victory goes to Menelaus dear to Ares.

You must surrender Helen and all her treasure with her.
At once—and pay us reparations fair and fitting,
a price to inspire generations still to come!"

So Atrides demanded. His armies roared assent.   540

BOOK FOUR

The Truce
Erupts in War

Now aloft by the side of Zeus the gods sat in council,
conferring across Olympus' golden floor as noble Hebe
poured them rounds of nectar. They lifted golden beakers,
pledging each other warmly, gazing down on Troy . . .
But abruptly Zeus was set on infuriating Hera,
courting her fire with cunning, mocking taunts: "So,
those two goddesses there are Menelaus' best defense,
Hera of Argos, Boeotian Athena, guard of armies.
Look at them—sitting apart, watching the dueling.
So they take their pleasure. But Aphrodite here   10
with her everlasting laughter always stands by Paris
and drives the deadly spirits from her man. Why,
just now she plucked him away, she saved his life
when he thought his end had come. Nevertheless—
clearly victory goes to Menelaus dear to Ares.

So now we plan how the war will all work out:
do we rouse the pain and grisly fighting once again
or hand down pacts of peace between both armies?
Ah if only it might prove well and good to all,
to every immortal god, men might still live on   20
in royal Priam's citadel. And Helen of Argos?
Menelaus just might lead her home again."

                                    So he mocked
as Athena and Queen Hera muttered between themselves,
huddled together, plotting Troy's destruction.
True, Athena held her peace and said nothing . . .
smoldering at the Father, seized with wild resentment.
But Hera could hold the anger in her breast no longer,
suddenly bursting out, "Dread majesty, son of Cronus,
what are you saying? How can you think of making
all my labor worthless, all gone for nothing?   30
Mortal labor—the sweat I poured, my horses panting,
spent from launching Achaea's armies, heaping pains
on Priam and Priam's sons.

                        Do as you please—
but none of the deathless gods will ever praise you."

    Rising in anger, Zeus who drives the storm clouds
thundered, "Insatiable Hera! How great are the pains
that Priam and Priam's sons have heaped on *you*
that you rage on, relentless, forever bent on razing
the well-built heights of Troy? Only if you could breach
their gates and their long walls and devour Priam   40
and Priam's sons and the Trojan armies raw—
then you just might cure your rage at last.
Well, do as *you* please. But in days to come
don't let this quarrel breed some towering clash
between us both, pitting you and me in conflict.
One more thing—take it to heart, I urge you.
Whenever *I* am bent on tearing down some city
filled with men you love—to please myself—
never attempt to thwart my fury, Hera,

give *me* my way. For I, I gave you this,   50
all of my own free will but hardly willing. No,
of all the cities under the sun and starry skies,
wherever men who walk the earth have dwelled,
I honor sacred Ilium most with my immortal heart:
Priam and men of Priam who hurls the strong ash spear.
Never once did my altar lack its share of victims,
winecups tipped and the deep smoky savor. These,
these are the gifts we claim—they are our rights."

    And Hera the Queen, her eyes wide, answered,
"Excellent! The three cities that I love best of all   60
are Argos and Sparta, Mycenae with streets as broad as Troy's.
Raze them—whenever they stir the hatred in your heart.
My cities . . . I will never rise in their defense,
not against you—I'd never grudge your pleasure.
What if I did protest, forbid you to raze their walls?
What good would protest do? You are far stronger than I.
Still, you must not make my labor come to nothing.
I am a god too. My descent the same as yours—
crooked-minded Cronus fathered me as well,
the first of all his daughters, first both ways: 70
both by birth and since I am called your consort
and you in turn rule all the immortal gods.
So come, let us yield to each other now
on this one point, I to you and you to me,
and the other deathless powers will fall in line.
But quickly, order Athena down to battle now,
into the killing-ground of Trojans and Achaeans—
and see that the Trojans break the sworn truce first
and trample on the Argives in their triumph!"

    The father of men and gods complied at once.   80
He winged Athena on with a flight of orders: "Quickly!
Down you go to Troy's and Achaea's armies now—
and see that the Trojans break the sworn truce first
and trample on the Argives in their triumph."

So he launched Athena already poised for action.
Down the goddess swept from Olympus' craggy peaks
and dove like a star the son of Cronus flings,
Cronus with all his turning, twisting ways—
a sign to men at sea or a massive army marching,
blazing on with a stream of sparks showering in its wake.   90
Like a shooting star Athena flashed across the earth,
plunging down in the midst of both camped forces.
Terror gripped the fighters looking on,
stallion-breaking Trojans, Argive men-at-arms.
One would glance at a comrade, groaning, "What next—
battle again, more pain and grisly fighting?
Or pacts between both armies? Peace from Zeus,
the great steward on high who rules our mortal wars?"

     As Achaeans and Trojans wondered what was coming,
Athena merged in the Trojan columns like a fighter,   100
like Antenor's son the rugged spearman Laodocus,
hunting for Pandarus, hoping to find the archer.
Find him she did, Lycaon's skilled, fearless son,
standing by, flanked by the bands of shielded men
who'd trooped with him from Aesepus' dark rapids.
Athena halted beside him, let her challenge fly:
"Here's glory, son of Lycaon—let me tempt you,
you with your archer's skill! Have you the daring
to wing an arrow at Menelaus? Just think what thanks,
what fame you'd win in the eyes of all the Trojans,   110
Prince Paris most of all. The first among all,
you'd bear off shining, priceless gifts from him.
Just let him see Menelaus, Atreus' fighting son
brought down by your shaft and hoisted onto his pyre,
mourned with grief and tears! Come, up with you,
whip an arrow at this invincible Menelaus—now!
But swear to Apollo, Wolf-god, glorious Archer,
you'll slaughter splendid victims, newborn lambs
when you march home to Zelea's sacred city."

     So Athena fired the fool's heart inside him.   120

Then and there he unstrapped his polished bow,
the horn of a wild goat he'd shot in the chest
one day as the springy ibex clambered down a cliff.
Lurking there under cover, he hit it in the heart
and the fine kill went sprawling down the rocks.
The horns on its head ran sixteen hands in length
and a bowyer good with goat-horn worked them up,
fitted, clasped them tight, sanded them smooth
and set the golden notch-rings at the tips.
Superb equipment—bending it back hard   130
the archer strung his bow . . .
propping an end against the ground as cohorts
braced their shields in a tight wedge to hide him,
fearing bands of Argives might just leap to their feet
before he could hit Menelaus, Atreus' fighting son.
He flipped the lid of his quiver, plucked an arrow
fletched and never shot, a shaft of black pain.
Quickly notching the sharp arrow on the string
he swore to Apollo, Wolf-god, glorious Archer,
he'd slaughter splendid victims, newborn lambs   140
when he marched home to Zelea's sacred city.
Squeezing the nock and string together, drawing
the gut back to his nipple, iron head to the handgrip
till he flexed the great weapon back in a half-circle curve—
the bow sprang! the string sang out, arrow shot away
razor-sharp and raging to whip through Argive ranks!

                                                    But you,
Menelaus, the blessed deathless gods did not forget you,
Zeus's daughter the queen of fighters first of all.
She reared before you, skewed the tearing shaft,
flicking it off your skin as quick as a mother   150
flicks a fly from her baby sleeping softly.
Athena's own hand deflected it down the belt
where the gold buckles clasp and breastplates overlap.
The shaft pierced the tight belt's twisted thongs,
piercing the blazoned plates, piercing the guard
he wore to shield his loins and block the spears,
his best defense—the shaft pierced even this,

the tip of the weapon grazing the man's flesh,
and dark blood came spurting from the wound.

Picture a woman dyeing ivory blood red . . .   160
a Carian or Maeonian staining a horse's cheekpiece,
and it's stored away in a vault and troops of riders
long to sport the ornament, true, but there it lies
as a king's splendor, kept and prized twice over—
his team's adornment, his driver's pride and glory.
So now, Menelaus, the fresh blood went staining down
your sturdy thighs, your shins and well-turned ankles.

The lord of men Agamemnon shuddered, frightened
to see the dark blood gushing from the wound.
And veteran Menelaus cringed himself but saw   170
the lashing-cords and barbs outside the gash
and his courage flooded back inside his chest.
Nevertheless, King Agamemnon, groaning heavily,
grasped Menelaus' hand and spoke out for the men
as friends around him groaned as well: "Dear brother—
that truce I sealed in blood was death for you,
setting you out alone . . .
exposed before our lines to fight the Trojans—
Look how the men of Troy have laid you low,
trampling down our solemn, binding truce!   180
But they will never go for nothing, the oaths,
the blood of the lambs, the unmixed wine we poured,
the firm clasp of the right hand we trusted.
                                              Never—
even if Zeus's wrath does not strike home at once,
he'll strike in his own good time with greater fury.
Transgressors will pay the price, a tremendous price,
with their own heads, their wives and all their children.
Yes, for in my heart and soul I know this well:
the day will come when sacred Troy must die,
Priam must die and all his people with him,   190
Priam who hurls the strong ash spear!
                                         The son of Cronus,

Zeus, throned aloft in the heavens where he lives,
Zeus himself will brandish over their heads
his black storm-shield, enraged at their deceit.
Nothing can stop it now. All this will come to pass.
But I will suffer terrible grief for you, Menelaus,
if you die now, if you fill out your destiny now—
and I go back to parching Argos in disgrace.
For the men will turn their minds toward home at once,
and we must leave Priam and all the men of Troy   200
a trophy to glory over, Helen, queen of Argos . . .
But the plowland here will rot your bones, my brother,
as you lie dead in Troy, your mission left unfinished.
Then some Trojan will glory, swaggering, arrogant,
leaping down on the grave of famous Menelaus:
'Let Agamemnon wreak his anger so on all his foes!
Just as he led his armies here for nothing, failure.
Now home he's gone to the dear land of his fathers,
his warships empty, leaving behind the hero Menelaus
moldering in his wake!'
                                        So some Trojan will trumpet—   210
let the great earth gape and take me down that day!"

    But the red-haired Menelaus tried to calm him:
"Courage. Don't alarm the men, not for a moment.
The point's not lodged in a mortal spot, you see?
My glittering war-belt stopped the shot in front,
my loin-piece and the plated guard below it,
gear the bronzesmiths hammered out for me."

    And marshal Agamemnon took his lead:
"Pray god you're right, dear brother Menelaus!
But the wound—a healer will treat it, apply drugs   220
and put a stop to the black waves of pain."

    Agamemnon turned to the sacred herald:
"Quick, Talthybius. Call Machaon here,
the son of Asclepius, that unfailing healer,
to see to Menelaus, Atreus' fighting son.

An archer's hit him, a good hand at the bow,
some Trojan or some Lycian—all glory to him,
a heavy blow to us."
                        The herald obeyed at once.
He ran through ranks of Achaeans armed in bronze,
searching for brave Machaon. Find him he did,   230
standing by, flanked by the bands of shielded men
who'd trooped with him from the stallion-land of Tricca.
He halted beside him there and let his message fly:
"Quickly, son of Asclepius, King Agamemnon calls!
Now see to Menelaus, Achaea's fighting captain.
An archer's hit him, a good hand at the bow,
some Trojan or some Lycian—all glory to him,
a heavy blow to us!"
                        So the herald shouted,
stirring Machaon's spirit. Back the two men ran
through crowds of troops in Achaea's vast encampment.   240
And gaining the place where red-haired Menelaus
nursed his wound and a growing ring of warlords
pressed around him, striding into their midst
the godsent healer reached the captain's side
and quickly drew the shaft from his buckled belt—
he pulled it clear, the sharp barbs broke back.
He loosed the glittering belt and slipped it off
and the loin-piece and the plated guard below it,
gear the bronzesmiths made. When he saw the wound
where the tearing arrow hit, he sucked out the blood   250
and deftly applied the healing salves that Chiron,
friend of Asclepius, gave his father long ago.

And all the while they worked over Menelaus
whose cry could marshal armies, on the Trojans came,
columns armed for assault, and again the Argives
donned their gear and roused their lust for war.

King Agamemnon's hour. You would not find him asleep,
not cringing a moment, hanging back from the struggle—
he pressed for battle now where men win glory.

He left his team and burnished bronze car   260
with an aide, Eurymedon, Ptolemaeus Piraïdes' son
reining off to the side his snorting pair of stallions.
He gave him strict orders to keep them close at hand
for the time his knees might buckle with fatigue
from bringing crowds of soldiers into line.
Then out he went on foot to range the ranks.
The charioteers he spotted, fast with teams,
he'd halt beside and spur them on: "My Argives,
never relax your nerve, your fighting strength!
Father Zeus, I swear, will never defend the Trojans,   270
liars—they were the first to trample on their oaths.
So vultures will eat them raw, their firm young flesh,
and we, we'll drag their dear wives and helpless children
back to the beaked ships, once we've seized their city!"

      But any men he saw retreating from hateful battle
he would lash with a sharp burst of rage: "You Argives—
glorious braggarts! Disgraces—have you no shame?
Just standing there, dumbstruck like fawns
done in from hightailing over some big meadow,
winded and teetering, heart inside them spent.   280
Standing there dazed, your fighting spirit dead—
what are you waiting for? You want these Trojans
to pin you against your high sterns beached in the surf?
To *see* if Zeus will stretch his hands above your heads
and save your craven lives?"

                              So the commander
ranged Achaea's ranks and brought them into line.
Moving on through the crowds he found the Cretans
arming for combat now, ringing brave Idomeneus.
Strong as a boar he urged his frontline troops
as Meriones brought the rear battalions up.   290
King Agamemnon, thrilled to watch them work,
was quick to salute the chief and sing his praises:
"You are the one I prize, Idomeneus, more than all
our Argive fighters fast with chariot-teams—
whether in war or action of any sort

or feasts where the ranking Argive warlords
mix their bowls with the shining wine of kings.
What if the rest of all the long-haired Achaeans
drink their measure off? Your cup stands filled, always,
brimmed like mine when the will stirs *you* to drink—   300
so now drink deep of battle. Be that fighter
you claimed to be in all the years gone by."

    The Cretan captain Idomeneus answered warmly,
"Trust me, Atrides—count on me, your comrade,
staunch as I swore at first, that day I bowed my head.
Now fire up the rest of your long-haired Achaeans.
On with the fighting, quickly!
The Trojans broke our binding truce just now—
death and grief to the men of Troy hereafter!
They were the first to trample on our pact."

                                    Hearing that,   310
the son of Atreus strode on. Elated and making way
through crowds of troops he found the two called Ajax,
Great and Little, both captains armed for attack
with a cloud of infantry forming up behind them.
Think how a goatherd off on a mountain lookout
spots a storm cloud moving down the sea . . .
bearing down beneath the rush of the West Wind
and miles away he sees it building black as pitch,
blacker, whipping the whitecaps, full hurricane fury—
the herdsman shudders to see it, drives his flocks to a cave—   320
so dense the battalions grouped behind the two Aeantes,
packed, massed with hardy fighters dear to the gods,
battalions black and bristling shields and spears,
fighters sweeping into the breaking storm of war.
And King Agamemnon, thrilled to see that sight,
sped them on with a rousing flight of praises:
"Ajax—Ajax! Chiefs of the Argives armed in bronze,
no orders for you—it's wrong to incite you two,
you lead your men to war in so much force.
Father Zeus, Athena, Apollo, if all my fighters   330

had such courage pounding inside their chests,
we'd bring King Priam's citadel crashing down
in an instant, sacked at our hands—annihilated."

He spun on his heels and left them there in place,
heading for other ranks and came on Nestor next,
the clear speaker of Pylos posting troops,
readying them for action, combat units forming
under the lanky Pelagon, Alastor and Chromius,
Haemon and stocky Bias, skilled captain of armies.
Forward he ranged the charioteers with teams and cars,   340
backed by infantry close behind them, milling, brave men,
the defensive line of battle—that would be their role.
But the known cowards he drove amidst the center:
a man might cringe but he'd be forced to fight.
And first he gave his drivers strict commands
to rein their teams back hard and never panic,
no fouling them in the onslaught: "Let no man,
so sure of his horsemanship and soldier's prowess,
dare to fight it out alone with the Trojans,
exposed in front of his lines. No heroics now!   350
But give no ground—the charge will go to pieces.
And any charioteer who reaches Trojan chariots,
thrust your spear from your own car, don't throw it!
Better that way—it's tighter, stronger fighting.
So men before your time stormed walls and cities,
holding fast to that tactic, warring on with heart."

The old soldier spurring his men with skills
from a lifetime spent campaigning, battles long ago.
And King Agamemnon, thrilled to see his efforts,
cheered him on with a flight of praise: "Old war-horse,   360
if only your knees could match the spirit in your chest
and your body's strength were planted firm as rock,
but the great leveler, age, has worn you down.
If only some other fighter had your years
and you could march with the younger, fitter men!"

    And Nestor the seasoned charioteer replied,
"True, Atrides, if only I were the man I was,
years ago, when I cut down rugged Ereuthalion . . .
but the gods won't give us all their gifts at once.
If I was a young man then, now old age dogs my steps.   370
Nevertheless, I'll still troop with the horsemen,
give them maneuvers, discipline and commands:
that is the right and pride of us old men.
The young spearmen will do the work with spears.
Younger than Nestor, the next generation up,
flush with their fresh strength."

                              So Nestor said
and Atrides ranged forward, glad at heart,
and came on Peteos' son the charioteer
Menestheus standing idle, and circling him
Athenian men who could raise the cry of battle.   380
And there beside them the great tactician Odysseus,
drawn up with his Cephallenians grouped around him,
bands of them, no mean fighters, watching, waiting.
The call to action had still not reached their ears
and the columns were only just now forming, moving out,
stallion-breaking Trojans and long lines of Achaeans.
So the Cephallenians held their ground there, poised . . .
when would some other Argive unit make its charge,
engage the Trojan front and open up in battle?
Spotting them now the lord of men Agamemnon   390
dressed them down with a winging burst of scorn:
"You there, Peteos' son, a king, dear to the gods!
And you, the captain of craft and cunning, shrewd with greed!
Why are you cowering here, skulking out of range?
Waiting for others to do your fighting for you?
You—it's your duty to stand in the front ranks
and take your share of the scorching blaze of battle.
First you are, when you hear of feasts from me,
when Achaeans set out banquets for the chiefs.
Then you're happy enough to down the roast meats   400
and cups of honeyed, mellow wine—all you can drink.
But now you'd gladly watch ten troops of Achaeans

beat you to this feast,
first to fight with the ruthless bronze before you!"

The great tactician Odysseus gave him a dark glance
and shot back at once, "Now what's this, Atrides,
this talk that slips through your clenched teeth?
How can you say I hang back from the fighting
when Argive units spur the slashing god of war
against these Trojan horsemen? Just you watch,   410
if you'll take the time and care to taste some action,
watch Telemachus' loving father lock and fight
with enemy champions, stallion-breaking Trojans.
You and your bluster—you are talking nonsense!"

Seeing his anger flare, field marshal Agamemnon
smiled broadly and took back his taunts at once:
"Royal son of Laertes, Odysseus, great tactician,
I must not bait you so beyond the limit . . .
must not give you orders. I know for a fact
the spirit in your heart is well-disposed   420
to me and all my efforts. We see eye-to-eye.
Come, we'll set these things to rights later—
if any offense has passed between us now.
May the gods make all our bluster come to nothing."

He left him there in place, heading for other chiefs.
And he came on Tydeus' son, impetuous Diomedes
standing by in his bolted car behind his team
with Sthenelus flanked beside him, Capaneus' son.
And spotting Tydides there, field marshal Agamemnon
gave him a winging burst of scorn: "What's this?—   430
you, the son of Tydeus, that skilled breaker of horses?
Why cringing here? Gazing out on the passageways of battle!
That was never Tydeus' way, shy behind the lines—
he'd grapple enemies, bolting ahead of comrades.
Or so they claim who watched him at his work.
I never met the man myself, never saw him,
but they say he had no equal. True enough,

he came to Mycenae once but not at war with us—
a guest, a friend, with the royal Polynices
raising troops that time they geared to attack   440
the holy walls of Thebes. They pressed us hard,
they begged us to give them battle-tested allies.
My kin were glad to oblige and grant them their requests—
till Zeus changed our minds with a flash of bad omens.
So off they went, getting some distance on their way
and reached the Asopus' grassy banks and reedbeds.
From that point the men sent Tydeus on ahead,
bearing their message. He marched out at once
and came on crowds, menacing bands of Thebans
feasting away in the halls of mighty Eteocles.

                       There,   450
a total stranger, the horseman Tydeus had no fear,
alone in the midst of Theban hordes. Undaunted,
Tydeus challenged them all to tests of strength
and beat them all with ease, in each event,
Athena urged him on with so much winning force.
But the Thebans rose in anger, lashed their teams
and packed an ambush to meet him heading back—
full fifty fighters with two chiefs in the lead,
Hunter the son of Bloodlust, strong as the gods,
and Killerman's son, the gifted cutthroat Slaughter.   460
But Tydeus treated them all to a shameful fate,
finished them all but let one run for home,
heeding the gods' signs he let the hunter off.
Now there was a man, that Tydeus, that Aetolian.
But he bore a son who's not the half of him in battle—
better only in wrangling, wars of words!"

                            Taunting so,
and steadfast Diomedes offered no reply . . .
overawed by the king's majestic scorn.
But Capaneus' headstrong son lashed back in style:
"Don't lie, Atrides! You know the truth—say it!   470
We claim we are far, far greater than our fathers.
We are the ones who stormed the seven gates of Thebes,
heading a weaker force and facing stronger walls

but obeying the gods' signs and backed by Zeus.
Our fathers? Fools. Their own bravado killed them.
Don't tell *me* you rank our fathers with ourselves!"

But resolute Diomedes gave him a dark glance:
"Sit down, my friend, be quiet. Listen to me.
I don't blame Agamemnon, our commander in chief,
for goading his combat-ready Argives into battle.   480
The glory goes to him if the Argive fighters
lay the Trojans low and take their sacred city,
but immense grief is his if comrades die in droves.
Up now, rouse our fighting-fury!"

                                   With that challenge
he sprang from his chariot fully armed and hit the ground.
A terrific din of bronze rang from the captain's chest,
striding toward attack. Fear would have gripped
the staunchest man and made his knees give way.

As a heavy surf assaults some roaring coast,
piling breaker on breaker whipped by the West Wind,   490
and out on the open sea a crest first rears its head
then pounds down on the shore with hoarse, rumbling thunder
and in come more shouldering crests, arching up and breaking
against some rocky spit, exploding salt foam to the skies—
so wave on wave they came, Achaean battalions ceaseless,
surging on to war. Each captain ordered his men
and the ranks moved on in silence . . .
You'd never think so many troops could march
holding their voices in their chests, all silence,
fearing their chiefs who called out clear commands,   500
and the burnished blazoned armor round their bodies flared,
the formations trampling on.

                              But not the Trojans, no . . .
like flocks of sheep in a wealthy rancher's steadings,
thousands crowding to have their white milk drained,
bleating nonstop when they hear their crying lambs—
so the shouts rose up from the long Trojan lines
and not one cry, no common voice to bind them

all together, their tongues mixed and clashed,
their men hailed from so many far-flung countries.
Ares drove them, fiery-eyed Athena drove the Argives,   510
and Terror and Rout and relentless Strife stormed too,
sister of manslaughtering Ares, Ares' comrade-in-arms—
Strife, only a slight thing when she first rears her head
but her head soon hits the sky as she strides across the earth.
Now Strife hurled down the leveler Hate amidst both sides,
wading into the onslaught, flooding men with pain.

At last the armies clashed at one strategic point,
they slammed their shields together, pike scraped pike
with the grappling strength of fighters armed in bronze
and their round shields pounded, boss on welded boss,   520
and the sound of struggle roared and rocked the earth.
Screams of men and cries of triumph breaking in one breath,
fighters killing, fighters killed, and the ground streamed blood.
Wildly as two winter torrents raging down from the mountains,
swirling into a valley, hurl their great waters together,
flash floods from the wellsprings plunging down in a gorge
and miles away in the hills a shepherd hears the thunder—
so from the grinding armies broke the cries and crash of war.

Antilochus was the first to kill a Trojan captain,
tough on the front lines, Thalysias' son Echepolus.   530
Antilochus thrust first, speared the horsehair helmet
right at the ridge, and the bronze spearpoint lodged
in the man's forehead, smashing through his skull
and the dark came whirling down across his eyes—
he toppled down like a tower in the rough assault.
As he fell the enormous Elephenor grabbed his feet,
Chalcodon's son, lord of the brave-hearted Abantes,
dragged him out from under the spears, rushing madly
to strip his gear but his rush was short-lived.
Just as he dragged that corpse the brave Agenor   540
spied his ribs, bared by his shield as he bent low—
Agenor stabbed with a bronze spear and loosed his limbs,
his life spirit left him and over his dead body now

the savage work went on, Achaeans and Trojans
mauling each other there like wolves, leaping,
hurtling into each other, man throttling man.

    And Telamonian Ajax struck Anthemion's son,
the hardy stripling Simoisius, still unwed . . .
His mother had borne him along the Simois' banks
when she trailed her parents down the slopes of Ida   550
to tend their flocks, and so they called him Simoisius.
But never would he repay his loving parents now
for the gift of rearing—his life cut short so soon,
brought down by the spear of lionhearted Ajax.
At the first charge he slashed his right nipple,
clean through the shoulder went the brazen point
and down in the dust he fell like a lithe black poplar
shot up tall and strong in the spreading marshy flats,
the trunk trimmed but its head a shock of branches.
A chariot-maker fells it with shining iron ax   560
as timber to bend for handsome chariot wheels
and there it lies, seasoning by the river . . .
So lay Anthemion's son Simoisius, cut down
by the giant royal Ajax.

                        Antiphus hurled at *him*—
the son of Priam wearing a gleaming breastplate
let fly through the lines but his sharp spear missed
and he hit Leucus instead, Odysseus' loyal comrade,
gouging his groin as the man hauled off a corpse—
it dropped from his hands and Leucus sprawled across it.
Enraged at his friend's death Odysseus sprang in fury,   570
helmed in fiery bronze he plowed through the front
and charging the enemy, glaring left and right
he hurled his spear—a glinting brazen streak—
and the Trojans gave ground, scattering back,
panicking there before his whirling shaft—
a direct hit! Odysseus struck Democoon,
Priam's bastard son come down from Abydos,
Priam's racing-stables. Incensed for the dead
Odysseus speared him straight through one temple

and out the other punched the sharp bronze point   580
and the dark came swirling thick across his eyes—
down he crashed, armor clanging against his chest.
And the Trojan front shrank back, glorious Hector too
as the Argives yelled and dragged away the corpses,
pushing on, breakneck on. But lord god Apollo,
gazing down now from the heights of Pergamus,
rose in outrage, crying down at the Trojans,
"Up and at them, you stallion-breaking Trojans!
Never give up your lust for war against these Argives!
What are their bodies made of, rock or iron to block   590
your tearing bronze? Stab them, slash their flesh!
Achilles the son of lovely sleek-haired Thetis—
the man's not even fighting, no, he wallows
in all his heartsick fury by the ships!"

                                              So he cried
from far on the city's heights, the awesome god Apollo.
But Zeus's daughter Athena spurred the Argives on—
Athena first in glory, third-born of the gods—
whenever she saw some slacker hanging back
as she hurtled through the onset.

                                   Now Amarinceus' son
Diores—fate shackled Diores fast and a jagged rock   600
struck him against his right shin, beside the ankle.
Pirous son of Imbrasus winged it hard and true,
the Thracian chief who had sailed across from Aenus . . .
the ruthless rock striking the bones and tendons
crushed them to pulp—he landed flat on his back,
slamming the dust, both arms flung out to his comrades,
gasping out his life. Pirous who heaved the rock
came rushing in and speared him up the navel—
his bowels uncoiled, spilling loose on the ground
and the dark came swirling down across his eyes.

                                        But Pirous—   610
Aetolian Thoas speared *him* as he swerved and sprang away,
the lancehead piercing his chest above the nipple
plunged deep in his lung, and Thoas, running up,
wrenched the heavy spear from the man's chest,

drew his blade, ripped him across the belly,
took his life but he could not strip his armor.
Look, there were Pirous' cohorts bunched in a ring,
Thracians, topknots waving, clutching their long pikes
and rugged, strong and proud as the Trojan Thoas was,
they shoved him back—he gave ground, staggering, reeling.   620
And so the two lay stretched in the dust, side-by-side,
a lord of Thrace, a lord of Epeans armed in bronze
and a ruck of other soldiers died around them.

                                    And now
no man who waded into that work could scorn it any longer,
anyone still not speared or stabbed by tearing bronze
who whirled into the heart of all that slaughter—
not even if great Athena led him by the hand,
flicking away the weapons hailing down against him.
That day ranks of Trojans, ranks of Achaean fighters
sprawled there side-by-side, facedown in the dust.   630

BOOK FIVE

Diomedes Fights the Gods

Then Pallas Athena granted Tydeus' son Diomedes
strength and daring—so the fighter would shine forth
and tower over the Argives and win himself great glory.
She set the man ablaze, his shield and helmet flaming
with tireless fire like the star that flames at harvest,
bathed in the Ocean, rising up to outshine all other stars.
Such fire Athena blazed from Tydides' head and shoulders,
drove him into the center where the masses struggled on.

    There was a Trojan, Dares, a decent, wealthy man,
the god Hephaestus' priest who had bred two sons,   10
Phegeus and Idaeus, trained for every foray . . .
Breaking ranks they rushed ahead in their chariot,
charging Diomedes already dismounted,
rearing up on foot.

They went for each other fast, close range—
Phegeus hurled first, his spear's shadow flew
and over Tydides' left shoulder the tip passed
and never touched his body. Tydides hurled next,
the bronze launched from his hand and not for nothing:
hitting Phegeus' chest between the nipples it pitched him out   20
behind his team. Idaeus leapt, abandoned the handsome car
but did not dare to stand and defend his dead brother—
and not even so would *he* have fled his black death
but the god of fire swept him off and saved him,
shrouding the man in night so the old priest
would not be wholly crushed with one son left.
But high-hearted Tydides drove away the team
and gave them to aides to lash both horses back
to the hollow ships. And now despite their courage
the Trojan fighters seeing the two sons of Dares,   30
one on the run, one dead beside his chariot—
all their hearts were stunned . . .
But Athena, eyes bright, taking Ares in hand,
called the violent god away with: "Ares, Ares,
destroyer of men, reeking blood, stormer of ramparts,
why not let these mortals fight it out for themselves?
Let Zeus give glory to either side he chooses.
We'll stay clear and escape the Father's rage."

    And so, luring the headlong Ares off the lines
Athena sat him down on Scamander's soft, sandy banks   40
while Argives bent the Trojans back. Each captain
killed his man. First Agamemnon lord of men
spilled the giant Odius, chief of the Halizonians
off his car—the first to fall, as he veered away
the spearhead punched his back between the shoulders,
gouging his flesh and jutting out through his ribs—
he fell with a crash, his armor rang against him.

    Idomeneus cut down Phaestus, Maeonian Borus' son
who shipped to Troy from the good rich earth of Tarne.

As he tried to mount behind his team the famous spearman   50
stabbed a heavy javelin deep in his right shoulder—
he dropped from his war-car, gripped by the hateful dark.

Then as Idomeneus' henchman stripped the corpse
Menelaus took Scamandrius down with a sharp spear—
Strophius' son, a crack marksman skilled at the hunt.
Artemis taught the man herself to track and kill
wild beasts, whatever breeds in the mountain woods,
but the Huntress showering arrows could not save him now
nor the archer's long shots, his forte in days gone by.
No, now Menelaus the great spearman ran him through,   60
square between the blades as he fled and raced ahead,
tearing into his flesh, drilling out through his chest—
he crashed facedown, his armor clanged against him.

Meriones killed Phereclus—son of Tecton,
son of the blacksmith Harmon—the fighter's hands
had the skill to craft all kinds of complex work
since Pallas Athena loved him most, her protégé
who had built Paris his steady, balanced ships,
trim launchers of death, freighted with death
for all of Troy and now for the shipwright too: 70
what could the man know of all the gods' decrees?
Meriones caught him quickly, running him down hard
and speared him low in the right buttock—the point
pounding under the pelvis, jabbed and pierced the bladder—
he dropped to his knees, screaming, death swirling round him.

Meges killed Pedaeus, Antenor's son, a bastard boy
but lovely Theano nursed him with close, loving care
like her own children, just to please her husband.
Closing, Meges gave him some close attention too—
the famous spearman struck behind his skull,   80
just at the neck-cord, the razor spear slicing
straight up through the jaws, cutting away the tongue—
he sank in the dust, teeth clenching the cold bronze.

Euaemon's son Eurypylus cut down brave Hypsenor,
son of lofty Dolopion, a man the Trojans made
Scamander's priest and worshipped like a god.
But Euaemon's royal son laid low his son—
Eurypylus, chasing Hypsenor fleeing on before him,
flailed with a sword, slashed the Trojan's shoulder
and lopped away the massive bulk of Hypsenor's arm . . .   90
the bloody arm dropped to the earth, and red death
came plunging down his eyes, and the strong force of fate.

So they worked away in the rough assaults, but Diomedes,
which side was the fighter on? You could not tell—
did he rampage now with the Trojans or the Argives?
Down the plain he stormed like a stream in spate,
a routing winter torrent sweeping away the dikes:
the tight, piled dikes can't hold it back any longer,
banks shoring the blooming vineyards cannot curb its course—
a flash flood bursts as the rains from Zeus pour down their power,   100
acre on acre the well-dug work of farmers crumbling under it—
so under Tydides' force the Trojan columns panicked now,
no standing their ground, massed, packed as they were.

But the shining archer Pandarus marked him storming
down the plain, smashing the Trojan lines before him.
Quickly he trained his reflex bow on Diomedes
charging straight ahead—he shot! he struck him full
in the right shoulder, under the breastplate's hollow
the ripping point tore deep, shearing its way through,
armor splattered with blood as Pandarus triumphed,   110
shouting over Tydides wildly, "Move up, attack,
my high-hearted Trojans, lash your stallions!
Look, the Achaean champion's badly wounded—
I shot him down, I swear he won't last long—
if the Archer really sped me here from Lycia!"

                                    Bragging so,
but the whizzing arrow had not brought him down.
Diomedes just drew back beside his car and team
and stood there calling Sthenelus, Capaneus' son:

"Quick, Sthenelus. Down from the car, my friend,
pull this wretched arrow from my shoulder!"   120

Sthenelus sprang from the car, hit the ground
and standing beside him, pulled the tearing arrow
clean on through the wound and blood came shooting out
like a red lance through the supple mesh shirt.
And Diomedes lord of the war cry prayed aloud,
"Hear me, daughter of Zeus whose shield is thunder,
tireless one, Athena! If you ever stood by father
with all your love amidst the blaze of battle,
stand by *me*—do me a favor now, Athena.
Bring that man into range and let me spear him!   130
He's wounded me off guard and now he triumphs—
he boasts I won't look long on the light of day."

So Tydides prayed and Athena heard his prayer,
put spring in his limbs, his feet, his fighting hands
and close beside him winged him on with a flight of orders:
"Now take heart, Diomedes, fight it out with the Trojans!
Deep in your chest I've put your father's strength.
He never quaked, that Tydeus, that great horseman—
what force the famous shieldsman used to wield!
Look, I've lifted the mist from off your eyes   140
that's blurred them up to now—
so you can tell a god from man on sight.
So now if a god comes up to test your mettle,
you must not fight the immortal powers head-on,
all but one of the deathless gods, that is—
if Aphrodite daughter of Zeus slips into battle,
she's the one to stab with your sharp bronze spear!"

Her eyes bright, Athena soared away and Tydeus' son
went charging back to the front line of champions.
Now, long ablaze as he was to fight the Trojans,   150
triple the fury seized him—claw-mad as a lion
some shepherd tending woolly flocks in the field
has just grazed, a lion leaping into the fold,

but he hasn't killed him, only spurred his strength
and helpless to beat him off the man scurries for shelter,
leaving his flocks panicked, lost as the ramping beast
mauls them thick-and-fast, piling corpse on corpse
and in one furious bound clears the fenced yard—
so raging Diomedes mauled the Trojans.

There—
he killed Astynous, then Hypiron, a frontline captain.   160
One he stabbed with a bronze lance above the nipple,
the other his heavy sword hacked at the collarbone,
right on the shoulder, cleaving the whole shoulder
clear of neck and back. And he left them there,
dead, and he made a rush at Abas and Polyidus,
sons of Eurydamas, an aged reader of dreams,
but the old prophet read no dreams for *them*
when they set out for Troy—Diomedes laid them low
then swung to attack the two sons of Phaenops,
hardy Xanthus and Thoon, both men grown tall   170
as their father shrank away with wasting age . . .
he'd never breed more sons to leave his riches to.
The son of Tydeus killed the two of them on the spot,
he ripped the dear life out of both and left their father
tears and wrenching grief. Now he'd never welcome
his two sons home from war, alive in the flesh,
and distant kin would carve apart their birthright.

Next Diomedes killed two sons of Dardan Priam
careening on in a single car, Echemmon and Chromius.
As a lion charges cattle, calves and heifers   180
browsing the deep glades and snaps their necks,
so Tydides pitched them both from the chariot,
gave them a mauling—gave them little choice—
quickly stripped their gear and passed their team
to his men to lash back to the ships.

Smashing
the lines of fighters now—

but Aeneas marked it all
and oblivious to the rain of spears he waded in,

hunting for Pandarus, hoping to find the archer.
Find him he did, Lycaon's skilled, fearless son,
and went right up and challenged him to his face: 190
"Pandarus, where's your bow, your winged arrows,
your archer's glory? No Trojan your rival here,
no Lycian can claim to be your better, no—
so up with you now! Lift your hands to Zeus,
you whip an arrow against that man, whoever he is
who routs us, wreaking havoc against us, cutting the legs
from under squads of good brave men. Unless it's a god
who smolders at our troops, enraged at a rite we failed—
when a god's enraged there's thunder at our heads."

     And Lycaon's shining son took up the challenge: 200
"Aeneas, counselor of the Trojans armed in bronze,
he looks like Tydeus' son to me in every way—
I know his shield, the hollow eyes of his visor,
his team, I've watched them closely.
And still I could never swear he's not a god . . .
but if he's the man I think he is, Tydeus' gallant son,
he rages so with a god beside him—not alone, no—
a god with his shoulders shrouded round in cloud
who deflects my shaft to a less mortal spot.
I had already whipped an arrow into him,   210
caught him square in the right shoulder too,
just where the breastplate leaves the armpit bare,
and I thought I'd sent him down to the House of Death
but I've still not laid him low. So it *is* some god rampaging!
And here I am, no chariot, no team to speed me on.
But back in Lycaon's halls are eleven war-cars,
beauties all, fresh from the smith and fire-new
and blankets spread across them. And beside each
a brace of stallions standing poised and pawing,
champing their oats and barley glistening white.   220
Over and over father, the old spearman Lycaon
urged me, setting out from his well-built halls,
'Take those teams and cars,' he told me, 'mount up,
lead the Trojans into the jolting shocks of battle!'

But would I listen? So much the better if I had . . .
I had to spare my teams. They'd never starve for fodder—
crammed with the fighters—bred to eat their fill.
So I left them there, I made it to Troy on foot,
trusting my bows and arrows, and a lot of good
I was to get from them. Already I've let fly   230
at two of their best men, Diomedes and Menelaus—
I've hit them both, and the blood gushed from both,
direct hits, but I only roused their fury.

                                   What bad luck—
to snatch this curved bow off its peg that day
I marched my Trojans hard to your lovely town of Troy,
to please Prince Hector. But if I get home again
and set my eyes on my native land, my wife
and my fine house with the high vaulting roof,
let some stranger cut my head off then and there
if I don't smash this bow and fling it in the fire—   240
the gear I packed is worthless as the wind."

     Aeneas the Trojan captain checked him sharply:
"No talk of turning for home! No turning the *tide*
till we wheel and face this man with team and car
and fight it out with weapons hand-to-hand.
Come, up with you now, climb aboard my chariot!
So you can see the breed of Tros's team, their flair
for their own terrain as they gallop back and forth,
one moment in flight, the next in hot pursuit.
They'll sweep us back to the city, back to safety   250
if Zeus hands Tydeus' son the glory once again.
Quick, take up the whip and glittering reins!
I'll dismount from the car and fight on foot—
or you engage the man and leave the team to me."

     The shining son of Lycaon made the choice:
"Take up the reins yourself, Aeneas. Do—
they're *your* team, they'll haul your curving chariot
so much better under the driver they know best
if we have to beat retreat from Diomedes.

God forbid they panic, skittish with fear,   260
buck and never pull us out of the fighting,
missing your own voice as Tydeus' son attacks—
he'll kill us both and drive them off as prizes.
So drive them yourself, your chariot and your team
and let him charge—I'll take him on with a sharp spear."

    Both men agreed, boarding the blazoned chariot,
wildly heading their racers at Diomedes now.
Capaneus' good son Sthenelus saw them coming
and quickly alerted Diomedes, warnings flying:
"Tydides, joy of my heart, dear comrade, look!   270
I see two men and they're bearing down to fight you!
Their power's enormous—one's a master archer,
Pandarus, son of Lycaon, so he boasts.
The other's Aeneas, claims Anchises' blood,
the noble Anchises, but his mother's Aphrodite.
Come, up you go in our chariot, give ground now!
No charging the front ranks—you might lose your life."

    But powerful Diomedes froze him with a glance:
"Not a word of retreat. You'll never persuade me.
It's not my nature to shrink from battle, cringe in fear   280
with the fighting strength still steady in my chest.
I shrink from mounting our chariot—no retreat—
on foot as I am, I'll meet them man-to-man.
Athena would never let me flinch. Those two?
Their horses will never sweep them clear of *us*,
not both men, though one or the other may escape.
One more thing—take it to heart, I tell you—
if part of Athena's plan gives *me* the honor
to kill them both, you check our racers here,
you lash them fast to our rails   290
then dash for Aeneas' horses—don't forget—
drive them out of the Trojan lines and into ours.
They are the very strain farseeing Zeus gave Tros,
payment in full for stealing Ganymede, Tros's son:
the purest, strongest breed of all the stallions

under the dawn and light of day. Lord Anchises
stole from that fine stock—behind Laomedon's back,
Tros's grandson and heir to Tros's teams—
he put some mares to the lusty stallions once
and they foaled him a run of six in his royal house.   300
Four he kept for himself, to rear in his own stalls,
but the two you see in action he gave Aeneas,
both of them driving terrors. Would to god
we'd take them both—we'd win ourselves great fame."

Wavering back and forth as their two attackers
closed in a rush, whipping that purebred team along
and Pandarus shouted first, "What mad bravado—
lofty Tydeus' boy will brave it out! So,
my arrow failed to bring you down, my tearing shot?
Now for a spear—we'll see if *this* can kill you!"   310

Shaft poised, he hurled and its long shadow flew
and it struck Tydides' shield, the brazen spearhead
winging, drilling right on through to his breastplate,
Pandarus yelling over him wildly now, "You're hit—
clean through the side! You won't last long, I'd say—
now the glory's mine!"

                But never shaken,
staunch Diomedes shot back, "No hit—you missed!
But the two of you will never quit this fight, *I'd* say,
till one of you drops and dies and gluts with blood
Ares who hacks at men behind his rawhide shield!"   320

With that he hurled and Athena drove the shaft
and it split the archer's nose between the eyes—
it cracked his glistening teeth, the tough bronze
cut off his tongue at the roots, smashed his jaw
and the point came ripping out beneath his chin.
He pitched from his car, armor clanged against him,
a glimmering blaze of metal dazzling round his back—
the purebreds reared aside, hoofs pawing the air
and his life and power slipped away on the wind.

Aeneas sprang down with his shield and heavy spear,   330
fearing the Argives might just drag away the corpse,
somehow, somewhere. Aeneas straddled the body—
proud in his fighting power like some lion—
shielded the corpse with spear and round buckler,
burning to kill off any man who met him face-to-face
and he loosed a bloodcurdling cry. Just as Diomedes
hefted a boulder in his hands, a tremendous feat—
no two men could hoist it, weak as men are now,
but all on his own he raised it high with ease,
flung it and struck Aeneas' thigh where the hipbone   340
turns inside the pelvis, the joint they call the cup—
it smashed the socket, snapped both tendons too
and the jagged rock tore back the skin in shreds.
The great fighter sank to his knees, bracing himself
with one strong forearm planted against the earth,
and the world went black as night before his eyes.

And now the prince, the captain of men Aeneas
would have died on the spot if Zeus's daughter
had not marked him quickly, his mother Aphrodite
who bore him to King Anchises tending cattle once.   350
Round her beloved son her glistening arms went streaming,
flinging her shining robe before him, only a fold
but it blocked the weapons hurtling toward his body.
She feared some Argive fast with chariot-team
might hurl bronze in his chest and rip his life out.

She began to bear her dear son from the fighting . . .
but Capaneus' son did not forget the commands
the lord of the war cry put him under. Sthenelus
checked his own racers clear of the crash of battle,
lashed them tight to his chariot-rails with reins   360
then dashed for Aeneas' glossy full-maned team
and drove them out of the Trojan lines and into his.
He passed them on to Deipylus, a friend-in-arms
he prized beyond all comrades his own age—
their minds worked as one—to drive to the ships

as Sthenelus mounted behind his own chariot now,
seized the glittering reins and whipped his team,
his strong-hoofed horses ahead at breakneck speed,
rearing, plunging to overtake his captain Diomedes
but *he* with his ruthless bronze was hunting Aphrodite—   370
Diomedes, knowing her for the coward goddess she is,
none of the mighty gods who marshal men to battle,
neither Athena nor Enyo raider of cities, not at all.
But once he caught her, stalking her through the onslaught,
gallant Tydeus' offspring rushed her, lunging out,
thrusting his sharp spear at her soft, limp wrist
and the brazen point went slashing through her flesh,
tearing straight through the fresh immortal robes
the Graces themselves had made her with their labor.
He gouged her just where the wristbone joins the palm   380
and immortal blood came flowing quickly from the goddess,
the ichor that courses through their veins, the blessed gods—
they eat no bread, they drink no shining wine, and so
the gods are bloodless, so we call them deathless.
A piercing shriek—she reeled and dropped her son.
But Phoebus Apollo plucked him up in his hands
and swathed him round in a swirling dark mist
for fear some Argive fast with chariot-team
might hurl bronze in his chest and rip his life out.
But Diomedes shouted after her, shattering war cries: 390
"Daughter of Zeus, give up the war, your lust for carnage!
So, it's not enough that you lure defenseless women
to their ruin? Haunting the fighting, are you?
Now I think you'll cringe at the hint of war
if you get wind of battle far away."

                              So he mocked
and the goddess fled the front, beside herself with pain.
But Iris quick as the wind took up her hand
and led her from the fighting . . .
racked with agony, her glowing flesh blood-dark.
And off to the left of battle she discovered Ares,   400
violent Ares sitting there at ease, his long spear
braced on a cloudbank, flanked by racing stallions.

Aphrodite fell to her knees, over and over begged
her dear brother to lend his golden-bridled team:
"Oh dear brother, help me! Give me your horses—
so I can reach Olympus, the gods' steep stronghold.
I'm wounded, the pain's too much, a mortal's speared me—
that daredevil Diomedes, *he*'d fight Father Zeus!"

Her brother Ares gave her the golden-bridled team.
Heart writhing in pain, she climbed aboard the car   410
and Iris climbed beside her, seized the reins,
whipped the team to a run and on the horses flew,
holding nothing back. In a moment they had reached
the immortals' stronghold, steep Olympus. Wind-quick Iris
curbed the team and loosing them from the chariot
threw ambrosial fodder down before their hoofs.
The deathless Aphrodite sank in Dione's lap
and her mother, folding her daughter in her arms,
stroked her gently, whispered her name and asked,
"Who has abused you now, dear child, tell me,   420
who of the sons of heaven so unfeeling, cruel?
Why, it's as if they had caught you in public,
doing something wrong . . ."

And Aphrodite who loves eternal laughter
sobbed in answer, "The son of Tydeus stabbed me,
Diomedes, that overweening, insolent—all because
I was bearing off my son from the fighting. Aeneas—
dearest to me of all the men alive. Look down!
It's no longer ghastly war for Troy and Achaea—
now, I tell you, the Argives fight the gods!"   430

Dione the light and loveliest of immortals
tried to calm her: "Patience, oh my child.
Bear up now, despite your heartsick grief.
How many gods who hold the halls of Olympus
have had to endure such wounds from mortal men,
whenever we try to cause each other pain . . .
Ares had to endure it, when giant Ephialtes and Otus,

sons of Aloeus, bound him in chains he could not burst,
trussed him up in a brazen cauldron, thirteen months.
And despite the god's undying lust for battle   440
Ares might have wasted away there on the spot
if the monsters' stepmother, beautiful Eriboea
had not sent for Hermes, and out of the cauldron
Hermes stole him away—the War-god breathing his last,
all but broken down by the ruthless iron chains.
And Hera endured it too, that time Amphitryon's son,
mighty Heracles hit her deep in the right breast
with a three-barbed shaft, and pain seized her,
nothing calmed the pain.

                                  Even tremendous Hades
had to endure that flying shaft like all the rest,   450
when the same man, the son of thunder-shielded Zeus,
shot him in Pylos—there with the troops of battle dead—
and surrendered Death to pain. But Hades made his way
to craggy Olympus, climbed to the house of Zeus,
stabbed with agony, grief-struck to the heart,
the shaft driven into his massive shoulder
grinding down his spirit . . .
But the Healer applied his pain-killing drugs
and sealed Hades' wound—he was not born to die.
Think of that breakneck Heracles, his violent work,   460
not a care in the world for all the wrongs he'd done—
he and his arrows raking the gods who hold Olympus!
But the man who attacked you? The great goddess
fiery-eyed Athena set him on, that fool—
Doesn't the son of Tydeus know, down deep,
the man who fights the gods does not live long?
Nor do his children ride his knees with cries of 'Father'—
home at last from the wars and heat of battle.

                                              So now
let Diomedes, powerful as he is, be on his guard
for fear a better soldier than you engage him—   470
for fear his wife, Aegialia, Adrastus' daughter,
for all her self-control, will wail through the nights
and wake her beloved servants out of sleep . . .

the gallant wife in tears, longing for him,
her wedded husband, the best of the Achaeans—
Diomedes breaker of horses."
                              Soothing words,
and with both her hands Dione gently wiped the ichor
from Aphrodite's arm and her wrist healed at once,
her stark pain ebbed away.
But Hera and great Athena were looking on   480
and with mocking words began to provoke the Father,
Athena leading off with taunts, her eyes bright:
"Father Zeus, I wonder if you would fume at me
if I ventured a bold guess? Our goddess of love—
I'd swear she's just been rousing another Argive,
another beauty to pant and lust for Trojans,
those men the goddess loves to such despair.
Stroking one of the Argive women's rippling gowns
she's pricked her limp wrist on a golden pinpoint!"

    So she mocked, and the father of gods and mortals   490
smiled broadly, calling the golden Aphrodite over:
"Fighting is not for you, my child, the works of war.
See to the works of marriage, the slow fires of longing.
Athena and blazing Ares will deal with all the bloodshed."

    And now as the high gods bantered back and forth
Diomedes, loosing his war cry, charged Aeneas—
though what he saw was lord Apollo himself,
guarding, spreading his arms above the fighter,
but even before the mighty god he would not flinch.
Tydides reared and hurled himself again and again,   500
trying to kill Aeneas, strip his famous armor.
Three times he charged, frenzied to bring him down,
three times Apollo battered his gleaming shield back—
then at Tydides' fourth assault like something superhuman,
the Archer who strikes from worlds away shrieked out—
a voice of terror—"Think, Diomedes, shrink back now!
Enough of this madness—striving with the gods.
We are not of the same breed, we never will be,

the deathless gods and men who walk the earth."

                                            Menacing so
that Tydeus' son pulled back, just a little, edging   510
clear of the distant deadly Archer's rage.
And Apollo swept Aeneas up from the onslaught
and set him down on the sacred heights of Pergamus,
the crest where the god's own temple had been built.
There in the depths of the dark forbidden chamber
Leto and Artemis who showers flights of arrows
healed the man and brought him back to glory.
But the lord of the silver bow devised a phantom—
like Aeneas to the life, wearing his very armor—
and round that phantom Trojans and brave Achaeans   520
went at each other, hacking the oxhides round their chests,
the bucklers full and round, skin-shields, tassels flying.
But Phoebus Apollo called to blazing Ares, "Ares, Ares,
destroyer of men, reeking blood, stormer of ramparts,
can't you go and drag that man from the fighting?
That daredevil Diomedes, *he'*d fight Father Zeus!
He's just assaulted Love, he stabbed her wrist—
like something superhuman he even charged at *me*!"

    With that, Apollo settled onto Pergamus heights
while murderous Ares, wading into the fighting,   530
spurred the Trojan columns on to mass attack.
Shaped like the runner Acamas, prince of Thrace,
Ares challenged the sons of Priam with a vengeance:
"You royal sons of Priam, monarch dear to the gods,
how long will you let Achaeans massacre your army?
Until they're battling round your well-built gates?
A man is down we prized on a par with noble Hector—
Aeneas, proud Anchises' son. Up with you now,
rescue him from the crash of battle! Save our comrade!"

    As Ares whipped the fighting spirit in each man   540
Sarpedon taunted Hector: "Hector, where has it gone—
that high courage you always carried in your heart?
No doubt you bragged that you could hold your city

without an army and Trojan allies—all on your own,
just with your sister's husbands and your brothers.
But where are they now? I look, I can't find one.
They cringe and cower like hounds circling a lion.
We—your allies here—we do your fighting for you.
And I myself, Hector, your ally-to-the-death,
a good long way I came from distant Lycia,   550
far from the Xanthus' rapids where I left
my loving wife, my baby son, great riches too,
the lasting envy of every needy neighbor.
And still I lead our Lycians into battle.
Myself? I chafe to face my man, full force,
though there's not a scrap of mine for looting here,
no cattle or gold the foe could carry off. But you,
you just stand there—don't even command the rest
to brace and defend their wives.

                              Beware the toils of war . . .
the mesh of the huge dragnet sweeping up the world,   560
before you're trapped, your enemies' prey and plunder—
soon they'll raze your sturdy citadel to the roots!
All this should obsess you, Hector, night and day.
You should be begging the men who lead your allies'
famous ranks to stand and fight for all they're worth—
you'll ward off all the blame they hurl against you."

    And Sarpedon's charge cut Hector to the core.
Down he leapt from his chariot fully armed, hit the ground
and brandishing two sharp spears went striding down his lines,
ranging flank to flank, driving his fighters into battle,   570
rousing grisly war—and round the Trojans whirled,
bracing to meet the Argives face-to-face:
but the Argives closed ranks, did not cave in.
Remember the wind that scatters the dry chaff,
sweeping it over the sacred threshing floor,
the men winnowing hard and blond Demeter culling
grain from dry husk in the rough and gusting wind
and under it all the heaps of chaff are piling white . . .
so white the Achaeans turned beneath the dust storm now,

pelting across their faces, kicked up by horses' hoofs   580
to the clear bronze sky—the battle joined again.
Charioteers swung chariots round,
thrust the powerful fist of fury straight ahead
and murderous Ares keen to help the Trojans
shrouded the carnage over in dense dark night—
lunging at all points, carrying out the commands
of Phoebus Apollo, lord of the golden sword,
who ordered Ares to whip the Trojans' war-lust
once he spotted Athena veering off the lines,
great Pallas who'd rushed to back the Argives.   590
Out of his rich guarded chamber the god himself
launched Aeneas now, driving courage into his heart
and the captain took his place amidst his men.
And how they thrilled to see him still alive,
safe, unharmed and marching back to their lines,
his soul ablaze for war, but his men asked him nothing.
The labor of battle would not let them, more labor urged
by the god of the silver bow and man-destroying Ares
and Strife flaring on, headlong on.

                                   The Achaeans?
The two Aeantes, Tydides and Odysseus spurred them   600
on to attack. The troops themselves had no fear,
no dread of the Trojans' power and breakneck charges,
no, they stood their ground like heavy thunderheads
stacked up on the towering mountaintops by Cronus' son,
stock-still in a windless calm when the raging North Wind
and his gusty ripping friends that had screamed down
to rout dark clouds have fallen dead asleep. So staunch
they stood the Trojan onslaught, never shrinking once
as Atrides ranged the ranks, shouting out commands:
"Now be men, my friends! Courage, come, take heart!   610
Dread what comrades say of you here in bloody combat!
When men dread that, more men come through alive—
when soldiers break and run, good-bye glory,
good-bye all defenses!"

                         A flash, a sudden hurl
and Atrides speared a champion out in front—

it was Prince Aeneas' comrade-in-arms Deicoon,
Pergasus' son the Trojans prized like Priam's sons,
quick as he always was to join the forward ranks.
Now his shield took powerful Agamemnon's spear
but failed to deflect it, straight through it smashed,   620
bronze splitting his belt and plunging down his guts—
he fell, thundering, armor ringing against him.

                                                         There—
Aeneas replied in kind and killed two Argive captains,
Diocles' two sons, Orsilochus flanking Crethon.
Their father lived in the fortress town of Phera,
a man of wealth and worth, born of Alpheus River
running wide through Pylian hills, the stream
that sired Ortilochus to rule their many men.
Ortilochus sired Diocles, that proud heart,
and Diocles bred Orsilochus twinned with Crethon   630
drilled for any fight. And reaching their prime
they joined the Argives sailing the black ships
outward bound for the stallion-land of Troy,
all for the sons of Atreus,
to fight to the end and win their honor back—
so death put an end to both, wrapped them both in night.
Fresh as two young lions off on the mountain ridges,
twins reared by a lioness deep in the dark glades,
that ravage shepherds' steadings, mauling the cattle
and fat sheep till it's their turn to die—hacked down   640
by the cleaving bronze blades in the shepherds' hands.
So here the twins were laid low at Aeneas' hands,
down they crashed like lofty pine trees axed.

                                                        Both down
but Menelaus pitied them both, yes, and out for blood
he burst through the front, helmed in fiery bronze,
shaking his spear, and Ares' fury drove him, Ares
hoping to see him crushed at Aeneas' hands.
Antilochus marked him now, great Nestor's son
went racing across the front himself, terrified
for the lord of armies—what if he were killed?   650
Their hard campaigning just might come to grief.

As Aeneas and Menelaus came within arm's reach,
waving whetted spears in each other's faces,
nerved to fight it out, Antilochus rushed in,
tensing shoulder-to-shoulder by his captain now—
and Aeneas shrank from battle, fast as he was in arms,
when he saw that pair of fighters side-by-side,
standing their ground against him . . .
Once they'd dragged the bodies back to their lines
they dropped the luckless twins in companions' open arms   660
and round they swung again to fight in the first ranks.

    And next they killed Pylaemenes tough as Ares,
a captain heading the Paphlagonian shieldsmen,
hot-blooded men. Menelaus the famous spearman
stabbed him right where he stood, the spearpoint
pounding his collarbone to splinters. Antilochus
killed his charioteer and steady henchman Mydon,
Atymnius' strapping son, just wheeling his racers round
as Antilochus winged a rock and smashed his elbow—
out of his grip the reins white with ivory flew   670
and slipped to the ground and tangled in the dust.
Antilochus sprang, he plunged a sword in his temple
and Mydon, gasping, hurled from his bolted car facefirst,
head and shoulders stuck in a dune a good long time
for the sand was soft and deep—his lucky day—
till his own horses trampled him down, down flat
as Antilochus lashed them hard and drove them back
to Achaea's waiting ranks.
                            But Hector marked them
across the lines and rushed them now with a cry
and Trojan shock troops backed him full strength.   680
And Ares led them in with the deadly Queen Enyo
bringing Uproar on, the savage chaos of battle—
the god of combat wielding his giant shaft in hand,
now ranging ahead of Hector, now behind him.
                                    Ares there—
and for all his war cries Diomedes shrank at the sight,
as a man at a loss, helpless, crossing a vast plain

halts short at a river rapids surging out to sea,
takes one look at the water roaring up in foam
and springs back with a leap. So he recoiled,
shouting out to comrades, "Oh my friends,   690
what fools we were to marvel at wondrous Hector,
what a spearman, we said, and what a daring fighter!
But a god goes with him always, beating off disaster—
look, that's Ares beside him now, just like a mortal!
Give ground, but faces fronting the Trojans always—
no use trying to fight the gods in force."

                                             So he warned
as the Trojans charged them, harder—and Hector, lunging,
leveled a pair of men who knew the joy of battle,
riding a single chariot, Menesthes and Anchialus.
Down they went and the Great Ajax pitied both,   700
he strode to their side and loomed there,
loosed a gleaming spear and struck down Amphius,
Selagus' son who had lived at ease in Paesus,
rich in possessions, rich in rolling wheatland . . .
But destiny guided Amphius on, a comrade sworn
to the cause of Priam and all of Priam's sons.
Now giant Ajax speared him through the belt,
deep in the guts the long, shadowy shaft stuck
and down he fell with a crash as glorious Ajax rushed
to strip his armor—Trojans showering spears against him,   710
points glittering round him, his shield taking repeated hits.
He dug his heel in the corpse, yanked his own bronze out
but as for the dead man's burnished gear—no hope.
The giant was helpless to rip it off his back.
Enemy weapons beating against him, worse,
he dreaded the Trojans too, swarming round him,
a tough ring of them, brave and bristling spears,
massing, rearing over their comrade's body now
and rugged, strong and proud as the Great Ajax was,
they shoved him back—he gave ground, staggering, reeling.   720

    So fighters worked away in the grim shocks of war.
And Heracles' own son, Tlepolemus tall and staunch . . .

his strong fate was driving him now against Sarpedon,
a man like a god. Closing quickly, coming head-to-head
the son and the son's son of Zeus who marshals storms,
Tlepolemus opened up to taunt his enemy first:
"Sarpedon, master strategist of the Lycians,
what compels you to cringe and cower here?
You raw recruit, green at the skills of battle!
They lie when they say you're born of storming Zeus.   730
Look at yourself. How short you fall of the fighters
sired by Zeus in the generations long before us!
Why, think what they say of mighty Heracles—
there was a man, my father,
that dauntless, furious spirit, that lionheart.
He once sailed here for Laomedon's blooded horses,
with just six ships and smaller crews than yours, true,
but he razed the walls of Troy, he widowed all her streets.
You with your coward's heart, your men dying round you!
You're no bulwark come out of Lycia, I can tell you—   740
no help to Trojans here. For all your power, soldier,
crushed at my hands you'll breach the gates of Death!"

But Sarpedon the Lycian captain faced him down:
"Right you are, Tlepolemus! Your great father
destroyed the sacred heights of Troy, thanks,
of course, to a man's stupidity, proud Laomedon.
That fool—he rewarded all his kindness with abuse,
never gave him the mares he'd come so far to win.
But the only thing you'll win at *my* hands here,
I promise you, is slaughter and black doom.   750
Gouged by my spear you'll give me glory now,
you'll give your life to the famous horseman Death!"

In fast reply Tlepolemus raised his ashen spear
and the same moment shafts flew from their hands
and Sarpedon hit him square across the neck,
the spear went ramming through—pure agony—
black night came swirling down across his eyes.
But Tlepolemus' shaft had struck Sarpedon too,

the honed tip of the weapon hitting his left thigh,
ferocious, razoring into flesh and scraping bone   760
but his Father beat off death a little longer.

                       Heroic Sarpedon—
his loyal comrades bore him out of the fighting quickly,
weighed down by the heavy spearshaft dragging on.
But hurrying so, no one noticed or even thought
to wrench the ashen javelin from his thigh
so the man could hobble upright. On they rushed,
bent on the work of tending to his body.

                       Tlepolemus—
far across the lines the armed Achaeans hauled him
out of the fight, and seasoned Odysseus saw it,
his brave spirit steady, ablaze for action now.   770
What should he do?—he racked his heart and soul—
lunge at Prince Sarpedon, son of storming Zeus,
or go at the Lycians' mass and kill them all?
But no, it was not the gallant Odysseus' fate
to finish Zeus's rugged son with his sharp bronze,
so Pallas swung his fury against the Lycian front.
Whirling, killing Coeranus, Chromius and Alastor,
killing Alcander and Halius, Prytanis and Noëmon—
and stalwart Odysseus would have killed still more
but tall Hector, his helmet flashing, marked him quickly,   780
plowed through the front, helmed in fiery bronze,
filling the Argives' hearts with sudden terror.
And Zeus's son Sarpedon rejoiced to see him
striding past and begged him in his pain,
"Son of Priam, don't leave me lying here,
such easy prey for the Danaans—protect me!
Later I'll bleed to death inside your walls.
Clearly it's not my fate
to journey home again to the fatherland I love,
to bring some joy to my dear wife, my baby son."

                       But Hector,   790
his helmet flashing, answered nothing—he swept past him,
Hector burning to thrust the Argives back at once
and tear the life and soul out of whole battalions.

But Sarpedon's loyal comrades laid him down,
a man like a god beneath a fine spreading oak
sacred to Zeus whose shield is banked with clouds.
The veteran Pelagon, one of his closest aides,
pushed the shaft of ashwood out through his wound—
his spirit left him—a mist poured down his eyes . . .
but he caught his breath again. A gust of the North Wind   800
blowing round him carried back the life breath
he had gasped away in pain.
                              But the Argive fighters?
Facing Ares' power and Hector helmed in bronze,
they neither turned and ran for their black ships
nor traded blows with enemies man-to-man.
Backing over and over, the Argives gave ground,
seeing the lord of battles lead the Trojan onset.

    Who was the first they slaughtered, who the last,
the brazen god of war and Hector son of Priam?
Teuthras first, Orestes lasher of stallions next,   810
an Aetolian spearman Trechus, Oenomaus and Helenus,
Oenops' son, and Oresbius cinched with shining belt
who had lived in Hyle hoarding his great wealth,
his estate aslope the shores of Lake Cephisus,
and round him Boeotians held the fertile plain.

    But soon as the white-armed goddess Hera saw them
mauling Argive units caught in the bloody press,
she winged her words at Pallas: "What disaster!
Daughter of storming Zeus, tireless one, Athena—
how hollow our vow to Menelaus that he would sack   820
the mighty walls of Troy before he sailed for home—
if we let murderous Ares rampage on this way. Up now,
set our minds on our own fighting-fury!"
                              Hera's challenge—
and goddess Athena, her eyes afire, could not resist.
Hera queen of the gods, daughter of giant Cronus,
launched the work, harnessed the golden-bridled team
and Hebe quickly rolled the wheels to the chariot,

paired wheels with their eight spokes all bronze,
and bolted them on at both ends of the iron axle.
Fine wheels with fellies of solid, deathless gold   830
and round them running rims of bronze clamped fast—
a marvel to behold! The silver hubs spin round
on either side of the chariot's woven body,
gold and silver lashings strapping it tight,
double rails sweeping along its deep full curves
and the yoke-pole jutting forward, gleaming silver.
There at the tip she bound the gorgeous golden yoke,
she fastened the gorgeous golden breast straps next
and under the yoke Queen Hera led the horses, racers
blazing for war and the piercing shrieks of battle.   840

     Then Athena, child of Zeus whose shield is thunder,
letting fall her supple robe at the Father's threshold—
rich brocade, stitched with her own hands' labor—
donned the battle-shirt of the lord of lightning,
buckled her breastplate geared for wrenching war
and over her shoulders slung her shield, all tassels
flaring terror—Panic mounted high in a crown around it,
Hate and Defense across it, Assault to freeze the blood
and right in their midst the Gorgon's monstrous head,
that rippling dragon horror, sign of storming Zeus.   850
Then over her brows Athena placed her golden helmet
fronted with four knobs and forked with twin horns,
engraved with the fighting men of a hundred towns.
Then onto the flaming chariot Pallas set her feet
and seized her spear—weighted, heavy, the massive shaft
she wields to break the battle lines of heroes
the mighty Father's daughter storms against.
                          A crack of the whip—
the goddess Hera lashed the team, and all on their own force
the gates of heaven thundered open, kept by the Seasons,
guards of the vaulting sky and Olympus heights empowered   860
to spread the massing clouds or close them round once more.
Now straight through the great gates she drove the team,
whipping them on full tilt until they came to Zeus

the son of Cronus sitting far from the other gods,
throned on the topmost crag of rugged ridged Olympus.
And halting her horses near, the white-armed Hera
called out at once to the powerful son of Cronus,
pressing home her questions: "Father Zeus, look—
aren't you incensed at Ares and all his brutal work?
Killing so many brave Achaeans for no good reason,   870
not a shred of decency, just to wound my heart!
While there they sit at their royal ease, exulting,
the goddess of love and Apollo lord of the silver bow:
they loosed this manic Ares—he has no sense of justice.
Father Zeus . . . I wonder if you would fume at me
if I hurled a stunning blow at the god of war
and drove him from the fighting?"

                      Zeus the Father
who marshals ranks of storm clouds gave commands,
"Leap to it then. Launch Athena against him—
the queen of plunder, she's the one—his match,   880
a marvel at bringing Ares down in pain."

So he urged and the white-armed goddess Hera
obeyed at once. And again she lashed her team
and again the stallions flew, holding nothing back,
careering between the earth and starry skies as far
as a man's glance can pierce the horizon's misting haze,
a scout on a watchtower who scans the wine-dark sea—
so far do the soaring, thundering horses of the gods
leap at a single stride. And once they reached
the plains of Troy where the two rivers flow,   890
where Simois and Scamander rush together,
the white-armed goddess Hera reined her team,
loosing them from the chariot-yoke and round them
poured a dense shrouding mist and before their hoofs
the Simois sprang ambrosial grass for them to graze.

The two immortals stepped briskly as wild doves,
quivering, keen to defend the fighting men of Argos.
Once they gained the spot where the most and bravest stood,

flanking strong Diomedes breaker of wild stallions—
massed like a pride of lions tearing raw flesh   900
or ramping boars whose fury never flags—
the white-armed goddess Hera rose and shouted
loud as the brazen voice of great-lunged Stentor
who cries out with the blast of fifty other men,
"Shame! Disgrace! You Argives, you degraded—
splendid in battle dress, pure sham!
As long as brilliant Achilles stalked the front
no Trojan would ever venture beyond the Dardan Gates,
they were so afraid of the man's tremendous spear.
Now they're fighting far away from the city,   910
right by your hollow ships!"
                            So Hera trumpeted,
lashing the nerve and fighting-fury in each man
as Athena, her eyes blazing, made for Diomedes.
Hard by his team and car she found the king,
cooling the wound that Pandarus' arrow dealt him.
Sweat from under the heavy buckler's flat strap
had rubbed him raw, he was chafed and his arm ached
from lifting up the strap, wiping off the blood
and the dark clots. Laying hold of the yoke
that bound his team, the goddess Pallas started,   920
"So, Tydeus' son is half the size of his father,
and *he* was short and slight—but Tydeus was a fighter!
Even then, when I forbade him to go to war
or make a show of himself in others' eyes . . .
that time, alone, apart from his men, he marched
the message into Thebes, filled with hordes of Thebans,
I told him to banquet in their halls and eat in peace.
But he always had that power, that courage from the first—
and so he challenged the brave young blades of Thebes
to tests of strength and beat them all with ease,   930
I urged him on with so much winning force.
But you, Tydides, I stand by you as well,
I guard you too. And with all good will I say,
fight it out with the Trojans here! But look at you—
fatigue from too much charging has sapped your limbs,

that or some lifeless fear has paralyzed you now.
So you're no offspring of Tydeus,
the gallant, battle-hardened Oeneus' son!"

And powerful Diomedes bowed to her at once:
"Well I know you, Goddess, daughter of storming Zeus,   940
and so I will tell you all, gladly. I'll hide nothing.
It's not some lifeless fear that paralyzes me now,
no flinching from combat either.
It's your own command still ringing in my ears,
forbidding me to fight the immortals head-on,
all but one of the blessed gods, that is—
if Aphrodite daughter of Zeus slips into battle,
she's the one to stab with my sharp bronze spear.
So now, you see, I have given ground myself
and told my comrades to mass around me here.   950
Too well I know that *Ares* leads the charge."

But the goddess roused him on, her eyes blazing:
"True son of Tydeus, Diomedes, joy of my heart!
Forget the orders—nothing to fear, my friend,
neither Ares nor any other god. You too,
I'll urge you on with so much winning force.
Up now! Lash your racing horses at Ares first,
strike him at close range, no shrinking away here
before that headlong Ares! Just look at the maniac,
born for disaster, double-dealing, lying two-faced god—   960
just now he promised me and Hera, the War-god swore
he'd fight the Trojans, stand behind the Argives.
But now, look, he's leading the Trojan rampage,
his pledges thrown to the winds!"

                              With that challenge
Athena levered Sthenelus out the back of the car.
A twist of her wrist and the man hit the ground,
springing aside as the goddess climbed aboard,
blazing to fight beside the shining Diomedes.
The big oaken axle groaned beneath the weight,
bearing a great man and a terrifying goddess—   970

and Pallas Athena seized the reins and whip,
lashing the racing horses straight at Ares.
The god was just stripping giant Periphas bare,
the Aetolians' best fighter, Ochesius' noble son—
the blood-smeared Ares was tearing off his gear
but Athena donned the dark helmet of Death
so not even stark Ares could see her now.
But the butcher did see Tydeus' rugged son
and he dropped gigantic Periphas on the spot
where he'd just killed him, ripped his life away   980
and Ares whirled at the stallion-breaking Diomedes—
the two of them closing fast, charging face-to-face
and the god thrust first, over Tydides' yoke and reins,
with bronze spear burning to take the fighter's life.
But Athena, her eyes afire, grabbed the flying shaft,
flicked it over the car and off it flew for nothing—
and after him Diomedes yelled his war cry, lunging out
with his own bronze spear and Pallas rammed it home,
deep in Ares' bowels where the belt cinched him tight.
There Diomedes aimed and stabbed, he gouged him down   990
his glistening flesh and wrenched the spear back out
and the brazen god of war let loose a shriek, roaring,
thundering loud as nine, ten thousand combat soldiers
shriek with Ares' fury when massive armies clash.
A shudder swept all ranks, Trojans and Argives both,
terror-struck by the shriek the god let loose,
Ares whose lust for slaughter never dies.

                                            But now,
wild as a black cyclone twisting out of a cloudbank,
building up from the day's heat, blasts and towers—
so brazen Ares looked to Tydeus' son Diomedes.   1000
Soaring up with the clouds to the broad sweeping sky
he quickly gained the gods' stronghold, steep Olympus,
and settling down by the side of Cronus' great son Zeus,
his spirit racked with pain, Ares displayed the blood,
the fresh immortal blood that gushed from his wound,
and burst out in a flight of self-pity: "Father Zeus,
aren't you incensed to see such violent brutal work?

We everlasting gods . . . Ah what chilling blows
we suffer—thanks to our own conflicting wills—
whenever we show these mortal men some kindness.   1010
And we all must battle *you*—
you brought that senseless daughter into the world,
that murderous curse—forever bent on crimes!
While all the rest of us, every god on Olympus
bows down to you, each of us overpowered.

                       But that girl—
you never block her way with a word or action, never,
you spur her on, since you, you gave her birth
from your own head, that child of devastation!
Just look at this reckless Diomedes now—
Athena spurred him on to rave against the gods.   1020
First he lunges at Aphrodite, stabs her hand at the wrist
then charges me—even me—like something superhuman!
But I, I'm so fast on my feet I saved my life.
Else for a good long while I'd have felt the pain,
writhing among the corpses there, or soldiered on,
weak as a breathless ghost, beaten down by bronze."

    But Zeus who marshals storm clouds lowered a dark glance
and let loose at Ares: "No more, you lying, two-faced . . .
no more sidling up to me, whining here before me.
You—I hate you most of all the Olympian gods.   1030
Always dear to your heart,
strife, yes, and battles, the bloody grind of war.
You have your mother's uncontrollable rage—incorrigible,
that Hera—say what I will, I can hardly keep her down.
Hera's urgings, I trust, have made you suffer this.
But I cannot bear to see you agonize so long.
You are *my* child. To me your mother bore you.
If you had sprung from another god, believe me,
and grown into such a blinding devastation,
long ago you'd have dropped below the Titans,   1040
deep in the dark pit."
                  So great Zeus declared
and ordered the healing god to treat the god of war.

And covering over his wound with pain-killing drugs
the Healer cured him: the god was never born to die.
Quickly as fig-juice, pressed into bubbly, creamy milk,
curdles it firm for the man who churns it round,
so quickly he healed the violent rushing Ares.
And Hebe washed him clean, dressed him in robes
to warm his heart, and flanking the son of Cronus
down he sat, Ares exultant in the glory of it all.   1050

    And now the two returned to the halls of mighty Zeus—
Hera of Argos, Boeotian Athena, guard of armies, both
had stopped the murderous Ares' cutting men to pieces.

BOOK SIX

Hector
Returns to Troy

So the clash of Achaean and Trojan troops was on its own,
the battle in all its fury veering back and forth,
careering down the plain
as they sent their bronze lances hurtling side-to-side
between the Simois' banks and Xanthus' swirling rapids.

That Achaean bulwark giant Ajax came up first,
broke the Trojan line and brought his men some hope,
spearing the bravest man the Thracians fielded,
Acamas tall and staunch, Eussorus' son.
The first to hurl, Great Ajax hit the ridge   10
of the helmet's horsehair crest—the bronze point
stuck in Acamas' forehead pounding through the skull
and the dark came swirling down to shroud his eyes.

A shattering war cry! Diomedes killed off Axylus,
Teuthras' son who had lived in rock-built Arisbe,
a man of means and a friend to all mankind,
at his roadside house he'd warm all comers in.
But who of his guests would greet his enemy now,
meet him face-to-face and ward off grisly death?
Diomedes killed the man and his aide-in-arms at once,   20
Axylus and Calesius who always drove his team—
both at a stroke he drove beneath the earth.

Euryalus killed Dresus, killed Opheltius,
turned and went for Pedasus and Aesepus, twins
the nymph of the spring Abarbarea bore Bucolion . . .
Bucolion, son himself to the lofty King Laomedon,
first of the line, though his mother bore the prince
in secrecy and shadow. Tending his flocks one day
Bucolion took the nymph in a strong surge of love
and beneath his force she bore him twin sons.   30
But now the son of Mecisteus hacked the force
from beneath them both and loosed their gleaming limbs
and tore the armor off the dead men's shoulders.

Polypoetes braced for battle killed Astyalus—
Winging his bronze spear Odysseus slew Pidytes
bred in Percote, and Teucer did the same
for the royal Aretaon—

                    Ablerus went down too,
under the flashing lance of Nestor's son Antilochus,
and Elatus under the lord of men Agamemnon's strength—
Elatus lived by the banks of rippling Satniois,   40
in Pedasus perched on cliffs—

                    The hero Leitus
ran Phylacus down to ground at a dead run
and Eurypylus killed Melanthius outright—

                    But Menelaus
lord of the war cry had caught Adrestus alive.
Rearing, bolting in terror down the plain
his horses snared themselves in tamarisk branches,

splintered his curved chariot just at the pole's tip
and breaking free they made a dash for the city walls
where battle-teams by the drove stampeded back in panic.
But their master hurled from the chariot, tumbling over the wheel   50
and pitching facedown in the dust, and above him now
rose Menelaus, his spear's long shadow looming.
Adrestus hugged his knees and begged him, pleading,
"Take me alive, Atrides, take a ransom worth my life!
Treasures are piled up in my rich father's house,
bronze and gold and plenty of well-wrought iron—
father would give you anything, gladly, priceless ransom
if only he learns I'm still alive in Argive ships!"

His pleas were moving the heart in Menelaus,
just at the point of handing him to an aide   60
to take him back to the fast Achaean ships . . .
when up rushed Agamemnon, blocking his way
and shouting out, "So soft, dear brother, why?
Why such concern for enemies? I suppose you got
such tender loving care at home from the Trojans.
Ah would to god not one of them could escape
his sudden plunging death beneath our hands!
No baby boy still in his mother's belly,
not even he escape—all Ilium blotted out,
no tears for their lives, no markers for their graves!"   70

And the iron warrior brought his brother round—
rough justice, fitting too.
Menelaus shoved Adrestus back with a fist,
powerful Agamemnon stabbed him in the flank
and back on his side the fighter went, faceup.
The son of Atreus dug a heel in his heaving chest
and wrenched the ash spear out.
                                        And here came Nestor
with orders ringing down the field: "My comrades—
fighting Danaans, aides of Ares—no plunder now!
Don't lag behind, don't fling yourself at spoils   80
just to haul the biggest portion back to your ship.

Now's the time for killing! Later, at leisure,
strip the corpses up and down the plain!''

So he ordered, spurring each man's nerve—
and the next moment crowds of Trojans once again
would have clambered back inside their city walls,
terror-struck by the Argives primed for battle.
But Helenus son of Priam, best of the seers
who scan the flight of birds, came striding up
to Aeneas and Hector, calling out, ''My captains!   90
You bear the brunt of Troy's and Lycia's fighting—
you are our bravest men, whatever the enterprise,
pitched battle itself or planning our campaigns,
so stand your ground right here!
Go through the ranks and rally all the troops.
Hold back our retreating mobs outside the gates
before they throw themselves in their women's arms in fear,
a great joy to our enemies closing for the kill.
And once you've roused our lines to the last man,
we'll hold out here and fight the Argives down,   100
hard-hit as we are—necessity drives us on.
                                        But you,
Hector, you go back to the city, tell our mother
to gather all the older noble women together
in gray-eyed Athena's shrine on the city's crest,
unlock the doors of the goddess' sacred chamber—
and take a robe, the largest, loveliest robe
that she can find throughout the royal halls,
a gift that far and away she prizes most herself,
and spread it out across the sleek-haired goddess' knees.
Then promise to sacrifice twelve heifers in her shrine,   110
yearlings never broken, if only she'll pity Troy,
the Trojan wives and all our helpless children,
if only she'll hold Diomedes back from the holy city—
that wild spearman, that invincible headlong terror!
He is the strongest Argive now, I tell you.
Never once did we fear Achilles so,
captain of armies, born of a goddess too,

or so they say. But here's a maniac run amok—
no one can match his fury man-to-man!"

                              So he urged
and Hector obeyed his brother start to finish.   120
Down he leapt from his chariot fully armed, hit the ground
and brandishing two sharp spears went striding down his lines,
ranging flank to flank, driving his fighters into battle,
rousing grisly war—and round the Trojans whirled,
bracing to meet the Argives face-to-face.
And the Argives gave way, they quit the slaughter—
they thought some god swept down from the starry skies
to back the Trojans now, they wheeled and rallied so.
Hector shouted out to his men in a piercing voice,
"Gallant-hearted Trojans and far-famed allies!   130
Now be men, my friends, call up your battle-fury!
Till I can return to Troy and tell them all,
the old counselors, all our wives, to pray to the gods
and vow to offer them many splendid victims."

    As Hector turned for home his helmet flashed
and the long dark hide of his bossed shield, the rim
running the metal edge, drummed his neck and ankles.

                                            And now

Glaucus son of Hippolochus and Tydeus' son Diomedes
met in the no man's land between both armies:
burning for battle, closing, squaring off   140
and the lord of the war cry Diomedes opened up,
"Who are you, my fine friend?—another born to die?
I've never noticed you on the lines where we win glory,
not till now. But here you come, charging out
in front of all the rest with such bravado—
daring to face the flying shadow of my spear.
Pity the ones whose sons stand up to me in war!
But if you are an immortal come from the blue,
I'm not the man to fight the gods of heaven.
Not even Dryas' indestructible son Lycurgus,   150
not even he lived long . . .
that fellow who tried to fight the deathless gods.

He rushed at the maenads once, nurses of wild Dionysus,
scattered them breakneck down the holy mountain Nysa.
A rout of them strewed their sacred staves on the ground,
raked with a cattle prod by Lycurgus, murderous fool!
And Dionysus was terrified, he dove beneath the surf
where the sea-nymph Thetis pressed him to her breast—
Dionysus numb with fear: shivers racked his body,
thanks to the raucous onslaught of that man.   160
But the gods who live at ease lashed out against him—
worse, the son of Cronus struck Lycurgus blind.
Nor did the man live long, not with the hate
of all the gods against him.
                          No, my friend,
I have no desire to fight the blithe immortals.
But if you're a man who eats the crops of the earth,
a mortal born for death—here, come closer,
the sooner you will meet your day to die!"

    The noble son of Hippolochus answered staunchly,
"High-hearted son of Tydeus, why ask about my birth?   170
Like the generations of leaves, the lives of mortal men.
Now the wind scatters the old leaves across the earth,
now the living timber bursts with the new buds
and spring comes round again. And so with men:
as one generation comes to life, another dies away.
But about my birth, if you'd like to learn it well,
first to last—though many people know it—
here's my story . . .
                          There is a city, Corinth,
deep in a bend of Argos, good stallion-country
where Sisyphus used to live, the wiliest man alive.   180
Sisyphus, Aeolus' son, who had a son called Glaucus,
and in his day Glaucus sired brave Bellerophon,
a man without a fault. The gods gave him beauty
and the fine, gallant traits that go with men.
But Proetus plotted against him. Far stronger,
the king in his anger drove him out of Argos,
the kingdom Zeus had brought beneath his scepter.

Proetus' wife, you see, was mad for Bellerophon,
the lovely Antea lusted to couple with him,
all in secret. Futile—she could never seduce   190
the man's strong will, his seasoned, firm resolve.
So straight to the king she went, blurting out her lies:
'I wish you'd die, Proetus, if you don't kill Bellerophon!
Bellerophon's bent on dragging me down with him in lust
though I fight him all the way!'
                        All of it false
but the king seethed when he heard a tale like that.
He balked at killing the man—he'd some respect at least—
but he quickly sent him off to Lycia, gave him tokens,
murderous signs, scratched in a folded tablet,
and many of them too, enough to kill a man.   200
He told him to show them to Antea's father:
that would mean his death.
                        So off he went to Lycia,
safe in the escort of the gods, and once he reached
the broad highlands cut by the rushing Xanthus,
the king of Lycia gave him a royal welcome.
Nine days he feasted him, nine oxen slaughtered.
When the tenth Dawn shone with her rose-red fingers,
he began to question him, asked to see his credentials,
whatever he brought him from his in-law, Proetus.
But then, once he received that fatal message   210
sent from his own daughter's husband, first
he ordered Bellerophon to kill the Chimaera—
grim monster sprung of the gods, nothing human,
all lion in front, all snake behind, all goat between,
terrible, blasting lethal fire at every breath!
But he laid her low, obeying signs from the gods.
Next he fought the Solymi, tribesmen bent on glory,
roughest battle of men he ever entered, so he claimed.
Then for a third test he brought the Amazons down,
a match for men in war. But as he turned back,   220
his host spun out the tightest trap of all:
picking the best men from Lycia far and wide
he set an ambush—that never came home again!

Fearless Bellerophon killed them all.
                                        Then, yes,
when the king could see the man's power at last,
a true son of the gods, he pressed him hard to stay,
he offered his own daughter's hand in marriage,
he gave him half his royal honors as the king.
And the Lycians carved him out a grand estate,
the choicest land in the realm, rich in vineyards   230
and good tilled fields for him to lord it over.
And his wife bore good Bellerophon three children:
Isander, Hippolochus and Laodamia. Laodamia
lay in the arms of Zeus who rules the world
and she bore the god a son, our great commander,
Sarpedon helmed in bronze.
                            But the day soon came
when even Bellerophon was hated by all the gods.
Across the Alean plain he wandered, all alone,
eating his heart out, a fugitive on the run
from the beaten tracks of men. His son Isander?   240
Killed by the War-god, never sated—a boy fighting
the Solymi always out for glory. Laodamia? Artemis,
flashing her golden reins, cut her down in anger.
But Hippolochus fathered me, I'm proud to say.
He sent me off to Troy . . .
and I hear his urgings ringing in my ears:
'Always be the best, my boy, the bravest,
and hold your head up high above the others.
Never disgrace the generation of your fathers.
They were the bravest champions born in Corinth,   250
in Lycia far and wide.'
                        There you have my lineage.
That is the blood I claim, my royal birth."

When he heard that, Diomedes' spirits lifted.
Raising his spear, the lord of the war cry drove it home,
planting it deep down in the earth that feeds us all
and with winning words he called out to Glaucus,
the young captain, "Splendid—you are my friend,

my guest from the days of our grandfathers long ago!
Noble Oeneus hosted your brave Bellerophon once,
he held him there in his halls, twenty whole days,   260
and they gave each other handsome gifts of friendship.
My kinsman offered a gleaming sword-belt, rich red,
Bellerophon gave a cup, two-handled, solid gold—
I left it at home when I set out for Troy.
My father, Tydeus, I really don't remember.
I was just a baby when father left me then,
that time an Achaean army went to die at Thebes.
So now I am your host and friend in the heart of Argos,
you are mine in Lycia when I visit in your country.
Come, let us keep clear of each other's spears,   270
even there in the thick of battle. Look,
plenty of Trojans there for me to kill,
your famous allies too, any soldier the god
will bring in range or I can run to ground.
And plenty of Argives too—kill them if you can.
But let's trade armor. The men must know our claim:
we are sworn friends from our fathers' days till now!"

　　Both agreed. Both fighters sprang from their chariots,
clasped each other's hands and traded pacts of friendship.
But the son of Cronus, Zeus, stole Glaucus' wits away.   280
He traded his gold armor for bronze with Diomedes,
the worth of a hundred oxen just for nine.

　　　　　　　　　　　　　　And now,
when Hector reached the Scaean Gates and the great oak,
the wives and daughters of Troy came rushing up around him,
asking about their sons, brothers, friends and husbands.
But Hector told them only, "Pray to the gods"—
all the Trojan women, one after another . . .
Hard sorrows were hanging over many.

　　　　　　　　　　　　　　And soon
he came to Priam's palace, that magnificent structure
built wide with porches and colonnades of polished stone.   290
And deep within its walls were fifty sleeping chambers
masoned in smooth, lustrous ashlar, linked in a line

where the sons of Priam slept beside their wedded wives,
and facing these, opening out across the inner courtyard,
lay the twelve sleeping chambers of Priam's daughters,
masoned and roofed in lustrous ashlar, linked in a line
where the sons-in-law of Priam slept beside their wives.
And there at the palace Hector's mother met her son,
that warm, goodhearted woman, going in with Laodice,
the loveliest daughter Hecuba ever bred. His mother   300
clutched his hand and urged him, called his name:
"My child—why have you left the bitter fighting,
why have you come home? Look how they wear you out,
the sons of Achaea—curse them—battling round our walls!
And that's why your spirit brought you back to Troy,
to climb the heights and stretch your arms to Zeus.
But wait, I'll bring you some honeyed, mellow wine.
First pour out cups to Father Zeus and the other gods,
then refresh yourself, if you'd like to quench your thirst.
When a man's exhausted, wine will build his strength—   310
battle-weary as *you* are, fighting for your people."

    But Hector shook his head, his helmet flashing:
"Don't offer me mellow wine, mother, not now—
you'd sap my limbs, I'd lose my nerve for war.
And I'd be ashamed to pour a glistening cup to Zeus
with unwashed hands. I'm splattered with blood and filth—
how could I pray to the lord of storm and lightning?
No, mother, you are the one to pray.
Go to Athena's shrine, the queen of plunder,
go with offerings, gather the older noble women   320
and take a robe, the largest, loveliest robe
that you can find throughout the royal halls,
a gift that far and away you prize most yourself,
and spread it out across the sleek-haired goddess' knees.
Then promise to sacrifice twelve heifers in her shrine,
yearlings never broken, if only she'll pity Troy,
the Trojan wives and all our helpless children,
if only she'll hold Diomedes back from the holy city—
that wild spearman, that invincible headlong terror!

Now, mother, go to the queen of plunder's shrine   330
and I'll go hunt for Paris, summon him to fight
if the man will hear what *I* have to say . . .
Let the earth gape and swallow him on the spot!
A great curse Olympian Zeus let live and grow in him,
for Troy and high-hearted Priam and all his sons.
That man—if I could see him bound for the House of Death,
I could say my heart had forgot its wrenching grief!"

But his mother simply turned away to the palace.
She gave her servants orders and out they strode
to gather the older noble women through the city.   340
Hecuba went down to a storeroom filled with scent
and there they were, brocaded, beautiful robes . . .
the work of Sidonian women. Magnificent Paris
brought those women back himself from Sidon,
sailing the open seas on the same long voyage
he swept Helen off, her famous Father's child.
Lifting one from the lot, Hecuba brought it out
for great Athena's gift, the largest, loveliest,
richly worked, and like a star it glistened,
deep beneath the others. Then she made her way   350
with a file of noble women rushing in her train.

Once they reached Athena's shrine on the city crest
the beauty Theano opened the doors to let them in,
Cisseus' daughter, the horseman Antenor's wife
and Athena's priestess chosen by the Trojans. Then—
with a shrill wail they all stretched their arms to Athena
as Theano, her face radiant, lifting the robe on high,
spread it out across the sleek-haired goddess' knees
and prayed to the daughter of mighty Father Zeus:
"Queen Athena—shield of our city—glory of goddesses!   360
Now shatter the spear of Diomedes! That wild man—
hurl him headlong down before the Scaean Gates!
At once we'll sacrifice twelve heifers in your shrine,
yearlings never broken, if only you'll pity Troy,
the Trojan wives and all our helpless children!"

But Athena refused to hear Theano's prayers.
And while they prayed to the daughter of mighty Zeus
Hector approached the halls of Paris, sumptuous halls
he built himself with the finest masons of the day,
master builders famed in the fertile land of Troy.   370
They'd raised his sleeping chamber, house and court
adjoining Priam's and Hector's aloft the city heights.
Now Hector, dear to Zeus, strode through the gates,
clutching a thrusting-lance eleven forearms long;
the bronze tip of the weapon shone before him,
ringed with a golden hoop to grip the shaft.
And there in the bedroom Hector came on Paris
polishing, fondling his splendid battle-gear,
his shield and breastplate, turning over and over
his long curved bow. And there was Helen of Argos,   380
sitting with all the women of the house, directing
the rich embroidered work they had in hand.

                                        Seeing Paris,
Hector raked his brother with insults, stinging taunts:
"What on earth are you doing? Oh how wrong it is,
this anger you keep smoldering in your heart! Look,
your people dying around the city, the steep walls,
dying in arms—and all for you, the battle cries
and the fighting flaring up around the citadel.
You'd be the first to lash out at another—anywhere—
you saw hanging back from this, this hateful war.   390
                                        Up with you—
before all Troy is torched to a cinder here and now!"

    And Paris, magnificent as a god, replied,
"Ah Hector, you criticize me fairly, yes,
nothing unfair, beyond what I deserve. And so
I will try to tell you something. Please bear with me,
hear me out. It's not so much from anger or outrage
at our people that I keep to my rooms so long.
I only wanted to plunge myself in grief.
But just now my wife was bringing me round,
her winning words urging me back to battle.   400

And it strikes me, even me, as the better way.
Victory shifts, you know, now one man, now another.
So come, wait while I get this war-gear on,
or you go on ahead and I will follow—
I think I can overtake you."
                                   Hector, helmet flashing,
answered nothing. And Helen spoke to him now,
her soft voice welling up: "My dear brother,
dear to me, bitch that I am, vicious, scheming—
horror to freeze the heart! Oh how I wish
that first day my mother brought me into the light   410
some black whirlwind had rushed me out to the mountains
or into the surf where the roaring breakers crash and drag
and the waves had swept me off before all this had happened!
But since the gods ordained it all, these desperate years,
I wish I had been the wife of a better man, someone
alive to outrage, the withering scorn of men.
This one has no steadiness in his spirit,
not now, he never will . . .
and he's going to reap the fruits of it, I swear.
But come in, rest on this seat with me, dear brother.   420
You are the one hit hardest by the fighting, Hector,
you more than all—and all for me, whore that I am,
and this blind mad Paris. Oh the two of us!
Zeus planted a killing doom within us both,
so even for generations still unborn
we will live in song."
                           Turning to go,
his helmet flashing, tall Hector answered,
"Don't ask me to sit beside you here, Helen.
Love me as you do, you can't persuade me now.
No time for rest. My heart races to help our Trojans—   430
they long for me, sorely, whenever I am gone.
But rouse this fellow, won't you?
And let him hurry himself along as well,
so he can overtake me before I leave the city.
For I must go home to see my people first,
to visit my own dear wife and my baby son.

Who knows if I will ever come back to them again?—
or the deathless gods will strike me down at last
at the hands of Argive fighters."

                        A flash of his helmet
and off he strode and quickly reached his sturdy,   440
well-built house. But white-armed Andromache—
Hector could not find her in the halls.
She and the boy and a servant finely gowned
were standing watch on the tower, sobbing, grieving.
When Hector saw no sign of his loyal wife inside
he went to the doorway, stopped and asked the servants,
"Come, please, tell me the truth now, women.
Where's Andromache gone? To my sisters' house?
To my brothers' wives with their long flowing robes?
Or Athena's shrine where the noble Trojan women   450
gather to win the great grim goddess over?"

    A busy, willing servant answered quickly,
"Hector, seeing you want to know the truth,
she hasn't gone to your sisters, brothers' wives
or Athena's shrine where the noble Trojan women
gather to win the great grim goddess over.
Up to the huge gate-tower of Troy she's gone
because she heard our men are so hard-pressed,
the Achaean fighters coming on in so much force.
She sped to the wall in panic, like a madwoman—   460
the nurse went with her, carrying your child."

    At that, Hector spun and rushed from his house,
back by the same way down the wide, well-paved streets
throughout the city until he reached the Scaean Gates,
the last point he would pass to gain the field of battle.
There his warm, generous wife came running up to meet him,
Andromache the daughter of gallant-hearted Eetion
who had lived below Mount Placos rich with timber,
in Thebe below the peaks, and ruled Cilicia's people.
His daughter had married Hector helmed in bronze.   470
She joined him now, and following in her steps

a servant holding the boy against her breast,
in the first flush of life, only a baby,
Hector's son, the darling of his eyes
and radiant as a star . . .
Hector would always call the boy Scamandrius,
townsmen called him Astyanax, Lord of the City,
since Hector was the lone defense of Troy.
The great man of war breaking into a broad smile,
his gaze fixed on his son, in silence. Andromache,   480
pressing close beside him and weeping freely now,
clung to his hand, urged him, called him: "Reckless one,
my Hector—your own fiery courage will destroy you!
Have you no pity for *him*, our helpless son? Or me,
and the destiny that weighs me down, your widow,
now so soon? Yes, soon they will kill you off,
all the Achaean forces massed for assault, and then,
bereft of you, better for me to sink beneath the earth.
What other warmth, what comfort's left for me,
once you have met your doom? Nothing but torment!   490
I have lost my father. Mother's gone as well.
Father . . . the brilliant Achilles laid him low
when he stormed Cilicia's city filled with people,
Thebe with her towering gates. He killed Eetion,
not that he stripped his gear—he'd some respect at least—
for he burned his corpse in all his blazoned bronze,
then heaped a grave-mound high above the ashes
and nymphs of the mountain planted elms around it,
daughters of Zeus whose shield is storm and thunder.
And the seven brothers I had within our halls . . .   500
all in the same day went down to the House of Death,
the great godlike runner Achilles butchered them all,
tending their shambling oxen, shining flocks.
                                        And mother,
who ruled under the timberline of woody Placos once—
he no sooner haled her here with his other plunder
than he took a priceless ransom, set her free
and home she went to her father's royal halls
where Artemis, showering arrows, shot her down.

You, Hector—you are my father now, my noble mother,
a brother too, and you are my husband, young and warm
        and strong!   510
Pity me, please! Take your stand on the rampart here,
before you orphan your son and make your wife a widow.
Draw your armies up where the wild fig tree stands,
there, where the city lies most open to assault,
the walls lower, easily overrun. Three times
they have tried that point, hoping to storm Troy,
their best fighters led by the Great and Little Ajax,
famous Idomeneus, Atreus' sons, valiant Diomedes.
Perhaps a skilled prophet revealed the spot—
or their own fury whips them on to attack."   520

    And tall Hector nodded, his helmet flashing:
"All this weighs on my mind too, dear woman.
But I would die of shame to face the men of Troy
and the Trojan women trailing their long robes
if I would shrink from battle now, a coward.
Nor does the spirit urge me on that way.
I've learned it all too well. To stand up bravely,
always to fight in the front ranks of Trojan soldiers,
winning my father great glory, glory for myself.
For in my heart and soul I also know this well: 530
the day will come when sacred Troy must die,
Priam must die and all his people with him,
Priam who hurls the strong ash spear . . .
                                Even so,
it is less the pain of the Trojans still to come
that weighs me down, not even of Hecuba herself
or King Priam, or the thought that my own brothers
in all their numbers, all their gallant courage,
may tumble in the dust, crushed by enemies—
That is nothing, nothing beside your agony
when some brazen Argive hales you off in tears,   540
wrenching away your day of light and freedom!
Then far off in the land of Argos you must live,
laboring at a loom, at another woman's beck and call,

fetching water at some spring, Messeis or Hyperia,
resisting it all the way—
the rough yoke of necessity at your neck.
And a man may say, who sees you streaming tears,
'There is the wife of Hector, the bravest fighter
they could field, those stallion-breaking Trojans,
long ago when the men fought for Troy.' So he will say   550
and the fresh grief will swell your heart once more,
widowed, robbed of the one man strong enough
to fight off your day of slavery.

                                No, no,
let the earth come piling over my dead body
before I hear your cries, I hear you dragged away!"

    In the same breath, shining Hector reached down
for his son—but the boy recoiled,
cringing against his nurse's full breast,
screaming out at the sight of his own father,
terrified by the flashing bronze, the horsehair crest,   560
the great ridge of the helmet nodding, bristling terror—
so it struck his eyes. And his loving father laughed,
his mother laughed as well, and glorious Hector,
quickly lifting the helmet from his head,
set it down on the ground, fiery in the sunlight,
and raising his son he kissed him, tossed him in his arms,
lifting a prayer to Zeus and the other deathless gods:
"Zeus, all you immortals! Grant this boy, my son,
may be like me, first in glory among the Trojans,
strong and brave like me, and rule all Troy in power   570
and one day let them say, 'He is a better man than his father!'—
when he comes home from battle bearing the bloody gear
of the mortal enemy he has killed in war—
a joy to his mother's heart."

                                So Hector prayed
and placed his son in the arms of his loving wife.
Andromache pressed the child to her scented breast,
smiling through her tears. Her husband noticed,
and filled with pity now, Hector stroked her gently,

trying to reassure her, repeating her name: "Andromache,
dear one, why so desperate? Why so much grief for me?   580
No man will hurl me down to Death, against my fate.
And fate? No one alive has ever escaped it,
neither brave man nor coward, I tell you—
it's born with us the day that we are born.
So please go home and tend to your own tasks,
the distaff and the loom, and keep the women
working hard as well. As for the fighting,
men will see to that, all who were born in Troy
but I most of all."
                        Hector aflash in arms
took up his horsehair-crested helmet once again.   590
And his loving wife went home, turning, glancing
back again and again and weeping live warm tears.
She quickly reached the sturdy house of Hector,
man-killing Hector,
and found her women gathered there inside
and stirred them all to a high pitch of mourning.
So in his house they raised the dirges for the dead,
for Hector still alive, his people were so convinced
that never again would he come home from battle,
never escape the Argives' rage and bloody hands.   600

   Nor did Paris linger long in his vaulted halls.
Soon as he buckled on his elegant gleaming bronze
he rushed through Troy, sure in his racing stride.
As a stallion full-fed at the manger, stalled too long,
breaking free of his tether gallops down the plain,
out for his favorite plunge in a river's cool currents,
thundering in his pride—his head flung back, his mane
streaming over his shoulders, sure and sleek in his glory,
knees racing him on to the fields and stallion-haunts he loves—
so down from Pergamus heights came Paris, son of Priam,   610
glittering in his armor like the sun astride the skies,
exultant, laughing aloud, his fast feet sped him on.
Quickly he overtook his brother, noble Hector
still lingering, slow to turn from the spot

where he had just confided in his wife . . .
Magnificent Paris spoke first: "Dear brother,
look at me, holding you back in all your speed—
dragging my feet, coming to you so late,
and you told me to be quick!"

A flash of his helmet as Hector shot back, 620
"Impossible man! How could anyone fair and just
underrate your work in battle? You're a good soldier.
But you hang back of your own accord, refuse to fight.
And that, that's why the heart inside me aches
when I hear our Trojans heap contempt on you,
the men who bear such struggles all for you.

                                       Come,
now for attack! We'll set all this to rights,
someday, if Zeus will ever let us raise
the winebowl of freedom high in our halls,
high to the gods of cloud and sky who live forever— 630
once we drive these Argives geared for battle out of Troy!"

BOOK SEVEN

Ajax Duels
with Hector

Vaunting, aflash in arms, Hector swept through the gates
with his brother Paris keeping pace beside him.
Both men bent on combat, on they fought like wind
when a god sends down some welcome blast to sailors
desperate for it, worked to death at the polished oars,
beating the heavy seas, their arms slack with the labor—
so welcome that brace of men appeared to the Trojans
desperate for their captains.
                              Each one killed his man.
Paris took Menesthius, one who had lived in Arne,
a son of King Areithous lord of the war-club   10
and his lady Phylomedusa with large lovely eyes.
Hector slashed Eioneus' throat with a sharp spear,
ripped him under the helmet's hammered bronze rim—

his legs collapsed in death.
                              Quick in the jolting onset
Lycia's captain Glaucus son of Hippolochus skewered
Dexius' son Iphinous just as he leapt behind
his fast mares—he stabbed his shoulder, hard,
and down from his car Iphinous crashed to earth
and his limbs went slack with death.
                                    Rampaging Trojans!
Yes, but as soon as fiery-eyed Athena marked them   20
killing Argive ranks in this all-out assault,
down she rushed from the peaks of Mount Olympus
straight for sacred Troy. But Phoebus Apollo
spotting her from Pergamus heights—the god grim set
on victory for the Trojans—rose to intercept her . . .
As the two came face-to-face beside the great oak,
lord Apollo the son of Zeus led off, "What next?—
what is the mighty Zeus's daughter blazing after now?
Down from Olympus, what heroics stir your heart?
No doubt you'll hand your Argives victory soon,   30
you'll turn the tide of battle!
You have no mercy, none for dying Trojans.
Come, listen to me—my plan is so much better:
let us halt the war and the heat of combat now,
at least for today. They'll fight again tomorrow,
until they win their way to the fixed doom of Troy,
since that is your only passion—you two goddesses—
to plunder Troy to rubble."
                            Athena's eyes lit up
and the goddess said, "So be it, archer of the sky!
Those were my very thoughts, winging down from Olympus   40
into the midst of Trojans and Achaeans. But tell me,
how do you hope to stop the men from fighting?"

"Hector!"—lord Apollo the son of Zeus replied—
"We'll spur his nerve and strength, that breaker of horses,
see if he'll challenge one of the Argives man-to-man
and they will duel in bloody combat to the death.

Achaeans armed in bronze will thrill to his call,
they'll put up a man to battle shining Hector."

    So Apollo staged the action. Her eyes afire
the goddess Pallas did not resist a moment.   50
She flashed the word in Helenus' mantic spirit—
the son of Priam sensed what pleased the immortals
hatching instant plans, and coming up to Hector
advised him quickly, "Hector, son of Priam,
a mastermind like Zeus, listen to me now—
let your brother guide you.
Have all Trojans and Argives take their seats,
and you, you challenge Achaea's bravest man
to duel in bloody combat to the death.
It's not the hour to meet your doom, not yet.   60
I heard a voice of the gods who live forever."

    When Hector heard that challenge he rejoiced
and right in the no man's land along his lines he strode,
gripping his spear mid-haft, staving men to a standstill
while Agamemnon seated his Argives geared for combat.
And Apollo lord of the silver bow and Queen Athena,
for all the world like carrion birds, like vultures,
slowly settled atop the broad towering oak
sacred to Zeus whose battle-shield is thunder,
relishing those men. Wave on wave of them settling,   70
close ranks shuddering into a dense, bristling glitter
of shields and spears and helmets—quick as a ripple
the West Wind suddenly risen shudders down the sea
and the deep sea swell goes dark beneath its force—
so settling waves of Trojan ranks and Achaeans
rippled down the plain . . .
And Hector rose and spoke between both sides:
"Hear me—Trojans, Achaeans geared for combat!
I'll speak out what the heart inside me urges.
Our oaths, our sworn truce—Zeus the son of Cronus   80
throned in the clouds has brought them all to nothing

and all the Father decrees is death for both sides at once.
Until you Argives seize the well-built towers of Troy
or you yourselves are crushed against your ships.

                                                    But now,
seeing the best of all Achaeans fill your ranks,
let one whose nerve impels him to fight with me
come striding from your lines, a lone champion
pitted against Prince Hector. Here are the terms
that I set forth—let Zeus look down, my witness!
If that man takes my life with his sharp bronze blade,   90
he will strip my gear and haul it back to his ships.
But give my body to friends to carry home again,
so Trojan men and Trojan women can do me honor
with fitting rites of fire once I am dead.
But if I kill *him* and Apollo grants me glory,
I'll strip his gear and haul it back to sacred Troy
and hang it high on the deadly Archer's temple walls.
But not his body: I'll hand it back to the decked ships,
so the long-haired Achaeans can give him full rites
and heap his barrow high by the broad Hellespont.   100
And someday one will say, one of the men to come,
steering his oar-swept ship across the wine-dark sea,
'There's the mound of a man who died in the old days,
one of the brave whom glorious Hector killed.'
So they will say, someday, and my fame will never die."

    A hushed silence went through all the Achaean ranks,
ashamed to refuse, afraid to take his challenge . . .
But at long last Menelaus leapt up and spoke,
lashing out at them, groaning, heartsick: "Oh no—
your threats, your bluster—women, not men of Achaea!   110
What disgrace it will be—shame, cringing shame
if not one Danaan now steps up to battle Hector.
You can all turn to earth and water—rot away!
Look at each of you, sitting there, lifeless,
lust for glory gone. I'll harness up,
I'll fight the man myself. The gods on high—
they hold the ropes of victory in their hands!"

With that he began to don his handsome gear.
And then and there, Menelaus,
the death-stroke would have blazed before your eyes—   120
dead at the hands of Hector, a far stronger man—
if Argive kings had not leapt up and caught you.
And Atreus' son himself, powerful Agamemnon
seized your right hand, shouting out your name:
"You're mad, my Prince! No need for such an outburst—
get a grip on yourself, distraught as you are.
Just for the sake of rivalry, soldier's pride,
don't rush to fight with a better man, with Hector
the son of Priam. Many others shrink before him.
Even Achilles dreads to pit himself against him   130
out on the battle lines where men win glory—
Achilles, far and away a stronger man than you.
Go back. Sit down with the comrades you command.
We'll put up another champion to go against this Hector.
Fearless, is he? and never sated with fighting?
He'll gladly sink to a knee and rest, I'd say,
if the man comes through alive
from the fight he begs for, dueling to the death."

Again the iron warrior brought his brother round—
good counsel, fitting too. Menelaus yielded at once.   140
His aides, elated, lifted the armor off his shoulders.
And then lord Nestor rose and spoke among the men:
"No more—or enormous sorrow comes to all Achaea!
How he would groan at this, the old horseman Peleus,
that fine speaker, the Myrmidons' famed commander.
How he rejoiced that day, questioning me in his halls,
when he learned the blood and birth of all the Argives.
Now if he heard how all cringe in the face of Hector,
time and again he'd stretch his hands to the gods
and pray that life breath would quit his limbs   150
and sink to the House of Death.
                              Oh if only—
Father Zeus, Athena, Apollo—I were young again!
Fresh as the day we fought by Celadon's rapids,

our Pylians in platoons against Arcadian spearmen
under Phia's ramparts, round the Iardanus' banks.
When Arcadia's champion Ereuthalion strode forth,
a man like a god for power, his shoulders decked
with King Areithous' armor, massive Areithous . . .
the Great War-club, so they called that hulk,
his men-at-arms and their sashed and lovely women.   160
He would never fight with a bow or long spear, no,
with his giant iron club he'd break battalions open.
That monster—Lycurgus cut him down by stealth,
not force at all, on a footpath so cramped
his iron club was useless fending off his death.
There—before he could heft it—a sudden lunge
and Lycurgus' spear had run him through the guts.
Flat on his back he went, slamming against the ground
and his killer stripped the armor brazen Ares gave him.
He donned it himself, for years of grueling war,   170
but then, when Lycurgus grew too old in his halls,
he passed it on to a favorite henchman, Ereuthalion,
and sporting that gear he challenged all our best.
And they, they shook from head to foot, terrified,
none with the nerve to face him then. Only I—
my hardened courage drove me to fight the man
in a hot burst of daring,
and I the youngest trooper of us all . . .
I took him on and Athena gave me glory. By heaven,
Ereuthalion was the biggest, strongest man I ever killed,   180
the huge lumbering sprawl of him stretching far and wide!
Oh make me young again, and the strength inside me
steady as a rock! Hector with that flashing helmet
would meet his match in combat in a moment.
You, the bravest of all Achaeans—and not one
with the spine to battle Hector face-to-face!"

     The old man's taunts brought nine men to their feet.
First by far Agamemnon lord of men sprang up
and following him Tydides, powerful Diomedes,
next the Great and Little Ajax armed in fury,   190

Idomeneus after them and Idomeneus' good aide,
Meriones, a match for the butcher god of war,
Eurypylus after them, Euaemon's gallant son,
Thoas son of Andraemon, Odysseus out for exploit:
all were roused to go up against Prince Hector.
Once more the fine old horseman gave commands:
"Now shake the lots for all,
the first to the last man—we'll see who wins.
He's the one to do his Achaean comrades proud,
do himself proud too, if he comes through alive   200
from the fight that waits him, dueling to the death."

    And each soldier scratched his mark on a stone
and threw it into Atrides Agamemnon's helmet.
Fighters prayed. Stretching hands to the gods
a man would murmur, scanning the wide sky,
"Father Zeus, let Ajax win, or Tydeus' son
or the proud king himself of all Mycenae's gold!"

    So they prayed as the old horseman shook the lots
and one leapt from the helmet, the one they wanted most—
Great Ajax' lot it was. And the herald took it round   210
through all the ranks, left to right for luck,
and showed it to all Achaea's bravest men.
None of them knew it, each denied the mark.
But once he'd passed it round and reached the man
who had scratched the stone and thrown it in the helmet—
Ajax bent on glory—out went his hand to take it,
the herald pausing beside him dropped it in
and Ajax knew his mark and thrilled to see it,
flung it down at his feet and shouted, "Friends—
the lot is mine and it fills my heart with joy!   220
I know I can overpower this dazzling Hector.
But come, while I strap my battle-armor on,
all of you pray to Cronus' son, almighty Zeus.
Pray to yourselves in silence, so Trojans cannot hear—
no, pray out loud!
No one at all to fear. No one can rout *me*—

his will against my will—not by force,
god knows, and not by a sly maneuver either.
I'm not such a raw recruit, I like to think,
born and bred on Salamis."

                So Great Ajax vaunted   230
and men prayed to the son of Cronus, King Zeus.
They'd call out, scanning the wide sky, "Father Zeus—
ruling over us all from Ida, god of greatness, glory!
Now let Ajax take this victory, shining triumph!
But if you love Hector, if you hold him dear,
at least give both men equal strength and glory."

                      So they prayed
as Ajax harnessed himself in burnished, gleaming bronze
and once he had strapped his legs and chest in armor,
out he marched like the giant god of battle wading
into the wars of men when Zeus drives them hard   240
to clash and soldier on with heart-devouring hate.
So giant Ajax marched, that bulwark of the Achaeans—
a grim smile curling below his dark shaggy brows,
under his legs' power taking immense strides,
shaking his spear high, its long shadow trailing.
The men of Argos exulted at the sight of him there
but terrible tremors shook each Trojan fighter's knees—
Hector himself, his heart pounding against his ribs.
But how could he shrink before the enemy, slip back
into a crowd of cohorts now? He was the challenger,   250
he with his lust for battle. Ajax strode on, closing,
bearing his huge body-shield like a rampart, heavy bronze
over seven layers of oxhide. Tychius made it for him,
laboring long, the finest leather-smith by far:
over in Hyle where the master had his home
he crafted that famous gleaming shield for Ajax,
layering seven welted hides of sturdy well-fed bulls
and hammered an eighth layer of bronze to top it off.
And now holding that great shield before his chest
Telamonian Ajax marched right up to Hector,   260
threatening with his deep resounding voice,
"Hector, now you'll learn, once and for all,

in combat man-to-man, what kind of champions
range the Argive ranks, even besides Achilles,
that lionheart who mauls battalions wholesale.
Off in his beaked seagoing ships Achilles lies,
raging away at Agamemnon, marshal of armies—
but here we are, strong enough to engage *you*,
and plenty of us too. Come—
lead off, if you can, with all your fighting power!''   270

A flash of his helmet as rangy Hector shook his head:
"Ajax, royal son of Telamon, captain of armies,
don't toy with me like a puny, weak-kneed boy
or a woman never trained in works of war!
War—I know it well, and the butchery of men.
Well I know, shift to the left, shift to the right
my tough tanned shield. That's what the real drill,
defensive fighting means to me. I know it all,
how to charge in the rush of plunging horses—
I know how to stand and fight to the finish,   280
twist and lunge in the War-god's deadly dance.
                              On guard!
Big and bluff as you are, I've no desire to hit you
sniping in on the sly—
I'd strike you out in the open, strike you now!''
                              He hurled—
his spear's long shadow flew and it struck Ajax' shield,
that awesome seven-layered buckler, right on the eighth,
the outside layer of bronze that topped it off,
through six hides it tore but the seventh stopped
the relentless brazen point.
                              But Great Ajax next—
dear to the gods he hurled and his spear's shadow flew   290
and the shaft hit Hector's round shield, hit full center—
straight through the gleaming hide the heavy weapon drove,
ripping down and in through the breastplate finely worked,
tearing the war-shirt, close by Hector's flank it jabbed
but the Trojan swerved aside and dodged black death.
Both seized their lances, wrenched them from the shields

and went for each other now like lions rending flesh
or a pair of wild boars whose power never flags.
Hector stabbed at the buckler, full center too,
not smashing through, the brazen point bent back—   300
and Ajax lunged at him, thrusting hard at his shield
and the shaft punched through, rammed him back in his fury
and grazed his neck and the dark blood gushed forth.
But not even then did Hector quit the battle . . .
backing, helmet flashing, his strong hand hefting
a rock from the field, dark, jagged, a ton weight—
he hurled it at Ajax, struck the gigantic shield,
seven oxhides thick, struck right on the jutting boss
and the bronze clanged, echoing round and round as Ajax
hoisting a boulder—far larger—wheeled and heaved it,   310
putting his weight behind it, tremendous force—
and the rock crashed home, Hector's shield burst in,
hit by a millstone—and Hector's fine knees buckled,
flat on his back he went, his shield crushing down on him
swept him off his feet. But Apollo quickly pulled him up—
and now they'd have closed with swords, hacked each other
if heralds of Zeus and men had not come rushing in,
one from the Trojans, one from the armed Achaeans,
Talthybius and Idaeus, both with good clear heads.
Parting them, holding their staffs between both men,   320
the herald Idaeus, cool, skilled in tactics, urged,
"No more, my sons—don't kill yourselves in combat!
Zeus who marshals the storm cloud loves you both.
You're both great fighters—we all know that full well.
The night comes on at last. Best to yield to night."

      But the giant Ajax answered briskly, "Wait,
Idaeus, tell Hector here to call the truce.
Mad for a fight, he challenged all our bravest.
Let him lead off. I'll take his lead, you'll see."

      His helmet flashed as Hector nodded: "Yes, Ajax,   330
since god has given you power, build and sense
and you are the strongest spearman of Achaea,

let us break off this dueling to the death,
at least for today. We'll fight again tomorrow,
until some fatal power decides between our armies,
handing victory down to one side or another. Look,
the night comes at last. Best to yield to night.
So you will bring some joy to Achaea's forces
camped beside their ships, and most of all
to your own troops, the comrades you command.   340
But I'll go back to the great city of King Priam
and bring some joy to the men of Troy and Trojan women
trailing their long robes. Thankful for my return
they'll go to meet the gods and sing their praises.

                                                  Come,
let us give each other gifts, unforgettable gifts,
so any man may say, Trojan soldier or Argive,
'First they fought with heart-devouring hatred,
then they parted, bound by pacts of friendship.' "

   With that he gave him his silver-studded sword,
slung in its sheath on a supple, well-cut sword-strap,   350
and Ajax gave his war-belt, glistening purple.
So both men parted, Ajax back to Achaea's armies,
Hector back to his thronging Trojans—overjoyed
to see him still alive, unharmed, striding back,
free of the rage and hands of Ajax still unconquered.
They escorted him home to Troy—saved, past all their hopes—
while far across the field the Achaean men-at-arms
escorted Ajax, thrilled with victory, back to Agamemnon.

   Soon as they had gathered within the warlord's tents
he sacrificed an ox in their midst, a full-grown ox,   360
five years old, to the towering son of Cronus, Zeus.
They skinned the animal quickly, butchered the carcass,
expertly cut the meat into pieces, pierced them with spits,
roasted them to a turn and pulled them off the fire.
The work done, the feast laid out, they ate well
and no man's hunger lacked a share of the banquet.
But the lord of far-flung kingdoms, hero Agamemnon,

honored giant Telamonian Ajax first and last
with the long savory cuts that line the backbone.
And when they had put aside desire for food and drink   ·   370
the old man began to weave his counsel among them:
Nestor was first to speak—from the early days
his plans and tactics always seemed the best.
With good will to the lords he rose and spoke:
"King Agamemnon, chiefs of all the Argives—
how many long-haired Achaeans lie here dead!
And now Ares the slashing god of war has swirled
their dark blood in Scamander's deep clear stream
and their souls have drifted down to the House of Death.
So at dawn you must call a halt to fighting by Achaeans,   380
form your units, bring on wagons, gather up the dead
and wheel the corpses back with mules and oxen. Then,
at a decent distance from the ships, we burn the bodies,
so every soldier here can carry back the bones
to a dead man's sons when he sails home again.
And let us heap a single great barrow over the pyre,
one great communal grave stretched out across the plain
and fronting it throw up looming ramparts quickly,
a landward wall for ships and troops themselves.
And amidst the wall build gateways fitted strong   390
to open a clear path for driving chariots through.
And just outside the wall we must dig a trench,
a deep ditch in a broad sweeping ring
to block their horse and men and break their charge—
then these headlong Trojans can never rush our armies."

So he advised. All the warlords sounded their assent.
And now the Trojans collected high on the crest of Troy.
They were shaken, distracted men at Priam's gates
but the clearheaded Antenor opened up among them:
"Hear me, Trojans, Dardans, all our loyal allies,   400
I must speak out what the heart inside me urges.
On with it—give Argive Helen and all her treasures
back to Atreus' sons to take away at last.
We broke our sworn truce. We fight as outlaws.

True, and what profit for us in the long run?
Nothing—unless we do exactly as I say."

    So he pressed the point, then took his seat.
But among them stood magnificent Paris now,
fair-haired Helen's lord, and he came back
with a winging burst in answer: "Stop, Antenor!   410
No more of your hot insistence—it repels me.
You must have something better than this to say.
But if you are serious, speaking from the heart,
the gods themselves have blotted out your senses.
Now I say this to our stallion-breaking Trojans,
I say No, straight out—I won't give up the woman!
But those treasures I once hauled home from Argos,
I'll return them all and add from my own stores."

    With that concession the prince sat down again.
Then Priam the son of Dardanus rose among them,   420
a man who could match the gods for strong advice,
and with good will toward all he swayed his people:
"Hear me, Trojans, Dardans, all our loyal allies—
I must speak out what the heart inside me urges.
Now take your evening meal throughout the city,
just as you always have, and stand your watches,
each man wide awake. And then, at first light,
let the herald Idaeus go to the beaked ships
and tell the Atridae, Agamemnon and Menelaus,
the offer of Paris who caused our long hard campaign.   430
Let Idaeus add this too, a good sound proposal:
see if they are willing to halt the brutal war
until we can burn the bodies of our dead.
We'll fight again tomorrow . . .
until some fatal power decides between us both,
handing victory down to our side—or the other."

    His people hung on his words and all obeyed the king.
They took their meal by ranks throughout the army.

At first light Idaeus went to the beaked ships
and out on the meeting grounds he found the Argives,   440
veterans close by the stern of Agamemnon's ship.
Taking his stand, right in the milling troops,
the herald called out in a high, firm voice,
"Son of Atreus! Captains of all Achaeans!
Priam and noble Trojans command me to report,
if it proves acceptable, pleasing to one and all,
the offer of Paris who caused our long hard campaign.
All the treasures that filled his hollow ships
and the prince hauled home to Troy—
would to god he'd drowned before that day!—   450
he'll return them all and add from his own stores.
But the lawful wife of Menelaus, renowned Menelaus,
he will not give her up, Paris makes that clear,
though all Troy commands him to do precisely that.
They tell me to add this too, a good sound proposal:
if you are willing, come, we'll halt the brutal war
until we can burn the bodies of our dead.
We'll fight again tomorrow—
until some fatal power decides between us both,
handing victory down to one side or the other."

So he spoke   460
and a hushed silence went through all the ranks.
Finally Diomedes lord of the war cry shouted out,
"No one touch the treasures of Paris, Helen either!
It's obvious—any fool can see it. Now, at last,
the neck of Troy's in the noose—her doom is sealed."

All the Achaean soldiers roared out their assent,
stirred by the stallion-breaking lord's reply,
and King Agamemnon rounded on Idaeus: "There,
there's the Achaeans' answer, Idaeus—a declaration—
you can hear for yourself. It is my pleasure too.   470
But about the dead, I'd never grudge their burning.
No holding back for the bodies of the fallen:
once they are gone, let fire soothe them quickly.
That is my sworn pledge. Zeus my witness now,

Hera's lord whose thunder drums the sky!"
                                    With that oath
he raised his scepter high in the eyes of all the gods
and Idaeus turned, trailing back to sacred Troy.
There they sat in assembly, Trojans, Dardans,
all collected together, waiting long and tense
for the herald to return. And home Idaeus came,   480
delivered his message standing in their midst
and they fell to making hurried preparations,
dividing the labors quickly—two detachments,
one to gather the bodies, one the timber.
And far on the other side Achaean troops
came streaming out of the well-benched ships,
some to gather the bodies, some the timber.

    Just as the sun began to strike the plowlands,
rising out of the deep calm flow of the Ocean River
to climb the vaulting sky, the opposing armies met.   490
And hard as it was to recognize each man, each body,
with clear water they washed the clotted blood away
and lifted them onto wagons, weeping warm tears.
Priam forbade his people to wail aloud. In silence
they piled the corpses on the pyre, their hearts breaking,
burned them down to ash and returned to sacred Troy.
And just so on the other side Achaean men-at-arms
piled the corpses on the pyre, their hearts breaking,
burned them down to ash and returned to the hollow ships.

    Then with the daybreak not quite risen into dawn,   500
the night and day still deadlocked, round the pyre
a work brigade of picked Achaeans grouped.
They heaped a single great barrow over the corpse-fire,
one great communal grave stretched out across the plain
and fronting it threw up looming ramparts quickly,
a landward wall for ships and troops themselves,
and amidst the wall built gateways fitted strong
to open a clear path for driving chariots through.
And against the fortress, just outside the wall,

the men dug an enormous trench, broad and deep,   510
and drove sharp stakes to guard it.
                    So they labored,
the long-haired Achaeans, while the gods aloft,
seated at ease beside the lord of lightning, Zeus,
gazed down on the grand work of Argives armed in bronze.
Poseidon the god whose breakers shake the land began,
"Father Zeus, is there a man on the whole wide earth
who still informs the gods of all his plans, his schemes?
Don't you see? Look there—the long-haired Achaeans
have flung that rampart up against their ships,
around it they have dug an enormous deep trench   520
and never offered the gods a hundred splendid bulls,
but its fame will spread as far as the light of dawn!
And men will forget those ramparts I and Apollo
reared for Troy in the old days—
for the hero Laomedon—we broke our backs with labor."

   But filled with anger, Zeus who marshals the thunderheads
let loose now: "Unbelievable! God of the earthquake,
you with your massive power, why are you moaning so?
Another god might fear their wall—their idle whim—
one far weaker than you in strength of hand and fury.   530
Your *own* fame goes spreading far as the light of dawn.
Come now, just wait till these long-haired Achaeans
sail back in their ships to the fatherland they love,
then batter their wall, sweep it into the salt breakers
and pile over the endless beach your drifts of sand again,
level it to your heart's content—the Argives' mighty wall."

   So they conferred together, building their resolve.
The sun went down. The Argives' work was finished.
They slew oxen beside the tents and took their meal.
And the ships pulled in from Lemnos bringing wine,   540
a big convoy sent across by Euneus, Jason's son
whom Hypsipyle bore the seasoned lord of armies.
An outright gift to Atrides Agamemnon and Menelaus,
Euneus gave a shipment of wine, a thousand measures full.

From the rest Achaean soldiers bought their rations,
some with bronze and some with gleaming iron,
some with hides, some with whole live cattle,
some with slaves, and they made a handsome feast.
Then all that night the long-haired Achaeans feasted
as Trojans and Trojan allies took their meal in Troy.   550
Yes, but all night long the Master Strategist Zeus
plotted fresh disaster for both opposing armies—
his thunder striking terror—
and blanching panic swept across the ranks.
They flung wine from their cups and wet the earth
and no fighter would dare drink until he'd poured
an offering out to the overwhelming son of Cronus.
Then down they lay at last and took the gift of sleep.

BOOK EIGHT

The Tide
of Battle Turns

Now as the Dawn flung out her golden robe across the earth
Zeus who loves the lightning summoned all the gods
to assembly on the topmost peak of ridged Olympus.
He harangued the immortals hanging on his words:
"Hear me, all you gods and all goddesses too,
as I proclaim what the heart inside me urges.
Let no lovely goddess—and no god either—
try to fight against my strict decree.
All submit to it now, so all the more quickly
I can bring this violent business to an end.   10
And any god I catch, breaking ranks with us,
eager to go and help the Trojans or Achaeans—
back he comes to Olympus, whipped by the lightning,
eternally disgraced. Or I will snatch and hurl him
down to the murk of Tartarus half the world away,

the deepest gulf that yawns beneath the ground,
there where the iron gates and brazen threshold loom,
as far below the House of Death as the sky rides over earth—
then he will know how far my power tops all other gods'
Come, try me, immortals, so all of you can learn.   20
Hang a great golden cable down from the heavens,
lay hold of it, all you gods, all goddesses too:
you can never drag me down from sky to earth,
not Zeus, the highest, mightiest king of kings,
not even if you worked yourselves to death.
But whenever I'd set my mind to drag you up,
in deadly earnest, I'd hoist you all with ease,
you and the earth, you and the sea, all together,
then loop that golden cable round a horn of Olympus,
bind it fast and leave the whole world dangling in mid-air—   30
that is how far I tower over the gods, I tower over men."

   A stunned silence seized them all, struck dumb—
Zeus's ringing pronouncements overwhelmed them so.
But finally clear-eyed Athena rose and spoke:
"Our Father, son of Cronus, high and mighty,
we already know your power, far too well . . .
who can stand against you?
Even so, we pity these Argive spearmen
living out their grim fates, dying in blood.
Yes, we'll keep clear of the war as you command.   40
We'll simply offer the Argives tactics that may save them—
so they won't all fall beneath your blazing wrath."

   Zeus who drives the storm clouds smiled and answered,
"Courage, Athena, third-born of the gods, dear child.
Nothing I said was meant in earnest—trust me,
I mean you all the good will in the world."
                                             With that,
he harnessed his bronze-hoofed horses onto his battle-car,
his pair that raced the wind with their golden manes
streaming on behind them, and strapping golden armor
around his body, Zeus himself took up his whip   50

that coils lithe and gold and climbed aboard.
A crack of the lash—the team plunged to a run
and on the stallions flew, holding nothing back
as they winged between the earth and starry skies
and gaining the slopes of Ida with all her springs,
the mother of wild beasts, they reached Gargaron peak
where the grove of Zeus and Zeus's smoking altar stand.
There the father of men and gods reined in his team,
set them free and around them poured a dense mist.
And Zeus assumed his throne on the mountaintop,   60
exulting in all his glory, gazing out over
the city walls of Troy and the warships of Achaea.

Quickly the long-haired Achaeans took their meal
throughout the shelters, then they armed at once.
And on their side the Trojans put on harness too,
mustering throughout the city, a smaller force
but nerved to engage in combat even so—
necessity pressed them to fight for sons and wives.
All the gates flung wide and the Trojan mass surged out,
horses, chariots, men on foot—a tremendous roar went up.   70

And now as the armies clashed at one strategic point
they slammed their shields together, pike scraped pike
with the grappling strength of fighters armed in bronze
and their round shields' bosses pounded hide-to-hide
and the thunder of struggle roared and rocked the earth.
Screams of men and cries of triumph breaking in one breath,
fighters killing, fighters killed, and the ground streamed blood.

As long as morning rose and the blessed day grew stronger,
the weapons hurtled side-to-side and men kept falling.
But once the sun stood striding at high noon,   80
then Father Zeus held out his sacred golden scales:
in them he placed two fates of death that lays men low—
one for the Trojan horsemen, one for Argives armed in bronze—
and gripping the beam mid-haft the Father raised it high ·
and down went Achaea's day of doom, Achaea's fate

settling down on the earth that feeds us all
as the fate of Troy went lifting toward the sky.
And Zeus let loose a huge crash of thunder from Ida,
hurling his bolts in a flash against Achaea's armies.
The men looked on in horror. White terror seized them all.   90

Neither Idomeneus nor Agamemnon dared stand his ground,
nor did the Great and Little Ajax, old campaigners,
Nestor alone held out,
the noble horseman, Achaea's watch and ward,
but not of his own will. One horse was finished,
hit by a shaft that fair-haired Helen's lord,
magnificent Paris winged at its brow's high peak
where the forelock crowns the skull—most fatal spot.
It reared in agony, arrow piercing its brain and flung
the team in panic, writhing round the brazen point   100
as the old horseman hewed the trace-horse clear,
hacked away the straps—sudden strokes of his sword.
But on came Hector's team in the rush-and-buck of battle,
sweeping their driver Hector on in fighting-fury
and then and there old Nestor would have died
if Diomedes had not marked him fast—
the lord of the war cry gave a harrowing shout,
trying to rouse Odysseus: "Where are you running,
the royal son of Laertes, cool tactician?
Turning your back in battle like some coward!   110
Cutting and running so—take care that no one
spears you in the back! Hold firm with me—
we'll fight this wild maniac off the old man here!"

But long-enduring Odysseus never heard him—
down he dashed to the hollow Argive ships.
So all on his own Diomedes charged the front,
lurched to a halt before old Nestor's team
and winged a flight of orders at the horseman:
"Old soldier, these young fighters wear you down—
your strength goes slack and old age dogs your steps,   120
your driver's worthless, your horses drag their weight.

Come, up with you now, climb aboard my chariot!
So you can see the breed of Tros's team, their flair
for their own terrain as they gallop back and forth,
one moment in flight, the next in hot pursuit—
I took them both from Aeneas, driving terrors.
Your own good team? Our aides will handle them—
we'll steer these racers straight at the Trojans now,
the great breakers of horses. We'll let Hector see
if the spear in *my* hand is mad for bloodshed too!"   130

    And the old charioteer rose to the challenge.
Aides caught his team, Sthenelus, loyal Eurymedon,
as the two commanders boarded Diomedes' car.
Nestor grasped the glistening reins in both fists,
lashed the team and they charged straight at Hector
charging straight at *them* as Tydides hurled a spear
and missed his man but he picked the driver off,
Eniopeus son of proud Thebaeus gripping the reins—
he slashed him beside the nipple, stabbed his chest
and off the car he pitched, his horses balking, rearing.   140
There on the spot the man's strength and life collapsed
and blinding grief for his driver overpowered Hector,
stunned for his friend but he left him lying there,
dead, and swept on, out for another hardy driver.
Nor did his team go long without a master,
Hector found one quickly—Iphitus' daring son,
Archeptolemus—mounted him up behind his racers,
thrust the reins in the fighting driver's hands.

    Now there would have been havoc, irreversible chaos,
the Trojans penned in the walls of Troy like sheep,   150
but the father of men and gods was quick to the mark.
A crash of thunder! Zeus let loose a terrific bolt
and blazing white at the hoofs of Diomedes' team
it split the earth, a blinding smoking flash—
molten sulphur exploding into the air,
stallions shying, cringing against the car—
and the shining reins flew free of Nestor's grip.

His heart quaking, he cried to Diomedes, "Quick, Tydides,
swing these stallions round and fly! Can't you see?
Victory comes from Zeus but not for you.   160
He hands the glory to Hector, today at least—
tomorrow it's ours, if he wants to give us glory.
There's not a man alive who can fight the will of Zeus,
even a man of iron—Zeus is so much stronger!"

But Diomedes lord of the war cry answered,
"Right, old soldier—all you say is true.
But here's the grief that cuts me to the quick:
one day this Hector will vaunt among his Trojans,
'Diomedes ran for his ships—I drove him back!'
So he'll boast, I know—   170
let the great earth gape and take me down that day!"

But the noble horseman Nestor shouted back,
"Nonsense, steady Tydeus' son—such loose talk!
Let Hector call you a coward, scorn your courage—
the Trojan and Dardan troops will never believe him,
nor will the wives of the lusty Trojan shieldsmen, never—
you flung their lords in the dust, laid them low in their prime!"

And with that he swung their racers round, mid-flight,
back again to the rout—Trojans and Hector after them,
shouting their savage cries and pelting both men now   180
with spears and painful arrows. Helmet flashing,
rangy Hector hurled a resounding yell: "Diomedes—
once the Danaan riders prized you first of men
with pride of place, choice meats and brimming cups.
Now they will disgrace you, a woman after all.
Away with you, girl, glittering little puppet!
I'll never yield, you'll never mount our towers,
never drag our women back to your ships of war—
I'll pack you off to the god of darkness first!"

                                                Fighting words,
and Diomedes was torn two ways—he'd half a mind   190
to turn the team and take him face-to-face . . .

Three times Tydides was tempted, heart and soul,
three times from the crags of Ida Zeus let loose his thunder,
the Master Strategist handing down a sign to the Trojans—
victory thunder turning the tide of war their way.
And Hector called to his men in a ringing voice,
"Trojans! Lycians! Dardan fighters hand-to-hand—
now be men, my friends, call up your battle-fury!
The Father nods his head in assent, I see, at last
he grants me glory, triumph—the Argives, bloody death.   200
Fools, erecting their rampart! Flimsy and futile,
not worth a second thought.
They'll never hold me back in my onslaught now,
with a bound my team will leap that trench they dug.
But soon as I reach their hollow ships, torches—
don't forget now, one of you bring me lethal fire!
I'll burn their ships, I'll slaughter all their men,
Argive heroes panicked in smoke along their hulls!"

    And with that threat he called out to his horses,
"Golden and Whitefoot, Blaze and Silver Flash!   210
Now repay me for all the loving care Andromache,
generous Eetion's daughter, showered on you aplenty.
First of the teams she gave you honey-hearted wheat,
she even mixed it with wine for you to drink
when the spirit moved her—before she'd serve *me*,
though I'm proud to say I am her loving husband.
After them, fast, full gallop! So we can seize
the shield of Nestor—its fame hits the skies,
solid gold, the handgrips and the shield itself—
and strip from the stallion-breaking Diomedes' back   220
the burnished armor Hephaestus forged with all his skill.
If only we lay our hands on these, I'm filled with hope
they'll take to their racing ships this very night!"

    So he gloried but Queen Hera stirred in outrage,
she shook on her throne and Mount Olympus quaked
as she cried in the face of the rugged god Poseidon,
"You ruthless—the Earth-shaker with all your power—

not even a twinge of pity deep inside your heart
for all these Argives dying! The same fighters
who pile your gifts at Aegae port and Helice,   230
gifts by the shipload, hoards to warm your heart.
And you used to plan their victory! If only we,
we gods who defend the Argives had the will to hurl
the Trojans back and hold off thundering Zeus—
there he would sit and smolder,
throned in desolate splendor up on Ida."

  Deeply shaken, the god who rocks the earth replied,
"Hera, what wild words! What are you saying?
I for one have no desire to battle Zeus,
not you and I and the rest of the gods together.   240
The King is far too strong—he'll crush us all."

  So they harangued each other to a standstill.
But as for Achaea's forces, all the ground
that the broad trench enclosed from ships to wall
was crammed with chariots, teams and men in armor
packed into close quarters, yes, and the one man
who packed them there, a match for rushing Ares,
Hector the son of Priam, now Zeus gave Hector glory.
And now he might have gutted the ships with fire,
blazing fire—but Queen Hera impelled Agamemnon,   250
out on the run already, to go and rouse his men.
He made his way through Achaea's ships and shelters,
flaring his great crimson cape with a strong hand
and stopped at Odysseus' huge black-bellied hull,
moored mid-line so a shout could reach both wings,
upshore to Telamonian Ajax' camp or down to Achilles'—
trusting so to their arms' power and battle-strength
they'd hauled their trim ships up on either flank.
Agamemnon's cry went piercing through the army:
"Shame! Disgrace! You Argives, you degraded—   260
splendid in battle dress, pure sham!
Where have the fighting taunts all gone? That time

you vaunted you were the finest force on earth—
all that empty bluster you let fly at Lemnos,
gorging yourselves on longhorn cattle meat
and drunk to the full on brimming bowls of wine,
bragging how each man could stand up to a hundred,
no, two hundred Trojan fighters in pitched battle.
Now our whole army is no match for one, for Hector—
he'll gut our ships with blazing fire at any moment!   270
Father Zeus, when did you ever strike a mighty king
with such mad blindness—then tear away his glory?

                                            Not once,
I swear, did I pass some handsome shrine of yours,
sailing my oar-swept ship on our fatal voyage here,
but on each I burned the fat and thighs of oxen,
longing to raze Troy's sturdy walls to the roots.
So, Father, at least fulfill this prayer for me:
let the men escape with their lives if nothing else—
don't let these Trojans mow us down in droves!"

                                        So he prayed
and the Father filled with pity, seeing Atrides weep.   280
The god bent his head that the armies must be saved,
not die in blood. That instant he launched an eagle—
truest of Zeus's signs that fly the skies—a fawn
clutched in its talons, sprung of a running doe,
but he dropped it free beside the handsome shrine
where Achaean soldiers always sacrificed to Zeus
whose voice rings clear with omens. Seeing the eagle
sent their way from Zeus, they roused their war-lust,
flung themselves on the Trojans with a vengeance.

                                                There,
massed in formation as they were, not a single man   290
could claim he outstripped Diomedes, Tydeus' son
lashing his high-strung team across the trench
to reach the front and battle hand-to-hand—
the first by far to kill a Trojan captain,
Agelaus the son of Phradmon. He'd just turned
his chariot round in flight and once he'd swerved

Diomedes' spear went punching through his back,
gouging his shoulder blade and driving through his chest—
he spilled from the chariot, armor clanging against him.

    Diomedes plowed on and after him came the Atridae,   300
Agamemnon and Menelaus, following in their wake
the Great and Little Ajax armed in fury,
Idomeneus after them and Idomeneus' good aide,
Meriones, a match for the butcher god of war,
Eurypylus after them, Euaemon's gallant son,
and Teucer came up ninth, tensing his reflex bow
and lurking under the wall of giant Ajax' shield.
As Ajax raised the rim, the archer would mark a target,
shoot through the lines—the man he hit dropped dead
on the spot—and quick as a youngster ducking under   310
his mother's skirts he'd duck under Ajax' shield
and the gleaming shield would hide him head to toe.

    Who was the first Trojan the marksman Teucer hit?
Orsilochus first, then Ormenus, Ophelestes,
Daetor and Chromius, princely Lycophontes,
Polyaemon's son Amopaon and Melanippus too—
corpse on corpse he dropped to the earth that rears us all.
And King Agamemnon, thrilled at the sight of Teucer
whipping arrows off his bow, reaping the Trojan ranks,
strode up and sang his praises: "Teucer, lovely soldier,   320
Telamon's son, pride of the armies—now you're shooting!
You'll bring a ray of hope to your men, your father too.
He raised you when you were little, a bastard boy,
no matter—Telamon tended you in his own house.
Far off as he is, you'll set him up in glory.
I tell you this, so help me it's the truth:
if Zeus with his storm-shield and Queen Athena
ever let me plunder the strong walls of Troy,
you are the first, the first after myself—
I'll place some gift of honor in your hands,   330
a tripod, or purebred team with their own car
or a fine woman to mount and share your bed."

   And Teucer gave his captain a faultless answer:
"Great field marshal, why bother to spur me on?
I go all-out as it is.
With all the power in me I've never quit,
not from the time we rolled them back to Troy.
I've stalked with my bow and picked them off in packs.
Eight arrows I've let fly, with long sharp barbs,
and all stuck in the flesh of soldiers quick to fight—   340
but I still can't bring this mad dog Hector down!"

   The archer loosed a fresh shaft from the bowstring
straight for Hector, his spirit longing to hit him—
but he missed and cut Gorgythion down instead,
a well-bred son of Priam, a handsome prince,
and the arrow pierced his chest, Gorgythion
whom Priam's bride from Aesyme bore one day,
lovely Castianira lithe as a deathless goddess . . .
As a garden poppy, burst into red bloom, bends,
drooping its head to one side, weighed down   350
by its full seeds and a sudden spring shower,
so Gorgythion's head fell limp over one shoulder,
weighed down by his helmet.
                            Quick with another arrow,
the archer let fly from his bowstring straight for Hector,
his spirit straining to hit him—shot and missed again
as Apollo skewed his shaft—
but he leveled Archeptolemus, Hector's daring driver
charging headlong, caught him square in the chest
beside the nipple and off his car he pitched
as his horses balked, rearing, pawing the air.   360
There on the spot his strength and life collapsed
and blinding grief for the driver overpowered Hector,
stunned for his friend but he left him lying there
and cried out to his brother Cebriones close by,
"Take the reins!" Cebriones rushed to obey—
but Hector leapt down from the burnished car,
he hit the earth with a yell, seized a rock
and went for Teucer, mad to strike the archer

just plucking a bitter arrow from his quiver,
notching it on the string and drawing back the bow   370
to his right shoulder, when Hector, helmet flashing,
caught him where the collarbone bridges neck and chest,
the deadliest spot of all. There Hector struck,
hurling the jagged rock at Teucer drawing in fury—
snapped the string and his hand went numb at the wrist,
he dropped to a knee, dazed . . . the bow slipped from his grip.
But giant Ajax would never fail his fallen brother—
he ran to straddle and hide him with his shield
as a brace of comrades shouldered up the fighter:
Echius' son Mecisteus helping good Alastor   380
bore him back to the hollow warships, groaning hard.

   And again the Olympian Father fired up the Trojans
ramming Argives back against their own deep trench.
Hector far in the lead, bristling in all his force
like a hound that harries a wild boar or lion—
hot pursuit, snapping quick at his heels,
hindquarters and flanks but still on alert
for him to wheel and fight—so Hector harried
the long-haired Argives, killing the last stragglers,
man after lagging man and they, they fled in panic.   390
Back through stakes and across the trench they fled,
and hordes were cut down at the Trojans' hands—the rest,
only after they reached the shipways, stood fast
and shouting out to each other, flung their arms
to all the immortals, each man crying out a prayer.
But Hector swerved his horses round at the trench's edge,
wheeling back and forth, tossing their gorgeous manes,
with Hector's eyes glaring bright as a Gorgon's eyes
or Ares', man-destroying Ares'.
                          A total rout—
and white-armed Hera saw it, and filled with pity   400
the goddess' words went winging toward Athena:
"Look, daughter of Zeus whose shield is thunder—
don't we care for them any longer? All our Argives
dying there in droves! This is our last chance.

They're filling out their fates to the last gasp,
hacked to pieces under a single man's assault.
This maniac, Hector—I cannot bear him any longer.
Look at the savage slaughter he has made!"

                                             Eyes blazing,
Athena answered, "Let him die a thousand deaths!—
Hector's life and his battle-frenzy blotted out   410
by the Argives here on Hector's native soil.
But Father rages now, that hard black heart,
always the old outrage, dashing all my plans!
Not a thought for the many times I saved his son
Heracles, worked to death by the labors of Eurystheus.
How he would whine to the high skies—till Father Zeus
would rush me down from the clouds to save his life.
If only I'd foreseen all this, I and my cunning—
that day Eurystheus sent him down to Death,
to the lord who guards the gates, to drag up   420
from the dark world the hound of grisly Death—
he would never have fled the steep cascading Styx.
But Zeus hates me now. He fulfills the plans of Thetis
who cupped his chin in her hand and kissed his knees,
begging Zeus to exalt Achilles scourge of cities.
But the day will come when Father, well I know,
calls me his darling gray-eyed girl again.
So now you harness the racing team for us
while I go into the halls of storming Zeus
and buckle on my gear and arm for combat.   430
Now I'll see if Hector, for all his flashing helmet,
leaps for joy when the two of us come blazing forth
on the passageways of battle—or one of his Trojans too
will glut the dogs and birds with his fat and flesh,
brought down in blood against the Argive ships!"

     The white-armed goddess Hera could not resist.
Hera queen of the gods, daughter of giant Cronus
launched the work, harnessed the golden-bridled team
while Athena, child of Zeus whose shield is thunder,
letting fall her supple robe at the Father's threshold—   440

rich brocade, stitched with her own hands' labor—
donned the battle-shirt of the lord of lightning,
buckled her breastplate geared for wrenching war.
Then onto the flaming chariot Pallas set her feet
and seized her spear—weighted, heavy, the massive shaft
she wields to break the battle lines of heroes
the mighty Father's daughter storms against.

                          A crack of the whip—
the goddess Hera lashed the team, and all on their own force
the gates of heaven thundered open, kept by the Seasons,
guards of the vaulting sky and Olympus heights empowered   450
to spread the massing clouds or close them round once more,
and straight through the great gates she drove the team.

    But as Father Zeus caught sight of them from Ida
the god broke into a sudden rage and summoned Iris
to run a message on with a rush of golden wings:
"Quick on your way now, Iris, shear the wind!
Turn them back, don't let them engage me here.
What an indignity for us to clash in arms.
I tell you this and I will fulfill it too:
I'll maim their racers for them,   460
right beneath their yokes, and those two goddesses,
I'll hurl them from their chariot, smash their car,
and not once in the course of ten slow wheeling years
will they heal the wounds my lightning bolt rips open.
So that gray-eyed girl of mine may learn what it means
to fight against her Father. But with Hera, though,
I am not so outraged, so irate—it's always her way
to thwart my will, whatever I command."

                             So he thundered
and Iris ran his message, racing with gale force
away from the peaks of Ida up to steep Olympus   470
cleft and craggy. There at the outer gates
she met them face-to-face and blocked their path,
sounding Zeus's orders: "Where are you rushing now?
What is this madness blazing in your hearts?
Zeus forbids you to fight for Achaea's armies!

Here is Father's threat—he will fulfill it too:
he'll maim your racers for you,
right beneath their yokes, and you two goddesses,
he'll hurl you from your chariot, smash your car,
and not once in the course of ten slow wheeling years   480
will you heal the wounds his lightning bolt rips open!
So you, his gray-eyed girl, may learn what it means
to fight against your Father. But with Hera, though,
he is not so outraged, so irate—it's always your way
to thwart his will, whatever Zeus commands. You,
you insolent brazen bitch—you really dare
to shake that monstrous spear in Father's face?"

And Iris racing the wind went veering past
and Hera turned to Pallas, calling off the conflict:
"Enough. Daughter of Zeus whose shield is thunder,   490
I cannot let us battle the Father any longer,
not for mortal men . . .
Men—let one of them die, another live,
however their luck may run. Let Zeus decide
the fates of the men of Troy and men of Argos both,
to his deathless heart's content—that is only right."

So she complied and turned their racers back.
The Seasons loosed the purebred sleek-maned team,
tethered them to their stalls, piled on ambrosia
and leaned the chariot up against the polished walls   500
that shimmered in the sun. The goddesses themselves
sat down on golden settles, mixing with the immortals,
Athena and Hera's hearts within them dashed.

                                        At the same time
Zeus the Father whipped his team and hurtling chariot
straight from Ida to Mount Olympus, soon to reach
the sessions of the gods. Quick at Zeus's side
the famous lord of earthquakes freed the team,
canted the battle-chariot firmly on its base
and wrapped it well with a heavy canvas shroud.
Thundering Zeus himself assumed his golden throne   510

as the massive range of Olympus shook beneath his feet.
Those two alone, Athena and Hera, sat apart from Zeus—
not a word would they send his way, not a question.
But the Father knew their feelings deep within his heart
and mocked them harshly: "Why so crushed, Athena, Hera?
Not overly tired, I trust, from all your efforts
there in glorious battle, slaughtering Trojans,
the men you break with all your deathless rage.
But I with *my* courage, *my* hands, never conquered—
for all their force not all the gods on Olympus heights   520
could ever turn me back. Ah but the two of you—
long ago the trembling shook your glistening limbs
before you could glimpse the horrid works of war.
I tell you this, and it would have come to pass:
once my lightning had blasted you in your chariot,
you could never have returned to Mount Olympus
where the immortals make their home."
                                                        So he mocked
as Athena and Queen Hera muttered between themselves,
huddled together, plotting Troy's destruction.
True, Athena held her peace and said nothing . . .   530
smoldering at the Father, seized with wild resentment.
But Hera could hold the anger in her breast no longer,
suddenly bursting out, "Dread majesty, son of Cronus,
what are you saying? We already know your power,
far too well . . . who can stand against you?
Even so, we pity these Argive spearmen
living out their grim fates, dying in blood.
Yes, we'll keep clear of the war as you command.
We'll simply offer the Argives tactics that may save them—
so they won't all fall beneath your blazing wrath."   540

    And Zeus who marshals the thunderheads replied,
"Tomorrow at dawn's your chance, my ox-eyed queen.
Look down then, if you have the taste for it, Hera,
and you will see the towering son of Cronus killing
still more hordes, whole armies of Argive soldiers.

This powerful Hector will never quit the fighting,
not till swift Achilles rises beside the ships
that day they battle against the high sterns,
pinned in the fatal straits
and grappling for the body of Patroclus.   550
So runs the doom of Zeus.
                              You and your anger—
rage away! I care nothing for that. Not even
if you go plunging down to the pit of earth and sea
where Cronus and Iapetus make their beds of pain,
where not a ray of the Sun can warm their hearts,
not a breeze, the depths of Tartarus wall them round.
Not if you ventured down as far as the black abyss itself—
I care nothing for you, you and your snarling anger,
none in the world a meaner bitch than you.''
                              So he erupted
but the white-armed goddess Hera answered not a word . . .   560
Now down in the Ocean sank the fiery light of day,
drawing the dark night across the grain-giving earth.
For the men of Troy the day went down against their will
but not the Argives—what a blessing, how they prayed
for the nightfall coming on across their lines.

     But again, still bent on glory, Hector mustered
his Trojan cohorts, pulled them back from the ships
toward the river rapids, to wide open ground
where they found a sector free and clear of corpses.
They swung down from their chariots onto earth   570
to hear what Hector dear to Zeus commanded now.
He clutched a thrusting-lance eleven forearms long;
the bronze tip of the weapon shone before him,
ringed with a golden hoop to grip the shaft.
Leaning on this, the prince addressed his men:
"Hear me, Trojans, Dardans, all our loyal allies!
I had hoped by now, once we destroyed them all—
all the Achaeans and all their hollow ships—
we might turn home to the windy heights of Troy.

But night came on too soon. That's what saved them,   580
that alone, they and their ships along the churning surf.
Very well then, let us give way to the dark night,
set out our supper, unyoke our full-maned teams
and pile the fodder down before their hoofs.
Drive cattle out of the city, fat sheep too,
quickly, bring on rations of honeyed, mellow wine
and bread from the halls, and heap the firewood high.
Then all night long till the breaking light of day
we keep the watch fires blazing, hundreds of fires
and the rising glare can leap and hit the skies,   590
so the long-haired Achaeans stand no chance tonight
to cut and run on the sea's broad back. Never,
not without a struggle, not at their royal ease
are they going to board those ships! No, no,
let every last man of them lick his wounds—
a memento at home—pierced by arrow or spear
as he vaults aboard his decks. So the next fool
will cringe at the thought of mounting hateful war
against our stallion-breaking Trojans.
                            Now let heralds
dear to Zeus cry out through the streets of Troy   600
that boys in their prime and old gray-headed men
must take up posts on the towers built by the gods,
in bivouac round the city. And as for our wives,
each in her own hall must set big fires burning.
The night watch too, it must be kept unbroken,
so no night raiders can slip inside the walls
with our armies camped afield.
                            That's our battle-order,
my iron-hearted Trojans, just as I command.
Let the order I issue now stand firm and clear
and the stirring call to arms I sound tomorrow morning,   610
my stallion-breaking Trojans!
                            My hopes are rising now—
I pray to Zeus and the great array of deathless gods
that we will whip the Achaeans howling out of Troy

and drive them off to death, those dogs of war
the deadly fates drove here in their black ships!
So now, for the night, we guard our own positions,
but tomorrow at daybreak, armed to the hilt for battle,
waken slashing war against their hollow hulls.
I'll soon see if the mighty Diomedes rams me
back from the ships and back against our walls   620
or I kill him with bronze and strip his bloody armor!
Tomorrow Tydeus' son will learn his own strength—
if he has the spine to stand the onrush of my spear.
In the front ranks he'll sprawl, I think, torn open,
a rout of his comrades down around their captain
just as the sun goes rising into dawn. If only
I were as sure of immortality, ageless all my days—
and I were prized as they prize Athena and Apollo—
as surely as this day will bring the Argives death!"

    So Hector urged his armies. The Trojans roared assent.   630
The fighters loosed their sweating teams from the yokes,
tethered them by the reins, each at his own chariot.
They herded cattle out of the city, fat sheep too,
quickly, brought on rations of honeyed, mellow wine
and bread from the halls, heaped the firewood high
and up from the plain the winds swept the smoke,
the sweetness and the savor swirling up the skies.

    And so their spirits soared
as they took positions down the passageways of battle
all night long, and the watchfires blazed among them.   640
Hundreds strong, as stars in the night sky glittering
round the moon's brilliance blaze in all their glory
when the air falls to a sudden, windless calm . . .
all the lookout peaks stand out and the jutting cliffs
and the steep ravines and down from the high heavens bursts
the boundless bright air and all the stars shine clear
and the shepherd's heart exults—so many fires burned
between the ships and the Xanthus' whirling rapids

set by the men of Troy, bright against their walls.
A thousand fires were burning there on the plain   650
and beside each fire sat fifty fighting men
poised in the leaping blaze, and champing oats
and glistening barley, stationed by their chariots,
stallions waited for Dawn to mount her glowing throne.

BOOK NINE

The Embassy to Achilles

So the Trojans held their watch that night but not the Achaeans—
godsent Panic seized them, comrade of bloodcurdling Rout:
all their best were struck by grief too much to bear.
As crosswinds chop the sea where the fish swarm,
the North Wind and the West Wind blasting out of Thrace
in sudden, lightning attack, wave on blacker wave, cresting,
heaving a tangled mass of seaweed out along the surf—
so the Achaeans' hearts were torn inside their chests.

Distraught with the rising anguish, Atreus' son
went ranging back and forth, commanding heralds   10
to sound out loud and clear and call the men to muster,
each by name, but no loud outcry now. The king himself
pitched in with the lead heralds, summoning troops.
They grouped on the meeting grounds, morale broken.

Lord marshal Agamemnon rose up in their midst,
streaming tears like a dark spring running down
some desolate rock face, its shaded currents flowing.
So, with a deep groan, the king addressed his armies:
"Friends . . . lords of the Argives, all my captains!
Cronus' son has entangled me in madness, blinding ruin—   20
Zeus is a harsh, cruel god. He vowed to me long ago,
he bowed his head that I should never embark for home
till I had brought the walls of Ilium crashing down.
But now, I see, he only plotted brutal treachery:
now he commands me back to Argos in disgrace,
whole regiments of my men destroyed in battle.
So it must please his overweening heart, who knows?
Father Zeus has lopped the crowns of a thousand cities,
true, and Zeus will lop still more—his power is too great.
So come, follow my orders. Obey me, all you Argives.   30
Cut and run! Sail home to the fatherland we love!
We'll never take the broad streets of Troy."

   Silence held them all, struck dumb by his orders.
A long while they said nothing, spirits dashed.
Finally Diomedes lord of the war cry broke forth:
"Atrides—I will be first to oppose you in your folly,
here in assembly, King, where it's the custom.
Spare me your anger. My courage—
mine was the first you mocked among the Argives,
branding me a coward, a poor soldier. Yes, well,   40
they know all about that, the Argives young and old.
But you—the son of Cronus with Cronus' twisting ways
gave you gifts by halves: with that royal scepter
the Father gave you honor beyond all other men alive
but he never gave you courage, the greatest power of all.
Desperate man! So certain, are you, the sons of Achaea
are cowards, poor soldiers, just because you say so?
Desert—if your spirit drives you to sail home,
then sail away, my King! The sea-lanes are clear,
there are your ships of war, crowded down the surf,   50
those that followed you from Mycenae, your own proud armada.

But the rest of the long-haired Achaeans will hold out,
right here, until we've plundered Troy. And they,
if they go running home to the land they love,
then the two of us, I and Sthenelus here
will fight our way to the fixed doom of Troy.
Never forget—we all sailed here with god."

　　And all the Achaeans shouted their assent,
stirred by the stallion-breaking Diomedes' challenge.
But Nestor the old driver rose and spoke at once: 60
"Few can match your power in battle, Diomedes,
and in council you excel all men your age.
So no one could make light of your proposals,
not the whole army—who could contradict you?
But you don't press on and reach a useful end.
How young you are . . . why, you could be my son,
my youngest-born at that, though you urge our kings
with cool clear sense: what you've said is right.
But it's my turn now, Diomedes.
I think I can claim to have some years on you.   70
So I *must* speak up and drive the matter home.
And no one will heap contempt on what I say,
not even mighty Agamemnon. Lost to the clan,
lost to the hearth, lost to the old ways, that one
who lusts for all the horrors of war with his own people.
But now, I say, let us give way to the dark night,
set out the evening meal. Sentries take up posts,
squads fronting the trench we dug outside the rampart.
That's the command I give the younger fighters.

　　　　　　　　　　　　　　　　Then,
Atrides, lead the way—you are the greatest king—   80
spread out a feast for all your senior chiefs.
That is your duty, a service that becomes you.
Your shelters overflow with the wine Achaean ships
bring in from Thrace, daily, down the sea's broad back.
Grand hospitality is yours, you rule so many men.
Come, gather us all and we will heed that man
who gives the best advice. That's what they need,

I tell you—all the Achaeans—good sound advice,
now our enemies, camping hard against the ships,
kindle their watchfires round us by the thousands.   90
What soldier could warm to that? Tonight's the night
that rips our ranks to shreds or pulls us through."

The troops hung on his words and took his orders.
Out they rushed, the sentries in armor, forming
under the son of Nestor, captain Thrasymedes,
under Ascalaphus, Ialmenus, sons of Ares,
under Meriones, Aphareus and Deipyrus,
under the son of Creon, trusty Lycomedes.
Seven chiefs of the guard, a hundred under each,
fighters marching, grasping long spears in their hands,   100
took up new positions between the trench and rampart.
There they lit their fires, each man made his meal.

Meanwhile marshal Agamemnon led his commanders,
a file of senior chiefs, toward his own lodge
and set before them a feast to please their hearts.
They reached out for the good things that lay at hand
but when they had put aside desire for food and drink
the old man began to weave his counsel among them:
Nestor was first to speak—from the early days
his plans and tactics always seemed the best.   110
With good will to the chiefs he rose and spoke,
"Great marshal Atrides, lord of men Agamemnon . . .
with you I will end, my King, with you I will begin,
since you hold sway over many warriors, vast armies,
and Zeus has placed in your hands the royal scepter
and time-honored laws, so you will advise them well.
So you above all must speak your mind, and listen,
and carry out the next man's counsel too,
whenever his spirit leads him on to speak
for the public good. Credit will go to you   120
for whatever he proposes.
Now I will tell you what seems best to me.
No one will offer a better plan than this . . .

the plan I still retain, and I've been forming,
well, for a good long while now, from the very day
that you, my illustrious King, infuriated Achilles—
you went and took from his tents the girl Briseis,
and not with any applause from us, far from it:
I for one, I urged you against it, strenuously.
But you, you gave way to your overbearing anger,   130
disgraced a great man the gods themselves esteem—
you seized his gift of honor and keep her still.
But even so, late as it is, let us contrive
to set all this to rights, to bring him round
with gifts of friendship and warm, winning words."

    And Agamemnon the lord of men consented quickly:
"That's no lie, old man—a full account you give
of all my acts of madness. Mad, blind I was!
Not even *I* would deny it.
Why look, that man is worth an entire army,   140
the fighter Zeus holds dear with all his heart—
how he exalts him now and mauls Achaea's forces!
But since I *was* blinded, lost in my own inhuman rage,
now, at last, I am bent on setting things to rights:
I'll give a priceless ransom paid for friendship.
                              Here,
before you all, I'll name in full the splendid gifts I offer.
Seven tripods never touched by fire, ten bars of gold,
twenty burnished cauldrons, a dozen massive stallions,
racers who earned me trophies with their speed.
He is no poor man who owns what they have won,   150
not strapped for goods with all that lovely gold—
what trophies those high-strung horses carried off for me!
Seven women I'll give him, flawless, skilled in crafts,
women of Lesbos—the ones I chose, my privilege,
that day he captured the Lesbos citadel himself:
they outclassed the tribes of women in their beauty.
These I will give, and along with them will go
the one I took away at first, Briseus' daughter,
and I will swear a solemn, binding oath in the bargain:

I never mounted her bed, never once made love with her—   160
the natural thing for mankind, men and women joined.
Now all these gifts will be handed him at once.
But if, later, the gods allow us to plunder
the great city of Priam, let him enter in
when we share the spoils, load the holds of his ship
with gold and bronze—as much as his heart desires—
and choose for his pleasure twenty Trojan women
second only to Argive Helen in their glory.
And then, if we can journey home to Achaean Argos,
pride of the breasting earth, he'll be my son-by-marriage!   170
I will even honor him on a par with my Orestes,
full-grown by now, reared in the lap of luxury.
Three daughters are mine in my well-built halls—
Chrysothemis and Laodice and Iphianassa—
and he may lead away whichever one he likes,
with no bride-price asked, home to Peleus' house.
And I will add a dowry, yes, a magnificent treasure
the likes of which no man has ever offered with his daughter!
Seven citadels I will give him, filled with people,
Cardamyle, Enope, and the grassy slopes of Hire,   180
Pherae the sacrosanct, Anthea deep in meadows,
rolling Aepea and Pedasus green with vineyards.
All face the sea at the far edge of sandy Pylos
and the men who live within them, rich in sheep-flocks,
rich in shambling cattle, will honor him like a god
with hoards of gifts and beneath his scepter's sway
live out his laws in sleek and shining peace.
                                              All this—
I would extend to him if he will end his anger.
Let him submit to me! Only the god of death
is so relentless, Death submits to no one—   190
so mortals hate him most of all the gods.
Let him bow down to me! I am the greater king,
I am the elder-born, I claim—the greater man."

Nestor the noble charioteer embraced his offer:
"Generous marshal Atrides, lord of men Agamemnon!

No one could underrate these gifts of yours, not now,
the treasure trove you offer Prince Achilles.
Come—we'll send a detail of picked men.
They'll go to Achilles' tent with all good speed.
Quick, whomever my eye will light on in review,   200
the mission's theirs. And old Phoenix first—
Zeus loves the man, so let him lead the way.
Then giant Ajax and tactful royal Odysseus.
Heralds? Odius and Eurybates, you escort them.
Water for their hands! A reverent silence now . . .
a prayer to Zeus. Perhaps he'll show us mercy."

The brisk commands he issued pleased them all.
Heralds brought the water at once and rinsed their hands,
and the young men brimmed the mixing bowls with wine
and tipping first drops for the god in every cup   210
they poured full rounds for all. Libations finished,
each envoy having drunk to his heart's content,
the party moved out from Atrides' shelters.
Nestor the old driver gave them marching orders—
a sharp glance at each, Odysseus most of all:
"Try hard now, bring him round—invincible Achilles!"

So Ajax and Odysseus made their way at once
where the battle lines of breakers crash and drag,
praying hard to the god who moves and shakes the earth
that they might bring the proud heart of Achilles   220
round with speed and ease.
Reaching the Myrmidon shelters and their ships,
they found him there, delighting his heart now,
plucking strong and clear on the fine lyre—
beautifully carved, its silver bridge set firm—
he won from the spoils when he razed Eetion's city.
Achilles was lifting his spirits with it now,
singing the famous deeds of fighting heroes . . .
Across from him Patroclus sat alone, in silence,
waiting for Aeacus' son to finish with his song.   230
And on they came, with good Odysseus in the lead,

and the envoys stood before him. Achilles, startled,
sprang to his feet, the lyre still in his hands,
leaving the seat where he had sat in peace.
And seeing the men, Patroclus rose up too
as the famous runner called and waved them on:
"Welcome! Look, dear friends have come our way—
I must be sorely needed now—my dearest friends
in all the Achaean armies, even in my anger."

So Prince Achilles hailed and led them in,   240
sat them down on settles with purple carpets
and quickly told Patroclus standing by, "Come,
a bigger winebowl, son of Menoetius, set it here.
Mix stronger wine. A cup for the hands of each guest—
here beneath my roof are the men I love the most."

He paused. Patroclus obeyed his great friend,
who put down a heavy chopping block in the firelight
and across it laid a sheep's chine, a fat goat's
and the long back cut of a full-grown pig,
marbled with lard. Automedon held the meats   250
while lordly Achilles carved them into quarters,
cut them well into pieces, pierced them with spits
and Patroclus raked the hearth, a man like a god
making the fire blaze. Once it had burned down
and the flames died away, he scattered the coals
and stretching the spitted meats across the embers,
raised them onto supports and sprinkled clean pure salt.
As soon as the roasts were done and spread on platters,
Patroclus brought the bread, set it out on the board
in ample wicker baskets. Achilles served the meat.   260
Then face-to-face with his noble guest Odysseus
he took his seat along the farther wall,
he told his friend to sacrifice to the gods
and Patroclus threw the first cuts in the fire.
They reached out for the good things that lay at hand
and when they had put aside desire for food and drink,
Ajax nodded to Phoenix. Odysseus caught the signal,

filled his cup and lifted it toward Achilles,
opening with this toast: "Your health, Achilles!
We have no lack of a handsome feast, I see that,   270
either in Agamemnon's tents, the son of Atreus,
or here and now, in yours. We can all banquet here
to our heart's content.

                     But it's not the flowing feast
that is on our minds now—no, a stark disaster,
too much to bear, Achilles bred by the gods,
that is what we are staring in the face
and we are afraid. All hangs in the balance now:
whether we save our benched ships or they're destroyed,
unless, of course, you put your fighting power in harness.
They have pitched camp right at our ships and rampart,   280
those brazen Trojans, they and their far-famed allies,
thousands of fires blaze throughout their armies . . .
Nothing can stop them now—that's their boast—
they'll hurl themselves against our blackened hulls.
And the son of Cronus sends them signs on the right,
Zeus's firebolts flashing. And headlong Hector,
delirious with his strength, rages uncontrollably,
trusting to Zeus—no fear of man or god, nothing—
a powerful rabid frenzy has him in its grip!
Hector prays for the sacred Dawn to break at once,   290
he threatens to lop the high horns of our sterns
and gut our ships with fire, and all our comrades
pinned against the hulls, panicked by thick smoke,
he'll rout and kill in blood!
A nightmare—I fear it, with all my heart—
I fear the gods will carry out his threats
and then it will be our fate to die in Troy,
far from the stallion-land of Argos . . .
                            Up with you—
now, late as it is, if you *want* to pull our Argives,
our hard-hit armies, clear of the Trojan onslaught.   300
Fail us now? What a grief it will be to you
through all the years to come. No remedy,
no way to cure the damage once it's done.

Come, while there's still time, think hard:
how can you fight off the Argives' fatal day?
Oh old friend, surely your father Peleus urged you,
that day he sent you out of Phthia to Agamemnon,
'My son, victory is what Athena and Hera will give,
if they so choose. But you, you hold in check
that proud, fiery spirit of yours inside your chest!   310
Friendship is much better. Vicious quarrels are deadly—
put an end to them, at once. Your Achaean comrades,
young and old, will exalt you all the more.'
That was your aged father's parting advice.
It must have slipped your mind.

                                    But now at last,
stop, Achilles—let your heart-devouring anger go!
The king will hand you gifts to match his insults
if only you'll relent and end your anger . . .
So come then, listen, as I count out the gifts,
the troves in his tents that Agamemnon vows to give you.   320
Seven tripods never touched by fire, ten bars of gold,
twenty burnished cauldrons, a dozen massive stallions,
racers who earned him trophies with their speed.
He is no poor man who owns what they have won,
not strapped for goods with all that lovely gold—
what trophies those high-strung horses carried off for him!
Seven women he'll give you, flawless, skilled in crafts,
women of Lesbos—the ones he chose, his privilege,
that day you captured the Lesbos citadel yourself:
they outclassed the tribes of women in their beauty.   330
These he will give, and along with them will go
the one he took away at first, Briseus' daughter,
and he will swear a solemn, binding oath in the bargain:
he never mounted her bed, never once made love with her . . .
the natural thing, my lord, men and women joined.
Now all these gifts will be handed you at once.
But if, later, the gods allow us to plunder
the great city of Priam, you shall enter in
when we share the spoils, load the holds of your ship
with gold and bronze—as much as your heart desires—   340

and choose for your pleasure twenty Trojan women
second only to Argive Helen in their glory.
And then, if we can journey home to Achaean Argos,
pride of the breasting earth, you'll be his son-by-marriage . . .
He will even honor you on a par with his Orestes,
full-grown by now, reared in the lap of luxury.
Three daughters are his in his well-built halls,
Chrysothemis and Laodice and Iphianassa—
and you may lead away whichever one you like,
with no bride-price asked, home to Peleus' house.   350
And he will add a dowry, yes, a magnificent treasure
the likes of which no man has ever offered with his daughter . . .
Seven citadels he will give you, filled with people,
Cardamyle, Enope, and the grassy slopes of Hire,
Pherae the sacrosanct, Anthea deep in meadows,
rolling Aepea and Pedasus green with vineyards.
All face the sea at the far edge of sandy Pylos
and the men who live within them, rich in sheep-flocks,
rich in shambling cattle, will honor you like a god
with hoards of gifts and beneath your scepter's sway   360
live out your laws in sleek and shining peace.

                                   All this . . .
he would extend to you if you will end your anger.
But if you hate the son of Atreus all the more,
him and his troves of gifts, at least take pity
on all our united forces mauled in battle here—
they will honor you, honor you like a god.
Think of the glory you will gather in their eyes!
Now you can kill Hector—seized with murderous frenzy,
certain there's not a single fighter his equal,
no Achaean brought to Troy in the ships—   370
now, for once, you can meet the man head-on!"

    The famous runner Achilles rose to his challenge:
"Royal son of Laertes, Odysseus, great tactician . . .
I must say what I have to say straight out,
must tell you how I feel and how all this will end—
so you won't crowd around me, one after another,

coaxing like a murmuring clutch of doves.
I hate that man like the very Gates of Death
who says one thing but hides another in his heart.
I will say it outright. That seems best to me.   380
Will Agamemnon win me over? Not for all the world,
nor will all the rest of Achaea's armies.
No, what lasting thanks in the long run
for warring with our enemies, on and on, no end?
One and the same lot for the man who hangs back
and the man who battles hard. The same honor waits
for the coward and the brave. They both go down to Death,
the fighter who shirks, the one who works to exhaustion.
And what's laid up for me, what pittance? Nothing—
and after suffering hardships, year in, year out,   390
staking my life on the mortal risks of war.

   Like a mother bird hurrying morsels back
to her unfledged young—whatever she can catch—
but it's all starvation wages for herself.
                                                So for me.
Many a sleepless night I've bivouacked in harness,
day after bloody day I've hacked my passage through,
fighting other soldiers to win their wives as prizes.
Twelve cities of men I've stormed and sacked from shipboard,
eleven I claim by land, on the fertile earth of Troy.
And from all I dragged off piles of splendid plunder,   400
hauled it away and always gave the lot to Agamemnon,
that son of Atreus—always skulking behind the lines,
safe in his fast ships—and he would take it all,
he'd parcel out some scraps but keep the lion's share.
Some he'd hand to the lords and kings—prizes of honor—
and they, they hold them still. From me alone, Achilles
of all Achaeans, he seizes, he keeps the bride I love . . .
Well *let* him bed her now—
enjoy her to the hilt!
                       Why must we battle Trojans,
men of Argos? Why did he muster an army, lead us here,   410
that son of Atreus? Why, why in the world if not

for Helen with her loose and lustrous hair?
Are *they* the only men alive who love their wives,
those sons of Atreus? Never! Any decent man,
a man with sense, loves his own, cares for his own
as deeply as I, I loved that woman with all my heart,
though I won her like a trophy with my spear . . .
But now that he's torn my honor from my hands,
robbed me, lied to me—don't let him try me now.
I know *him* too well—he'll never win me over!

                                          No, Odysseus,   420
let him rack his brains with you and the other captains
how to fight the raging fire off the ships. Look—
what a mighty piece of work he's done without *me*!
Why, he's erected a rampart, driven a trench around it,
broad, enormous, and planted stakes to guard it. No use!
He still can't block the power of man-killing Hector!
No, though as long as *I* fought on Achaea's lines
Hector had little lust to charge beyond his walls,
never ventured beyond the Scaean Gates and oak tree.
There he stood up to me alone one day—   430
and barely escaped my onslaught.

                                   Ah but now,
since I have no desire to battle glorious Hector,
tomorrow at daybreak, once I have sacrificed
to Zeus and all the gods and loaded up my holds
and launched out on the breakers—watch, my friend,
if you'll take the time and care to see me off,
and you will see my squadrons sail at dawn,
fanning out on the Hellespont that swarms with fish,
my crews manning the oarlocks, rowing out with a will,
and if the famed god of the earthquake grants us safe passage,   440
the third day out we raise the dark rich soil of Phthia.
There lies my wealth, hoards of it, all I left behind
when I sailed to Troy on this, this insane voyage—
and still more hoards from here: gold, ruddy bronze,
women sashed and lovely, and gleaming gray iron,
and I will haul it home, all I won as plunder.
All but my prize of honor . . .

he who gave that prize has snatched it back again—
what outrage! That high and mighty King Agamemnon,
that son of Atreus!

                       Go back and tell him all,   450
all I say—out in the open too—so other Achaeans
can wheel on him in anger if he still hopes—
who knows?—to deceive some other comrade.

                                     Shameless,
inveterate—armored in shamelessness! Dog that he is,
he'd never dare to look me straight in the eyes again.
No, I'll never set heads together with that man—
no planning in common, no taking common action.
He cheated me, did me damage, wrong! But never again,
he'll never rob me blind with his twisting words again!
Once is enough for him. Die and be damned for all I care!   460
Zeus who rules the world has ripped his wits away.
His gifts, I loathe his gifts . . .
I wouldn't give you a splinter for that man!
Not if he gave me ten times as much, twenty times over, all
he possesses now, and all that could pour in from the world's end—
not all the wealth that's freighted into Orchomenos, even into Thebes,
Egyptian Thebes where the houses overflow with the greatest troves
    of treasure,
Thebes with the hundred gates and through each gate battalions,
two hundred fighters surge to war with teams and chariots—
no, not if his gifts outnumbered all the grains of sand   470
and dust in the earth—no, not even then could Agamemnon
bring my fighting spirit round until he pays me back,
pays full measure for all his heartbreaking outrage!

      His daughter . . . I will marry no daughter of Agamemnon.
Not if she rivaled Aphrodite in all her golden glory,
not if she matched the crafts of clear-eyed Athena,
not even then would I make *her* my wife! No,
let her father pitch on some other Argive—
one who can please *him*, a greater king than I.
If the gods pull me through and I reach home alive,   480
Peleus needs no help to fetch a bride for me himself.

Plenty of Argive women wait in Hellas and in Phthia,
daughters of lords who rule their citadels in power.
Whomever I want I'll make my cherished wife—at home.
Time and again my fiery spirit drove me to win a wife,
a fine partner to please my heart, to enjoy with her
the treasures my old father Peleus piled high.
I say no wealth is worth my life! Not all they claim
was stored in the depths of Troy, that city built on riches,
in the old days of peace before the sons of Achaea came—   490
not all the gold held fast in the Archer's rocky vaults,
in Phoebus Apollo's house on Pytho's sheer cliffs!
Cattle and fat sheep can all be had for the raiding,
tripods all for the trading, and tawny-headed stallions.
But a man's life breath cannot come back again—
no raiders in force, no trading brings it back,
once it slips through a man's clenched teeth.

                                        Mother tells me,
the immortal goddess Thetis with her glistening feet,
that two fates bear me on to the day of death.
If I hold out here and I lay siege to Troy,   500
my journey home is gone, but my glory never dies.
If I voyage back to the fatherland I love,
my pride, my glory dies . . .
true, but the life that's left me will be long,
the stroke of death will not come on me quickly.

    One thing more. To the rest I'd pass on this advice:
sail home now! You will never set your eyes
on the day of doom that topples looming Troy.
Thundering Zeus has spread his hands above her—
her armies have taken heart!

                        So you go back   510
to the great men of Achaea. You report my message—
since this is the privilege of senior chiefs—
let *them* work out a better plan of action,
use their imaginations now to save the ships
and Achaea's armies pressed to their hollow hulls.
This maneuver will never work for them, this scheme

they hatched for the moment as I raged on and on.
But Phoenix can stay and rest the night with us,
so he can voyage home, home in the ships with me
to the fatherland we love. Tomorrow at dawn.   520
But only if Phoenix wishes.
I will never force the man to go."

                                        He stopped.
A stunned silence seized them all, struck dumb—
Achilles' ringing denials overwhelmed them so.
At last Phoenix the old charioteer spoke out,
he burst into tears, terrified for Achaea's fleet:
"Sail home? Is *that* what you're turning over in your mind,
my glorious one, Achilles? Have you no heart at all
to fight the gutting fire from the fast trim ships?
The spirit inside you overpowered by anger!   530
How could I be severed from you, dear boy,
left behind on the beachhead here—alone?
The old horseman Peleus had me escort you,
that day he sent you out of Phthia to Agamemnon,
a youngster still untrained for the great leveler, war,
still green at debate where men can make their mark.
So he dispatched me, to teach you all these things,
to make you a man of words and a man of action too.
Cut off from you with a charge like that, dear boy?
I have no heart to be left behind, not even   540
if Zeus himself would swear to scrape away
the scurf of age and make me young again . . .
As fresh as I was that time I first set out
from Hellas where the women are a wonder,
fleeing a blood feud with my father, Amyntor,
Ormenus' son. How furious father was with me,
over his mistress with her dark, glistening hair.
How he would dote on *her* and spurn his wedded wife,
my own mother! And time and again she begged me,
hugging my knees, to bed my father's mistress down   550
and kill the young girl's taste for an old man.
Mother—I did your bidding, did my work . . .
But father, suspecting at once, cursed me roundly,

he screamed out to the cruel Furies—'Never,
never let me bounce on my knees a son of his,
sprung of his loins!'—and the gods drove home that curse,
mighty Zeus of the Underworld and grim Persephone.
So I, I took it into my head to lay him low
with sharp bronze! But a god checked my anger,
he warned me of what the whole realm would say,   560
the loose talk of the people, rough slurs of men—
they must not call me a father-killer, our Achaeans!
Then nothing could keep me there, my blood so fired up.
No more strolling about the halls with father raging.
But there was a crowd of kin and cousins round me,
holding me in the house, begging me to stay . . .
they butchered plenty of fat sheep, banquet fare,
and shambling crook-horned cattle, droves of pigs,
succulent, rich with fat—they singed the bristles,
splaying the porkers out across Hephaestus' fire,   570
then wine from the old man's jars, all we could drink.
Nine nights they passed the hours, hovering over me,
keeping the watch by rounds. The fires never died,
one ablaze in the colonnade of the walled court,
one in the porch outside my bedroom doors.

                              But then,
when the tenth night came on me, black as pitch,
I burst the doors of the chamber bolted tight
and out I rushed, I leapt the walls at a bound,
giving the slip to guards and women servants.
And away I fled through the whole expanse of Hellas   580
and gaining the good dark soil of Phthia, mother of flocks,
I reached the king, and Peleus gave me a royal welcome.
Peleus loved me as a father loves a son, I tell you,
his only child, the heir to his boundless wealth,
he made me a rich man, he gave me throngs of subjects,
I ruled the Dolopes, settling down on Phthia's west frontier.
And I made you what you are—strong as the gods, Achilles—
I loved you from the heart. You'd never go with another
to banquet on the town or feast in your own halls.
Never, until I'd sat you down on my knees   590

and cut you the first bits of meat, remember?
You'd eat your fill, I'd hold the cup to your lips
and all too often you soaked the shirt on my chest,
spitting up some wine, a baby's way . . . a misery.
Oh I had my share of troubles for you, Achilles,
did my share of labor. Brooding, never forgetting
the gods would bring no son of mine to birth,
not from my own loins.
                    So you, Achilles—
great godlike Achilles—I made you my son, I tried,
so someday *you* might fight disaster off my back.   600
But now, Achilles, beat down your mounting fury!
It's wrong to have such an iron, ruthless heart.
Even the gods themselves can bend and change,
and theirs is the greater power, honor, strength.
Even the gods, I say, with incense, soothing vows,
with full cups poured and the deep smoky savor
men can bring them round, begging for pardon
when one oversteps the mark, does something wrong.
We do have Prayers, you know, Prayers for forgiveness,
daughters of mighty Zeus . . . and they limp and halt,   610
they're all wrinkled, drawn, they squint to the side,
can't look you in the eyes, and always bent on duty,
trudging after Ruin, maddening, blinding Ruin.
But Ruin is strong and swift—
She outstrips them all by far, stealing a march,
leaping over the whole wide earth to bring mankind to grief.
And the Prayers trail after, trying to heal the wounds.
And then, if a man reveres these daughters of Zeus
as they draw near him, they will help him greatly
and listen to his appeals. But if one denies them,   620
turns them away, stiff-necked and harsh—off they go
to the son of Cronus, Zeus, and pray that Ruin
will strike the man down, crazed and blinded
until he's paid the price.
                    Relent, Achilles—you too!
See that honor attend these good daughters of Zeus,
honor that sways the minds of others, even heroes.

If Agamemnon were not holding out such gifts,
with talk of more to come, that son of Atreus,
if the warlord kept on blustering in his anger, why,
I'd be the last to tell you, 'Cast your rage to the winds!   630
Defend your friends!'—despite their desperate straits.
But now, look, he gives you a trove of treasures
right away, and vows there are more to follow.
He sends the bravest captains to implore you,
leaders picked from the whole Achaean army,
comrades-in-arms that you love most yourself.
Don't dismiss their appeal, their expedition here—
though no one could blame your anger, not before.
So it was in the old days too. So we've heard
in the famous deeds of fighting men, of heroes,   640
when seething anger would overcome the great ones.
Still you could bring them round with gifts and winning words.
There's an old tale I remember, an ancient exploit,
nothing recent, but this is how it went . . .
We are all friends here—let me tell it now.

     The Curetes were fighting the combat-hard Aetolians,
armies ringing Calydon, slaughtering each other,
Aetolians defending their city's handsome walls
and Curetes primed to lay them waste in battle.
It all began when Artemis throned in gold   650
loosed a disaster on them, incensed that Oeneus
offered her no first fruits, his orchard's crowning glory.
The rest of the gods had feasted full on oxen, true,
but the Huntress alone, almighty Zeus's daughter—
Oeneus gave her nothing. It slipped his mind
or he failed to care, but what a fatal error!
How she fumed, Zeus's child who showers arrows,
she loosed a bristling wild boar, his tusks gleaming,
crashing his savage, monstrous way through Oeneus' orchard,
ripping up whole trunks from the earth to pitch them headlong,   660
rows of them, roots and all, appleblossoms and all!
But the son of Oeneus, Meleager, cut him down—
mustering hunters out of a dozen cities,

packs of hounds as well. No slim band of men
could ever finish him off, that rippling killer,
he stacked so many men atop the tear-soaked pyre.
But over his body the goddess raised a terrific din,
a war for the prize, the huge beast's head and shaggy hide—
Curetes locked to the death with brave Aetolians.

                                                    Now,

so long as the battle-hungry Meleager fought,   670
it was deadly going for the Curetes. No hope
of holding their ground outside their *own* city walls,
despite superior numbers. But then, when the wrath
came sweeping over the man, the same anger that swells
the chests of others, for all their care and self-control—
then, heart enraged at his own dear mother Althaea,
Meleager kept to his bed beside his wedded wife,
Cleopatra . . . that great beauty. Remember her?
The daughter of trim-heeled Marpessa, Euenus' child,
and her husband Idas, strongest man of the men   680
who once walked the earth—he even braved Apollo,
he drew his bow at the Archer, all for Marpessa
the girl with lovely ankles. There in the halls
her father and mother always called Cleopatra Halcyon,
after the seabird's name . . . grieving once for her own fate
her mother had raised the halcyon's thin, painful cry,
wailing that lord Apollo the distant deadly Archer
had whisked her far from Idas.

                          Meleager's Cleopatra—
she was the one he lay beside those days,
brooding over his heartbreaking anger.   690
He was enraged by the curses of his mother,
volleys of curses she called down from the gods.
So racked with grief for her brother he had killed
she kept pounding fists on the earth that feeds us all,
kept crying out to the god of death and grim Persephone,
flung herself on the ground, tears streaking her robes
and she screamed out, 'Kill Meleager, kill my son!'
And out of the world of darkness a Fury heard her cries,

stalking the night with a Fury's brutal heart, and suddenly—
thunder breaking around the gates, the roar of enemies,   700
towers battered under assault. And Aetolia's elders
begged Meleager, sent high priests of the gods,
pleading, 'Come out now! defend your people now!'—
and they vowed a princely gift.
Wherever the richest land of green Calydon lay,
there they urged him to choose a grand estate,
full fifty acres, half of it turned to vineyards,
half to open plowland, and carve it from the plain.
And over and over the old horseman Oeneus begged him,
he took a stand at the vaulted chamber's threshold,   710
shaking the bolted doors, begging his own son!
Over and over his brothers and noble mother
implored him—he refused them all the more—
and troops of comrades, devoted, dearest friends.
Not even they could bring his fighting spirit round
until, at last, rocks were raining down on the chamber,
Curetes about to mount the towers and torch the great city!
And then, finally, Meleager's bride, beautiful Cleopatra
begged him, streaming tears, recounting all the griefs
that fall to people whose city's seized and plundered—   720
the men slaughtered, citadel burned to rubble, enemies
dragging the children, raping the sashed and lovely women.
How his spirit leapt when he heard those horrors—
and buckling his gleaming armor round his body,
out he rushed to war. And so he saved them all
from the fatal day, he gave way to his own feelings,
but too late. No longer would they make good the gifts,
those troves of gifts to warm his heart, and even so
he beat off that disaster . . . empty-handed.

But you, you wipe such thoughts from your mind.   730
Don't let your spirit turn you down that path, dear boy.
Harder to save the warships once they're up in flames.
Now—while the gifts still wait—go out and fight!
Go—the Achaeans all will honor you like a god!

But enter this man-killing war without the gifts—
your fame will flag, no longer the same honor,
even though you hurl the Trojans home!"

  But the swift runner Achilles answered firmly,
"Phoenix, old father, bred and loved by the gods,
what do I need with honor such as that?   740
I say my honor lies in the great decree of Zeus.
That gift will hold me here by the beaked ships
as long as the life breath remains inside my chest
and my springing knees will lift me. Another thing—
take it to heart, I urge you. Stop confusing
my fixed resolve with this, this weeping and wailing
just to serve his pleasure, Atreus' mighty son.
It degrades you to curry favor with that man,
and I will hate you for it, I who love you.
It does you proud to stand by me, my friend,   750
to attack the man who attacks me—
be king on a par with me, take half my honors!
These men will carry their message back, but you,
you stay here and spend the night in a soft bed.
Then, tomorrow at first light, we will decide
whether we sail home or hold out here."
                                            With that,
he gave Patroclus a sharp glance, a quiet nod
to pile the bedding deep for Phoenix now,
a sign to the rest to think of leaving quickly.
Giant Ajax rose to his feet, the son of Telamon,   760
tall as a god, turned and broke his silence:
"Ready, Odysseus? Royal son of Laertes,
great tactician—come, home we go now.
There's no achieving our mission here, I see,
not with this approach. Best to return at once,
give the Achaeans a full report, defeating as it is.
They must be sitting there, waiting for us now.
                                            Achilles—
he's made his own proud spirit so wild in his chest,
so savage, not a thought for his comrades' love—

we honored him past all others by the ships.   770
Hard, ruthless man . . .
Why, any man will accept the blood-price paid
for a brother murdered, a child done to death.
And the murderer lives on in his own country—
the man has paid enough, and the injured kinsman
curbs his pride, his smoldering, vengeful spirit,
once he takes the price.

         You—the gods have planted
a cruel, relentless fury in your chest! All for a girl,
just one, and here we offer you seven—outstanding beauties—
that, and a treasure trove besides. Achilles,   780
put some human kindness in your heart.
Show respect for your own house. Here we are,
under your roof, sent from the whole Achaean force!
Past all other men, all other Achaean comrades,
we long to be your closest, dearest friends."

   And the swift runner Achilles answered warmly,
"Ajax, royal son of Telamon, captain of armies,
all well said, after my own heart, or mostly so.
But my heart still heaves with rage
whenever I call to mind that arrogance of his—   790
how he mortified me, right in front of the Argives—
that son of Atreus treating me like some vagabond,
like some outcast stripped of all my rights!
You go back to him and declare my message:
I will not think of arming for bloody war again,
not till the son of wise King Priam, dazzling Hector
batters all the way to the Myrmidon ships and shelters,
slaughtering Argives, gutting the hulls with fire.
But round my own black ship and camp this Hector
blazing for battle will be stopped, I trust—   800
stopped dead in his tracks!"

         So he finished.
Then each man, lifting his own two-handled cup,
poured it out to the gods, and back they went
along the ships, Odysseus in the lead.

Patroclus told his friends and serving-women
to pile a deep warm bed for Phoenix, quickly.
They obeyed and spread the bed as he ordered,
with fleeces, woolen throws and soft linen sheets.
There the old man lay, awaiting shining Dawn.
And deep in his well-built lodge Achilles slept   810
with the woman he brought from Lesbos, Phorbas' daughter,
Diomede in all her beauty sleeping by his side.
And over across from him Patroclus slept
with the sashed and lovely Iphis by his side,
whom Prince Achilles gave him the day he took
the heights of Scyros, Enyeus' rocky stronghold.

But once the envoys reached Atrides' shelters,
comrades leapt to their feet, welcomed them back
and clustering round them, lifted golden cups.
One after another pressed them with questions,   820
King Agamemnon most urgent of all: "Come—
tell me, famous Odysseus, Achaea's pride and glory—
will he fight the fire off the ships? Or does he refuse,
does rage still grip his proud, mighty spirit?"

And the steady, long-enduring Odysseus replied,
"Great marshal Atrides, lord of men Agamemnon,
that man has no intention of quenching his rage.
He's still bursting with anger, more than ever—
he spurns you, spurns all your gifts. Work out
your own defense, he says, you and your captains   830
save the Argive armies and the ships. Himself?
Achilles threatens, tomorrow at first light,
to haul his well-benched warships out to sea.
And what's more, he advises all the rest,
'Sail home now. You will never set your eyes
on the day of doom that topples looming Troy.
Thundering Zeus has spread his hands above her . . .
her armies have taken heart.'
                                                    That's his answer.
And here are men to confirm it, fellow envoys.

Ajax and two heralds, both clear-headed men.   840
But old Phoenix passes the night in camp
as Achilles bids him, so he can voyage home,
home in the ships with him to the fatherland they love.
Tomorrow at dawn. But only if Phoenix wishes.
He will never force the man to go."

                                    So he reported.
Silence held them all, struck dumb by his story,
Odysseus' words still ringing in their ears.
A long while they said nothing, spirits dashed.
Finally Diomedes lord of the war cry broke forth:
"Great marshal Atrides, lord of men Agamemnon—   850
if only you'd never begged the dauntless son of Peleus,
holding out to Achilles trove on trove of gifts!
He's a proud man at the best of times, and now
you've only plunged him deeper in his pride.
I say have done with the man—
whether he sails for home or stays on here.
He'll fight again—in his own good time—whenever
the courage in him flares and a god fires his blood.
So come, follow my orders. And all of us unite.
Go to sleep now, full to your heart's content   860
with food and wine, a soldier's strength and nerve.
Then when the Dawn's red fingers shine in all their glory,
quickly deploy your chariots and battalions, Agamemnon,
out in front of the ships—you spur them on
and you yourself, you fight in the front ranks!"

     And Achaea's kings all shouted their assent,
stirred by the stallion-breaking Diomedes' challenge.
Pouring cups to the gods, each warlord sought his shelter.
There they spent the night and took the gift of sleep.

BOOK TEN

Marauding
Through the Night

So by the ships the other lords of Achaea's armies
slept all night long, overcome by gentle sleep . . .
But not the great field marshal Agamemnon—
the sweet embrace of sleep could not hold him:
his mind kept churning, seething. Like Zeus's bolts
when the lord of bright-haired Hera flashes lightning,
threatening to loose torrential rain or pelting hail
or snow when a blizzard drifts on fields—or driving on,
somewhere on earth, the giant jaws of rending war—
so thick-and-fast the groans came from Atrides,   10
wrenching his chest, heaving up from his heart
and rocked his very spirit to the core.
Now as he scanned across the Trojan plain
Agamemnon marveled in horror at those fires,
a thousand fires blazing against the walls of Troy,

and the shrill of pipes and flutes and low roar of men.
And now as he glanced back at Achaea's troops and ships
he tore out his hair by the roots, he looked to Zeus on high,
groaning from the depths of his proud, embattled heart.
But soon this recourse struck his mind as best: 20
he would go and approach the son of Neleus first
and see if Nestor could work out something with him,
some foolproof plan that just might ward disaster
off the Achaean forces.

                  He rose up quickly
and over his chest he pulled a battle-shirt,
under his smooth feet he fastened supple sandals,
round him slung the glossy hide of a big tawny lion,
swinging down to his heels, and grasped a spear.

    And the same anguish shook Menelaus too—
no sleep could settle over his eyes, not now.   30
He feared his men might meet the worst at last,
comrades who crossed a waste of seas for him
to raise Troy and mount their fierce assault.
First he covered his broad back with leopard skin,
a fine spotted hide, then lifting a round helmet
of good sturdy bronze, he fitted it to his head,
he took a spear in his grip and off he strode
to rouse his brother, king of all the Argives,
the armies that prized him in his power like a god.
And Menelaus found him alongside his ship's stern,   40
strapping his handsome gear around his shoulders.
Agamemnon warmed with pleasure as he came up
but Menelaus lord of the war cry ventured first,
"Why arming now, my brother? To spur a volunteer
to spy on Trojan lines? Not a man in sight will take
that mission on, I fear, and go against our enemies,
scout them out alone in the bracing godsent night—
it will take a daring man to do the job."

    King Agamemnon answered crisply, "Tactics,
my noble Menelaus. That's what we need now,   50

you and I both, and cunning tactics too.
Something to shield and save our men and ships
since Zeus's heart has turned—his mighty heart
is set on Hector's offerings more than ours.
I've never seen or heard tell of a single man
wreaking so much havoc in one day as Hector,
Zeus's favorite, wreaks against our troops,
and all on his own—no son of god or goddess.
He's made a slaughter, I tell you. Pain for Achaeans,
enough to last us down the years to come . . .   60
what blows he's dealt our men!
Go now, call Ajax, Idomeneus, quickly,
make a run for it down along the ships.
I'll go after Nestor, wake and rouse him,
see if the good man wants to join the guard,
that strong contingent, and give them orders.
He's the one they'll obey. His own son commands
the sentry-line, he and Idomeneus' aide Meriones.
They above all—we put those men in charge."

The lord of the war cry nodded, "Yes, fine,   70
but what orders for me? Do I stay with them,
waiting for you to come? Or follow you on the run,
once I've given the captains your command?"

The marshal made things clearer: "You stay there—
so we don't miss one another rushing back and forth
in the endless maze of pathways up and down the camp.
But shout wherever you go, tell them to stay awake.
And call each man by his name and father's line,
show them all respect. Not too proud now.
We are the ones who ought to do the work.   80
On our backs, from the day that we were born,
it seems that Zeus has piled his pack of hardships."

With his order clear, he sent his brother off
while he went after Nestor, the old commander.
He found him beside his black ship and shelter,

stretched on a fleecy bed, his blazoned gear at hand,
his shield and two long spears and burnished helmet.
His war-belt lay beside him, gleaming in all its fire.
The old man cinched it on whenever he'd harness up,
marching his men to war where fighters die—   90
Nestor gave no ground to withering old age.
He propped himself on an elbow, craned his head
and probed sharply, whispering through the dark,
"Who goes there? Stalking along the ships,
alone through camp in the very dead of night
when other mortals try to catch some sleep.
Tracking a stray mule or a lost companion? Speak!
Don't steal on me in silence—what do you want?"

    The lord of men Agamemnon reassured him:
"Nestor, son of Neleus, glory of Achaea,   100
don't you recognize Agamemnon? The one man,
past all others, Zeus has plunged in troubles,
year in, year out, for as long as the life breath
fills my lungs and the spring in my knees will lift me.
I roam this way since sleep won't close my eyes—
war's my worry, the agonies of our Achaeans.
How I fear for our comrades, fear the worst!
My mind is torn, I'm harried back and forth,
the heart inside me pounding through my chest
and the sturdy legs beneath me giving way.   110
But if you want action now—
sleeping is just as hard for you, it seems—
come, let's go down to the sentry-line and see
if numb with exhaustion, lack of sleep, they've nodded off,
all duty wiped from their minds, the watch dissolved.
Our blood enemies camp hard by. How do we know
they're not about to attack us in the night?"

    And the old charioteer warmed to his challenge:
"Great marshal Atrides, lord of men Agamemnon—
Hector and Hector's high hopes? Not a chance.   120
The plans of Zeus will never bring them off,

those dreams of glory inspiring Hector now.
Oh I think he'll have his troubles to shoulder,
plenty of them too, if Achilles ever turns away
from the heartbreaking anger deep inside him.
Follow you? Surely. Let's wake others also,
Diomedes famed for his spear, Odysseus,
quick Little Ajax and Phyleus' brave son.
And if only one would go and call the rest,
giant Ajax strong as a god and King Idomeneus—   130
they're hardly close, their ships last on the line.
But I *will* blame Menelaus, loved as he is and honored,
even if you will wheel on me in anger—I must,
I can't hide it now. How that fellow sleeps!
Turning over the work to you alone.
Now is the time for him to work, to hunt
the leading captains and beg them all for help.
Desperate straits—we can't hold out much longer."

    The lord of men replied, "You're right, old soldier.
I'd even *urge* you to fault him any other day.   140
So often he hangs back, with no heart for the work,
not that he shrinks from action, skittish or off guard—
it's just that he looks to me, waiting for me
to make the first move. This time, though,
he woke before me, came and roused me first
and I sent him off to call the men you're after.
So let's move out, overtake the rest at the gates,
with the sentries where I ordered them to group."

    And Nestor the noble charioteer assented gladly:
"True, when the man leaps in the breach that way   150
no one can blame or disobey him, no Achaean,
not when he spurs the troops and gives commands."

    With that he slipped his tunic over his chest,
under his smooth feet he fastened supple sandals,
pinned with a brooch his crimson cape around him,
flowing in double folds and topped with thick fleece,

and gripping a tough spear tipped with a brazen point,
he strode along the ships of the Argives armed in bronze.
And reaching Odysseus first, a mastermind like Zeus,
the old driver roused him from sleep, shouting out,   160
"Wake up!" The cry went ringing through his ears
and out of his tent he came, shouting in return,
"Why, why prowling along the ships and camp,
you alone in the bracing godsent night—
what's the crisis now? What trouble's come?"

    And Nestor the noble charioteer replied,
"Royal son of Laertes, Odysseus, great tactician,
no time for anger now—
such misery has overcome our Argives.
Follow us, come, so we can wake the next man,   170
some captain fit to map our strategy here,
whether we break and run or stand and fight."

    Backing into his tent, the great tactician slung
his wrought shield on his back and joined the party
striding toward the son of Tydeus, Diomedes.
They found him with all his gear outside his shelter,
cohorts sleeping round him, shields beneath their heads,
spears stuck straight in the ground on butt-end spikes
and the bronze points flashing into the distance
like forked lightning flung by Father Zeus.   180
But the veteran fighter lay there fast asleep,
the cured hide of a field ox spread beneath him,
a lustrous blanket stretched beneath his head . . .
The old charioteer moved in and woke him roughly,
dug a heel in his ribs, chiding him to his face,
"Up with you, Diomedes! What, sleep all night?
Haven't you heard? Trojans hold the high ground,
over the beachhead there, camped against the ships—
only a narrow strip to keep off sudden death."

    So he prodded and Diomedes woke from sleep   190
with a quick start and burst of winging words:

"A hard man you are, old soldier—hard.
You never give up the good fight, do you?
Where are the younger troopers now we need them?
Why don't *they* go wake each king in turn—
padding softly up and down through camp?
You, old man, you'd overpower us all!"

And Nestor the noble driver answered warmly,
"Right you are, my friend, straight to the point.
Sons I have, and they're hardy, handsome boys,   200
and comrades too, men aplenty—one of the lot
could light out now and summon up the kings.
But now a crisis has overwhelmed our armies.
Our fate, I tell you, stands on a razor's edge:
life or death for Achaea, gruesome death at that.
Up with you! Wake quick Little Ajax, Meges too.
You're so much younger—come, pity an old man."

And round his back Diomedes slung the hide
of a big tawny lion, swinging down to his heels,
he grasped a spear and the fighter strode away   210
and roused those men to leave their beds and march.

And now as they filed among the mustered guard
they found the chief sentries far from sleep—
on the alert, all stationed set with weapons.
Like sheepdogs keeping watch on flocks in folds,
a nervous, bristling watch when the dogs get wind
of a wild beast rampaging down through mountain timber,
crashing toward the pens, and the cries break as he charges,
a din of men and dogs, and their sleep is broken, gone—
and so the welcome sleep was routed from their eyes,   220
guardsmen keeping the long hard watch that night.
Always turning toward the plain, tense to catch
some sign of the Trojans launching an attack.
The old chariot-driver warmed to the sight
and cheered them on with urgings flying fast:

"Keep it up, my boys, that's the way to watch!
Not one of you submit to the grip of sleep—
you'd give great joy to the men who'd take our lives."

    With that the driver clambered through the trench.
They took the old captain's lead, the Argive kings   230
all called to the muster now. And flanking them
Meriones came in haste with Nestor's handsome son—
the kings had summoned both to share their counsel.
Crossing out over the deep trench they grouped
on open ground, where they chanced to find a sector
free and clear of corpses, in fact the very place
where Hector in all his power had veered and turned away
from cutting Argives down when night closed in.
There they settled, conferring among themselves
till the noble horseman opened with his plan: 240
"My friends, isn't there one man among us here,
so sure of himself, his soldier's nerve and pluck,
he'd infiltrate these overreaching Trojans?
Perhaps he'd seize a straggler among the foe
or catch some rumor floating along their lines.
What plans are they mapping, what maneuvers next?
Are they bent on holding tight by the ships, exposed?—
or heading home to Troy, now they've trounced our armies?
If a man could gather that, then make it back unharmed,
why, what glory he'd gain across the whole wide earth   250
in the eyes of every man—and what a gift he'd win!
All the lords who command the ships of battle,
each and every one will give him a black ewe
suckling a young lamb—no prize of honor like it.
They'll ask that man to every feast and revel."

    So Nestor proposed. All ranks held their peace
but Diomedes lord of the war cry spoke up briskly:
"Nestor, the mission stirs my fighting blood.
I'll slip right into enemy lines at once—
these Trojans, camped at our flank.   260

If another comrade would escort me, though,
there'd be more comfort in it, confidence too.
When two work side-by-side, one or the other
spots the opening first if a kill's at hand.
When one looks out for himself, alert but alone,
his reach is shorter—his sly moves miss the mark."

At that a crowd volunteered to go with Diomedes.
The two Aeantes, old campaigners, volunteered,
Meriones volunteered and Nestor's son leapt up
and Menelaus the famous spearman volunteered   270
and battle-hardened Odysseus too, to foray
into the Trojan units camped for the night—
Odysseus' blood was always up for exploit.
But King Agamemnon interceded quickly,
"Diomedes, soldier after my own heart,
pick your comrade now, whomever you want,
the best of the volunteers—how many long to go!
But no false respect. Don't pass over the better man
and pick the worse. Don't bow to a soldier's rank,
an eye to his birth—even if he's more kingly."   280

He suddenly feared for red-haired Menelaus
but Diomedes strong with the war cry answered,
"Is that an order? Pick my own comrade?
Then how could I pass up royal Odysseus here?
His heart's so game, his fighting edge so keen,
the best of us all in every combat mission—
Athena loves the man. With him at my side
we'd go through fire and make it back alive—
no one excels the mastermind of battle."

But much-enduring Odysseus cut him short: 290
"Not too long on the praise—don't fault me either.
You're talking to Argive men who know my record.
Let's move out. The night is well on its way

and daybreak's near. The stars go wheeling by,
the full of the dark is gone—two watches down
but the third's still ours for action."

                           On that note
both men harnessed up in the grim gear of war . . .
Thrasymedes staunch in combat handed Tydeus' son
a two-edged sword—he'd left his own at the ship—
a shield too, and over his head he set a helmet,   300
bull's-hide, bare of ridge and crest, a skullcap,
so it's called, and made to protect the heads
of tough young-blooded fighters.
Meriones gave Odysseus bow, quiver and sword
and over his head he set a helmet made of leather.
Inside it was crisscrossed taut with many thongs,
outside the gleaming teeth of a white-tusked boar
ran round and round in rows stitched neat and tight—
a master craftsman's work, the cap in its center
padded soft with felt. The Wolf Himself Autolycus   310
lifted that splendid headgear out of Eleon once,
he stole it from Ormenus' son Amyntor years ago,
breaching his sturdy palace walls one night
then passed it on to Amphidamas, Cythera-born,
Scandia-bound. Amphidamas gave it to Molus,
a guest-gift once that Molus gave Meriones
his son to wear in battle. And now it encased
Odysseus' head, snug around his brows.

                           And so,
both harnessed up in the grim gear of war,
the two men moved out, leaving behind them   320
all the captains clustered on the spot.
Athena winged a heron close to their path
and veering right. Neither man could see it,
scanning the dark night, they only heard its cry.
Glad for the lucky sign, Odysseus prayed to Pallas,
"Hear me, daughter of Zeus whose shield is thunder!
Standing by me always, in every combat mission—
no maneuver of mine slips by you—now, again,

give me your best support, Athena, comrade!
Grant our return in glory back to the warships   330
once we've done some feat that brings the Trojans pain!''

Next Diomedes lord of the war cry prayed aloud,
"Hear me too, daughter of Zeus, tireless goddess!
Be with me now, just as you went with father,
veteran Tydeus, into Thebes that day
he ran ahead of the Argives with his message.
He left his armored men along the Asopus banks
and carried a peaceful word to Theban cohorts
crowded in their halls. But turning back he bent
to some grand and grisly work with you, Goddess,   340
and you stood by him then, a steadfast ally.
So come, stand by me now, protect me now!
I will make you a sacrifice, a yearling heifer
broad in the brow, unbroken, never yoked by men.
I'll offer it up to you—I'll sheathe its horns in gold!''

Their prayers rose and Pallas Athena heard them.
Once they'd appealed to Zeus's mighty daughter,
into the black night they went like two lions
stalking through the carnage and the corpses,
through piles of armor and black pools of blood.   350

But no sleep for the headstrong Trojans either.
Hector would not permit it. He summoned all his chiefs
to a council of war, all Trojan lords and captains.
Mustering them he launched his own crafty plan:
"Who will undertake a mission and bring it off
for a princely gift? A prize to match the exploit!
I'll give him a chariot, two horses with strong necks,
the best of the breeds beside Achaea's fast ships.
Whoever will dare—what glory he can win—
a night patrol by the ships to learn at once   360
if the fleet's still guarded as before or now,
battered down at our hands, huddling together,

they plan a quick escape, their morale too low
to mount the watch tonight—bone-weary from battle."

    So Hector proposed. All ranks held their peace.
But there was a man among the troops, one Dolon,
a son of the sacred Trojan herald Eumedes.
He was rich in bronze, rich in bars of gold,
no feast for the eyes but lightning on his feet
and an only son in the midst of five sisters.   370
This one volunteered among the Trojans:
"Hector, the mission stirs my fighting blood—
I'll reconnoiter the ships and gather all I can.
Come, raise that scepter and swear you'll give me
the battle-team and the burnished brazen car
that carry great Achilles—I will be your spy.
And no mean scout, I'll never let you down.
I'll infiltrate their entire army, I will,
all the way till I reach the ship of Agamemnon!
That's where the captains must be mapping tactics now,   380
whether they'll break and run or stand and fight."

    How he bragged and Hector, grasping his scepter,
swore a binding oath: "Now Zeus my witness,
thundering lord of Hera—no other Trojan fighter
will ride behind that team, none but you, I swear—
they will be your glory all your life to come!"

    So Hector vowed—with an oath he swore in vain
but it spurred the man to action. Dolon leapt to it,
he quickly slung a reflex bow on his back,
over it threw the pelt of a gray wolf   390
and set on his head a cap of weasel skin
and taking a sharp spear, moved out from camp,
heading toward the fleet—but he was never to come back
from the enemy's beaked ships, bringing Hector news.
Putting the mass of horse and men behind him
Dolon picked up speed, hot for action now,
but keen as a god Odysseus saw him coming

and alerted Diomedes: "Who is this?
A man heading out of the Trojan camp!
Why? I can't be sure—to spy on our ships   400
or loot the fallen, one of the fighters' corpses?
Let him get past us first, into the clear a bit,
then rush him and overtake him double-quick!
If he outruns us, crowd him against the ships,
cut him off from his lines, harry him with your spear
and never stop—so he can't bolt back to Troy."

No more words. Swerving off the trail
they both lay facedown with the corpses now
as Dolon sped by at a dead run, the fool.
Soon as he got a furlong's lead ahead,   410
the plowing-range of a good team of mules—
faster than draft oxen dragging a bolted plow
through deep fallow ground—the two raced after
and Dolon, hearing their tread, froze stock-still,
his heart leaping—here were friends, yes,
fellow Trojans coming to turn him back,
yes, Hector had just called off the mission!
But soon as they were a spear-cast off or less
he saw them—enemies—
                    quick as a flash he sprang,
fleeing for dear life—
                    they sprang in pursuit   420
as a pair of rip-tooth hounds
bred for the hunt and flushing fawn or hare
through a woody glen keep closing for the kill,
nonstop and the prey goes screaming on ahead—
so Odysseus raider of cities and Diomedes
cut him off from his own lines, coursing him,
closing nonstop with the Trojan about to break in
on the line of sentries, racing fast for the ships—
when Athena poured fresh strength in Tydeus' son
so no Achaean could beat him out for the glory   430
of hitting Dolon first, Diomedes come in second.

Rushing him with his spear in a sudden surge
Tydides shouted, "Stop or I'll run you through!
You'll never escape my spear—headlong death—
I swear I'll send it hurling from my fist!"

He flung his shaft, missing the man on purpose—
over his right shoulder the sharp spearpoint winged
and stabbed the earth. Dead in his tracks he stopped,
terrified, stammering, teeth chattering in his mouth,
bled white with fear as the two men overtook him   440
and panting hard, yanked and pinned his arms.
He burst into tears, pleading, "Take me alive!
I'll ransom myself! Treasures cram our house,
bronze and gold and plenty of well-wrought iron—
father would give you anything, gladly, priceless ransom—
if only he learns I'm still alive in Argive ships!"

Odysseus quick with tactics answered, "Courage.
Death is your last worry. Put your mind at rest.
Come, tell me the truth now, point by point.
Why prowling among the ships, cut off from camp,   450
alone in the dead of night when other men are sleeping?
To loot the fallen, one of the fighters' corpses?
Or did Hector send you out to spy on our ships,
reconnoiter them stem to stern?
Or did your own itch for glory spur you on?"

Dolon answered, his legs shaking under him,
"Hector—he duped me so—so many mad, blind hopes!
He swore he'd give me the great Achilles' stallions,
purebred racers, his burnished bronze chariot too!
He told me to go through the rushing dark night,   460
to patrol the enemy lines and learn at once
if the fleet's still guarded as before or now,
battered down at our hands, huddling together,
you plan a quick escape, your morale too low
to mount the watch tonight—bone-weary from battle."

Breaking into a smile the cool tactician laughed,
"By god, what heroic gifts you set your heart on—
the great Achilles' team!
They're hard for mortal men to curb or drive,
for all but Achilles—his mother is immortal.   470
Now out with it, point by point. Hector—
where did you leave the captain when you came?
Where's his war-gear lying? where's his chariot?
How are the other Trojans posted—guards, sleepers?
What plans are they mapping, what maneuvers next?
Are they bent on holding tight by the ships, exposed?—
or heading home to Troy, now they've trounced our armies?"

And Dolon son of the herald blurted out, "Yes, yes,
I'll tell you everything, down to the last detail!
Hector's holding council with all his chiefs,   480
mapping plans on old King Ilus' barrow,
clear of the crowds at camp. Guards, my lord?
Nothing. No one's picked to defend the army.
Only our native Trojans hold their posts—
many as those with hearth fires back in Troy—
our men have no choice, shouting out to each other,
'Stay awake! keep watch!' But our far-flung friends,
they're fast asleep, they leave the watch to us—
their wives and children are hardly camped nearby."

But the shrewd tactician kept on pressing: "Be precise.   490
Where are they sleeping? Mixed in with the Trojans?
Separate quarters? Tell me. I must know it all."

And Dolon son of the herald kept on blurting,
"Everything—anything—whatever will satisfy you!
To seaward, Carians, Paeonian men with bent bows,
Leleges and Cauconians, crack Pelasgians—inland,
toward Thymbra, camp the Lycians, swaggering Mysians,
fighting Phrygian horsemen, Maeonian chariot-drivers—
but why interrogate me down to the last platoon?
You really want to raid some enemy units?   500

There are the Thracians, look, just arrived,
exposed on the flank, apart from all the rest
and right in their midst Eioneus' son, King Rhesus.
His are the best horses I ever saw, the biggest,
whiter than snow, and speed to match the wind!
His chariot's finished off with gold and silver,
the armor he's brought in with him, gold too,
tremendous equipment—what a marvelous sight.
No gear for a mortal man to wear, I'd say,
it's fit for the deathless gods!   510
There. *Now* will you take me to your ships
or leave me here—bound and gagged right here?—
till you can make your raid and test my story,
see if I've told the truth or I've been lying."

      But rugged Diomedes gave him a grim look:
"Escape? Take my advice and wipe it from your mind,
good as your message is—you're in *my* hands now.
What if we set you free or you should slip away?
Back you'll slink to our fast ships tomorrow,
playing the spy again or fighting face-to-face.   520
But if I snuff your life out in my hands,
you'll never annoy our Argive lines again."

      With that, just as Dolon reached up for his chin
to cling with a frantic hand and beg for life,
Diomedes struck him square across the neck—
a flashing hack of the sword—both tendons snapped
and the shrieking head went tumbling in the dust.
They tore the weasel-cap from the head, stripped
the wolf pelt, the reflex bow and long tough spear
and swinging the trophies high to Pallas queen of plunder,   530
exultant royal Odysseus shouted out this prayer:
"Here, Goddess, rejoice in these, they're yours!
You are the first of all the gods we'll call!
Now guide us again, Athena, guide us against
that Thracian camp and horses!"

                                                So Odysseus prayed

and hoisting the spoils over his head, heaved them
onto a tamarisk bush nearby and against it heaped
a good clear landmark, clumping together reeds
and fresh tamarisk boughs they'd never miss
as they ran back through the rushing dark night.   540
On they stalked through armor and black pools of blood
and suddenly reached their goal, the Thracian outpost.
The troops were sleeping, weary from pitching camp,
their weapons piled beside them on the ground,
three neat rows of the burnished well-kept arms
and beside each man his pair of battle-horses.
Right in the midst lay Rhesus dead asleep,
his white racers beside him, strapped by thongs
to his chariot's outer rail. Spotting him first
Odysseus quickly pointed him out to Diomedes: 550
"Look, here's our man, here are his horses.
The ones marked out by the rascal we just killed.
On with it now—show us your strength, full force.
Don't just stand there, useless with your weapons.
Loose those horses—or you go kill the men
and leave the team to me!"

                Athena, eyes blazing,
breathed fury in Diomedes and he went whirling
into the slaughter now, hacking left and right
and hideous groans broke from the dying Thracians
slashed by the sword—the ground ran red with blood.   560
As a lion springs on flocks unguarded, shepherd gone,
pouncing on goats or sheep and claw-mad for the kill,
so Tydeus' son went tearing into that Thracian camp
until he'd butchered twelve. Each man he'd stand above
and chop with the sword, the cool tactician Odysseus
grappled from behind, grabbing the fighter's heels,
dragging him out of the way with one thought in mind:
that team with their flowing manes must get through fast,
not quake at heart and balk, trampling over the dead,
those purebred horses still not used to corpses.   570
But now the son of Tydeus came upon the king,
the thirteenth man, and ripped away his life,

his sweet life as he lay there breathing hard.
A nightmare hovered above his head that night—
Diomedes himself! sped by Athena's battle-plan—
while staunch Odysseus loosed the stamping horses,
hitched them together tight with their own reins
and drove them through the ruck,
lashing them with his bow: he forgot to snatch
the shining whip that lay in the well-wrought car.   580
He whistled shrill, his signal to rugged Diomedes
pausing, deep in thought . . . what was the worst,
most brazen thing he could do? Seize the car
where the handsome armor lay and pull it out
by the pole or prize it up, bodily, haul it off—
or tear the life from still more Thracian troops?
His mind swarming with all this, Pallas Athena
swept to his side and cautioned Diomedes, "Back—
think only of getting back, great son of Tydeus!
Back to the ships, quick, or you'll run for your life!   590
Some other god—who knows?—may wake the Trojans."

          The goddess' voice—he knew it, mounted at once
as Odysseus whacked the stallions smartly with his bow
and they made a run for Achaea's rapid ships.

          But Apollo lord of the silver bow kept watch.
No blind man's watch, no, Apollo saw Athena
take Tydides in hand, and raging against her
plunged into the main mass of Trojan fighters
to rouse a Thracian captain called Hippocoon,
a loyal kinsman of Rhesus. He woke with a jolt   600
and seeing empty ground where the fast team had stood,
men gasping out their lives, retching in all that carnage,
he wailed out, sobbing, crying his dear companion's name
and piercing wails broke as the Trojans swirled in panic—
a desperate rout of them rushing up to the bloodbath there
stood staring down at the grisly work the marauders did
before they made their dash for the beaked ships.

Reaching the place where they'd killed Hector's spy,
Odysseus dear to Zeus reined in the headlong team
and leaping down to the ground Tydides heaved   610
the bloody spoils into his comrade's arms.
He mounted again and flogged the horses hard
and on they flew to the ships, holding nothing back—
that's where their spirits drove them on to go.
Nestor, the first to hear their thunder, shouted,
"Friends—lords of the Argives, all our captains,
right or wrong, what can I say? My heart tells me,
my ears ring with the din of drumming hoofs . . .
If only Odysseus and rugged Diomedes were driving
racers off the Trojan lines, here, here and fast!   620
I'm cold with fear—what if they've met the worst,
our ranking Argives killed in a Trojan charge?"

Before he could say the last, the two raced in,
leapt to the ground and comrades hugged them warmly,
with handclasps all around and words of welcome.
Nestor the noble horseman led with questions:
"Tell me, Odysseus, Achaea's pride and glory,
famous Odysseus, how did you get these horses?
How—stealing behind the Trojans' main lines
or meeting up with a god who gave them to you?   630
What terrific sheen—silver afire like sunbeams!
Day after day I've gone against the Trojans,
never hanging back by the ships, I swear,
old warrior that I am—
But I've never seen such horses, never dreamed . . .
I'd say an immortal came your way and gave you these.
Zeus who marshals the storm cloud loves you both,
Zeus's daughter too with the shield of thunder.
Athena's eyes are shining on you both!"

The cool tactician set the record straight: 640
"No, no, Nestor—Achaea's greatest glory—
any god, if he really set his mind to it,
could give us an even finer pair than this.

Easily. The gods are so much stronger.
Now these horses you ask about, old soldier,
they're newcomers, just arrived from Thrace.
Their master? Brave Diomedes killed him off,
twelve of his cohorts too, all men of rank.
And a thirteenth man besides, a scout we took—
prowling along the ships, spying on our positions—   650
Hector and all his princely Trojans sent him out."

    And across the trench he drove the purebred team
with a rough exultant laugh as comrades cheered,
crowding in his wake.
And once they reached Tydides' sturdy lodge
they tethered the horses there with well-cut reins,
hitching them by the trough where Diomedes' stallions
pawed the ground, champing their sweet barley.
Then away in his ship's stern Odysseus stowed
the bloody gear of Dolon, in pledge of the gift   660
they'd sworn to give Athena. The men themselves,
wading into the sea, washed off the crusted sweat
from shins and necks and thighs. And once the surf
had scoured the thick caked sweat from their limbs
and the two fighters cooled, their hearts revived
and into the polished tubs they climbed and bathed.
And rinsing off, their skin sleek with an olive oil rub,
they sat down to their meal and dipping up their cups
from an overflowing bowl, they poured them forth—
honeyed, mellow wine to the great goddess Athena.   670

BOOK ELEVEN

Agamemnon's
Day of Glory

Now Dawn rose up from bed by her lordly mate Tithonus,
bringing light to immortal gods and mortal men.
But Zeus flung Strife on Achaea's fast ships,
the brutal goddess flaring his storm-shield,
his monstrous sign of war in both her fists.
She stood on Odysseus' huge black-bellied hull,
moored mid-line so a shout could reach both wings,
upshore to Telamonian Ajax' camp or down to Achilles'—
trusting so to their arms' power and battle-strength
they'd hauled their trim ships up on either flank.   10
There Strife took her stand, raising her high-pitched cry,
great and terrible, lashing the fighting-fury
in each Achaean's heart—no stopping them now,
mad for war and struggle. Now, suddenly,

battle thrilled them more than the journey home,
than sailing hollow ships to their dear native land.

    Agamemnon cried out too, calling men to arms
and harnessed up in gleaming bronze himself.
First he wrapped his legs with well-made greaves,
fastened behind the heels with silver ankle-clasps,   20
and next he strapped the breastplate round his chest
that Cinyras gave him once, a guest-gift long ago.
The rousing rumor of war had carried far as Cyprus—
how the Achaean ships were launching war on Troy—
so he gave the king that gear to please his spirit.
Magnificent! Ten bands of blue enamel spanned it,
spaced by twelve of gold and twenty of beaten tin
and dark blue serpents writhed toward the throat,
three each side, shimmering bright as rainbows arched
on the clouds by Cronus' son, a sign to mortal men.   30
Then over his shoulder Agamemnon slung his sword,
golden studs at the hilt, the blade burnished bright
and the scabbard sheathed in silver swung on golden straps,
and he grasped a well-wrought shield to encase his body,
forged for rushing forays—beautiful, blazoned work.
Circling the center, ten strong rings of bronze
with twenty disks of glittering tin set in,
at the heart a boss of bulging blue steel
and there like a crown the Gorgon's grim mask—
the burning eyes, the stark, transfixing horror—   40
and round her strode the shapes of Rout and Fear.
The shield-belt glinted silver and rippling on it ran
a dark blue serpent, two heads coiling round a third,
reared from a single neck and twisting left and right.
Then over his broad brow Agamemnon set his helmet
fronted with four knobs and forked with twin horns
and the horsehair crest atop it tossing, bristling terror.
And last he picked up two tough spears, tipped in bronze,
honed sharp, and the glare flashed off their brazen points
and pierced the high skies—and awestruck at the sight   50
Athena and Hera loosed a crack of thunder, exalting

the great king of Mycenae rich in gold.
                                    At once
each captain shouted out commands to his driver:
"Rein the team by the trench, good battle-order now!"
While the men themselves, armed for full assault,
leapt down and swarmed to the trench's edge on foot
and a long undying roar went up in the early dawn.
Well ahead of the war-cars they reached the brink,
closed ranks as drivers backed them yards behind.
But Zeus drove a swirl of panic deep in their lines   60
and down from the vaulting skies released a shower
raining blood, for Zeus was bent on hurling down
to the House of Death a rout of sturdy fighters.

    Trojans—the other side on the plain's high ground—
formed around tall Hector, staunch Polydamas, Aeneas
loved by the Trojans like a god, and Antenor's sons,
Polybus, Prince Agenor and Acamas still unwed,
three men in their prime like gods who never die.
Hector bore his round shield in the forefront, blazing out
like the Dog Star through the clouds, all withering fire,   70
then plunging back in the cloud-rack massed and dark—
so Hector ranged on, now flaring along the front,
now shouting his orders back toward the rear,
all of him armed in bronze aflash like lightning
flung by Father Zeus with his battle-shield of thunder.

    And the men like gangs of reapers slashing down
the reaping-rows and coming closer, closer across
the field of a warlord rich in wheat or barley—
swaths by the armfuls falling thick-and-fast—
so Achaeans and Trojans closed and slashed,   80
lunging into each other and neither side now
had a thought of flight that would have meant disaster.
No, the pressure of combat locked them head-to-head,
lunging like wolves, and Strife with wild groans
exulted to see them, glaring down at the melee,
Strife alone of immortals hovering over fighters.

The other gods kept clear, at their royal ease,
reclining off in the halls where the roofs of each
were built for the ages high on rugged ridged Olympus.
And all were blaming Zeus with his storming dark clouds   90
because the Father decreed to hand the Trojans glory.
But the Father paid no heed to them. Retiring
peaks apart from the other gods, he sat aloof,
glorying in his power, gazing out over
the city walls of Troy and the warships of Achaea,
the flash of bronze, fighters killing, fighters killed . . .

As long as morning rose and the blessed day grew stronger,
the weapons hurtled side-to-side and men kept falling.
But just when the woodsman makes his morning meal,
deep in a mountain forest, arm-weary from chopping   100
the big heavy trunks and his heart has had enough
and sudden longing for tempting food overtakes the man
and makes his senses whirl—just at the height of morning
the Argives smashed battalions, their courage breaking through
and they shouted ranks of cohorts on along the lines.
And right in the midst sprang Agamemnon first
and killed a fighter, Bienor, veteran captain,
then his aide Oileus lashing on their team.
Down from the car he'd leapt, squaring off,
charging in full fury, full face, straight   110
into Agamemnon's spearhead ramming sharp—
the rim of the bronze helmet could not hold it,
clean through heavy metal and bone the point burst
and the brains splattered all inside the casque.
He battered Oileus down despite the Trojan's rage
and the lord of fighters left them lying there, both dead
and their chests gleamed like bronze as he stripped them bare.
Then on he went for Isus and Antiphus, killed and stripped
the two sons of Priam, one a bastard, one royal blood
and both riding a single car, the bastard driving,   120
the famous Antiphus standing poised beside him . . .
Achilles had caught them once on the spurs of Ida,
bound them with willow ropes as they watched their flocks

and set them free for ransom. But now it was Agamemnon
lord of the far-flung kingdoms catching up with Isus—
he stabbed his chest with a spear above the nipple,
Antiphus he hacked with a sword across the ear
and hurled him from his chariot, rushing fast
to rip the splendid armor off their bodies.
He knew them both, he'd seen them once by the ships   130
when the swift Achilles dragged them in from Ida.
Think how a lion, mauling the soft weak young
of a running deer, clamped in his massive jaws,
cracks their backbones with a snap—he's stormed in,
invading the lair to tear their tender hearts out
and the mother doe, even if she's close by,
what can she do to save her fawns? She's helpless—
terrible trembling racks her body too—and suddenly
off she bounds through the glades and the thick woods,
drenched in sweat, leaping clear of the big cat's pounce.   140
So not a single Trojan could save those two from death,
they fled themselves before the Argive charge.

                                        But next
Agamemnon killed Pisander and combat-hard Hippolochus,
two sons of Antimachus, that cunning, politic man
whom Paris bribed with gold and sumptuous gifts,
so he was the first to fight the return of Helen
to red-haired Menelaus. Now powerful Agamemnon
caught his two sons riding the same chariot,
both struggling to curb their high-strung team—
the reins slipped their grasp, both horses panicked   150
as Agamemnon ramped up in their faces like a lion—
both fighters shouting from their chariot, pleading,
"Take us alive, Atrides, take a ransom worth our lives!
Vast treasures are piled up in Antimachus' house,
bronze and gold and plenty of well-wrought iron—
father would give you anything, gladly, priceless ransom
if only he learns we're still alive in Argive ships!"

     So they cried to the king, cries for mercy,
but only heard a merciless voice in answer:

"Cunning Antimachus! So you're that man's sons?   160
Once in the Trojan council he ordered Menelaus,
there on an embassy joined by King Odysseus,
murdered right on the spot—no safe-conduct
back to the land of Argos. You're his sons?
Now pay for your father's outrage, blood for blood!"

And he pitched Pisander off the chariot onto earth
and plunged a spear in his chest—the man crashed on his back
as Hippolochus leapt away, but *him* he killed on the ground,
slashing off his arms with a sword, lopping off his head
and he sent him rolling through the carnage like a log.   170
He left them there for dead and just at the point
where most battalions scattered Agamemnon charged,
the rest of his troops in armor quick behind him now,
infantry killing infantry fleeing headlong, hard-pressed,
drivers killing drivers—under the onrush dust in whirlwinds
driven up from the plain, hoofs of stallions rumbling thunder,
bronze flashing, immense slaughter and always King Agamemnon
whirling to kill, crying his Argives on, breakneck on.
Like devouring fire roaring down onto dry dead timber,
squalls hurling it on, careening left and right and   180
brush ripped up by the roots goes tumbling under
crushed by the blasting fire rampaging on—
so under Atrides' onslaught Trojans dropped in flight,
stampedes of massive stallions dragged their empty chariots
clattering down the passageways of battle, stallions
yearning to feel their masters' hands at the reins
but there they lay, sprawled across the field,
craved far more by the vultures than by wives.

But Zeus drew Hector out of range of the weapons,
out of the dust storm, out of the mounting kills,   190
the blood and rout of war as Atrides followed hard,
shouting his Argives on, furious, never stopping.
The Trojans streaked in flight past Ilus' barrow,
ancient son of Dardanus, past the mid-field mark
of the plain and past the wild fig and struggling

to reach Troy and always in hot pursuit and shrieking,
Agamemnon splattered with gore, his hands, invincible hands.
But once they reached the Scaean Gates and the great oak,
there the two sides halted, waiting each other's charge.
Yet stragglers still stampeded down the plain   200
like cattle driven wild by a lion lunging
in pitch darkness down on the whole herd
but to one alone a sudden death comes flashing—
first he snaps its neck, clamped in his huge jaws,
then down in gulps he bolts its blood and guts.
So King Agamemnon coursed his quarry, always cutting
the straggler from the mass and they, they fled in terror,
squads amok, spilling out of their chariots facefirst
or slammed on their backs beneath Atrides' hands—
storming and thrusting his spear and lunging on.   210
But just as he was about to reach the steep city,
up under the walls, the father of men and gods,
descending out of the heavens, took his throne
on the high ridge of Ida with all her springs.
Holding fast in his grip a lightning bolt
he drove Iris down in a rush of golden wings
to bear his message: "Away with you now, Iris—
quick as the wind and speed this word to Hector.
So long as he sees lord marshal Agamemnon storming
among the champions, mowing columns down in blood,   220
Hector must hold back, command the rest of his men
to fight the enemy, stand their headlong charge.
But soon as a spear or bowshot wounds the king
and Atrides mounts his chariot once again,
then I will hand Hector the power to kill and kill
till he cuts his way to the benched ships and the sun sinks
and the blessed darkness sweeps across the earth."

   So he commanded. Wind-quick Iris obeyed at once
and down from Ida's peaks she dove to sacred Troy,
found the son of wise King Priam, shining Hector   230
standing amidst his teams and bolted cars,
and swift as a breeze beside him Iris called,

"Hector, son of Priam—a mastermind like Zeus!
The Father has sped me down to tell you this:
so long as you see lord marshal Agamemnon storming
among the champions, mowing columns down in blood,
you must hold back, command the rest of your men
to fight the enemy, stand their headlong charge!
But soon as a spear or bowshot wounds the king
and Atrides mounts his chariot once again—   240
then Zeus will hand you the power to kill and kill
till you cut your way to the benched ships and the sun sinks
and the blessed darkness sweeps across the earth!"

      And Iris racing the wind went veering off.
Hector leapt to ground from his chariot fully armed
and brandishing two sharp spears went striding down his lines,
ranging flank to flank, driving his fighters into battle,
rousing grisly war—and round the Trojans whirled,
bracing to meet the Argives face-to-face:
but against their mass the Argives closed ranks,   250
the fighting about to break, the troops squaring off
and Atrides, tense to outfight them all, charged first.

      Sing to me now, you Muses who hold the halls of Olympus,
who was the first to go up against King Agamemnon,
who of the Trojans or famous Trojan allies?

      Iphidamas, the rough and rangy son of Antenor
bred in the fertile land of Thrace, mother of flocks.
Cisseus reared him at home when he was little—
his mother's father who sired the fine beauty Theano—
but once he hit the stride of his youth and ached for fame,   260
Cisseus tried to hold him back, gave him a daughter's hand
but warm from the bridal chamber marched the groom,
fired up by word that Achaea's troops had landed.
Twelve beaked ships sailed out in his command,
trim vessels he left behind him in Percote,
making his way to Troy to fight on foot
and here he came now, up against Agamemnon,

closer, closing . . .
                    Atrides hurled and missed,
his spearshaft just slanting aside the man's flank
as Iphidamas went for the waist beneath the breastplate—   270
he stabbed home, leaning into the blow full weight,
trusting his heavy hand but failed to pierce
the glittering belt, failed flat-out—the point,
smashing against the silver, bent back like lead.
And seizing the spearshaft powerful Agamemnon
dragged it toward him, tussling like some lion
and wrenching it free from Iphidamas' slack grasp
he hacked his neck with a sword and loosed his limbs.
And there he dropped and slept the sleep of bronze,
poor soldier, striving to help his fellow Trojans,   280
far from his wedded wife, his new bride . . .
No joy had he known from her for all his gifts,
the full hundred oxen he gave her on the spot
then promised a thousand head of goats and sheep
from the boundless herds he'd rounded up himself.
Now the son of Atreus stripped him, robbed his corpse
and strode back to his waiting Argive armies,
hoisting the gleaming gear.
                         But Coon marked him, Coon,
Antenor's eldest son, a distinguished man-at-arms,
and stinging grief went misting down his eyes   290
for his fallen brother. In from the blind side
he came—
          Agamemnon never saw him—
                             tensed with a spear
and slashed him under the elbow, down the forearm—
a glint of metal—the point ripped through his flesh
and the lord of fighting men Atrides shuddered.
Not that he quit the foray even then—
he sprang at Coon, gripping his big spearshaft
tough from the gusting wind that whipped its tree.
Coon was just dragging his brother footfirst,
wild now to retrieve his own father's son,   300
calling for help from all the bravest men—

but as Coon hauled the body through the press
Agamemnon lunged up, under his bossed shield,
thrust home hard with the polished bronze point,
unstrung his limbs and reared and lopped his head
and the head tumbled onto his fallen brother's corpse.
So then and there under royal Agamemnon's hands
the two sons of Antenor filled out their fates
and down they plunged to the strong House of Death.

But the king kept ranging, battling ranks on ranks   310
and thrusting his spear and sword and hurling heavy rocks
so long as the blood came flowing warm from his wound.
But soon as the gash dried and firm clots formed,
sharp pain came bursting in on Atrides' strength—
spear-sharp as the labor-pangs that pierce a woman,
agonies brought on by the harsh, birthing spirits,
Hera's daughters who hold the stabbing power of birth—
so sharp the throes that burst on Atrides' strength.
And back he sprang in the car and told his driver
to make for the hollow ships, racked with pain   320
but he loosed a shrill cry to all his men:
"Friends—lords of the Argives, O my captains!
Your turn now—keep on shielding our fast ships
from this latest mass attack. Zeus who rules the world
forbids me to battle Trojans all day long."

                                        A crack of the lash
and his driver whipped the team with streaming manes
straight for the curved ships, and on they flew,
holding nothing back, their heaving chests foaming,
bellies pelted with dust, rushing the wounded warlord
free and clear of battle.

                            There—Hector's signal!   330
Seeing Atrides hurt and speeding off the lines
he gave a ringing shout to his troops and allies:
"Trojans! Lycians! Dardan fighters hand-to-hand—
now be men, my friends, call up your battle-fury!
Their best man cuts and runs—
Zeus is handing me glory, awesome glory.

Drive your horses right at these mighty Argives,
seize the higher triumph—seize it now!"
                                                    Hector—
whipping the fight and fire in each man like a huntsman
crying on his hounds, their white fangs flashing,   340
harrying savage game, some wild boar or lion—
so at Achaea's ranks he drove his fearless Trojans,
Hector son of Priam, a match for murderous Ares.
The prince himself went wading into the front lines,
his hopes soaring, and down he hurled on the fray
like a sudden killer-squall that blasts down
on the dark blue sea to whip and chop its crests.

  Who was the first he slaughtered, who the last,
Hector the son of Priam, now Zeus gave him glory?
Asaeus first, Autonous next and then Opites,   350
Dolops, Clytius' son, and Opheltius, Agelaus,
Aesymnus and Orus, Hipponous staunch in combat.
These were the Argive captains Hector killed
then went for the main mass
like the West Wind battering soft shining clouds
the South Wind wafts along—in deep explosive blasts
it strikes and the great swelling waves roll on and on
and the spray goes shooting up from under the wind's hurl
swerving, roaring down the sea—so wildly Hector routed
the packed lines of fighters caught in his onslaught.   360

  Now there would have been havoc, irreversible chaos,
fleeing bands of Achaeans flung back on their ships
if Odysseus had not shouted out to Diomedes,
"What's wrong with us? Forgetting our battle-fury?
Come here, old friend, stand by me! What humiliation—
if Hector with that flashing helmet takes our ships!"

  Powerful Diomedes took his challenge quickly:
"I'll stand and fight, by god, and take the worst
but little joy it will bring our comrades now.
Zeus the king of the clouds has pitched on victory   370

for the Trojans, not for us."
                                  But all the same
he hurled Thymbraeus down to ground from his car—
Diomedes speared his left breast as Odysseus killed
the warlord's aide-in-arms Molion tall as a god
and left them there for dead, their fighting finished.
Then both went thrashing into the lines to make a slaughter
as two wild boars bristling, ramping back for the kill,
fling themselves on the yelping packs that hunt them—
back they whirled on attack and laid the Trojans low
while Achaeans just in flight from Hector's onset   380
leapt at the chance to gather second wind.

                                            At once
they took two lords of the realm and seized their car,
the two good sons of Merops out of Percote harbor,
Merops adept beyond all men in the mantic arts.
He refused to let his two boys march to war,
this man-killing war, but the young ones fought him
all the way—the forces of black death drove them on
and Diomedes a marvel with a spear destroyed them both,
stripped them of life breath and tore their gear away
and Odysseus killed Hippodamus, killed Hypirochus.

                                            And there,   390
gazing down from his ridge on Ida, the son of Cronus
stretched the rope of battle tense and taut
as the fighters kept on killing side-to-side.
Diomedes hurled a spear that struck Agastrophus,
Paeon's warrior son, and smashed the joint of his hip
but his team was not close by for fast escape—
a big mistake, the fool.
His driver held them reined off at the side
while he advanced through the front ranks on foot,
plowing on and on till he lost his own life . . .   400
But Hector quickly marked them across the lines—
he charged them both full force with a savage shout
and Trojan battalions churning in his wake.
Diomedes shuddered to see him coming on,
the lord of the war cry called out to Odysseus

quickly, close beside him, "We're in for shipwreck—
a breaker rolling down on us, look, this massive Hector!
Brace for him, stand our ground together—beat him back!"

He aimed and hurled and his spear's long shadow flew—
a clean hit, no miss, trained at the head of Hector,   410
his helmet ridge. But bronze glanced off bronze
and never grazed firm flesh, the helmet blocked it,
triple-ply with the great blank hollow eyes,
a gift of Apollo. Sprinting a long way back,
downfield and fast, Hector rejoined his men
and sinking down onto one knee, propped himself
with a strong hand planted against the earth—
and the world went black as night across his eyes.
But soon as Tydides followed up his spear,
tracking its flight far down along the front   420
where it stuck in sand, Hector caught his breath
and boarding his car, drove for his own main force
as he hurtled clear of the dark fates of death—
Diomedes shouting after him, shaking his spear,
"Now, again, you've escaped your death, you dog,
but a good close brush with death it was, I'd say!
Now, again, your Phoebus Apollo pulls you through,
the one you pray to, wading into our storm of spears.
We'll fight again—I'll finish you off next time
if one of the gods will only urge *me* on as well.   430
But now I'll go for the others, anyone I can catch."

And he set to stripping his kill, Paeon's spearman son.
But at once Paris the lord of fair-haired Helen
drew his bow at the rugged captain Diomedes . . .
the archer leaning firmly against a pillar
raised on the man-made tomb of Dardan's son,
Ilus an old lord of the realm in ancient days.
As Diomedes was stripping strong Agastrophus bare,
tearing the burnished breastplate off his victim's chest,
the shield from his shoulders and heavy crested helmet,   440
Paris, clenching the grip and drawing back his bow,

shot!—no wasted shot, it whizzed from his hand
and punched the flat top of Tydides' right foot,
the shaft dug through and stuck fast in the ground.
And loosing a heady laugh of triumph Paris leapt
from his hiding-place and shouted out in glory,
"Now you're hit—no wasted shot, my winging arrow!
But would to god I'd hit you deep in the guts
and ripped your life away! Then my Trojans
could catch their breath again, reprieved from death—   450
they cringed at you like bleating goats before some lion."

   But never flinching, staunch Diomedes countered,
"So brave with your bow and arrows—big bravado—
glistening lovelocks, roving eye for girls!
Come, try me in combat, weapons hand-to-hand—
bow and spattering shafts will never help you then.
You scratch my foot and you're vaunting all the same—
but who cares? A woman or idiot boy could wound me so.
The shaft of a good-for-nothing coward's got no point
but mine's got heft and edge. Let it graze a man—   460
my weapon works in a flash and drops him dead.
And his good wife will tear her cheeks in grief,
his sons are orphans and he, soaking the soil
red with his own blood, he rots away himself—
more birds than women flocking round his body!"

   So he yelled and the famous spearman Odysseus
rushed in close and reared up to shield him.
Slipping behind, Tydides dropped to a knee
and yanked the winged arrow from his foot
as the raw pain went stabbing through his flesh.   470
Back Diomedes jumped on his car and told his driver
to make for the hollow ships—Tydides racked with pain.

   That left the famous spearman Odysseus on his own,
not a single Argive comrade standing by his side
since panic seized them all. Unnerved himself,

Odysseus probed his own great fighting heart:
"O dear god, what becomes of Odysseus now?
A disgraceful thing if I should break and run,
fearing their main force—but it's far worse
if I'm taken all alone. Look, Zeus just drove   480
the rest of my comrades off in panic flight.
But why debate, my friend, why thrash things out?
Cowards, I know, would quit the fighting now
but the man who wants to make his mark in war
must stand his ground and brace for all he's worth—
suffer his wounds or wound his man to death."

Weighing it all, heart and soul, as on they came,
waves of Trojan shieldsmen crowding him tighter,
closing in on their own sure destruction . . .
like hounds and lusty hunters closing, ringing   490
a wild boar till out of his thicket lair he crashes,
whetting his white tusks sharp in his bent, wrenching jaws
and they rush in to attack and under the barks and shouts
you can hear the gnash of tusks but the men stand firm—
terrible, murderous as he is—so the Trojans ringed
Odysseus dear to Zeus, rushing him straight on.
But *he* lunged first, wounding lordly Deiopites,
spearshaft slicing into the Trojan's shoulder,
then cut down Thoon and Ennomus in their blood,
Chersidamas next, vaulting down from his car—   500
Odysseus caught him up under the bulging shield
with a jabbing spear that split him crotch to navel—
the man writhed in the dust, hands clutching the earth.
Odysseus left them dead and skewered Hippasus' son,
one Charops the blood brother of wealthy Socus
but Socus moved in quick as a god to shield his kin,
standing up to his enemy, crying out, "Odysseus—
wild for fame, glutton for cunning, glutton for war,
today you can triumph over the two sons of Hippasus,
killing such good men and stripping off their gear—   510
or beaten down by my spear you'll breathe your last!"

    With that he stabbed at Odysseus' balanced shield,
straight through the gleaming hide the heavy weapon drove,
ripping down and in through the breastplate finely worked
and it flayed the skin clean off Odysseus' ribs
but Pallas Athena would never let it pierce
her hero's vitals. Odysseus knew the end
had not yet come—no final, fatal wound—
and drawing back he hurled his boast at Socus:
"Poor man, headlong death is about to overtake you!   520
You've stopped my fighting against the Trojans, true,
but I tell you here and now that a dark, bloody doom
will take you down today—gouged by my spear
you'll give me glory now,
you'll give your life to the famous horseman Death!"

    And spinning in terror off he ran but as he spun
Odysseus plunged a spear in his back between the shoulders—
straight through his chest the shaft came jutting out
and down Socus crashed, Odysseus vaunting over him:
"Socus, son of Hippasus, skilled breaker of horses,   530
so, Death in its rampage outraced you—no escape.
No, poor soldier. Now your father and noble mother
will never close your eyes in death—screaming vultures
will claw them out of you, wings beating your corpse!
But I, if I should die,
my comrades-in-arms will bury me in style!"

    He dragged the heavy spear of hardened Socus
squelching out of his own wound and bulging shield.
As the fighter tore it out the blood came gushing forth
and his heart sank. And seeing Odysseus bleeding there   540
the Trojan troops exulted, calling across the melee,
charging him in a mass as edging, backing off
he gave ground now, calling his own companions.
Three shattering cries he loosed at full pitch
till Odysseus' head would burst—three times
Menelaus tense for combat heard his cries

and at once he called to Ajax standing near,
"Ajax, royal son of Telamon, captain of armies,
my ears ring with his cries—Odysseus never daunted.
He sounds like a man cut off and overpowered,   550
mauled by Trojan ranks in the rough assault.
Quick through the onset—better save him now!
I'm afraid he may be hurt, alone with the Trojans,
brave as Odysseus is—a blow to all our troops."

    And Atrides led the way and Ajax took his lead,
striding on like a god until they found Odysseus
dear to Zeus but round him Trojans thronged
like tawny jackals up in the mountains swarming
round a horned stag just wounded—a hunter's hit him
with one fast shaft from his bow and the stag's escaped,   560
sprinting at top speed so long as his blood runs warm
and the spring in his knees still lasts . . .
But soon as the swift arrow saps his strength
the ravening carrion packs begin their feasting
off on a ridge in twilight woods until some god,
some power drives a lion down against them—claw-mad
and the panicked jackals scatter, the lion rends their prey.
So packed around Odysseus skilled and quick to maneuver
swarmed the brave bulk of Trojans—but still the hero
kept on lunging, spearing, keeping death at bay.   570
And in moved Ajax now, planted right beside him,
bearing that shield of his like a wall, a tower—
Trojans scattered in panic, bolting left and right
while the fighting son of Atreus led Odysseus
through the onslaught, bracing him with an arm
till a reinsman drove his team and car up close.

    But charging down on the Trojans Ajax killed Doryclus,
bastard son of Priam—he wounded Pandocus next,
wounded Lysander, Pyrasus, then Pylartes.
Wild as a swollen river hurling down on the flats,   580
down from the hills in winter spate, bursting its banks
with rain from storming Zeus, and stands of good dry oak,

whole forests of pine it whorls into itself and sweeps along
till it heaves a crashing mass of driftwood out to sea—
so glorious Ajax swept the field, routing Trojans,
shattering teams and spearmen in his onslaught.
Nor had Hector once got wind of the rampage . . .
far off on the left flank of the whole campaign
he fought his way, powering past Scamander's banks
where the heads of fighters fell in biggest numbers   590
and grim incessant war cries rose around tall Nestor
and battle-hard Idomeneus. Hector amidst them now
engaged them with a vengeance, doing bloody work
with lances flung and a master's horsemanship,
destroying young battalions. Still the Achaeans
never would have yielded before the prince's charge
if Paris the lord of lovely fair-haired Helen
had not put a stop to Machaon's gallant fighting,
striking the healer squarely with an arrow
triple-flanged that gouged his right shoulder.   600
Achaeans breathing fury feared for Machaon now:
what if the tide turned and Trojans killed the healer?
Idomeneus suddenly called to Nestor, "Pride of Achaea!
Quick, mount your chariot, mount Machaon beside you—
lash your team to the warships, fast, full gallop!
A man who can cut out shafts and dress our wounds—
a good healer is worth a troop of other men."

Nestor the noble charioteer did not resist.
He mounted his car at once as Asclepius' son,
Machaon born of the famous healer swung aboard.   610
He lashed the team and on they flew to the ships,
holding nothing back—that's where their spirits
drove them on to go.

                 But riding on with Hector
Cebriones saw the Trojan rout and shouted, "Hector!
Look at us here, engaging Argives with a vengeance,
true, but off on the fringe of brutal all-out war
while our central force is routed pell-mell,
men and chariots flung against each other.

Giant Ajax drives them—I recognize the man,
that wall of a buckler slung around his shoulders.   620
Hurry, head our chariot right where the fighting's thickest,
there—horse and infantry hurling into the slaughter,
hacking each other down, terrific war cries rising!"

     With that, Cebriones flogged their sleek team
and leaping under the whistling, crackling whip
they sped the careering car into both milling armies,
trampling shields and corpses, axle under the chariot splashed
with blood, blood on the handrails sweeping round the car,
sprays of blood shooting up from the stallions' hoofs
and churning, whirling rims. And Hector straining   630
to wade into the press and panicked ruck of men,
charge them, break them down—he flung terror
and stark disaster square in the Argive lines,
never pausing, giving his spear no rest.
Hector kept on ranging, battling ranks on ranks,
slashing his spear and sword and flinging heavy rocks
but he stayed clear of attacking Ajax man-to-man.

     But Father Zeus on the heights forced Ajax to retreat.
He stood there a moment, stunned,
then swinging his seven-ply oxhide shield behind him,   640
drew back in caution, throwing a fast glance
at his own Achaean troops like a trapped beast,
pivoting, backpedaling, step by short step . . .
Like a tawny lion when hounds and country field hands
drive him out of their steadings filled with cattle—
they'll never let him tear the rich fat from the oxen,
all night long they stand guard but the lion craves meat,
he lunges in and in but his charges gain him nothing,
thick-and-fast from their hardy arms the javelins
rain down in his face, and waves of blazing torches—   650
these the big cat fears, balking for all his rage,
and at dawn he slinks away, his spirits dashed.
So Ajax slowly drew back from the Trojans,
spirits dashed, and much against his will,

fearing the worst for Achaea's waiting ships.
Like a stubborn ass some boys lead down a road . . .
stick after stick they've cracked across his back
but he's too much for them now, he rambles into a field
to ravage standing crops. They keep beating his ribs,
splintering sticks—their struggle child's play   660
till with one final shove they drive him off
but not before he's had his fill of feed.
So with Telamon's son Great Ajax then—
vaunting Trojans and all their far-flung allies
kept on stabbing his shield, full center, no letup.
And now the giant fighter would summon up his fury,
wheeling on them again, beating off platoons
of the stallion-breaking Trojans—and now again
he'd swerve around in flight. But he blocked them all
from hacking passage through to the fast trim ships   670
as Ajax all alone, battling on mid-field between
Achaean and Trojan lines, would stand and fight.
Some spears that flew from the Trojans' hardy arms,
hurtling forward, stuck fast in his huge shield
but showers of others, cut short
halfway before they could graze his gleaming skin,
stuck in the ground, still lusting to sink in flesh.

But Euaemon's shining son Eurypylus saw him
overwhelmed by the Trojans' dense barrage of spears.
Up to his side he dashed and flanked Great Ajax tight,   680
let fly with a spear and the glinting spearpoint hit
the son of Phausias, Apisaon captain of armies,
square in the liver, up under the midriff—
his knees went limp as Eurypylus rushed in,
starting to rip the armor off his shoulders.
But now Paris spotted him stripping Apisaon,
drew his bow at Eurypylus, fast—he shot well
and the arrow struck him full in the right thigh
but the shaft snapped, the thigh weighed down with pain.
Eurypylus staggered back to his massing comrades,   690
dodging death, and shouted a stark piercing cry:

"Friends—lords of the Argives, all our captains!
Come, wheel round—stand firm!
Beat the merciless day of death from Ajax,
overpowered, look, by a pelting rain of spears.
He can't escape, I tell you, not this wrenching battle.
Stand up to them—ring Great Ajax, Telamon's son."

    So wounded Eurypylus pleaded, friends around him
crowding, bracing shields against their shoulders,
spears brandished high   700
and back to the bulking front came giant Ajax now.
The fighter turned on his heels and took his stand,
once he reached that wedge of Argive comrades.

    So on they fought like a mass of swirling fire
as Neleus' foaming mares bore Nestor clear of battle
and bore Machaon the expert healer too . . .
                                                    But now
the brilliant runner Achilles watched and marked him—
there he stood on the stern of his looming hollow hull,
looking out over the uphill work and heartsick rout of war.
He called at once to his friend-in-arms Patroclus,   710
shouting down from the decks. Hearing Achilles,
forth he came from his shelter,
striding up like the deathless god of war
but from that moment on his doom was sealed.
The brave son of Menoetius spoke out first:
"Why do you call, Achilles? Do you need me?"
And the swift runner Achilles answered quickly,
"Son of Menoetius, soldier after my own heart,
now I think they will grovel at my knees,
our Achaean comrades begging for their lives.   720
The need has reached them—a need too much to bear.
Go now, Patroclus dear to Zeus, and question Nestor.
Who's that wounded man he's bringing in from the fighting?
He looks to me like Machaon from behind, clearly,
Machaon head to foot, Asclepius' only son.
But I never saw his eyes—the team sped by me,

tearing on full tilt."
                              Patroclus obeyed his great friend
and off at a run he went along the ships and shelters.

    Now, as soon as the others reached Nestor's tent
they climbed down on the earth that feeds us all.   730
The driver Eurymedon freed the old man's team.
The men themselves dried off their sweat-soaked shirts,
standing against the wind that whipped along the surf,
then entered the tent and took their seats on settles.
And well-kempt Hecamede mixed them a bracing drink,
the woman that old King Nestor won from Tenedos
when Achilles stormed it, proud Arsinous' daughter,
the prize the Achaeans chose to give to Nestor
because he excelled them all at battle-tactics.
First Hecamede pushed a table up toward them,   740
handsome, sanded smooth, with blue enamel legs,
and on it she set a basket, braided in bronze
with onions in it, a relish for the drink,
and pale gold honey along with barley meal,
the grain's blessed yield. And there in the midst
the grand, glowing cup the old king brought from home,
studded with golden nails, fitted with handles,
four all told and two doves perched on each,
heads bending to drink and made of solid gold
and twin supports ran down to form the base.   750
An average man would strain to lift it off the table
when it was full, but Nestor, old as he was,
could hoist it up with ease.
In this cup the woman skilled as a goddess
mixed them a strong drink with Pramnian wine,
over it shredded goat cheese with a bronze grater
and scattered barley into it, glistening pure white,
then invited them to drink when she had mulled it all.
Now as the two men drank their parching thirst away
and had just begun to please themselves with talk,   760
confiding back and forth—there stood Patroclus
tall at the threshold, vivid as a god . . .

Old Nestor saw him at once and started up
from his polished chair, warmly grasped his hand
and led Patroclus in, pressing him to sit.
But standing off to the side his guest declined:
"No time to sit, old soldier dear to the gods.
You won't persuade me. Awesome and quick to anger,
the man who sent me here to find out who's been wounded,
the one you've just brought in. But I can see him—   770
I recognize Machaon myself, the expert healer.
So back I go to give Achilles the message.
Well you know, old soldier loved by the gods,
what sort of man *he* is—that great and terrible man.
Why, he'd leap to accuse a friend without a fault."

But Nestor the noble charioteer replied at length,
"Now why is Achilles so cast down with grief
for this or that Achaean winged by a stray shaft?
He has no idea of the anguish risen through the army!
Look—our finest champions laid up in the ships,   780
all hit by arrows or run through by spears . . .
there's powerful Diomedes brought down by an archer,
Odysseus wounded, and Agamemnon too, the famous spearman,
and Eurypylus took a shaft in the thigh, and here,
Machaon—I just brought him in from the fighting,
struck down by an arrow whizzing off the string.
But Achilles, brave as he is, he has no care,
no pity for our Achaeans. How long will he wait?
Till our ships that line the shore go up in flames,
gutted, despite a last-ditch stand? And we ourselves   790
are mowed down in droves?
                              And I, what good am I?
My limbs are gnarled now, the old power's gone.
Oh make me young again,
and the strength inside me steady as a rock!
As fresh as I was that time the feud broke out . . .
fighting Epeans over a cattle-raid I killed Itymoneus,
Hypirochus' gallant son who used to live in Elis.
I was rustling their cattle in reprisal, you see,

and he defending his herds, when a spear I hurled
caught him right in the front ranks of herdsmen—   800
down he went and round him his yokel drovers
scattered home in panic. And what a lovely haul,
what plunder we rounded up and herded off the plain!
Fifty herds of cattle, as many head of sheep,
as many droves of pigs and as many goat-flocks
ranging free, a hundred and fifty horses too,
strong and tawny, broodmares every one
and under the flanks of many, nursing foals.

                    The whole lot—
we drove them all into Pylos then, that very night,
corraling them all inside the walls of Neleus.   810
And father beamed, seeing how much I'd won,
a young soldier out on his first campaign.
And the heralds cried out at the break of day,
'Pylians—come collect your debts from wealthy Elis!'
And a troop of Pylian chiefs turned out in force
to carve up the spoils. The Epeans owed us all,
few as we were in Pylos, hard-pressed as well.
For mighty Heracles came against us years before,
he ground our lives out, killing off our best.
Twelve sons we were of the noble old Neleus   820
and I alone was left . . .
the rest of my brothers perished in that rout.
Riding high on our loss the Epeans rose in arms,
lording over us, harassing us with outrage after outrage.
So now, out of Epean spoils, the old king chose
a herd of cattle and handsome flock of sheep,
three hundred head he picked, the herdsmen too.
For wealthy Elis owed my father a heavy debt:
four prizewinning thoroughbreds, chariot and all.
They'd gone to the games, primed to race for the tripod,   830
but Augeas the warlord commandeered them on the spot
and sent the driver packing, sick for his team.
So now old Neleus, still enraged at it all—
the threats to his man, the naked treachery—
helped himself to a priceless treasure trove

but gave the rest to his people to divide,
so none would go deprived of his fair share.
But just as we were parceling out the plunder
and offering victims to the gods around the city,
right on the third day they came, the Epeans massed   840
in a swarm of men and plunging battle-stallions struck
at the border, full force—and square in their midst
the two Moliones armed to the hilt, and still boys,
not quite masters yet in the ways of combat.

                                                    Now then,
there's a frontier fortress, Thryoëssa perched on cliffs,
far off above the Alpheus, at the edge of sandy Pylos.
The Epeans ringed that fort, keen to raze its walls,
but once their troops had swept the entire plain,
down Athena rushed to us in the night, a herald
down from Olympus crying out, 'To arms! to arms!'   850
Nor did Pallas muster a slow, unwilling army
there in Pylos, all of us spoiling for a fight.
But Neleus would not let me arm for action—
he'd hidden away my horses,
thought his boy still green at the work of war.
So I had to reach the front lines on foot
but I shone among our horsemen all the same—
that's how Athena called the turns of battle.
Listen. There is a river, the Minyeos
emptying into the sea beside Arene's walls,   860
and there we waited for Goddess Dawn to rise,
the Pylian horse in lines while squads of infantry
came streaming up behind. Then, from that point on,
harnessed in battle-armor, moving at forced march
our army reached the Alpheus' holy ford at noon.
There we slaughtered fine victims to mighty Zeus,
a bull to Alpheus River, a bull to lord Poseidon
and an unyoked cow to blazing-eyed Athena.
And then through camp we took our evening meal
by rank and file, and caught what sleep we could,   870
each in his gear along the river rapids.

                                    And all the while

those vaunting Epeans were closing round the fortress,
burning to tear it down. But before they got the chance
a great work of the War-god flashed before their eyes!
Soon as the sun came up in flames above the earth
we joined battle, lifting a prayer to Zeus and Pallas.
And just as our two opposing armies clashed
I was the first to kill a man and seize his team,
the spearman Mulius, son-in-law to their king
and wed to his eldest daughter, blond Agamede,   880
skilled with as many drugs as the wide world grows.
Just as he lunged I speared the man with a bronze lance
and Mulius pitched in the dust as I, I swung aboard his car
and I took my place in our front ranks of champions.
How those hot-blooded Epeans scattered in terror!
Scuttling left and right when they saw him down,
their chariot captain who'd outfought them all.
Now I charged their lines like a black tornado,
I captured fifty chariots there, and each time
two men bit the dust, crushed beneath my spear.   890
Now I would have destroyed the young Moliones,
Actor's sons—if their real father, Poseidon,
lord god of the open sea who shakes the earth,
had not snatched them out of the fighting then,
shrouded them round in clouds.
But now Zeus gave our Pylians stunning triumph!
Pushing Epeans north on the spreading plain we went,
killing their troops, gathering up their burnished gear,
far as Buprasion rich in wheat our chariots rolled,
all the way to Olenian Rock and the high ground   900
they call Alesion Hill—but there, at last,
Pallas Athena turned our forces back.
I killed my last man there, I left him dead.
There our Achaeans swung round from Buprasion,
heading their high-strung horses back to Pylos
where all gave glory to Zeus among the gods
and among all men to Nestor.
                                  So, such was I
in the ranks of men . . . or was it all a dream?

                                                    This Achilles—
he'll reap the rewards of that great courage of his
alone, I tell you—weep his heart out far too late,   910
when our troops are dead and gone.
My friend, remember your father's last commands?
That day he sent you out of Phthia to Agamemnon.
We were both there inside, I and Prince Odysseus
heard it all in the halls, all your father told you.
We'd come to the strong and storied house of Peleus,
out for recruits across Achaea's good green land.
There inside we found the old soldier Menoetius,
found you too, and Achilles close beside you,
and the old horseman Peleus tending, burning   920
the fat thighs of an ox to thundering Zeus,
deep in the walled enclosure of his court.
He was lifting a golden cup and pouring wine,
glistening wine to go with the glowing victim.
You two were busy over the carcass, carving meat
when we both appeared and stood at the broad doors.
Achilles sprang to his feet, he seemed startled,
clasped the two of us by the hand and led us in—
he pressed us to take a seat and set before us
sumptuous stranger's fare, the stranger's right.   930
And once we'd had our fill of food and drink,
I led off with our plan, inviting the two of you
to come campaign with us. How willing you were!
And your fathers filled your ears with marching orders.
The old horseman Peleus urging his son Achilles,
'Now always be the best, my boy, the bravest,
and hold your head up high above the others.'
And Actor's son Menoetius urging you, 'My child,
Achilles is nobler than you with his immortal blood
but you are older. He has more power than you, by far,   940
but give him sound advice, guide him, even in battle.
Achilles will listen to you—for his own good.'
So the old man told you. You've forgotten.
                                    But even now,
late as it is, you could tell your Achilles all this

and your fiery friend might listen. Who knows?
With a god's help you just might rouse him now,
bring his fighting spirit round at last.
The persuasion of a comrade has its powers.
But if down deep some prophecy makes him balk,
some doom his noble mother revealed to him from Zeus,   950
at least let Achilles send *Patroclus* into battle.
Let the whole Myrmidon army follow your command—
you might bring some light of victory to our Argives!
And let him give you his own fine armor to wear in war
so the Trojans might take *you* for him, Patroclus, yes,
hold off from attack, and Achaea's fighting sons
get second wind, exhausted as they are . . .
Breathing room in war is all too brief.
You're fresh, unbroken. They're bone-weary from battle—
you could roll those broken Trojans back to Troy,   960
clear of our ships and shelters!"

                        So old Nestor urged
and the fighting spirit leapt inside Patroclus—
he dashed back by the ships toward Achilles.
But sprinting close to King Odysseus' fleet
where the Argives met and handed down their laws,
the grounds where they built their altars to the gods,
there he met Eurypylus, Euaemon's gallant son,
wounded, the arrow planted deep in his thigh,
and limping out of battle . . .
The sweat was streaming down his face and back   970
and the dark blood still flowed from his ugly wound
but the man's will was firm, he never broke his stride.
And moved at the sight, the good soldier Patroclus
burst out in grief with a flight of winging words,
"Poor men! Lords of the Argives, O my captains!
How doomed you are, look—far from your loved ones
and native land—to glut with your shining fat
the wild dogs of battle here in Troy . . .
But come, tell me, Eurypylus, royal fighter,
can the Achaeans, somehow, still hold monstrous Hector?—   980
or must they all die now, beaten down by his spear?"

Struggling with his wound, Eurypylus answered,
"No hope, Patroclus, Prince. No bulwark left.
They'll all be hurled back to the black ships.
All of them, all our best in the old campaigns
are laid up in the hulls, they're hit by arrows,
pierced by spears, brought down by Trojan hands
while the Trojans' power keeps on rising, rising!
Save me at least. Take me back to my black ship.
Cut this shaft from my thigh. And the dark blood—   990
wash it out of the wound with clear warm water.
And spread the soothing, healing salves across it,
the powerful drugs they say you learned from Achilles
and Chiron the most humane of Centaurs taught your friend.
And as for our own healers, Podalirius and Machaon,
one is back in the shelters, wounded, I think—
Machaon needs a good strong healer himself,
he's racked with pain. The other's still afield,
standing up to the Trojans' slashing onslaught."

The brave son of Menoetius answered quickly,   1000
"Impossible. Eurypylus, hero, what shall we do?
I am on my way with a message for Achilles,
our great man of war—the plan that Nestor,
Achaea's watch and ward, urged me to report.
But I won't neglect you, even so, with such a wound."

And bracing the captain, arm around his waist,
he helped him toward his shelter. An aide saw them
and put some oxhides down. Patroclus stretched him out,
knelt with a knife and cut the sharp, stabbing arrow
out of Eurypylus' thigh and washed the wound clean   1010
of the dark running blood with clear warm water.
Pounding it in his palms, he crushed a bitter root
and covered over the gash to kill his comrade's pain,
a cure that fought off every kind of pain . . .
and the wound dried and the flowing blood stopped

BOOK TWELVE

The Trojans
Storm the Rampart

And so under shelter now Menoetius' fighting son
was healing Eurypylus' wounds. But hordes of men fought on,
the Achaean and Trojan infantry going hand-to-hand.
The Argive trench could not hold out much longer,
nor could the rampart rearing overhead, the wide wall
they raised to defend the ships and the broad trench
they drove around it all—they never gave the gods
the splendid sacrifice the immortals craved,
that the fortress might protect the fast ships
and the bulking plunder heaped behind its shield.   10
Defying the deathless gods they built that wall
and so it stood there steadfast no long time.
While Hector still lived and Achilles raged on
and the warlord Priam's citadel went unstormed,
so long the Achaeans' rampart stood erect.

But once the best of the Trojan captains fell,
and many Achaeans died as well while some survived,
and Priam's high walls were stormed in the tenth year
and the Argives set sail for the native land they loved—
then, at last, Poseidon and Lord Apollo launched their plan   20
to smash the rampart, flinging into it all the rivers' fury.
All that flow from the crests of Ida down to breaking surf,
the Rhesus and the Heptaporus, Caresus and the Rhodius,
Grenicus and Aesepus, and the shining god Scamander
and Simois' tides where tons of oxhide shields
and horned helmets tumbled deep in the river silt
and a race of men who seemed half god, half mortal.
The channels of all those rivers—Apollo swung them round
into one mouth and nine days hurled their flood against the wall
and Zeus came raining down, cloudburst powering cloudburst,   30
the faster to wash that rampart out to open sea.
The Earth-shaker himself, trident locked in his grip,
led the way, rocking loose, sweeping up in his breakers
all the bastion's strong supports of logs and stones
the Achaeans prized in place with grueling labor . . .
He made all smooth along the rip of the Hellespont
and piled the endless beaches deep in sand again
and once he had leveled the Argives' mighty wall
he turned the rivers flowing back in their beds again
where their fresh clear tides had run since time began.   40

    So in the years to come Poseidon and god Apollo
would set all things to rights once more.
                                 But now
the war, the deafening crash of battle blazed
around the strong-built work, and rampart timbers
thundered under the heavy blows as Argive fighters
beaten down by the lash of Zeus were rolled back,
pinned to their beaked ships in dread of Hector,
that invincible headlong terror.
On he fought like a whirlwind, staunch as always—
think of the hounds and huntsmen circling round   50
some lion or boar when the quarry wheels at bay,

rippling in strength as the men mass like a bastion
standing up to his charge and hurl their pelting spears
and the boar's brave spirit never flinches, never bolts
and his own raw courage kills him—time and again
he wheels around, testing the huntsmen's ranks
and where he lunges out the ranks of men give way.
So Hector lunged into battle, rallying cohorts now,
spurring them on to cross the gaping trench—
but his own rearing stallions lacked the nerve.   60
They balked, whinnying shrill at the edge, the brink—
a dead stop—frightened off by the trench so broad
the team could never leap it, not at a single bound,
nor could they plunge on through with any ease.
Steep banks overhung its whole length, jutting up
on either side and topped by stabbing rows of stakes,
planted there by the Argives, thickset and huge
to block the enemy's onslaught.
No light work for the teams that trundled chariots
churning massive wheels to make it through in stride   70
but the Trojans strained to bring it off on foot.
So Polydamas stood by headstrong Hector, warning,
"Hector—and all our Trojan captains, allies-in-arms!
It's madness to drive our teams across that trench,
impossible to traverse it. Look, the sharp stakes
jutting right at the edge, and just beyond that
the Achaeans' sturdy rampart. No room there
for charioteers to dismount and fight it out,
the strait's too narrow, cramped—
we'll take a mauling there, I see it all!   80
If mighty Zeus, thundering up on high, is bent
on wiping out the Argives, down to the last man,
if he longs to back our Trojan forces to the hilt,
by heaven I hope the Father works his will at once
and the Argives die here, their memory blotted out,
a world away from Argos!
                 But what if they round on us?
If the Argives roll us back away from the ships,
trapped and tangled there in the yawning trench,

no runner, I tell you, pressed by an Argive rally,
could struggle free and bear the news to Troy.   90
So come, do as I say, and let us all unite.
Drivers, rein your horses hard by the trench—
the men themselves, armed for assault on foot,
we all follow Hector, all in a mass attack.
And the Argives? They cannot hold their line,
not if the ropes of death are knotted round their necks!"

So Polydamas urged. His plan won Hector over—
less danger, more success—and down he leapt
from his chariot fully armed and hit the ground.
Nor did the other chariot-drivers hold formation—   100
all dismounted, seeing shining Hector leap to earth.
Each man shouted out commands to his driver, quickly,
"Rein the team by the trench, good battle-order now!"
And the fighters split apart and then closed ranks,
marshaled in five battalions, captains leading each.

The men who trooped with Hector and Prince Polydamas—
they were the greatest force, the best and bravest,
grim set above all the rest to breach the wall
and go for the beaked ships and fight it out.
Cebriones followed close, third in command   110
since Hector left another to rein his team,
a driver less than Cebriones, less a fighter.
The second Trojan battalion Paris led in arms
with Alcathous and Agenor. Helenus led the third
with Deiphobus striding on like a god beside him,
two sons of Priam; captain Asius third in command,
Asius son of Hyrtacus—hulking, fiery stallions
bore him in from Arisbe, from the Selleis River.
The fourth battalion marched with gallant Aeneas,
Anchises' offspring flanked by Antenor's two sons,   120
Acamas and Archelochus drilled for every foray.
Sarpedon marshaled the famous allies, placing Glaucus
next in command with the combat veteran Asteropaeus,
head and shoulders the best men, Sarpedon thought,

after himself of course: he outshone the rest.
Now shield against oxhide shield, wedging tight,
with a wild rush they charged the Argives head-on,
never thinking the Argive line could still hold out—
they'd all be hurled back on their blackened hulls.

So all the Trojans and famous friends-in-arms   130
embraced Polydamas' plan, the faultless chieftain.
But Asius captain of armies, Hyrtacus' son refused
to leave his horses there with a driver reining back—
and on he drove at the fast trim ships, chariot and all,
the fool. Vaunting along the hulls with team and car
but never destined to slip past the deadly spirits,
never to ride in glory home to windswept Troy.
Long before, his accursed doom blacked him out
with Idomeneus' spear, Deucalion's noble son.
Now left of the ships he sped where Argive ranks   140
would head home from the plain with teams and cars.
Here Asius flogged his team and chariot hard,
nor did he find the gates shut, the bolt shot home,
not yet, the men still held them wide, hoping to save
some comrade fleeing the onset, racing for the ships.
Straight at the gates he lashed his team, hell-bent,
his troops crowding behind him shouting war cries,
never thinking the Argive line could still hold out—
they'd all be hurled back on their blackened hulls.
Idiots. There in the gates they found two men,   150
a brace of two great fighters,
lionhearted sons of the Lapith spearmen,
one Pirithous' offspring, rugged Polypoetes,
the other Leonteus, a match for murderous Ares.
Both warriors planted there before the towering gates
rose like oaks that rear their crests on a mountain ridge,
standing up to the gales and driving rains, day in, day out,
their giant roots branching, gripping deep in the earth:
so these two, trusting all to their arms, their power,
stood up to Asius' headlong charge and never shrank.   160
On the Trojans came, straight for the rock-tight wall,

raising rawhide shields and yelling their lungs out,
grouped under captain Asius, Iamenus and Orestes
and Asius' own son Adamas, Thoon and Oenomaus.
The Lapiths had just been rousing Argives packed
behind the rampart: "Close in a ring—defend the ships!"
But soon as the Lapiths saw the Trojans storm the wall,
and cries broke from the Argives lost in sudden panic,
then the two burst forth to fight before the gates
like wild boars, a pair of them up on the hilltops   170
bracing to take some breakneck rout of men and dogs
and the two go slanting in on the charge, shattering timber
round about them, shearing off the trunks at the roots
and a grinding, screeching clatter of tusks goes up
till a hunter spears them, tears their lives out—
so the clatter screeched from the gleaming bronze
that cased their chests as blows piled on blows.
Deadly going, fighting now for all they were worth,
staking all on their own strength and friends overhead
as they ripped off rocks from the rampart's sturdy ledge   180
and hurled them down, defending themselves, their shelters,
their fast ships—the rocks pelted the ground like snow
that a sudden squall in fury, driving the dark clouds,
heaps thick-and-fast on the earth that feeds us all.
So the missiles showering from their hands—Achaeans,
Trojans, helmets and bossed shields clashing, ringing
shrilly under the blows of boulders big as millstones.
And now with a deep groan and pounding both thighs
Asius son of Hyrtacus cried in anguish, "Father Zeus—
so even *you* are an outright liar after all!   190
I never dreamed these heroic Argive ranks
could hold back our charge, our invincible arms.
Look, like wasps quick and pinched at the waist
or bees who build their hives on a rocky path,
they never give up their hollow house, they hold on,
keep the honey-hunters at bay, fight for their young.
So these men will never budge from the gates
though they're only two defenders—
not till they kill us all or we kill them!"

But his wailing failed to move the heart of Zeus: 200
it was Zeus's pleasure to hand the prize to Hector.

Now squad on squad, gate to gate they fought—
but how can I tell it all, sing it all like a god?
The strain is far too great. Everywhere round the wall
the surging inhuman blaze of war leapt up the rocks—
the Argives, desperate, had no choice, they struggled now
to defend the ships, and the gods were cast down in spirit,
all who had urged the Argive soldiers on in battle . . .
But the Lapiths still kept fighting, slaughtering on.

There—Pirithous' son the rugged Polypoetes   210
skewered Damasus, pierced his bronze-sided helmet.
None of the bronze plate could hold it, boring through
the metal and skull the brazen spearpoint pounded,
Damasus' brains splattered all inside his casque—
Polypoetes beat him down despite the Trojan's rage,
then Pylon and Ormenus, killed and stripped them both.
And the tested veteran Leonteus speared Hippomachus,
gouged Antimachus' offspring down across the belt,
then drawing his long sharp sword from its sheath
he rushed the front and took Antiphates first   220
with a quick thrust, stabbing at close range—
he slammed on his back, sprawled along the ground.
Then Menon, Orestes, Iamenus—Leonteus killed the lot,
crowding corpse on corpse on the earth that rears us all.

While the Lapiths stripped their kills of gleaming gear
the fighters trooping behind Polydamas and Hector,
the greatest force, the best and bravest, grim set
above all to breach the wall and torch the ships,
still halted up at the trench, torn with doubt.
For suddenly, just as the men tried to cross,   230
a fatal bird-sign flashed before their eyes,
an eagle flying high on the left across their front
and clutching a monstrous bloody serpent in both talons,
still alive, still struggling—it had not lost its fight,

writhing back to strike it fanged the chest of its captor
right beside the throat—and agonized by the bites
the eagle flung it away to earth, dashed it down
amidst the milling fighters, loosed a shriek
and the bird veered off along the gusting wind.
The Trojans shuddered to see the serpent glistening,   240
wriggling at their feet, a sign from storming Zeus.
And Polydamas stood by headstrong Hector, saying,
"Hector, you always seem to attack me in assembly,
despite my good advice. Never right, is it,
for a common man to speak against you, King,
never in open council, and god forbid in war.
Our part is always to magnify your power. Well,
once again I am bound to say what I think best.
Stop the attack, don't fight them at their ships!
All will end as the omen says, I do believe,   250
if the bird-sign really came to us, the Trojans,
just as our fighters tried to cross the trench.
That eagle flying high on the left across our front,
clutching this bloody serpent in both its talons,
still alive—but he let the monster drop at once,
before he could sweep it back to his own home . . .
he never fed his nestlings in the end.
                                              Nor will we.
Even if we can breach the Argives' gates and wall,
assaulting in force, and the Argives give ground,
back from the ships we'll come,   260
back the way we went but our battle-order ruined,
whole battalions of Trojans left behind and killed—
the Achaeans will cut us down with bronze to save their fleet!
So a knowing seer of the gods would read this omen,
someone clear in his mind and skilled with signs,
a man the Trojan armies would obey."

                                              His helmet flashing,
Hector wheeled with a dark glance: "Enough, Polydamas!
Your pleading repels me now—
you must have something better than this to say.
But if you are serious, speaking from the heart,   270

the gods themselves have blotted out your senses.
You tell *me* to forget the plans of storming Zeus,
all he promised me when he nodded in assent?
You tell *me* to put my trust in birds,
flying off on their long wild wings? Never.
I would never give them a glance, a second thought,
whether they fly on the right toward the dawn and sunrise
or fly on the left toward the haze and coming dark!
No, no, put our trust in the will of mighty Zeus,
king of the deathless gods and men who die.

                                    Bird-signs!   280
Fight for your country—that is the best, the only omen!
You, why are you so afraid of war and slaughter?
Even if all the rest of us drop and die around you,
grappling for the ships, you'd run no risk of death:
you lack the heart to last it out in combat—coward!
But if you hold back from the bloody foray here
or turn some other soldier back from battle,
winning him over—you with your soft appeals—
at one quick stroke my spear will beat you down,
you'll breathe your last!"

                            Shouting he led the charge   290
and his armies swarmed behind with blood-chilling cries.
And above their onset Zeus who loves the lightning
launched from Ida's summits a sudden howling gale
that whipped a dust storm hard against the ships,
spellbinding Achaean units in their tracks,
handing glory to Hector and Hector's Trojans.
Inspired by the signs and their own raw power
all pitched in to smash the Achaeans' massive wall.
They tore at the towers' outworks, pulled at battlements,
heaving, trying to pry loose with levers the buttress stakes   300
Achaeans first drove in the earth to shore the rampart up—
they struggled to root these out, hoping to break down
the Achaean wall itself. But not yet did the Argives
give way to assault—no, they stopped the breaches up
with oxhide shields and down from the breastwork heights
they hurled rocks at the enemy coming on beneath the wall.

    And the two Aeantes ranged all points of the rampart,
    calling out commands to spur their comrades' fury.
    Now cheering a soldier on, tongue-lashing the next
    if they marked a straggler hanging back from battle: 310
    "Friends—you in the highest ranks of Argives,
    you in the midst and you in rank and file,
    we cannot all be equal in battle, ever,
    but now the battle lies before us all—
    come, see for yourselves, look straight down.
    Now let no fighter be turned back to the ships,
    not with his captain's orders ringing in his ears—
    keep pressing forward, shouting each other on!
    If only Olympian Zeus the lord of lightning
    grants us strength to repel this Trojan charge   320
    then carve a passage through to Troy's high walls!"

    So their cries urged on the Achaeans' war-lust.
    Thick-and-fast as the snows that fall on a winter dawn
    when Zeus who rules the world brings on a blizzard,
    displaying to all mankind his weaponry of war . . .
    and he puts the winds to sleep, drifting on and on
    until he has shrouded over the mountains' looming peaks
    and the headlands jutting sharp, the lowlands deep in grass
    and the rich plowed work of farming men, and the drifts fall
    on the gray salt surf and the harbors and down along the beaches   330
    and only breakers beating against the drifts can hold them off
    but all else on the earth they cover over, snows from the sky
    when Zeus comes storming down—now so thick-and-fast
    they volleyed rocks from both sides, some at the Trojans,
    some from Trojans against the Argives, salvos landing,
    the whole long rampart thundering under blows.

    But not even now would Trojans and Prince Hector
    have burst apart the rampart's gates and huge bar
    if Zeus the Master Strategist had not driven
    his own son Sarpedon straight at the Argives,   340
    strong as a lion raiding crook-horned cattle.

Quickly Sarpedon swung his shield before him—
balanced and handsome beaten bronze a bronzesmith
hammered out with layer on layer of hide inside
and stitched with golden rivets round the rim.
That splendid shield he gripped before his chest
and shaking a pair of spears went stalking out
like a mountain lion starved for meat too long
and the lordly heart inside him fires him up
to raid some stormproof fold, to go at the sheep,   350
and even if he should light on herdsmen at the spot,
guarding their flocks with dogs and bristling spears,
the marauder has no mind to be driven off that steading,
not without an attack. All or nothing—he charges flocks
and hauls off bloody prey or he's run through himself
at the first assault with a fast spear driven home.
So now the heart of Sarpedon stalwart as a god
impelled him to charge the wall and break it down.
He quickly called Hippolochus' son: "Glaucus,
why do they hold us both in honor, first by far   360
with pride of place, choice meats and brimming cups,
in Lycia where all our people look on us like gods?
Why make us lords of estates along the Xanthus' banks,
rich in vineyards and plowland rolling wheat?
So that now the duty's ours—
we are the ones to head our Lycian front,
brace and fling ourselves in the blaze of war,
so a comrade strapped in combat gear may say,
'Not without fame, the men who rule in Lycia,
these kings of ours who eat fat cuts of lamb   370
and drink sweet wine, the finest stock we have.
But they owe it all to their own fighting strength—
our great men of war, they lead our way in battle!'
Ah my friend, if you and I could escape this fray
and live forever, never a trace of age, immortal,
I would never fight on the front lines again
or command you to the field where men win fame.
But now, as it is, the fates of death await us,
thousands poised to strike, and not a man alive

can flee them or escape—so in we go for attack!   380
Give our enemy glory or win it for ourselves!"

Glaucus did not turn back or shun that call—
on they charged, leading the Lycians' main mass.
And Peteos' son Menestheus cringed to see them
heading straight for his bastion, hurling ruin on . . .
He scanned the Achaean rampart: where could he find
some chief, some captain to fight disaster off his men?
He spotted the Great and Little Ajax, gluttons for battle,
flanking Teucer fresh from his shelter, side-by-side.
But Menestheus could not reach them with a shout—   390
the din was deafening, war cries hitting the skies,
spears battering shields and helmets' horsehair crests
and the huge gates all bolted shut, but against them there
the Trojans tensed and heaved, trying to smash them down
and force a passage through. At once Menestheus
sped a herald to Ajax: "Run for it, quick one,
call Great Ajax here—
both of them, better yet, that's best of all.
Headlong ruin's massing against us quickly.
Lycia's captains are bearing down too hard,   400
fierce as they always were in past attacks.
But if fighting's flaring up in their own sector,
at least let the rugged giant Ajax come alone
with Teucer the master archer at his side."

A brisk command, and the runner snapped to it—
he dashed along the wall of the Argive men-at-arms
till he reached the two Aeantes, stopped and shouted,
"Ajax—Ajax! Chiefs of the Argives armed in bronze,
the favorite son of Peteos dear to immortals
needs you at his strongpoint—hurry, come,   410
just for a moment, meet the crisis there.
Both of you, better yet, that's best of all.
Headlong ruin's massing against us quickly.
Lycia's captains are bearing down too hard,
fierce as they always were in past attacks.
But if fighting's flaring up in your own sector,

at least let the rugged giant Ajax come alone
with Teucer the master archer at his side!"

And Telamon's giant son agreed at once.
He called out to his smaller, faster brother   420
with orders flying, "Ajax, you stay here,
you and the burly Lycomedes stand your ground,
keep our Danaans fighting here with all they've got.
I'm on my way over there to meet this new assault—
I'll soon be back, once I've helped our friends."

And with that Telamonian Ajax strode off
with his brother Teucer, his own father's son,
and Pandion cradling Teucer's long curved bow.
Holding close to the wall, they picked their way
until they reached the brave Menestheus' bastion.   430
There they found the defenders packed, hard-pressed
as the Lycians' stalwart lords and captains stormed
like a black tornado up against the breastworks—
both men flung themselves in attack, the war cries broke.

And Telamon's son was the first to kill his man,
Sarpedon's comrade, Epicles great with heart.
He brought him down with a glinting jagged rock,
massive, top of the heap behind the rampart's edge,
no easy lift for a fighter even in prime strength,
working with both hands, weak as men are now.   440
Giant Ajax hoisted it high and hurled it down,
crushed the rim of the fighter's four-horned helmet
and cracked his skull to splinters, bloody pulp—
and breakneck down like a diver went the Trojan
plunging off and away from the steep beetling tower
as life breath left his bones.
                              And Glaucus next . . .
Hippolochus' brawny son was scrambling up the wall
when Teucer's arrow winged him from high aloft,
just where he saw his shoulder blade laid bare,
and stopped his lust for battle. Down he jumped   450

from the wall in secret, fast, so no Achaean
could see him hit and bellow out in triumph.
Soon as he noticed Glaucus slipping clear,
the pain overcame Sarpedon
but even so he never forgot *his* lust for battle.
He lunged in with a spear at Thestor's son Alcmaon,
stabbed him, dragged out the shaft as the victim,
caving into the spear's pull, pitched headfirst
and his fine bronze armor clashed against his corpse.
And Sarpedon clawing the rampart now with powerful hands,   460
wrenched hard and the whole wall came away, planks and all
and the rampart stood exposed, top defenses stripped—
Sarpedon had made a gaping breach for hundreds.

But Teucer and Ajax, aiming at him together,
shot!—Teucer's arrow hitting the gleaming belt
that cinched his body-shield around his chest—
but Zeus brushed from his son the deadly spirits:
not by the ships' high sterns would his Sarpedon die.
Ajax lunged at the man, he struck his shield but the point
would not pierce through, so he beat him back in rage   470
and he edged away from the breastwork just a yard.
Not that Sarpedon yielded all the way, never,
his heart still raced with hopes of winning glory,
whirling, shouting back to his splendid Lycians,
"Lycians—why do you slack your fighting-fury now?
It's hard for me, strong as I am, single-handed
to breach the wall and cut a path to the ships—
come, shoulder-to-shoulder!
The more we've got, the better the work will go!"

So he called, and dreading their captain's scorn   480
they bore down fiercer, massing round Sarpedon now
but against their bulk the Argives closed ranks,
packed tight behind the wall,
and a desperate battle flared between both armies.
Lycian stalwarts could not force the Achaeans back,
breach their wall and burst through to the ships,

nor could Achaean spearmen hurl the Lycians back,
clear of the rampart, once they'd made their stand.
As two farmers wrangle hard over boundary-stones,
measuring rods in hand, locked in a common field,   490
and fight it out on the cramped contested strip
for equal shares of turf—so now the rocky bastion
split the troops apart and across the top they fought,
hacked at each other, chopped the oxhides round their chests,
the bucklers full and round, skin-shields, tassels flying.
Many were wounded, flesh ripped by the ruthless bronze
whenever some fighter wheeled and bared his back
but many right through the buckler's hide itself.
Everywhere—rocks, ramparts, breastworks swam
with the blood of Trojans, Argives, both sides,   500
but still the Trojans could not rout the Argives.
They held tight as a working widow holds the scales,
painstakingly grips the beam and lifts the weight
and the wool together, balancing both sides even,
struggling to win a grim subsistence for her children.
So powerful armies drew their battle line dead even
till, at last, Zeus gave Hector the son of Priam
the greater glory—the first to storm the wall.
Hector loosed a piercing cry at his men:
"Drive, drive, my stallion-breaking Trojans!   510
Breach the Achaean rampart! Hurl your fire now—
a blazing inferno of fire against their ships!"

                                    So he cried,
driving them on, and all ears rang with his cries
and a tight phalanx launched straight at the wall,
brandishing sharp spears, swarming the bastions
as Hector grappled a boulder, bore it up and on.
It stood at the gates, huge, blunt at the base
but spiked to a jagged point
and no two men, the best in the whole realm,
could easily prize it up from earth and onto a wagon,   520
weak as men are now—but he quickly raised and shook it
as Zeus the son of Cronus with Cronus' twisting ways
made it a light lift for Hector all on his own.

As a shepherd lifts a ram's fleece with ease,
plucks it up with a hand—no weight at all to him—
so Hector raised the rock, bore it straight for the doors
that blocked the gateway, powerful, thickset, the pair
towering up with two bars on the inside, crossing over
each other, shot home with a bolt to pin them firm.
Planting his body right in front, legs spread wide,   530
his weight in the blow to give it total impact,
Hector hurled at the gates, full center, smashing
the hinges left and right and the boulder tore through,
dropped with a crash and both gates groaned and thundered—
the doorbars could not hold, the planking shattered up
in a flying storm of splinters under the rock's force
and Hector burst through in glory, his face dark
as the sudden rushing night but he blazed on in bronze
and terrible fire broke from the gear that wrapped his body,
two spears in his fists. No one could fight him, stop him,   540
none but the gods as Hector hurtled through the gates
and his eyes flashed fire. And whirling round
he cried to his Trojans, shouting through the ruck,
"The wall, storm the wall!"

                                        They rushed to obey him,
some swarming over the top at once, others streaming in
through the sturdy gateways—Argives scattering back in terror,
back by the hollow hulls, the uproar rising, no way out, no end—

BOOK THIRTEEN

Battling
for the Ships

But once Zeus had driven Hector and Hector's Trojans
hard against the ships, he left both armies there,
milling among the hulls to bear the brunt
and wrenching work of war—no end in sight—
while Zeus himself, his shining eyes turned north,
gazed a world away to the land of Thracian horsemen,
the Mysian fighters hand-to-hand and the lordly Hippemolgi
who drink the milk of mares, and the Abii, most decent men alive.
But not a moment more would he turn his shining eyes to Troy.
Zeus never dreamed in his heart a single deathless god   10
would go to war for Troy's or Achaea's forces now.

But the mighty god of earthquakes was not blind.
He kept his watch, enthralled by the rush of battle,

aloft the summit of timbered Samos facing Thrace.
From there the entire Ida ridge swung clear in view,
the city of Priam clear and the warships of Achaea.
Climbing out of the breakers, there Poseidon sat
and pitied the Argives beaten down by Trojan troops
and his churning outrage rose against the Father.

Suddenly down from the mountain's rocky crags   20
Poseidon stormed with giant, lightning strides
and the looming peaks and tall timber quaked
beneath his immortal feet as the sea lord surged on.
Three great strides he took, on the fourth he reached his goal,
Aegae port where his famous halls are built in the green depths,
the shimmering golden halls of the god that stand forever.
Down Poseidon dove and yoked his bronze-hoofed horses
onto his battle-car, his pair that raced the wind
with their golden manes streaming on behind them,
and strapping the golden armor round his body,   30
seized his whip that coils lithe and gold
and boarded his chariot launching up and out,
skimming the waves, and over the swells they came,
dolphins leaving their lairs to sport across his wake,
leaping left and right—well they knew their lord.
And the sea heaved in joy, cleaving a path for him
and the team flew on in a blurring burst of speed,
the bronze axle under the war-car never flecked with foam,
the stallions vaulting, speeding Poseidon toward Achaea's fleet.

There is a vast cave, down in the dark sounding depths,   40
mid-sea between Tenedos and Imbros' rugged cliffs . . .
Here the god of the earthquake drove his horses down,
he set them free of the yoke and flung before them
heaps of ambrosia, fodder for them to graze.
Round their hoofs he looped the golden hobbles
never broken, never slipped, so there they'd stand,
stock-still on the spot to wait their lord's return
and off Poseidon strode to Achaea's vast encampment.

But the Trojans swarmed like flame, like a whirlwind
following Hector son of Priam blazing on nonstop,   50
their war cries shattering, crying as one man—
their hopes soaring to take the Argive ships
and slaughter all their best against the hulls.
But the ocean king who grips and shakes the earth,
rising up from the offshore swell, urged the Argives,
taking the build and tireless voice of Calchas.
First the god commanded the Great and Little Ajax,
hungry for war as both men were already, "Ajax, Ajax!
Both of you—fight to save the Achaean armies,
call up your courage, no cringing panic now!   60
At other points on the line I have no fear
of the Trojans' hands, invincible as they seem—
troops who had stormed our massive wall in force—
our men-at-arms will hold them all at bay.
But here I fear the worst, I dread a breakthrough.
Here this firebrand, rabid Hector leads the charge,
claiming to be the son of high and mighty Zeus.
But the two of you, if only a god could make you
stand fast yourselves, tense with all your power,
and command the rest of your men to stand fast too—   70
then you could hurl him back from the deep-sea ships,
hard as he hurls against you, even if Zeus himself
impels the madman on."
                              In the same breath the god
who shakes the mainland struck both men with his staff
and filled their hearts with strength and striking force,
put spring in their limbs, their feet and fighting hands.
Then off he sped himself with the speed of a darting hawk
that soaring up from a sheer rock face, hovering high,
swoops at the plain to harry larks and swallows—
so the lord of the earthquake sped away from both.   80
First of the two to know the god was rapid Ajax.
Oileus' son alerted Telamon's son at once:
"Ajax, since one of the gods who hold Olympus,
a god in a prophet's shape, spurs us on to fight
beside the ships—and I tell you he's not Calchas,

seer of the gods who scans the flight of birds . . .
The tracks in his wake, his stride as he sped away—
I know him at once, with ease—no mistaking the gods.
And now, what's more, the courage inside my chest
is racing faster for action, full frontal assault—   90
feet quiver beneath me, hands high for the onset!"

And Telamonian Ajax joined him, calling out,
"I can feel it too, now, the hands on my spear,
invincible hands quivering tense for battle, look—
the power rising within me, feet beneath me rushing me on!
I even long to meet this Hector in single combat,
blaze as he does nonstop for bloody war!"

So they roused each other, exulting in the fire,
the joy of battle the god excited in their hearts.
And he sped to the rear to stir more ranks of Argives,   100
men refreshing their strength against the fast ships,
dead on their feet from the slogging work of war—
and anguish caught their hearts to see the Trojans,
troops who had stormed their massive wall in force.
They watched that assault, weeping freely now . . .
they never thought they would fight free of death.
But a light urging sent by the god of earthquakes
rippled through their lines and whipped battalions on.
Spurring Teucer and Leitus first with bracing orders,
then the fighting Peneleos, Thoas and Deipyrus,   110
Meriones and Antilochus, both strong with the war cry,
Poseidon pressed them on with winging charges: "Shame—
you Argives, raw recruits—and I, I trusted in you,
certain that if you fight you'll save our ships!
But if *you* hang back from the grueling battle now,
your day has dawned to be crushed by Trojans. What disgrace—
a marvel right before my eyes! A terrible thing . . .
and I never dreamed the war would come to this:
the Trojans advancing all the way to our ships,
men who up till now had panicked like deer,   120
food in the woods for jackals, leopards, wolves—

helpless, racing for dear life, all fight gone.
For months on end the Trojans would have no heart
to stand and face the Argives' rage and bloody hands.
Not for a moment. Ah but now, quite exposed,
far from Troy they battle around our hollow ships,
thanks to our leader's weakness, our armies' slacking off.
Our men fight with *him*. They'd rather drop and die
by our fast trim ships than rise to their defense.
And what if it's all true and the man's to blame—   130
lord of the far-flung kingdoms, hero Agamemnon—
because he spurned the famous runner Achilles?
How on earth can we hang back from combat now?
Heal our feuds at once! Surely they *can* be healed,
the hearts of the brave. How can you hold back
your combat-fury any longer? Not with honor—
you, the finest men in all our ranks . . .
Why, not even I would rail against that man,
that worthless coward who cringes from the fighting.
But you, I round on you with all my heart. Weaklings!   140
You'll make the crisis worse at any moment with this,
this hanging back. Each of you get a grip on yourself—
where's your pride, your soldier's sense of shame?
A great battle rises before us! Look—Hector
the king of the war cry fights beside our ships,
assaulting in all his force. Hector's crashed our gates,
he's burst the tremendous bar!"

                                        His voice like a shock wave,
the god of the earthquake spurred the Argive fighters on—
battalions forming around the two Aeantes, full strength,
crack battalions the god of war would never scorn,   150
rearing midst their ranks, nor would Pallas Athena
driver of armies. Here were the best picked men
detached in squads to stand the Trojan charge
and shining Hector: a wall of them bulked together,
spear-by-spear, shield-by-shield, the rims overlapping,
buckler-to-buckler, helm-to-helm, man-to-man massed tight
and the horsehair crests on glittering helmet horns brushed
as they tossed their heads, the battalions bulked so dense,

shoulder-to-shoulder close, and the spears they shook
in daring hands packed into jagged lines of battle—   160
single-minded fighters facing straight ahead,
Achaeans primed for combat.
                              Trojans pounded down on them!
Tight formations led by Hector careering breakneck on
like a deadly rolling boulder torn from a rock face—
a river swollen with snow has wrenched it from its socket,
immense floods breaking the bank's grip, and the reckless boulder
bounding high, flying with timber rumbling under it,
nothing can stop it now, hurtling on undaunted
down, down till it hits the level plain
and then it rolls no more for all its wild rush.   170
So Hector threatened at first to rampage through
the Argives' ships and shelters and reach the sea
with a single sudden charge, killing all the way.
But once he crashed against those dense battalions
dead in his tracks he stopped, crushed up against them:
sons of Achaea faced him now, stabbing away with swords,
with two-edged spears, hoisting him off their lines—
and he gave ground, staggering, reeling, shouting out
to his troops with shrill cries, "Trojans! Lycians!
Dardan skirmishers hand-to-hand—stand by me here!   180
They cannot hold me off any longer, these Achaeans,
not even massed like a wall against me here—
they'll crumble under my spear, well I know,
if the best of immortals really drives me on,
Hera's lord whose thunder drums the sky!"
                                        So he shouted,
lashing the rage and fighting-fury in every Trojan.
And breaking out of their ranks Deiphobus strode,
the son of Priam fired for feats of arms, there,
thrusting his balanced round buckler before him,
step by springy step on the balls of his feet,   190
pressing forward under his shield. But Meriones,
taking aim at Deiphobus, hurled his flashing spear
and struck—no miss!—right in the bull's-hide boss
but the spear did not ram through, far from it,

the long shaft snapped at the spearhead's socket—
the Trojan had thrust his shield at arm's length,
shrinking before the expert marksman's lance.
But now Meriones pulled back to his cohorts,
stung with rage for two defeats at once:
victory shattered, spearshaft smashed to bits.   200
He went on the run to Achaea's ships and shelters,
out for the heavy lance he'd left aslant his hut.

The rest fought on with deafening war cries rising.
Teucer was first to kill his man, a son of Mentor,
breeder of stallions, the rugged spearman Imbrius.
He had lived in Pedaeon, before the Argives came,
and wed a bastard daughter of Priam, Medesicaste,
but once the rolling ships of Achaea swept ashore,
home he came to Troy where he shone among the Trojans,
living close to Priam, who prized him like his sons.   210
Under his ear the son of Telamon stabbed with a heavy lance,
wrenched the weapon out and down he went like a tall ash
on a landmark mountain ridge that glistens far and wide—
chopped down by an ax, its leaves running with sap,
strewn across the earth . . . So Imbrius fell,
the fine bronze armor clashing against him hard.
Teucer charged forward, mad to strip that gear
but as Teucer charged, Hector flung his lance—
a glint of bronze—but the Argive saw it coming,
dodged to the side and it missed him by an inch   220
and hit Amphimachus, Cteatus' son and Actor's heir,
the shaft slashed his chest as he ran toward the front
and down he went, thundering, armor clanging round him.
And Hector rushed to tear the helmet off his head,
snug on Amphimachus' brows, the gallant soldier—
Hector rushing in and Ajax lunged with a spear
yet the burnished weapon could not pierce his skin,
Hector's whole body was cased in tremendous bronze.
But Ajax did stab home at the shield's jutting bulge,
beating Hector back with enormous driving force   230
and he gave ground, back and away from both corpses

as Argives hauled them from the fighting by the heels.
The captains of Athens, Stichius, staunch Menestheus,
bore Amphimachus back to Achaea's waiting lines.
But the two Aeantes blazing in battle-fury
saw to Imbrius now . . . as two lions seizing a goat
from under the guard of circling rip-tooth hounds,
lugging the carcass on through dense matted brush,
hoist it up from the earth in their big grinding jaws.
So the ramping, crested Aeantes hoisted Imbrius high,   240
stripping his gear in mid-air, and the Little Ajax,
raging over Amphimachus' death, lopped the head
from the corpse's limp neck and with one good heave
sent it spinning into the milling fighters like a ball,
right at the feet of Hector, tumbling in the dust.

And then the heart of Poseidon quaked with anger—
his own grandson brought down in the bloody charge.
He surged along the Achaean ships and shelters,
spurring Argives, piling griefs on Trojans.
The famous spearman Idomeneus crossed his path—   250
he'd come from a friend who just emerged from battle
gashed in back of the kneecap, gouged by whetted bronze.
That soldier the comrades carried off but Idomeneus,
giving the healers orders, made for his own tent
though he still yearned for action face-to-face.
And the god of earthquakes only fueled his fire,
taking the voice of Thoas, son of Andraemon,
king over all Pleuron, craggy Calydon too
and Aetolian men he ruled revered him like a god:
"Idomeneus, captain of Cretans under arms—   260
where have the threats all gone
that sons of Achaea leveled at these Trojans?"

The Cretan captain Idomeneus answered, "Thoas—
no man's to blame now, so far as I can tell.
Every one of us knows the ropes in war.
No one here's in the grip of bloodless fear,
collapsing in cowardice, ducking the grim assault.

No, this is the pleasure of overweening Zeus, it seems—
to kill the Achaeans here, our memory blotted out
a world away from Argos. But you, Thoas,   270
you who were always rock-steady in battle
and braced the ones you saw go slack and flinch—
don't quit now, Thoas, urge each man you find!"

The god of earthquakes answered back, "Idomeneus—
may that man, that coward never get home from Troy—
let him linger here, ripping sport for the dogs,
whoever shirks the fight while this day lasts.
Quick, take up your gear and off we go.
Shoulder-to-shoulder, swing to the work, we must—
just two as we are—if we hope to make some headway.   280
The worst cowards, banded together, have their power
but you and I have got the skill to fight their best!"

With that he strode away, a god in the wars of men.
As soon as Idomeneus reached his well-built shelter
he strapped his burnished armor round his body,
grasped two spears and out he ran like a lightning bolt
the Father grips and flings from brilliant Olympus,
a dazzling sign to men—a blinding forked flash.
So the bronze flared on his chest as out he rushed
but his rough-and-ready aide-in-arms Meriones   290
intercepted him just outside the tent . . .
He was on his way for a new bronze spear to use
and staunch Idomeneus shouted out, "Meriones—
racing son of Molus, brother-in-arms, old friend,
why back from the lines, why leave the fight behind?
Taken a wound, some spearhead sapped your strength?
Or come with a word for me? Does someone need me?
I have no mind to sit it out in the shelters—
what I love is battle!"

                Never flustered,
the cool-headed Meriones took his point: 300
"Idomeneus, captain of Cretans under arms,
I've come for a spear to fight with,

if you still have one left inside your tents.
I've just splintered the lance I used to carry,
smashed it against his shield—swaggering Deiphobus."

But the Cretan captain Idomeneus countered, "Spears?
If it's spears you want, you'll find not one but twenty,
all propped on my shelter's shining inner wall:
Trojan weapons, stripped from the men I kill.
It's not *my* way, I'd say, to fight at a distance,   310
out of enemy range.
So I take my plunder—spears, bossed shields,
helmets and breastplates, gleaming, polished bright."

"And so do I, by god!"—the cool Meriones blazed up
in his own defense—"They crowd my ship and shelter,
hoards of Trojan plunder, but out of reach just now.
Though I never forgot my courage, I can tell you—
not I, there at the front where we win glory,
there I take my stand whenever a pitched battle
rears its head. Another Achaean armed in bronze   320
may well be blind to the way I fight. Not you—
you are the one who knows me best, I'd say."

And the Cretan captain Idomeneus answered warmly,
"I *know* your style, your courage. No need for you to tell it.
If we all formed up along the ships right now,
our best men picked for an ambush—
that's where you really spot a fighter's mettle,
where the brave and craven always show their stripes.
The skin of the coward changes color all the time,
he can't get a grip on himself, he can't sit still,   330
he squats and rocks, shifting his weight from foot to foot,
his heart racing, pounding inside the fellow's ribs,
his teeth chattering—he dreads some grisly death.
But the skin of the brave soldier never blanches.
He's all control. Tense but no great fear.
The moment he joins his comrades packed in ambush
he prays to wade in carnage, cut-and-thrust at once.

Who could deny your nerve there, your fighting hands?
Why, even if you were badly wounded in battle,
winged by a shaft or gored by a blade close-up,   340
the weapon would never hit you behind, in neck or back—
it would pierce your chest or guts as you press forward,
lusting for all the champions' lovely give-and-take.
On with it! No more standing round like bragging boys—
someone will dress us down, and roughly too.
Off you go to my shelter. Choose a sturdy spear."

    Meriones a match for the rapid god of battles
ran for the tent, seized a fine bronze lance
and hot for action rushed to catch his captain.
And *he* went on to war as grim as murderous Ares,   350
his good son Panic stalking beside him, tough, fearless,
striking terror in even the combat-hardened veteran, yes,
both of them marching out of Thrace, geared to fight the Ephyri
or Phlegians great with heart, but they turn deaf ears
to the prayers of both sides at once, handing glory
to either side they choose. So on they marched,
Meriones and Idomeneus commanders of armies
strode to battle helmed in gleaming bronze,
Meriones first to ask, "Son of Deucalion,
where do you say we join the fighting now?   360
Right of the whole engagement, work the center
or go at the left flank? That's the place, I think—
nowhere else are the long-haired Argives so outfought."

    The Cretan captain Idomeneus answered quickly,
"Plenty of others can shield the ships mid-line,
the two Aeantes, Teucer the best Achaean archer,
an expert too at fighting head-to-head.
They'll give royal Hector his fill of blows,
strong on attack, glutton for battle as he is.
Berserk for blood, he'll find it uphill work   370
to beat their valor down, matchless hands at war,
and gut our ships with fire—unless almighty Zeus
should fling a torch at the fast trim ships himself.

When it comes to men, Great Ajax yields to no one,
no mortal who eats Demeter's grain, I tell you,
one you can break with bronze and volleyed rocks.
Not even Achilles who smashes whole battalions—
he would never yield to him in a stand-up fight
though in downfield racing none can touch the man.
So lead us on to the left flank—we'll soon see   380
if we give our enemy glory or win it for ourselves."

And quick as the god of war Meriones led the way
till they reached the front his captain pointed out.

When the Trojans saw Idomeneus fierce as fire,
him and his aide-in-arms in handsome blazoned gear,
they all cried out and charged them through the press
and a sudden, pitched battle broke at the ships' sterns.
As gale-winds swirl and shatter under the shrilling gusts
on days when drifts of dust lie piled thick on the roads
and winds whip up the dirt in a dense whirling cloud—   390
so the battle broke, storming chaos, troops inflamed,
slashing each other with bronze, carnage mounting,
manslaughtering combat bristling with rangy spears,
the honed lances brandished in hand and ripping flesh
and the eyes dazzled now, blind with the glare of bronze,
glittering helmets flashing, breastplates freshly burnished,
shields fiery in sunlight, fighters plowing on in a mass.
Only a veteran steeled at heart could watch that struggle
and still thrill with joy and never feel the terror.

The two powerful sons of Cronus, Zeus and Poseidon,   400
their deathless spirits warring against each other,
were building mortal pains for seasoned heroes.
Zeus willing a Trojan victory, Hector's victory,
lifting the famous runner Achilles' glory higher,
but he had no lust to destroy the whole Argive force
before the walls of Troy—all the Father wanted
was glory for Thetis and Thetis' strong-willed son.
But Poseidon surging in secret out of the gray surf

went driving into the Argive ranks and lashed them on,
agonized for the fighters beaten down by Trojans,   410
and his churning outrage rose against great Zeus.
Both were gods of the same line, a single father,
but Zeus was the elder-born and Zeus knew more.
And so Poseidon shrank from defending allies
out in the open—all in secret, always
armed like a man the god kept urging armies on.
Both gods knotted the rope of strife and leveling war,
strangling both sides at once by stretching the mighty cable,
never broken, never slipped, that snapped the knees of thousands.

    And there, grizzled gray as he was, he spurred his men,   420
Idomeneus ramping amidst the Trojans, striking panic.
He finished Othryoneus, a man who'd lived in Cabesus,
one who had just come at the rousing word of war
and asked for Priam's loveliest daughter, Cassandra—
with no bride-price offered—
but Othryoneus promised a mighty work of battle:
he would rout the unwilling Argives out of Troy.
And old King Priam bent his head in assent,
promised the man his daughter, so on he fought,
trusting his life to oaths taken, promises struck—   430
till Idomeneus took his life with a glinting spear,
struck him coming on with his high, swaggering strides.
His breastplate could not save him, the bronze he always wore,
and the shaft pierced his bowels. He fell with a crash
as Idomeneus boasted, shouting over him, "Bravo,
Othryoneus, bravo to you beyond all men alive!
If you can really keep your promise to Priam now,
who promised his daughter—a true blood-wedding day!
Look, we'll make you a promise—we'll keep it too.
We'll hand you Agamemnon's loveliest daughter,   440
lead her here from Argos, marry her off to you
if you'll just help us raze the walls of Troy.
Just step this way! So we can come to terms
by the deep-sea ships and strike our marriage pact—
you'll find *our* price for brides not quite so killing!"

The hero seized his foot, dragging him through the rout.
But Asius leapt down to defend his comrade, just ahead
of his chariot-horses still held close by a driver,
the team snorting, panting over his shoulders—
Asius strained in fury to spear Idomeneus   450
but the Cretan took him first.
A spearhead punched his gullet under the chin
and the bronze point went ripping through his nape
and down the Trojan fell as an oak or white poplar falls
or towering pine that shipwrights up on a mountain
hew down with whetted axes for sturdy ship timber—
so he stretched in front of his team and chariot,
sprawled and roaring, clawing the bloody dust.
His driver out of his mind, what mind he had,
lost all nerve to wheel his horses round   460
and give the slip to his enemy's deadly hands
and staunch Antilochus speared him through the midriff.
His breastplate could not save him, the bronze he always wore,
and the lance impaled his guts—he gasped, convulsed
and out of his well-made car the Trojan pitched—
and as for his team, proud Nestor's son Antilochus
drove them out of the Trojans into Argive lines.

But raging in tears for Asius came Deiphobus
charging against Idomeneus, heaving a flashing spear—
but Idomeneus saw it coming, dodged the bronze point   470
by crouching under his buckler's full round cover.
He always carried it, layered with hide and ringed
with gleaming bronze, fitted with double cross-stays—
under it low he hunched and the brazen spear flew past
with a grating screech as the shaft grazed the shield.
But Deiphobus' strong swift hurl was not for nothing,
no, he caught Hypsenor, Hippasus' son the captain,
struck him under the midriff, slit his liver
and that instant the man's knees went limp.
Deiphobus shouted, vaunting in wild glory,   480
"Asius dies, but not without revenge!
Down to the god of death he goes, I tell you,

down to the mighty gates but thrilled at heart—
look at the escort I have sent him for the journey!"

The more he gloried, the more grief swept the Argives,
brave Antilochus most, his battle-passion rising,
stunned with pain but he would not fail Hypsenor.
He ran to straddle and hide him with his shield
as a brace of comrades shouldered up the fighter:
Echius' son Mecisteus helping good Alastor   490
bore him back to the hollow warships, groaning hard.

But Idomeneus never slacked his fury, always struggling
to plunge some Trojan soldier in deep shrouding night
or fall himself, beating disaster off his lines.
And here was a royal kill, the son of Aesyetes,
the hero Alcathous, son-in-law to Anchises,
wed to his eldest daughter, Hippodamia . . .
Her father and noble mother loved her dearly,
the pride of their halls excelling all her age
in beauty, works of the loom and good clear sense.   500
So the bravest man in the broad realm of Troy
took her hand in marriage, true, the very man
Poseidon crushed at the hands of Idomeneus here,
spellbinding his shining eyes, crippling his fine legs.
He couldn't escape—no retreat, no dodging the stroke,
like a pillar or tree crowned with leaves, rearing,
standing there stock-still as the hero Idomeneus
stabbed him square in the chest
and split the bronze plate that cased his ribs,
gear that had always kept destruction off his flesh   510
but it cracked and rang out now, ripped by the spear.
Down Alcathous crashed and the point stuck in his heart
and the heart in its last throes jerked and shook the lance—
the butt-end quivering into the air till suddenly
rugged Ares snuffed its fury out, dead still.
And Idomeneus shouted, vaunting in wild glory,
"Now, Deiphobus, now shall we call it quits at last?
Three men killed for the one you bragged about so much!

Come here, you idiot—stand up to me yourself
so you can see what cut of man I am. Look,   520
a son of Zeus come here to face you down.
He first bore Minos, watch and ward of Crete,
then Minos bore an illustrious son Deucalion, yes,
and Deucalion fathered me to command a race of men
through the length and breadth of Crete, and now our ships
have borne me here to your shores to be your curse,
a curse to your father, curse to the men of Troy!"

So he taunted. Deiphobus' mind was torn—
should he pull back and call a friend to his side,
some hardy Trojan, or take the Argive on alone?   530
As he thought it out, the first way seemed the best.
He went for Aeneas, found him out on the flank
and fringe of battle, standing idle, forever
angered at Priam who always scrimped his honors,
brave as Aeneas was among the Trojan fighters.
Deiphobus reached him soon with winging words:
"Aeneas, captain, counselor, how we need you now!
Shield your sister's husband—if grief can touch your heart.
Follow me, fight for Alcathous, your brother-in-law
who reared you at home when you were just a boy.   540
The famous spearman Idomeneus cut him down."
                                                       Fighting words—
that began to stir the rage inside Aeneas' chest
and out for blood he charged Idomeneus now.
But nothing could make *him* panic—no green boy,
he stood his ground like a wild mountain boar,
trusting his strength, standing up to a rout of men
that scream and swoop against him off in a lonely copse,
the ridge of his back bristling, his eyes flashing fire,
he grinds his teeth, champing to beat back dogs and men.
So Idomeneus, famous spearman, stood his ground,   550
he never gave an inch with Aeneas charging in,
quick to the rescue. Idomeneus called his comrades,
glancing fast at Ascalaphus, Aphareus, Deipyrus,
Meriones and Antilochus, both strong with the war cry—

he called them closer, his winging orders flying:
"Over here, my friends! I'm all alone, defend me!
I fear Aeneas—terribly—coming on, top speed,
bearing down on me now and filled with power,
enormous power to take men down in battle.
He's just in the first flush of youth, what's more,   560
the greatest power of all. If we were the same age,
I tell you, just as the same fury fills us both—
at a single stroke he'd bear off glory now
or I'd bear it off myself!"
           So the Cretan yelled
and all his comrades came in a pack with one will,
massing round him, bracing shields to shoulders.
But across the lines Aeneas called *his* comrades,
glancing fast at Deiphobus, Paris, brave Agenor,
all the Trojan captains who backed Aeneas here,
and fighters followed close behind like flocks   570
that follow the lead ram, leaving the pastureland
to drink at springs, and the shepherd's heart exults.
So now the heart of Aeneas leapt inside his chest
when he saw the flocks of fighters crowding in his wake.

    Round Alcathous' corpse they lunged in hand-to-hand
with their long spears, and the bronze around their chests
clashed out, a terrific din as they struck each other fiercely,
the lines jamming and two fighters rearing above the rest,
Idomeneus and Aeneas, both a match for Ares, charged
with their ruthless bronze to hack each other's flesh.   580
Aeneas was first—he aimed and hurled at Idomeneus
but the Cretan saw it coming, dodged the brazen tip
and Aeneas' lance plunged in the earth, quivering,
his arm's power poured in a wasted shot.
                Idomeneus—
he hurled and speared Oenomaus through the belly,
smashing his corslet just where the plates join
and the bronze spearhead spilled his entrails out
and down the Trojan crashed, grasping, clawing the dust.
Idomeneus wrenched his dark shaft from the corpse

but as for the dead man's burnished gear—no use.   590
The chief was helpless to rip it off his shoulders—
enemy weapons jolted him back with so much force
his legs buckled, the old driving power lost,
no dash left to dive for a spear or dodge one.
So there he stood, taking it all, beating away
the ruthless day of death. No more running now,
no quick leaps to sweep him clear of the fighting,
just backing, step by step . . .
                And Deiphobus taking aim
with his big glinting spear, forever hating the man
and he hurled and missed again—   600
but Deiphobus hit Ascalaphus with that shaft,
Ascalaphus son of the butcher god of battles—
the heavy spearshaft ran him through the shoulder
and down he thundered, scraping, clutching the dust.
But the giant bellowing Ares had heard nothing yet
of how his son went down in the mounting carnage.
On a crest of Olympus under golden clouds he sat,
the god of war held fast by the will of Zeus, aloof
where the other deathless gods were kept back from battle.

Still round Ascalaphus fighters kept on lunging in.   610
Deiphobus stripped away the corpse's gleaming helmet
but quick as the god of war Meriones leapt at *him,*
stabbed his outstretched arm and the blank-eyed helmet
slipped from his grasp, pounding the ground and clanging.
Meriones back on attack—a savage swoop like a vulture—
yanked the spear from the Trojan's shoulder joint
and back he drew into crowds of waiting troops.
But Polites swept up close to Deiphobus' side,
caught his brother around the waist with both arms
and dragged him clear of the heartbreaking skirmish,   620
far downfield till they reached his team of racers
standing behind the rear lines and rush of battle,
their driver and handsome chariot held in tow . . .
Then back to Troy they bore Deiphobus, groaning hard,
in agony, blood from his fresh wound pouring down his arm.

And still the rest fought on, relentless war cries rising.
Aeneas charging Aphareus, son of Caletor, slit open
his throat just turning toward Aeneas' ripping blade—
his head slumped to the side, shield crushing in on him,
helmet too, and courage-shattering death engulfed his corpse.   630
Next Antilochus, watching Thoon veer for a quick escape,
sprang and stabbed him, slashing away the whole vein
that runs the length of the back to reach the neck—
he severed it, sheared it clear
and the man went sprawling, back flat in the dust
and stretching out both hands to his friends-in-arms.
Antilochus closed to tear the gear from his shoulders,
glancing left and right as Trojans massed against him,
plunging from every side to batter down his shield
but they could not pierce that broad glistening hide—   640
no scoring his tender young flesh with ruthless bronze.
Not Antilochus, guarded now by the god of earthquakes
shielding, ringing the son of Nestor round, even in this,
this storm of spears. Antilochus never clear of enemies,
always wheeling, bracing to face them, his own spear
never resting, always brandished, quivering tense,
his courage primed to cut men down with a hurl
or charge them face-to-face.

                        His spear aimed in the melee—
but Adamas, Asius' son missed nothing, he saw it all,
rushed him, rammed Antilochus' buckler dead center   650
with sharp bronze but the blue-haired god Poseidon
crushed the spear, denied him the Argive's life.
Half his lance hung there in Antilochus' shield
like a charred stake, half dropped to the ground.
And back he shrank to his cohorts, dodging death
but hounding him as he went Meriones speared him
between the genitals and the navel—hideous wound,
the worst the god of battles deals to wretched men.
There the spear stuck. Hugging the shaft he writhed,
gasping, shuddering like some wild bull in the hills   660
that herdsmen shackle, trapping the beast with twisted ropes
and he fights them all the way as the men drag him off—

so he gasped with his wound. A little, not for long.
Till the hero Meriones moved in where he sprawled,
wrenched the spear from his corpse
and the dark came shrouding down across his eyes.

Helenus charged Deipyrus, cleft the side of his head
with a massive Thracian sword, smashed his helmet
and knocked it off. It fell to earth and an Argive
snatched it up as it rolled at soldiers' feet—   670
and the night came blinding down Deipyrus' eyes.

And anguish seized Menelaus lord of the war cry.
He went on the run at the fighting prophet Helenus,
all menace, madly shaking his whetted javelin
just as Helenus seized his bow by the handgrip.
Both let fly at each other, one launching out
with a sharp lance, one a shaft from the string—
and Helenus' arrow hit Atrides right on the chest,
on the breastplate's curve but the arrow sprang away.
High as the black-skin beans and chickpeas bounce and leap   680
from a big bladed shovel, flying across the threshing floor,
sped by a whistling wind and a winnower's sweeping stroke—
so the arrow flew from fighting Atrides' breastplate,
the keen shaft glancing, skittering off downfield.
But the lord of the war cry aimed for Helenus' hand
gripping his polished bow—and clean through his fist
the bronze spearhead drove and cracked the tensed weapon.
Back he fell to his massed companions, dodging death,
his hand dangling, dragging the long ashen shaft.
And gallant Agenor drew the spear from his hand   690
and bound it up in a band of tightly twisted wool,
a sling his aide retained for the good commander.

And now Pisander rushed Menelaus famed in arms
but a grim fate was rushing *him* to the stroke of death—
to be crushed in this hell of war by you, Menelaus.
Just as the two men closed, heading into each other,

Atrides missed—his spearshaft hooking off to the side—
Pisander stabbed his shield but the bronze could not bore through—
the huge hide blocked it, the shaft snapped at the socket.
Still the Trojan exulted, wild with hopes of triumph   700
as Menelaus, drawing his sword with silver studs,
leapt at Pisander, who clutched beneath his shield
his good bronze ax with its cleaving blade
set on a long smooth olive haft—

                                   A clash!
Both fighters at one great stroke
chopped at each other—Pisander hacked the horn
of the horsehair-crested helmet right at its ridge,
lunging as Menelaus hacked Pisander between the eyes,
the bridge of the nose, and bone cracked, blood sprayed
and both eyes dropped at his feet to mix in the dust—   710
he curled and crashed. Digging a heel in his chest
Menelaus stripped his gear and vaunted out in glory,
"So home you'll run from our racing ships, by god,
all as corpses—see, you death-defying Trojans?
Never sated with shattering war cries, are you?
Nor do you lack the other brands of outrage,
all that shame you heaped on me, you rabid dogs!
No fear in your hearts for the quaking rage of Zeus,
the thundering god of host and welcome stranger—
one day he'll raze your lofty city for you.   720
You Trojans who stole away my wedded wife
and hoards of riches too—for no reason, none—
my queen of the realm who hosted you with kindness.
And now you rampage on among our deep-sea ships,
wild to torch our hulls and kill our heroes—well,
you'll be stopped, somewhere, mad as you are for combat!
Zeus, Father Zeus, they say you excel all others . . .
all men and gods, in wisdom clear and calm—
but all this brutal carnage comes from *you*.
Look how you favor them, these reckless Trojans,   730
their fury always in uproar—no one can ever slake
their thirst for blood, for the great leveler, war!
One can achieve his fill of all good things,

even of sleep, even of making love . . .
rapturous song and the beat and sway of dancing.
A man will yearn for his fill of all these joys
before his fill of war. But not these Trojans—
no one can glut their lust for battle!"
                                        So he cried
and staunch Atrides stripped the gear from the corpse
and heaving the bloody bronze to eager comrades   740
swung to attack again, frontline assault.
                                There—
Harpalion charged Menelaus—King Pylaemenes' son
who'd followed his father into war at Troy
but he never reached his fatherland again.
He closed on Atrides, spear stabbing his shield
right on the boss but the bronze could not drive through,
so back he drew to his ranks, dodging death, glancing
left and right, fearing a lance would graze his flesh.
But Meriones caught him in full retreat, he let fly
with a bronze-tipped arrow, hitting his right buttock   750
up under the pelvic bone so the lance pierced the bladder.
He sank on the spot, hunched in his dear companion's arms,
gasping out his life as he writhed along the ground
like an earthworm stretched out in death, blood pooling,
soaking the earth dark red. Hardy Paphlagonians,
working over him, hoisting him onto a chariot,
bore him back to the sacred walls of Troy . . .
deep in grief while his father, weeping freely,
walked beside them now. No blood-price came his way.
Not for his son who breathed his last in battle.   760

    But Paris flared in rage at his comrade's death,
his friend and guest among all the Paphlagonians.
Incensed, he let loose with a bronze-tipped arrow
aimed at one Euchenor, son of the prophet Polyidus,
a decent, wealthy man who made his home in Corinth.
Well Euchenor knew that boarding the ships for Troy
meant certain death: his father told him so . . .
Time and again the strong old prophet said

he'd die in his own halls of a fatal plague
or go with the ships and die at Trojan hands.   770
So off Euchenor sailed, both to save his wealth
from the heavy fine the Argives made deserters pay
and himself from wasting illness—no slow plague for him.
Suddenly Paris struck him under the jaw and ear—
and life flew from his limbs
and the hateful darkness had him in its grip.

　　The rest fought on like a mass of whirling fire.
But Hector dear to Zeus had no idea, Hector
heard nothing of how his men, left of the ships,
were torn and mauled in the Argives' rough response.   780
The glory might even have gone to *them* at any moment,
so intent was the god who grips and shakes the earth
as he surged his Argives on and the god surged too,
adding his own immortal force in their defense.
But Hector kept on driving too—just at the point
where he first broke through the gates and wall he charged,
he smashed the Achaean lines, dense with armed men,
there where Protesilaus' and giant Ajax' ships
lay hauled up in the breaking, churning surf
and the wall to landward dipped low to the ground,   790
the weakest point where the fiercest fighting raged—
waves of Trojans, Trojan horse in assault.
　　　　　　　　　　　　　　　　Bulked against them,
Boeotian troops, Ionian troops with their long war-shirts,
Locrians, Phthians and men of Epea famed in battle
fought to stop this Hector hurtling at the ships.
Nothing they did could thrust him off their lines,
Prince Hector roaring on like a torch—not even
the picked Athenians led by Menestheus, Peteos' son
and backing him came Phidas, Stichius, brave Bias,
then the Epean units led by Meges, Phyleus' son,   800
Amphion, Dracius, and leading the Phthian ranks
came Medon flanking Podarces tough in skirmish.
Medon the bastard son of royal King Oileus,
Little Ajax' brother, but Medon lived in Phylace,

banished from native land—he'd killed a kinsman
dear to Oileus' wife, his stepmother Eriopis—
but Iphiclus son of Phylacus bore Podarces . . .
Brothers-in-arms, he and Medon led the Phthians,
out in the forefront of those gallant soldiers
fighting beside Boeotians now to save the ships.   810
But Oileus' son the racing Ajax—not for a moment,
not at all would he leave his giant brother Ajax,
shoulder-to-shoulder they fought together here:
close as a brace of wine-dark oxen matched in power,
dragging a bolted plow through packed fallow land
and the sweat rushes up at the roots of both their horns
and only the width of polished yoke keeps both beasts apart,
struggling up the furrow to cut the field's last strip.
So both men stood their ground, bracing man-to-man
and a flock of comrades, hardened combat veterans   820
followed the Great Ajax, ready to take his shield
whenever sweat and labor sapped his knees.
But no Locrians followed the hearty Little Ajax.
They had no love for stand-and-fight encounters—
had no crested bronze helmets to guard their heads,
no balanced shields in their grasp, no ashen spears,
only their bows and slings of springy, twisted wool.
Trusting these, they followed their chief to Troy,
shooting with these, salvo on pelting salvo,
they tore the Trojan battle lines to pieces.   830
So the men in heavy armor fought at the front,
they grappled Trojans and Hector helmed in bronze
while Locrians slung from the rear, safe, out of range,
till the Trojan troops forgot their lust for blood
as showering arrows raked their ranks with panic.

                                        Deadly going—
then and there the Trojans might have been rolled back,
far away from the ships and tents to wind-torn Troy
if Polydamas had not rushed to headstrong Hector:
"Impossible man! Won't you listen to reason?
Just because some god exalts you in battle   840
you think you can beat the rest at tactics too.

How can you hope to garner all the gifts at once?
One man is a splendid fighter—a god has made him so—
one's a dancer, another skilled at lyre and song,
and deep in the next man's chest farseeing Zeus
plants the gift of judgment, good clear sense.
And many reap the benefits of that treasure:
troops of men he saves, as he himself knows best.
So now I will tell you what seems best to me. Look,
the battle burns like a swirling crown around your head   850
but our valiant Trojans, once they scaled the wall—
some fall back from the front, idling in armor,
others soldier on, squads against mass formations,
scattering helter-skelter round the hulls.

                                 Draw back now!
Call the best of our captains here, this safe ground.
Then we can all fall in and plan our tactics well:
whether we fling ourselves against the ships—
if Zeus would care to hand us victory now—
or beat retreat from the beach and cut our losses.
I fear they'll pay us back for yesterday's triumph.   860
He waits by the ships, a man never sated with battle . . .
I doubt he'll keep from the fighting any longer,
not with all his war-lust!"

     So he urged. His plan won Hector over—
less danger, more success—and down he leapt
from his chariot fully armed and hit the ground,
calling out to Polydamas brisk, winged orders:
"You stay here, hold back our captains here.
I'm on my way over there to meet this new assault—
I'll soon be back, once I've given them clear commands."   870

     And out like a flashing snowcapped peak he moved,
shouting, sweeping on through his ranks and Trojan allies.
Squads of others swarmed and rallied around Polydamas,
Panthous' friendly son—they'd heard Hector's orders.
But Hector ranged the front to find his leaders,

hunting Deiphobus and the rugged warlord Helenus,
Adamas, Asius' son, and Asius son of Hyrtacus.
Where could he find them now? Find them he did,
no longer free of wounds, unhurt—not at all . . .
Adamas, Asius, both sprawled at Achaea's sterns,   880
dead at the Argives' hands. The others at home,
behind the walls, were gouged by shaft or sword.
But he quickly found one more, on the left flank
of the heart-wrenching carnage—royal Paris,
fair-haired Helen's consort was rousing comrades,
driving them back to battle. Once he gained his side
Hector raked his brother with insults, stinging taunts:
"Paris, appalling Paris! Our prince of beauty—
mad for women, you lure them all to ruin!
Where's Deiphobus? Helenus, rugged warlord?   890
Adamas, Asius' son, and Asius son of Hyrtacus—
where's Othryoneus, tell me.
Now all towering Troy is ruined top to bottom!
Now one thing's certain—your own headlong death!"

        And Paris, magnificent as a god, replied,
"Hector, bent on faulting a man without a fault?
At other times I might have shrunk from the fighting,
true, but not today. Mother bore me—even me—
not to be a coward through and through. Think,
since you fired our comrades' fury against the ships,   900
from that hour we've held our ground right here,
taking the Argives on, and nonstop, no rest.
Our comrades are dead, Hector,
those you inquire about with such concern . . .
Only Deiphobus and the rugged warlord Helenus
have made it back alive, wounded with sturdy spears,
both in the hand too, but Zeus beat off their deaths.
Now lead the way, wherever your fighting spirit bids you.
All of us right behind you, hearts intent on battle.
Nor do I think you'll find us short on courage,   910
long as our strength will last. Past his strength
no man can go, though he's set on mortal combat."

That brought his brother's warrior spirit round.
On they went where the thickest fighting broke,
churning round Cebriones, dauntless Polydamas,
Phalces, Orthaeus and veteran Polyphetes,
Palmys, Hippotion's two sons—Ascanius, Morys—
fresh reserves just come from Ascania's fertile soil,
just last morning, but now great Zeus incited all-out war.
Down the Trojans came like a squall of brawling gale-winds   920
blasting down with the Father's thunder, loosed on earth
and a superhuman uproar bursts as they pound the heavy seas,
the giant breakers seething, battle lines of them roaring,
shoulders rearing, exploding foam, waves in the vanguard,
waves rolling in from the rear. So on the Trojans came,
waves in the vanguard, waves from the rear, closing,
bronze men glittering, following captains, closing
and Hector led the way, a match for murderous Ares—
Priam's son holding his balanced shield before him,
tough with oxhides, studded thick with bronze   930
and round his temples the flashing helmet shook.
He plowed forward, testing enemy lines at all points
to see if they'd crack before him—charging under his shield
but he could not overpower the Argives' stiff resolve
and Ajax hulking forward with big strides, the first
to challenge Hector: "Madman! Here, come closer—
trying to frighten Argives? Why waste your breath?
No, no, it's not that we lack the skill in battle,
it's just the brutal lash of Zeus that beats us down.
Your hopes soar, I suppose, to gut and crush our ships?   940
Well *we* have strong arms too, arms to defend those ships—
and long before *that* your city packed with people
will fall beneath our hands, plundered to rubble.
And you, I say, the day draws near when off you run
and pray to Father Zeus and the other deathless gods
to make your full-maned horses swifter than hawks—
whipping dust from the plain to sweep you back to Troy!"

     Clear on the right a bird winged past to seal those words,
a soaring eagle swooping. Spirits high with the sign,

the Argive armies cheered. But bent on glory   950
Hector answered the giant Ajax taunt for taunt:
"Enough of your blustering threats, you clumsy ox—
what loose talk, what rant!
I wish I were as surely the son of storming Zeus
for all my days—and noble Hera gave me birth
and I were prized as they prize Athena and Apollo—
as surely as this day will bring your Argives death,
down to the last man. And you will die with the rest.
If you *have* the daring to stand against my heavy spear
its point will rip your soft warm skin to shreds!   960
Then, then you'll glut the dogs and birds of Troy
with your fat and flesh—cut down by the beaked ships!"

And loosing a savage yell, Hector led the way
and his captains followed close with unearthly cries
and Trojan ranks behind them crying shrill.
But facing them the Achaean ranks cried back,
not forgetting their courage, braced hard for assault
as the Trojans' bravest charged and roars from both armies
struck the high clear skies, the lightning world of Zeus.

BOOK FOURTEEN

Hera
Outflanks Zeus

But the mounting cries of war could not escape old Nestor,
pausing over his wine. He turned to Asclepius' son
with an urgent, winged word:
"Think, noble Machaon, what shall we do now?
The cries are fiercer—fighters beside the ships!
You sit here, keep drinking the shining wine now,
till well-kempt Hecamede draws you a warm bath,
steaming hot, and washes away that clotted blood.
But I am off to a lookout point to learn the truth."

With that he seized the well-wrought shield of his son, 10
Thrasymedes breaker of horses—it lay in a corner,
all glowing bronze, while the boy used his father's.
Gripping a sturdy spear, bronze-edged and sharp,
he no sooner left his tent than stopped at once—

what a grim, degrading piece of work he saw.
Friends routed, enemies harrying friends in panic,
the Trojans riding high—the Argive wall in ruins.
Nestor stood there, stunned.
As a huge ground swell boils up on the open seas,
soundless, foreboding a hurricane's howling onslaught,   20
rearing but never rolling back or forth . . . all adrift
till one steady, decisive blast comes down from Zeus—
so the old man thrashed things out, torn two ways,
to join his Argives fast with chariot-teams
or go and find Agamemnon lord of armies.
His mind in turmoil, this way seemed the best:
he'd head for Atreus' son. But other soldiers
kept on flailing, cutting each other to pieces,
the tough bronze casing their bodies clanging out,
fighters stabbing with swords, flinging two-edged spears.   30

    And now the royal kings fell in with Nestor.
Back they came, trailing along the shipways,
all who had taken wounds from the sharp bronze,
Diomedes, Odysseus, and Atreus' son Agamemnon.
Their ships were drawn up far away from the fighting,
moored in a group along the gray churning surf—
first ships ashore they'd hauled up on the plain
then built a defense to landward off their sterns.
Not even the stretch of beach, broad as it was,
could offer berths to all that massed armada,   40
troops were crammed in a narrow strip of coast.
So they had hauled their vessels inland, row on row,
while the whole shoreline filled and the bay's gaping mouth
enclosed by the jaws of the two jutting headlands.
Now up they came for a better view of the battle,
a slow file of kings, leaning on their spears,
hearts in their chests weighed down with anguish—
and the sight of the old horseman coming toward them
struck them all with a sharper sense of dread.
The king of men Agamemnon hailed him quickly: 50
"Nestor, son of Neleus, great pride of Achaea,

why turn your back on the lines where men are dying?
Why come back here to shore? I'm filled with fear
that breakneck Hector will bring his word to pass—
the threat he hurled against me once in a Trojan muster
that he would never leave our ships and return to Troy
till he'd torched our hulls and slaughtered all our men.
That was the prince's threat . . .
and now, look, by god, it all comes to pass!
How shameful—and now the rest of our men-at-arms   60
must harbor anger against me deep inside their hearts,
just like Achilles. And they have no stomach left
to fight to the end against the warships' sterns."

     The noble old horseman could only bear him out:
"True, too true. A disaster's right upon us.
Not even thundering Zeus himself could turn the tide.
The rampart's down, there, the great wall we trusted,
our impregnable shield for the ships and men themselves.
The enemy storms down on the rolling hulls nonstop,
desperate, life or death. Hard as you scan the lines,   70
there's no more telling from which side we're harried—
carnage left and right. Death-cries hit the skies!
Put heads together—what shall we do now?—
if strategy's any use. Struggle's clearly not.
The last thing I'd urge is to throw ourselves into battle.
How on earth can a wounded man make war?"

     So the lord of men Agamemnon staged the action:
"Since they are fighting against the sterns, old friend,
and the wall we built is useless, the trench a waste
where our Argive forces took such heavy losses . . .   80
always hoping against hope it was indestructible,
our impregnable shield for ships and men themselves—
so it must please the Father's overweening heart
to kill the Achaeans here, our memory blotted out
a world away from Argos! I knew it then,
even when Zeus defended *us* with all his might,
and I know it now, when he glorifies these Trojans—

he lifts them high as the blessed deathless gods
but ties our hands and lames our fighting spirit.
So come, follow my orders. All obey me now.   90
All vessels beached on the front along the shore—
haul them down and row them out on the bright sea,
ride them over the anchor-stones in the offshore swell
till the bracing godsent night comes down and then,
if the Trojans will refrain from war at night,
we haul down all the rest. No shame in running,
fleeing disaster, even in pitch darkness.
Better to flee from death than feel its grip."

    With a dark glance the shrewd tactician. Odysseus
wheeled on his commander: "What's this, Atrides,   100
this talk that slips from your clenched teeth?
You are the disaster.
Would to god you commanded another army,
a ragtag crew of cowards, instead of ruling us,
the men whom Zeus decrees, from youth to old age,
must wind down our brutal wars to the bitter end
until we drop and die, down to the last man.
So this is how you'd bid farewell to Troy,
yearning to kiss her broad streets good-bye—
Troy that cost our comrades so much grief?

                                        Quiet!   110
What if one of the men gets wind of your brave plan?
No one should ever let such nonsense pass his lips,
no one with any skill in fit and proper speech—
and least of all yourself, a sceptered king.
Full battalions hang on your words, Agamemnon—
look at the countless loyal fighters you command!
Now where's your sense? You fill me with contempt—
what are you saying? With the forces poised to clash
you tell us to haul our oar-swept vessels out to sea?
Just so one more glory can crown these Trojans—   120
god help us, they have beaten us already—
and the scales of headlong death can drag us down.
Achaean troops will never hold the line, I tell you,

not while the long ships are being hauled to sea.
They'll look left and right—where can they run?—
and fling their lust for battle to the winds. Then,
commander of armies, your plan will kill us all!"

At that the king of men Agamemnon backed down:
"A painful charge, Odysseus, straight to the heart.
I am hardly the man to order men, against their will,   130
to haul the oar-swept vessels out to sea. So now,
whoever can find a better plan, let him speak up,
young soldier or old. I would be pleased to hear him."

And Diomedes lord of the war cry stepped forward,
"Here is your man. Right here, not far to seek.
If you'll only hear me out and take my lead,
not glare at me in resentment, each of you,
since I am the youngest-born in all our ranks.
I too have a noble birth to boast—my father,
Tydeus, mounded over now by the earth of Thebes.   140
Three brave sons were born of the loins of Portheus:
they made their homes in Pleuron and craggy Calydon,
Agrius first, then Melas, the horseman Oeneus third,
my father's father, the bravest of them all.
There Oeneus stayed, on his own native soil,
but father wandered far, driven to live in Argos . . .
by the will of Zeus, I suppose, and other deathless gods.
He married one of Adrastus' daughters, settled down
in a fine wealthy house, with plenty of grainland
ringed with row on row of blooming orchards   150
and pastures full of sheep, his own herds.
And he excelled all Argives with his spear—
you must have heard the story, know it's true.
So you cannot challenge my birth as low, cowardly,
or spurn the advice I give, if the plan is really sound.
I say go back to the fighting, wounded as we are—
we must, we have no choice. But once at the front,
hold off from the spear-play, out of range ourselves
since who of us wants to double wounds on wounds?

But we can spur the rest of them into battle,   160
all who had nursed some private grudge before,
kept to the rear and shunned the grueling forays."

    The others listened closely and fell in line,
moving out, and marshal Agamemnon led them on.

    But the famous god of earthquakes was not blind.
No, Poseidon kept his watch and down he came
to the file of kings like an old veteran now,
he tugged at the right hand of Atreus' son
and sent his message flying: "Agamemnon—
now, by heaven, Achilles' murderous spirit   170
must be leaping in his chest, filled with joy
to behold his comrades slain and routed in their blood.
That man has got no heart in him, not a pulsebeat.
So let him die, outright—let a god wipe him out!
But with you the blessed gods are not enraged,
not through and through, Agamemnon . . .
A day will come when the Trojan lords and captains
send an immense dust storm swirling down the plain—
with your own eyes you'll see them break for Troy,
leaving your ships and shelters free and clear!"   180

    A shattering cry, and he surged across the plain,
thundering loud as nine, ten thousand combat soldiers
shriek with Ares' fury when massive armies clash—so huge
that voice the god of the earthquake let loose from his lungs,
planting enormous martial power in each Achaean's heart
to urge the battle on, to fight and never flinch.

    Now Hera poised on her golden throne looked down,
stationed high at her post aloft Olympus' peak.
At once she saw the sea lord blustering strong
in the war where men win glory, her own brother   190
and husband's brother too, and her heart raced with joy.
But then she saw great Zeus at rest on the ridge
and the craggy heights of Ida gushing cold springs

and her heart filled with loathing. What could she do?—
Queen Hera wondered, her eyes glowing wide . . .
how could she outmaneuver Zeus the mastermind,
this Zeus with his battle-shield of storm and thunder?
At last one strategy struck her mind as best:
she would dress in all her glory and go to Ida—
perhaps the old desire would overwhelm the king   200
to lie by her naked body and make immortal love
and she might drift an oblivious, soft warm sleep
across his eyes and numb that seething brain.
So off she went to her room,
the chamber her loving son Hephaestus built her,
hanging the doors from doorposts snug and tight,
locked with a secret bolt no other god could draw.
She slipped in, closing the polished doors behind her.
The ambrosia first. Hera cleansed her enticing body
of any blemish, then she applied a deep olive rub,   210
the breath-taking, redolent oil she kept beside her . . .
one stir of the scent in the bronze-floored halls of Zeus
and a perfumed cloud would drift from heaven down to earth.
Kneading her skin with this to a soft glow and combing her hair,
she twisted her braids with expert hands, and sleek, luxurious,
shining down from her deathless head they fell, cascading.
Then round her shoulders she swirled the wondrous robes
that Athena wove her, brushed out to a high gloss
and worked into the weft an elegant rose brocade.
She pinned them across her breasts with a golden brooch   220
then sashed her waist with a waistband
floating a hundred tassels, and into her earlobes,
neatly pierced, she quickly looped her earrings,
ripe mulberry-clusters dangling in triple drops
and the silver glints they cast could catch the heart.
Then back over her brow she draped her headdress,
fine fresh veils for Hera the queen of gods,
their pale, glimmering sheen like a rising sun,
and under her smooth feet she fastened supple sandals.
Now, dazzling in all her rich regalia, head to foot,   230
out of her rooms she strode and beckoned Aphrodite

away from the other gods and whispered, "Dear child,
would you do me a favor . . . whatever I might ask?
Or would you refuse me, always fuming against me
because I defend the Argives, you the Trojans?"

Aphrodite the daughter of Zeus replied at once,
"Hera, queen of the skies, daughter of mighty Cronus,
tell me what's on your mind. I am eager to do it—
whatever I *can* do . . . whatever can be done."

Quick with treachery noble Hera answered,   240
"Give me Love, give me Longing now, the powers
you use to overwhelm all gods and mortal men!
I am off to the ends of the fruitful, teeming earth
to visit Ocean, fountainhead of the gods, and Mother Tethys
who nourished me in their halls and reared me well.
They received me from Rhea, when thundering Zeus
drove Cronus under the earth and the barren salt sea.
I go to visit them and dissolve their endless feud—
how long they have held back from each other now,
from making love, since anger struck their hearts.   250
But if words of mine could lure them back to love,
back to bed, to lock in each other's arms once more . . .
they would call me their honored, loving friend forever."

Aphrodite, smiling her everlasting smile, replied,
"Impossible—worse, it's *wrong* to deny your warm request,
since you are the one who lies in the arms of mighty Zeus."

With that she loosed from her breasts the breastband,
pierced and alluring, with every kind of enchantment
woven through it . . . There is the heat of Love,
the pulsing rush of Longing, the lover's whisper,   260
irresistible—magic to make the sanest man go mad.
And thrusting it into Hera's outstretched hands
she breathed her name in a throbbing, rising voice:
"Here now, take this band, put it between your breasts—
ravishing openwork, and the world lies in its weaving!

You won't return, I know, your mission unfulfilled,
whatever your eager heart desires to do."

Hera broke into smiles now, her eyes wide—
with a smile she tucked the band between her breasts.

And Aphrodite the daughter of Zeus went home   270
but Hera sped in a flash from Mount Olympus' peak
and crossing Pieria's coast and lovely Emathia
rushed on, over the Thracian riders' snowy ridges,
sweeping the highest summits, feet never touching the earth
and east of Athos skimmed the billowing, foaming sea
and touched down on Lemnos, imperial Thoas' city.
There she fell in with Sleep, twin brother of Death,
clung to his hand and urged him, called his name:
"Sleep, master of all gods and all mortal men,
if you ever listened to me in the old days,   280
do what I ask you now—
and you shall have my everlasting thanks.
Put Zeus to sleep for me! Seal his shining eyes
as soon as I've gone to bed with him, locked in love,
and I will give you gifts—a magnificent throne,
never tarnished, always glittering, solid gold.
My own son Hephaestus, the burly crippled Smith
will forge it finely and under it slide a stool
where you can prop your glistening feet and rest,
stretching out at feasts."

             And the voice of Sleep   290
the soft and soothing drifted back . . . "Hera, Hera,
queen of the gods and daughter of mighty Cronus—
any other immortal god who lives forever,
believe me, I would put to sleep in a wink,
even the rolling tides of the great Ocean River,
the fountainhead that brought them all to birth.
But *Zeus*? Not I—I would not get too close
to the son of Cronus, much less put him under,
not unless the Father gave the command himself.
A commission of yours taught *me* my lesson once,   300

the day that Heracles, the insolent son of Zeus
sailed out from Troy, having razed her to the ground.
And then I put the brain of thundering Zeus to sleep,
pouring myself in a soft, soothing slumber round him.
But you and your anger! You were bent on trouble,
whipping a howling killer-squall across the sea,
bearing Heracles off to the crowded town of Cos,
far from all his friends. But Zeus woke up,
furious, flinging immortal gods about his house
to hunt for me—I was the culprit, the worst of all—   310
and out of the skies he would have sunk me in the sea,
wiped me from sight, if the Night had failed to save me,
old Night that can overpower all gods and mortal men.
I reached her in flight and Father called it quits
despite his towering anger. True, Zeus shrank
from doing a thing to outrage rushing Night.
But now you are back, Hera—
you ask me to do the impossible once again."

     Eyes widening, noble Hera coaxed him further:
"So troubled, Sleep, why torture yourself with that?   320
You think that thundering Zeus, shielding the men of Troy,
will rage as he raged for great Heracles, his own son?
Come now, I will give you one of the younger Graces—
Wed her at once and she'll be called your wife."

     "On with it!"—Sleep cried, thrilled by the offer—
"Swear to me by the incorruptible tides of Styx,
one hand grasping the earth that feeds mankind,
the other the bright sea, that all may be our witness,
all gods under earth that gather round King Cronus!
Swear you will give me one of the younger Graces,   330
Pasithea, she's the one—
all my days I've tossed and turned for *her*!"

     The white-armed goddess Hera complied at once.
She swore as he urged and sounded out the names

of all the gods in the Tartarean Pit we call the Titans.
As soon as she'd sworn and sealed her binding oath,
away they launched from Imbros' walls and Lemnos,
swathed in a thick mist and nimbly made their way
until they reached Mount Ida with all her springs,
the mother of wild beasts, and making Lectos headland,   340
left the sea for the first time and swept over dry land
as the treetops swayed and shook beneath their feet.
There Sleep came to a halt—
before the eyes of the Father could detect him—
and climbed up softly into a towering pine tree.
The tallest trunk there was on the heights of Ida,
it pierced the low-hung mist and shot up through the sky.
There he nestled, hidden deep in the needling boughs,
for all the world like the bird with a shrill cry,
the mountain bird the immortals call Bronze Throat   350
and mortals call the Nighthawk.

                       But not Hera—
quick on her feet she scaled Gargaron peak,
the highest crest of Ida. And Zeus spotted her now,
Zeus who gathers the breasting clouds. And at one glance
the lust came swirling over him, making his heart race,
fast as the first time—all unknown to their parents—
they rolled in bed, they locked and surged in love.
He rose before her now, he savored her name:
"Hera—where are you rushing?
What wild desire brings you here from Olympus?   360
Where are the team and car you always ride?"

    And filled with guile the noble Hera answered,
"I am off to the ends of the fruitful, teeming earth
to visit Ocean, fountainhead of the gods, and Mother Tethys
who nourished me in their halls and reared me well . . .
I go to visit them and dissolve their endless feud—
how long they have held back from each other now,
from making love, since anger struck their hearts.
My team stands at the foot of Ida with all her springs,
they wait to bear me over the good dry land and sea.   370

But now it is you, you I have come to visit, Zeus—
speeding here from the heights of Mount Olympus,
afraid you'll flare in anger against me later
if I should go in secret toward the halls
of the deep, flowing Ocean."

                              "Why hurry, Hera?"—
Zeus who gathers the breasting clouds replied,
"that is a journey you can make tomorrow. Now—
come, let's go to bed, let's lose ourselves in love!
Never has such a lust for goddess or mortal woman
flooded my pounding heart and overwhelmed me so.   380
Not even then, when I made love to Ixion's wife
who bore me Pirithous, rival to all the gods in wisdom . . .
not when I loved Acrisius' daughter Danaë—marvelous ankles—
and Perseus sprang to life and excelled all men alive . . .
not when I stormed Europa, far-famed Phoenix' daughter
who bore me Minos and Rhadamanthys grand as gods . . .
not even Semele, not even Alcmena queen of Thebes
who bore me a son, that lionheart, that Heracles,
and Semele bore Dionysus, ecstasy, joy to mankind—
not when I loved Demeter, queen of the lustrous braids—   390
not when I bedded Leto ripe for glory—

                              Not even *you*!
That was nothing to how I hunger for you now—
irresistible longing lays me low!"

    Teeming with treachery noble Hera led him on:
"Dread majesty, son of Cronus, what are you saying?
You are eager for bed now, burning to make love,
here on Ida's heights for all the world to see?
What if one of the deathless gods observes us,
sleeping together, yes—
and runs off to the rest and points us out to all?   400
I have no desire to rise from a bed like that
and steal back home to your own high halls—
think of the shocking scandal there would be!
But if you're on fire, overflowing with passion,
there's always your own bedroom. Hephaestus built it,

your own dear son, and the doors fit snug and tight . . .
There we can go to bed at once—since love is now your pleasure!"

And Zeus who gathers the breasting clouds assured her,
"Hera—nothing to fear, no god or man will see us—
I will wrap us round in a golden cloud so dense   410
not even the Sun's rays, the sharpest eyes in the world,
will pierce the mist and glimpse us making love!"

With that the son of Cronus caught his wife in his arms
and under them now the holy earth burst with fresh green grass,
crocus and hyacinth, clover soaked with dew, so thick and soft
it lifted their bodies off the hard, packed ground . . .
Folded deep in that bed they lay and round them wrapped
a marvelous cloud of gold, and glistening showers of dew
rained down around them both.
                                    And so, deep in peace,
the Father slept on Gargaron peak, conquered by Sleep   420
and strong assaults of Love, his wife locked in his arms.
Soothing Sleep went rushing off to the ships at once,
running a message to Poseidon. Approaching the god
who shakes the earth, Sleep sent a winged urging:
"Fight for the Argives now with all your might!
Now give them glory, if only a moment's glory—
long as Zeus still slumbers. I've covered him over,
sent him into a deep, soothing sleep as soon as Hera
seduced great Zeus to lose himself in love."
                                          With that
Sleep went drifting off to the famous tribes of men,   430
stirring Poseidon even more to defend the Argives.
He suddenly sprang forward, into the front ranks,
the god's voice rippling strong: "Again, you Argives?
You're handing victory over to Hector, Priam's son,
so he can seize the ships and reap the glory?
That's his hope, his prayer, thanks to Achilles,
ironbound by the ships and filled with anger still.
But Achilles won't be missed so sorely, not a bit,
if the rest of us can rouse and defend each other.

So come, follow my orders. All obey me now.   440
Gear up with the best and biggest shields in camp
and encase our heads in helmets, burnished, fire-bright
and take in hand the longest javelins we can find—
then in for attack! And I, I will lead the way
and the son of Priam won't stand up against us,
not for long, I tell you, not for all his fury.
Let any rugged fighter who shoulders a small buckler
pass it on to a weaker man—put on the bigger shield."

The men hung on his words and they obeyed at once.
And the kings themselves, overcoming their wounds,   450
arrayed them all in proper battle-order.
Diomedes, Odysseus, Atreus' son Agamemnon
ranged the ranks, made them exchange their armor.
The best men donned the best, the worst the worst
and soon as they strapped the bronze around their bodies,
out they moved and the god of earthquakes led them on,
grasping his terrible long sword in his massive hand,
the grip of power, the blade like a lightning flash.
There is no way in the world a man can meet its edge
and still survive the slashing—fear holds all men back.   460

But over against them glorious Hector ranged his Trojans . . .
and now they stretched the line of battle strangling tight,
the blue-haired god of the sea and Hector fired in arms,
he driving the Trojans, the god driving the Argives—
and a wild surf pounded the ships and shelters,
squadrons clashed with shattering war cries rising.
Not so loud the breakers bellowing out against the shore,
driven in from open sea by the North Wind's brutal blast,
not so loud the roar of fire whipped to a crackling blaze
rampaging into a mountain gorge, raging up through timber,   470
not so loud the gale that howls in the leafy crowns of oaks
when it hits its pitch of fury tearing branches down—
Nothing so loud as cries of Trojans, cries of Achaeans,
terrible war cries, armies storming against each other.

And shining Hector was first to hurl his spear—
at the giant Ajax veering into him, full face—
a direct hit! where two straps crossed his chest,
one for the shield, one for the silver-studded sword
but both flexed taut to guard his glistening skin.
Hector seethed in anger—his hurtling spear   480
and his whole arm's power poured in a wasted shot—
and back in his massing ranks he shrank, dodging death.
But as Hector backed away Great Ajax seized a rock—
countless holding-stones for the fast trim ships
were rolling round among the fighters' feet—
he hoisted one and heaved it at Hector's chest
and struck him over the shield-rim, close to his throat
and the blow sent Hector whirling off like a whipping-top,
reeling round and round. As a huge oak goes down
at a stroke from Father Zeus, ripped up by the roots   490
and a grim reek of sulphur bursts forth from the trunk
and a passerby too close, looking on, loses courage—
the bolt of mighty Zeus is hell on earth—so in a flash,
for all his fighting power, Hector plunged in the dust,
his spear dropped from his fist, shield and helmet '
crushing in on him, bronze gear clashing round him.
And shouting squads of Achaeans raced in for the kill,
hoping to drag him off and hurling showers of spears
but none could stab or strike the lord of armies now.
Too fast for them, here was a ring of Trojan chiefs: 500
Aeneas, Polydamas and the royal prince Agenor,
Sarpedon the Lycians' captain, valiant Glaucus—
and all their troops spared nothing, pitching in,
bracing their thick bulging shields to cover Hector.
Comrades heaved him up and swept him clear of the fighting,
far downfield till they gained his team of racers
standing behind the rear lines and rush of battle,
their driver and blazoned chariot held in tow . . .
Then back to Troy they bore him, groaning hard.

But once they reached the ford where the river runs clear,   510
the strong, whirling Xanthus sprung of immortal Zeus,

they lifted him off his car and laid him down
on the level bank, splashing water over him.
Hector caught his breath and his eyes cleared,
he crouched down on his knees to vomit dark clots
then slumped back down, stretched on the ground again
and the world went black as night across his eyes.
The force of the blow still overwhelmed his senses.

But Argive units, spotting Hector in full retreat,
charged the Trojans harder, their lust for battle rising.   520
And first by far was Oïleus' son, quick Little Ajax—
he lunged out and his spearhead skewered Satnius,
Enops' son the lithe nymph of the ford once bore
to Enops tending his flocks by Satniois' banks . . .
Now the renowned spearman Ajax rushed against him,
slashing him down the flank, knocking him backward—
Trojans and Argives swarming over him, out for blood.
Shaking a spear Polydamas moved in fast to the rescue,
Panthous' son lancing the right shoulder of Prothoënor,
Arielycus' son, and the heavy shaft impaled his upper arm—   530
he pitched in the dust, clawing the earth with both hands
and Polydamas shouted over him, wild with glory now:
"Here is another spear that leaps from my strong arm,
from Panthous' brave son, and hits its mark, by god!
It's found its home in an Argive's waiting flesh—
a crutch in his grip, I'd say,
as he trudges down now to the House of Death!"

The Argives rose in horror to hear that boast,
veteran Ajax most of all, the anger leapt inside him—
Prothoënor had dropped at the feet of Telamon's son.   540
Ajax suddenly spun a glinting spear at Polydamas,
fast, but the Trojan dodged black fate himself
with a quick spring to the side—
but Antenor's son Archelochus caught the shaft
for the gods had doomed that fighting man to death.
Ajax struck him right where the head and neckbone join,
the last link in the spine, he cut both tendons through

so the mouth and brow and nostrils hit the ground
before the shins and knees as the man dropped dead.
And now it was Ajax' turn to shout at brave Polydamas, 550
"Think it over, Polydamas, tell the truth, my friend—
a decent bargain, no? This man's body for Prothoënor's!
No coward, to judge by his looks, no coward's stock,
no doubt some brother of stallion-breaking Antenor,
that or his own son—the blood-likeness is striking!"

So Ajax vaunted, knowing his victim full well,
and a raw revulsion seized the Trojans' hearts.
Straddling his brother, Acamas thrust and speared
Boeotian Promachus, trying to drag the corpse by the feet,
and Acamas loosed his cry of exultation, "Argives— 560
glorious braggarts, you, insatiate with your threats!
Don't think struggle and pain will be ours alone—
your day will come to die in blood like him.
Think how Promachus sleeps at your feet now,
beaten down by my spear—with no long wait
to pay the price for my brother dead and gone.
That's why a fighter prays for kin in his halls,
blood kin to survive and avenge his death in battle!"

But the Argives rose in grief to avenge that boast—
skilled Peneleos most of all, anger blazed inside him. 570
He charged Acamas—Acamas could not stand the attack,
he ran—and Peneleos stabbed at Ilioneus instead,
a son of the herdsman Phorbas rich in flocks,
Hermes' favorite Trojan: Hermes gave him wealth
but Ilioneus' mother gave him just one son . . .
the one Peneleos lanced beneath the brows,
down to the eyes' roots and scooped an eyeball out—
the spear cut clean through the socket, out behind the nape
and backward down he sat, both hands stretched wide
as Peneleos, quickly drawing his whetted sword, 580
hacked him square in the neck and lopped his head
and down on the ground it tumbled, helmet and all.
But the big spear's point still stuck in the eye socket—

hoisting the head high like a poppy-head on the shaft
he flourished it in the eyes of all the Trojans now,
yelling out his boast: "Go tell them from me,
you Trojans, tell the loving father and mother
of lofty Ilioneus to start the dirges in the halls!
The wife of Promachus, Alegenor's son, will never thrill
to her dear husband striding home from the wars   590
that day the sons of Achaea sail from Troy!"

And the knees of every Trojan shook with fear,
each veteran frantic, glancing left and right—
how to escape his sudden, plunging death?

Sing to me now, you Muses who hold the halls of Olympus,
who was the first Achaean to drag off bloody spoils
as the famous god of earthquakes turned the tide?
Telamonian Ajax first, Ajax brought down Hyrtius,
Gyrtius' son, a lord of the ironhearted Mysians.
Next Antilochus slaughtered Phalces, Mermerus—   600
Meriones killed off Morys, killed Hippotion,
Teucer cut down Periphetes and Prothoon.
Menelaus took the hardened captain Hyperenor,
gouged his flank and the bronze ripped him open,
spurting his entrails out—and his life, gushing forth
through the raw, yawning wound, went pulsing fast
and the dark came swirling down across his eyes.
But Oileus' son, quick Ajax killed the most—
no one alive could run men down in flight like him
once Zeus whipped enemy ranks in blinding, panic rout.   610

BOOK FIFTEEN

The Achaean
Armies at Bay

Back through jutting stakes and across the trench they fled,
and hordes were cut down at the Argives' hands—the rest,
only after they reached the chariots, stood fast,
blanched with fear, whipped in desperate flight.
That moment Zeus awoke on the heights of Ida,
stretched out by Hera, queen of the golden throne—
he leapt to his feet, he saw the Trojans and Achaeans,
one side routed, the other harrying them in panic,
Achaeans attacking, and god Poseidon led the way.
And Zeus saw Hector sprawled on the battlefield,   10
his comrades kneeling round him as he panted,
struggling hard for breath, his senses stunned,
vomiting blood . . . The man who'd struck him down
was not the weakest Argive. At the sight of Hector
the father of men and gods filled with pity now

and shooting a terrible dark glance down at Hera,
burst out at her, "What a disaster you create!
Uncontrollable Hera—you and your treachery—
halting Hector's assault and routing Hector's armies.
I wouldn't be surprised, my Queen, if you were the first   20
to reap the pernicious whirlwind you have sown—
I'll whip you stroke on stroke.
Don't you recall the time I strung you in mid-air
and slung those two massive anvils down from your feet
and lashed both hands with a golden chain you could not break?
There, there in the clouds and high clear sky you dangled.
And the mighty gods on steep Olympus raged away,
impotent—what could they do to set you free?
Standing there, helpless. And any god I caught
I'd seize and send him plunging over the ramparts,   30
headfirst till he hit the earth, barely alive.
Not even then would the stark grief for Heracles
release my breaking heart—my own godlike son . . .
You with the North Wind's help had coaxed the gales
to send him scudding over the barren salt sea—
you, always plotting miseries for my son,
you bore him off to the crowded town of Cos.
But there I saved him, whisked him away to safety,
back to the stallion-land of Argos, worn with torment.
I will help you remember—you'll give up your treacheries,   40
you will see if your warm embraces serve you then,
your bed of lust where you sank me in your arms.
Down from the gods you came to waylay me—
you seduced me blind."
                                          Her eyes wide,
Queen Hera shuddered before his thunder,
protesting, swearing a flight of winged oaths:
"Earth be my witness now, the vaulting Sky above
and the dark cascading waters of the Styx—I swear
by the greatest, grimmest oath that binds the happy gods!
By your sacred head, by the bed of our own marriage   50
that I, at least, would never take in vain . . .
Never by will of mine did the god of earthquakes

wreak havoc among the Trojan ranks and Hector
and surge to help their foes!
It *must* be his own great rage that drives him on—
he pitied the sight of Argives pinned against their ships.
Not I . . . why, I'd be the first to counsel him
to take your lead, Zeus, wherever you command,
my king of the black cloud!"

　　　　　　　　　　A rousing appeal,
and the father of men and gods looked down and smiled   60
and took command with a flight of winging orders:
"Excellent, Hera. Now, if in the years to come
you will accord with me, my wide-eyed Queen,
throned with me in the gods' decisive sessions,
then Poseidon, bent as he is to go his own way,
must change at once and wrench his will to ours,
to yours and mine united.

　　　　　　　　　So then, Hera,
if you mean what you say, down to the last word,
go back now to the deathless tribes of gods
and summon Iris to come before my presence,   70
summon Apollo too, lord of the famous bow.
Iris will fly to Achaea's bronze-armed troops
and direct the god who shakes the earth to stop,
to quit the war and return to his own ocean halls.
And let Apollo drive Prince Hector back to battle,
breathe power back in his lungs, make him forget
the pains that rack his heart. Let him whip the Achaeans
in headlong panic rout and roll them back once more,
tumbling back on the oar-swept ships of Peleus' son Achilles.
And he, he will launch his comrade Patroclus into action   80
and glorious Hector will cut him down with a spear
in front of Troy, once Patroclus has slaughtered
whole battalions of strong young fighting men
and among them all, my shining son Sarpedon.
But then—enraged for Patroclus—
brilliant Achilles will bring Prince Hector down.
And then, from that day on, I'll turn the tide of war:
back the fighting goes, no stopping it, ever, all the way

till Achaean armies seize the beetling heights of Troy
through Athena's grand design.
                                    But till that hour   90
I will never cease my anger. Nor will I permit
a single immortal god to save the Argive forces,
not till Achilles' prayer has been fulfilled.
So I vowed at first. I bowed my head in assent
that day the goddess Thetis clutched my knees,
begging me to exalt Achilles scourge of cities."

    And the white-armed goddess Hera obeyed at once—
clearing Ida's peaks she soared for sheer Olympus.
Quick as a thought goes flashing through a man
who's traveled the world—"Ah to be there, or there!"—   100
as his mind swarms with journeys, fresh desires—
so quick in her eager flight flew noble Hera now
and scaling steep Olympus went among the gods,
the immortal powers thronging Zeus's halls.
They all sprang to their feet at sight of Hera,
lifting cups to greet her, crowding round the queen.
But she passed the rest and took a cup from Themis,
flushed with beauty, who ran to meet her first
and hailed her now with winged words of welcome:
"Hera, what brings you back? You look so harried.   110
Oh I know it, the son of Cronus has terrified you—
your everlasting husband!"
                                    "Please, Themis,"
the white-armed goddess Hera answered firmly,
"don't ask me to go through that ordeal again.
You know his rage yourself. So rigid, unrelenting.
But you keep on presiding over the gods, Themis,
the feasting in the halls. You'll hear it all,
and with you all the immortals—
what a chain of disasters Zeus brings to light!
Nothing to lift all spirits alike, I warn you . . .   120
not among men, not among gods, if one's still left
who warms to feasts, his heart at peace, these days."

With those bleak words Queen Hera took her seat.
The gods looked grim throughout the halls of Zeus.
She smiled with her lips only,
her forehead furrowed over her dark brows
as her anguish rose and she addressed them all:
"What fools we are, storming against Zeus—we're mad!
And still we engage him, trying to block his way
with a word or show of force. But there he sits,   130
off and away—with never a care or qualm for us—
claiming that he among the deathless gods on high
is first in strength and power, none in the world his rival.
So each of you here must take what blows he sends.
Why, Ares, I gather, has just received his share . . .
his son is dead in battle, his dearest son, Ascalaphus—
doesn't invincible Ares claim to be his father?"

     Fighting words, and Ares pounded his sturdy thighs
with the flats of both hands and let loose in grief:
"Now, you gods of Olympus—who could blame me now   140
if I descend on Achaea's ships to avenge my son,
my butchered son? Even if fate will crush me,
striking me down with the thunderbolt of Zeus—
sprawled in the blood and dust with dead men's corpses!"

     With that he called his henchmen Rout and Terror
to yoke his team as the god strapped on his shining gear.
And now some greater disaster might have come from Zeus,
some wrath, some harsher rage to break the gods on high—
if Pallas Athena, fearing the worst for all immortals,
had not leapt from her throne, bolted through the gates,   150
torn the helmet off his head, the shield from his back
and snatching the brazen spear from his burly grip,
propped it against a pillar
and dressed the War-god down in all his fury:
"Maniac, out of your senses! You, you're ruined!
What are your ears for, Ares, can't you hear the truth?
Your wits are gone—where's your respect for others?

Can't you grasp what the white-armed goddess tells us?—
and she's just returned from Olympian Zeus, just now.
What's your pleasure? To fill your own cup of pain   160
then slink back to Olympus, whipped and fuming—forced?
You're planting the seeds of endless trouble for us all!
He will leave those men in a flash, Achaeans, Trojans,
overweening Trojans, and back great Zeus will come
to batter *us* on Olympus, seize one after another—
gods guilty and innocent routed all together.
So now, I tell you, drop this anger for your son.
By now some fighter better than he, a stronger hand
has gone down in his own blood, or soon will go.
It is no small labor to rescue all mankind,   170
every mother's son."

                        With that sharp warning
Athena seated headlong Ares on his throne.
But Queen Hera summoned Apollo from the halls
and Iris too, the messenger of the immortals,
and gave them both their winged marching orders:
"Zeus directs you to Ida with all good speed!
But once you arrive and meet great Zeus's glance,
do whatever the Father drives you on to do."

    And with that command Queen Hera strode home
and regained her throne. But the two launched out in flight   180
and reaching Ida with all her springs, mother of flocks,
they found the thundering son of Cronus seated high
on Gargaron peak, crowned with a fragrant cloud.
Coming before the lord of storm and lightning
the two just stood there, waiting . . .
Nor was his heart displeased to see them both—
how fast they'd obeyed his loving wife's commands—
and first he issued Iris winging orders: "Away, Iris!
Quick as you can to the grand sea lord Poseidon.
Go, give him my message, start to finish—   190
and see that every word of it rings exactly so.
Command Poseidon to quit the war and slaughter now,
go back to the tribes of gods or down to his bright sea.

But if he will not obey my orders, if he spurns them,
let him beware, heart and soul—for all his power
he can never muster the will to stand my onslaught.
I claim I am far greater than he in striking force,
I am the first-born too. Yet the spirit inside him
never shrinks from claiming to be my equal, never,
though other gods will cringe from me in terror."   200

    And Iris riding the wind obeyed his orders,
swooping down from Ida's peaks to sacred Troy.
Like the snow or freezing hail that pelts from clouds
when the North Wind born in the clear heaven blasts it on—
so in an eager rush of speed the wind-swift Iris flew
and stopped beside the famous god of earthquakes,
calling out to him, "Here is a message for you,
god of the sea-blue mane who grips the earth.
I speed this word to you from storming Zeus.
He commands you to quit the war and slaughter now,   210
go back to the tribes of gods or down to your bright sea!
But if you will not obey his orders, if you spurn them,
he threatens to come here in person, fight you down,
power against power. Avoid his grasp, he warns.
He claims he is far greater than you in striking force,
he is the first-born too! Yet the spirit inside you
never shrinks from claiming to be his equal, never—
though other gods will cringe from him in terror."

    But the glorious god of earthquakes shook in anger:
"What outrage! Great as he is, what overweening arrogance!   220
So, force me, will he, to wrench my will to his?
I with the same high honors?
Three brothers we are, all sprung from Cronus,
all of us brought to birth by Rhea—Zeus and I,
Hades the third, lord of the dead beneath the earth.
The world was split three ways. Each received his realm.
When we shook the lots I drew the sea, my foaming eternal home,
and Hades drew the land of the dead engulfed in haze and night
and Zeus drew the heavens, the clouds and the high clear sky,

but the earth and Olympus heights are common to us all.   230
So I will never live at the beck and call of Zeus!
No, at his royal ease, and powerful as he is,
let him rest content with *his* third of the world.
Don't let him try to frighten *me* with his mighty hands—
what does he take me for, some coward out-and-out?
He'd better aim his terrible salvos at his own,
all his sons and daughters. He's their father—
they *have* to obey his orders. It's their fate.''

    Iris quick as the breezes tried to soothe him:
''Wait, god of the sea-blue mane who grips the earth—   240
you really want me to take that harsh, unbending answer
back to Zeus? No change of heart, not even a little?
The hearts of the great, you know, can always change . . .
you know how the Furies always stand by older brothers.''

    The lord of the earthquake yielded ground in answer:
''True, Iris, immortal friend, how right you are—
it's a fine thing when a messenger knows what's proper.
Ah but how it galls me, it wounds me to the quick
when the Father tries to revile *me* with brute abuse,
his equal in rank, our fated shares of the world the same!   250
Still, this time I will yield, for all my outrage . . .
but I tell you this, and there's anger in my threat:
if ever—against my will and Athena queen of armies,
Hera and Hermes, and the god of fire Hephaestus—
if Zeus ever spares the towering heights of Troy,
if he ever refuses to take her walls by force
and give the Argive troops resounding triumph,
let Zeus know this full well—
the breach between us both will never heal!''

                                A sharp tremor
and the massive god of earthquakes left Achaea's lines,   260
into the surf he dove and heroes missed him sorely.
That very instant storming Zeus dispatched Apollo:
''Go, my friend, to the side of Hector armed in bronze.
The god of the quakes who grips and pounds the earth

has just this moment plunged in his own bright sea,
diving away from all my mounting anger. Just think
what the gods would have heard if we had come to blows,
even those beneath the ground who circle Cronus.
Better for me this way, Poseidon too, to yield
before my mighty hands—outraged as he is: 270
not without sweat would we have called it quits.
But now take up in your hands my storm-cloud shield,
its dark tassels flying, shake it over the Argives,
stampede their heroes in panic, Archer of the Sky.
But make this glorious Hector your main concern,
rouse his breakneck courage till, racing in terror,
the Argives reach the fleet and the Hellespont in rout.
From that point on I plan my tactics, give commands
to grant the Argives breathing room in battle."

Apollo did not neglect the Father's orders.   280
Down from Ida's peaks he swooped like a hawk,
the killer of doves, the fastest thing on wings.
He found Prince Hector, the son of wise King Priam,
sitting up now, sprawled on the ground no longer,
just regaining his strength, just beginning
to recognize his comrades round about him . . .
His heavy sweating, his hard breathing stopped
the moment the will of storming Zeus revived him.
Apollo the Archer stood beside him, taunting,
"Hector, son of Priam, why so far from your troops?   290
Sitting here, half dead—some trouble's come your way?"

Hector struggled for words, his helmet flashing:
"Who are you, my lord—who of the high gods—
to probe me face-to-face?
Haven't you heard? I was killing his friends
against the ships when the lord of the war cry Ajax
struck me down with a boulder square across my chest—
he took the fight right out of me, I can tell you . . .
I thought for certain I'd go to join the dead,

descend to the House of Death this very day—   300
I thought I'd breathed my last."
                                        But lord Apollo
the distant deadly Archer reassured him: "Courage!
Look what a strong support the son of Cronus
speeds from Ida to take your side and shield you—
I am Phoebus Apollo, lord of the golden sword!
I who saved you before, and along with you
your towering city too. So up now, Hector—
command your drivers here in all their hundreds
to lash their plunging teams at the hollow ships.
And I'll surge on ahead, clearing the whole way   310
for the teams' assault—I'll bend the Argives back!"

That breathed tremendous strength in the famous captain.
As a stallion full-fed at the manger, stalled too long,
breaking free of his tether gallops down the plain,
out for his favorite plunge in a river's cool currents,
thundering in his pride—his head flung back, his mane
streaming over his shoulders, sure and sleek in his glory,
knees racing him on to the fields and stallion-haunts he loves—
so Hector hurtled on, his legs driving, his knees pumping,
spurring his reinsmen once he heard the god's command.   320
And the Argives wheeled and gave ground quickly.
Think how dogs and huntsmen off in the wilds
rush some antlered stag or skittish mountain goat
but a rocky gorge or shadowed forest gives him shelter—
they see it's not their lot to bring that quarry down,
their shouting only flushes a great bearded lion
ramping across their path, suddenly charging them,
scattering men and packs despite their lust for battle—
so up till now the Achaeans kept advancing, close formation,
stabbing away with swords and rugged two-edged spears   330
but once they saw tall Hector attack the ranks again
they wheeled in terror—hearts collapsed at their heels.

But Thoas son of Andraemon spurred them on,
Aetolia's best by far, skilled with the spear,

superb at cut-and-thrust
and few Achaeans could put him down in debate
when the young men vie and struggle over points.
Now forth he came with calls to back his comrades:
"Look—a genuine miracle right before my eyes!
Hector's escaped again, he's risen from the dead!   340
And just as each of us hoped with all his heart
he'd dropped and died at the hands of giant Ajax.
But again some god swoops down and saves this Hector—
and hasn't he wiped enough of us out already?
Now he'll make more slaughter, well I know.
He'd never *be* at the front, smashing our lines
unless Old Thunder, Zeus, had put him on his feet.
So come, friends, do as I say—all take my lead.
The rank and file go back, withdraw to the ships,
but we who claim to be the armies' finest champions   350
stand our ground—face him first, try to beat him off!
Spears at the ready! For all his fury, trust me,
he'll quake before he penetrates our front."

                                                 Sound tactics—
the captains hung on his words and all fell in line.
Squads forming around Great Ajax, King Idomeneus,
Teucer, Meriones and Meges a match for Ares
closed tight for the onset, calling all their best
to brace and face Prince Hector and Hector's Trojans.
Behind them rank and file withdrew to Achaea's ships.

    But packed in a mass the Trojans came on pounding,   360
Hector leading the way with long, leaping strides
and heading the van in person came the god Apollo,
shoulders wrapped in cloud, gripping the storm-shield,
the tempest terror, dazzling, tassels flaring along its front—
The bronzesmith god of fire gave it to Zeus to bear
and strike fear in men and Apollo gripped it now,
locked in his two fists as he led the Trojans on.

    But packed in a mass the Argives stood their ground,
deafening cries of battle breaking from both sides

as whipping arrows leapt away from bowstrings.   370
Showers of spears raining from daring, hardy arms
went deep into soldiers' bodies quick to fight
but showers of others, cut short
halfway before they could graze glistening skin,
stuck in the ground, still lusting to sink in flesh.
Long as Apollo held the storm-shield firm in his grasp
the weapons hurtled side-to-side and men kept falling . . .
But once he looked the fast Achaean drivers square in the eyes,
shook the shield and loosed an enormous battle cry himself,
Apollo stunned the high courage in all their chests—   380
they lost their grip, forgot their fighting-fury.
Routed like herds of cattle or big flocks of sheep
when two wild beasts stampede them away in terror,
suddenly pouncing down in their midst—pitch darkness,
the shepherd off and gone—so the defenseless Argives
panicked, routed. Apollo hurled fear in their hearts
and handed Hector and all his Trojans instant glory.

   There man killed man in the mad scatter of battle.
Hector finished Stichius, finished Arcesilaus off,
the one a chief of Boeotians armed in bronze,   390
the other, brave Menelaus' trusty comrade.
Aeneas slaughtered Medon and Iasus outright,
Medon the bastard son of royal King Oileus,
Little Ajax' brother, but Medon lived in Phylace,
banished from native land—he'd killed a kinsman
dear to Oileus' wife, his stepmother Eriopis.
But Iasus became a captain of Athens' troops,
Sphelus' son he was called and Bucolus' grandson.
Polydamas killed Mecisteus—
                       Polites cut down Echius,
first in the onset—
                       dashing Agenor cut down Clonius—   400
and Paris lanced Deiochus deep below the shoulder,
ran him through from behind as he fled the front
and the bronze spear came jutting out his chest.

While the Trojans tore the war-gear off the bodies
Argives clambered back in a tangled mass, scrambling back
through the sharp stakes and deep pit of the trench,
fleeing left and right, forced inside the rampart.
So Hector commanded his Trojans, sounding out,
"Now storm the ships! Drop those bloody spoils!
Any straggler I catch, hanging back from the fleet,   410
right here on the spot I'll put that man to death.
No kin, no women commit his corpse to the flames—
the dogs will tear his flesh before our walls!"

With a full-shoulder stroke he flogged his horses on,
loosing a splitting war cry down the Trojan ranks
and all cried back in answer—a savage roar rising—
driving teams and chariots close in line with his.
And Apollo far in the lead, the god's feet kicking
the banks of the deep trench down with a god's ease,
tumbled earth in the pit between, bridging it with a dike   420
immense and wide and long as a hurtling spear will fly
when a man makes practice casts to test his strength.
Holding formation now the Trojans rolled across it,
Apollo heading them, gripping the awesome storm-shield
and he tore that Argive rampart down with the same ease
some boy at the seashore knocks sand castles down—
he no sooner builds his playthings up, child's play,
than he wrecks them all with hands and kicking feet,
just for the sport of it. God of the wild cry, Apollo—
so you wrecked the Achaeans' work and drove the men   430
who had built it up with all that grief and labor
into headlong panic rout.
                                   Achaeans stampeding back
till they reined in hard, huddling tight by the sterns
and shouting out to each other, flung their arms
to all the immortals, each man crying out a prayer.
But none as rapt as Nestor, Achaea's watch and ward,
who stretched his hands to the starry skies and prayed,
"Father Zeus! If ever in Argos' golden wheatlands

one of us burned the fat thighs of sheep or bulls
and begged a safe return and you promised with a nod—   440
remember it now, Olympian. Save us from this ruthless day!
Don't let these Trojans mow us down in droves!''

                      So he pleaded
and hearing the old man's prayers, Zeus who rules the world
let loose a great crack of thunder, rending the skies.
But Trojans, thrilled at the sound of Zeus's thunder,
pitched themselves at the Argives still more fiercely,
summoning up their fiery lust for battle.
Like a giant breaker rearing up on the rangy seas,
crashing over a ship's sides, driven in by the winds
and the blast builds the comber's crushing impact—   450
a hoarse roar!—Trojans stormed over the rampart,
lashing their teams to fight against the ships,
hurling their two-edged spears at close range there,
Trojans from lurching cars but Achaeans from high decks,
scrambling aloft black hulls, lunged down with the long pikes—
jointed and clinched and tipped with ripping bronze—
they'd kept on board for bloody fights at sea.

                          Now,
as long as the armies fought to take the rampart,
far from the fast ships, Patroclus sat it out
in his friend Eurypylus' shelter . . .   460
trying to lift the soldier's heart with stories,
applying soothing drugs to his dreadful wound
as he sought to calm the black waves of pain.
But soon as he heard the Trojans storm the wall
and shouts rise from Achaeans lost in panic rout,
Patroclus gave a groan and slapping his thighs hard
with the flats of both hands, burst forth in anguish:
''I can't stay here with you any longer, Eurypylus,
much as you need me—there, a great battle breaks!
No, let an aide attend you here while I rush back   470
to Achilles, spur him into combat. Who knows?
With a god's help I just might rouse him now,
bring his fighting spirit round at last.
The persuasion of a comrade has its powers.''

With the last words his feet sped him on.
Meanwhile the Argives blocked the Trojan assault
but they still could not repel them from the fleet,
outnumbering them as they did. Nor could the Trojans
once break through the Argives' bulking forward mass
and force their passage through to ships and shelters.   480
Tense as a chalk-line marks the cut of a ship timber,
drawn taut and true in a skilled shipwright's hands—
some master craftsman trained in Athena's school—
so tense the battle line was drawn, dead even . . .
Some forces at some ships, some clashing at others,
but Hector charged head-on at Ajax braced for battle
and both warriors fought it out for a single vessel,
nor could Hector burst through and ignite the hull
nor Ajax drive him back—a god drove Hector on.
And here came Caletor son of Trojan Clytius   490
sweeping fire against the prow but famous Ajax
stopped him short with a spear that stabbed his chest.
Down he crashed, the torch dropped from his fist,
right before Hector's eyes—he watched his cousin
sprawl in the dust before the huge black ship
and gave a stirring cry to all his units:
"Trojans! Lycians! Dardan fighters hand-to-hand,
don't yield an inch, not in these bloody straits!
Rescue Caletor before the Argives strip his gear—
he's down, he's dead by the ships that crowd the beach!"   500

As he raised that cry he flung his spear at Ajax—
but the glinting metal missed and he hit Mastor's son,
Lycophron, Ajax' friend-in-arms, Cythera-born
yet he lived with Ajax once he'd killed a man
on Cythera's holy shores. Hector killed him now
with whetted bronze, cleaving his skull above the ear
as he stood by Ajax. Down off the ship's stern he dropped,
his back slamming the ground, his limbs slack in death,
and Ajax shuddered, calling out to his brother,
"Teucer, my friend—our trusted comrade's dead,   510
Mastor's son who came our way from Cythera.

We lived in our halls together, prized the man
as we prize our beloved parents—Hector's killed him!
Hurry, where are your arrows fletched with death?
Where is the bow that god Apollo gave you?"

Teucer took the challenge, rushed to his side
and reflex bow in hand and quiver bristling shafts
he loosed a splattering burst against the Trojans.
He picked off Clitus, Pisenor's shining son—
the charioteer to noble Panthous' son Polydamas—   520
wrestling the reins, struggling to head his horses
straight for the point where most battalions panicked,
eager to please Prince Hector and all his Trojans,
Clitus raced on but his death came even faster.
No one could save him now, strain as they did—
a sudden arrow jabbed him behind the neck,
pierced him with pain and out the car he hurtled—
horses rearing in terror, empty chariot clattering off.
But their master Polydamas marked the kill at once,
ran and planted himself across the horses' path   530
and handed them on to Protiaon's son Astynous,
shouting strict commands—"Watch my every move!
Keep the team close by!"—then veering away himself,
back again to grapple frontline troops.
                                        But Teucer—
quick with his next shaft the archer aimed at Hector,
at Hector's brazen crest, and would have stopped
his assault on Argive ships, hit him squarely
and torn his life out just as his courage peaked.
But he could not dodge the lightning mind of Zeus—
standing guard over Hector   540
Zeus tore the glory right from Teucer's grasp,
he snapped the twisted cord on his handsome bow
just as the archer drew it taut against his man
and the weighted bronze shaft skittered off to the side,
the bow dropped from his hand and Teucer shuddered,
calling out to his brother, "Oh what luck—look,
some power cuts us out of the fighting, foils our plans!

He's knocked the bow from my grip, snapped the string,
the fresh gut I tied to the weapon just at dawn
to launch the showers of arrows I'd let fly."   550

    "Too bad, my friend," said Ajax. "Leave them there,
that bow and spill of arrows down on the ground—
a god with a grudge against us wrecks them all.
Take up a long spear, shield on your shoulder,
go for the Trojans, urge your troops to battle.
Maybe they've whipped us here but not without a fight
will they take our benched ships. Call up the joy of war!"

    At that his brother dropped his bow in a shelter,
slung a shield on his shoulder, four plies thick,
over his powerful head he set a well-forged helmet,   560
the horsehair crest atop it tossing, bristling terror.
And taking a rugged spearshaft tipped with whetted bronze
the archer went on the run to stand by Ajax' side.

    But Hector, seeing Teucer's arrows in disarray,
let fly a resounding shout to all his units:
"Trojans! Lycians! Dardan fighters hand-to-hand!
Fight like men, my friends, call up your battle-fury—
make for the hollow ships! I see with my own eyes
how Zeus has blocked their finest archer's arrows.
Easy to see what help Zeus lends to mortals,   570
either to those he gives surpassing glory
or those he saps and wastes, refuses to defend,
just as he wastes the Argives' power but backs us now.
So fight by the ships, all together. And that comrade
who meets his death and destiny, speared or stabbed,
let him die! He dies fighting for fatherland—
no dishonor there!
He'll leave behind him wife and sons unscathed,
his house and estate unharmed—once these Argives
sail for home, the fatherland they love."
                                        That was his cry   580
as Hector put fresh fighting spirit in each man.

But Ajax fired the troops on his side too:
"Shame, you Argives! All or nothing now—
die, or live and drive defeat from the ships!
You want this flashing Hector to take the fleet
then each man walk the waves to regain his native land?
Can't you hear him calling his armies on, full force,
this Hector, wild to gut our hulls with fire?
He's not inviting them to a dance, believe me—
he commands them into battle! No better tactics now   590
than to fight them hand-to-hand with all our fury.
Quick, better to live or die, once and for all,
than die by inches, slowly crushed to death—
helpless against the hulls in the bloody press—
by far inferior men!"
                    And that was Ajax' cry
as the giant put fresh fighting spirit in each man.
But Hector cut down Schedius now, Perimedes' son,
a Phocian chieftain—and Ajax killed Laodamas,
captain of infantry, Antenor's splendid son—
and Polydamas killed Cyllenian Otus outright,   600
Meges' friend, one of the proud Epeans' leaders.
Meges saw him drop, he lunged at Polydamas, fast,
but he ducked and veered away and Meges missed him—
Apollo was not about to let him fall at the front,
not Panthous' son. But Meges did hit Croesmus,
stabbed him square in the chest with a thrusting-lance
and down he crashed—with Meges tearing the armor off his back
as the Trojan Dolops lunged at *him*. A crack spearman—
Laomedon's grandson, Lampus' big and brawny son,
the strongest he sired, the best trained for assault—   610
Dolops quickly went for Meges at close range,
he speared his bulging shield
but the solid breastplate warded off the blow
with both plates fitted tight to bind his body.
The gear his father brought from Ephyra once . . .
the Selleis banks where his host the lord Euphetes
gave him that sturdy bronze to wear in battle,

to beat off the bloody attacks of desperate men
and now it saved his son's young flesh from death.
So Meges chopped at the crown of Dolops' bronze helmet,   620
split its spiny ridge with a sharp cleaving spear
and sheared away its bristling horsehair crest.
Down in the dust the war-gear tumbled, all
still glistening bright in its fresh purple dye
but the man stood his ground, still rearing to fight,
his hopes still soaring for triumph. But now Menelaus,
Atrides out for blood, moved in to fight for Meges—
spear poised in his grip—in from the blind side
and struck from behind the Trojan's shoulder so hard
the spear came jutting out through his chest in all its fury   630
and Dolops reeled and sank, facedown on the ground.
The two men swarmed over him, ripping the armor
off his back as Hector called his kinsmen on,
all his kinsmen, but marked out Hicetaon's son
the strong Melanippus, railing first at him . . .
He used to graze his shambling herds in Percote,
long ago when the enemy's forces stood far off
but once the rolling ships of Achaea swept ashore,
home he came to Troy where he shone among the Trojans,
living close to Priam, who prized him like his sons.   640
But Hector rebuked him now, shouting out his name:
"Melanippus—how can we take things lying down this way?
No qualm in your heart for *this*? Your cousin's dead!
Can't you see how they're clawing over Dolops' armor?
Follow me now. No more standing back, no fighting
these Argives at a distance—kill them hand-to-hand.
Now—before they topple towering Ilium down,
all our people slaughtered!"
                So with a shout
he surged ahead and his gallant cohort followed.
But Great Telamonian Ajax spurred his Argives on: 650
"Be men, my friends! Discipline fill your hearts!
Dread what comrades say of you here in bloody combat!
When men dread that, more men come through alive—

when soldiers break and run, good-bye glory,
good-bye all defenses!''
                             Up in arms as they were
to shield themselves, they took his word to heart
and round the ships they raised a wall of bronze.
But against them Zeus impelled the Trojan ranks
as Menelaus lord of the war cry urged Antilochus,
"None of the younger troops, Antilochus, none   660
is faster of foot than you or tougher in combat—
why not leap right in and lay some Trojan out?''

    Menelaus withdrew as he drove Antilochus on.
Out of the front he sprang, glaring left and right
and hurled his spear—a glinting brazen streak—
and the Trojans scattered, cringing before his shaft . . .
no wasted shot! Antilochus hit Hicetaon's son,
impetuous Melanippus sweeping into battle,
slashed him across the chest beside the nipple.
Down he crashed and the darkness swirled his eyes   670
with Antilochus rushing over him like some hound
pouncing down on a deer that's just been wounded—
leaping out of its lair a hunter's speared it,
a lethal hit that's loosed its springy limbs. ·
So staunch Antilochus leapt at you, Melanippus,
stripping away your gear, but Hector marked it now
and straight through the ruck he charged Antilochus hard.
Quick as that fighter was, he could not hold his ground,
not there—he turned tail and broke like a rogue beast
that's done some serious damage, mauled a dog to death   680
or a herdsman tending flocks, and takes to his heels
before the gangs of men can group and go against him.
So Antilochus turned and ran as a savage cry went up
and Hector and all his Trojans showered deadly shafts
in hot pursuit, but he wheeled and stood his ground
when he reached his thronging cohorts.
                                        Now to the ships—
now like a pride of man-eating lions the Trojan forces
stormed the fleet, fulfilling Zeus's strict commands

as Zeus kept building their fury higher, stunned
the Argives' spirit and wrenched away their glory,   690
lashing Trojans on. The Father's will was set
on giving glory over to Hector son of Priam
that he might hurl his torch at the beaked ships—
the force of fire, quenchless, ravening fire, yes,
and bring to its bitter end the disastrous prayer of Thetis.
For that alone he waited, the god who rules the world,
to see with his own eyes the first Achaean ship
go up in a blaze of flames. Then, from that point on
he'd thrust the Trojans breakneck back from the fleet
and give the Argives glory. Dead set now on that,   700
he drove Prince Hector against the hollow hulls
though the son of Priam raged in his own right,
raged like Ares with brandished spear, or flash fire
roaring down from a ridge into thick stands of timber.
The foam flecked his mouth and his eyes shot flame,
glaring under his shaggy brows and round his head
his helmet shook and clashed, a terrific wild din—
Hector on the attack! And high in the clear sky
Zeus himself defended his champion—Hector alone
he prized and glorified among hordes of men   710
for Hector's life would be cut short so soon . . .
Why, even now Athena was speeding the fatal day
when he would fall to the power of great Achilles.
But now he was bent on breaking men, probing the lines
wherever he saw the largest mass and the finest gear
but he could not smash through yet for all his fury.
They closed ranks, they packed like a stone wall,
a granite cliff that towers against the churning surf,
standing up to the screaming winds, their sudden assaults
and the breaking waves they spawn that crash against its base—   720
so the Danaans stood the Trojan onslaught, rock-solid
and never flinched in fear. But Hector all afire,
blazing head to foot, charged at their main force,
bursting down as a wave bursts down on a veering ship,
down from under the clouds it batters, bred by gale-winds—
showers of foam overwhelm the hull, blot it all from sight,

the hurricane's killing blast thundering into the sails
and scudding clear of death by the skin of their teeth
the sailors quake, their hearts race on with terror—
so the Achaeans' courage quaked. And Hector lunged again   730
like a murderous lion mad for kills, charging cattle
grazing across the flats of a broad marshy pasture,
flocks by the hundred led by an unskilled herdsman
helpless to keep the marauder off a longhorn heifer—
no fighting that bloody slaughter—all he can do
is keep pace with the lead or straggling heads,
leaving the center free for the big cat's pounce
and it eats a heifer raw as the rest stampede away.
And so the Achaeans stampeded now, unearthly terror,
all of them routed now by Father Zeus and Hector—   740
though Hector killed just one . . .
Periphetes, a Mycenaean, favorite son of Copreus,
Eurystheus' herald who summoned rugged Heracles
time and again to grinding labors. Copreus, yes,
that worthless father who sired a better son,
better at every skill, primed for speed and war
and his wits outstripped the best in all Mycenae,
but all of it went now to build Prince Hector's glory.
As the Argive spun in retreat his shield-rim tripped him—
down to his feet that shield he bore to keep off spears—   750
he stumbled over it now, pitched back, helmet clanging
harshly against his brows as the man hit the ground.
But Hector marked him at once, rushed up to his side
and staked a spear in his chest to kill the fighter
right in the eyes of loyal comrades standing by.
Sick for their friend but what could *they* do? Nothing—
just shake with dread in the face of mighty Hector.

Now the Achaeans milled among the shipways,
shielded round by the looming superstructures,
stern on stern drawn up on the first line inland.   760
But the Trojans stormed them there and back they fell,
they had no choice, edging away from the front ships
but once at the tents nearby they held their ground,

massing ranks, no scattering back through camp.
Their proud discipline gripped them, terror too—
they rallied each other, nonstop, war cries rising.
Noble Nestor was first, Achaea's watch and ward,
pleading, begging each man for his parents' sake,
"Be men, my friends! Discipline fill your hearts,
maintain your pride in the eyes of other men!   770
Remember, each of you, sons, wives, wealth, parents—
are mother and father dead or alive? No matter,
I beg you for *their* sakes, loved ones far away—
now stand and fight, no turning back, no panic."

With that he put new strength in each man's spirit.
Athena thrust from their eyes the blinding battle-haze,
the darkness sent by the gods, and a hard bright light
burst down in both directions, out to the ships
and down the lines where fighting drew dead even.
Now they could make out Hector lord of the war cry,   780
all his troops, squads in reserve and clear of battle,
forward squads that fought at the fast trim ships. ·

Ajax' challenge—how could it please his courage still
to hang back now where other Achaeans held the rear?
No more. Up and down the decks of the ships he went
with his great plunging strides, swinging in hand
his enormous polished pike for fights at sea,
clamped with clinchers, twenty-two forearms long.
Ajax skilled as a show-rider, a virtuoso horseman
who picks from the herd four stallions, yokes them tight   790
and galloping off the plain comes racing toward a large city,
over a trafficked road and the crowds gaze in wonder,
men and women watching, as sure-footed, never a slip,
the rider keeps on leaping, swinging from back to back
and the pounding team flies on. So Ajax swung now,
leaping from deck to deck on the fast trim ships,
ranging with huge strides as his voice hit the skies,
keeping up a terrific bellowing, calling Argives on

to defend the ships and shelters.
                              And Hector too—
how could he hold back with his massing, armored Trojans?   800
Now like a flashing eagle swooping down on bird-flocks,
winged thousands feeding, swarming a river's banks,
geese, cranes or swans with their long lancing necks—
so swooping Hector went headfirst at a warship,
charged its purple prow, and Zeus behind him
thrust him on with his mighty, deathless hand,
urging the soldiers on who crowded Hector's back.

And again a desperate battle broke at the ships.
You'd think they waded into the fighting, fresh troops,
unbruised, unbroken, they fought with such new fire.   810
And what were the fighters thinking? Only this:
the Argives certain they'd never flee the worst,
they'd perish then and there,
but the hopes soared in every Trojan's heart
to torch the ships and slaughter Argive heroes—
so ran their thoughts, closing for the kill. At last
Hector grappled a ship's stern, a beauty built for speed—
it swept the seas with Protesilaus, bore him to Troy
but never bore him back to his fatherland again.
Now churning round that ship Achaeans and Trojans   820
hacked each other at close range. No more war at a distance,
waiting to take the long flights of spears and arrows—
they stood there man-to-man and matched their fury,
killing each other now with hatchets, battle-axes,
big swords, two-edged spears, and many a blade,
magnificent, heavy-hilted and thonged in black
lay strewn on the ground—some dropped from hands,
some fell as the fighters' shoulder-straps were cut—
and the earth ran black with blood. And Hector held fast,
he never let go of the high stern, he hugged its horn,   830
arms locked in a death-grip, crying out to Trojans,
"Bring fire! Up with the war cries, all together!
Now Zeus hands *us* a day worth all the rest,
today we seize these ships—

they stormed ashore against the will of the gods,
they came here freighted with years of pain for us,
and all thanks to our city elders. What cowards!
Whenever I longed to fight at the ships' high sterns
the old men kept me back, they held the troops in check.
Oh but if Zeus's lightning blinded us those days,   840
it's Zeus who drives us, hurls us on today!"

> The harder he cried
the harder his forces charged against the Argives.
Not even Ajax held his post, no longer now:
forced by the shafts he backed away by inches,
certain he'd die there—down he leapt from the decks,
down to bestride the seven-foot bridge amidships.
There he stood, tensing, braced to take them on—
his huge pike kept beating the Trojans off the hulls,
any attacker flinging tireless fire, and all the time
that terrible voice of his, bellowing out to cohorts,   850
"Friends! Fighting Danaans! Aides-in-arms of Ares!
Fight like men, my comrades—call up your battle-fury!
You think we have reserves in the rear to back us up?
Some stronger wall to shield our men from disaster?
No, there's no great citadel standing near with towers
where *we* could defend ourselves and troops could turn the tide.
No—we're here on the plain of Troy—all Troy's in arms!
Dug in, backs to the sea, land of our fathers far away!
Fight—the light of safety lies in our fighting hands,
not spines gone soft in battle!"

> And with each cry   860
he thrust his slashing pike with a fresh new fury.
And any Trojan crashing against the beaked ships,
torch ablaze in hand, straining to please Hector
who urged him on . . . Ajax ready and waiting there
would stab each man with his long, rugged pike—
twelve he impaled point-blank, struggling up the hulls.

BOOK SIXTEEN

Patroclus
Fights and Dies

So they fought to the death around that benched beaked ship
as Patroclus reached Achilles, his great commander,
and wept warm tears like a dark spring running down
some desolate rock face, its shaded currents flowing.
And the brilliant runner Achilles saw him coming,
filled with pity and spoke out winging words:
"Why in tears, Patroclus?
Like a girl, a baby running after her mother,
begging to be picked up, and she tugs her skirts,
holding her back as she tries to hurry off—all tears,   10
fawning up at her, till she takes her in her arms . . .
That's how you look, Patroclus, streaming live tears.
But why? Some news for the Myrmidons, news for me?
Some message from Phthia that you alone have heard?
They tell me Menoetius, Actor's son, is still alive,

and Peleus, Aeacus' son, lives on among his Myrmidons—
if both our fathers had died, we'd have some cause for grief.
Or weeping over the Argives, are you? Seeing them die
against the hollow ships, repaid for their offenses?
Out with it now! Don't harbor it deep inside you.   20
We must share it all."

                  With a wrenching groan
you answered your friend, Patroclus O my rider:
"Achilles, son of Peleus, greatest of the Achaeans,
spare me your anger, please—
such heavy blows have overwhelmed the troops.
Our former champions, all laid up in the ships,
all are hit by arrows or run through by spears.
There's powerful Diomedes brought down by an archer,
Odysseus wounded, and Agamemnon too, the famous spearman,
and Eurypylus took an arrow-shot in the thigh . . .   30
Healers are working over them, using all their drugs,
trying to bind the wounds—

                  But *you* are intractable, Achilles!
Pray god such anger never seizes *me*, such rage you nurse.
Cursed in your own courage! What good will a man,
even one in the next generation, get from you
unless you defend the Argives from disaster?
You heart of iron! He was not your father,
the horseman Peleus—Thetis was not your mother.
Never. The salt gray sunless ocean gave you birth
and the towering blank rocks—your temper's so relentless.   40
But still, if down deep some prophecy makes you balk,
some doom your noble mother revealed to you from Zeus,
well and good: at least send *me* into battle, quickly.
Let the whole Myrmidon army follow my command—
I might bring some light of victory to our Argives!
And give me your own fine armor to buckle on my back,
so the Trojans might take *me* for you, Achilles, yes,
hold off from attack, and Achaea's fighting sons
get second wind, exhausted as they are . . .
Breathing room in war is all too brief.   50
We're fresh, unbroken. The enemy's battle-weary—

we could roll those broken Trojans back to Troy,
clear of the ships and shelters!"
                              So he pleaded,
lost in his own great innocence . . .
condemned to beg for his own death and brutal doom.
And moved now to his depths, the famous runner cried,
"No, no, my prince, Patroclus, what are you saying?
Prophecies? None that touch me. None I know of.
No doom my noble mother revealed to me from Zeus,
just this terrible pain that wounds me to the quick—   60
when one man attempts to plunder a man his equal,
to commandeer a prize, exulting so in his own power.
That's the pain that wounds me, suffering such humiliation.
That girl—the sons of Achaea picked her as my prize,
and I'd sacked a walled city, won her with my spear
but right from my grasp he tears her, mighty Agamemnon,
that son of Atreus! Treating me like some vagabond,
some outcast stripped of all my rights . . .
                                   Enough.
Let bygones be bygones now. Done is done.
How on earth can a man rage on forever?   70
Still, by god, I said I would not relax my anger,
not till the cries and carnage reached my own ships.
So you, you strap my splendid armor on your back,
you lead our battle-hungry Myrmidons into action!—
if now, in fact, the black cloud of the Trojans
blasts down on the ships with full gale force,
our backs to the breaking surf but clinging still
to a cramped strip of land—the Argives, lost.
The whole city of Troy comes trampling down on us,
daring, wild—why? They cannot see the brow of my helmet   80
flash before their eyes—Oh they'd soon run for their lives
and choke the torrent-beds of the field with all their corpses
if only the mighty Agamemnon met me with respect:
now, as it is, they're fighting round our camp!
No spear rages now in the hand of Diomedes,
keen to save the Argives from disaster . . .
I can't even hear the battle cry of Agamemnon

break from his hated skull. But it's man-killing Hector
calling his Trojans on, his war cries crashing round me,
savage cries of his Trojans sweeping the whole plain,   90
victors bringing the Argive armies to their knees.
Even so, Patroclus, fight disaster off the ships,
fling yourself at the Trojans full force—
before they gut our hulls with leaping fire
and tear away the beloved day of our return.
But take this command to heart—obey it to the end.
So you can win great honor, great glory for me
in the eyes of all the Argive ranks, and they,
they'll send her back, my lithe and lovely girl,
and top it off with troves of glittering gifts.   100
Once you have whipped the enemy from the fleet
you must come back, Patroclus. Even if Zeus
the thundering lord of Hera lets you seize your glory,
you must not burn for war against these Trojans,
madmen lusting for battle—not without *me*—
you will only make *my* glory that much less . . .
You must not, lost in the flush and fire of triumph,
slaughtering Trojans outright, drive your troops to Troy—
what if one of the gods who never die comes down
from Olympus heights to intervene in battle?   110
The deadly Archer loves his Trojans dearly.
No, you must turn back—
soon as you bring the light of victory to the ships.
Let the rest of them cut themselves to pieces on the plain!
Oh would to god—Father Zeus, Athena and lord Apollo—
not one of all these Trojans could flee his death, not one,
no Argive either, but we could stride from the slaughter
so we could bring Troy's hallowed crown of towers
toppling down around us—you and I alone!"

     And so the comrades roused each other now.   120
But Ajax could hold his post on the decks no longer.
He was overwhelmed by the latest salvos, driven back
by the will of Zeus and the fearless Trojan spearmen
hurling blows nonstop—a terrific din at his temples,

his shining helmet clashing under repeated blows,
relentless blows beating his forged cheek-irons.
And the joint of his left shoulder ached with labor,
forever bracing his huge burnished shield rock-steady,
but they could not wrench it loose from round his body
for all their pelting weapons. Again and again   130
he fought for breath, gasping, bathed in sweat
rivering down his body, his limbs soaked and sleek . . .
where could he find some breathing room in battle?
Wherever he looked, pains heaped on pains.

                              Sing to me now,
you Muses, you who hold Olympus' vaulting halls,
how fire was first pitched on Achaea's ships!

    Hector lunged at Ajax toe-to-toe,
hacked his ash-wood pike with a heavy sword
and striking the socket just behind the point
he slashed the head clean off, leaving the shaft,   140
the lopped stump dangling in Ajax' fist, useless,
bronze head bounding away, clanging along the ground.
And deep in his heart brave Ajax knew and shuddered—
here was work of the gods, thundering Zeus on high,
cutting him off from battle, dashing all his plans,
Zeus, determined to grant the Trojans triumph now.
So Ajax drew back, out of range, and then—
they flung their tireless fire at a fast trim ship.
She was up in flames at once, engulfed in quenchless fire,
in a flash the blaze went swirling round the stern   150
and Achilles slapped his thighs and urged Patroclus,
"To arms—Patroclus, prince and master horseman!
I can see the blaze go roaring up the ships.
They *must* not destroy them. No escape-route then.
Quick, strap on my gear—I'll rouse the troops."

                              That was all,
and Patroclus armed himself in Achilles' gleaming bronze.
First he wrapped his legs with the well-made greaves,
fastened behind the heels with silver ankle-clasps,
next he strapped the breastplate round his chest,

blazoned with stars—swift Achilles' own—   160
then over his shoulder Patroclus slung the sword,
the fine bronze blade with its silver-studded hilt,
and then the shield-strap and the sturdy, massive shield
and over his powerful head he set the well-forged helmet,
the horsehair crest atop it tossing, bristling terror,
and he took two rugged spears that fit his grip.
And Achilles' only weapon Patroclus did not take
was the great man's spear, weighted, heavy, tough.
No other Achaean fighter could heft that shaft,
only Achilles had the skill to wield it well: 170
Pelian ash it was, a gift to his father Peleus
presented by Chiron once, hewn on Pelion's crest
to be the death of heroes.
                            Now the war-team.
Patroclus ordered Automedon to yoke them quickly—
a man he honored next to Achilles breaker of men,
always firmest in battle, nerved to wait the call.
So at his command Automedon yoked the horses,
the rapid stallions Roan Beauty and Dapple,
the team that raced the gales, magnificent team
the storm-wind filly Lightfoot foaled for the West Wind,   180
grazing the lush green grass along the Ocean's tides.
And into the traces he ran the purebred Bold Dancer—
Achilles seized him once when he stormed Eetion's city,
a mortal war-horse pacing immortal horses now.

   Prince Achilles, ranging his ranks of Myrmidons,
arrayed them along the shelters, all in armor.
Hungry as wolves that rend and bolt raw flesh,
hearts filled with battle-frenzy that never dies—
off on the cliffs, ripping apart some big antlered stag
they gorge on the kill till all their jaws drip red with blood,   190
then down in a pack they lope to a pooling, dark spring,
their lean sharp tongues lapping the water's surface,
belching bloody meat, but the fury, never shaken,
builds inside their chests though their glutted bellies burst—
so wild the Myrmidon captains, Myrmidon field commanders

swarming round Achilles' dauntless friend-in-arms.
And there in the midst Achilles stood like the god of war,
urging his charioteers and fighters bracing shields..

There were fifty fast black ships that bore his troops
when Achilles dear to Zeus sailed east for Troy.   200
Fifty fighters aboard each, manning the oarlocks,
five captains he named, entrusted with command,
but he himself in his martial power ruled them all . . .
The first battalion was led by Menesthius bright in bronze,
son of Spercheus River swelled by the rains of Zeus
and born by the lovely Polydora, Peleus' daughter,
when a girl and the god of a tireless river bedded down.
But they called him the son of Borus, Perieres' son
who showered the girl with countless bridal gifts,
his wedded bride in the sight of all the world.   210
The next battalion was led by fighting Eudorus,
born out of wedlock too. Phylas' daughter,
Polymela the gorgeous dancer bore the man
when irresistible Hermes, Hermes the giant-killer
lusted for her once—she ravished the god's bright eyes,
swaying among the dancers singing goddess Artemis
with arrow of gold and cry that halloos the hunt.
And straightway up to her chamber Hermes climbed,
the Healer, in secret, lay in her arms in love
and the woman bore the god a radiant son, Eudorus—   220
lightning on his feet and a crack man of war.
But soon as the Lady of Labor's birthing pangs
brought him to light and he saw the blaze of day,
Actor's majestic son the powerful lord Echecles
led her home to his house with troves of bridal gifts
while old King Phylas reared the boy with kindness,
tending, embracing the young Eudorus like a son.
The third battalion was led by brave Pisander,
Maemalus' son, who outfought them all with spears,
all the Myrmidons after Achilles' friend Patroclus.   230
The fourth was led by the old horseman Phoenix,
Alcimedon led the fifth, Laerces' gallant son.

But soon as Achilles mustered all battalions,
positioned in battle-order led by captains,
he imposed this stern command on all his troops:
"Myrmidons! Not one of you dare forget those threats
you hurled from the fast trim ships against the Trojans
all the while I raged, and I was the one you blamed,
down to the last fighter: 'Brutal son of Peleus—
your mother nursed you on gall! Merciless, iron man—   240
confining your own men to the ships against their will!
So home we go in those ships and cut the seas again,
since now such deadly anger strikes our captain.'
                                        Denouncing *me*—
my comrades, clustered together, always grumbling.
Well, here's a tremendous work of battle, look,
blazing before your eyes
and just the sort you longed for all those days.
So each man tense with courage—fight the Trojans down!"

    That was the cry that fired each soldier's heart.
Hearing the king's command the ranks pulled closer,   250
tight as a mason packs a good stone wall,
blocks on granite blocks for a storied house
that fights the ripping winds—crammed so close
the crested helmets, the war-shields bulging, jutting,
buckler-to-buckler, helm-to-helm, man-to-man massed tight
and the horsehair crests on glittering helmet horns brushed
as they tossed their heads, the battalions bulked so dense.
And out before them all, two men took battle-stations,
Patroclus and Automedon, seized with a single fury
to fight in the comrades' vanguard, far in front.   260

    But Achilles strode back to his shelter now
and opened the lid of the princely inlaid sea chest
that glistening-footed Thetis stowed in his ship to carry,
filled to the brim with war-shirts, windproof cloaks
and heavy fleecy rugs. And there it rested . . .
his handsome, well-wrought cup. No other man
would drink the shining wine from its glowing depths,

nor would Achilles pour the wine to any other god,
none but Father Zeus. Lifting it from the chest
he purified it with sulphur crystals first   270
then rinsed it out with water running clear,
washed his hands and filled it bright with wine.
And then, taking a stand before his lodge, he prayed,
pouring the wine to earth and scanning the high skies
and the god who loves the lightning never missed a word:
"King Zeus—Pelasgian Zeus, lord of Dodona's holy shrine,
dwelling far away, brooding over Dodona's bitter winters!
Your prophets dwelling round you, Zeus, the Selli
sleeping along the ground with unwashed feet . . .
If you honored me last time and heard my prayer   280
and rained destruction down on all Achaea's ranks,
now, once more, I beg you, bring my prayer to pass!
I myself hold out on shore with the beached ships here
but I send my comrade forth to war with troops of Myrmidons—
Launch glory along with him, high lord of thunder, Zeus!
Fill his heart with courage—so even Hector learns
if Patroclus has the skill to fight his wars alone,
my friend-in-arms, or his hands can rage unvanquished
only when *I* go wading in and face the grind of battle.
But once he repels the roaring onslaught from the ships   290
let him come back to me and our fast fleet—unharmed—
with all my armor round him, all our comrades
fighting round my friend!"
                              So Achilles prayed
and Zeus in all his wisdom heard those prayers.
One prayer the Father granted, the other he denied:
Patroclus would drive the onslaught off the ships—
that much Zeus granted, true,
but denied him safe and sound return from battle.
Once Achilles had poured the wine and prayed to Zeus,
he returned to his shelter, stowed the cup in the chest   300
then took his stand outside, his spirit yearning still
to watch Achaeans and Trojans struggle to the death.
                                                    Myrmidons,
battalions ranged in armor with greathearted Patroclus,

moving out now, the fury bursting inside them,
suddenly chargéd the Trojans—
they swarmed forth like wasps from a roadside nest
when boys have made it their sport to set them seething,
day after day tormenting them round their wayside hive—
idiot boys! they make a menace for every man in sight.
Any innocent traveler passing them on that road   310
can stir them accidentally—up in arms in a flash,
all in a swarm come pouring, each one raging down
to fight for home and children—

                          Such frenzy seized their hearts,
Myrmidons pouring out of the ships, ceaseless shouts rising
and over them all Patroclus' war cries rousing comrades:
"Myrmidons! Brothers-in-arms of Peleus' son Achilles!
Fight like men, my friends, call up your battle-fury!
Now we must win high honor for Peleus' royal son,
far the greatest fighter among the Argive fleet,
and we who fight beside him the bravest troops—   320
so even mighty Atrides can see how mad he was
to disgrace Achilles, the best of the Achaeans!"

He closed with a shout and fired each fighter's heart
and down in a mass they launched against the Trojans,
ships around them echoing back their shattering cries.

The Trojans, soon as they saw Menoetius' gallant son,
himself and his loyal driver flare in brazen gear—
all their courage quaked, their columns buckled,
thinking swift Achilles had tossed to the winds
his hard rage that held him back by the ships   330
and chosen friendship toward the Argives now.
Each Trojan soldier glancing left and right—
how could he run from sudden, plunging death?

Patroclus was first to hurl his glinting spear,
right at the center mass—the fighters milling
round the stern of Protesilaus' blazing ship—
and hit Pyraechmes, firebrand who led the Paeonians,

the master riders from Amydon, from Axius' broad currents.
Patroclus slashed his right shoulder and down he went,
his back slamming the dust with a jolting groan   340
as companions panicked round him—brave Paeonians—
Patroclus whipped the terror in all their hearts
when he killed the chief who topped them all in battle.
He rode them off the ships, he quenched the leaping fire,
leaving Protesilaus' hulk half-burnt but upright still
and the Trojans scattered back with high, shrill cries.
The Argives poured against them, back by the hollow hulls,
the din of battle incessant—
                            an Argive breakthrough—
bright as the moment Zeus the lord of lightning moves
from a craggy mountain ridge a storm cloud massing dense   350
and all the lookout peaks stand out and the jutting cliffs
and the steep ravines and down from the high heavens bursts
the boundless bright air . . . So now the Argives
drove the ravening fire clear of the warships,
winning a little breathing room, not much,
no real halt to the buck-and-rush of battle.
For despite the surge of the Argives primed for war
the Trojans were still not wheeling round in headlong rout
away from the black hulls. Forced back from them, true,
they braced for battle still and made a stand.
                            Deadlock: 360
there man killed man in the pell-mell clash of battle,
captains going at captains. Brave Patroclus first—
just as Areilycus swerved in sudden flight
he gored him in the hip with a slashing spear
and the bronze lancehead hammered through his flesh,
the shaft splintering bone as he pitched face-first,
pounding the ground—
                    And veteran Menelaus wounded Thoas,
raking his chest where the shield-rim left it bare,
and loosed his limbs—
                    And Amphiclus went for Meges
but Meges saw him coming and got in first by far,   370
spearing him up the thigh where it joins the body,

the spot where a man's muscle bunches thickest:
the tough sinews shredded around the weapon's point
as the dark swirled down his eyes—

                    Nestor's sons on attack!
Antilochus struck Atymnius hard with a whetted spear,
the bronze ripping into his flank and clean through—
he crashed at his feet—

                But Maris charged Antilochus,
sweeping in with his lance, enraged for his brother,
planted himself before his corpse but Thrasymedes,
quick as a god, beat him to it—he stabbed   380
before Maris stabbed—no miss! right in the shoulder,
the Argive's spearpoint cracked through the bony socket,
shearing away the tendons, wrenched the whole arm out
and down he thundered, darkness blanked his eyes.
So these two brothers, laid low by the two brothers,
dropped to the world of night: Sarpedon's stalwart cohorts,
spearmen sons of Amisodarus—he who bred the Chimaera,
the grim monster that sent so many men to death.
There—quick Oilean Ajax rushed Cleobulus,
took him alive, stumbling blind in the rout   390
but took his life at once, snapped his strength
with a sword that hewed his neckbone—up to the hilt
so the whole blade ran hot with blood, and red death
came flooding down his eyes, and the strong force of fate.
And now in a breakneck charge Peneleos closed with Lycon—
they'd missed each other with spears, two wasted casts,
so now both clashed with swords. Lycon, flailing,
chopped the horn of Peneleos' horsehair-crested helmet
but round the socket the sword-blade smashed to bits—
just as Peneleos hacked his neck below the ear   400
and the blade sank clean through, nothing held
but a flap of skin, the head swung loose to the side
as Lycon slumped down to the ground . . . There—
at a dead run Meriones ran down Acamas, Acamas
mounting behind his team, and gouged his right shoulder—
he pitched from the car and the mist whirled down his eyes.
Idomeneus skewered Erymas straight through the mouth,

the merciless brazen spearpoint raking through,
up under the brain to split his glistening skull—
teeth shattered out, both eyes brimmed to the lids   410
with a gush of blood and both nostrils spurting,
mouth gaping, blowing convulsive sprays of blood
and death's dark cloud closed down around his corpse.

    So in a rush each Argive captain killed his man.
As ravenous wolves come swooping down on lambs or kids
to snatch them away from right amidst their flock—all lost
when a careless shepherd leaves them straggling down the hills
and quickly spotting a chance the wolf pack picks them off,
no heart for the fight—so the Achaeans mauled the Trojans.
Shrieking flight the one thing on the Trojans' minds,   420
they forgot their fighting-fury . . .

    Great Ajax now—forever aiming at Hector,
trying to strike his helmet flashing bronze
but Hector was far too seasoned, combat-tested,
broad shoulders hunching under his bull's-hide shield,
his eyes peeled for a whistling shaft or thudding spear.
Hector knew full well the tide of battle had turned
but still stood firm, defending die-hard comrades.

    Wild as a storm cloud moving off Olympus into heaven
out of a clear blue sky when Zeus brings cyclones on—   430
so wild the rout, the cries that came from the ships
as back through the trench they ran, formations wrecked.
And Hector? Hector's speeding horses swept him away,
armor and all, leaving his men to face their fate,
Trojans trapped but struggling on in the deep trench.
Hundreds of plunging war-teams dragging chariots down,
snapping the yoke-poles, ditched their masters' cars
and Patroclus charged them, heart afire for the kill,
shouting his Argives forward—"Slaughter Trojans!"
Cries of terror breaking as Trojans choked all roads,   440
their lines ripped to pieces, up from under the hoofs
a dust storm swirling into the clouds as rearing horses

broke into stride again and galloped back to Troy,
leaving ships and shelters in their wake. Patroclus—
wherever he saw the biggest masses dashing before him,
there he steered, plowing ahead with savage cries
and fighters tumbled out of their chariots headfirst,
crushed under their axles, war-cars crashing over, yes,
but straight across the trench went his own careering team
at a superhuman bound. Magnificent racing stallions,   450
gifts of the gods to Peleus, shining immortal gifts,
straining breakneck on as Patroclus' high courage
urged him against Prince Hector, keen for the kill
but Hector's veering horses swept him clear.
And all in an onrush dark as autumn days
when the whole earth flattens black beneath a gale,
when Zeus flings down his pelting, punishing rains—
up in arms, furious, storming against those men
who brawl in the courts and render crooked judgments,
men who throw all rights to the winds with no regard   460
for the vengeful eyes of the gods—so all their rivers
crest into flood spate, ravines overflowing cut the hilltops
off into lonely islands, the roaring flood tide rolling down
to the storm-torn sea, headlong down from the foothills
washes away the good plowed work of men—

                                        Rampaging so,
the gasping Trojan war-teams hurtled on.

                                        Patroclus—
soon as the fighter cut their front battalions off
he swerved back to pin them against the warships,
never letting the Trojans stream back up to Troy
as they struggled madly on—but there mid-field   470
between the ships, the river and beetling wall
Patroclus kept on sweeping in, hacking them down,
making them pay the price for Argives slaughtered.
There, Pronous first to fall—a glint of the spear
and Patroclus tore his chest left bare by the shield-rim,
loosed his knees and the man went crashing down.
And next he went for Thestor the son of Enops
cowering, crouched in his fine polished chariot,

crazed with fear, and the reins flew from his grip—
Patroclus rising beside him stabbed his right jawbone,   480
ramming the spearhead square between his teeth so hard
he hooked him by that spearhead over the chariot-rail,
hoisted, dragged the Trojan out as an angler perched
on a jutting rock ledge drags some fish from the sea,
some noble catch, with line and glittering bronze hook.
So with the spear Patroclus gaffed him off his car,
his mouth gaping round the glittering point
and flipped him down facefirst,
dead as he fell, his life breath blown away.
And next he caught Erylaus closing, lunging in—   490
he flung a rock and it struck between his eyes
and the man's whole skull split in his heavy helmet,
down the Trojan slammed on the ground, head-down
and courage-shattering Death engulfed his corpse.
Then in a blur of kills, Amphoterus, Erymas, Epaltes,
Tlepolemus son of Damastor, and Echius and Pyris,
Ipheus and Euippus and Polymelus the son of Argeas—
he crowded corpse on corpse on the earth that rears us all.

But now Sarpedon, watching his comrades drop and die,
war-shirts billowing free as Patroclus killed them,   500
dressed his godlike Lycians down with a harsh shout:
"Lycians, where's your pride? Where are you running?
Now be fast to attack! I'll take him on myself,
see who he is who routs us, wreaking havoc against us—
cutting the legs from under squads of good brave men."

With that he leapt from his chariot fully armed
and hit the ground and Patroclus straight across,
as soon as he saw him, leapt from his car too.
As a pair of crook-clawed, hook-beaked vultures
swoop to fight, screaming above some jagged rock—   510
so with their battle cries they rushed each other there.
And Zeus the son of Cronus with Cronus' twisting ways,
filling with pity now to see the two great fighters,

said to Hera, his sister and his wife, "My cruel fate . . .
my Sarpedon, the man I love the most, my own son—
doomed to die at the hands of Menoetius' son Patroclus.
My heart is torn in two as I try to weigh all this.
Shall I pluck him up, now, while he's still alive
and set him down in the rich green land of Lycia,
far from the war at Troy and all its tears?   520
Or beat him down at Patroclus' hands at last?"

   But Queen Hera, her eyes wide, protested strongly:
"Dread majesty, son of Cronus—what are you saying?
A man, a mere mortal, his doom sealed long ago?
You'd set him free from all the pains of death?
Do as you please, Zeus . . .
but none of the deathless gods will ever praise you.
And I tell you this—take it to heart, I urge you—
if you send Sarpedon home, living still, beware!
Then surely some other god will want to sweep   530
his own son clear of the heavy fighting too.
Look down. Many who battle round King Priam's
mighty walls are sons of the deathless gods—
you will inspire lethal anger in them all.
                                                    No,
dear as he is to you, and your heart grieves for him,
leave Sarpedon there to die in the brutal onslaught,
beaten down at the hands of Menoetius' son Patroclus.
But once his soul and the life force have left him,
send Death to carry him home, send soothing Sleep,
all the way till they reach the broad land of Lycia.   540
There his brothers and countrymen will bury the prince
with full royal rites, with mounded tomb and pillar.
These are the solemn honors owed the dead."
                                          So she pressed
and Zeus the father of men and gods complied at once.
But he showered tears of blood that drenched the earth,
showers in praise of him, his own dear son,
the man Patroclus was just about to kill
on Troy's fertile soil, far from his fatherland.

Now as the two came closing on each other
Patroclus suddenly picked off Thrasymelus   550
the famous driver, the aide who flanked Sarpedon—
he speared him down the guts and loosed his limbs.
But Sarpedon hurled next with a flashing lance
and missed his man but he hit the horse Bold Dancer,
stabbing his right shoulder and down the stallion went,
screaming his life out, shrieking down in the dust
as his life breath winged away. And the paired horses
reared apart—a raspy creak of the yoke, the reins flying,
fouled as the trace horse thrashed the dust in death-throes.
But the fine spearman Automedon found a cure for that—   560
drawing his long sharp sword from his sturdy thigh
he leapt with a stroke to cut the trace horse free—
it worked. The team righted, pulled at the reins
and again both fighters closed with savage frenzy,
dueling now to the death.
                              Again Sarpedon missed—
over Patroclus' left shoulder his spearhead streaked,
it never touched his body. Patroclus hurled next,
the bronze launched from his hand—no miss, a mortal hit.
He struck him right where the midriff packs the pounding heart
and down Sarpedon fell as an oak or white poplar falls   570
or towering pine that shipwrights up on a mountain
hew down with whetted axes for sturdy ship timber—
so he stretched in front of his team and chariot,
sprawled and roaring, clawing the bloody dust.
As the bull a marauding lion cuts from the herd,
tawny and greathearted among the shambling cattle,
dies bellowing under the lion's killing jaws—
so now Sarpedon, captain of Lycia's shieldsmen,
died at Patroclus' hands and died raging still,
crying out his beloved comrade's name: "Glaucus—   580
oh dear friend, dear fighter, soldier's soldier!
Now is the time to prove yourself a spearman,
a daring man of war—now, if you are brave,
make grueling battle your one consuming passion.

First find Lycia's captains, range the ranks,
spur them to fight and shield Sarpedon's body.
Then you, Glaucus, you fight for me with bronze!
You'll hang your head in shame—every day of your life—
if the Argives strip my armor here at the anchored ships
where I have gone down fighting. Hold on, full force—   590
spur all our men to battle!"
                              Death cut him short.
The end closed in around him, swirling down his eyes,
choking off his breath. Patroclus planted a heel
against his chest, wrenched the spear from his wound
and the midriff came out with it—so he dragged out both
the man's life breath and the weapon's point together.
Close by, the Myrmidons clung to the panting stallions
straining to bolt away, free of their masters' chariot.

     But grief came over Glaucus, hearing his comrade's call.
His heart was racing—what could he do to help him?   600
Wounded himself, he gripped his right arm hard,
aching where Teucer's arrow had hit him squarely,
assaulting the Argive wall, when Teucer saved his men.
Glaucus cried a prayer to the distant deadly Archer:
"Hear me, Lord Apollo! Wherever you are now—
in Lycia's rich green country or here in Troy,
wherever on earth, you can hear a man in pain,
you have that power, and pain comes on me now.
Look at this ugly wound—
my whole arm rings with the stabbing pangs,   610
the blood won't clot, my shoulder's a dead weight.
I can't take up my spear, can't hold it steady—
no wading into enemy ranks to fight it out . . .
and our bravest man is dead, Sarpedon, Zeus's son—
did Zeus stand by him? Not even his own son!
I beg you, Apollo, heal this throbbing wound,
lull the pain now, lend me power in battle—
so I can rally our Lycians, drive them into war
and fight to save my comrade's corpse myself."

So Glaucus prayed and Apollo heard his prayer.   620
He stopped the pains at once, stanched the dark blood
in his throbbing wound and filled his heart with courage.
And Glaucus sensed it all and the man glowed with joy
that the mighty god had heard his prayer so quickly.
First he hurried to spur his Lycian captains on,
ranging his own ranks, to fight around Sarpedon,
then he ran for the Trojan lines with long strides.
He found Polydamas, Panthous' son, and Prince Agenor
and reaching Aeneas and Hector helmed in bronze,
shoulder-to-shoulder let his challenge fly: 630
"Hector, you've wiped your allies from your mind!
And all for you, Hector, far from their loved ones,
far from native land they bleed their lives away.
But you won't lift a hand to fight beside them.
There lies Sarpedon, lord of Lycia's shieldsmen,
who defended his realm with just decrees and power—
Ares has cut him down with Patroclus' brazen spear.
Quick, my friends, stand by him! Cringe with shame
at the thought they'll strip his gear and maim his corpse—
these Myrmidons, seething for all the Argive troops we killed,   640
we speared to death against their fast trim ships!"

Hard grief came sweeping over the Trojans' heads—
unbearable, irrepressible. He was their city's bastion,
always, even though he came from foreign parts,
and a mass of allies marched at his command
but he excelled them all in battle, always.
So now they went at the Argives, out for blood,
and furious for Sarpedon Hector swung them round.
But the Argives surged to Patroclus' savage spirit—
he spurred the Aeantes first, both ablaze for battle: 650
"Ajax, Ajax! Come—now thrill to fight as before,
brave among the brave, but now be braver still!
Their captain's down, the first to storm our wall,
the great Sarpedon. If only we could seize his body,
mutilate him, shame him, tear his gear from his back
and any comrade of his who tries to shield his corpse—

bring that enemy down witn ruthless bronze!"

> Urging so

but his men already burned to drive the Trojans off.
And both armies now, pulling their lines tighter,
Trojans and Lycians, Myrmidons and Achaeans   660
closed around the corpse to lunge in battle—,
terrible war cries, stark clashing of armored men.
And across the onslaught Zeus swept murderous night
to make the pitched battle over his own dear son
a brutal, blinding struggle.

> Here at the first assault

the Trojans shouldered back the fiery-eyed Achaeans—
a Myrmidon had been hit, and not their least man,
dauntless Agacles' son, renowned Epigeus . . .
He ruled Budion's fortress town in the old days
but then, having killed some highborn cousin, fled   670
to Peleus and glistening Thetis, begged for his own life
and they sent him off with Achilles, breaker of men,
east to stallion-country to fight and die in Troy.
He had just grasped the corpse
when shining Hector smashed his head with a rock
and his whole skull split in his massive helmet—
down he slammed on Sarpedon's body, facefirst
and courage-shattering Death engulfed his corpse.
Grief for his dead companion seized Patroclus now,
he tore through frontline fighters swift as a hawk   680
diving to scatter crows and fear-struck starlings—
straight at the Lycians, Patroclus O my rider,
straight at the pressing Trojan ranks you swooped,
enraged at your comrade's death! and struck Sthenelaus,
Ithaemenes' favorite son—a big rock to the neck
snapped the tendons strung to the skull's base.
So the front gave ground and flashing Hector too,
though only as far as a long slim spear can fly
when a man tests his hurling strength in the games
or in war when enemy fighters close to crush his life—   690
so far the Trojans gave as the Argives drove them back.
But Glaucus was first, lord of Lycia's shieldsmen now,

the first to turn and he killed the gallant Bathycles,
Chalcon's prize son who had made his home in Hellas,
excelling the Myrmidons all in wealth and fortune.
Now, just as the man was about to catch Glaucus
Glaucus suddenly spun and struck, he stabbed his chest,
ripped him down with a crash. A heavy blow to the Argives,
one of the brave ones down. A great joy to the Trojans,
massing packs of them swarming round the corpse   700
but Achaean forces never slacked their drive,
their juggernaut fury bore them breakneck on.
And there—Meriones killed a Trojan captain,
Laogonus, daring son of Onetor, priest of Zeus,
Idaean Zeus, and his land revered him like a god—
Meriones gouged him under the jaw and ear, his spirit
flew from his limbs and the hateful darkness gripped him.
Just then Aeneas hurled his brazen spear at Meriones,
hoping to hit the man as he charged behind his shield.
But he eyed Aeneas straight on, he dodged the bronze,   710
ducking down with a quick lunge, and behind his back
the heavy spearshaft plunged and stuck in the earth,
the butt end quivering into the air till suddenly
rugged Ares snuffed its fury out, dead still.
The weapon shaking, planted fast in the ground,
his whole arm's power poured in a wasted shot,
Aeneas flared in anger, shouting out, "Meriones—
great dancer as you are, my spear would have stopped
your dancing days for good if only I had hit you!"

The hardy spearman Meriones shot back, "Aeneas—   720
great man of war as you are, you'll find it hard
to quench the fire of every man who fights you.
You too are made of mortal stuff, I'd say. And I,
if I'd lanced your guts with bronze—strong as you are
and cocksure of your hands—you'd give me glory now,
you'd give your life to the famous horseman Death!"

But Patroclus nerved for battle dressed him down:
"Meriones, brave as you are, why bluster on this way?

Trust me, my friend, you'll never force the Trojans
back from this corpse with a few stinging taunts—
Earth will bury many a man before that. Come—   730
the proof of battle is action, proof of words, debate.
No time for speeches now, it's time to fight."

Breaking off, he led the way as Meriones followed,
staunch as a god. And loud as the roar goes up
when men cut timber deep in the mountain glades
and the pounding din of axes echoes miles away—
so the pound and thud of blows came rising up
from the broad earth, from the trampled paths of war
and the bronze shields and tough plied hides struck hard   740
as the swords and two-edged spearheads stabbed against them.
Not even a hawk-eyed scout could still make out Sarpedon,
the man's magnificent body covered over head to toe,
buried under a mass of weapons, blood and dust.
But they still kept swarming round and round the corpse
like flies in a sheepfold buzzing over the brimming pails
in the first spring days when the buckets flood with milk.
So veteran troops kept swarming round that corpse,
never pausing—nor did mighty Zeus for a moment
turn his shining eyes from the clash of battle.   750
He kept them fixed on the struggling mass forever,
the Father's spirit churning, thrashing out the ways,
the numberless ways to cause Patroclus' slaughter . . .
To kill him too in this present bloody rampage
over Sarpedon's splendid body? Hector in glory
cutting Patroclus down with hacking bronze
then tearing the handsome war-gear off his back?
Or let him take still more, piling up his kills?
As Zeus turned things over, that way seemed the best:
the valiant friend-in-arms of Peleus' son Achilles
would drive the Trojans and Hector helmed in bronze   760
back to Troy once more, killing them by platoons—
and Zeus began with Hector, he made the man a coward.
Hector leaping back in his chariot, swerving to fly,
shouted out fresh orders—"Retreat, Trojans, now!"

He knew that Zeus had tipped the scales against him.
A rout—not even the die-hard Lycians stood their ground,
they all scattered in panic, down to the last man
when they saw their royal king speared in the heart,
Sarpedon sprawled there in the muster of the dead,   770
for men by the squad had dropped across his corpse
once Zeus stretched tight the lethal line of battle.
So then the Achaeans ripped the armor off his back,
Sarpedon's gleaming bronze that Menoetius' son
the brave Patroclus flung in the arms of cohorts
poised to speed those trophies back to the beaked ships.
And storming Zeus was stirring up Apollo: "On with it now—
sweep Sarpedon clear of the weapons, Phoebus my friend,
and once you wipe the dark blood from his body,
bear him far from the fighting, off and away,   780
and bathe him well in a river's running tides
and anoint him with deathless oils . . .
dress his body in deathless, ambrosial robes.
Then send him on his way with the wind-swift escorts,
twin brothers Sleep and Death, who with all good speed
will set him down in the broad green land of Lycia.
There his brothers and countrymen will bury the prince
with full royal rites, with mounded tomb and pillar.
These are the solemn honors owed the dead."
                                            So he decreed
                                                                      790
and Phoebus did not neglect the Father's strong desires.
Down from Ida's slopes he dove to the bloody field
and lifting Prince Sarpedon clear of the weapons,
bore him far from the fighting, off and away,
and bathed him well in a river's running tides
and anointed him with deathless oils . . .
dressed his body in deathless, ambrosial robes
then sent him on his way with the wind-swift escorts,
twin brothers Sleep and Death, who with all good speed
set him down in Lycia's broad green land.
                                            But Patroclus,
                                                                      800
giving a cry to Automedon whipping on his team,
Patroclus went for Troy's and Lycia's lines,

blind in his fatal frenzy—luckless soldier.
If only he had obeyed Achilles' strict command
he might have escaped his doom, the stark night of death.
But the will of Zeus will always overpower the will of men,
Zeus who strikes fear in even the bravest man of war
and tears away his triumph, all in a lightning flash,
and at other times he will spur a man to battle,
just as he urged Patroclus' fury now.

        Patroclus—
who was the first you slaughtered, who the last   810
when the great gods called you down to death?
First Adrestus, then Autonous, then Echeclus,
then Perimus, Megas' son, Epistor and Melanippus,
then in a flurry Elasus, Mulius and Pylartes—
he killed them all but the rest were bent on flight.

  And then and there the Achaeans might have taken Troy,
her towering gates toppling under Patroclus' power
heading the vanguard, storming on with his spear.
But Apollo took his stand on the massive rampart,
his mind blazing with death for him but help for Troy. 820
Three times Patroclus charged the jut of the high wall,
three times Apollo battered the man and hurled him back,
the god's immortal hands beating down on the gleaming shield.
Then at Patroclus' fourth assault like something superhuman,
the god shrieked down his winging words of terror: "Back—
Patroclus, Prince, go back! It is not the will of fate
that the proud Trojans' citadel fall before your spear,
not even before Achilles—far greater man than you!"

  And Patroclus gave ground, backing a good way off,
clear of the deadly Archer's wrath.

        But now Hector, 830
reining his high-strung team at the Scaean Gates,
debated a moment, waiting . . .
should he drive back to the rout and soldier on?
Or call his armies now to rally within the ramparts?

As he turned things over, Apollo stood beside him,
taking the shape of that lusty rugged fighter
Asius, an uncle of stallion-breaking Hector,
a blood brother of Hecuba, son of Dymas
who lived in Phrygia near Sangarius' rapids.
Like him, Apollo the son of Zeus incited Hector: 840
"Hector, why stop fighting? Neglecting your duty!
If only I outfought *you* as you can outfight *me*,
I'd soon teach you to shirk your work in war—
you'd pay the price, I swear. Up with you—fast!
Lash those pounding stallions straight at Patroclus—
you might kill him still—Apollo might give you glory!"

And back Apollo strode, a god in the wars of men
while glorious Hector ordered skilled Cebriones,
"Flog the team to battle!" Apollo pressed on,
wading into the ruck, hurling Argives back in chaos   850
and handing glory to Hector and all the Trojan forces.
But Hector ignored the Argive masses, killing none,
he lashed his pounding stallions straight at Patroclus.
Patroclus, over against him, leapt down from his car
and hit the ground, his left hand shaking a spear
and seized with his right a jagged, glittering stone
his hand could just cover—Patroclus flung it hard,
leaning into the heave, not backing away from Hector,
no, and no wasted shot. But he hit his driver—
a bastard son of famed King Priam, Cebriones   860
yanking the reins back taut—right between the eyes.
The sharp stone crushed both brows, the skull caved in
and both eyes burst from their sockets, dropping down
in the dust before his feet as the reinsman vaulted,
plunging off his well-wrought car like a diver—
Cebriones' life breath left his bones behind
and you taunted his corpse, Patroclus O my rider:
"Look what a springy man, a nimble, flashy tumbler!
Just think what he'd do at sea where the fish swarm—
why, the man could glut a fleet, diving for oysters!   870
Plunging overboard, even in choppy, heaving seas,

just as he dives to ground from his war-car now.
Even these Trojans have their tumblers—what a leap!"

   And he leapt himself at the fighting driver's corpse
with the rushing lunge of a lion struck in the chest
as he lays waste pens of cattle—
his own lordly courage about to be his death.
So you sprang at Cebriones, full fury, Patroclus,
as Hector sprang down from his chariot just across
and the two went tussling over the corpse as lions   880
up on the mountain ridges over a fresh-killed stag—
both ravenous, proud and savage—fight it out to the death.
So over the driver here and both claw-mad for battle,
Patroclus son of Menoetius, Hector ablaze for glory
strained to slash each other with ruthless bronze.
Hector seized the corpse's head, would not let go—
Patroclus clung to a foot and other fighters clashed,
Trojans, Argives, all in a grueling, maiming onset.

   As the East and South Winds fight in killer-squalls
deep in a mountain valley thrashing stands of timber,   890
oak and ash and cornel with bark stretched taut and hard
and they whip their long sharp branches against each other,
a deafening roar goes up, the splintered timber crashing—
so Achaeans and Trojans crashed,
hacking into each other, and neither side now
had a thought of flight that would have meant disaster.
Showers of whetted spears stuck fast around Cebriones,
bristling winged arrows whipped from the bowstrings,
huge rocks by the salvo battering shields on shields
as they struggled round the corpse. And there he lay   900
in the whirling dust, overpowered in all his power
and wiped from memory all his horseman's skills.

   So till the sun bestrode the sky at high noon
the weapons hurtled side-to-side and men kept falling.
But once the sun wheeled past the hour for unyoking oxen,
then the Argives mounted a fiercer new attack,

fighting beyond their fates . . .
They dragged the hero Cebriones out from under
the pelting shafts and Trojans' piercing cries
and they tore the handsome war-gear off his back   910
and Patroclus charged the enemy, fired for the kill.
Three times he charged with the headlong speed of Ares,
screaming his savage cry, three times he killed nine men.
Then at the fourth assault Patroclus like something superhuman—
then, Patroclus, the end of life came blazing up before you,
yes, the lord Apollo met you there in the heart of battle,
the god, the terror! Patroclus never saw him coming,
moving across the deadly rout, shrouded in thick mist
and on he came against him and looming up behind him now—
slammed his broad shoulders and back with the god's flat hand   920
and his eyes spun as Apollo knocked the helmet off his head
and under his horses' hoofs it tumbled, clattering on
with its four forged horns and its hollow blank eyes
and its plumes were all smeared in the bloody dust.
Forbidden before this to defile its crest in dust,
it guarded the head and handsome brow of a god,
a man like a god, Achilles. But now the Father
gave it over to Hector to guard his head in war
since Hector's death was closing on him quickly.
Patroclus though—the spear in his grip was shattered,   930
the whole of its rugged bronze-shod shadow-casting length
and his shield with straps and tassels dropped from his shoulders,
flung down on the ground—and lord Apollo the son of Zeus
wrenched his breastplate off. Disaster seized him—
his fine legs buckling—

                          he stood there, senseless—
                                                  And now,
right at his back, close-up, a Dardan fighter speared him
squarely between the shoulder blades with a sharp lance.
Panthous' son Euphorbus, the best of his own age
at spears and a horseman's skill and speed of foot,
and even in this, his first attack in chariots—   940
just learning the arts of war—
he'd brought down twenty drivers off their cars.

He was the first to launch a spear against you,
Patroclus O my rider, but did not bring you down.
Yanking out his ashen shaft from your body,
back he dashed and lost himself in the crowds—
the man would not stand up to Patroclus here
in mortal combat, stripped, defenseless as he was.
Patroclus stunned by the spear and the god's crushing blow
was weaving back to his own thronging comrades,   950
trying to escape death . . .
                              Hector waiting, watching
the greathearted Patroclus trying to stagger free,
seeing him wounded there with the sharp bronze
came rushing into him right across the lines
and rammed his spearshaft home,
stabbing deep in the bowels, and the brazen point
went jutting straight out through Patroclus' back.
Down he crashed—horror gripped the Achaean armies.
As when some lion overpowers a tireless wild boar
up on a mountain summit, battling in all their fury   960
over a little spring of water, both beasts craving
to slake their thirst, but the lion beats him down
with sheer brute force as the boar fights for breath—
so now with a close thrust Hector the son of Priam
tore the life from the fighting son of Menoetius,
from Patroclus who had killed so many men in war,
and gloried over him, wild winging words: "Patroclus—
surely you must have thought you'd storm my city down,
you'd wrest from the wives of Troy their day of freedom,
drag them off in ships to your own dear fatherland—   970
you fool! Rearing in their defense my war-team,
Hector's horses were charging out to battle,
galloping, full stretch. And I with my spear,
Hector, shining among my combat-loving comrades,
I fight away from *them* the fatal day—but you,
the vultures will eat your body raw!
                              Poor, doomed . . .
not for all his power could Achilles save you now—
and how he must have filled your ears with orders

as you went marching out and the hero stayed behind:
'Now don't come back to the hollow ships, you hear?—   980
Patroclus, master horseman—
not till you've slashed the shirt around his chest
and soaked it red in the blood of man-killing Hector!'
So he must have commanded—you maniac, you obeyed."

   Struggling for breath, you answered, Patroclus O my rider,
"Hector! Now is your time to glory to the skies . . .
now the victory is yours.
A gift of the son of Cronus, Zeus—Apollo too—
they brought me down with all their deathless ease,
they are the ones who tore the armor off my back.   990
Even if twenty Hectors had charged against me—
they'd all have died here, laid low by my spear.
No, deadly fate in league with Apollo killed me.
From the ranks of men, Euphorbus. You came third,
and all you could do was finish off my life . . .
One more thing—take it to heart, I urge you—
you too, you won't live long yourself, I swear.
Already I see them looming up beside you—death
and the strong force of fate, to bring you down
at the hands of Aeacus' great royal son . . .
                              Achilles!"   1000

   Death cut him short. The end closed in around him.
Flying free of his limbs
his soul went winging down to the House of Death,
wailing his fate, leaving his manhood far behind,
his young and supple strength. But glorious Hector
taunted Patroclus' body, dead as he was, "Why, Patroclus—
why prophesy my doom, my sudden death? Who knows?—
Achilles the son of sleek-haired Thetis may outrace me—
struck by *my* spear first—and gasp away his life!"

   With that he planted a heel against Patroclus' chest,   1010
wrenched his brazen spear from the wound, kicked him over,
flat on his back, free and clear of the weapon.

At once he went for Automedon with that spear—
quick as a god, the aide of swift Achilles—
keen to cut him down but his veering horses
swept him well away—magnificent racing stallions,
gifts of the gods to Peleus, shining immortal gifts.

BOOK SEVENTEEN

Menelaus'
Finest Hour

But Atreus' son the fighting Menelaus marked it all—
the Trojans killing Patroclus there in the brutal carnage—
and crested now in his gleaming bronze gear Atrides
plowed through the front to stand astride the body,
braced like a mother cow lowing over a calf,
her first-born, first labor-pangs she'd felt.
So the red-haired captain bestrode Patroclus now,
shielding his corpse with spear and round buckler,
burning to kill off any man who met him face-to-face.
But Euphorbus who hurled the lethal ashen spear   10
would not neglect his kill, Patroclus' handsome body.
Halting close beside it, he taunted fighting Menelaus:
"Back, high and mighty Atrides, captain of armies—
back from the corpse, and leave the bloody gear!
I was the first Trojan, first of the famous allies

to spear Patroclus down in the last rough charge.
So let me seize my glory among the Trojans now—
or I'll spear you too, I'll rip your own sweet life away!"

But the red-haired captain flared back in anger:
"Father Zeus—listen to this indecent, reckless bluster!   20
Not even the leopard's fury makes the beast so proud,
not even the lion's, not the murderous wild boar's,
the greatest pride of all, bursting the boar's chest—
they're nothing next to the pride of Panthous' sons
with their strong ashen spears. But no, no joy
did even powerful Hyperenor, breaker of horses,
get from *his* young strength when he scorned *me*,
stood up to *me*, reviling *me* as the weakest fighter
in all Achaea's armies. Home he went, I'd say,
but not on his own two feet, and brought no cheer   30
to his loyal, loving wife and devoted parents.
And you, I'll break your courage for you too
if you try to take me on.
Go back to your own rank and file, I tell you!
Don't stand up against me—or you will meet your death.
Even a fool learns something once it hits him."

                                    So he warned
but failed to shake Euphorbus who shot right back,
"Now, high and mighty Atrides, now by heaven
you pay in blood for the brother you laid low!
You glory over it too—making his wife a widow   40
lost in the depths of their new bridal chamber,
bringing his parents cursed tears and grief.
But I could stop that wretched couple's pain
if only I brought your head and bloody armor home
and laid them in Panthous' arms, in lovely Phrontis' arms!
We're wasting time. Our fight's unfought, untested—
we'll see who stands his ground, who cuts and runs."

    And he stabbed Menelaus' round shield, full center,
not battering through—the brazen point bent back
in the tough armor.

But his turn next, Menelaus   50
rose with a bronze lance and a prayer to Father Zeus
and lunging out at Euphorbus just dropping back,
pierced the pit of his throat—leaning into it hard,
his whole arm's weight in the stroke to drive it home
and the point went slicing through the tender neck.
He fell with a crash, armor ringing against his ribs,
his locks like the Graces' locks splashed with blood,
still braided tight with gold and silver clips,
pinched in like a wasp's waist. There he lay
like an olive slip a farmer rears to strength   60
on a lonely hilltop, drenching it down with water,
a fine young stripling tree, and the winds stir it softly,
rustling from every side, and it bursts with silver shoots—
then suddenly out of nowhere a wind in gale force comes storming,
rips it out of its trench, stretches it out on the earth—
so Panthous' stripling son lay sprawled in death,
Euphorbus who hurled the strong ashen spear . . .
Menelaus cut him down, was stripping off his armor—

Menelaus fierce as a mountain lion sure of his power,
seizing the choicest head from a good grazing herd.   70
First he cracks its neck, clamped in his huge jaws,
mauling the kill then down in gulps he bolts it,
blood and guts, and around him dogs and shepherds
raise a fierce din but they keep their distance,
lacking nerve to go in and take the lion on—
the fear that grips their spirit makes them blanch.
So now not a single Trojan fighter had the spine
to go and face Atrides tensing in all his strength.
Then and there Menelaus might have stripped Euphorbus
and swept the Trojan's glittering armor off with ease   80
if Apollo had not grudged him all that glory,
rousing Hector against him, swift as Ares.
Taking a man's shape, the Cicones' captain Mentes,
Apollo spurred him on with winged orders: "Hector—
you're chasing the wild wind, fiery Achilles' team!

They're hard for mortal men to curb and drive,
for all but Achilles—his mother is immortal.
But all the while Menelaus, Atreus' fighting son
bestrides Patroclus—he's killed the Trojans' best,
Panthous' son Euphorbus, stopped his fury cold." 90

And back Apollo strode, a god in the wars of men.
But grief bore down on Hector, packing his dark heart
as he scanned the battle lines and saw the worst at once:
the two men there, one stripping the gleaming armor,
the other sprawled on the ground,
blood still spurting warm from his slashed throat.
Down the front he charged, crested in flashing bronze,
Hector loosing a savage cry and flaring on like fire,
like the god of fire, the blaze that never dies.
And the cry pierced Menelaus, deeply torn now 100
as he probed his own great heart: "What can I do?
If I leave this splendid gear and desert Patroclus—
who fell here fighting, all to redeem my honor—
won't any comrade curse me, seeing me break away?
But if I should take on Hector and Hector's Trojans
alone, in single combat—trying to save my pride—
won't they encircle me, one against so many?
This flashing Hector has all Troy at his back!
But why debate, my friend, why thrash things out?
When you fight a man against the will of the gods, 110
a man they have sworn to honor—then look out,
a heavy wave of ruin's about to overwhelm you.
Surely no Achaean will curse me, seeing me now,
giving ground to Hector . . .
since fighting Hector's flanked by god almighty.
Ah if only I knew where Ajax could be found,
that man with his ringing war cry—we two together
would go back to the melee calling up our fury,
even fight in the teeth of every god on high
and haul the body back to Achilles—somehow. 120
Things are bad, but that would be the best."

Working it out, his heart racing as on they came,
waves of Trojan soldiers and Hector led them in.
And Atrides gave ground, he left the corpse
but kept on turning round to face an attack—
like a great bearded lion the dogs and field hands
drive back from the folds with spears and sharp cries
and the brave, battling heart in his chest freezes tight
and the big cat, all reluctance, pulls back from the sheds.
So the red-haired captain backed away from Patroclus' corpse   130
but wheeled at bay when he reached his waiting allies,
glancing round and round for Ajax' massive hulk.
All at once on the left flank he marked him,
spurring companions, urging them to fight,
for Phoebus had filled each man with quaking fear.
Atrides went on the run and reached him, shouting, "Ajax!
Hurry, my friend, this way—fight for dead Patroclus!
At least we could bring his body back to Achilles,
stripped as Patroclus is—but not Achilles' armor:
Hector with that flashing helmet has seized it all."   140

So he roused the fury in battling Ajax' heart
and down the front he stalked with the red-haired king.
Hector, tearing the famous armor off Patroclus,
tugged hard at the corpse,
mad to hack the head from the neck with bronze
and drag the trunk away to glut the dogs of Troy.
But in charged Ajax, shield like a tower before him
and Hector, falling back on a crowd of comrades,
leapt to his chariot, flinging the burnished gear
to his waiting troops to haul away to Troy—   150
trophies to be his own enormous glory. But Ajax,
shielding Patroclus round with his broad buckler,
stood fast now like a lion cornered round his young
when hunters cross him, leading his cubs through woods—
he ramps in all the pride of his power, bristling strength,
the heavy folds of his forehead frowning down his eyes.
So Ajax stood his ground over brave Patroclus now—

the fighting Atrides right beside him, standing fast,
his grief mounting, every waiting moment.

But Glaucus,
Hippolochus' son and lord of Lycia's forces now,   160
scowled at Hector, lashing out at him: "Hector—
our prince of beauty, in battle all a sham!
That empty glory of yours a runner's glory,
a scurrying girl's at that.
Now you'd better plan how to save your city,
you alone and your native troopers born in Troy.
Now not a single Lycian goes to fight the Argives,
not to save your Troy. What lasting thanks for us,
for warring with your enemies, on and on, no end?
What hope has the common soldier in your ranks   170
to be saved by you, Hector, you heart of iron?—
if you could quit Sarpedon, your guest and friend-in-arms
abandoned there as carrion fit for the Argive maws.
Think what a staunch support Sarpedon was to you
and to all Troy while the man was still alive!
Now you lack the daring to save him from the dogs.
So now, if any Lycian troops will obey my orders,
home we go—and headlong death can come and topple Troy.
If the Trojans had that courage, unswerving courage
that fires men who fight for their own country,   180
beating their enemies down in war and struggle,
then we could drag Patroclus back to Troy at once.
If we could haul him from battle, dead as he is,
and lodge him behind King Priam's looming walls,
our enemies would release Sarpedon's gear at once
and then, then we could bring *his* body back to Troy.
For the man we cut down here was the loyal friend
of Prince Achilles—far the greatest among the Argive ships
and at his command go rugged fighters hand-to-hand.
But you—with enemy war cries ringing in your ears—   190
you lacked the nerve to go up against Great Ajax,
that fierce heart, to look him straight in the eye
and fight the man head-on—he's a better man than you!"

With a dark glance from under his flashing helmet
Hector lashed back, "Glaucus, such brazen insolence
from a decent man like you, but why? Ah too bad,
and I always thought you excelled the rest in sense,
all who hale from Lycia's fertile soil. But now—
you fill me with contempt—what are you saying?
You tell *me* that I can't stand up to monstrous Ajax?   200
I tell *you* I never cringe at war and thundering horses!
But the will of Zeus will always overpower the will of men,
Zeus who strikes fear in even the bravest man of war
and tears away his triumph, all in a lightning flash,
and at other times he will spur a man to battle.
Come on, my friend, stand by me, watch me work!
See if I prove a coward dawn to dusk—your claim—
or I stop some Argive, blazing in all his power,
from fighting on to shield Patroclus' corpse!"

With that he loosed a shrill cry to his Trojans,   210
"Trojans! Lycians! Dardan fighters hand-to-hand—
now be men, my friends, call up your battle-fury!
I'll strap on the brave Achilles' armor, burnished armor
I stripped from strong Patroclus when I killed him!"

So he cried and his own bronze helmet flashed
as Hector veered away from the heavy fighting,
running after his men and caught them quickly.
They'd not gone far and he ran with eager strides
as they bore Achilles' famous arms toward Troy.
Standing far from the war and all its heartbreak   220
Hector exchanged his armor, handing his own gear
to his battle-hungry troops to return to holy Troy,
and donned the deathless arms of Peleus' son Achilles,
arms the gods of the sky once gave his loving father—
and Peleus passed them on to his son when he grew old
but the son would not grow old in his father's armor.

                                                    Now,
when Zeus who arrays the clouds saw Hector from afar,
strapping on the gear of Peleus' godlike son,

he shook his head and addressed his own deep heart:
"Poor soldier. Never a thought of death weighs down   230
your spirit now, yet death is right beside you . . .
You don the deathless arms of a great fighter—
and all other fighters tremble before him, true,
but you, you killed his comrade, gentle, strong,
and against all rights you ripped the immortal armor
off his head and shoulders. So great power for the moment
I will grant you to compensate for all that is to come:
never again will you return from battle, Hector,
nor will Andromache take that famous armor,
Achilles' deathless armor, from your hands."

                        So he decreed   240
and the son of Cronus bowed his craggy dark brows.
Zeus fitted the armor tightly on Hector's body
and Ares surged in his heart with awesome force,
filling his limbs with power and fighting strength.
And on he strode amidst his illustrious Trojan allies—
calling out with wild cries, now flashing before them all
in the gleaming battle-gear of greathearted Achilles.
He ranged their ranks, inspiriting every captain,
commanding Mesthles, Glaucus, Medon, Thersilochus,
Asteropaeus, Disenor, Hippothous, Phorcys, Chromius,   250
Ennomus too, who could read the flight of birds.
Hector drove them on with winging orders: "Hear me—
numberless tribes of allies living round our borders—
I neither sought nor needed enormous hordes of men
that day I called you here, each from your own city.
What I needed was men to shield our helpless children,
fighting men to defend our Trojan women—all-out—
against these savage Argives. That goal in mind,
I bleed my own people for gifts and food
so I can build your courage, each and every man.   260
So now, each of you, turn straight for the enemy,
live or die—that is the lovely give-and-take of war.
That man who drags Patroclus back to Trojan charioteers,
dead as Patroclus is, and makes Great Ajax yield—
to him I will give one half the bloody spoils,

keep half for myself—his glory will equal mine!"
                                                    Strong vow—
and they bore straight down on the Argives full force,
shaking their spears, their hearts fired with hopes
of dragging Patroclus' body out from under Ajax—
fools! Over the corpse he'd cut down crowds of men,   270
though now, at this point, Ajax warned Menelaus,
lord of the battle cry, "Old friend, my Prince,
I lose hope that we alone, on our own power,
can make it back from the fighting.
I not only fear for our comrade's body—
Patroclus will glut the dogs and birds of Troy
and all too soon—but I fear for my own head,
for my own life. And yours too, Menelaus—
look at this cloud of war that blots out all the field,
this Hector, this headlong death that stares us in the face!   280
Quick, call to the chiefs—if one can hear you now."

    At that the prince of the battle cry complied
with a high piercing shout that reached all troops:
"Friends—lords of the Argives, O my captains!
All who join the Atridae, Agamemnon and Menelaus,
who drink wine at the king's expense and hold command
of your own troops, your rank and fame from Zeus!
Impossible now to pick you out, my captains,
man by man—the battle blazes up so wildly.
Forward, each on his own! You'll die of shame   290
if the dogs of Ilium make Patroclus ripping sport."

    And the quick Oilean Ajax heard him clearly,
first on the run along the fighting front to meet him—
Idomeneus after him and Idomeneus' good aide,
Meriones, a match for the butcher god of war.
For the rest who followed, waking Achaea's war-lust,
what man has spirit strong enough to sing their names?

    Down in a mass the Trojans pounded—Hector led them in,
charging in as a heavy surf roars in against the rip

at a river's mouth, swelled with rains from Zeus,   300
and on either side the jutting headlands bellow back
at the booming sea with matching thunder—in they came,
the Trojans roaring in. But the Argives faced them,
standing fast in a ring around Patroclus, one fury
seizing their hearts, packing a wall of bronze shields
and round about their glittering crested helmets now
the son of Cronus spread a dense, deepening mist.
He had never hated Menoetius' son in the past,
while he was alive and still Achilles' aide,
and now the Father loathed to see him prey   310
to Troy's marauders, the ravening dogs of Troy—
so he drove his comrades on to shield his corpse.

    At first the Trojans could ram the Argives back
and they abandoned the corpse, their fiery-eyed battalions
fled away in panic. But still the breakneck Trojans,
up in arms as they were,
killed off none of the Argives with their spears—
instead they began to drag away Patroclus' corpse.
But not for long would his comrades give him up:
in a swift maneuver Ajax wheeled them round,   320
Ajax, greatest in build, greatest in works of war
of all the Argives after Peleus' matchless son.
Right through the front he plowed like a wild boar
ramping in power up on the high mountain ridges,
scattering dogs and reckless hunters at one charge
when he wheels at bay and drives them down the glades.
So now the son of noble Telamon, dauntless Ajax
scattered the massing Trojan packs at a charge,
all who bestrode Patroclus now, high with hopes
of dragging him back to Troy to win the glory—

                                Trying hardest,   330
Hippothous out for fame . . . Pelasgian Lethus' son,
lashing a shield-strap round the ankle tendons,
was hauling Patroclus footfirst through the melee,
hoping to please Prince Hector and all the Trojans,
Hippothous rushing on but death came just as fast.

No Trojans could save him now, strain as they might—
Ajax son of Telamon charging quickly into the carnage
speared him at close range through the bronze-cheeked helmet,
the horsehair crest cracked wide open around the point,
smashed by the massive spear and hand that drove it.   340
His brains burst from the wound in sprays of blood,
soaking the weapon's socket—
his strength dissolved on the spot, his grip loosed
and he dropped the foot of brave Patroclus' corpse.
There on the ground it lay—he rushed to join it,
pitching over the dead man's body face-to-face,
a world away from Larissa's dark rich soil . . .
Never would he repay his loving parents now
for the gift of rearing—his life cut short so soon,
brought down by the spear of lionhearted Ajax.   350

    Hector hurled at *him*—a sudden glint of the spear—
but Ajax saw it coming and dodged the bronze shaft,
just by a hair, and the weapon caught Schedius,
gallant Iphitus' son and Phocia's finest man,
who made his home in the famous town of Panopeus,
ruling tribes of men. Hector speared him now—
the point split the collarbone, slashing through
and out by the shoulder's base, sticking out the back.
He fell with a crash, his armor clanging round him.
                                              Ajax next—
with a lunge he stabbed Phorcys, Phaenops' warrior son   360
bestriding Hippothous' corpse—he ripped his belly,
smashing the corslet just where the plates join
and the bronze spearhead spilled his entrails out
and down went Phorcys, grasping, clawing the dust.
The Trojan front gave ground, glorious Hector too
and the Argives yelled wildly, dragging the bodies,
hauling Hippothous' corpse along with Phorcys' now
and tearing the bloody armor off their backs.
                              Then, once more,
Trojan troops would have clambered back inside their walls,
whipped weak with fear by the Argives primed for battle   370

and they, they would have seized enormous glory—
yes, defying even the great decree of Zeus—
by dint of their own power and striking force.
But god Apollo himself spurred on Aeneas,
taking the build of Periphas, Summoner's son
who had grown old as herald to Aeneas' father
the aged king—a loving, loyal herald too . . .
Like him to the life, Apollo provoked Aeneas:
"Aeneas—how could you and your men save Troy
with the gods *against* you? As I've seen other men   380
who trust to their own power and striking force,
their own valor, their own troop-strength—
even badly outmanned—defend their country well.
But Zeus is *with* us here! Decreeing triumph for us,
not for the Argives now. But you, you're all frightened
out of your minds—you cannot fight."

                                The deadly Archer—
Aeneas knew him at once, looking straight in his eyes
and the fighter loosed a rousing shout at Hector:
"Hector—all you captains of Trojans, Trojan allies—
shame, what shame! Clambering back into Troy now,   390
whipped weak with fear by the Argive forces? Look—
one of the gods comes up beside me, tells me Zeus
the supreme commander still impels us all in battle.
So go for the Argives—head-on! Don't let them bear
Patroclus' body back to their ships without a fight!"

    And springing out of the lines Aeneas took his stand
as the rest swung round and braced to meet the Argives.
There—Aeneas lunged and speared Leocritus through,
a son of Arisbas, Lycomedes' die-hard friend.
And veteran Lycomedes pitied him as he dropped,   400
sweeping beside him, rearing—a flash of his lance
and he hit a captain, Hippasus' son Apisaon,
slitting open his liver, up under the midriff . . .
His knees went limp, a man who'd marched from Paeonia,
good fertile soil where he excelled all fighters,
all but Asteropaeus—

                    Down to the ground he went
but battling Asteropaeus pitied his comrade's pain
and charged the Argives hard, mad to fight it out—
no use, too late. They'd packed behind their shields,
ringing Patroclus round on all sides, spears jutting   410
as Ajax ranged them all and shouted out commands:
"No one back away from the body! No heroes either,
bolting out of the Argive pack for single combat!
Cluster round Patroclus, shoulder-to-shoulder,
fight them at close range!" At the giant's command
the earth ran red with blood, slithering dark now
and the soldiers' corpses tumbling thick-and-fast,
Trojans and breakneck allies piled alongside Argives—
how could the Argives fight without some bloody losses?
But far fewer of them went down, remembering always   420
to fight in tight formation,
friend defending friend from headlong slaughter.

    So on they fought like a swirl of living fire—
you could not say if the sun and moon still stood secure,
so dense the battle-haze that engulfed the brave
who stood their ground around Patroclus' body.
But the other Trojans and Argive men-at-arms
fought on at their ease beneath a clear blue sky—
sharp brilliance of sunlight glittering round them,
not a cloud in sight to shadow the earth and mountains.   430
Men who fought at a distance worked with frequent breaks,
dodging painful arrows that showered side-to-side.
But men who held the center suffered agonies,
thanks to the haze and carnage—
ruthless bronze hacking their lines to pieces,
there where the bravest fought. Yet two men there,
famous fighters, Antilochus flanking Thrasymedes
still had not caught word of Patroclus' death:
they thought the gallant soldier still alive,
fighting Trojans up on the clashing front lines.   440
But the two men kept their lookout, always alert
to their comrades' deaths or signs of instant flight

as the two fought out on the flank—just as Nestor ordered,
sending both sons forth from the black ships to battle.

So all day long for the men of war the fighting raged,
grim and grueling, relentless, drenching labor, nonstop,
and the knees, shins and feet that upheld each fighter,
their hands, their eyes, ran with the sweat of struggle
over the great runner Achilles' steadfast aide-in-arms—
an enormous tug-of-war. As when some master tanner   450
gives his crews the hide of a huge bull for stretching,
the beast's skin soaked in grease and the men grab hold,
bracing round in a broad circle, tugging, stretching hard
till the skin's oils go dripping out as the grease sinks in,
so many workers stretch the whole hide tough and taut—
so back and forth in a cramped space they tugged,
both sides dragging the corpse and hopes rising,
Trojans hoping to drag Patroclus back to Troy,
Achaeans to drag him back to the hollow ships
and round him always the brutal struggle raging.   460
Not even Ares, lasher of armies, not even Athena
watching the battle here could scorn its fury,
not even in their most savage lust for combat, no—
so tense the work of war for the men and chariot-teams
that Zeus stretched taut across Patroclus this one day . . .

But great Achilles knew nothing yet of Patroclus' death.
They were fighting far afield of the deep-sea ships,
beneath the Trojan wall, so Achilles never feared
his friend was dead—he must be still alive,
pressing on to the very gates, but he'd come back.   470
Achilles never dreamed Patroclus would storm all Troy
without him, not even *with* him. No, time and again
his mother Thetis told him this was not to be,
she told him alone, in secret . . .
always bringing word of mighty Zeus's plans,
but not this time. One thing she never told him—
his own mother—what a terrible thing had taken place:

his dearest friend-in-arms on earth lay dead.
                                    Over his corpse
no letup, the fighters kept on thrusting whetted spears,
locked in endless struggle, cutting each other down.   480
And an Argive armed in bronze would call out, "Friends!
Our glory's gone if we fall back now on the ships—
let the black earth gape and take us all at once,
here and now! Better for us that way, by far,
if we yield his corpse to the stallion-breaking Trojans,
all to drag him back to Troy and win the glory."

    And a hardy Trojan would call on his side, "Friends!
What if it's fated for us to die beside this body—
all dead in a mass? Let no man quit the battle!"

    So they would say, fueling comrades' courage.   490
And so they fought and the iron din went rising up
to the bronze sky through the barren breathless air.
But standing clear of the fray Achilles' horses wept
from the time they first had sensed their driver's death,
brought down in the dust by man-killing Hector.
Diores' rugged son Automedon did his best,
lashed them over and over with stinging whip—
coaxing them gently now, now shouting oath on oath.
But both balked at returning now to the ships
moored at the Hellespont's far-reaching shore   500
or galloping back to fight beside the Argives.
Staunch as a pillar planted tall above a barrow,
standing sentry over some lord or lady's grave-site,
so they stood, holding the blazoned chariot stock-still,
their heads trailing along the ground, warm tears flowing
down from their eyes to wet the earth . . . the horses mourned,
longing now for their driver, their luxurious manes soiled,
streaming down from the yoke-pads, down along the yoke.

    And Zeus pitied them, watching their tears flow.
He shook his head and addressed his own deep heart: 510
"Poor creatures, why did we give you to King Peleus,

a mortal doomed to death . . .
you immortal beasts who never age or die?
So you could suffer the pains of wretched men?
There is nothing alive more agonized than man
of all that breathe and crawl across the earth.
But Hector, at least, will never ride behind you,
you and your blazoned chariot. I will never permit it.
What more does he want? The arms are enough for him—
Priam's son with his empty, futile boasting.   520
But I will fill your legs and hearts with strength
so you can save Automedon, bear him from the fighting
back to the fleet. For still I will give the Trojans glory—
killing all the way to the benched ships till the sun sinks
and the blessed darkness sweeps across the earth."

   And with that he breathed fresh fire in the team.
They shook the dust from their manes and galloped off,
speeding the fast chariot just where the armies clashed.
Automedon fought as he rode, though grieving for his friend,
swooping in with the team like a vulture after geese.   530
Now he'd veer from the Trojan melee in a flash
then dart back in a charge, pursuing mobs of men
but he could not kill the ones he rushed in force—
no way for him now, alone in the hurtling car,
to lunge with a spear and still control those racers.
But at last a cohort marked the driver's straits,
Alcimedon the son of Laerces, Haemon's grandson
coming behind the chariot, shouted out, "Automedon!
What god has put such a tactic in your head?
It's good-for-nothing—he's torn your wits away.   540
Taking the Trojans on alone, on the front lines
but your comrade's dead, look, and Hector himself,
strapped in Achilles' armor, swaggers on in glory!"

   Diores' son Automedon shouted back, "Alcimedon!
What other Achaean driver could match your skill
at curbing this deathless team or spurring on their fury?
Only Patroclus, skilled as the gods themselves

while the man was still alive—
now death and fate have got him in their grip.
On with it! Take up the whip and shining reins,   550
I'll dismount the car and fight on foot."

Alcimedon sprang aboard the hurtling chariot,
quickly grasping the whip and reins in both fists
as Automedon leapt to ground. But Hector saw them
and called at once to Aeneas posted close beside him,
"Aeneas, counselor of the Trojans armed in bronze,
I can see the great runner Achilles' team—look there—
heading into the fight but reined by feeble drivers.
So my hopes ride high that we can seize them now
if you have the heart to join me.   560
Charge! Those two will flinch, they'd never dare
stand up to us man-to-man in all-out battle!"

And Anchises' gallant son did not resist.
They went straight on, shoulders shielded in oxhide
tanned and tough and hammered thick with bronze.
And a brace of fighters, Chromius, strong Aretus
flanked their attack and the Trojans had high hopes
of killing the men and driving off the massive stallions.
Reckless fools! They'd never disengage from Automedon,
not without some bloodshed. No, with a prayer to Zeus   570
some new fighting power had filled his dark heart
and he quickly called his trusted friend Alcimedon:
"Alcimedon, keep those horses close beside me,
breathing down my neck. Nothing can hold him back,
this Hector in all his fury—nothing, I tell you—
not till he leaps behind Achilles' long-maned team
and kills us both and routs our forward line—
or he goes down himself in the first assault."

And he called the two Aeantes and Menelaus:
"Ajax, Ajax—lords of the Argives—Menelaus!   580
Leave Patroclus now to the best men you can find,
they'll straddle the corpse and fight off Trojan packs—

you fight the fatal day from us, we're still alive.
Here they come, full tilt, Aeneas and Hector,
Troy's best men, bearing down on us here—
this point of tears and attack!
But all lies in the lap of the great gods.
I'll fling a spear myself and leave the rest to Zeus."

He aimed and hurled and his spear's long shadow flew
and hit Aretus square in the balanced round shield—   590
no blocking the shaft, the bronze rammed through,
piercing his belt and gouging down his belly.
As a burly farmhand wielding a whetted ax,
chopping a field-ranging bull behind the horns,
hacks through its whole hump and the beast heaves up
then topples forward—so Aretus reared, heaving up
then toppled down on his back. The slashing spear
shuddered tense in his guts and the man was gone.
A flash of a lance—Hector hurled at Automedon
who kept his eyes right on him, dodged the bronze,   600
ducking down with a quick lunge, and behind his back
the heavy spearshaft plunged and stuck in the earth,
the butt end quivering into the air till suddenly
rugged Ares snuffed its fury out, dead still . . .
Now they would have attacked with swords, close-up,
incensed, but the two Aeantes drove a wedge between them,
plowing through the press at their comrade's call.
Cowering backward fast the Trojans gave ground,
Hector, Aeneas and Chromius, noble prince,
deserted Aretus there, his life torn out,   610
sprawled on the spot. Automedon rushed in,
wild as the god of war to strip the armor off,
shouting in savage exultation, "Now, by heaven,
I've eased the grief of Patroclus' ghost a little—
though the man I battered down was half as great as he!"

With that he tossed the bloody gear in the chariot,
climbed aboard with his hands and feet dripping gore

like a lion that rends and bolts a bull.
                              And now, again,
the fight for Patroclus flared, stretched to the breaking point,
mounting in tears, in fury, since Pallas fired their blood,   620
sweeping down from the heavens, sent by the Father
thundering far and wide to drive the Argives on,
for now his mind had changed, at least for a moment.
Yes, down like a lurid rainbow Zeus sends arching
down to mortal men from the high skies, a sign of war
or blizzard to freeze the summer's warmth and put a halt
to men's work on the face of the earth and harry flocks—
so shrouded round in a lurid cloud came Pallas now
and dove in the Argive ranks to fire up each man.
And the first one she roused was Atreus' son   630
powerful Menelaus—he stood right at hand—
she took the build and tireless voice of Phoenix:
"Yours is the shame, Atrides. You will hang your head
if under the walls of Troy the dogs in all their frenzy
drag and maul the proud Achilles' steadfast friend.
Hold on, full force—spur all our men to battle!"

    The lord of the war cry told the goddess quickly,
"Phoenix, father, good old soldier—if only Pallas
would give me power and drive the weapons off me!
Then I'd gladly stand and fight for Patroclus.   640
My comrade's death has cut me to the quick.
But Hector keeps his terrible fury blazing,
keeps his bronze spear stabbing
and never stops the slaughter—Zeus hands him glory!"

    Her gray eyes afire, the goddess Pallas thrilled
that the man had prayed to her before all other gods.
She put fresh strength in his back, spring in his knees
and filled his heart with the horsefly's raw daring—
brush it away from a man's flesh and back it comes,
biting, attacking, crazed for sweet human blood.   650
With such raw daring she filled his dark heart
and he bestrode Patroclus, flung a gleaming spear—

and there was a Trojan, Eetion's son called Podes,
well-bred, wealthy, and Hector prized him most
in all the realm—a first-rate drinking friend . . .
As he sprang in flight the red-haired captain hit him,
splitting his belt, and bronze went ripping through his flesh
and down he went with a crash. Atrides hauled his corpse
from under the Trojans toward his own massing friends.

But Hector—Apollo stood by *him* and drove him on,   660
disguised as Phaenops, Asius' son Abydos-born,
dearest to Hector of all his foreign guests.
Like him to the life, the deadly Archer taunted,
"Hector, what Achaean will ever fear you now?
Look how you cringe in the face of Menelaus,
no great fighter before this—a weakling, soft.
He's gone and snatched a corpse from under our noses,
single-handed he's taken down your trusted comrade
brave in the front ranks, Podes, Eetion's son."

A black cloud of grief came shrouding over Hector   670
but helmed in flashing bronze he hurtled through the front.
That very moment the son of Cronus seized his storm-shield—
rippling and flaring bright—and shrouding Ida in dark clouds,
loosed a bolt with a huge crack of thunder, shook the shield,
gave the Trojans triumph and routed fear-struck Argives.

And the first to beat retreat, a Boeotian, Peneleos.
Charging forward as always, head-on, until Polydamas
speared his shoulder—just grazing its ridge
but grating bone—he thrust at point-blank range.
Close range too, Hector stabbed the wrist of Leitus,   680
brave Alectryon's son, and knocked him out of action.
No hope left he could wield a spear against the Trojans,
no more fighting now—Leitus looked around and ran.
But as Hector rushed him, Idomeneus speared *Hector*,
struck the plate on his chest beside the nipple—
his long spearshaft splintered off at the head
and the Trojans shouted out. And Hector hurled

at Idomeneus now aboard a chariot—missed by a hair
but he caught Meriones' aide and driver Coeranus,
one who'd come with his lord from rock-built Lyctus.   690
Idomeneus had left the ships on foot that morning
and would have offered the Trojans a fine triumph now
if Coeranus had not rushed to the rescue, lashed his team
and come like light to the king—
                              he saved his life that day
but he quickly lost his own to man-killing Hector—
                                                    Hector
speared him under the jaw and ear, knocking teeth out,
shattering roots and all and split his tongue in half.
He pitched from his car, the reins poured to the ground
and on foot Meriones grabbed them up in his hands,
shouting out at Idomeneus, "Whip them hard now!   700
Back to the fast ships! You see for yourself—
no power left in the Argives."
                              So Meriones yelled
and Idomeneus whipped the team with their manes streaming,
back to the hollow ships—fear seized the king at last.

    Lionhearted Ajax and Menelaus were not blind . . .
they saw Zeus turn the tide toward the Trojans.
Telamonian Ajax voiced frustration first:
"Dear god, enough! Any idiot boy could see
how Father Zeus himself supports these Trojans.
All their weapons land, no matter who flings them,   710
brave fighter or bad—Zeus guides them all to the mark.
Ours all clatter to ground. Wasted, harmless shots.
So come, alone as we are, find the best way out:
how do we pull the body clear and save ourselves,
make it back to our lines and bring our friends some joy?
They look our way in despair, they must. All hope gone
that murderous Hector's rage and invincible spear-arm
can be stopped—not now—
he'll hurl himself against our blackened hulls!
If only an aide could speed the word to Achilles.   720
I'm certain he has not heard the dreadful news

that his dear friend lies dead. Wherever I look,
no use, I cannot see the Achaean for the mission,
such swirling mist blots out the men and horses both.
O Father Zeus—draw our armies clear of the cloud,
give us a bright sky, give us back our sight!
Kill us all in the light of day at least—
since killing's now your pleasure!"

                                So he prayed
and the Father filled with pity, seeing Ajax weep.
He dispelled the mist at once,   730
drove off the cloud and the sun came blazing forth
and the whole war swung into view, clear, that instant—
and Ajax called the lord of the war cry, Menelaus:
"Look hard for Antilochus now, my royal friend.
If you see him still alive, brave Nestor's son,
tell him to run the news to great Achilles quickly—
his dearest friend-in-arms on earth lies dead."

    And the lord of the battle cry could not refuse
but dragged his heels like a lion leaving sheepfolds,
bone-weary from harrying hounds and field hands.   740
They'll never let him tear the rich fat from the oxen,
all night long they stand their guard but the lion craves meat,
he lunges in and in but his charges gain him nothing,
thick-and-fast from their hardy hands the javelins
rain down in his face, and waves of roaring torches—
these the big cat fears, balking for all his rage,
and at dawn he slinks away, his spirits dashed.
And so the lord of the war cry left Patroclus,
resisting all the way—he feared the worst:
stampeded in terror, his men would leave the body   750
easy prey for the Trojans. So here Menelaus paused
with much to command Meriones and the Aeantes:
"Ajax and Ajax, captains of Achaea, Meriones too,
remember Patroclus now, our stricken comrade!
That gentle man, the soul of kindness to all
while the man was still alive . . .
Now death and fate have got him in their grip."

And with that the red-haired captain moved ahead
like an eagle scanning left and right, the bird men say
has the sharpest eyes of all that fly the heavens: 760
high as he soars he'll never miss the racing hare
cowering down low in the dense, shaggy brush—
down on its head he swoops
and pins it fast and rips its life away. So now,
Menelaus O my King, you turned your shining eyes,
scanning the crowds of comrades front and rear,
trying to see if Nestor's son was still alive.
He marked him quickly, out on the left flank
and rousing cohorts, driving them back to war,
and the red-haired captain halted near and called,   770
"Turn this way, Antilochus, Prince, and hear the news,
dreadful news—would to god it had never happened!
You see for yourself, I know, how Father Zeus
sends waves of ruin breaking down our lines—
victory goes to Troy. Our best Achaean's dead—
Patroclus, a stunning loss to all our armies!
Quick, run to Achilles' moorings up the beach
and tell him all. Perhaps—but he must be fast—
he can bring the body safely back to his ship,
stripped as Patroclus is—   780
Hector with that flashing helmet has his armor."

Antilochus listened closely, hating every word.
He stood there speechless a while, struck dumb . . .
tears filling his eyes, his strong voice choked.
But he still would not neglect Atrides' order.
So handing his gear to a loyal aide Laodocus,
who maneuvered his pawing horses close by,
he set off at a run.
                    But he wept freely now
as his feet swept him clear of the close fighting,
bearing the dreadful news to Peleus' son Achilles.   790
But you, Menelaus O my King, you had no heart
to defend the Pylians, hard-pressed as they were,
once their leader left, a heavy blow to his troops.

And putting the veteran Thrasymedes in command,
he ran back to bestride Patroclus' corpse again
and flanking the two Aeantes now, reported briskly,
"I sent Antilochus. He's off to the fast ships
to tell the swift Achilles. But I've little hope
he'll come at all—for all his rage at Hector.
How can he fight the Trojans without armor?   800
So come, alone as we are, find the best way out:
how do we pull the body clear and save ourselves
from the Trojan uproar, flee our death, our fate?"

The Great Telamonian Ajax answered firmly,
"All true, straight to the point, Lord Menelaus.
Quickly, you and Meriones shoulder up the body,
carry it off the lines. We're right behind you,
fighting the Trojans, fighting this Prince Hector.
The two Aeantes bearing the same fury, the same name—
and no strangers at standing up to slashing Ares,   810
each defending the other side-by-side."
                                   So he urged
and up from the earth they caught the body in their arms,
hoisting it high above their heads with a great heave—
and Trojan forces crowding behind them shouted out
when they saw the Argive fighters lift the corpse.
They swept in like hounds that fling themselves
at a wounded boar before young hunters reach him,
darting in for a moment, keen to rip the boar apart
till he wheels at bay, ramping into the pack with all his power
and the hounds cringe and bolt and scatter left and right.   820
And so the Trojans kept on pressing, squad on squad,
stabbing away with swords and two-edged spears
till the two called Ajax wheeled against them hard
to make a stand—and they turned white, none had nerve
to charge forth now and fight it out for the corpse.

So they labored to haul Patroclus from the war,
back to the beaked ships as fighting flared behind them
wild as a flash fire, sprung out of nowhere, storming down

on a teeming city, houses caving in to the big blaze
as gale-winds whip it into a roaring conflagration.   830
So rose the relentless din of horse and fighting men
breaking against them now as they struggled back to shore.
Dead set as mules who put their backs in the labor . . .
dragging down from the cliffs along a stony trail
some roof-beam or a heavy ship timber, slogging on
till they nearly burst their hearts with sweat and labor—
so they strained to carry off the corpse. Right behind them
the two Aeantes held the Trojans off as a wooded rocky ridge
stretched out across an entire plain holds back a flood,
fighting off the killer-tides of the mounting rivers,   840
beating them all back to swamp the lowland flats—
none of their pounding waves can make a breakthrough.
So the two Aeantes kept on beating the Trojans off
but on they came, assaulting the rear, two in the lead,
Aeneas the son of Anchises flanking glorious Hector.
Flying before them now like clouds of crows or starlings
screaming murder, seeing a falcon dive in for the kill,
the hawk that wings grim death at smaller birds—
so pursued by Aeneas and Hector Argive fighters
raced, screaming death-cries, lust for battle lost   850
and masses of fine armor littered both sides of the trench
as the Argives fled in fear, no halt in the fighting, not now—

BOOK EIGHTEEN

The Shield of Achilles

So the men fought on like a mass of whirling fire
as swift Antilochus raced the message toward Achilles.
Sheltered under his curving, beaked ships he found him,
foreboding, deep down, all that had come to pass.
Agonizing now he probed his own great heart:
"Why, why? Our long-haired Achaeans routed again,
driven in terror off the plain to crowd the ships, but why?
Dear gods, don't bring to pass the grief that haunts my heart—
the prophecy that mother revealed to me one time . . .
she said the best of the Myrmidons—while I lived—   10
would fall at Trojan hands and leave the light of day.
And now he's dead, I know it. Menoetius' gallant son,
my headstrong friend! And I told Patroclus clearly,
'Once you have beaten off the lethal fire, quick,
come back to the ships—you must not battle Hector!' "

As such fears went churning through his mind
the warlord Nestor's son drew near him now,
streaming warm tears, to give the dreaded message:
"Ah son of royal Peleus, what you must hear from me!
What painful news—would to god it had never happened!   20
Patroclus has fallen. They're fighting over his corpse.
He's stripped, naked—Hector with that flashing helmet,
Hector has your arms!"
                            So the captain reported.
A black cloud of grief came shrouding over Achilles.
Both hands clawing the ground for soot and filth,
he poured it over his head, fouled his handsome face
and black ashes settled onto his fresh clean war-shirt.
Overpowered in all his power, sprawled in the dust,
Achilles lay there, fallen . . .
tearing his hair, defiling it with his own hands.   30
And the women he and Patroclus carried off as captives
caught the grief in their hearts and keened and wailed,
out of the tents they ran to ring the great Achilles,
all of them beat their breasts with clenched fists,
sank to the ground, each woman's knees gave way.
Antilochus kneeling near, weeping uncontrollably,
clutched Achilles' hands as he wept his proud heart out—
for fear he would slash his throat with an iron blade.
Achilles suddenly loosed a terrible, wrenching cry
and his noble mother heard him, seated near her father,   40
the Old Man of the Sea in the salt green depths,
and she cried out in turn. And immortal sea-nymphs
gathered round their sister, all the Nereids dwelling
down the sounding depths, they all came rushing now—
Glitter, blossoming Spray and the swells' Embrace,
Fair-Isle and shadowy Cavern, Mist and Spindrift,
ocean nymphs of the glances pooling deep and dark,
Race-with-the-Waves and Headlands' Hope and Safe Haven,
Glimmer of Honey, Suave-and-Soothing, Whirlpool, Brilliance,
Bounty and First Light and Speeder of Ships and buoyant Power, 50
Welcome Home and Bather of Meadows and Master's Lovely
     Consort,

Gift of the Sea, Eyes of the World and the famous milk-white Calm
and Truth and Never-Wrong and the queen who rules the tides
    in beauty
and in rushed Glory and Healer of Men and the one who rescues
    kings
and Sparkler, Down-from-the-Cliffs, sleek-haired Strands of Sand
and all the rest of the Nereids dwelling down the depths.
The silver cave was shimmering full of sea-nymphs,
all in one mounting chorus beating their breasts
as Thetis launched the dirge: "Hear me, sisters,
daughters of Nereus, so you all will know it well—   60
listen to all the sorrows welling in my heart!
I am agony—
          mother of grief and greatness—O my child!
Yes, I gave birth to a flawless, mighty son . . .
the splendor of heroes, and he shot up like a young branch,
like a fine tree I reared him—the orchard's crowning glory—
but only to send him off in the beaked ships to Troy
to battle Trojans! Never again will I embrace him
striding home through the doors of Peleus' house.
And long as I have him with me, still alive,
looking into the sunlight, he is racked with anguish.   70
And I, I go to his side—nothing I do can help him.
Nothing. But go I shall, to see my darling boy,
to hear what grief has come to break his heart
while he holds back from battle."
                    So Thetis cried
as she left the cave and her sisters swam up with her,
all in a tide of tears, and billowing round them now
the ground swell heaved open. And once they reached
the fertile land of Troy they all streamed ashore,
row on row in a long cortege, the sea-nymphs
filing up where the Myrmidon ships lay hauled,   80
clustered closely round the great runner Achilles . . .
As he groaned from the depths his mother rose before him
and sobbing a sharp cry, cradled her son's head in her hands
and her words were all compassion, winging pity: "My child—
why in tears? What sorrow has touched your heart?

Tell me, please. Don't harbor it deep inside you.
Zeus has accomplished everything you wanted,
just as you raised your hands and prayed that day.
All the sons of Achaea are pinned against the ships
and all for want of you—they suffer shattering losses."   90

And groaning deeply the matchless runner answered,
"O dear mother, true! All those burning desires
Olympian Zeus has brought to pass for me—
but what joy to me now? My dear comrade's dead—
Patroclus—the man I loved beyond all other comrades,
loved as my own life—I've lost him—Hector's killed him,
stripped the gigantic armor off his back, a marvel to behold—
my burnished gear! Radiant gifts the gods presented Peleus
that day they drove you into a mortal's marriage bed . . .
I wish you'd lingered deep with the deathless sea-nymphs,   100
lived at ease, and Peleus carried home a mortal bride.
But now, as it is, sorrows, unending sorrows must surge
within your heart as well—for your own son's death.
Never again will you embrace him striding home.
My spirit rebels—I've lost the will to live,
to take my stand in the world of men—unless,
before all else, Hector's battered down by my spear
and gasps away his life, the blood-price for Patroclus,
Menoetius' gallant son he's killed and stripped!"

But Thetis answered, warning through her tears,   110
"You're doomed to a short life, my son, from all you say!
For hard on the heels of Hector's death your death
must come at once—"
                    "Then let me die at once"—
Achilles burst out, despairing—"since it was not my fate
to save my dearest comrade from his death! Look,
a world away from his fatherland he's perished,
lacking me, my fighting strength, to defend him.
But now, since I shall not return to my fatherland . . .
nor did I bring one ray of hope to my Patroclus,
nor to the rest of all my steadfast comrades,   120

countless ranks struck down by mighty Hector—
No, no, here I sit by the ships . . .
a useless, dead weight on the good green earth—
I, no man my equal among the bronze-armed Achaeans,
not in battle, only in wars of words that others win.
If only strife could die from the lives of gods and men
and anger that drives the sanest man to flare in outrage—
bitter gall, sweeter than dripping streams of honey,
that swarms in people's chests and blinds like smoke—
just like the anger Agamemnon king of men   130
has roused within me now . . .
                              Enough.
Let bygones be bygones. Done is done.
Despite my anguish I will beat it down,
the fury mounting inside me, down by force.
But now I'll go and meet that murderer head-on,
that Hector who destroyed the dearest life I know.
For my own death, I'll meet it freely—whenever Zeus
and the other deathless gods would like to bring it on!
Not even Heracles fled his death, for all his power,
favorite son as he was to Father Zeus the King.   140
Fate crushed him, and Hera's savage anger.
And I too, if the same fate waits for me . . .
I'll lie in peace, once I've gone down to death.
But now, for the moment, let me seize great glory!—
and drive some woman of Troy or deep-breasted Dardan
to claw with both hands at her tender cheeks and wipe away
her burning tears as the sobs come choking from her throat—
they'll learn that I refrained from war a good long time!
Don't try to hold me back from the fighting, mother,
love me as you do. You can't persuade me now."   150

    The goddess of the glistening feet replied,
"Yes, my son, you're right. No coward's work,
to save your exhausted friends from headlong death.
But your own handsome war-gear lies in Trojan hands,
bronze and burnished—and Hector in that flashing helmet,
Hector glories in your armor, strapped across his back.

Not that he will glory in it long, I tell you:
his own destruction hovers near him now. Wait—
don't fling yourself in the grind of battle yet,
not till you see me coming back with your own eyes.   160
Tomorrow I will return to you with the rising sun,
bearing splendid arms from Hephaestus, god of fire!"

With that vow she turned away from her son
and faced and urged her sisters of the deep,
"Now down you go in the Ocean's folding gulfs
to visit father's halls—the Old Man of the Sea—
and tell him all. I am on my way to Olympus heights,
to the famous Smith Hephaestus—I pray he'll give my son
some fabulous armor full of the god's great fire!"

And under a foaming wave her sisters dove   170
as glistening-footed Thetis soared toward Olympus
to win her dear son an immortal set of arms.
                                          And now,
as her feet swept her toward Olympus, ranks of Achaeans,
fleeing man-killing Hector with grim, unearthly cries,
reached the ships and the Hellespont's long shore.
As for Patroclus, there seemed no hope that Achaeans
could drag the corpse of Achilles' comrade out of range.
Again the Trojan troops and teams overtook the body
with Hector son of Priam storming fierce as fire.
Three times illustrious Hector shouted for support,   180
seized his feet from behind, wild to drag him off,
three times the Aeantes, armored in battle-fury
fought him off the corpse. But Hector held firm,
staking all on his massive fighting strength—
again and again he'd hurl himself at the melee,
again and again stand fast with piercing cries
but he never gave ground backward, not one inch.
The helmed Aeantes could no more frighten Hector,
the proud son of Priam, back from Patroclus' corpse
than shepherds out in the field can scare a tawny lion   :90
off his kill when the hunger drives the beast claw-mad.

And now Hector would have hauled the body away
and won undying glory . . .
if wind-swift Iris had not swept from Olympus
bearing her message—Peleus' son must arm—
but all unknown to Zeus and the other gods
since Hera spurred her on. Halting near
she gave Achilles a flight of marching orders:
"To arms—son of Peleus! Most terrifying man alive!
Defend Patroclus! It's all for him, this merciless battle   200
pitched before the ships. They're mauling each other now,
Achaeans struggling to save the corpse from harm,
Trojans charging to haul it back to windy Troy.
Flashing Hector's far in the lead, wild to drag it off,
furious to lop the head from its soft, tender neck
and stake it high on the city's palisade.
                              Up with you—
no more lying low! Writhe with shame at the thought
Patroclus may be sport for the dogs of Troy!
Yours, the shame will be yours
if your comrade's corpse goes down to the dead defiled!"   210

       But the swift runner replied, "Immortal Iris—
what god has sped you here to tell me this?"

       Quick as the wind the rushing Iris answered,
"Hera winged me on, the illustrious wife of Zeus.
But the son of Cronus throned on high knows nothing,
nor does any other immortal housed on Olympus
shrouded deep in snow."
                              Achilles broke in quickly—
"How can I go to war? The Trojans have my gear.
And my dear mother told me I must not arm for battle,
not till I see her coming back with my own eyes—   220
she vowed to bring me burnished arms from the god of fire.
I know of no other armor. Whose gear could I wear?
None but Telamonian Ajax' giant shield.
But he's at the front, I'm sure, engaging Trojans,
slashing his spear to save Patroclus' body."

Quick as the wind the goddess had a plan:
"We know—we too—they hold your famous armor.
Still, just as you are, go out to the broad trench
and show yourself to the Trojans. Struck with fear
at the sight of you, they might hold off from attack   230
and Achaea's fighting sons get second wind,
exhausted as they are . . .
Breathing room in war is all too brief."

And Iris racing the wind went veering off
as Achilles, Zeus's favorite fighter, rose up now
and over his powerful shoulder Pallas slung the shield,
the tremendous storm-shield with all its tassels flaring—
and crowning his head the goddess swept a golden cloud
and from it she lit a fire to blaze across the field.
As smoke goes towering up the sky from out a town   240
cut off on a distant island under siege . . .
enemies battling round it, defenders all day long
trading desperate blows from their own city walls
but soon as the sun goes down the signal fires flash,
rows of beacons blazing into the air to alert their neighbors—
if only they'll come in ships to save them from disaster—
so now from Achilles' head the blaze shot up the sky.
He strode from the rampart, took his stand at the trench
but he would not mix with the milling Argive ranks.
He stood in awe of his mother's strict command.   250
So there he rose and loosed an enormous cry
and off in the distance Pallas shrieked out too
and drove unearthly panic through the Trojans.
Piercing loud as the trumpet's battle cry that blasts
from murderous raiding armies ringed around some city—
so piercing now the cry that broke from Aeacides.
And Trojans hearing the brazen voice of Aeacides,
all their spirits quaked—even sleek-maned horses,
sensing death in the wind, slewed their chariots round
and charioteers were struck dumb when they saw that fire,   260
relentless, terrible, burst from proud-hearted Achilles' head,
blazing as fiery-eyed Athena fueled the flames. Three times

the brilliant Achilles gave his great war cry over the trench,
three times the Trojans and famous allies whirled in panic—
and twelve of their finest fighters died then and there,
crushed by chariots, impaled on their own spears.
And now the exultant Argives seized the chance
to drag Patroclus' body quickly out of range
and laid him on a litter . . .
Standing round him, loving comrades mourned,   270
and the swift runner Achilles joined them, grieving,
weeping warm tears when he saw his steadfast comrade
lying dead on the bier, mauled by tearing bronze,
the man he sent to war with team and chariot
but never welcomed home again alive.

    Now Hera the ox-eyed queen of heaven drove the sun,
untired and all unwilling, to sink in the Ocean's depths
and the sun went down at last and brave Achaeans ceased
the grueling clash of arms, the leveling rout of war.

    And the Trojans in turn, far across the field,   280
pulling forces back from the last rough assault,
freed their racing teams from under chariot yokes
but before they thought of supper, grouped for council.
They met on their feet. Not one of them dared to sit
for terror seized them all—the great Achilles
who held back from the brutal fray so long
had just come blazing forth.
Panthous' son Polydamas led the debate,
a good clear head, and the only man who saw
what lay in the past and what the Trojans faced.   290
He was Hector's close comrade, born on the same night,
but excelled at trading words as he at trading spear-thrusts.
And now, with all good will, Polydamas rose and spoke:
"Weigh both sides of the crisis well, my friends.
What I urge is this: draw back to the city now.
Don't wait for the holy Dawn to find us here afield,
ranged by the ships—we're too far from our walls.
As long as that man kept raging at royal Agamemnon

the Argive troops were easier game to battle down.
I too was glad to camp the night on the shipways,   300
hopes soaring to seize their heavy rolling hulls.
But now racing Achilles makes my blood run cold.
So wild the man's fury he will never rest content,
holding out on the plain where Trojans and Argives
met halfway, exchanging blows in the savage onset—
never: *he* will fight for our wives, for Troy itself!
So retreat to Troy. Trust me—we will face disaster.
Now, for the moment, the bracing godsent night
has stopped the swift Achilles in his tracks.
But let him catch us lingering here tomorrow,   310
just as he rises up in arms—there may be some
who will sense his fighting spirit all too well.
You'll thank your stars to get back to sacred Troy,
whoever escapes him. Dogs and birds will have their fill—
of Trojan flesh, by heaven. Battalions of Trojans!
Pray god such grief will never reach my ears.
So follow my advice, hard as it may seem . . .
Tonight conserve our strength in the meeting place,
and the great walls and gates and timbered doors we hung,
well-planed, massive and bolted tight, will shield the city.   320
But tomorrow at daybreak, armed to the hilt for battle,
we man the towering ramparts. All the worse for him—
if Achilles wants to venture forth from the fleet,
fight us round our walls. Back to the ships he'll go,
once he's lashed the power out of his rippling stallions,
whipping them back and forth beneath our city walls.
Not even *his* fury will let him crash our gates—
he'll never plunder Troy.
Sooner the racing dogs will eat him raw!"

    Helmet flashing, Hector wheeled with a dark glance: 33ɔ
"No more, Polydamas! Your pleading repels me now.
You say go back again—be crammed inside the city.
Aren't you sick of being caged inside those walls?
Time was when the world would talk of Priam's Troy
as the city rich in gold and rich in bronze—but now

our houses are stripped of all their sumptuous treasures,
troves sold off and shipped to Phrygia, lovely Maeonia,
once great Zeus grew angry . . .
But now, the moment the son of crooked Cronus
allows me to seize some glory here at the ships   340
and pin these Argives back against the sea—
you fool, enough! No more thoughts of retreat
paraded before our people. Not that one Trojan
will ever take your lead—I'll never permit it.
Come, follow my orders! All obey me now.
Take supper now. Take your posts through camp.
And no forgetting the watch, each man wide awake.
And any Trojan so weighed down, so oppressed
by his own possessions, let him collect the lot,
pass them round to the people—a grand public feast.   350
Far better for one of ours to reap the benefits
than all the marauding Argives. Then, as you say,
'tomorrow at daybreak, armed to the hilt for battle'—
we slash to attack against their deep curved hulls!
If it really *was* Achilles who reared beside the ships,
all the worse for him—if he wants his fill of war.
I for one, I'll never run from his grim assault,
I'll stand up to the man—see if he bears off glory
or I bear it off myself! The god of war is impartial:
he hands out death to the man who hands out death."   360

So Hector finished. The Trojans roared assent,
lost in folly. Athena had swept away their senses.
They gave applause to Hector's ruinous tactics,
none to Polydamas, who gave them sound advice.
And now their entire army settled down to supper
but all night long the Argives raised Patroclus' dirge.
And Achilles led them now in a throbbing chant of sorrow,
laying his man-killing hands on his great friend's chest,
convulsed with bursts of grief. Like a bearded lion
whose pride of cubs a deer-hunter has snatched away,   370
out of some thick woods, and back he comes, too late,
and his heart breaks but he courses after the hunter,

hot on his tracks down glen on twisting glen—
where can he find him?—gripped by piercing rage . . .
so Achilles groaned, deeply, crying out to his Myrmidons,
"O my captains! How empty the promise I let fall
that day I reassured Menoetius in his house—
I promised the king I'd bring him back his son,
home to Opois, covered in glory, Troy sacked,
hauling his rightful share of plunder home, home.   380
But Zeus will never accomplish all our best-laid plans.
Look at us. Both doomed to stain red with our blood
the same plot of earth, a world away in Troy!
For not even *I* will voyage home again. Never.
No embrace in his halls from the old horseman Peleus
nor from mother, Thetis—this alien earth I stride
will hold me down at last.
                                    But now, Patroclus,
since I will follow you underneath the ground,
I shall not bury you, no, not till I drag back here
the gear and head of Hector, who slaughtered you,   390
my friend, greathearted friend . . .
Here in front of your flaming pyre I'll cut the throats
of a dozen sons of Troy in all their shining glory,
venting my rage on them for your destruction!
Till then you lie as you are beside my beaked ships
and round you the Trojan women and deep-breasted Dardans
will mourn you night and day, weeping burning tears,
women we fought to win—strong hands and heavy lance—
whenever we sacked rich cities held by mortal men."

With that the brilliant Achilles ordered friends   400
to set a large three-legged cauldron over the fire
and wash the clotted blood from Patroclus' wounds
with all good speed. Hoisting over the blaze
a cauldron, filling it brimful with bathing water,
they piled fresh logs beneath and lit them quickly.
The fire lapped at the vessel's belly, the water warmed
and soon as it reached the boil in the glowing bronze
they bathed and anointed the body sleek with olive oil,

closed each wound with a soothing, seasoned unguent
and then they laid Patroclus on his bier . . .   410
covered him head to foot in a thin light sheet
and over his body spread the white linen shroud.
Then all night long, ringing the great runner Achilles,
Myrmidon fighters mourned and raised Patroclus' dirge.

But Zeus turned to Hera, his wife and sister, saying,
"So, my ox-eyed Queen, you've had your way at last,
setting the famous runner Achilles on his feet.
Mother Hera—look, these long-haired Achaeans
must be sprung of your own immortal loins."

But her eyes widening, noble Hera answered,   420
"Dread majesty, son of Cronus, what are you saying?
Even a mortal man will act to help a friend,
condemned as a mortal always is to death
and hardly endowed with wisdom deep as ours.
So how could I, claiming to be the highest goddess—
both by birth and since I am called your consort
and you in turn rule all the immortal gods—
how could I hold back from these, these Trojans,
men I loathe, and fail to weave their ruin?"

Now as the King and Queen provoked each other,   430
glistening-footed Thetis reached Hephaestus' house,
indestructible, bright as stars, shining among the gods,
built of bronze by the crippled Smith with his own hands.
There she found him, sweating, wheeling round his bellows,
pressing the work on twenty three-legged cauldrons,
an array to ring the walls inside his mansion.
He'd bolted golden wheels to the legs of each
so all on their own speed, at a nod from him,
they could roll to halls where the gods convene
then roll right home again—a marvel to behold.   440
But not quite finished yet . . .
the god had still to attach the inlaid handles.

These he was just fitting, beating in the rivets.
As he bent to the work with all his craft and cunning,
Thetis on her glistening feet drew near the Smith.
But Charis saw her first, Charis coming forward,
lithe and lovely in all her glittering headdress,
the Grace the illustrious crippled Smith had married.
Approaching Thetis, she caught her hand and spoke her name:
"Thetis of flowing robes! What brings you to our house?   450
A beloved, honored friend—but it's been so long,
your visits much too rare. Follow me in, please,
let me offer you all a guest could want."

                                      Welcome words,
and the radiant goddess Charis led the way inside.
She seated her on a handsome, well-wrought chair,
studded with silver, under it slipped a stool
and called the famous Smith: "Hephaestus, come—
look who's here! Thetis would ask a favor of you!"

    And the famous crippled Smith exclaimed warmly,
"Thetis—here? Ah then a wondrous, honored goddess   460
comes to grace our house! Thetis saved my life
when the mortal pain came on me after my great fall,
thanks to my mother's will, that brazen bitch,
she wanted to hide me—because I was a cripple.
What shattering anguish I'd have suffered then
if Thetis had not taken me to her breast, Eurynome too,
the daughter of Ocean's stream that runs around the world.
Nine years I lived with both, forging bronze by the trove,
elegant brooches, whorled pins, necklaces, chokers, chains—
there in the vaulted cave—and round us Ocean's currents   470
swirled in a foaming, roaring rush that never died.
And no one knew. Not a single god or mortal,
only Thetis and Eurynome knew—they saved me.
And here is Thetis now, in our own house!
So I *must* do all I can to pay her back,
the price for the life she saved . . .
the nymph of the sea with sleek and lustrous locks.
Quickly, set before her stranger's generous fare

while I put away my bellows and all my tools."

                                        With that
he heaved up from the anvil block—his immense hulk   480
hobbling along but his shrunken legs moved nimbly.
He swung the bellows aside and off the fires,
gathered the tools he'd used to weld the cauldrons
and packed them all in a sturdy silver strongbox.
Then he sponged off his brow and both burly arms,
his massive neck and shaggy chest, pulled on a shirt
and grasping a heavy staff, Hephaestus left his forge
and hobbled on. Handmaids ran to attend their master,
all cast in gold but a match for living, breathing girls.
Intelligence fills their hearts, voice and strength their frames,   490
from the deathless gods they've learned their works of hand.
They rushed to support their lord as he went bustling on
and lurching nearer to Thetis, took his polished seat,
reached over to clutch her hand and spoke her name:
"Thetis of flowing robes! What brings you to our house?
A beloved, honored friend—but it's been so long,
your visits much too rare.
Tell me what's on your mind. I am eager to do it—
whatever I *can* do . . . whatever can be done."

    But Thetis burst into tears, her voice welling: 500
"Oh Hephaestus—who of all the goddesses on Olympus,
who has borne such withering sorrows in her heart?
Such pain as Zeus has given me, above all others!
Me out of all the daughters of the sea he chose
to yoke to a mortal man, Peleus, son of Aeacus,
and I endured his bed, a mortal's bed, resisting
with all my will. And now he lies in the halls,
broken with grisly age, but now my griefs are worse.
Remember? Zeus also gave me a son to bear and breed,
the splendor of heroes, and he shot up like a young branch,   510
like a fine tree I reared him—the orchard's crowning glory—
but only to send him off in the beaked ships to Troy
to battle Trojans! Never again will I embrace him
striding home through the doors of Peleus' house.

And long as I have him with me, still alive,
looking into the sunlight, he is racked with anguish.
I go to his side—nothing I do can help him. Nothing.
That girl the sons of Achaea picked out for his prize—
right from his grasp the mighty Agamemnon tore her,
and grief for her has been gnawing at his heart.   520
But then the Trojans pinned the Achaeans tight
against their sterns, they gave them no way out,
and the Argive warlords begged my son to help,
they named in full the troves of glittering gifts
they'd send his way. But at that point he refused
to beat disaster off—refused himself, that is—
but he buckled his own armor round Patroclus,
sent him into battle with an army at his back.
And all day long they fought at the Scaean Gates,
that very day they would have stormed the city too,   530
if Apollo had not killed Menoetius' gallant son
as he laid the Trojans low—Apollo cut him down
among the champions there and handed Hector glory.
So now I come, I throw myself at your knees,
please help me! Give my son—he won't live long—
a shield and helmet and tooled greaves with ankle-straps
and armor for his chest. All that he had was lost,
lost when the Trojans killed his steadfast friend.
Now he lies on the ground—his heart is breaking."

  And the famous crippled Smith replied, "Courage!   540
Anguish for all that armor—sweep it from your mind.
If only I could hide him away from pain and death,
that day his grim destiny comes to take Achilles,
as surely as glorious armor shall be his, armor
that any man in the world of men will marvel at
through all the years to come—whoever sees its splendor."

  With that he left her there and made for his bellows,
turning them on the fire, commanding, "Work—to work!"
And the bellows, all twenty, blew on the crucibles,
breathing with all degrees of shooting, fiery heat   550

as the god hurried on—a blast for the heavy work,
a quick breath for the light, all precisely gauged
to the god of fire's wish and the pace of the work in hand.
Bronze he flung in the blaze, tough, durable bronze
and tin and priceless gold and silver, and then,
planting the huge anvil upon its block, he gripped
his mighty hammer in one hand, the other gripped his tongs.

   And first Hephaestus makes a great and massive shield,
blazoning well-wrought emblems all across its surface,
raising a rim around it, glittering, triple-ply   560
with a silver shield-strap run from edge to edge
and five layers of metal to build the shield itself,
and across its vast expanse with all his craft and cunning
the god creates a world of gorgeous immortal work.

   There he made the earth and there the sky and the sea
and the inexhaustible blazing sun and the moon rounding full
and there the constellations, all that crown the heavens,
the Pleiades and the Hyades, Orion in all his power too
and the Great Bear that mankind also calls the Wagon:
she wheels on her axis always fixed, watching the Hunter,   570
and she alone is denied a plunge in the Ocean's baths.

   And he forged on the shield two noble cities filled
with mortal men. With weddings and wedding feasts in one
and under glowing torches they brought forth the brides
from the women's chambers, marching through the streets
while choir on choir the wedding song rose high
and the young men came dancing, whirling round in rings
and among them flutes and harps kept up their stirring call—
women rushed to the doors and each stood moved with wonder.
And the people massed, streaming into the marketplace   580
where a quarrel had broken out and two men struggled
over the blood-price for a kinsman just murdered.
One declaimed in public, vowing payment in full—
the other spurned him, he would not take a thing—
so both men pressed for a judge to cut the knot.

The crowd cheered on both, they took both sides,
but heralds held them back as the city elders sat
on polished stone benches, forming the sacred circle,
grasping in hand the staffs of clear-voiced heralds,
and each leapt to his feet to plead the case in turn.   590
Two bars of solid gold shone on the ground before them,
a prize for the judge who'd speak the straightest verdict.

But circling the other city camped a divided army
gleaming in battle-gear, and two plans split their ranks:
to plunder the city or share the riches with its people,
hoards the handsome citadel stored within its depths.
But the people were not surrendering, not at all.
They armed for a raid, hoping to break the siege—
loving wives and innocent children standing guard
on the ramparts, flanked by elders bent with age   600
as men marched out to war. Ares and Pallas led them,
both burnished gold, gold the attire they donned, and great,
magnificent in their armor—gods for all the world,
looming up in their brilliance, towering over troops.
And once they reached the perfect spot for attack,
a watering place where all the herds collected,
there they crouched, wrapped in glowing bronze.
Detached from the ranks, two scouts took up their posts,
the eyes of the army waiting to spot a convoy,
the enemy's flocks and crook-horned cattle coming . . .   610
Come they did, quickly, two shepherds behind them,
playing their hearts out on their pipes—treachery
never crossed their minds. But the soldiers saw them,
rushed them, cut off at a stroke the herds of oxen
and sleek sheep-flocks glistening silver-gray
and killed the herdsmen too. Now the besiegers,
soon as they heard the uproar burst from the cattle
as they debated, huddled in council, mounted at once
behind their racing teams, rode hard to the rescue,
arrived at once, and lining up for assault   620
both armies battled it out along the river banks—
they raked each other with hurtling bronze-tipped spears.

And Strife and Havoc plunged in the fight, and violent Death—
now seizing a man alive with fresh wounds, now one unhurt,
now hauling a dead man through the slaughter by the heels,
the cloak on her back stained red with human blood.
So they clashed and fought like living, breathing men
grappling each other's corpses, dragging off the dead.

    And he forged a fallow field, broad rich plowland
tilled for the third time, and across it crews of plowmen   630
wheeled their teams, driving them up and back and soon
as they'd reach the end-strip, moving into the turn,
a man would run up quickly
and hand them a cup of honeyed, mellow wine
as the crews would turn back down along the furrows,
pressing again to reach the end of the deep fallow field
and the earth churned black behind them, like earth churning,
solid gold as it was—that was the wonder of Hephaestus' work.

    And he forged a king's estate where harvesters labored,
reaping the ripe grain, swinging their whetted scythes.   640
Some stalks fell in line with the reapers, row on row,
and others the sheaf-binders girded round with ropes,
three binders standing over the sheaves, behind them
boys gathering up the cut swaths, filling their arms,
supplying grain to the binders, endless bundles.
And there in the midst the king,
scepter in hand at the head of the reaping-rows,
stood tall in silence, rejoicing in his heart.
And off to the side, beneath a spreading oak,
the heralds were setting out the harvest feast,   650
they were dressing a great ox they had slaughtered,
while attendant women poured out barley, generous,
glistening handfuls strewn for the reapers' midday meal.

    And he forged a thriving vineyard loaded with clusters,
bunches of lustrous grapes in gold, ripening deep purple
and climbing vines shot up on silver vine-poles.
And round it he cut a ditch in dark blue enamel

and round the ditch he staked a fence in tin.
And one lone footpath led toward the vineyard
and down it the pickers ran   660
whenever they went to strip the grapes at vintage—
girls and boys, their hearts leaping in innocence,
bearing away the sweet ripe fruit in wicker baskets.
And there among them a young boy plucked his lyre,
so clear it could break the heart with longing,
and what he sang was a dirge for the dying year,
lovely . . . his fine voice rising and falling low
as the rest followed, all together, frisking, singing,
shouting, their dancing footsteps beating out the time.

And he forged on the shield a herd of longhorn cattle,   670
working the bulls in beaten gold and tin, lowing loud
and rumbling out of the farmyard dung to pasture
along a rippling stream, along the swaying reeds.
And the golden drovers kept the herd in line,
four in all, with nine dogs at their heels,
their paws flickering quickly—a savage roar!—
a crashing attack—and a pair of ramping lions
had seized a bull from the cattle's front ranks—
he bellowed out as they dragged him off in agony.
Packs of dogs and the young herdsmen rushed to help   680
but the lions ripping open the hide of the huge bull
were gulping down the guts and the black pooling blood
while the herdsmen yelled the fast pack on—no use.
The hounds shrank from sinking teeth in the lions,
they balked, hunching close, barking, cringing away.

And the famous crippled Smith forged a meadow
deep in a shaded glen for shimmering flocks to graze,
with shepherds' steadings, well-roofed huts and sheepfolds.

And the crippled Smith brought all his art to bear
on a dancing circle, broad as the circle Daedalus   690
once laid out on Cnossos' spacious fields
for Ariadne the girl with lustrous hair.

Here young boys and girls, beauties courted
with costly gifts of oxen, danced and danced,
linking their arms, gripping each other's wrists.
And the girls wore robes of linen light and flowing,
the boys wore finespun tunics rubbed with a gloss of oil,
the girls were crowned with a bloom of fresh garlands,
the boys swung golden daggers hung on silver belts.
And now they would run in rings on their skilled feet,   700
nimbly, quick as a crouching potter spins his wheel,
palming it smoothly, giving it practice twirls
to see it run, and now they would run in rows,
in rows crisscrossing rows—rapturous dancing.
A breathless crowd stood round them struck with joy
and through them a pair of tumblers dashed and sprang,
whirling in leaping handsprings, leading on the dance.

     And he forged the Ocean River's mighty power girdling
round the outmost rim of the welded indestructible shield.

     And once the god had made that great and massive shield   710
he made Achilles a breastplate brighter than gleaming fire,
he made him a sturdy helmet to fit the fighter's temples,
beautiful, burnished work, and raised its golden crest
and made him greaves of flexing, pliant tin.
                                        Now,
when the famous crippled Smith had finished off
that grand array of armor, lifting it in his arms
he laid it all at the feet of Achilles' mother Thetis—
and down she flashed like a hawk from snowy Mount Olympus
bearing the brilliant gear, the god of fire's gift.

BOOK NINETEEN

The Champion Arms for Battle

As Dawn rose up in her golden robe from Ocean's tides,
bringing light to immortal gods and mortal men,
Thetis sped Hephaestus' gifts to the ships.
She found her beloved son lying facedown,
embracing Patroclus' body, sobbing, wailing,
and round him crowded troops of mourning comrades.
And the glistening goddess moved among them now,
seized Achilles' hand and urged him, spoke his name:
"My child, leave your friend to lie there dead—
we must, though it breaks our hearts . . .
The will of the gods has crushed him once for all.
But here, Achilles, accept this glorious armor, look,
a gift from the god of fire—burnished bright, finer
than any mortal has ever borne across his back!"

                                              Urging,

10

the goddess laid the armor down at Achilles' feet
and the gear clashed out in all its blazoned glory.
A tremor ran through all the Myrmidon ranks—none dared
to look straight at the glare, each fighter shrank away.
Not Achilles. The more he gazed, the deeper his anger went,
his eyes flashing under his eyelids, fierce as fire—   20
exulting, holding the god's shining gifts in his hands.
And once he'd thrilled his heart with looking hard
at the armor's well-wrought beauty,
he turned to his mother, winged words flying:
"Mother—armor sent by the god—you're right,
only immortal gods could forge such work,
no man on earth could ever bring it off!
Now, by heaven, I'll arm and go to war.
But all the while my blood runs cold with fear—
Menoetius' fighting son . . . the carrion blowflies   30
will settle into his wounds, gouged deep by the bronze,
worms will breed and seethe, defile the man's corpse—
his life's ripped out—his flesh may rot to nothing."

      But glistening-footed Thetis reassured him:
"O my child, wipe these worries from your mind.
I'll find a way to protect him from those swarms,
the vicious flies that devour men who fall in battle.
He could lie there dead till a year has run its course
and his flesh still stand firm, even fresher than now . . .
So go and call the Argive warriors to the muster: 40
renounce your rage at the proud commander Agamemnon,
then arm for battle quickly, don your fighting power!"

      With that she breathed in her son tremendous courage
then instilled in Patroclus' nostrils fresh ambrosia,
blood-red nectar too, to make his flesh stand firm.

      But brilliant Achilles strode along the surf,
crying his piercing cry and roused Achaean warriors.
Even those who'd kept to the beached ships till now,
the helmsmen who handled the heavy steering-oars

and stewards left on board to deal out rations—   50
even they trooped to the muster: great Achilles
who held back from the brutal fighting so long
had just come blazing forth.
And along came two aides of Ares limping in,
the battle-hard Tydides flanked by good Odysseus
leaning on their spears, still bearing painful wounds,
and slowly found their seats in the front ranks.
And the lord of men Agamemnon came in last of all,
weighed down by the wound he took in the rough charge
when Coon, son of Antenor, slashed his arm with bronze.   60
And now, as all the Achaean armies massed together,
the swift runner Achilles rose among them, asking,
"Agamemnon—was it better for both of us, after all,
for you and me to rage at each other, raked by anguish,
consumed by heartsick strife, all for a young girl?
If only Artemis had cut her down at the ships—
with one quick shaft—
that day I destroyed Lyrnessus, chose her as my prize.
How many fewer friends had gnawed the dust of the wide world,
brought down by enemy hands while I raged on and on.   70
Better? Yes—for Hector and Hector's Trojans!
Not for the Argives. For years to come, I think,
they will remember the feud that flared between us both.
Enough. Let bygones be bygones. Done is done.
Despite my anguish I will beat it down,
the fury mounting inside me, down by force.
Now, by god, I call a halt to all my anger—
it's wrong to keep on raging, heart inflamed forever.
Quickly, drive our long-haired Achaeans to battle now!
So I can go at the Trojans once again and test their strength   80
and see if they still long to camp the night at the ships.
They'll gladly sink to a knee and rest at home, I'd say—
whoever comes through alive from the heat of combat,
out from under my spear!"
                          Welcome, rousing words,
and Achaeans-at-arms roared out with joy to hear
the greathearted Achilles swearing off his rage.

Now it was King Agamemnon's turn to address them.
He rose from his seat, not moving toward the center.
The lord of men spoke out from where he stood:
"My friends, fighting Danaans, aides of Ares . . .   90
when a man stands up to speak, it's well to listen.
Not to interrupt him, the only courteous thing.
Even the finest speaker finds intrusions hard.
Yet how can a person hear or say a word?—
this howling din could drown the clearest voice.
But I will declare my inmost feelings to Achilles.
And you, the rest of you Argives, listen closely:
every man of you here, mark each word I say.
Often the armies brought this matter up against me—
they would revile me in public. But I am not to blame!   100
Zeus and Fate and the Fury stalking through the night,
they are the ones who drove that savage madness in my heart,
that day in assembly when I seized Achilles' prize—
on my own authority, true, but what could *I* do?
A god impels all things to their fulfillment:
Ruin, eldest daughter of Zeus, she blinds us all,
that fatal madness—she with those delicate feet of hers,
never touching the earth, gliding over the heads of men
to trap us all. She entangles one man, now another.
Why, she and her frenzy blinded *Zeus* one time,   110
highest, greatest of men and gods, they say:
even Father Zeus! Hera deceived him blind—
feminine as she is, and only armed with guile—
that day in Thebes, ringed with tower on tower,
Alcmena was poised to bear invincible Heracles.
So the proud Father declared to all immortals,
'Hear me, all you gods and all goddesses too,
as I proclaim what's brooding deep inside me.
Today the goddess of birth pangs and labor
will bring to light a human child, a man-child   120
born of the stock of men who spring from *my* blood,
one who will lord it over all who dwell around him.'
But teeming with treachery noble Hera set her trap,
'You will prove a liar . . .

when the time arrives to crown your words with action.
Come now, my Olympian, swear your inviolate oath
that he shall lord it over all who dwell around him—
that child who drops between a woman's knees today,
born of the stock of men who spring from Zeus's blood.'
And Zeus suspected nothing, not a word of treachery.   130
He swore his mighty oath—blinded, from that hour on.
Speeding down in a flash from Mount Olympus' summit
Hera reached Achaean Argos in no time, where,
she knew for a fact, the hardy wife of Sthenelus,
Perseus' own son, was about to bear her child,
but only seven months gone. So into the light
Queen Hera brought the baby, two months shy,
and the goddess stopped Alcmena's hour of birth,
she held back the Lady of Labor's birthing pangs
and rushed in person to give the word to Zeus: 140
'Zeus, Father, lord of the lightning bolt—
here is a piece of news to warm your heart!
Today an illustrious son is born to rule the Argives . . .
Eurystheus, son of Sthenelus, descended of Perseus—
so he is born of your own stock and immortal blood
and it's only right for *him* to rule the Argives!'
With that, a stab of agony struck his deep heart.
Suddenly seizing Ruin by her glossy oiled braids—
he was furious, raging—now he swore his inviolate oath
that never again would she return to Olympus' starry skies,   150
that maddening goddess, Ruin, Ruin who blinds us all.
With that he whirled her round in his massive hand
and flung her out of the brilliant, starry skies
and she soon found herself in the world of men.
But Zeus could never think of Ruin without a groan
whenever he saw Heracles, his own dear son endure
some shameful labor Eurystheus forced upon him.

      And so with me, I tell you!
When tall Hector with that flashing helmet of his
kept slaughtering Argives pinned against our ships—   160
how could I once forget that madness, that frenzy,

the Ruin that blinded *me* from that first day?
But since I *was* blinded and Zeus stole my wits,
I am intent on setting things to rights, at once:
I'll give that priceless ransom paid for friendship.
Gear up for battle now! And rouse the rest of your armies!
As for the gifts, here I am to produce them all,
all that good Odysseus promised you in full,
the other day, when he approached your tents.
Or if you prefer, hold off a moment now . . .   170
much as your heart would spur you on to war.
Aides will fetch that treasure trove from my ship,
they'll bring it here to you, so you can behold
what hoards I'll give to set your heart at peace."

    But the swift runner Achilles broke in sharply—
"Field marshal Atrides, lord of men Agamemnon,
produce the gifts if you like, as you see fit,
or keep them back, it's up to you. But now—
quickly, call up the wild joy of war at once!
It's wrong to malinger here with talk, wasting time—   180
our great work lies all before us, still to do.
Just as you see Achilles charge the front once more,
hurling his bronze spear, smashing Troy's battalions—
so each of you remember to battle down your man!"

    But Odysseus fine at tactics answered firmly,
"Not so quickly, brave as you are, godlike Achilles.
Achaea's troops are hungry: don't drive them against Troy
to fight the Trojans. It's no quick skirmish shaping,
once the massed formations of men begin to clash
with a god breathing fury in both sides at once.   190
No, command them now to take their food and wine
by the fast ships—a soldier's strength and nerve.
No fighter can battle all day long, cut-and-thrust
till the sun goes down, if he is starved for food.
Even though his courage may blaze up for combat,
his limbs will turn to lead before he knows it,
thirst and hunger will overtake him quickly,

his knees will cave in as the man struggles on.
But the one who takes his fill of food and wine
before he grapples enemies full force, dawn to dusk—   200
the heart in his chest keeps pounding fresh with courage,
nor do his legs give out till all break off from battle.
Come, dismiss your ranks, have them make their meal.
As for the gifts, let the king of men Agamemnon
have the lot of them hauled amidst our muster,
so all the troops can see the trove themselves
and you, Achilles, you can warm your heart.
And let the king stand up before the entire army,
let Agamemnon swear to you his solemn, binding oath:
he never mounted her bed, never once made love with her,   210
the natural thing, my lord, men and women joined.
And you, Achilles, show some human kindness too,
in your own heart. Then, as a peace offering,
let him present you a lavish feast in his tents
so you won't lack your just deserts at last.
And you, great son of Atreus . . .
you be more just to others, from now on.
It is no disgrace for a king to appease a man
when the king himself was first to give offense."

    The lord of men Agamemnon answered warmly,   220
"Son of Laertes, I delight to hear your counsel!
You have covered it all fairly, point by point.
I'll gladly swear your oath—the spirit moves me now—
nor will I break that oath in the eyes of any god.
But let Achilles remain here, for the moment,
much as his heart would race him into war.
The rest remain here too, all in strict formation,
till the treasure trove is hauled forth from my tents
and we can seal our binding oaths in blood.
And you, Odysseus, I tell you, I command you: 230
pick out young men, the best in our joint forces,
bring forth the gifts from my ship, all we promised
Achilles just the other day, and bring the women too.
Here in the presence of our united armed contingents

let Talthybius quickly prepare a wild boar for me—
we must sacrifice to the Sun and Father Zeus."

    But the swift runner Achilles interjected,
"Field marshal Atrides, lord of men Agamemnon,
better busy yourself with that some other time,
when a sudden lull in the fighting lets us rest   240
and the fury's not such fire inside my heart.
Now our men are lying mauled on the field—
all that Hector the son of Priam overwhelmed
when Zeus was handing Hector his high glory—
but you, you and Odysseus urge us to a banquet!
I, by god, I'd drive our Argives into battle *now*,
starving, famished, and only then, when the sun goes down,
lay on a handsome feast—once we've avenged our shame.
Before then, for me at least, neither food nor drink
will travel down my throat, not with my friend dead,   250
there in my shelter, torn to shreds by the sharp bronze . . .
His feet turned to the door, stretched out for burial,
round him comrades mourning.
                        You talk of food?
I have no taste for food—what I really crave
is slaughter and blood and the choking groans of men!"

    But Odysseus, cool tactician, tried to calm him:
"Achilles, son of Peleus, greatest of the Achaeans,
greater than I, stronger with spears by no small edge—
yet I might just surpass you in seasoned judgment
by quite a lot, since I have years on you   260
and I know the world much better . . .
So let your heart be swayed by what I say.
Now fighting men will sicken of battle quickly:
the more dead husks the bronze strews on the ground
the sparser the harvest then, when Zeus almighty
tips his scales and the tide of battle turns—
the great steward on high who rules our mortal wars.
You want the men to grieve for the dead by *starving*?
Impossible. Too many falling, day after day—battalions!

When could we find a breathing space from fasting?   270
No. We must steel our hearts. Bury our dead,
with tears for the day they die, not one day more.
And all those left alive, after the hateful carnage,
remember food and drink—so all the more fiercely
we can fight our enemies, nonstop, no mercy,
durable as the bronze that wraps our bodies.
Let no one hold back now, waiting further summons—
these *are* your summons: pain and death to the man
who skulks beside the ships! Now, all in a mass,
drive hard against them—rousing battering war   280
against these stallion-breaking Trojans!"
                                        He led an escort
formed of the brave old soldier Nestor's sons,
Meges the son of Phyleus, Meriones and Thoas,
Lycomedes the son of Creon, Melanippus too.
Off they went to the tents of Agamemnon—
a few sharp commands and the work was done.
Seven tripods hauled from the tents, as promised,
twenty burnished cauldrons, a dozen massive stallions.
They quickly brought out women, flawless, skilled in crafts,
seven, and Briseis in all her beauty made the eighth.   290
Then Odysseus weighed out ten full bars of gold
and led the princes back, laden with other gifts,
and they set them down amid the meeting grounds.
Agamemnon rose to his feet.
The crier Talthybius, his voice clear as a god's,
holding the boar in his arms, flanked the great commander.
And Atreus' son drew forth the dagger always slung
at his battle-sword's big sheath, he cut some hairs
from the boar's head, first tufts to start the rite,
and lifting up his arms to Zeus on high he prayed   300
while the armies held fast to their seats in silence,
all by rank and file, listening to their king.
He scanned the vaulting skies as his voice rang in prayer:
"Zeus be my witness first, the highest, best of gods!
Then Earth, the Sun, and Furies stalking the world below
to wreak revenge on the dead who broke their oaths—

I swear I never laid a hand on the girl Briseis,
I never forced her to serve my lust in bed
or perform some other task . . .
Briseis remained untouched within my tents.   310
True. If a word of what I say is falsely sworn,
may the gods deal out such blows to me, such agonies
as they deal out to the men who break sworn oaths
and take their names in vain!"
                              On those terms
he dragged his ruthless dagger across the boar's throat.
Talthybius whirled the carcass round about his head
and slung it into the yawning gulf of the gray sea
for swarming fish to eat. Then Prince Achilles stood
and addressed the Argives keen for battle: "Father Zeus—
great are the blinding frenzies you deal out to men!   320
If not, I swear, Atrides could never have roused
the fury in me, the rage that would not die,
or wrenched the girl away against my will—
stubborn, implacable man. But Zeus, somehow,
was bent on this awesome slaughter of Achaeans.
Go now, take your meal—the sooner to bring on war."

    This brusque command dispersed the muster quickly.
The contingents scattered, each to its own ship.
Exultant Myrmidons took charge of the gifts
and bore them off to their royal captain's moorings.   330
They stowed them safe in his shelters, settled the women
and proud henchmen drove the teams to his herds.

    And so Briseis returned, like golden Aphrodite,
but when she saw Patroclus lying torn by the bronze
she flung herself on his body, gave a piercing cry
and with both hands clawing deep at her breasts,
her soft throat and lovely face, she sobbed,
a woman like a goddess in her grief, "Patroclus—
dearest joy of my heart, my harrowed, broken heart!
I left you alive that day I left these shelters,   340
now I come back to find you fallen, captain of armies!

So grief gives way to grief, my life one endless sorrow!
The husband to whom my father and noble mother gave me,
I saw him torn by the sharp bronze before our city,
and my three brothers—a single mother bore us:
my brothers, how I loved you!—
you all went down to death on the same day . . .
But you, Patroclus, you would not let me weep,
not when the swift Achilles cut my husband down,
not when he plundered the lordly Mynes' city—   350
not even weep! No, again and again you vowed
you'd make me godlike Achilles' lawful, wedded wife,
you would sail me west in your warships, home to Phthia
and there with the Myrmidons hold my marriage feast.
So now I mourn your death—I will never stop—
you were always kind."

                       Her voice rang out in tears
and the women wailed in answer, grief for Patroclus
calling forth each woman's private sorrows.
But Achaea's warlords clustered round Achilles,
begging him to eat. He only spurned them, groaning,   360
"I beg *you*—if any comrade will hear me out in this—
stop pressing me now to glut myself with food and drink,
now such painful grief has come and struck my heart!
I'll hold out till the sun goes down—enduring—
fasting—despite your appeals."

                         His voice so firm
that Achilles caused the other kings to scatter.
But the two Atridae stayed, and good Odysseus,
Nestor, Idomeneus, Phoenix the old charioteer,
all trying to comfort Achilles deep in sorrow.
But no comfort could reach the fighter's heart   370
till he went striding into the jaws of bloody war.
The memories swept over him . . .
sighs heaved from his depths as Achilles burst forth,
"Ah god, time and again, my doomed, my dearest friend,
you would set before us a seasoned meal yourself,
here in our tents, in your quick and expert way,
when Argive forces rushed to fight the Trojans,

stampeding those breakers of horses into rout.
But now you lie before me, hacked to pieces here
while the heart within me fasts from food and drink   380
though stores inside are full—
                           I'm sick with longing for you!
There is no more shattering blow that I could suffer.
Not even if I should learn of my own father's death,
who, this moment, is weeping warm tears in Phthia,
I know it, bereft of a son as loved as this . . .
and here I am in a distant land, fighting Trojans,
and all for that blood-chilling horror, Helen!—
or the death of my dear son, reared for me in Scyros,
if Prince Neoptolemus is still among the living.
Till now I'd hoped, hoped with all my heart   390
that I alone would die
far from the stallion-land of Argos, here in Troy,
but you, Patroclus, would journey back to Phthia
and then you'd ferry Neoptolemus home from Scyros,
fast in your black ship, and show him all my wealth,
my servingmen, my great house with the high vaulting roof.
For father, I fear—if he's not dead and buried yet—
just clings, perhaps, to his last breath of life,
ground down now by the hateful siege of years,
waiting, day after day, for painful news of me—   400
until he learns his only son is dead."

     His voice rang out in tears and the warlords mourned in answer,
each remembering those he had left behind at home.
Seeing their grief the Father, filled with pity,
quickly turned to Athena with winging words:
"My child, have you abandoned him forever?
Your favorite man of war. Is it all lost now?—
no more care for Achilles left inside your heart?
There he huddles before his curving, beaked ships,
racked with grief for his dear friend while others scatter,   410
settling down to their meal. He's fasting, never fed.
Go. Run and instill some nectar and sweet ambrosia
deep within his chest. Stave off his hunger now."

   So he urged Athena already poised for action.
Down the sky she swooped through the clear bright air
like a shrieking, sharp-winged hawk, and while Achaeans
quickly armed throughout the encampment, she instilled
some nectar and sweet ambrosia deep in Achilles' chest
so the stabbing pangs of hunger could not sap his knees.
Then back to her mighty Father's sturdy halls she went   420
as troops moved out, pouring out of the fast trim ships.
Thick-and-fast as the snow comes swirling down from Zeus,
frozen sharp when the North Wind born in heaven blasts it on—
so massed, so dense the glistening burnished helmets shone,
streaming out of the ships, and shields with jutting bosses,
breastplates welded front and back and the long ashen spears.
The glory of armor lit the skies and the whole earth laughed,
rippling under the glitter of bronze, thunder resounding
under trampling feet of armies. And in their midst
the brilliant Achilles began to arm for battle . . .   430
A sound of grinding came from the fighter's teeth,
his eyes blazed forth in searing points of fire,
unbearable grief came surging through his heart
and now, bursting with rage against the men of Troy,
he donned Hephaestus' gifts—magnificent armor
the god of fire forged with all his labor.
First he wrapped his legs with well-made greaves,
fastened behind his heels with silver ankle-clasps,
next he strapped the breastplate round his chest
then over his shoulder Achilles slung his sword,   440
the fine bronze blade with its silver-studded hilt,
then hoisted the massive shield flashing far and wide
like a full round moon—and gleaming bright as the light
that reaches sailors out at sea, the flare of a watchfire
burning strong in a lonely sheepfold up some mountain slope
when the gale-winds hurl the crew that fights against them
far over the fish-swarming sea, far from loved ones—
so the gleam from Achilles' well-wrought blazoned shield
shot up and hit the skies. Then lifting his rugged helmet
he set it down on his brows, and the horsehair crest   450
shone like a star and the waving golden plumes shook

that Hephaestus drove in bristling thick along its ridge.
And brilliant Achilles tested himself in all his gear,
Achilles spun on his heels to see if it fitted tightly,
see if his shining limbs ran free within it, yes,
and it felt like buoyant wings lifting the great captain.
And then, last, Achilles drew his father's spear
from its socket-stand—weighted, heavy, tough.
No other Achaean fighter could heft that shaft,
only Achilles had the skill to wield it well: 460
Pelian ash it was, a gift to his father Peleus
presented by Chiron once, hewn on Pelion's crest
to be the death of heroes.
                    Now the war-team—
Alcimus and Automedon worked to yoke them quickly.
They cinched the supple breast-straps round their chests
and driving the bridle irons home between their jaws,
pulled the reins back taut to the bolted chariot.
Seizing a glinting whip, his fist on the handgrip,
Automedon leapt aboard behind the team and behind him
Achilles struck his stance, helmed for battle now,   470
glittering in his armor like the sun astride the skies,
his ringing, daunting voice commanding his father's horses:
"Roan Beauty and Charger, illustrious foals of Lightfoot!
Try hard, do better this time—bring your charioteer
back home alive to his waiting Argive comrades
once we're through with fighting. Don't leave Achilles
there on the battlefield as you left Patroclus—dead!"

      And Roan Beauty the horse with flashing hoofs
spoke up from under the yoke, bowing his head low
so his full mane came streaming down the yoke-pads,   480
down along the yoke to sweep the ground . . .
The white-armed goddess Hera gave him voice:
"Yes! we will save your life—this time too—
master, mighty Achilles! But the day of death
already hovers near, and we are not to blame
but a great god *is* and the strong force of fate.
Not through our want of speed or any lack of care

did the Trojans strip the armor off Patroclus' back.
It was all that matchless god, sleek-haired Leto's son—
he killed him among the champions and handed Hector glory.   490
Our team could race with the rush of the West Wind,
the strongest, swiftest blast on earth, men say—
still *you* are doomed to die by force, Achilles,
cut down by a deathless god and mortal man!"

He said no more. The Furies struck him dumb.
But the fiery runner Achilles burst out in anger,
"Why, Roan Beauty—why prophesy my doom?
Don't waste your breath. I know, well I know—
I am destined to die here, far from my dear father,
far from mother. But all the same I will never stop   500
till I drive the Trojans to their bloody fill of war!"

A high stabbing cry—
and out in the front ranks he drove his plunging stallions.

BOOK TWENTY

Olympian Gods
in Arms

So by the beaked ships the Argives formed for battle,
arming round you, Achilles—Achilles starved for war—
and faced by the Trojan ranks along the plain's high ground.
At the same time, from the peak of rugged ridged Olympus
Zeus commanded Themis to call the gods to council.
Themis made her rounds, ranging far and wide
and summoned all to march to Father's halls.
Not a single river failed to come, none apart
from the Ocean stream that holds the earth in place,
nor a single nymph who haunts the rustling groves   10
and the river springs and the lush, grassy meadows.
All flocked to the halls of Zeus who gathers storms
and found their seats in the colonnades of polished stone
Hephaestus built for Father Zeus with all his craft and cunning.

And so the powers assembled deep in Zeus's halls.
Nor did the god of earthquakes fail to hear the goddess.
Surging up from the sea he came to join their ranks,
took a seat in their midst and probed Zeus's plans:
"Why now, great king of the lightning,
why summon the gods to council once again?   20
Still some concern for Troy's and Achaea's armies?—
now that battle is set to burst in flames between them!"

But Zeus who marshals the thunderheads replied,
"God of the earthquake, well you know my plans,
the strategy in my mind, and why I call you here
These mortals do concern me, dying as they are.
Still, here I stay on Olympus throned aloft,
here in my steep mountain cleft, to feast my eyes
and delight my heart. The rest of you: down you go,
go to Trojans, go to Achaeans. Help either side   30
as the fixed desire drives each god to act.
If Achilles fights the Trojans—unopposed by us—
not for a moment will they hold his breakneck force.
Even before now they'd shake to see him coming.
Now, with his rage inflamed for his friend's death,
I fear he'll raze the walls against the will of fate."

And with that command Zeus roused incessant battle.
Down the immortals launched to the field of action—
their warring spirits split the gods two ways.
Hera went to the massed ships with Pallas Athena,   40
Poseidon who grips the earth, and Hermes god of luck
who excels them all at subtle twists and tactics—
and the god of fire flanked them, seething power,
hobbling along but his shrunken legs moved nimbly.
But Ares swept down to the Trojans, helmet flashing,
and pacing him went Phoebus with long hair streaming
and Artemis showering arrows, Leto and River Xanthus
and goddess Aphrodite strong with eternal laughter.

Now, while the gods had still kept clear of mortal men,
the Achaeans kept on gaining glory—great Achilles   50
who held back from the brutal fighting so long
had just come blazing forth. Chilling tremors
shook the Trojans' knees, down to the last man,
terrified at the sight: the headlong runner coming,
gleaming in all his gear, afire like man-destroying Ares.
But once the Olympians merged with mortal fighters,
Strife the mighty driver of armies rose in strength
and Athena bellowed her stunning war cry—standing now
at the edge of the deep-dug trench outside the rampart,
now at thundering cliffs she loosed her vibrant cry.   60
And Ares bellowed his cry from far across the lines,
churning black as a whirlwind, roaring down now
from the city's crest, commanding Trojans on and now
rushing along the Simois banks and scaling Sunlight Hill.

So the blissful gods were rousing both opposing armies,
clashing front to front but then, in their own ranks,
their overpowering strife broke out in massive war.
Down from the high skies the father of men and gods
let loose tremendous thunder—from down below Poseidon
shook the boundless earth and towering heads of mountains.   70
The whole world quaked, the slopes of Ida with all her springs
and all her peaks and the walls of Troy and all Achaea's ships.
And terror-struck in the underworld, Hades lord of the dead
cringed and sprang from his throne and screamed shrill,
fearing the god who rocks the ground above his realm,
giant Poseidon, would burst the earth wide open now
and lay bare to mortal men and immortal gods at last
the houses of the dead—the dank, moldering horrors
that fill the deathless gods themselves with loathing.
So immense the clash as the war of gods erupted.   80
There, look, rearing against the lord Poseidon
Phoebus Apollo loomed, bristling winged arrows,
rearing against Ares, blazing-eyed Athena,
rearing against Hera, Artemis with arrow of gold

and cry that halloos the hunt, the goddess raining shafts,
Huntress sister of Phoebus the distant deadly Archer—
rearing against Leto, Hermes the running god of luck
and against the Fire-god rose the great deep-swirling river
immortals call the Xanthus, mankind calls Scamander.

So god went up against god. But blazing Achilles   90
strained to engage Prince Hector, plunge in battle
with him beyond all others—Achilles yearning now
to glut with Hector's blood, his, no other,
Ares who hacks at men behind his rawhide shield.
But Aeneas it was whom Phoebus, urger of armies,
filled with power now and drove against Achilles.
Phoebus, masking his voice like Priam's son Lycaon,
like him to the life the son of Zeus called out,
"Captain of Trojan councils—where have they gone,
those threats you made in your cups before the kings?   100
Boasting you'd face Achilles man-to-man in battle!"

But Aeneas turned and gave the god an answer:
"Son of Priam, why press me to go against Achilles?
It's much against my will—his fury is overwhelming.
Nor would it be the first time I have had to face
the matchless, headlong runner. Once before
he chased me hard with his spear, down from Ida
the day he raided our flocks and sacked Lyrnessus,
Pedasus fort as well. But Zeus saved me then,
put force in my heart, spring in my racing knees.   110
Else I'd gone down at Achilles' hands, Athena's too—
the goddess sweeping before him lent the light of safety,
calling Achilles on that day with his bronze spear
to slaughter Leleges and Trojans. That is why
no mortal can fight Achilles head-to-head:
at every foray one of the gods goes with him,
beating back his death. Even without that power
his spear flies straight to the mark, never stops,
not till it bores clean through some fighter's flesh.
But if only Zeus would stretch the ropes of war dead even   120

the man would have no easy victory then, believe me—
not though he claims he's built of solid bronze!"

Apollo son of Zeus encouraged him still more:
"Hero, why not invoke the deathless gods yourself?
They say you're a son of Aphrodite, Zeus's daughter,
but Achilles sprang from a lesser goddess' loins—
Aphrodite's a child of Zeus,
Thetis comes from the Old Man of the Sea.
So ram him straight on with your tough bronze!
Now—and not for a moment let him turn you back   130
with his stinging proud contempt and brazen threats!"

That breathed enormous strength in the good captain—
right through the front he went, helmed in flashing bronze.
Nor did the white-armed Hera fail to see Anchises' son
advancing there through the press to face Achilles.
And rallying other gods around her, Hera shouted,
"Bend to the work, you two, Poseidon, Athena,
decide in your hearts how this assault will go!
Here comes Aeneas, look, helmed in flashing bronze
to oppose Achilles now and Phoebus speeds him on.   140
Come, spin him round in his tracks and drive him back.
That, or else one of *us* might stand beside Achilles
and lend him winning force—his courage must not flag.
Let him know he's loved by the greatest gods on high
while the gods who up till now have shielded Troy
from war and death are worthless as the wind!
We swept down from Olympus, all to join this fight
so Achilles might not fall at Trojan hands today.
Afterward he must suffer what the Fates spun out
on the doomed fighter's life line drawn that day   150
his mother gave him birth. If Achilles fails
to learn all this from our own immortal voices
he will quail when a god attacks him face-to-face.
The gods are hard to handle—
when they come blazing forth in their true power."

But the god who grips the earth restrained the Queen:
"Hera, so hard, so senseless! Don't leap to extremes.
I, at least, have no real lust to drive our forces
against the gods of Troy. Our side is so much stronger.
Come now, let us move off and settle down together   160
far from the trampled field, take a lookout post
and leave the war to mortals . . .
But if Ares or Phoebus cares to start things off,
if they block Achilles and keep him out of action,
they will have a fight on their hands, then and there,
an all-out fight with us. But not for long, I trust—
they will soon break off and slink back to Olympus,
home to the gathered gods who wait their coming,
overwhelmed by the crushing power of our fists!"

And with that threat the god of the sea-blue mane   170
led the way to the fortress raised for godlike Heracles:
earth piled on both sides, a high imposing breastwork
men of Troy and Pallas Athena flung up for the man
where he could race and escape that sea monster
whenever it charged him hard from shore to plain.
There Poseidon sat at ease with his deathless friends
who spread unbroken shrouds of mist around their shoulders,
while far on the other side the gods of Troy sat down
on the brows of Sunlight Hill, flanking you, Apollo,
god of the wild cry, and Ares scourge of cities.   180

So either side of the lines they took positions,
weighing tactics, each Olympian force reluctant now
to launch out first on the wrenching horrors of war . . .
while Zeus on the heights sat poised to thunder orders.

But the whole plain filled with men and flashed with bronze,
with troops and horse and beneath their feet the earth quaked
as armies rushed together. And now in the no man's land
two champions, greatest of all, strode and closed,
both men burning for battle,
Aeneas son of Anchises and brilliant Achilles.   190

Aeneas came up first with long, menacing strides,
head tossing his heavy helmet, his charging shield
thrust out to defend his chest, and shook his bronze spear.
But over against him came Achilles rearing like some lion
out on a rampage, and a whole town of men has geared
for the hunt to cut him down: but at first he lopes along,
all contempt, till one of the fast young hunters spears him—
then . . . crouched for attack, his jaws gaping, over his teeth
the foam breaks out, deep in his chest the brave heart groans,
he lashes his ribs, his flanks and hips with his tail,   200
he whips himself into fighting-fury, eyes glaring,
hurls himself head-on—kill one of the men or die,
go down himself at the first lethal charge!
So now magnificent pride and fury lashed Achilles
to go against Aeneas the greathearted fighter.
As they closed on each other, both in range,
the matchless runner Achilles opened up: "Aeneas—
why so far from your own ranks, standing all exposed?
Does your courage really drive you to challenge *me*?
In hopes of ruling your stallion-breaking friends   210
and filling Priam's throne? Even if you killed me,
would Priam drop his crown in your hands—for that?
The king has sons. He's sound of limb. No half-wit either.
Or have the Trojans sworn to carve you a fine estate?
The choicest land in the realm, rich in vineyards
and good tilled fields for you to lord it over—
if only you kill *me*!
Ah but I think you'll find the work quite taxing.
I seem to remember once before you fled my spear . . .
Or have you forgot the time I caught you all alone,   220
I cut you off from your flocks and sent you scurrying down
the slopes of Ida? Running for dear life, legs driving,
never a look behind. And you escaped that time,
you fled to Lyrnessus' walls, but at one charge
I sacked the place with Athena's help and Father Zeus,
I tore the day of freedom away from all the women,
dragged them off as slaves. Zeus saved you then
and other gods joined in. But he won't save you now,

I'd say—though the hope goes racing through your mind.
Go back to your own rank and file, I tell you!   230
Don't stand up against me—or you will meet your death.
Even a fool learns something once it hits him.''

But Aeneas, taking a long, deep breath, replied,
"Don't think for a moment, Achilles, son of Peleus,
you can frighten me with words like a child, a fool—
I'm an old hand myself at trading taunts and insults.
We both know each other's birth, each other's parents,
we've heard their far-flung fame on the lips of mortal men,
though you have never set eyes on mine, or I on yours.
They say you are Peleus' son, that fine, flawless man;   240
your mother, Thetis, sleek-haired child of the Sea.
And I am Aeneas, and I can boast Anchises' blood,
the proud Anchises, but my mother is Aphrodite.
Our parents—one pair or the other will mourn
a dear son today. Certain it is, I warn you,
we won't break off from battle and leave the field
with no more than a youngster's banter light as this.
But about my birth, if you'd like to learn it well,
first to last—though many people know it—
here's my story, Achilles . . .   250
Starting with Dardanus, Storm-king Zeus's son
who founded Dardania, long before holy Troy arose,
that city reared on the plain to shelter all our people.
They still camped on the slopes of Ida wet with springs.
Then Dardanus had a son in turn, King Erichthonius,
and he was the richest man in all the world—
three thousand mares he owned, grazing the marshes,
brood-mares in their prime, proud of their leaping foals.
And the North Wind, lusting once for the herd at pasture,
taking on the build of a black stallion, mounted several   260
and swelling under his force they bore him twelve colts.
And when they'd frisk on the tilled fields ripe with grain
they'd brush the crests of the corn and never snap a stalk,
but when they'd frisk and vault on the sea's broad back
they'd skim the crests of whitecaps glistening foam.

Now Erichthonius sired Tros, a lord of the Trojans,
and Tros, in turn, had three distinguished sons:
Ilus, Assaracus and Ganymede radiant as a god,
and he was the handsomest mortal man on earth—
and so the immortals, awestruck by his beauty,   270
snatched him away to bear the cup of Zeus
and pour out wine for all the deathless gods.
And Ilus, in turn, sired a valiant son Laomedon,
Laomedon had his sons as well, Tithonus and Priam,
Lampus and Clytius, Hicetaon the gallant aide of Ares,
and Assaracus fathered Capys, and he had a son Anchises
and Anchises fathered me, but Priam had Prince Hector.
There you have my lineage.
That is the blood I claim, my royal birth.
As for strength in war, Zeus lends power to some,   280
others he wastes away, whatever his pleasure—
the strongest god of all.
                            Come, Achilles,
no more bragging on this way like boys,
standing here in the thick of a pitched battle.
Plenty of insults we could fling against each other,
enough to sink a ship with a hundred benches!
A man's tongue is a glib and twisty thing . . .
plenty of words there are, all kinds at its command—
with all the room in the world for talk to range and stray.
And the sort you use is just the sort you'll hear.   290
What do we need with wrangling, hurling insults?
Cursing each other here like a pair of nagging women
boiling over with petty, heartsick squabbles, blustering
into the streets to pelt themselves with slander,
much of it true, much not. Anger stirs up lies.
I blaze for battle—your taunts can't turn me back,
not till we've fought it out with bronze. On with it—
taste the bite of each other's brazen spears!"
                                        With that
he hurled a heavy lance at the great and awesome shield
and its massive surface clanged as it took the point.   300
Achilles had thrust it forth with his strong fist,

fearing staunch Aeneas' spear with its long shadow
would drive its whole length lightly through his buckler—
groundless fears. The fighter had no idea at all
that famous gifts of the gods do not break lightly,
can't be crushed when a mortal hand assails them.
So now not even seasoned Aeneas' heavy shaft
could smash Achilles' shield:
the gold blocked it, forged in the god's gift.
It did bore through two plies but three were left,   310
since the crippled Smith had made it five plies thick
with two of bronze on the outside, inside two of tin,
between them one of gold where the ashen spear held fast.

   Achilles next—he hurled his spear and its long shadow flew
and the weapon struck the balanced round shield of Aeneas
under the outer rim where the bronze ran thinnest,
backed by the thinnest bull's-hide. Straight through
the Pelian ash burst, the shield rang out with a screech—
but Aeneas crouched low, holding the buckler off his chest,
terrified as the shaft shot past his back, hurled so hard   320
it plunged deep in the ground, even after it tore up
two round plies of the shield that cased his body.
Dodging the big spear, Aeneas got to his feet . . .
a dizzying swirl of anguish rushing down his eyes,
blind with fear, the point had stuck so close.
But drawing his sharp sword, Achilles charged, wild,
hurtling toward him, loosing a savage cry as Aeneas
hefted a boulder in his hands, a tremendous feat—
no two men could hoist it, weak as men are now,
but all on his own he raised it high with ease.   330
Then and there he'd have struck Achilles lunging in,
the rock would have hit him square in casque or shield,
the gear would have warded off grim death, and Achilles, closing,
would have slashed his life away with a well-honed blade—
if the god of earthquakes had not marked it quickly
and called the gods at once who grouped around him:
"Now, I tell you, my heart aches for great Aeneas!
He'll go down to the House of Death this instant,

overwhelmed by Achilles—all because he trusted
the distant deadly Archer's urgings. Poor fool—   340
as if Apollo would lift a hand to save him now
from death, grim death. Aeneas the innocent!
Why should Aeneas suffer here, for no good reason,
embroiled in the quarrels of others, not his own?
He always gave us gifts to warm our hearts,
gifts for the gods who rule the vaulting skies.
So come, let us rescue him from death ourselves,
for fear the son of Cronus might just tower in rage
if Achilles kills this man. He is destined to survive.
Yes, so the generation of Dardanus will not perish,   350
obliterated without an heir, without a trace:
Dardanus, dearest to Zeus of all the sons
that mortal women brought to birth for Father.
Now he has come to hate the generation of Priam,
and now Aeneas will rule the men of Troy in power—
his sons' sons and the sons born in future years."

But Hera the Queen broke in, her eyes open wide:
"Decide in your own mind, god of the earthquake,
whether to save Aeneas now or let him die,
crushed by Achilles, for all his fighting heart.   360
But time and again we two have sworn our oaths
in the eyes of all the gods—I and Pallas Athena—
never to drive the fatal day away from the Trojans,
not even when all Troy burns in the ramping flames
when the warring sons of Achaea burn her down!"

As soon as he heard that, the god of earthquakes
surged through the clashing troops and raining spears
to reach the place where the two famed heroes fought.
Quickly he poured a mist across Achilles' eyes,
wrenched the spear from stalwart Aeneas' shield,   370
laid the bronze-shod ashen shaft at Achilles' feet
and hoisting Aeneas off the earth he slung him far . . .
And over the massing lines of men and massing chariots,
high in the air Aeneas vaulted, hurled by the god's hand

till he came to ground at the battle's churning flank
where Cauconian units braced themselves for action.
The god of the earthquake swept beside him there
and gave the man a burst of winging orders: "Aeneas—
what god on high commands you to play the madman?
Fighting against Achilles' overwhelming fury!—   380
both a better soldier and more loved by the gods.
Pull back at once, whenever you're thrown against him—
or go down to the House of Death against the will of fate.
But once Achilles has met his death, his certain doom,
take courage then, go fight on the front lines then—
no other Achaean can bring you down in war."

                                        With that,
with destiny made clear, he left him there on the spot
and turning back to Achilles quickly brushed away
the mist from his eyes, the magic, godsent haze.
And Achilles stared with all his might, dazzled,   390
disgusted too, and addressed his own great heart:
"Impossible—look, a marvel right before my eyes!
That spear I hurled is lying here on the ground.
That man—I cannot see him—
the one I hurled at, wild to cut him down.
Ah, so the deathless gods must love Aeneas too.
And I thought his vaunts were empty, hollow boasting.
Well let him go, I say! Never, never again
will he have the nerve to test my fighting power—
even now he was glad to save himself from death.   400
Now, quick, I'll marshal our battle-hungry Argives—
face the rest of the Trojans, test them, fight them down!"

    And back to the lines he leapt and urged each man,
"No more standing back from the Trojans, brave Achaeans!
Now fighter go against fighter, out for bloodshed!
It's hard for me, strong as I am, single-handed
to make for such a force and fight them all.
Why, not even Ares the deathless god of war,
not even Athena—for all their heavy labor—
could hack a passage through such jaws of battle.   410

But I—whatever fists and feet and strength can do,
that I will do, I swear, not hang back, not one inch.
Straight through enemy columns I go plowing now—
and no Trojan, I guarantee, will thrill with pleasure
once he meets my spearshaft head-to-head!"

                                        Spurring his men
while Hector aflash in armor urged his Trojans—
thinking he'd even go up against Achilles:
"No fear of Pelides now, my gallant Trojans!
I too could battle the deathless gods with words—
it's hard with a spear, the gods are so much stronger.   420
Not even Achilles can bring off all his boasts:
some he'll accomplish, some cut short, half done.
I'm off to engage the man, though his fists are fire,
though his fists are fire and his fury burnished iron!"

    Spurring them on to raise their spears for full assault
and the Trojans' fury massed and mounted, war cries broke
but Apollo suddenly stood by Hector, shouting,
"Don't for a moment duel Achilles, Hector,
out in front of your ranks!
Withdraw to your main lines and wait him there,   430
out of the crash of battle. Else he'll spear you down
or close for the kill and hack you with his sword."

    So Hector drew back to his thronging comrades,
terrified to hear the voice of god. Not Achilles—
armored in battle-power down he flung on the Trojans,
loosed barbaric cries, and his first kill was Iphition,
Otrynteus' hardy son and a chief of large contingents,
born of a river nymph to Otrynteus, scourge of towns,
below Tmolus' snows in the wealthy realm of Hyde . . .
As the Trojan charged head-on Achilles speared him   440
square in the brows—his whole skull split in half
and down he crashed, Achilles exulting over him:
"Here you lie, Otrynteus' son—most terrible man alive!
Here's your deathbed! Far from your birthplace, Gyge Lake

where your father's fine estate lies next to the Hyllus
stocked with fish and next to the whirling Hermus!"

Vaunting over the dark that swept his quarry's eyes
and the running-rims of Argive war-cars cut him to shreds
at the onset's breaking edge. And next Achilles lunged
at Demoleon, son of Antenor, a tough defensive fighter—   450
he stabbed his temple and cleft his helmet's cheekpiece.
None of the bronze plate could hold it—boring through
the metal and skull the bronze spearpoint pounded,
Demoleon's brains splattered all inside his casque,
the Trojan beaten down in his fury. Hippodamas next,
he leapt from his chariot fleeing before Achilles—
Achilles' spearshaft rammed him through the back
and he gasped his life away, bellowing like some bull
that chokes and grunts when the young boys drag him round
the lord of Helice's shrine and the earthquake god   460
delights to see them dragging—so he bellowed now
and the man's proud spirit left his bones behind.
Achilles rushed with his spear at noble Polydorus
son of Priam. His father would not let him fight,
ever, he was the youngest-born of all his sons—
Priam loved him most, the fastest runner of all
but now the young fool, mad to display his speed,
went dashing along the front to meet his death.
Just as he shot past the matchless runner Achilles
speared him square in the back where his war-belt clasped,   470
golden buckles clinching both halves of his breastplate—
straight on through went the point and out the navel,
down on his knees he dropped—
screaming shrill as the world went black before him—
ciutched his bowels to his body, hunched and sank.

But Hector seeing his own brother Polydorus
clutching his entrails, sinking limp to the ground—
the mist came swirling down his eyes as well . . .
He could bear no more, wheeling off at a distance—
shaking his whetted spear he charged Achilles now,   480

coming fierce as fire but Achilles marked him quickly
and springing forth to take him, triumphed to himself,
"Here is the man who's raked my heart the most,
who killed my cherished comrade! No more delay,
dodging each other down the passageways of battle!"

Under his brows he glared at royal Hector, shouting,
"Quick, charge me—the sooner to meet your death!"

But Hector, his helmet flashing, never flinched:
"Don't think for a moment, Achilles, son of Peleus,
you can frighten me with words like a child, a fool—   490
I'm an old hand myself at trading taunts and insults.
Well I know you are brave, and I am far weaker.
True—but all lies in the lap of the great gods.
Weaker I am, but I still might take your life
with one hurl of a spear—my weapon can cut too,
long before now its point has found its mark!"
                                           Grim reminder—
he brandished the shaft and hurled with all his might
but Athena blew it back from Achilles bent on glory—
a quick light breath and the shaft flew back again
to tall Prince Hector and fell before his feet.   500
Achilles blazed, charging, raging to cut him down,
loosing savage cries—but Phoebus whisked him away,
easy work for a god, and wrapped him round in mist.
Three times the brilliant runner Achilles charged him,
lunged with his bronze spear, three times he slashed at cloud—
then at Achilles' fourth assault like something superhuman
his terrifying voice burst out in winging words:
"Now, again, you've escaped your death, you dog,
but a good close brush with death it was, I'd say!
Now, again, your Phoebus Apollo pulls you through,   510
the one you pray to, wading into our storm of spears.
We'll fight again—I'll finish you off next time
if one of the gods will only urge *me* on as well.
But now I'll go for the others, anyone I can catch."
                                           Whirling

he stabbed Dryops, speared him right through the neck—
he dropped at his feet and Achilles left him dead
and smashed Demuchus' knee, Philetor's strapping son,
stopped him right in his tracks with a well-flung spear
then sprang with his great sword and ripped his life away.
Then on he rushed at the sons of Bias—Laogonus, Dardanus—   520
hurled them off their chariot, slammed them both to ground,
one with a spear-thrust, one chopped down with a blade.
Then Tros, Alastor's son, crawled to Achilles' knees
and clutched them, hoping he'd spare him,
let Tros off alive, no cutting him down in blood,
he'd pity Tros, a man of his own age—the young fool,
he'd no idea, thinking *Achilles* could be swayed!
Here was a man not sweet at heart, not kind, no,
he was raging, wild—as Tros grasped his knees,
desperate, begging, Achilles slit open his liver,   530
the liver spurted loose, gushing with dark blood,
drenched his lap and the night swirled down his eyes
as his life breath slipped away.
                              And Mulius next—
he reared and jammed his lance through the man's ear
so the lance came jutting out through the other ear,
bronze point glinting.
                       Echeclus son of Agenor next—
Achilles split his head at the brow with hilted sword
so the whole blade ran hot with blood, and red death
came plunging down his eyes, and the strong force of fate.
Deucalion next—he lanced his arm with a bronze-shod spear,   540
he spitted the Trojan through where the elbow-tendons grip
and there he stood, waiting Achilles, arm dangling heavy,
staring death in the face—and Achilles chopped his neck
and his sword sent head and helmet flying off together
and marrow bubbling up from the clean-cut neckbone.
Down he went, his corpse full length on the ground—
just as Achilles charged at Piras' handsome son,
Rhigmus who'd sailed from the fertile soil of Thrace—
Achilles pierced his belly, the bronze impaled his guts
and out of his car he pitched as his driver Areithous   550

swung the horses round but Achilles speared his back
and the spearshaft heaved him off the chariot too
and the panicked stallions bolted.

                              Achilles now
like inhuman fire raging on through the mountain gorges
splinter-dry, setting ablaze big stands of timber,
the wind swirling the huge fireball left and right—
chaos of fire—Achilles storming on with brandished spear
like a frenzied god of battle trampling all he killed
and the earth ran black with blood. Thundering on,
on like oxen broad in the brow some field hand yokes   560
to crush white barley heaped on a well-laid threshing floor
and the grain is husked out fast by the bellowing oxen's hoofs—
so as the great Achilles rampaged on, his sharp-hoofed stallions
trampled shields and corpses, axle under his chariot splashed
with blood, blood on the handrails sweeping round the car,
sprays of blood shooting up from the stallions' hoofs
and churning, whirling rims—and the son of Peleus
charioteering on to seize his glory, bloody filth
splattering both strong arms, Achilles' invincible arms—

BOOK TWENTY-ONE

Achilles
Fights the River

But once they reached the ford where the river runs clear,
the strong, whirling Xanthus sprung of immortal Zeus,
Achilles split the Trojan rout, driving one half
back toward the city, scattering up the plain
where Achaeans themselves stampeded off in terror
just the day before when Hector raged unchecked.
Now back in their tracks the Trojans fled pell-mell
while Hera spread dense cloud ahead to block their way.
But the other half were packed in the silver-whirling river,
into its foaming depths they tumbled, splashing, flailing—   10
the plunging river roaring, banks echoing, roaring back
and the men screamed, swimming wildly, left and right,
spinning round in the whirlpools. Spun like locusts
swarming up in the air, whipped by rushing fire,
flitting toward a river—the tireless fire blazes,

scorching them all with hard explosive blasts of flame
and beaten down in the depths the floating locusts huddle—
so at Achilles' charge the Xanthus' swirling currents
choked with a spate of horse and men—the river roared.

And the god-sprung hero left his spear on the bank,   20
propped on tamarisks—in he leapt like a frenzied god,
his heart racing with slaughter, only his sword in hand,
whirling in circles, slashing—hideous groans breaking,
fighters stabbed by the blade, water flushed with blood.
Like shoals of fish darting before some big-bellied dolphin,
escaping, cramming the coves of a good deepwater harbor,
terrified for their lives—he devours all he catches—
so the Trojans down that terrible river's onrush
cowered under its bluffs. But soon as Achilles
grew arm-weary from killing, twelve young Trojans   30
he rounded up from the river, took them all alive
as the blood-price for Patroclus' death, Menoetius' son.
He dragged them up on the banks, dazed like fawns,
lashed their hands behind them with well-cut straps—
their own belts that cinched their billowing war-shirts—
gave them to friends to lead away to the beaked ships
and back he whirled, insane to hack more flesh.

And first he met a son of Dardan Priam
just escaping the rapids—Lycaon, the very man
Achilles seized himself, once on a midnight raid,   40
and hauled from his father's orchard, resisting all the way.
He was pruning a young fig with his sharp bronze hook,
cutting green branches to bend for chariot-rails
when a sudden blow came down on him in the dark—
the grim marauder Achilles. That was the time
he shipped him to Lemnos fortress, sold him off
and the son of Jason paid the price for the slave,
but a stranger there released him from his chains,
Eetion out of Imbros paid a princely ransom
and sent him off to Arisbe's shining walls.   50
From there he slipped away to his father's house,

struggling home from Lemnos, but only eleven days
he cheered his heart with friends. Then on the twelfth
some god cast him into Achilles' hands again
and now he would send him off on a new journey,
resisting all the way to the House of Death.
The swift runner recognized him at once—
disarmed, no shield, no helmet, no spear left,
he'd scattered all his gear on the bank, sweating,
clambering out of the ford exhausted, knees buckling . . .   60
Achilles, filled with rage, addressed his own great heart:
"By heaven, an awesome miracle right before my eyes!
These gallant, die-hard Trojans, even those I've killed,
they'll all come rising back from the western gloom!
Look at this fellow here, back he comes again,
fleeing his fatal day—
and I'd sold him off as a slave in holy Lemnos
but the heaving gray salt sea can't hold him back,
though it stops whole fleets of men who buck its tides.
Let's try again—this time he'll taste my spearpoint.   70
Now we'll see, once and for all we'll know
if he returns as fast from his newest destination—
or the firm life-giving earth can hold him down,
the grave that hugs the strongest man alive."
                                                    Waiting,
plotting, the other stumbling toward him, stunned,
wild to grasp his knees, wild with all his heart
to escape his death and grueling black fate
as the great Achilles raised his massive spear,
wild to run him through—
                                        He ducked, ran under the hurl
and seized Achilles' knees as the spear shot past his back   80
and stuck in the earth, still starved for human flesh.
And begging now, one hand clutching Achilles' knees,
the other gripping the spear, holding for dear life,
Lycaon burst out with a winging prayer: "Achilles!
I hug your knees—mercy!—spare my life!
I am your suppliant, Prince, you must respect me!
Yours was the first bread I broke, Demeter's gift,

that day you seized me in Priam's well-fenced orchard,
hauled me away from father, loved ones, sold me off
in holy Lemnos and I, I fetched you a hundred bulls—   90
and once released I brought three times that price.
And it's just twelve days that I've been home in Troy—
all I've suffered! But now, again, some murderous fate
has placed me in your hands, your prisoner twice over—
Father Zeus must hate me, giving me back to you!
Ah, to a short life you bore me, mother—mother,
she was Laothoë, aged Altes' daughter . . .
Altes who rules the Leleges always keen for war,
who holds the Pedasus heights along the Satniois—
and Priam wed his daughter, with many other wives,   100
and she produced two sons, and you, you'll butcher both!
One you killed in the ranks of frontline fighters,
noble Polydorus, ran him down with your lance
and a gruesome death awaits me here and now—
no hope of escape for me, from *your* clutches,
not when destiny drives me up against you.
Listen, this too—take it to heart, I beg you—
don't kill me! I'm not from the same womb as Hector,
Hector who killed your friend, your strong, *gentle* friend!"

So the illustrious son of Priam begged for life   110
but only heard a merciless voice in answer: "Fool,
don't talk to me of ransom. No more speeches.
Before Patroclus met his day of destiny, true,
it warmed my heart a bit to spare some Trojans:
droves I took alive and auctioned off as slaves.
But now not a single Trojan flees his death,
not one the gods hand over to me before your gates,
none of all the Trojans, sons of Priam least of all!
Come, friend, you too must die. Why moan about it so?
Even Patroclus died, a far, far better man than you.   120
And look, you see how handsome and powerful I am?
The son of a great man, the mother who gave me life
a deathless goddess. But even for me, I tell you,
death and the strong force of fate are waiting.

There will come a dawn or sunset or high noon
when a man will take my life in battle too—
flinging a spear perhaps
or whipping a deadly arrow off his bow."
                                        At that
Lycaon's knees gave way on the spot, his heart too.
He let go of the spear, he sank back down . . .   130
spreading both arms wide. Drawing his sharp sword
Achilles struck his collarbone just beside the neck
and the two-edged blade drove home, plunging to the hilt—
and down on the ground he sprawled, stretched facefirst
and dark blood pouring out of him drenched the earth.
Achilles grabbed a foot, slung him into the river,
washed away downstream as he cried above him
savage words to wing him on his way: "There—
lie there! Make your bed with the fishes now,
they'll dress your wound and lick it clean of blood—   140
so much for your last rites! Nor will your mother
lay your corpse on a bier and mourn her darling son—
whirling Scamander will roll you down the sea's broad bosom!
And many a fish, leaping up through the waves, breaking
the cold ripples shivering dark will dart and bolt
Lycaon's glistening fat! Die, Trojans, die—
till I butcher all the way to sacred Troy—
run headlong on, I'll hack you from behind!
Nothing can save you now—
not even your silver-whirling, mighty-tiding river—   150
not for all the bulls you've slaughtered to it for years,
the rearing stallions drowned alive in its eddies . . . die!—
even so—writhing in death till all you Trojans pay
for Patroclus' blood and the carnage of Achaeans
killed by the racing ships when I was out of action!"

    The more he vaunted the more the river's anger rose,
churning at heart for a way to halt his rampage,
godlike Achilles, and stop the Trojans' rout.
But now Pelides shaking his long-shadowed spear
was charging Asteropaeus, mad to cut him down—   160

Pelegon's son, himself a son of the Axius River
broad and fast and Acessamenus' eldest daughter,
Periboea, loved by the deep-swirling stream.
Achilles went for Asteropaeus fresh from the ford,
braced to face him there and brandishing two spears
and the Xanthus filled the Trojan's heart with courage,
the river seething for all the youths Achilles slaughtered,
chopped to bits in its tide without a twinge of pity.
Closing against each other, just about in range,
the magnificent runner Achilles opened up,   170
"Who on earth are you? Where do you hail from?—
you with the gall to go against my onslaught.
Pity the ones whose sons stand up to me in war!"

     But the noble son of Pelegon answered firmly,
"High-hearted son of Peleus, why ask about my birth?
I hail from Paeonia's rich soil, a far cry from here,
heading Paeonian troops with their long spears,
and this my eleventh day since raising Troy.
My birth? I come from the Axius' broad currents—
Axius floods the land with the clearest stream on earth   180
and Axius fathered the famous spearman Pelegon.
Men say I am his son.
Now on with it, great Pelides, let us fight!"
                                                  Menacing so
as brilliant Achilles raised the Pelian ash spear
but the fighting Asteropaeus, quick, ambidextrous,
hurled both spears at once—one shaft hit the shield,
no breakthrough, the shaft could not smash through,
the gold blocked it, forged in the god's gift.
But the other grazed Achilles' strong right arm
and dark blood gushed as the spear shot past his back,   190
stabbing the earth hard, still lusting to sink in flesh . . .
But next Achilles, burning to cut down Asteropaeus
hurled his ashen shaft—it flew straight as a die
but a clean miss—it struck the river's high bank
and half the length of the lance stuck deep in soil.
So Achilles, drawing the sharp sword at his hip,

sprang at the man in rage as *he* tried to wrench
Pelides' spear from the bank but his grip failed.
Three times he tried to wrench it free, tugging madly,
thrice gave up the struggle—the fourth with all his might   200
he fought to bend Aeacides' shaft and break it off
but before it budged the hero was all over him,
slashing out his life, slitting his belly open—
a scooping slice at the navel and all his bowels
spilled out on the ground, darkness swirled his eyes
as he gasped his breath away. And trampling his chest
Achilles tore his gear off, glorying over him now:
"Lie there with the dead! Punishing work, you see,
to fight the sons of invincible Cronus' son,
even sprung from a river as you are! You—   210
you claimed your birth from a river's broad stream?
Well I can boast my birth from powerful Zeus himself!
My father's the man who rules the hordes of Myrmidons,
Peleus, son of Aeacus, and Aeacus sprang from Zeus
and as Zeus is stronger than rivers surging out to sea,
so the breed of Zeus is stronger than any stream's.
Here is a great river flowing past you, look—
what help can he give you? None!
Nothing can fight the son of Cronus, Zeus,
not even Achelous king of rivers vies with Zeus,   220
not even the overpowering Ocean's huge high tides,
the source of all the rivers and all the seas on earth
and all springs and all deep wells—all flow from the Ocean
but even the Ocean shrinks from the mighty Father's bolt
when terrible thunder crashes down the skies!"

                                              With that
Achilles pulled his bronze spear from the river bluff
and left him there, the Trojan's life slashed out,
sprawled in the sand, drenched by the black tide—
eels and fish the corpse's frenzied attendants
ripping into him, nibbling kidney-fat away.   230
But Achilles went for Paeonians, helmets plumed,
still running in panic along the river's rapids
once they saw their finest fall in the onslaught,

beaten down by Pelides' hands and hacking sword.
He killed in a blur of kills—Thersilochus, Mydon,
Astypylus, Mnesus, Thrasius, Aenius and Ophelestes—
still more Paeonian men the runner would have killed
if the swirling river had not risen, crying out in fury,
taking a man's shape, its voice breaking out of a whirlpool:
"Stop, Achilles! Greater than any man on earth,   240
greater in outrage too—
for the gods themselves are always at your side!
But if Zeus allows you to kill off all the Trojans,
drive them out of my depths at least, I ask you,
out on the plain and do your butchery there.
All my lovely rapids are crammed with corpses now,
no channel in sight to sweep my currents out to sacred sea—
I'm choked with corpses and still you slaughter more,
you blot out more! Leave me alone, have done—
captain of armies, I am filled with horror!"   250

      And the breakneck runner only paused to answer,
"So be it, Scamander sprung of Zeus—as you command.
But I, I won't stop killing these overweening Trojans,
not till I've packed them in their walls and tested Hector,
strength against strength—he kills me or I kill him!"

      Down on the Trojan front he swept like something superhuman
and now from his deep whirls the river roared to Phoebus,
"Disgrace—god of the silver bow and born of Zeus!
You throw to the winds the will of Cronus' son—
time and again Zeus gave you strict commands: 260
Stand by the Trojan ranks and save their lives
till the sun goes down at last and darkness shrouds
the plowlands ripe with grain!"
                                    When he heard *that*
Achilles the famous spearman, leaping down from the bluff,
plunged in the river's heart and the river charged against him,
churning, surging, all his rapids rising in white fury
and drove the mass of corpses choking tight his channel,
the ruck Achilles killed—Scamander heaved them up

and bellowing like a bull the river flung them out
on the dry land but saved the living, hiding them down   270
the fresh clear pools of his thundering whirling current
but thrashing over Achilles' shoulders raised a killer-wave—
the tremendous thrust of it slammed against his shield
and he staggered, lost his footing, his arms flung out
for a tall strong elm, he clung but out it came by the roots,
toppling down, ripping away the whole cliff, blocking the stream
with a tangled snarl of branches crashing into it full length
to dam the river bank to bank—Bursting up from a whirlpool
Achilles dashed for the plain, his feet flying in terror
but the great god would not let up, hurling against him,   280
Scamander looming into a murderous breaker, dark, over him,
dead set on stopping the brilliant Achilles' rampage here
and thrusting disaster off the struggling Trojan force—
But the hero sprang away, far as a hard-flung spear,
swooping fast as the black eagle, the fierce marauder,
both the strongest and swiftest bird that flies the sky—
on he streaked and the bronze rang out against his chest,
clashing grimly—slipping out from under the wave he fled
with the river rolling on behind him, roaring, huge . . .
As a farmhand runs a ditch from a dark spring, sluicing   290
the gushing stream through plants and gardens, swinging
his mattock to knock the clods out down the shoot
and the water rushes on, tearing the pebbles loose
and what began as a trickle hits a quick slope and
down it goes, outstripping the man who guides it—
so the relentless tide kept overtaking Achilles,
yes, for all his speed—gods are stronger than men.
Again and again the brilliant swift Achilles whirled,
trying to stand and fight the river man-to-man and see
if all the immortal gods who rule the vaulting skies   300
were after him, putting him to rout—again and again
the mighty crest of the river fed by the rains of Zeus
came battering down his shoulders, down from high above
but Achilles kept on leaping, higher, desperate now
as the river kept on dragging down his knees, lunging
under him, cutting the ground from under his legs . . .

Pelides groaned, scanning the arching blank sky:
"Father Zeus! To think in all my misery not one god
can bring himself to rescue me from this river!
Then I'd face any fate. And no god on high,   310
none is to blame so much as my dear mother—
how she lied, she beguiled me, she promised me
I'd die beneath the walls of the armored Trojans,
cut down in blood by Apollo's whipping arrows!
I wish Hector had killed me,
the best man bred in Troy—the killer a hero then
and a hero too the man whose corpse he stripped!
Now look what a wretched death I'm doomed to suffer,
trapped in this monstrous river like some boy, some pig-boy
swept away, trying to ford a winter torrent in a storm!"   320

    Quick to his cry Poseidon and Pallas moved in close,
stood at his shoulder now and taking human form,
grasped him hand-to-hand, spoke bracing words,
Poseidon who shakes the mainland first to say,
"Courage, Achilles! Why such fear, such terror?
Not with a pair like us to urge you on—gods-in-arms
sent down with Zeus's blessings, I and Pallas Athena.
It's not your fate to be swallowed by a river:
he'll subside, and soon—you'll see for yourself.
But we do have sound advice, if only you will yield.   330
Never rest your hands from the great leveler war,
not till you pack and cram the Trojan armies tight
in the famous walls of Troy—whoever flees your onset.
But once you've ripped away Prince Hector's life,
back to the ships you go! We give you glory—
seize it in your hands!"
                              With that challenge
both went soaring home to the deathless ones on high
but Achilles rampaged on with the gods' strong command
driving him down the plain where the river flooded now,
an immense, cresting outrush bursting with burnished gear   340
and troops of battle dead, men cut down in their prime,
floating corpses rolling—But Achilles surged on too

with high hurdling strides, charging against the river,
on, breakneck on and the river could not stop him,
not for all its reach and tide race, not with Athena
pumping enormous strength deep down Achilles' heart—
But the Xanthus River would not slack his fury either,
he raged at Achilles all the more, he marshaled up
a mountainous ridge of water, roaring out to Simois,
"Oh dear brother, rise! Both of us rush together   350
to halt this mortal's onslaught! At any moment
he'll storm King Priam's mighty stronghold down—
the Trojans can't stand up to the man in battle.
Beat him back, quickly! Deluge all your channels
from all your gushing springs—muster all your torrents—
raise up a tremendous wave, rumbling, booming with timber,
boulders crashing—we'll stop this wild man in his tracks,
lording it in his power now and raging like some god!
Neither his strength nor splendid build can save him,
not now, I tell you—nor all that glorious armor: 360
now, somewhere under our floods that gear will sink,
immersed deep in slime, and I, I'll roil his body
round in sand and gravel, tons of spills of silt.
Achaeans will never know where to find his bones,
never collect them now—
I'll bury that man so deep in mud and rocks!
That's where his grave-mound will be piled and then
no need in the world to raise his barrow high
when comrades come to give him royal rites!"
                                                        So he vaunted,
rearing against Achilles, seething, heaving up in fury,   370
thundering out now in foam and blood and corpses—
the bloodred crest of the river swelled by Zeus
came arching higher, ready to tear Pelides down
but Hera, struck with fear for Achilles, screamed out,
dreading he might be swept away by the giant churning river
and quickly cried to the god of fire, her own dear son,
"To arms, my child—god of the crooked legs!
You are the one we'd thought a worthy match
for the whirling river Xanthus!

Quick, rescue Achilles! Explode in a burst of fire!   380
I'll drive the West and South Winds white with clouds
and sweep in from the open seas a tearing gale to sear
the Trojan bodies and gear and spread your lethal flames!
And you, you make for the Xanthus banks and burn the trees,
hurl the stream itself into conflagration—not for a moment
let him turn you back with his winning words or threats.
Never abate your fury! Not till I let loose my shout—
then halt your withering fire!"

                              Hera's command—
and Hephaestus launched his grim inhuman blaze.
First he shot into flames and burned the plain,   390
ignited hordes of corpses, squads Achilles slaughtered—
he scorched the whole plain and the shining river shrank.
Hard as the autumn North Wind hits a leveled field
just drenched in a downpour, quickly dries it off
and the farmer is glad and starts to till his soil—
so the whole plain was parched and the god of fire devoured
all the dead, then blazing in all his glory veered for the river—
an inferno—the elms burned, the willows and tamarisks burned
and the lotus burned and the galingale and reeds and rushes,
all that flourished along the running river's lush banks   400
and the eels writhed and fish in the whirlpools leapt high,
breaking the surface left and right in a sheen of fire,
gasping under the Master Smith Hephaestus' blast
and now the river's strength was burning out,
he panted the god's name: "Hephaestus—stop!
Not a single god can stand against you—no, not I—
can't fight such fire, such fury—hold your attack, stop!
Brilliant Achilles can drive them out of Ilium now!
What's this war to me? Why should I help Troy?"

    He screamed in flames, his clear currents bubbling up   410
like a cauldron whipped by crackling fire as it melts down
the lard of a fat swine, splattering up around the rim—
dry logs blazing under it, lashing it to the boil—
so the river burned, his clear currents seethed
and lost all will to flow. He stopped—overwhelmed

by the torrid blast of the Master Craftsman god of fire—
and Xanthus cried to Hera, pouring out his heart
in a flood of supplication, "Oh Hera—why?
Why does your son attack me, whip my waters more
than all the others? Why, what have I done to *you*?   420
Nothing beside those other powers, all who rush
to defend the Trojan armies. Oh I'll stop—
if that is your command—
but let your son stop too! I'll swear, what's more,
never to drive the fatal day away from the Trojans,
not even when all Troy burns in the ramping flames
when the warring sons of Achaea burn her down!"

And Hera heard him, the radiant white-armed goddess
quickly cried to the god of fire, her own dear son,
"Hephaestus, stop! Stop, my glorious blazing boy!   430
It's not right to batter another deathless god,
not for the sake of these *mortals*."
                                        She ceased
and the god of fire quenched his grim inhuman blaze
and back in its channel ran the river's glistening tides.

And now with the strength of Xanthus beaten down
the two called off their battle. Hera held them back,
still enraged as she was. But now for total war,
bearing down on the other gods, disastrous, massive,
their fighting-fury blasting loose from opposing camps—
the powers collided! A mammoth clash—the wide earth roared   440
and the arching vault of heaven echoed round with trumpets!
And Zeus heard the chaos, throned on Olympus heights,
and laughed deep in his own great heart, delighted
to see the gods engage in all-out conflict.
They did not waste a moment, closed at once—
Ares stabber of shields led off, charging Athena,
shaking his brazen spear and dressed the goddess down:
"You dog-fly, why drive the gods to battle once again
with that stormy bluster driving your wild heart?
Don't you recall the time you drove Tydides' son   450

to spear me through? In the eyes of all the world
you seized his lance and rammed it home yourself,
tearing into my rippling, deathless flesh—so now
I think I'll pay you back for all your outrage!"

With that he stabbed at her battle-shield of storm,
its dark tassels flaring, packing tremendous force—
not even Zeus's lightning bolt can break its front.
Bloody Ares lunged at it now with giant lance
and Athena backed away, her powerful hand hefting
a boulder off the plain, black, jagged, a ton weight   460
that men in the old days planted there to mark off plowland—
Pallas hurled that boundary-stone at Ares, struck his neck,
loosed his limbs, and down he crashed and out over seven acres
sprawled the enormous god and his mane dragged in the dust,
his armor clashed around him. Athena laughed aloud,
glorying over him, winging insults: "Colossal fool—
it never even occurred to you, not even now
when you matched your strength with mine,
just how much greater I claim to be than you!
So now you feel the weight of your mother's curses—   470
Hera plotted against you, Hera up in arms
because you left the Achaean forces in the lurch
and rushed to defend these reckless, headlong Trojans!"

Triumphant Athena turned her shining eyes away
and Aphrodite daughter of Zeus took Ares' hand
and led him off the field, racked with groans,
barely able to gather back his strength . . .
But the white-armed Hera saw her move at once
and winged Athena on: "Just look at them there—
daughter of Zeus whose shield is storm and thunder,   480
tireless one, Athena. There she goes again,
that dog-fly, leading her man-destroying Ares clear
of the rampage, through the slaughter! After her, quick!"

Athena's heart leapt high, she charged at Aphrodite,
overtook her and beat her breasts with clenched fists.

Down she sank with Ares, resistance quite dissolved,
two immortals spread on the earth that rears us all
with Pallas trumpeting over them winged exultations:
"Down you go! May all the gods who help the Trojans
fall as hard when they battle Argives armed for war—   490
all as courageous, all as steadfast as Aphrodite
when she sped to Ares' side and faced my fury!
Then we'd have done with fighting long ago,
razed the rugged walls of Troy and laid her waste."

        So Athena vaunted and white-armed Hera smiled
but the mighty god of earthquakes challenged Phoebus:
"Apollo—why hold back from each other? It's not fair
when the other gods have launched themselves in war.
What disgrace for us—to return without a fight
to the bronze-floored house of Zeus on Mount Olympus!   500
You lead off. You are the younger-born, and I—
it's wrong for me, since I have years on you
and I know the world much better.
Fool, what short-lived memory you must have!
Don't you remember? Have you forgotten—even now?—
all those troubles we suffered here alongside Troy,
we alone of the gods when Zeus dispatched us down
to slave for proud Laomedon one whole year,
for stated wages—at that man's beck and call.
I erected the rampart round the Trojans' city,   510
a massive ashlar wall to make the place impregnable.
You, Phoebus, herded his shambling crook-horned cattle
along the spurs of Ida's timbered ridges. Ah but then,
when the happy spring brought time for payment round,
that outrageous man Laomedon robbed us blind.
He stole our wages, cursed us, sent us packing—
he threatened to bind us both, hand and foot,
ship us off and away as slaves to distant islands—
he was all for lopping off our ears with a brazen ax!
So we made our way back home, hearts smoldering,   520
furious for the sum he swore but never paid—
and that, that is the one whose men you favor now."

No joining ranks with us as we fight to wipe them out,
these insolent Trojans, stretch them out in the dust
with all their sons and all their honored wives!"

　　But the distant deadly Archer volleyed back,
"God of the earthquake—you'd think me hardly sane
if I fought with you for the sake of wretched mortals . . .
like leaves, no sooner flourishing, full of the sun's fire,
feeding on earth's gifts, than they waste away and die.　　　530
Stop. Call off this skirmish of ours at once—
let these mortals fight themselves to death."

　　With that he turned and left, filled with shame
to grapple his own father's brother hand-to-hand.
But his sister Artemis, Huntress, queen of beasts,
inveighed against him now with stinging insults:
"So, the deadly immortal Archer runs for dear life!—
turning over victory to Poseidon, total victory,
giving him all the glory here without a fight.
Why do you sport that bow, you spineless fool?—　　　540
it's worthless as the wind!
Don't let me hear you boast in Father's halls,
ever again, as you bragged among the gods till now,
that you would fight Poseidon strength for strength."

　　Not a word in reply to *that* from the Archer-god
but Zeus's regal consort flew into rage at once
and her outburst raked the Huntress armed with arrows:
"How do you have the gall, you shameless bitch,
to stand and fight me here? You and your archery!
Zeus made you a lion against all women, true,　　　550
he lets you kill off mothers in their labor—
but you'll find it painful, matching force with me.
Better to slaughter beasts on rocky mountain slopes
and young deer in the wild than fight a higher goddess!
But since you'd like a lesson in warfare, Artemis,
just to learn, to savor how much stronger I am

when you engage my power—"
                              She broke off,
her left hand seizing both wrists of the goddess,
right hand stripping the bow and quiver off her shoulders—
Hera boxed the Huntress' ears with her own weapons,   560
smiling broadly now as her victim writhed away
and showering arrows scattered. Bursting into tears
the goddess slipped from under her clutch like a wild dove
that flies from a hawk's attack to a hollow rocky cleft
for it's not the quarry's destiny to be caught—
so she fled in tears, her archery left on the spot.
But Hermes the guide of souls and giant-killer
reassured her mother, Leto, "Nothing to fear,
I'd never fight you, Leto. An uphill battle it is,
trading blows with the wives of Zeus who rules the clouds.   570
No, go boast to your heart's content and tell the gods
you triumphed over *me* with your superhuman power!"

    So Leto gathered the reflex bow and arrows
scattered left and right in the swirling dust,
and bearing her daughter's archery in her arms
withdrew from the field of battle trailing Artemis.
By now the Huntress had reached Olympus heights
and made her way to the bronze-floored house of Zeus.
And down she sat on her Father's lap, a young girl,
sobbing, her deathless robe quivering round her body.   580
But her Father, son of Cronus, hugged her tight
and giving a low warm laugh inquired gently,
"Who has abused you now, dear child, tell me,
who of the sons of heaven so unfeeling, cruel?
Why, it's as if they had caught you in public,
doing something wrong . . ."
                              Wreathed in flowers
the one who halloos the hunt cried out at once,
"Your own wife, Father! The white-armed Hera beat me!
This strife, this warfare plaguing all the immortals—
Hera's all to blame!"   590

And now as the powers wrangled back and forth
the lord god Apollo entered holy Troy,
filled with dread for the city's sturdy walls:
what if the Argive forces stormed them down today—
against the will of fate? The rest of the gods
who live forever soon returned to Mount Olympus,
some enraged, some in their proud, new-won glory,
and sat beside the Father, king of the black cloud.
But Achilles slaughtered on and on, never pausing,
killing Trojans and skittish battle-teams at once.   600
As smoke goes towering into the broad vaulting sky
from a burning town and the gods' wrath drives it on,
dealing struggle to all, to many searing grief—
so Achilles dealt the Trojans struggle, grief.

But there on the god-built heights stood aged Priam.
He saw the monstrous Achilles and racing on before him
Trojans whipped in headlong flight, all rescue gone.
The king cried out and clambered down to ground
from the high tower, issuing quick commands
to veteran gateway guards beside the walls: 610
"Spread the great gates wide—all hands now—
till our routed troops can straggle back to Troy!
Achilles swarms over them—they're stampeding,
a terrible mauling's coming . . . I can see it now!
Once they're packed in the walls and catch their breath,
close the thickset gates and bolt them tight again.
I dread this murderous man—he'll burst right through our walls."

They spread the gates and rammed the doorbars back
and the spreading gates made way for a ray of hope
as Phoebus Apollo hurtled forth to meet Achilles,   620
to fight disaster off the Trojan troops.
Heading straight for the city's lofty ramparts,
ragged with thirst, choked with dust from the plain
they fled as Achilles stormed them, shaking his spear,
that wild rabid frenzy always gripping his heart,

blazing to seize his glory.
                    And then and there
the Achaeans would have taken the lofty gates of Troy
if Apollo had not driven Prince Agenor at them,
Antenor's son, a courageous, rugged soldier.
He inspired his heart with daring, standing near—   630
in person, to beat away the dragging fates of death—
leaning against an oak, concealed in swirls of mist.
And now, as soon as Agenor saw Achilles coming,
there he stood, poised for the scourge of cities
while the heart inside him heaved like heavy seas.
Waiting, tense, he probed his own brave spirit:
"Ah dear god—if I run from Achilles' onslaught,
taking the route the rest have fled, stampeding,
he'll catch me even so and slash my coward's throat.
But if I leave my comrades panicked before his charge,   640
this Prince Achilles—slip away from the wall on foot
and race the other way, out to Ilium's plain and
reach the spurs of Ida, hide in the underbrush
and then, in the dying light . . .
once I've washed my sweat away in the river,
yes, I just might make it back again to Troy—
but why debate, my friend, why thrash things out?
God forbid that Achilles sees me turning tail,
heading from town and out to open country—
he'll come after me full tilt and run me down!   650
And then no way to escape my death, my certain doom—
Achilles is far too strong for any man on earth.
Wait . . . what if I face him out before the walls?
Surely his body can be pierced by bronze, even his—
he *has* only one life, and people say he's mortal:
it's only the son of Cronus handing him the glory."

Filled with resolve, he braced, waiting Achilles,
his warrior blood incensed. He'd fight to the death
as a panther springs forth from her thicket lair
to stand and face the huntsman: no fear in her heart,   660

no thought of flight when she hears the baying packs—
and even if he's too quick with spear or lunging sword,
even if she's run through, she never slacks her fury
until she's charged him hard or gone down fighting.
And so the noble son of Antenor, brave Agenor
would never run until he'd tested Achilles.
He steadied his balanced shield before his chest,
aimed his spear at the man and flung this challenge:
"Surely you must have hoped with all your heart—
the great glorious Achilles—that you would raze   670
the proud Trojans' city this very day! You fool—
you still have plenty of pain to suffer for *her* sake.
We have fighting men by the hundreds still inside her,
forming a wall before our loving parents, wives and sons
to defend Troy—where you rush on to meet your doom,
headlong man as you are, breakneck man of war!"

    And he hurled his sharp spear from a strong hand—
a hard true hit on Achilles' shin below the knee!
But the tin of the fire-new armor round his leg
let loose an unearthly ring—back the spear sprang   680
from the wondrous gear it struck, not punching through:
the gift of the god Hephaestus blocked its force.
Achilles next, he leapt at Prince Agenor—
but Phoebus refused to let him seize the glory—
he whisked Agenor off, wrapped in swirls of mist
and sped him out of the fighting safely on his way
and then with trickery kept Achilles off the Trojans.
True, just like Agenor head to foot the deadly Archer
stood in Achilles' path and Achilles sprang in chase,
feet racing, coursing him far across the wheat-fields,   690
heading him out toward Scamander's whirling depths
as the god led *him* a little, luring him on and on—
always hoping to catch the god with bursts of speed.
But all the while the rest of the Trojans fled en masse,
thrilled to reach the ramparts, crowding, swarming in,
no daring left to remain outside the city walls

and wait for each other, learn who made it through,
who died in battle—no, in a driving rout they came,
streaming into Troy,
any fighter whose racing legs could save his life.   700

BOOK TWENTY-TWO

The Death of Hector

So all through Troy the men who had fled like panicked fawns
were wiping off their sweat, drinking away their thirst,
leaning along the city's massive ramparts now
while Achaean troops, sloping shields to shoulders,
closed against the walls. But there stood Hector,
shackled fast by his deadly fate, holding his ground,
exposed in front of Troy and the Scaean Gates.
And now Apollo turned to taunt Achilles:
"Why are you chasing *me*? Why waste your speed?—
son of Peleus, you a mortal and I a deathless god.   10
You still don't know that I am immortal, do you?—
straining to catch me in your fury! Have you forgotten?
There's a war to fight with the Trojans you stampeded,
look, they're packed inside their city walls, but you,
you've slipped away out here. You can't kill *me*—

I can never die—it's not my fate!"
                              Enraged at that,
Achilles shouted in mid-stride, "You've blocked my way,
you distant, deadly Archer, deadliest god of all—
you made me swerve away from the rampart there.
Else what a mighty Trojan army had gnawed the dust
before they could ever straggle through their gates!
Now you've robbed me of great glory, saved their lives
with all your deathless ease. Nothing for you to fear,
no punishment to come. Oh I'd pay you back
if I only had the power at my command!"

    No more words—he dashed toward the city,
heart racing for some great exploit, rushing on
like a champion stallion drawing a chariot full tilt,
sweeping across the plain in easy, tearing strides—
so Achilles hurtled on, driving legs and knees.   30

    And old King Priam was first to see him coming,
surging over the plain, blazing like the star
that rears at harvest, flaming up in its brilliance,—
far outshining the countless stars in the night sky,
that star they call Orion's Dog—brightest of all
but a fatal sign emblazoned on the heavens,
it brings such killing fever down on wretched men.
So the bronze flared on his chest as on he raced—
and the old man moaned, flinging both hands high,
beating his head and groaning deep he called,   40
begging his dear son who stood before the gates,
unshakable, furious to fight Achilles to the death.
The old man cried, pitifully, hands reaching out to him,
"Oh Hector! Don't just stand there, don't, dear child,
waiting that man's attack—alone, cut off from friends!
You'll meet your doom at once, beaten down by Achilles,
so much stronger than you—that hard, headlong man.
Oh if only the gods loved him as much as I do . . .
dogs and vultures would eat his fallen corpse at once!—
with what a load of misery lifted from my spirit.   50

That man who robbed me of many sons, brave boys,
cutting them down or selling them off as slaves,
shipped to islands half the world away . . .
Even now there are two, Lycaon and Polydorus—
I cannot find them among the soldiers crowding Troy,
those sons Laothoë bore me, Laothoë queen of women.
But if they are still alive in the enemy's camp,
then we'll ransom them back with bronze and gold.
We have hoards inside the walls, the rich dowry
old and famous Altes presented with his daughter.   60
But if they're dead already, gone to the House of Death,
what grief to their mother's heart and mine—we gave them life.
For the rest of Troy, though, just a moment's grief
unless you too are battered down by Achilles.
Back, come back! Inside the walls, my boy!
Rescue the men of Troy and the Trojan women—
don't hand the great glory to Peleus' son,
bereft of your own sweet life yourself.

                        Pity me too!—
still in my senses, true, but a harrowed, broken man
marked out by doom—past the threshold of old age . . .   70
and Father Zeus will waste me with a hideous fate,
and after I've lived to look on so much horror!
My sons laid low, my daughters dragged away
and the treasure-chambers looted, helpless babies
hurled to the earth in the red barbarity of war . . .
my sons' wives hauled off by the Argives' bloody hands!
And I, I last of all—the dogs before my doors
will eat me raw, once some enemy brings me down
with his sharp bronze sword or spits me with a spear,
wrenching the life out of my body, yes, the very dogs   80
I bred in my own halls to share my table, guard my gates—
mad, rabid at heart they'll lap their master's blood
and loll before my doors.

                      Ah for a young man
all looks fine and noble if he goes down in war,
hacked to pieces under a slashing bronze blade—
he lies there dead . . . but whatever death lays bare,

all wounds are marks of glory. When an old man's killed
and the dogs go at the gray head and the gray beard
and mutilate the genitals—that is the cruelest sight
in all our wretched lives!"
                              So the old man groaned   90
and seizing his gray hair tore it out by the roots
but he could not shake the fixed resolve of Hector.
And his mother wailed now, standing beside Priam,
weeping freely, loosing her robes with one hand
and holding out her bare breast with the other,
her words pouring forth in a flight of grief and tears:
"Hector, my child! Look—have some respect for *this*!
Pity your mother too, if I ever gave you the breast
to soothe your troubles, remember it now, dear boy—
beat back that savage man from safe inside the walls!   100
Don't go forth, a champion pitted against him—
merciless, brutal man. If he kills you now,
how can I ever mourn you on your deathbed?—
dear branch in bloom, dear child I brought to birth!—
Neither I nor your wife, that warm generous woman . . .
Now far beyond our reach, now by the Argive ships
the rushing dogs will tear you, bolt your flesh!"

    So they wept, the two of them crying out
to their dear son, both pleading time and again
but they could not shake the fixed resolve of Hector.   110
No, he waited Achilles, coming on, gigantic in power.
As a snake in the hills, guarding his hole, awaits a man—
bloated with poison, deadly hatred seething inside him,
glances flashing fire as he coils round his lair . . .
so Hector, nursing his quenchless fury, gave no ground,
leaning his burnished shield against a jutting wall,
but harried still, he probed his own brave heart:
"No way out. If I slip inside the gates and walls,
Polydamas will be first to heap disgrace on me—
he was the one who urged me to lead our Trojans   120
back to Ilium just last night, the disastrous night
Achilles rose in arms like a god. But did I give way?

Not at all. And how much better it would have been!
Now my army's ruined, thanks to my own reckless pride,
I would die of shame to face the men of Troy
and the Trojan women trailing their long robes . . .
Someone less of a man than I will say, 'Our Hector—
staking all on his own strength, he destroyed his army!'
So they will mutter. So now, better by far for me
to stand up to Achilles, kill him, come home alive   130
or die at his hands in glory out before the walls.
But wait—what if I put down my studded shield
and heavy helmet, prop my spear on the rampart
and go forth, just as I am, to meet Achilles,
noble Prince Achilles . . .
why, I could promise to give back Helen, yes,
and all her treasures with her, all those riches
Paris once hauled home to Troy in the hollow ships—
and they were the cause of all our endless fighting—
Yes, yes, return it all to the sons of Atreus now   140
to haul away, and then, at the same time, divide
the rest with all the Argives, all the city holds,
and then I'd take an oath for the Trojan royal council
that we will hide nothing! Share and share alike the hoards
our handsome citadel stores within its depths and—
Why debate, my friend? Why thrash things out?
I must not go and implore him. He'll show no mercy,
no respect for me, my rights—he'll cut me down
straight off—stripped of defenses like a woman
once I have loosed the armor off my body.   150
No way to parley with that man—not now—
not from behind some oak or rock to whisper,
like a boy and a young girl, lovers' secrets
a boy and girl might whisper to each other . . .
Better to clash in battle, now, at once—
see which fighter Zeus awards the glory!"

                                        So he wavered,
waiting there, but Achilles was closing on him now
like the god of war, the fighter's helmet flashing,
over his right shoulder shaking the Pelian ash spear,

that terror, and the bronze around his body flared   160
like a raging fire or the rising, blazing sun.
Hector looked up, saw him, started to tremble,
nerve gone, he could hold his ground no longer,
he left the gates behind and away he fled in fear—
and Achilles went for him, fast, sure of his speed
as the wild mountain hawk, the quickest thing on wings,
launching smoothly, swooping down on a cringing dove
and the dove flits out from under, the hawk screaming
over the quarry, plunging over and over, his fury
driving him down to beak and tear his kill—   170
so Achilles flew at him, breakneck on in fury
with Hector fleeing along the walls of Troy,
fast as his legs would go. On and on they raced,
passing the lookout point, passing the wild fig tree
tossed by the wind, always out from under the ramparts
down the wagon trail they careered until they reached
the clear running springs where whirling Scamander
rises up from its double wellsprings bubbling strong—
and one runs hot and the steam goes up around it,
drifting thick as if fire burned at its core   180
but the other even in summer gushes cold
as hail or freezing snow or water chilled to ice . . .
And here, close to the springs, lie washing-pools
scooped out in the hollow rocks and broad and smooth
where the wives of Troy and all their lovely daughters
would wash their glistening robes in the old days,
the days of peace before the sons of Achaea came . . .
Past these they raced, one escaping, one in pursuit
and the one who fled was great but the one pursuing
greater, even greater—their pace mounting in speed   190
since both men strove, not for a sacrificial beast
or oxhide trophy, prizes runners fight for, no,
they raced for the life of Hector breaker of horses.
Like powerful stallions sweeping round the post for trophies,
galloping full stretch with some fine prize at stake,
a tripod, say, or woman offered up at funeral games
for some brave hero fallen—so the two of them

whirled three times around the city of Priam,
sprinting at top speed while all the gods gazed down,
and the father of men and gods broke forth among them now: 200
"Unbearable—a man I love, hunted round his own city walls
and right before my eyes. My heart grieves for Hector.
Hector who burned so many oxen in my honor, rich cuts,
now on the rugged crests of Ida, now on Ilium's heights.
But now, look, brilliant Achilles courses him round
the city of Priam in all his savage, lethal speed.
Come, you immortals, think this through. Decide.
Either we pluck the man from death and save his life
or strike him down at last, here at Achilles' hands—
for all his fighting heart."

                   But immortal Athena,   210
her gray eyes wide, protested strongly: "Father!
Lord of the lightning, king of the black cloud,
what are you saying? A man, a mere mortal,
his doom sealed long ago? You'd set him free
from all the pains of death?

                   Do as you please—
but none of the deathless gods will ever praise you."

    And Zeus who marshals the thunderheads replied,
"Courage, Athena, third-born of the gods, dear child.
Nothing I said was meant in earnest, trust me,
I mean you all the good will in the world. Go.   220
Do as your own impulse bids you. Hold back no more."

    So he launched Athena already poised for action—
down the goddess swept from Olympus' craggy peaks.

    And swift Achilles kept on coursing Hector, nonstop
as a hound in the mountains starts a fawn from its lair,
hunting him down the gorges, down the narrow glens
and the fawn goes to ground, hiding deep in brush
but the hound comes racing fast, nosing him out
until he lands his kill. So Hector could never throw
Achilles off his trail, the swift racer Achilles—   230

time and again he'd make a dash for the Dardan Gates,
trying to rush beneath the rock-built ramparts, hoping
men on the heights might save him, somehow, raining spears
but time and again Achilles would intercept him quickly,
heading him off, forcing him out across the plain
and always sprinting along the city side himself—
endless as in a dream . . .
when a man can't catch another fleeing on ahead
and he can never escape nor his rival overtake him—
so the one could never run the other down in his speed   240
nor the other spring away. And how could Hector have fled
the fates of death so long? How unless one last time,
one final time Apollo had swept in close beside him,
driving strength in his legs and knees to race the wind?
And brilliant Achilles shook his head at the armies,
never letting them hurl their sharp spears at Hector—
someone might snatch the glory, Achilles come in second.
But once they reached the springs for the fourth time,
then Father Zeus held out his sacred golden scales:
in them he placed two fates of death that lays men low—   250
one for Achilles, one for Hector breaker of horses—
and gripping the beam mid-haft the Father raised it high
and down went Hector's day of doom, dragging him down
to the strong House of Death—and god Apollo left him.
Athena rushed to Achilles, her bright eyes gleaming,
standing shoulder-to-shoulder, winging orders now:
"At last our hopes run high, my brilliant Achilles—
Father Zeus must love you—
we'll sweep great glory back to Achaea's fleet,
we'll kill this Hector, mad as he is for battle!   260
No way for him to escape us now, no longer—
not even if Phoebus the distant deadly Archer
goes through torments, pleading for Hector's life,
groveling over and over before our storming Father Zeus.
But you, you hold your ground and catch your breath
while I run Hector down and persuade the man
to fight you face-to-face."
                          So Athena commanded

and he obeyed, rejoicing at heart—Achilles stopped,
leaning against his ashen spearshaft barbed in bronze.
And Athena left him there, caught up with Hector at once,   270
and taking the build and vibrant voice of Deiphobus
stood shoulder-to-shoulder with him, winging orders:
"Dear brother, how brutally swift Achilles hunts you—
coursing you round the city of Priam in all his lethal speed!
Come, let us stand our ground together—beat him back."

      "Deiphobus!"—Hector, his helmet flashing, called out to her—
"dearest of all my brothers, all these warring years,
of all the sons that Priam and Hecuba produced!
Now I'm determined to praise you all the more,
you who dared—seeing me in these straits—   280
to venture out from the walls, all for *my* sake,
while the others stay inside and cling to safety."

      The goddess answered quickly, her eyes blazing,
"True, dear brother—how your father and mother both
implored me, time and again, clutching my knees,
and the comrades round me begging me to stay!
Such was the fear that broke them, man for man,
but the heart within me broke with grief for you.
Now headlong on and fight! No letup, no lance spared!
So now, now we'll *see* if Achilles kills us both   290
and hauls our bloody armor back to the beaked ships
or *he* goes down in pain beneath your spear."

      Athena luring him on with all her immortal cunning—
and now, at last, as the two came closing for the kill
it was tall Hector, helmet flashing, who led off:
"No more running from you in fear, Achilles!
Not as before. Three times I fled around
the great city of Priam—I lacked courage then
to stand your onslaught. Now my spirit stirs me
to meet you face-to-face. Now kill or be killed!   300
Come, we'll swear to the gods, the highest witnesses—
the gods will oversee our binding pacts. I swear

I will never mutilate you—merciless as you are—
if Zeus allows me to last it out and tear your life away.
But once I've stripped your glorious armor, Achilles,
I will give your body back to your loyal comrades.
Swear you'll do the same."

                              A swift dark glance
and the headstrong runner answered, "Hector, stop!
You unforgivable, you . . . don't talk to me of pacts.
There are no binding oaths between men and lions—   310
wolves and lambs can enjoy no meeting of the minds—
they are all bent on hating each other to the death.
So with you and me. No love between us. No truce
till one or the other falls and gluts with blood
Ares who hacks at men behind his rawhide shield.
Come, call up whatever courage you can muster.
Life or death—now prove yourself a spearman,
a daring man of war! No more escape for you—
Athena will kill you with my spear in just a moment.
Now you'll pay at a stroke for all my comrades' grief,   320
all you killed in the fury of your spear!"

                                        With that,
shaft poised, he hurled and his spear's long shadow flew
but seeing it coming glorious Hector ducked away,
crouching down, watching the bronze tip fly past
and stab the earth—but Athena snatched it up
and passed it back to Achilles
and Hector the gallant captain never saw her.
He sounded out a challenge to Peleus' princely son:
"You missed, look—the great godlike Achilles!
So you knew nothing at all from Zeus about my death—   330
and yet how sure you were! All bluff, cunning with words,
that's all you are—trying to make me fear you,
lose my nerve, forget my fighting strength.
Well, you'll never plant your lance in my back
as I flee *you* in fear—plunge it through my chest
as I come charging in, if a god gives you the chance!
But now it's for you to dodge *my* brazen spear—

I wish you'd bury it in your body to the hilt.
How much lighter the war would be for Trojans then
if you, their greatest scourge, were dead and gone!"   340

    Shaft poised, he hurled and his spear's long shadow flew
and it struck Achilles' shield—a dead-center hit—
but off and away it glanced and Hector seethed,
his hurtling spear, his whole arm's power poured
in a wasted shot. He stood there, cast down . . .
he had no spear in reserve. So Hector shouted out
to Deiphobus bearing his white shield—with a ringing shout
he called for a heavy lance—
                   but the man was nowhere near him,
vanished—
           yes and Hector knew the truth in his heart
and the fighter cried aloud, "My time has come!   350
At last the gods have called me down to death.
I thought he was at my side, the hero Deiphobus—
he's safe inside the walls, Athena's tricked me blind.
And now death, grim death is looming up beside me,
no longer far away. No way to escape it now. This,
this was their pleasure after all, sealed long ago—
Zeus and the son of Zeus, the distant deadly Archer—
though often before now they rushed to my defense.
So now I meet my doom. Well let me die—
but not without struggle, not without glory, no,   360
in some great clash of arms that even men to come
will hear of down the years!"
                   And on that resolve
he drew the whetted sword that hung at his side,
tempered, massive, and gathering all his force
he swooped like a soaring eagle
launching down from the dark clouds to earth
to snatch some helpless lamb or trembling hare.
So Hector swooped now, swinging his whetted sword
and Achilles charged too, bursting with rage, barbaric,
guarding his chest with the well-wrought blazoned shield,   370

head tossing his gleaming helmet, four horns strong
and the golden plumes shook that the god of fire
drove in bristling thick along its ridge.
Bright as that star amid the stars in the night sky,
star of the evening, brightest star that rides the heavens,
so fire flared from the sharp point of the spear Achilles
brandished high in his right hand, bent on Hector's death,
scanning his splendid body—where to pierce it best?
The rest of his flesh seemed all encased in armor,
burnished, brazen—*Achilles'* armor that Hector stripped   380
from strong Patroclus when he killed him—true,
but one spot lay exposed,
where collarbones lift the neckbone off the shoulders,
the open throat, where the end of life comes quickest—*there*
as Hector charged in fury brilliant Achilles drove his spear
and the point went stabbing clean through the tender neck
but the heavy bronze weapon failed to slash the windpipe—
Hector could still gasp out some words, some last reply . . .
he crashed in the dust—
                          godlike Achilles gloried over him:
"Hector—surely you thought when you stripped Patroclus' armor   390
that you, you would be safe! Never a fear of me—
far from the fighting as I was—you fool!
Left behind there, down by the beaked ships
his great avenger waited, a greater man by far—
that man was I, and I smashed your strength! And you—
the dogs and birds will maul you, shame your corpse
while Achaeans bury my dear friend in glory!"

    Struggling for breath, Hector, his helmet flashing,
said, "I beg you, beg you by your life, your parents—
don't let the dogs devour me by the Argive ships!   400
Wait, take the princely ransom of bronze and gold,
the gifts my father and noble mother will give you—
but give my body to friends to carry home again,
so Trojan men and Trojan women can do me honor
with fitting rites of fire once I am dead."

Staring grimly, the proud runner Achilles answered,
"Beg no more, you fawning dog—begging me by my parents!
Would to god my rage, my fury would drive me now
to hack your flesh away and eat you raw—
such agonies you have caused me! Ransom?   410
No man alive could keep the dog-packs off you,
not if they haul in ten, twenty times that ransom
and pile it here before me and promise fortunes more—
no, not even if Dardan Priam should offer to weigh out
your bulk in gold! Not even then will your noble mother
lay you on your deathbed, mourn the son she bore . . .
The dogs and birds will rend you—blood and bone!"

At the point of death, Hector, his helmet flashing,
said, "I know you well—I see my fate before me.
Never a chance that I could win you over . . .   420
Iron inside your chest, that heart of yours.
But now beware, or my curse will draw god's wrath
upon your head, that day when Paris and lord Apollo—
for all your fighting heart—destroy you at the Scaean Gates!"

Death cut him short. The end closed in around him.
Flying free of his limbs
his soul went winging down to the House of Death,
wailing his fate, leaving his manhood far behind,
his young and supple strength. But brilliant Achilles
taunted Hector's body, dead as he was, "Die, die!   430
For my own death, I'll meet it freely—whenever Zeus
and the other deathless gods would like to bring it on!"

With that he wrenched his bronze spear from the corpse,
laid it aside and ripped the bloody armor off the back.
And the other sons of Achaea, running up around him,
crowded closer, all of them gazing wonder-struck
at the build and marvelous, lithe beauty of Hector.
And not a man came forward who did not stab his body,

glancing toward a comrade, laughing: "Ah, look here—
how much softer he is to handle now, this Hector,   440
than when he gutted our ships with roaring fire!"

Standing over him, so they'd gloat and stab his body.
But once he had stripped the corpse the proud runner Achilles
took his stand in the midst of all the Argive troops
and urged them on with a flight of winging orders:
"Friends—lords of the Argives, O my captains!
Now that the gods have let me kill this man
who caused us agonies, loss on crushing loss—
more than the rest of all their men combined—
come, let us ring their walls in armor, test them,   450
see what recourse the Trojans still may have in mind.
Will they abandon the city heights with this man fallen?
Or brace for a last, dying stand though Hector's gone?
But wait—what am I saying? Why this deep debate?
Down by the ships a body lies unwept, unburied—
Patroclus . . . I will never forget him,
not as long as I'm still among the living
and my springing knees will lift and drive me on.
Though the dead forget their dead in the House of Death,
I will remember, even there, my dear companion.

                                              Now,   460
come, you sons of Achaea, raise a song of triumph!
Down to the ships we march and bear this corpse on high—
we have won ourselves great glory. We have brought
magnificent Hector down, that man the Trojans
glorified in their city like a god!"

                                  So he triumphed
and now he was bent on outrage, on shaming noble Hector.
Piercing the tendons, ankle to heel behind both feet,
he knotted straps of rawhide through them both,
lashed them to his chariot, left the head to drag
and mounting the car, hoisting the famous arms aboard,   470
he whipped his team to a run and breakneck on they flew,
holding nothing back. And a thick cloud of dust rose up
from the man they dragged, his dark hair swirling round

that head so handsome once, all tumbled low in the dust—
since Zeus had given him over to his enemies now
to be defiled in the land of his own fathers.

So his whole head was dragged down in the dust.
And now his mother began to tear her hair . . .
she flung her shining veil to the ground and raised
a high, shattering scream, looking down at her son.   480
Pitifully his loving father groaned and round the king
his people cried with grief and wailing seized the city—
for all the world as if all Troy were torched and smoldering
down from the looming brows of the citadel to her roots.
Priam's people could hardly hold the old man back,
frantic, mad to go rushing out the Dardan Gates.
He begged them all, groveling in the filth,
crying out to them, calling each man by name,
"Let go, my friends! Much as you care for me,
let me hurry out of the city, make my way,   490
all on my own, to Achaea's waiting ships!
I must implore that terrible, violent man . . .
Perhaps—who knows?—he may respect my age,
may pity an old man. He has a father too,
as old as I am—Peleus sired him once,
Peleus reared him to be the scourge of Troy
but most of all to me—he made my life a hell.
So many sons he slaughtered, just coming into bloom . . .
but grieving for all the rest, one breaks my heart the most
and stabbing grief for him will take me down to Death—   500
my Hector—would to god he had perished in my arms!
Then his mother who bore him—oh so doomed,
she and I could glut ourselves with grief."

So the voice of the king rang out in tears,
the citizens wailed in answer, and noble Hecuba
led the wives of Troy in a throbbing chant of sorrow:
"O my child—my desolation! How can I go on living?
What agonies must I suffer now, now you are dead and gone?
You were my pride throughout the city night and day—

a blessing to us all, the men and women of Troy: 510
throughout the city they saluted you like a god.
You, you were their greatest glory while you lived—
now death and fate have seized you, dragged you down!"

    Her voice rang out in tears, but the wife of Hector
had not heard a thing. No messenger brought the truth
of how her husband made his stand outside the gates.
She was weaving at her loom, deep in the high halls,
working flowered braiding into a dark red folding robe.
And she called her well-kempt women through the house
to set a large three-legged cauldron over the fire   520
so Hector could have his steaming hot bath
when he came home from battle—poor woman,
she never dreamed how far he was from bathing,
struck down at Achilles' hands by blazing-eyed Athena.
But she heard the groans and wails of grief from the rampart now
and her body shook, her shuttle dropped to the ground,
she called out to her lovely waiting women, "Quickly—
two of you follow me—I must see what's happened.
That cry—that was Hector's honored mother I heard!
My heart's pounding, leaping up in my throat,   530
the knees beneath me paralyzed—Oh I know it . . .
something terrible's coming down on Priam's children.
Pray god the news will never reach my ears!
Yes but I dread it so—what if great Achilles
has cut my Hector off from the city, daring Hector,
and driven him out across the plain, and all alone?—
He may have put an end to that fatal headstrong pride
that always seized my Hector—never hanging back
with the main force of men, always charging ahead,
giving ground to no man in his fury!"
                                    So she cried,   540
dashing out of the royal halls like a madwoman,
her heart racing hard, her women close behind her.
But once she reached the tower where soldiers massed
she stopped on the rampart, looked down and saw it all—
saw him dragged before the city, stallions galloping,

dragging Hector back to Achaea's beaked warships—
ruthless work. The world went black as night
before her eyes, she fainted, falling backward,
gasping away her life breath . . .
She flung to the winds her glittering headdress,   550
the cap and the coronet, braided band and veil,
all the regalia golden Aphrodite gave her once,
the day that Hector, helmet aflash in sunlight,
led her home to Troy from her father's house
with countless wedding gifts to win her heart.
But crowding round her now her husband's sisters
and brothers' wives supported her in their midst,
and she, terrified, stunned to the point of death,
struggling for breath now and coming back to life,
burst out in grief among the Trojan women: "O Hector—   560
I am destroyed! Both born to the same fate after all!
You, you at Troy in the halls of King Priam—
I at Thebes, under the timberline of Placos,
Eetion's house . . . He raised me as a child,
that man of doom, his daughter just as doomed—
would to god he'd never fathered *me*!

                          Now you go down
to the House of Death, the dark depths of the earth,
and leave me here to waste away in grief, a widow
lost in the royal halls—and the boy only a baby,
the son we bore together, you and I so doomed.   570
Hector, what help are you to him, now you are dead?—
what help is he to you? Think, even if he escapes
the wrenching horrors of war against the Argives,
pain and labor will plague him all his days to come.
Strangers will mark his lands off, stealing his estates.
The day that orphans a youngster cuts him off from friends.
And he hangs his head low, humiliated in every way . . .
his cheeks stained with tears, and pressed by hunger
the boy goes up to his father's old companions,
tugging at one man's cloak, another's tunic,   580
and some will pity him, true,
and one will give him a little cup to drink,

enough to wet his lips, not quench his thirst.
But then some bully with both his parents living
beats him from the banquet, fists and abuses flying:
'You, get out—you've got no father feasting with us here!'
And the boy, sobbing, trails home to his widowed mother . . .
Astyanax!

    And years ago, propped on his father's knee,
he would only eat the marrow, the richest cuts of lamb,
and when sleep came on him and he had quit his play,   590
cradled warm in his nurse's arms he'd drowse off,
snug in a soft bed, his heart brimmed with joy.
Now what suffering, now he's lost his father—
           Astyanax!
The Lord of the City, so the Trojans called him,
because it was you, Hector, you and you alone
who shielded the gates and the long walls of Troy.
But now by the beaked ships, far from your parents,
glistening worms will wriggle through your flesh,
once the dogs have had their fill of your naked corpse—
though we have such stores of clothing laid up in the halls, 600
fine things, a joy to the eye, the work of women's hands.
Now, by god, I'll burn them all, blazing to the skies!
No use to you now, they'll never shroud your body—
but they will be your glory
burned by the Trojan men and women in your honor!"

Her voice rang out in tears and the women wailed in answer.

BOOK TWENTY-THREE

Funeral Games
for Patroclus

So they grieved at Troy while Achaea's troops pulled back.
Once they reached the warships moored at the Hellespont
the contingents scattered, each man to his own ship,
but Achilles still would not dismiss his Myrmidons,
he gave his battle-loving comrades strict commands:
"Charioteers in fast formation—friends to the death!
We must not loose our teams from the war-cars yet.
All in battle-order drive them past Patroclus—
a cortege will mourn the man with teams and chariots.
These are the solemn honors owed the dead. And then,   10
after we've eased our hearts with tears and dirge,
we free the teams and all take supper here."
                                      All as one
the armies cried out in sorrow, and Achilles led the chant.
Three times they drove their full-maned stallions round the body,

Myrmidon soldiers mourning, and among them Thetis stirred
a deep desire to grieve. And the sands grew wet,
the armor of fighting men grew wet with tears,
such bitter longing he roused . . .
Patroclus, that terror who routed Trojans headlong.
Achilles led them now in a throbbing chant of sorrow,   20
laying his man-killing hands on his great friend's chest:
"Farewell, Patroclus, even there in the House of Death!
Look—all that I promised once I am performing now:
I've dragged Hector here for the dogs to rip him raw—
and here in front of your flaming pyre I'll cut the throats
of a dozen sons of Troy in all their shining glory,
venting my rage on them for your destruction!"

                                                        So he triumphed
and again he was bent on outrage, on shaming noble Hector—
he flung him facedown in the dust beside Patroclus' bier.
And down to the last unit all eased off their armor,   30
fine burnished bronze, and released their neighing teams
and took their seats by the swift runner Achilles' ship,
Myrmidons in their thousands, and he set before them all
a handsome funeral feast to meet their hearts' desire.
And many pale-white oxen sank on the iron knife,
gasping in slaughter, many sheep and bleating goats
and droves of swine with their long glinting tusks,
succulent, rich with fat. They singed the bristles,
splaying the porkers out across Hephaestus' fire
then poured the blood in cupfuls all around the corpse.   40

    But now their commander, swift Achilles was led away
by Achaea's kings, barely able to bring him round—
still raging for his friend—to feast with Agamemnon.
As soon as the party reached the warlord's tents
they ordered the clear-voiced heralds straightaway
to set a large three-legged cauldron over the fire,
still in hopes of inducing Peleus' royal son
to wash the clotted bloodstains from his body.
He spurned their offer, firmly, even swore an oath:
"No, no, by Zeus—by the highest, greatest god!   50

It's sacrilege for a single drop to touch my head
till I place Patroclus on his pyre and heap his mound
and cut my hair for him—for a second grief this harsh
will never touch my heart while I am still among the living . . .
But now let us consent to the feasting that I loathe.
And at daybreak, marshal Agamemnon, rouse your troops
to fell and haul in timber, and furnish all that's fitting,
all the dead man needs for his journey down the western dark.
Then, by heaven, the tireless fire can strike his corpse—
the sooner to burn Patroclus from our sight—   60
and the men turn back to battles they must wage."

So he insisted. They hung on his words, complied,
rushed to prepare the meal, and each man feasted well
and no man's hunger lacked a share of the banquet.
When they had put aside desire for food and drink
each went his way and slept in his own shelter.
But along the shore as battle lines of breakers
crashed and dragged, Achilles lay down now,
groaning deep from the heart,
near his Myrmidon force but alone on open ground   70
where over and over rollers washed along the shore.
No sooner had sleep caught him, dissolving all his grief
as mists of refreshing slumber poured around him there—
his powerful frame was bone-weary from charging Hector
straight and hard to the walls of windswept Troy—
than the ghost of stricken Patroclus drifted up . . .
He was like the man to the life, every feature,
the same tall build and the fine eyes and voice
and the very robes that used to clothe his body.
Hovering at his head the phantom rose and spoke: 80
"Sleeping, Achilles? You've forgotten me, my friend.
You never neglected me in life, only now in death.
Bury me, quickly—let me pass the Gates of Hades.
They hold me off at a distance, all the souls,
the shades of the burnt-out, breathless dead,
never to let me cross the river, mingle with them . . .
They leave me to wander up and down, abandoned, lost

at the House of Death with the all-embracing gates.
Oh give me your hand—I beg you with my tears!
Never, never again shall I return from Hades   90
once you have given me the soothing rites of fire.
Never again will you and I, alive and breathing,
huddle side-by-side, apart from loyal comrades,
making plans together—never . . . Grim death,
that death assigned from the day that I was born
has spread its hateful jaws to take me down.

                                        And you too,
your fate awaits you too, godlike as you are, Achilles—
to die in battle beneath the proud rich Trojans' walls!
But one thing more. A last request—grant it, please.
Never bury my bones apart from yours, Achilles,   100
let them lie together . . .
just as we grew up together in your house,
after Menoetius brought me there from Opois,
and only a boy, but banished for bloody murder
the day I killed Amphidamas' son. I was a fool—
I never meant to kill him—quarreling over a dice game.
Then the famous horseman Peleus took me into his halls,
he reared me with kindness, appointed me your aide.
So now let a single urn, the gold two-handled urn
your noble mother gave you, hold our bones—together!"   110

    And the swift runner Achilles reassured him warmly:
"Why have you returned to me here, dear brother, friend?
Why tell me of all that I must do? I'll do it all.
I will obey you, your demands. Oh come closer!
Throw our arms around each other, just for a moment—
take some joy in the tears that numb the heart!"

    In the same breath he stretched his loving arms
but could not seize him, no, the ghost slipped underground
like a wisp of smoke . . . with a high thin cry.
And Achilles sprang up with a start and staring wide,   120
drove his fists together and cried in desolation, "Ah god!
So even in Death's strong house there is something left,

a ghost, a phantom—true, but no real breath of life.
All night long the ghost of stricken Patroclus
hovered over me, grieving, sharing warm tears,
telling me, point by point, what I must do.
Marvelous—like the man to the life!"

                        So he cried
and his outcry stirred in them all a deep desire to grieve,
and Dawn with her rose-red fingers shone upon them weeping
round the wretched corpse. At daybreak King Agamemnon   130
ordered parties of men and mules to haul in timber,
pouring from the tents with a good man in charge,
the lordly Idomeneus' aide-in-arms Meriones.
The troops moved out with loggers' axes in hand
and sturdy cabled ropes as mules trudged on ahead.
Uphill, downhill, crisscross, zigzag on they tramped
and once they reached the slopes of Ida with all her springs,
quickly pitching themselves at towering, leaf-crowned oaks,
they put their backs into strokes of the whetted bronze axes
and huge trunks came crashing down. They split them apart,   140
lashed the logs to the mules and their hoofs tore up the earth,
dragging them down to level ground through dense brush.
And all the woodcutters hoisted logs themselves—
by command of Idomeneus' good aide Meriones—
and they heaved them down in rows along the beach
at the site Achilles chose to build an immense mound
for Patroclus and himself.

                   With boundless timber piled
on all sides of the place, down they sat, waiting, massed.
And at once Achilles called his Myrmidons keen for battle:
"Belt yourselves in bronze! Each driver yoke his team!   150
Chariots harnessed!" Up they rose and strapped on armor
and swung aboard the war-cars, drivers, fighters beside them—
and the horse moved out in front, behind came clouds of infantry,
men by thousands, and in their midst his comrades bore Patroclus.
They covered his whole body deep with locks of hair they cut
and cast upon him, and just behind them brilliant Achilles
held the head, in tears—this was his steadfast friend
whom he escorted down to the House of Death.

When they reached the site Achilles had pointed out
they laid Patroclus down and swiftly built his body   160
a fitting height of timber.
And now the great runner remembered one more duty.
Stepping back from the pyre he cut the red-gold lock
he'd let grow long as a gift to the river god Spercheus—
scanning the wine-dark sea he prayed in anguish, "Spercheus!
All in vain my father Peleus vowed to you that there,
once I had journeyed home to my own dear fatherland,
I'd cut this lock for you and offer splendid victims,
dedicate fifty young ungelded rams to your springs,
there at the spot where your grove and smoking altar stand!   170
So the old king vowed—but you've destroyed his hopes.
Now, since I shall not return to my fatherland,
I'd give my friend this lock . . .
and let the hero Patroclus bear it on his way."
                                                        With that,
Achilles placed the lock in his dear comrade's hands
and stirred in the men again a deep desire to grieve.
And now the sunlight would have set upon their tears
if Achilles had not turned to Agamemnon quickly:
"Atrides—you are the first the armies will obey.
Even of sorrow men can have their fill. So now   180
dismiss them from the pyre, have them prepare
an evening meal. We are the closest to the dead,
we'll see to all things here.
But I'd like the leading captains to remain."

   Hearing his wish, the lord of men Agamemnon
dismissed the troops at once to the balanced ships.
But the chief mourners stayed in place, piled timber
and built a pyre a hundred feet in length and breadth
and aloft it laid the corpse with heavy, aching hearts.
And droves of fat sheep and shambling crook-horned cattle   190
they led before the pyre, skinned and dressed them well.
And the greathearted Achilles, flensing fat from all,
wrapped the corpse with folds of it, head to foot,
then heaped the flayed carcasses round Patroclus.

He set two-handled jars of honey and oil beside him,
leaned them against the bier—and then with wild zeal
slung the bodies of four massive stallions onto the pyre
and gave a wrenching groan. And the dead lord Patroclus
had fed nine dogs at table—he slit the throats of two,
threw them onto the pyre and then a dozen brave sons   200
of the proud Trojans he hacked to pieces with his bronze . . .
Achilles' mighty heart was erupting now with slaughter—
he loosed the iron rage of fire to consume them all
and cried out, calling his dear friend by name,
"Farewell, Patroclus, even there in the House of Death!
All that I promised once I have performed at last.
Here are twelve brave sons of the proud Trojans—
all, the fire that feeds on you devours them all
but not Hector the royal son of Priam, Hector
I will never give to the hungry flames—   210
wild dogs will bolt his flesh!"
                              So he threatened
but the dogs were not about to feed on Hector.
Aphrodite daughter of Zeus beat off the packs,
day and night, anointing Hector's body with oil,
ambrosial oil of roses, so Achilles could not rip
the prince's skin as he dragged him back and forth.
And round him Phoebus Apollo brought a dark cloud down
from high sky to the plain to shroud the entire space
where Hector's body lay, before the sun's white fury
could sear away his flesh, his limbs and sinews.   220

    But the pyre of dead Patroclus was not burning—
and the swift runner Achilles thought of what to do.
Stepping back from the pyre he prayed to the two winds—
Zephyr and Boreas, West and North—promised splendid victims
and pouring generous, brimming cups from a golden goblet,
begged them to come, so the wood might burst in flame
and the dead burn down to ash with all good speed.
And Iris, hearing his prayers, rushed the message on
to the winds that gathered now in stormy Zephyr's halls
to share his brawling banquet. Iris swept to a stop   230

and once they saw her poised at the stone threshold
all sprang up, each urged her to sit beside him
but she refused, pressing on with her message:
"No time for sitting now. No, I must return
to the Ocean's running stream, the Aethiopians' land.
They are making a splendid sacrifice to the gods—
I must not miss my share of the sacred feast.
But I bring Achilles' prayers!
He begs you to come at once, Boreas, blustering Zephyr,
he promises splendid victims—come with a strong blast   240
and light the pyre where Patroclus lies in state
and all the Argive armies mourn around him!"

    Message delivered, off she sped as the winds rose
with a superhuman roar, stampeding clouds before them.
Suddenly reaching the open sea in gale force,
whipping whitecaps under a shrilling killer-squall
they raised the good rich soil of Troy and struck the pyre
and a huge inhuman blaze went howling up the skies.
All night long they hurled the flames—massed on the pyre,
blast on screaming blast—and all night long the swift Achilles,   250
lifting a two-handled cup, dipped wine from a golden bowl
and poured it down on the ground and drenched the earth,
calling out to the ghost of stricken, gaunt Patroclus.
As a father weeps when he burns his son's bones,
dead on his wedding day,
and his death has plunged his parents in despair . . .
so Achilles wept as he burned his dear friend's bones,
dragging himself around the pyre, choked with sobs.

    At that hour the morning star comes rising up
to herald a new day on earth, and riding in its wake   260
the Dawn flings out her golden robe across the sea,
the funeral fires sank low, the flames died down.
And the winds swung round and headed home again,
over the Thracian Sea, and the heaving swells moaned.
And at last Achilles, turning away from the corpse-fire,
sank down, exhausted. Sweet sleep overwhelmed him.

But Agamemnon's followers grouped together now
and as they approached Achilles
the din and trampling of their feet awoke him.
He sat up with a start and made his wishes known: 270
"Atrides—chiefs of Achaea's united forces—
first put out the fires with glistening wine,
wherever the flames still burn in all their fury.
Then let us collect the bones of Menoetius' son Patroclus,
pick them out with care—but they cannot be mistaken:
he lay amidst the pyre, apart from all the others
burned at the edge, the ruck of men and horses.
Then let us place his bones in a golden urn,
sealed tight and dry with a double fold of fat,
till I myself lie hid in the strong House of Death.   280
For his barrow, build him nothing large, I ask you,
something right for the moment. And then, later,
Achaeans can work to make it broad and lofty,
all who survive me here,
alive in the benched ships when I am gone."

    And the men obeyed the swift runner's orders.
They first put out the fires with glistening wine,
far as the flames had spread and the ashes bedded deep.
In tears they gathered their gentle comrade's white bones,
all in a golden urn, sealed with a double fold of fat,   290
and stowed the urn in his shelter, covered well
with a light linen shroud, then laid his barrow out.
Around the pyre they planted a ring of stone revetments,
piled the loose earth high in a mound above the ring
and once they'd heaped the barrow turned to leave.
But Achilles held the armies on the spot.
He had them sit in a great and growing circle—
now for funeral games—and brought from his ships
the trophies for the contests: cauldrons and tripods,
stallions, mules and cattle with massive heads,   300
women sashed and lovely, and gleaming gray iron.

                                                              First,
for the fastest charioteers he set out glittering prizes:

a woman to lead away, flawless, skilled in crafts,
and a two-eared tripod, twenty-two measures deep—
all that for the first prize.
Then for the runner-up he brought forth a mare,
unbroken, six years old, with a mule foal in her womb.
For the third he produced a fine four-measure cauldron
never scorched by flames, its sheen as bright as new.
For the fourth he set out two gold bars, for the fifth,   310
untouched by fire as well, a good two-handled jar.
And he rose up tall and challenged all the Argives:
"Atrides—Achaeans-at-arms! Let the games begin!
The trophies lie afield—they await the charioteers.
If we held our games now in another hero's honor,
surely I'd walk off to my tent with first prize.
You know how my team outstrips all others' speed.
Immortal horses they are, Poseidon gave them himself
to my father Peleus, Peleus passed them on to me.
But I and our fast stallions will not race today,   320
so strong his fame, the charioteer they've lost,
so kind—always washing them down with fresh water,
sleeking their long manes with smooth olive oil.
No wonder they stand here, mourning . . .
look, trailing those very manes along the ground.
They both refuse to move, saddled down with grief.
But all the rest of you, come, all Achaeans in camp
who trust to your teams and bolted chariots—
take your places now!"
                              Achilles' call rang out
and it brought the fastest drivers crowding forward.   330
The first by far, Eumelus lord of men sprang up,
Admetus' prized son who excelled in horsemanship
and following him Tydides, powerful Diomedes,
yoking the breed of Tros he'd wrested from Aeneas
just the other day when Apollo saved their master.
Then Atreus' son Menelaus, the red-haired captain
born of the gods, leading under the yoke his racers,
Blaze, Agamemnon's mare, and his own stallion Brightfoot.
Anchises' son Echepolus gave Agamemnon Blaze,

a gift that bought him off from the king's armies   340
bound for windy Troy: he'd stay right where he was,
a happy man, since Zeus had given him vast wealth
and he lived in style on Sicyon's broad dancing rings.
His was the mare Atrides harnessed, champing for the race.
And the fourth to yoke his full-maned team was Antilochus,
the splendid son of Nestor the old high-hearted king,
lord Neleus' offspring. A team of Pylian purebreds
drew his chariot. His father stood at his side,
lending sound advice to the boy's own good sense:
"Young as you are, Antilochus, how the gods have loved you!   350
Zeus and Poseidon taught you horsemanship, every sort,
so there's no great need for me to set you straight.
Well you know how to double round the post . . .
but you've got the slowest nags—a handicap, I'd say.
Yet even if other teams are faster, look at their drivers:
there's not a trick in their whips that you don't have at hand.
So plan your attack, my friend, muster all your skills
or watch the prize slip by!
It's skill, not brawn, that makes the finest woodsman.
By skill, too, the captain holds his ship on course,   360
scudding the wine-dark sea though rocked by gales.
By skill alone, charioteer outraces charioteer.
The average driver, leaving all to team and car,
recklessly makes his turn, veering left and right,
his pair swerving over the course—he can't control them.
But the cunning driver, even handling slower horses,
always watches the post, turns it close, never loses
the first chance to relax his reins and stretch his pair
but he holds them tight till then, eyes on the leader.
Now, the turn itself—it's clear, you cannot miss it.   370
There's a dead tree-stump standing six feet high,
it's oak or pine, not rotted through by the rains,
and it's propped by two white stones on either side.
That's your halfway mark where the homestretch starts
and there's plenty of good smooth racing-room around it—
it's either the grave-mound of a man dead long ago
or men who lived before us set it up as a goal.

Now, in any event, swift Achilles makes it
his turning-post. And you must hug it close
as you haul your team and chariot round but you   380
in your tight-strung car, you lean to the left yourself,
just a bit as you whip your right-hand horse, hard,
shout him on, slacken your grip and give him rein.
But make your left horse hug that post so close
the hub of your well-turned wheel will almost seem
to scrape the rock—just careful not to graze it!
You'll maim your team, you'll smash your car to pieces.
A joy to your rivals, rank disgrace to yourself . . .
So keep your head, my boy, be on the lookout.
Trail the field out but pass them all at the post,   390
no one can catch you then or overtake you with a surge—
not if the man behind you were driving huge Arion,
Adrastus' lightning stallion sired by the gods,
or Laomedon's team, the greatest bred in Troy.''

Nestor sat down again. He'd shown his son the ropes,
the last word in the master horseman's skills.

Now after Meriones yoked his sleek horses fifth,
they boarded their cars and dropped lots in a helmet.
Achilles shook it hard—Antilochus' lot leapt out
so he drew the inside track.   400
Next in the draw came hardy lord Eumelus,
Atrides Menelaus the famous spearman next
and Meriones drew the fourth starting-lane
and Tydides Diomedes drew the fifth and last,
the best of them all by far at driving battle-teams.
All pulled up abreast as Achilles pointed out the post,
far off on the level plain, and stationed there beside it
an umpire, old lord Phoenix, his father's aide-in-arms,
to mark the field at the turn and make a true report.

Ready—
          whips raised high—
                              at the signal all together   410

lashed their horses' backs and shouted, urging them on—
they broke in a burst of speed, in no time swept the plain,
leaving the ships behind and lifting under their chests
the dust clung to the teams like clouds or swirling gales
as their manes went streaming back in the gusty tearing wind.
The cars shot on, now jouncing along the earth that rears us all,
now bounding clear in the air but the drivers kept erect
in the lurching cars and the heart of each man raced,
straining for victory—each man yelled at his pair
as they flew across the plain in a whirl of dust.   420
But just out of the turn,
starting the homestretch back to sunlit sea
the horses lunged, each driver showed his form,
the whole field went racing full tilt and at once
the fast mares of Eumelus surged far out in front—
And after him came Diomedes' team, Tros's stallions
hardly a length behind now, closing at each stride
and at any moment it seemed they'd mount Eumelus' car,
their hot breath steaming his back and broad shoulders,
their heads hovering over him, breakneck on they flew—   430
and now he'd have passed him or forced a dead heat
if Apollo all of a sudden raging at Diomedes
had not knocked the shining whip from his fist.
Tears of rage came streaming down his cheeks
as he watched Eumelus' mares pulling farther ahead
and his team losing pace, no whip to lash them on . . .
But Athena, missing nothing of Phoebus' foul play
that robbed Diomedes, sped to the gallant captain,
handed him back his whip, primed his team with power
and flying after Admetus' son in full immortal fury   440
the goddess smashed his yoke. His mares bolted apart,
careening off the track and his pole plowed the ground
and Eumelus hurled from the chariot, tumbling over the wheel,
the skin was ripped from his elbows, mouth and nostrils,
his forehead battered in, scraped raw at the brows,
tears filling his eyes, his booming voice choked—
But veering round the wreck Diomedes steered his racers
shooting far ahead of the rest, leaving them in the dust

as Athena fired his team and gave the man his glory.
And after him came Atrides, red-haired Menelaus,   450
next Antilochus, urging his father's horses:
"Drive, the two of you—full stretch and fast!
I don't tell you to match the leader's speed,
skilled Diomedes' team—look, Athena herself
just fired their pace and gave their master glory.
But catch Menelaus' pair—fast—don't get left behind—
or Blaze will shower the two of you with disgrace—
Blaze is a mare! Why falling back, my brave ones?
I warn you both—so help me it's the truth—
no more grooming for you at Nestor's hands!   460
The old driver will slaughter you on the spot
with a sharp bronze blade if you slack off now
and we take a lesser prize. After them, faster—
full gallop—I'll find the way, I've got the skill
to slip past him there where the track narrows—
I'll never miss my chance!"
                              Whipped with fear
by their master's threats they put on a fresh burst
for a length or two but suddenly brave Antilochus
saw the narrow place where the road washed out—
a sharp dip in the land where massing winter rains   470
broke off the edge, making it all one sunken rut.
There Atrides was heading—no room for two abreast—
but Antilochus swerved to pass him, lashing his horses
off the track then swerving into him neck-and-neck
and Atrides, frightened, yelled out at the man,
"Antilochus—you drive like a maniac! Hold your horses!
The track's too narrow here—it widens soon for passing—
watch out—you'll crash your chariot, wreck us both!"

So he cried but Antilochus drove on all the wilder,
cracking his lash for more speed like a man stone deaf.   480
As far as a full shoulder-throw of a whirling discus
hurled by a young contender testing out his strength,
so far they raced dead even. But then Menelaus' pair
dropped back as he yielded, cut the pace on purpose—

he feared the massive teams would collide on the track
and the tight-strung cars capsize, the men themselves
go sprawling into the dust, striving, wild for triumph.
As his rival passed the red-haired captain cursed him:
"Antilochus—no one alive more treacherous than you!
Away with you, madman—damn you!   490
How wrong we were when we said you had good sense.
You'll never take the prize unless you take the oath!"

  Turning back to his team, calling, shouting them on:
"Don't hold back, don't stop now—galled as you are—
that team in the lead will sag in the leg before you—
robbed of their prime, their racing days are done!"
And lashed with fear by their master's angry voice
they put on a surge, closing on them fast.

                                        And all the while
the armies tense in a broad circle watched for horses
flying back on the plain in a rising whirl of dust.   500
The first to make them out was the Cretan captain.
Idomeneus sat perched on a rise outside the ring,
a commanding lookout point, and hearing a driver
shouting out in the distance, recognized the voice,
could see a stallion too—far in the lead, unmistakable—
a big chestnut beauty, all but the blaze he sported
stark white on his forehead, round as a full moon.
He sprang to his feet, calling down to cohorts,
"Friends—lords of the Argives, O my captains—
am I the only one who can spot that pair   510
or can you see them too?
Seems to me it's a new team out in front,
a new driver as well, just coming into sight.
The mares of Eumelus must have come to grief,
somewhere downfield—they led on the way out.
I saw them heading first for the turn, by god,
but I can't find them now—anywhere—hard as I look,
left and right, scanning the whole Trojan plain.
He lost his reins, he lost control of his horses
round the post and they failed to make the turn—   520

that's where he got thrown, I'd say, his chariot smashed
and his horses went berserk and bolted off.
                                    Stand up,
look for yourselves! I can't make them out . . .
not for certain, no, but the leader seems to me
an Aetolian man by birth—he's king of the Argives,
horse-breaking Tydeus' son, rugged Diomedes!"

But quick Little Ajax rounded on him roughly:
"Loose talk, Idomeneus—why are you always sounding off?
They still have a way to go out there, those racing teams.
You too, you're a far cry from the youngest Argive here,   530
nor are the eyes in your head our sharpest scouts
but you're always blustering, you, you foul-mouthed—
why must we have you blurting out this way
in the face of keener men?
Those mares in front are the same that led before—
they're Eumelus' mares, look, and there's Eumelus now,
astride his chariot, gripping the reins himself!"

But the Cretan captain burst back in answer,
"Ajax, champion wrangler in all the ranks! Stupid too,
first and last the worst man in the Argive armies—   540
stubborn, bullnecked fool. Come now,
let's both put up a tripod or a cauldron,
wager which horses are really out in front
and we'll make Atrides Agamemnon our referee—
you'll learn, don't worry, once you pay the price!"

Ajax rose in fury to trade him taunt for taunt,
and now the two of them might have come to blows
if Achilles himself had not stood up to calm them:
"Enough! No more trading your stinging insults now,
Ajax, Idomeneus! It's offensive—this is not the time.   550
You'd be the first to blame a man who railed this way.
Sit down in the ring, you two, and watch the horses—
they'll be home in a moment, racing hard to win.
Then each can see for himself who comes in second,

who takes off first prize."
                                In the same breath
Diomedes came on storming toward them—closer, look,
closing—lashing his team nonstop, full-shoulder strokes,
making them kick high as they hurtled toward the goal.
Constant sprays of dust kept pelting back on the driver,
the chariot sheathed in gold and tin careering on   560
in the plunging stallions' wake, its spinning rims
hardly leaving a rut behind in the thin dust
as the team thundered in—a whirlwind finish!
He reined them back in the ring with drenching sweat,
lather streaming down to the ground from necks and chests.
Their master leapt down from the bright burnished car,
propped his whip on the yoke. His aide lost no time—
the hardy Sthenelus rushed to collect the prizes,
gave their proud troops the woman to lead away
and they carried off the handsome two-eared tripod   570
as he was loosing the horses from the harness . . .

        Antilochus next—the son of Nestor drove in second,
beating Atrides not by speed but cunning—
but still Menelaus kept his racers close behind.
Tight as the closing gap between the wheel and horse
when he hauls his master's car top speed across the flats,
the very tip of his tail brushing the running-rim
and the wheel spins closer, hardly a gap between
as he sweeps the open plain—that much, no more,
Menelaus trailed Antilochus, dauntless driver.   580
At first he'd trailed him a full discus-throw
but now he was closing, gaining on him fast—
yes, Blaze with all her fury and flowing mane,
Agamemnon's mare was coming on with a strong surge
and now if the two teams had a longer course to run
Menelaus would have passed him—no dead heat about it.
Then Idomeneus' good aide Meriones came in fourth,
trailing the famed Atrides by a spear-throw.
His team had sleek manes but the slowest pace afield
and the man himself was the poorest racing-driver.   590

But Admetus' son Eumelus came in last of all . . .
dragging his fine chariot, flogging his team before him.
Seeing him there the swift Achilles filled with pity,
rose in their midst and said these winging words:
"The best man drives his purebred team home last!
Come, let's give him a prize, it's only right—
but second prize, of course—
Tydeus' son must carry off the first."
                              So he said
and the armies called assent to what he urged.
And now, spurred by his comrades' quick approval,   600
Achilles was just about to give the man the mare
when Antilochus, son of magnanimous old Nestor,
leapt to his feet and lodged a formal protest:
"Achilles—I'll be furious if you carry out that plan!
Do you really mean to strip me of my prize?—
so concerned that his team and car were wrecked,
and the fellow too, for all his racing skills.
Why, he should have prayed to the deathless gods!
Then he would never have finished last of all.
You pity the man? You're fond of him, are you?   610
You have hoards of gold in your tents, bronze, sheep,
serving-girls by the score and purebred racers too:
pick some bigger trophy out of the whole lot
and hand it on to the man, but do it later—
or now, at once, and win your troops' applause.
I won't give up the mare! The one who wants her—
step this way and try—
he'll have to fight me for her with his fists!"

    He flared up and the swift runner Achilles smiled,
delighting in Antilochus—he liked the man immensely.   620
He answered him warmly, winged words: "Antilochus,
you want me to fetch an extra gift from my tents,
a consolation prize for Eumelus? I'm glad to do it.
I'll give him the breastplate I took from Asteropaeus.
It's solid bronze with a glittering overlay of tin,
rings on rings. A gift he'll value highly."

He asked Automedon, ready aide, to bring
the breastplate from his tents. He went and brought it,
handed it to Eumelus. The man received it gladly.

But now Menelaus rose, his heart smoldering,   630
still holding a stubborn grudge against Antilochus.
A crier put a staff in his hands and called for silence.
And with all his royal weight Atrides thundered, "Antilochus—
you used to have good sense! Now see what you've done!
Disgraced my horsemanship—you've fouled my horses,
cutting before me, you with your far slower team.
Quickly, lords of the Argives, all my captains,
judge between us—impartially, no favoritism—
so none of our bronze-armed men can ever say,
'Only with lies did Atrides beat Antilochus out   640
and walk off with the mare—his team was far slower
but the king's own rank and power took the prize!'
Wait, I'll settle things myself. I have no fear
that any Achaean will accuse me: I'll be fair.
Come over here, Antilochus, royal prince—
this is the old custom. Come, stand in front
of your team and chariot, grasp the coiling whip
that lashed them home, lay your hand on their manes
and swear by the mighty god who grips and shakes the earth
you never blocked my chariot—not by deliberate foul."   650

Antilochus came to his senses, backed off quickly:
"No more, please. I am much younger than you are,
lord Menelaus—you're my senior, you the greater man.
Well you know how the whims of youth break all the rules.
Our wits quicker than wind, our judgment just as flighty.
Bear with me now. I'll give you this mare I won—
of my own accord. And any finer trophy you'd ask
from my own stores, I'd volunteer at once,
gladly, Atrides, my royal king—*anything*
but fall from your favor all my days to come   660
and swear a false oath in the eyes of every god."

   With that the son of magnanimous old Nestor
led the mare and turned her over to Menelaus' hands.
And his heart melted now like the dew that wets the corn
when the fresh stalks rise up and the ripe fields ripple—
so the heart in your chest was melted now, Menelaus,
and you gave your friend an answer, winged words:
"Antilochus, now it is my turn to yield to you,
for all my mounting anger . . .
you who were never wild or reckless in the past.   670
It's only youth that got the better of your discretion,
just this once—but the next time be more careful.
Try to refrain from cheating your superiors.
No other Achaean could have brought me round so soon,
but seeing that you have suffered much and labored long,
your noble father, your brother too—all for my sake—
I'll yield to your appeal, I'll even give you the mare,
though she is mine, so our people here will know
the heart inside me is never rigid, unrelenting."

   He handed back the mare to Antilochus' man.   680
Noëmon led her off while Atrides took instead
the polished cauldron bright in all its sheen.
Meriones, who had come in fourth took fourth prize,
the two bars of gold. That left the fifth unclaimed,
the jar with double handles. Bearing it through the crowd
Achilles gave it to Nestor, standing close beside him,
urging, "Here, old friend—a trophy for you too!
Lay it away as a treasure . . .
let it remind you of the burial of Patroclus.
Never again will you see him among the Argives.   690
I give you this prize, a gift for giving's sake,
for now you will never fight with fists or wrestle,
or enter the spear-throw, or race on sprinting feet.
The burdens of old age already weigh you down."

   And Achilles placed the trophy in Nestor's hands.
He thrilled to have it and spoke out winging words:
"True, true, my son, all of it, right on the mark.

My legs no longer firm, my friend, dead on my feet,
nor do my arms go shooting from my shoulders—
the stunning punch, the left and right are gone.   700
Oh make me young again, and the strength inside me
steady as a rock! As fresh as I was that day
the Epeans buried lord Amarynceus in Buprasion
and his sons held games to celebrate the king . . .
No one could match me there, none among the Epeans,
not even our own Pylians, or Aetolia's hardy men.
At boxing I destroyed Clytomedes, Enops' boy.
Ancaeus of Pleuron wrestled against me—down he went.
Fast as Iphiclus was, I raced him to his knees,
with a spear I outhurled Phyleus, Polydorus too.   710
Only at chariot-racing the sons of Actor beat me—
two against one, cutting before me, hellbent to win,
for the biggest prize was left for the last event.
But it took twins—one with the reins rock-steady,
holding them rock-steady, the other lashed the team.
So that's the man I was . . . but now's the time
for the younger men to lock in rough encounters,
time for me to yield to the pains of old age.
But there was a day I shone among the champions.

                                        Well,

you must get on with your friend's burial now—   720
the games must go on—
but I accept this gladly, my old heart rejoices.
You never forget my friendship, never miss a chance
to pay me the honor I deserve among our comrades.
For all that you have done for me, Achilles,
may the immortals fill your cup with joy!"

    He savored every word of Nestor's story.
Then Achilles made his way through crowds of troops
and set out prizes next for the bruising boxing-match.
He fetched and tethered a heavy-duty mule in the ring,   730
six years old, unbroken—the hardest kind to break—
and offered the loser a cup with double handles.
He rose up tall and challenged all the Argives:

"Son of Atreus—all you Achaean men-at-arms!
We invite two men—our best—to compete for these.
Put up your fists, fight for what you're worth.
The man that Apollo helps outlast the other—
clearly witnessed here by Achaea's armies—
he takes this beast of burden back to his tents
but the one he beats can have the two-eared cup."   740

And a powerful, huge man loomed up at once,
Panopeus' son Epeus, the famous boxing champion.
He clamped a hand on the draft mule and shouted,
"Step right up and get it—whoever wants that cup!
This mule is mine, I tell you. No Achaean in sight
will knock me out and take her—I am the greatest!
So what if I'm not a world-class man of war?
How can a man be first in all events?
I warn you, soldiers—so help me it's the truth—
I'll crush you with body-blows, I'll crack your ribs to splinters!   750
You keep your family mourners near to cart you off—
once my fists have worked you down to pulp!"

Dead silence. So the armies met his challenge.
Only Euryalus rose to take him on, heroic volunteer,
bred of Talaus' blood and a son of King Mecisteus
who went to Thebes in the old days, when Oedipus fell,
and there at his funeral games defeated all the Thebans.
The spearman Diomedes served as the man's second,
goading him on, intent to see him win.
First he cinched him round with the boxer's belt   760
then taking rawhide thongs, cut from a field-ox,
wrapped his knuckles well.
                              Both champions, belted tight,
stepped into the ring squared off at each other and let loose,
trading jabs with their clenched fists then slugged it out—
flurries of jolting punches, terrific grinding of jaws,
sweat rivering, bodies glistening—suddenly Euryalus
glanced for an opening, dropped his guard and Epeus hurled
his smashing roundhouse hook to the head—a knockout blow!

He could keep his feet no longer, knees caved in on the spot—
as under the ruffling North Wind a fish goes arching up   770
and flops back down on a beach-break strewn with seaweed
and a dark wave blacks him out. So he left his feet
and down he went—out cold—but big-hearted Epeus
hoisted him in his arms and stood him upright.
A band of loyal followers rushed to help him,
led him out of the ring, his feet dragging,
head lolling to one side, spitting clots of blood . . .
still senseless after they propped him in their corner,
and they had to fetch the two-eared cup themselves.

                                                Quickly
Achilles displayed before the troops the prizes set   780
for the third event, the grueling wrestling-match.
For the winner a large tripod made to stride a fire
and worth a dozen oxen, so the soldiers reckoned.
For the loser he led a woman through their midst,
worth four, they thought, and skilled in many crafts.
And he rose up tall and challenged all the Achaeans:
"Now two come forward—fight to win this prize!"
And the giant Ajax got to his feet at once,
Odysseus stood up too,
an expert at every subtle, cunning hold.   790
Both champions, belted tight, stepped into the ring
and grappling each other hard with big burly arms,
locked like rafters a master builder bolts together,
slanting into a pitched roof to fight the ripping winds.
And their backbones creaked as scuffling hands tugged
for submission-holds and sweat streamed down their spines
and clusters of raw welts broke out on ribs and shoulders
slippery, red with blood, and still they grappled, harder,
locking for victory, locked for that burnished tripod:
Odysseus no more able to trip and bring to ground   800
his man than Ajax could—Odysseus' brawn held out.
A stalemate. And the troops were growing bored,
so at last the giant Ajax spurred his rival,
grunting, "Son of Laertes—resourceful one, enough—
you hoist me or I hoist you—and leave the rest to Zeus."

As Ajax heaved him up Odysseus never missed a trick—
he kicked him behind the knee, clipping the hollow,
cut his legs from under him, knocked him backward—
pinned as Odysseus flung himself across his chest!
That roused the crowd, they leaned to look and marveled.   810
The next throw now—long-enduring Odysseus' turn . . .
he tried to hoist Great Ajax, budged him a little
off the ground, true, but he could not heave him clear,
then hooked him round a knee and down they sprawled together,
both men clenched in a death-lock, tussling round in dust.
And now they'd have jumped up, gone for the third fall
if Achilles himself had not stepped in and stopped them:
"No more struggling—don't kill yourselves in sport!
Victory goes to both. Share the prizes. Off you go,
so the rest of the men can have a crack at contests."   820

And they listened gladly, nodding at his decision,
wiped the dust from their backs and pulled their shirts on.

Achilles quickly set out prizes for the footrace.
A silver bowl, gorgeous, just six measures deep
but the finest mixing bowl in all the world.
Nothing could match its beauty—a masterpiece
that skilled Sidonian craftsmen wrought to perfection,
Phoenician traders shipped across the misty seas
and mooring in Thoas' roads, presented to the king.
Euneus son of Jason gave it to Prince Patroclus,   830
the ransom paid to release Lycaon, Priam's son.
This was the bowl Achilles offered up at games
to commemorate his great friend—for the one racer
who proved the fastest on his feet. For the runner-up
he produced a massive ox with rippling folds of fat
and half a bar of gold for him who came in last.
He rose up tall and challenged all the Achaeans:
"Now men come forward, fight to win this prize!"
And the racing Oilean Ajax sprang up at once,
Odysseus quick at tactics too, then Nestor's son,   840
Antilochus, fastest of all the young men in the ranks.

Achilles pointed out the post . . .
                               They toed the line—
and broke flat out from the start and Ajax shot ahead
with quick Odysseus coming right behind him, close
as the weaver's rod to a well-sashed woman's breast
when she deftly pulls it toward her, shooting the spool
across the warp, still closer, pressing her breast—
so close Odysseus sprinted, hot on Ajax' heels,
feet hitting his tracks before the dust could settle
and quick Odysseus panting, breathing down his neck,   850
always forcing the pace and all the Argives shouting,
cheering him on as he strained for triumph, sprinting on
and fast in the homestretch, spurting toward the goal
Odysseus prayed in his heart to blazing-eyed Athena,
"Hear me, Goddess, help me—hurry, urge me on!"
So Odysseus prayed and Athena heard his prayer,
put spring in his limbs, his feet, his fighting hands
and just as the whole field came lunging in for the trophy
Ajax slipped at a dead run—Athena tripped him up—
right where the dung lay slick from bellowing cattle   860
the swift runner Achilles slew in Patroclus' honor.
Dung stuffed his mouth, his nostrils dripped muck
as shining long-enduring Odysseus flashed past him
to come in first by far and carry off the cup
while Ajax took the ox. The racer in all his glory
just stood there, clutching one of the beast's horns,
spitting out the dung and sputtering to his comrades,
"Foul, by heaven! The goddess fouled my finish!
Always beside Odysseus—just like the man's mother,
rushing to put his rivals in the dust."   870

   They all roared with laughter at his expense.
Antilochus came in last and carried off his prize
with a broad smile and a joke to warm his comrades:
"I'll tell you something you've always known, my friends—
down to this very day the gods prefer old-timers.
Look at Ajax now, with only a few years on me.
But Odysseus—why, *he*'s out of the dark ages,

one of the old relics—
but in green old age, they say. No mean feat
to beat him out in a race, for all but our Achilles."   880

Bantering so, but he flattered swift Achilles
and the matchless runner paid him back in kind:
"Antilochus, how can I let your praise go unrewarded?
Here's more gold—a half-bar more in the bargain."

He placed it in his hands, and he was glad to have it.
Then Achilles carried into the armies' broad ring
a spear trailing its long shadow, laid it down
and beside it placed a battle-shield and helmet,
the arms Patroclus stripped from lord Sarpedon.
And Achilles rose and challenged all the Argives: 890
"We invite two men—our best—to compete for these.
Full battle-gear, take up your slashing bronze lances.
Fight it out with each other, duel before the troops!
The soldier who gets in first and cuts a rival's flesh,
who pierces armor to draw blood and reach his entrails—
I'll give that man this broadsword, silver-studded,
handsome Thracian work I stripped from Asteropaeus.
But both fighters will share this armor, bear it off,
and we'll give them a victor's banquet in our tents."

Huge Telamonian Ajax rose to meet the challenge,   900
Tydeus' son rose too, the powerful Diomedes.
Both men armed at opposite sides of the forces,
into the ring they strode and met, burning for battle,
glances menacing, wild excitement seizing all their comrades.
And just coming in range, just closing on each other . . .
they made three rapid charges, three lunges and then—
Ajax stabbed through Tydides' round balanced shield
but failed to reach his flesh—saved by the breastplate
just behind the buckler! But now Diomedes thrusting
over the giant's massive shield, again and again,   910
threatened to graze his throat—the spearpoint glinting sharp—
and such terror for Ajax struck his Argive friends

they cried for them to stop, to divide the prizes,
"Share and share alike!" But the hero Achilles
took the great long sword and gave it to Diomedes,
slung in its sheath on a supple, well-cut sword-strap.

And now Achilles set out a lump of pig iron,
the shot Eetion used to put with all his power
before the swift runner Pelides brought him down
and hauled it off in the ships with all his other wealth.   920
Achilles rose up tall and challenged every Achaean:
"Now men come forward—compete to win this prize!
An ingot big enough to keep the winner in iron
for five wheeling years. Though his rich estates
lie far away in the country, it won't be want of iron
that brings his shepherd or plowman into town—
he'll be well-stocked at home."
                              That was his offer.
Up stood Polypoetes, always braced for battle,
Leonteus flanked him, strong, intense as a god,
then Telamon's son Great Ajax, lord Epeus too.   930
They stood in a row. Big Epeus hefted the iron,
swung and heaved it—and comrades burst out laughing.
Next the veteran Leonteus gave the weight a hurl,
then Ajax came up third and the giant flung it hard
with his rippling brawny arm to pass all other marks.
But then Polypoetes braced for battle took the weight
and far as a seasoned herdsman flings his throwing staff,
whirling in flight across his cows to keep them all in line—
so far he outhurled the whole field. The armies roared.
And the powerful Polypoetes' men sprang up to bear   940
the king's trophy back to their hollow ships.
                              Archery next—
and again Achilles set out iron, dark gray trophies,
ten double-headed axes, ten with single heads.
He stepped the mast of a dark-prowed man-of-war
far down the beach and tethered a fluttering dove
atop the pole, its foot looped with a light cord,
then challenged men to shoot and hit that mark:

"The man who hits the fluttering dove up there
can carry the whole array of double-axes home!
Whoever misses the bird but still hits the cord—   950
he's the loser, true, but he takes the single heads."

Teucer the master archer rose to meet the challenge,
Meriones joined him, Idomeneus' rough-and-ready aide.
They dropped lots in a bronze helmet, shook it hard
and the lot fell to Teucer to shoot first . . .
He quickly loosed an arrow, full-draw force
but never swore to the Archer
he'd slaughter splendid victims, newborn lambs,
so he missed the dove—Apollo grudged him that—
but he hit the cord that tethered the bird's foot,   960
the tearing arrow split the cord straight through
and the bird shot into the sky and left the tether
dangling down to ground. The armies roared applause.
But already clutching a shaft while Teucer aimed
Meriones leapt to snatch the bow from his hand
and quickly swore to the distant deadly Archer
he'd slaughter splendid victims, newborn lambs—
Up under the clouds he glimpsed the fluttering dove
and there as she wheeled he hit her right beneath the wing
and straight through the heart and out the arrow passed,   970
plunged at Meriones' foot and stabbed the earth hard.
The dove settled onto the mast of the dark-prowed ship,
her neck wrenched awry, her beating wings went slack
and life breath flew from her limbs that instant—
down she dropped, a long drop down to the ground.
The armies looked on wonder-struck and marveled.
Meriones carried off the double-axes, all ten,
Teucer took the singles back to his hollow ships.

                                                        Finally
Achilles produced a spear that trailed its long shadow,
a cauldron too, untouched by fire, chased with flowers   980
and worth an ox, and set them down in the ring.
And now the spear-throwers rose up to compete,
Atrides Agamemnon, lord of the far-flung kingdoms,

flanked by Idomeneus' rough-and-ready aide Meriones
but the swift runner Achilles interceded at once:
"Atrides—well we know how far you excel us all:
no one can match your strength at throwing spears,
you are the best by far!
Take first prize and return to your hollow ships
while we award this spear to the fighter Meriones,   990
if that would please your heart. That's what I propose."

And Agamemnon the lord of men could not resist.
Achilles gave the bronze-shod spear to Meriones.
And the winning hero Atrides gave his own prize
to his herald Talthybius—the king's burnished trophy.

BOOK TWENTY-FOUR

Achilles and Priam

The games were over now. The gathered armies scattered,
each man to his fast ship, and fighters turned their minds
to thoughts of food and the sweet warm grip of sleep.
But Achilles kept on grieving for his friend,
the memory burning on . . .
and all-subduing sleep could not take him,
not now, he turned and twisted, side to side,
he longed for Patroclus' manhood, his gallant heart—
What rough campaigns they'd fought to an end together,
what hardships they had suffered, cleaving their way   10
through wars of men and pounding waves at sea.
The memories flooded over him, live tears flowing,
and now he'd lie on his side, now flat on his back,
now facedown again. At last he'd leap to his feet,
wander in anguish, aimless along the surf, and dawn on dawn

flaming over the sea and shore would find him pacing.
Then he'd yoke his racing team to the chariot-harness,
lash the corpse of Hector behind the car for dragging
and haul him three times round the dead Patroclus' tomb,
and then he'd rest again in his tents and leave the body   20
sprawled facedown in the dust. But Apollo pitied Hector—
dead man though he was—and warded all corruption off
from Hector's corpse and round him, head to foot,
the great god wrapped the golden shield of storm
so his skin would never rip as Achilles dragged him on.

And so he kept on raging, shaming noble Hector,
but the gods in bliss looked down and pitied Priam's son.
They kept on urging the sharp-eyed giant-killer Hermes
to go and steal the body, a plan that pleased them all,
but not Hera, Poseidon or the girl with blazing eyes.   30
They clung to their deathless hate of sacred Troy,
Priam and Priam's people, just as they had at first
when Paris in all his madness launched the war.
He offended Athena and Hera—both goddesses.
When they came to his shepherd's fold he favored Love
who dangled before his eyes the lust that loosed disaster.
But now, at the twelfth dawn since Hector's death,
lord Apollo rose and addressed the immortal powers:
"Hard-hearted you are, you gods, you live for cruelty!
Did Hector never burn in your honor thighs of oxen   40
and flawless, full-grown goats? Now you cannot
bring yourselves to save him—even his corpse—
so his wife can see him, his mother and his child,
his father Priam and Priam's people: how they'd rush
to burn his body on the pyre and give him royal rites!
But murderous Achilles—you gods, you *choose* to help Achilles.
That man without a shred of decency in his heart . . .
his temper can never bend and change—like some lion
going his own barbaric way, giving in to his power,
his brute force and wild pride, as down he swoops   50
on the flocks of men to seize his savage feast.
Achilles has lost all pity! No shame in the man,

shame that does great harm or drives men on to good.
No doubt some mortal has suffered a dearer loss than this,
a brother born in the same womb, or even a son . . .
he grieves, he weeps, but then his tears are through.
The Fates have given mortals hearts that can endure.
But this Achilles—first he slaughters Hector,
he rips away the noble prince's life
then lashes him to his chariot, drags him round   60
his beloved comrade's tomb. But why, I ask you?
What good will it do him? What honor will he gain?
Let that man beware, or great and glorious as he is,
we mighty gods will wheel on him in anger—look,
he outrages the senseless clay in all his fury!"

But white-armed Hera flared at him in anger:
"Yes, there'd be some merit even in what *you* say,
lord of the silver bow—if all you gods, in fact,
would set Achilles and Hector high in equal honor.
But Hector is mortal. He sucked a woman's breast.   70
Achilles sprang from a goddess—one I reared myself:
I brought her up and gave her in marriage to a man,
to Peleus, dearest to all your hearts, you gods.
All you gods, you shared in the wedding rites,
and so did you, Apollo—there you sat at the feast
and struck your lyre. What company you keep now,
these wretched Trojans. You—forever faithless!"

But Zeus who marshals the storm clouds warned his queen,
"Now, Hera, don't fly into such a rage at fellow gods.
These two can never attain the same degree of honor.   80
Still, the immortals loved Prince Hector dearly,
best of all the mortals born in Troy . . .
so *I* loved him, at least:
he never stinted with gifts to please my heart.
Never once did my altar lack its share of victims,
winecups tipped and the deep smoky savor. These,
these are the gifts we claim—they are our rights.
But as for stealing courageous Hector's body,

we must abandon the idea—not a chance in the world
behind Achilles' back. For Thetis is always there,   90
his mother always hovering near him night and day.
Now, would one of you gods call Thetis to my presence?—
so I can declare to her my solemn, sound decree:
Achilles must receive a ransom from King Priam,
Achilles must give Hector's body back."

                         So he decreed
and Iris, racing a gale-wind down with Zeus's message,
mid-sea between Samos and Imbros' rugged cliffs
dove in a black swell as groaning breakers roared.
Down she plunged to the bottom fast as a lead weight
sheathed in a glinting lure of wild bull's horn,   100
bearing hooked death to the ravenous fish.
And deep in a hollow cave she came on Thetis.
Gathered round her sat the other immortal sea-nymphs
while Thetis amidst them mourned her brave son's fate,
doomed to die, she knew, on the fertile soil of Troy,
far from his native land. Quick as the wind now
Iris rushed to the goddess, urging, "Rise, Thetis—
Zeus with his everlasting counsels calls you now!"
Shifting on her glistening feet, the goddess answered,
"Why . . . what does the great god want with me?   110
I cringe from mingling with the immortals now—
Oh the torment—never-ending heartbreak!
But go I shall. A high decree of the Father
must not come to nothing—whatever he commands."

    The radiant queen of sea-nymphs seized a veil,
blue-black, no robe darker in all the Ocean's depths,
and launched up and away with wind-swift Iris leading—
the ground swell round them cleaved and opened wide.
And striding out on shore they soared to the high sky
and found farseeing Zeus, and around him all the gods   120
who live in bliss forever sat in a grand assembly.
And Thetis took a seat beside the Father,
a throne Athena yielded. Hera placed in her hand
a burnished golden cup and said some words of comfort,

and taking a few quick sips, Thetis gave it back . . .
The father of men and gods began to address them:
"You have come to Olympus now, immortal Thetis,
for all your grief—what unforgettable sorrow
seizes on your heart. I know it well myself.
Even so, I must tell you why I called you here.   130
For nine whole days the immortals have been feuding
over Hector's corpse and Achilles scourge of cities.
They keep urging the sharp-eyed giant-killer Hermes
to go and steal the body. But that is not my way.
I will grant Achilles glory and so safeguard
your awe and love of me for all the years to come.
Go at once to the camp, give your son this order:
tell him the gods are angry with him now
and I am rising over them all in deathless wrath
that he in heartsick fury still holds Hector's body,   140
there by his beaked ships, and will not give him back—
perhaps in fear of me he'll give him back at once.
Then, at the same time, I am winging Iris down
to greathearted Priam, commanding the king
to ransom his dear son, to go to Achaea's ships,
bearing gifts to Achilles, gifts to melt his rage."

                                            So he decreed
and Thetis with her glistening feet did not resist a moment.
Down the goddess flashed from the peaks of Mount Olympus,
made her way to her son's camp, and there he was,
she found him groaning hard, choked with sobs.   150
Around him trusted comrades swung to the work,
preparing breakfast, steadying in their midst
a large fleecy sheep just slaughtered in the shelter.
But his noble mother, settling down at his side,
stroked Achilles gently, whispering his name: "My child—
how long will you eat your heart out here in tears and torment?
All wiped from your mind, all thought of food and bed?
It's a welcome thing to make love with a woman . . .
You don't have long to live now, well I know:
already I see them looming up beside you—death   160
and the strong force of fate. Listen to me,

quickly! I bring you a message sent by Zeus:
he says the gods are angry with you now
and he is rising over them all in deathless wrath
that you in heartsick fury still hold Hector's body,
here by your beaked ships, and will not give him back.
O give him back at once—take ransom for the dead!"

The swift runner replied in haste, "So be it.
The man who brings the ransom can take away the body,
if Olympian Zeus himself insists in all earnest."   170

While mother and son agreed among the clustered ships,
trading between each other many winged words,
Father Zeus sped Iris down to sacred Troy:
"Quick on your way now, Iris, shear the wind!
Leave our Olympian stronghold—
take a message to greathearted Priam down in Troy:
he must go to Achaea's ships and ransom his dear son,
bearing gifts to Achilles, gifts to melt his rage.
But let him go alone, no other Trojan attend him,
only a herald with him, a seasoned, older one   180
who can drive the mules and smooth-running wagon
and bring the hero's body back to sacred Troy,
the man that brilliant Achilles killed in battle.
Let him have no fear of death, no dread in his heart,
such a powerful escort we will send him—the giant-killer
Hermes will guide him all the way to Achilles' presence.
And once the god has led him within the fighter's shelter,
Achilles will not kill him—he'll hold back all the rest:
Achilles is no madman, no reckless fool, not the one
to defy the gods' commands. Whoever begs his mercy   190
he will spare with all the kindness in his heart."

So he decreed
and Iris ran his message, racing with gale force
to Priam's halls where cries and mourning met her.
Sons huddled round their father deep in the courtyard,
robes drenched with tears, and the old man amidst them,
buried, beaten down in the cloak that wrapped his body . . .

Smeared on the old man's head and neck the dung lay thick
that he scraped up in his own hands, groveling in the filth.
Throughout the house his daughters and sons' wives wailed,
remembering all the fine brave men who lay dead now,   200
their lives destroyed at the fighting Argives' hands.
And Iris, Zeus's crier, standing alongside Priam,
spoke in a soft voice, but his limbs shook at once—
"Courage, Dardan Priam, take heart! Nothing to fear.
No herald of doom, I come on a friendly mission—
I come with all good will.
I bring you a message sent by Zeus, a world away
but he has you in his heart, he pities you now . . .
Olympian Zeus commands you to ransom royal Hector,
to bear gifts to Achilles, gifts to melt his rage.   210
But you must go alone, no other Trojan attend you,
only a herald with you, a seasoned, older one
who can drive the mules and smooth-running wagon
and bring the hero's body back to sacred Troy,
the man that brilliant Achilles killed in battle.
But have no fear of death, no dread in your heart,
such a powerful escort will conduct you—the giant-killer
Hermes will guide you all the way to Achilles' presence.
And once the god has led you within the fighter's shelter,
Achilles will not kill you—he'll hold back all the rest: 220
Achilles is no madman, no reckless fool, not the one
to defy the gods' commands. Whoever begs his mercy
he will spare with all the kindness in his heart!"

And Iris racing the wind went veering off
and Priam ordered his sons to get a wagon ready,
a good smooth-running one, to hitch the mules
and strap a big wicker cradle across its frame.
Then down he went himself to his treasure-chamber,
high-ceilinged, paneled, fragrant with cedarwood
and a wealth of precious objects filled its chests.   230
He called out to his wife, Hecuba, "Dear woman!
An Olympian messenger came to me from Zeus—
I must go to Achaea's ships and ransom our dear son,

bearing gifts to Achilles, gifts to melt his rage.
Tell me, what should I do? What do *you* think?
Myself—a terrible longing drives me, heart and soul,
down to the ships, into the vast Achaean camp."

But his wife cried out in answer, "No, no—
where have your senses gone?—that made you famous once,
both among outland men and those you rule in Troy!   240
How can you think of going down to the ships, alone,
and face the glance of the man who killed your sons,
so many fine brave boys? You have a heart of iron!
If he gets you in his clutches, sets his eyes on you—
that savage, treacherous man—he'll show no mercy,
no respect for your rights!

                    Come, all we can do now
is sit in the halls, far from our son, and wail for Hector . . .
So this, this is the doom that strong Fate spun out,
our son's life line drawn with his first breath—
the moment I gave him birth—   250
to glut the wild dogs, cut off from his parents,
crushed by the stronger man. Oh would to god
that I could sink my teeth in his liver, eat him raw!
That would avenge what he has done to Hector—
no coward the man Achilles killed—my son stood
and fought for the men of Troy and their deep-breasted wives
with never a thought of flight or run for cover!"

But the old and noble Priam answered firmly,
"I will go. My mind's made up. Don't hold me back.
And don't go flying off on your own across the halls,   260
a bird of evil omen—you can't dissuade me now.
If someone else had commanded me, some mortal man,
some prophet staring into the smoke, some priest,
I'd call it a lie and turn my back upon it.
Not now. I heard her voice with my own ears,
I looked straight at the goddess, face-to-face.
So I am going—her message must not come to nothing.
And if it is my fate to die by the beaked ships

of Achaeans armed in bronze, then die I shall.
Let Achilles cut me down straightway—   270
once I've caught my son in my arms and wept my fill!"

He raised back the carved lids of the chests
and lifted out twelve robes, handsome, rich brocades,
twelve cloaks, unlined and light, as many blankets,
as many big white capes and shirts to go with them.
He weighed and carried out ten full bars of gold
and took two burnished tripods, four fine cauldrons
and last a magnificent cup the Thracians gave him once—
he'd gone on an embassy and won that priceless treasure—
but not even *that* did the old man spare in his halls,   280
not now, consumed with desire to ransom back his son.
Crowds of Trojans were mobbing his colonnades—
he gave them a tongue-lashing, sent them packing:
"Get out—you good-for-nothings, public disgraces!
Haven't you got enough to wail about at home
without coming here to add to all my griefs?
You think it nothing, the pain that Zeus has sent me?—
he's destroyed my best son! You'll learn too, in tears—
easier game you'll be for Argive troops to slaughter,
now my Hector's dead. But before I have to see   290
my city annihilated, laid waste before my eyes—
oh let me go down to the House of Death!"

He herded them off with his staff—they fled outside
before the old man's fury. So he lashed out at his sons,
cursing the sight of Helenus, Paris, noble Agathon,
Pammon, Antiphonus, Polites loud with the war cry,
Deiphobus and Hippothous, even lordly Dius—
the old man shouted at all nine, rough commands:
"Get to your work! My vicious sons—my humiliations!
If only you'd all been killed at the fast ships   300
instead of my dear Hector . . .
But I—dear god, my life so cursed by fate!—
I fathered hero sons in the wide realm of Troy
and now, now not a single one is left, I tell you.

Mestor the indestructible, Troilus, passionate horseman
and Hector, a god among men—no son of a mortal man,
he seemed a deathless god's. But Ares killed them all
and all he left me are these, these disgraces—liars,
dancers, heroes only at beating the dancing-rings,
you plunder your own people for lambs and kids!   310
Why don't you get my wagon ready—now, at once?
Pack all these things aboard! We must be on our way!"

    Terrified by their father's rough commands
the sons trundled a mule-wagon out at once,
a good smooth-running one,
newly finished, balanced and bolted tight,
and strapped a big wicker cradle across its frame.
They lifted off its hook a boxwood yoke for the mules,
its bulging pommel fitted with rings for guide-reins,
brought out with the yoke its yoke-strap nine arms long   320
and wedged the yoke down firm on the sanded, tapered pole,
on the front peg, and slipped the yoke-ring onto its pin,
strapped the pommel with three good twists, both sides,
then lashed the assembly round and down the shaft
and under the clamp they made the lashing fast.
Then the priceless ransom for Hector's body:
hauling it up from the vaults they piled it high
on the wagon's well-made cradle, then they yoked the mules—
stamping their sharp hoofs, trained for heavy loads—
that the Mysians once gave Priam, princely gifts.   330
And last they yoked his team to the king's chariot,
stallions he bred himself in his own polished stalls.

    No sooner were both men harnessed up beneath the roofs,
Priam and herald, minds set on the coming journey,
than Hecuba rushed up to them, gaunt with grief,
her right hand holding a golden cup of honeyed wine
so the men might pour libations forth at parting.
She stood in front of the horses, crying up at Priam,
"Here, quickly—pour a libation out to Father Zeus!
Pray for a safe return from all our mortal enemies,   340

seeing you're dead set on going down to the ships—
though you go against my will. But if go you must,
pray, at least, to the great god of the dark storm cloud,
up there on Ida, gazing down on the whole expanse of Troy!
Pray for a bird of omen, Zeus's wind-swift messenger,
the dearest bird in the world to his prophetic heart,
the strongest thing on wings—clear on the right
so you can see that sign with your own eyes
and trust your life to *it* as you venture down
to Achaea's ships and the fast chariot-teams.   350
But if farseeing Zeus does *not* send you that sign—
his own messenger—then I urge you, beg you,
don't go down to the ships—
not for all the passion in your heart!"

The old majestic Priam gave his answer:
"Dear woman, surely I won't resist your urging now.
It's well to lift our hands and ask great Zeus for mercy."

And the old king motioned a steward standing by
to pour some clear pure water over his hands,
and she came forward, bearing a jug and basin.   360
He rinsed his hands, took the cup from his wife
and taking a stand amidst the forecourt, prayed,
pouring the wine to earth and scanning the high skies,
Priam prayed in his rich resounding voice: "Father Zeus!
Ruling over us all from Ida, god of greatness, god of glory!
Grant that Achilles will receive me with kindness, mercy.
Send me a bird of omen, your own wind-swift messenger,
the dearest bird in the world to your prophetic heart,
the strongest thing on wings—clear on the right
so I can see that sign with my own eyes   370
and trust my life to *it* as I venture down
to Achaea's ships and the fast chariot-teams!"

And Zeus in all his wisdom heard that prayer
and straightaway the Father launched an eagle—
truest of Zeus's signs that fly the skies—

the dark marauder that mankind calls the Black-wing.
Broad as the door of a rich man's vaulted treasure-chamber,
well-fitted with sturdy bars, so broad each wing of the bird
spread out on either side as it swept in through the city
flashing clear on the right before the king and queen.   380
All looked up, overjoyed—the people's spirits lifted.

        And the old man, rushing to climb aboard his chariot,
drove out through the gates and echoing colonnades.
The mules in the lead hauled out the four-wheeled wagon,
driven on by seasoned Idaeus. The horses came behind
as the old man cracked the lash and urged them fast
throughout the city with all his kinsmen trailing . . .
weeping their hearts out, as if he went to his death.
But once the two passed down through crowded streets
and out into open country, Priam's kin turned back,   390
his sons and in-laws straggling home to Troy.
But Zeus who beholds the world could hardly fail
to see the two men striking out across the plain.
As he watched the old man he filled with pity
and quickly summoned Hermes, his own dear son:
"Hermes—escorting men is your greatest joy,
you above all the gods,
and you listen to the wish of those you favor.
So down you go. Down and conduct King Priam there
through Achaea's beaked ships, so none will see him,   400
none of the Argive fighters recognize him now,
not till he reaches Peleus' royal son."
                                        So he decreed
and Hermes the giant-killing guide obeyed at once.
Under his feet he fastened the supple sandals,
never-dying gold, that wing him over the waves
and boundless earth with the rush of gusting winds.
He seized the wand that enchants the eyes of men
whenever Hermes wants, or wakes them up from sleep.
That wand in his grip he flew, the mighty giant-killer
touching down on Troy and the Hellespont in no time   410
and from there he went on foot, for all the world

like a young prince, sporting his first beard,
just in the prime and fresh warm pride of youth.
                                        And now,
as soon as the two drove past the great tomb of Ilus
they drew rein at the ford to water mules and team.
A sudden darkness had swept across the earth
and Hermes was all but on them when the herald
looked up, saw him, shouted at once to Priam,
"Danger, my king—think fast! I see a man—
I'm afraid we'll both be butchered on the spot—   420
into the chariot, hurry! Run for our lives
or fling ourselves at his knees and beg for mercy!"

    The old man was stunned, in a swirl of terror,
the hairs stood bristling all over his gnarled body—
he stood there, staring dumbly. Not waiting for welcome
the running god of luck went straight up to Priam,
clasped the old king's hands and asked him warmly,
"Father—where do you drive these mules and team
through the godsent night while other mortals sleep?
Have you no fear of the Argives breathing hate and fury?   430
Here are your deadly enemies, camping close at hand.
Now what if one of them saw you, rolling blithely on
through the rushing night with so much tempting treasure—
how would you feel then? You're not so young yourself,
and the man who attends you here is far too old
to drive off an attacker spoiling for a fight.
But I would never hurt you—and what's more,
I'd beat off any man who'd do you harm:
you remind me of my dear father, to the life."

    And the old and noble Priam said at once,   440
"Our straits are hard, dear child, as you say.
But a god still holds his hands above me, even me.
Sending such a traveler here to meet me—
what a lucky omen! Look at your build . . .
your handsome face—a wonder. And such good sense—
your parents must be blissful as the gods!"

The guide and giant-killer answered quickly,
"You're right, old man, all straight to the mark.
But come, tell me the truth now, point by point:
this treasure—a king's ransom—do you send it off   450
to distant, outland men, to keep it safe for you?
Or now do you all abandon sacred Troy,
all in panic—such was the man who died,
your finest, bravest man . . . your own son
who never failed in a fight against the Argives.''

But the old majestic Priam countered quickly,
"Who are *you*, my fine friend?—who are your parents?
How can you speak so well of my doomed son's fate?''

And the guide and giant-killer answered staunchly,
"You're testing me, old man—asking of noble Hector.   460
Ah, how often I watched him battling on the lines
where men win glory, saw the man with my own eyes!
And saw him drive Achaeans against the ships that day
he kept on killing, cutting them down with slashing bronze
while we stood by and marveled—Achilles reined us in:
no fighting for us while *he* raged on at Agamemnon.
I am Achilles' aide, you see,
one and the same good warship brought us here.
I am a Myrmidon, and my father is Polyctor,
and a wealthy man he is, about as old as you . . .   470
He has six sons—I'm the seventh—we all shook lots
and it fell to me to join the armies here at Troy.
I've just come up from the ships to scout the plain—
at dawn the fiery-eyed Achaeans fight around the city.
They chafe, sitting in camp, so bent on battle now
the kings of Achaea cannot hold them back.''

And the old and noble Priam asked at once,
"If you really are the royal Achilles' aide,
please, tell *me* the whole truth, point by point.
My son—does he still lie by the beached ships,   480

or by now has the great Achilles hacked him
limb from limb and served him to his dogs?"

   The guide and giant-killer reassured him:
"So far, old man, no birds or dogs have eaten him.
No, there he lies—still there at Achilles' ship,
still intact in his shelters.
This is the twelfth day he's lain there, too,
but his body has not decayed, not in the least,
nor have the worms begun to gnaw his corpse,
the swarms that devour men who fall in battle.   490
True, dawn on fiery dawn he drags him round
his beloved comrade's tomb, drags him ruthlessly
but he cannot mutilate his body. It's marvelous—
go see for yourself how he lies there fresh as dew,
the blood washed away, and no sign of corruption.
All his wounds sealed shut, wherever they struck . . .
and many drove their bronze blades through his body.
Such pains the blissful gods are lavishing on your son,
dead man though he is—the gods love him dearly!"

   And the old man rejoiced at that, bursting out,   500
"O my child, how good it is to give the immortals
fit and proper gifts! Now take my son—
or was he all a dream? Never once in his halls
did he forget the gods who hold Olympus, never,
so now they remember *him* . . . if only after death.
Come, this handsome cup: accept it from me, I beg you!
Protect me, escort me now—if the gods will it so—
all the way till I reach Achilles' shelter."

   The guide and giant-killer refused him firmly,
"You test me again, old man, since I am young,   510
but you will not persuade me,
tempting me with a gift behind Achilles' back.
I fear the man, I'd die of shame to rob him—
just think of the trouble I might suffer later.
But I'd escort you with all the kindness in my heart,

all the way till I reached the shining hills of Argos
bound in a scudding ship or pacing you on foot—
and no marauder on earth, scorning your escort,
would dare attack you then."

                              And the god of luck,
leaping onto the chariot right behind the team,   520
quickly grasped the whip and reins in his hands
and breathed fresh spirit into the mules and horses.
As they reached the trench and rampart round the fleet,
the sentries had just begun to set out supper there
but the giant-killer plunged them all in sleep . . .
he spread the gates at once, slid back the bars
and ushered Priam in with his wagon-load of treasure.
Now, at last, they approached royal Achilles' shelter,
the tall, imposing lodge the Myrmidons built their king,
hewing planks of pine, and roofed it high with thatch,   530
gathering thick shaggy reeds from the meadow banks,
and round it built their king a spacious courtyard
fenced with close-set stakes. A single pine beam
held the gates, and it took three men to ram it home,
three to shoot the immense bolt back and spread the doors—
three average men. Achilles alone could ram it home himself.
But the god of luck now spread the gates for the old man,
drove in the glinting gifts for Peleus' swift son,
climbed down from behind the team and said to Priam,
"Old man, look, I am a god come down to you,   540
I am immortal Hermes—
my Father sent me here to be your escort.
But now I will hasten back. I will not venture
into Achilles' presence: it would offend us all
for a mortal man to host an immortal face-to-face.
But you go in yourself and clasp Achilles' knees,
implore him by his father, his mother with lovely hair,
by his own son—so you can stir his heart!"

                                    With that urging
Hermes went his way to the steep heights of Olympus.
But Priam swung down to earth from the battle-car   550
and leaving Idaeus there to rein in mules and team,

the old king went straight up to the lodge
where Achilles dear to Zeus would always sit.
Priam found the warrior there inside . . .
many captains sitting some way off, but two,
veteran Automedon and the fine fighter Alcimus
were busy serving him. He had just finished dinner,
eating, drinking, and the table still stood near.
The majestic king of Troy slipped past the rest
and kneeling down beside Achilles, clasped his knees   560
and kissed his hands, those terrible, man-killing hands
that had slaughtered Priam's many sons in battle.
Awesome—as when the grip of madness seizes one
who murders a man in his own fatherland and flees
abroad to foreign shores, to a wealthy, noble host,
and a sense of marvel runs through all who see him—
so Achilles marveled, beholding majestic Priam.
His men marveled too, trading startled glances.
But Priam prayed his heart out to Achilles:
"Remember your own father, great godlike Achilles—   570
as old as I am, past the threshold of deadly old age!
No doubt the countrymen round about him plague him now,
with no one there to defend him, beat away disaster.
No one—but at least he hears you're still alive
and his old heart rejoices, hopes rising, day by day,
to see his beloved son come sailing home from Troy.
But I—dear god, my life so cursed by fate . . .
I fathered hero sons in the wide realm of Troy
and now not a single one is left, I tell you.
Fifty sons I had when the sons of Achaea came,   580
nineteen born to me from a single mother's womb
and the rest by other women in the palace. Many,
most of them violent Ares cut the knees from under.
But one, one was left me, to guard my walls, my people—
the one you killed the other day, defending his fatherland,
my Hector! It's all for him I've come to the ships now,
to win him back from you—I bring a priceless ransom.
Revere the gods, Achilles! Pity me in my own right,
remember your own father! I deserve more pity . . .

I have endured what no one on earth has ever done before—   590
I put to my lips the hands of the man who killed my son.''

Those words stirred within Achilles a deep desire
to grieve for his own father. Taking the old man's hand
he gently moved him back. And overpowered by memory
both men gave way to grief. Priam wept freely
for man-killing Hector, throbbing, crouching
before Achilles' feet as Achilles wept himself,
now for his father, now for Patroclus once again,
and their sobbing rose and fell throughout the house.
Then, when brilliant Achilles had had his fill of tears   600
and the longing for it had left his mind and body,
he rose from his seat, raised the old man by the hand
and filled with pity now for his gray head and gray beard,
he spoke out winging words, flying straight to the heart:
''Poor man, how much you've borne—pain to break the spirit!
What daring brought you down to the ships, all alone,
to face the glance of the man who killed your sons,
so many fine brave boys? You have a heart of iron.
Come, please, sit down on this chair here . . .
Let us put our griefs to rest in our own hearts,   610
rake them up no more, raw as we are with mourning.
What good's to be won from tears that chill the spirit?
So the immortals spun our lives that we, we wretched men
live on to bear such torments—the gods live free of sorrows.
There are two great jars that stand on the floor of Zeus's halls
and hold his gifts, our miseries one, the other blessings.
When Zeus who loves the lightning mixes gifts for a man,
now he meets with misfortune, now good times in turn.
When Zeus dispenses gifts from the jar of sorrows only,
he makes a man an outcast—brutal, ravenous hunger   620
drives him down the face of the shining earth,
stalking far and wide, cursed by gods and men.
So with my father, Peleus. What glittering gifts
the gods rained down from the day that he was born!
He excelled all men in wealth and pride of place,
he lorded the Myrmidons, and mortal that he was,

they gave the man an immortal goddess for a wife.
Yes, but even on him the Father piled hardships,
no powerful race of princes born in his royal halls,
only a single son he fathered, doomed at birth,   630
cut off in the spring of life—
and I, I give the man no care as he grows old
since here I sit in Troy, far from my fatherland,
a grief to you, a grief to all your children . . .
And you too, old man, we hear you prospered once:
as far as Lesbos, Macar's kingdom, bounds to seaward,
Phrygia east and upland, the Hellespont vast and north—
that entire realm, they say, you lorded over once,
you excelled all men, old king, in sons and wealth.
But then the gods of heaven brought this agony on you—   640
ceaseless battles round your walls, your armies slaughtered.
You must bear up now. Enough of endless tears,
the pain that breaks the spirit.
Grief for your son will do no good at all.
You will never bring him back to life—
sooner you must suffer something worse."

   But the old and noble Priam protested strongly:
"Don't make me sit on a chair, Achilles, Prince,
not while Hector lies uncared-for in your camp!
Give him back to me, now, no more delay—   650
I must see my son with my own eyes.
Accept the ransom I bring you, a king's ransom!
Enjoy it, all of it—return to your own native land,
safe and sound . . . since now you've spared my life."

   A dark glance—and the headstrong runner answered,
"No more, old man, don't tempt my wrath, not now!
My own mind's made up to give you back your son.
A messenger brought me word from Zeus—my mother,
Thetis who bore me, the Old Man of the Sea's daughter.
And what's more, I can see through you, Priam—   660
no hiding the fact from me: one of the gods

has led you down to Achaea's fast ships.
No man alive, not even a rugged young fighter,
would dare to venture into our camp. Never—
how could he slip past the sentries unchallenged?
Or shoot back the bolt of my gates with so much ease?
So don't anger me now. Don't stir my raging heart still more.
Or under my own roof I may not spare your life, old man—
suppliant that you are—may break the laws of Zeus!"

The old man was terrified. He obeyed the order.   670
But Achilles bounded out of doors like a lion—
not alone but flanked by his two aides-in-arms,
veteran Automedon and Alcimus, steady comrades,
Achilles' favorites next to the dead Patroclus.
They loosed from harness the horses and the mules,
they led the herald in, the old king's crier,
and sat him down on a bench. From the polished wagon
they lifted the priceless ransom brought for Hector's corpse
but they left behind two capes and a finely-woven shirt
to shroud the body well when Priam bore him home.   680
Then Achilles called the serving-women out:
"Bathe and anoint the body—
bear it aside first. Priam must not see his son."
He feared that, overwhelmed by the sight of Hector,
wild with grief, Priam might let his anger flare
and Achilles might fly into fresh rage himself,
cut the old man down and break the laws of Zeus.
So when the maids had bathed and anointed the body
sleek with olive oil and wrapped it round and round
in a braided battle-shirt and handsome battle-cape,   690
then Achilles lifted Hector up in his own arms
and laid him down on a bier, and comrades helped him
raise the bier and body onto the sturdy wagon . . .
Then with a groan he called his dear friend by name:
"Feel no anger at me, Patroclus, if you learn—
even there in the House of Death—I let his father
have Prince Hector back. He gave me worthy ransom
and you shall have your share from me, as always,

your fitting, lordly share."
                    So he vowed
and brilliant Achilles strode back to his shelter,   700
sat down on the well-carved chair that he had left,
at the far wall of the room, leaned toward Priam
and firmly spoke the words the king had come to hear:
"Your son is now set free, old man, as you requested.
Hector lies in state. With the first light of day
you will see for yourself as you convey him home.
Now, at last, let us turn our thoughts to supper.
Even Niobe with her lustrous hair remembered food,
though she saw a dozen children killed in her own halls,
six daughters and six sons in the pride and prime of youth.   710
True, lord Apollo killed the sons with his silver bow
and Artemis showering arrows killed the daughters.
Both gods were enraged at Niobe. Time and again
she placed herself on a par with their own mother,
Leto in her immortal beauty—how she insulted Leto:
'All you have borne is two, but I have borne so many!'
So, two as they were, they slaughtered all her children.
Nine days they lay in their blood, no one to bury them—
Cronus' son had turned the people into stone . . .
then on the tenth the gods of heaven interred them.   720
And Niobe, gaunt, worn to the bone with weeping,
turned her thoughts to food. And now, somewhere,
lost on the crags, on the lonely mountain slopes,
on Sipylus where, they say, the nymphs who live forever,
dancing along the Achelous River run to beds of rest—
there, struck into stone, Niobe still broods
on the spate of griefs the gods poured out to her.

So come—we too, old king, must think of food.
Later you can mourn your beloved son once more,
when you bear him home to Troy, and you'll weep many tears."   730

Never pausing, the swift runner sprang to his feet
and slaughtered a white sheep as comrades moved in
to skin the carcass quickly, dress the quarters well.

Expertly they cut the meat in pieces, pierced them with spits,
roasted them to a turn and pulled them off the fire.
Automedon brought the bread, set it out on the board
in ample wicker baskets. Achilles served the meat.
They reached out for the good things that lay at hand
and when they had put aside desire for food and drink,
Priam the son of Dardanus gazed at Achilles, marveling   740
now at the man's beauty, his magnificent build—
face-to-face he seemed a deathless god . . .
and Achilles gazed and marveled at Dardan Priam,
beholding his noble looks, listening to his words.
But once they'd had their fill of gazing at each other,
the old majestic Priam broke the silence first:
"Put me to bed quickly, Achilles, Prince.
Time to rest, to enjoy the sweet relief of sleep.
Not once have my eyes closed shut beneath my lids
from the day my son went down beneath your hands . . .   750
day and night I groan, brooding over the countless griefs,
groveling in the dung that fills my walled-in court.
But now, at long last, I have tasted food again
and let some glistening wine go down my throat.
Before this hour I had tasted nothing."

                                      He shook his head
as Achilles briskly told his men and serving-women
to make beds in the porch's shelter, to lay down
some heavy purple throws for the beds themselves
and over them spread some blankets, thick woolly robes,
a warm covering laid on top. Torches in hand,   760
they left the hall and fell to work at once
and in no time two good beds were spread and made.
Then Achilles nodded to Priam, leading the king on
with brusque advice: "Sleep outside, old friend,
in case some Achaean captain comes to visit.
They keep on coming now, huddling beside me,
making plans for battle—it's their duty.
But if one saw you here in the rushing dark night
he'd tell Agamemnon straightaway, our good commander.
Then you'd have real delay in ransoming the body.   770

One more point. Tell me, be precise about it—
how many days do you need to bury Prince Hector?
I will hold back myself
and keep the Argive armies back that long."

And the old and noble Priam answered slowly,
"If you truly want me to give Prince Hector burial,
full, royal honors, you'd show me a great kindness,
Achilles, if you would do exactly as I say.
You know how crammed we are inside our city,
how far it is to the hills to haul in timber,   780
and our Trojans are afraid to make the journey.
Well, nine days we should mourn him in our halls,
on the tenth we'd bury Hector, hold the public feast,
on the eleventh build the barrow high above his body—
on the twelfth we'd fight again . . . if fight we must."

The swift runner Achilles reassured him quickly:
"All will be done, old Priam, as you command.
I will hold our attack as long as you require."

With that he clasped the old king by the wrist,
by the right hand, to free his heart from fear.   790
Then Priam and herald, minds set on the journey home,
bedded down for the night within the porch's shelter.
And deep in his sturdy well-built lodge Achilles slept
with Briseis in all her beauty sleeping by his side.

Now the great array of gods and chariot-driving men
slept all night long, overcome by gentle sleep.
But sleep could never hold the running Escort—
Hermes kept on turning it over in his mind . . .
how could he convoy Priam clear of the ships,
unseen by devoted guards who held the gates?   800
Hovering at his head the Escort rose and spoke:
"Not a care in the world, old man? Look at you,
how you sleep in the midst of men who'd kill you—
and just because Achilles spared your life. Now, yes,

you've ransomed your dear son—for a king's ransom.
But wouldn't the sons you left behind be forced
to pay three times as much for *you* alive?
What if Atrides Agamemnon learns you're here—
what if the whole Achaean army learns you're here?"

The old king woke in terror, roused the herald.   810
Hermes harnessed the mules and team for both men,
drove them fast through the camp and no one saw them.

Once they reached the ford where the river runs clear,
the strong, whirling Xanthus sprung of immortal Zeus,
Hermes went his way to the steep heights of Olympus
as Dawn flung out her golden robe across the earth,
and the two men, weeping, groaning, drove the team
toward Troy and the mules brought on the body.
No one saw them at first, neither man nor woman,
none before Cassandra, golden as goddess Aphrodite.   820
She had climbed to Pergamus heights and from that point
she saw her beloved father swaying tall in the chariot,
flanked by the herald, whose cry could rouse the city.
And Cassandra saw *him* too . . .
drawn by the mules and stretched out on his bier.
She screamed and her scream rang out through all Troy:
"Come, look down, you men of Troy, you Trojan women!
Behold Hector now—if you ever once rejoiced
to see him striding home, home alive from battle!
He was the greatest joy of Troy and all our people!"   830

Her cries plunged Troy into uncontrollable grief
and not a man or woman was left inside the walls.
They streamed out at the gates to meet Priam
bringing in the body of the dead. Hector—
his loving wife and noble mother were first
to fling themselves on the wagon rolling on,
the first to tear their hair, embrace his head
and a wailing throng of people milled around them.
And now, all day long till the setting sun went down

they would have wept for Hector there before the gates   840
if the old man, steering the car, had not commanded,
"Let me through with the mules! Soon, in a moment,
you can have your fill of tears—once I've brought him home."

    So he called and the crowds fell back on either side,
making way for the wagon. Once they had borne him
into the famous halls, they laid his body down
on his large carved bed and set beside him singers
to lead off the laments, and their voices rose in grief—
they lifted the dirge high as the women wailed in answer.
And white-armed Andromache led their songs of sorrow,   850
cradling the head of Hector, man-killing Hector
gently in her arms: "O my husband . . .
cut off from life so young! You leave me a widow,
lost in the royal halls—and the boy only a baby,
the son we bore together, you and I so doomed.
I cannot think he will ever come to manhood.
Long before *that* the city will be sacked,
plundered top to bottom! Because you are dead,
her great guardian, you who always defended Troy,
who kept her loyal wives and helpless children safe,   860
all who will soon be carried off in the hollow ships
and I with them—
                And you, my child, will follow me
to labor, somewhere, at harsh, degrading work,
slaving under some heartless master's eye—that,
or some Achaean marauder will seize you by the arm
and hurl you headlong down from the ramparts—horrible death—
enraged at *you* because Hector once cut down his brother,
his father or his son, yes, hundreds of armed Achaeans
gnawed the dust of the world, crushed by Hector's hands!
Your father, remember, was no man of mercy . . .   870
not in the horror of battle, and that is why
the whole city of Troy mourns you now, my Hector—
you've brought your parents accursed tears and grief
but to me most of all you've left the horror, the heartbreak!
For you never died in bed and stretched your arms to me

or said some last word from the heart I can remember,
always, weeping for you through all my nights and days!"

Her voice rang out in tears and the women wailed in answer
and Hecuba led them now in a throbbing chant of sorrow:
"Hector, dearest to me by far of all my sons . . .   880
and dear to the gods while we still shared this life—
and they cared about you still, I see, even after death.
Many the sons I had whom the swift runner Achilles
caught and shipped on the barren salt sea as slaves
to Samos, to Imbros, to Lemnos shrouded deep in mist!
But you, once he slashed away your life with his brazen spear
he dragged you time and again around his comrade's tomb,
Patroclus whom you killed—not that he brought Patroclus
back to life by that. But I have you with me now . . .
fresh as the morning dew you lie in the royal halls   890
like one whom Apollo, lord of the silver bow,
has approached and shot to death with gentle shafts."

Her voice rang out in tears and an endless wail rose up
and Helen, the third in turn, led their songs of sorrow:
"Hector! Dearest to me of all my husband's brothers—
my husband, Paris, magnificent as a god . . .
he was the one who brought me here to Troy—
Oh how I wish I'd died before that day!
But this, now, is the twentieth year for me
since I sailed here and forsook my own native land,   900
yet never once did I hear from *you* a taunt, an insult.
But if someone else in the royal halls would curse me,
one of your brothers or sisters or brothers' wives
trailing their long robes, even your own mother—
not your father, always kind as my own father—
why, you'd restrain them with words, Hector,
you'd win them to my side . . .
you with your gentle temper, all your gentle words.
And so in the same breath I mourn for you and me,
my doom-struck, harrowed heart! Now there is no one left   910

in the wide realm of Troy, no friend to treat me kindly—
all the countrymen cringe from me in loathing!"

Her voice rang out in tears and vast throngs wailed
and old King Priam rose and gave his people orders:
"Now, you men of Troy, haul timber into the city!
Have no fear of an Argive ambush packed with danger—
Achilles vowed, when he sent me home from the black ships,
not to do us harm till the twelfth dawn arrives."

At his command they harnessed oxen and mules to wagons,
they assembled before the city walls with all good speed   920
and for nine days hauled in a boundless store of timber.
But when the tenth Dawn brought light to the mortal world
they carried gallant Hector forth, weeping tears,
and they placed his corpse aloft the pyre's crest,
flung a torch and set it all aflame.
                              At last,
when young Dawn with her rose-red fingers shone once more,
the people massed around illustrious Hector's pyre . . .
And once they'd gathered, crowding the meeting grounds,
they first put out the fires with glistening wine,
wherever the flames still burned in all their fury.   930
Then they collected the white bones of Hector—
all his brothers, his friends-in-arms, mourning,
and warm tears came streaming down their cheeks.
They placed the bones they found in a golden chest,
shrouding them round and round in soft purple cloths.
They quickly lowered the chest in a deep, hollow grave
and over it piled a cope of huge stones closely set,
then hastily heaped a barrow, posted lookouts all around
for fear the Achaean combat troops would launch their attack
before the time agreed. And once they'd heaped the mound   940
they turned back home to Troy, and gathering once again
they shared a splendid funeral feast in Hector's honor,
held in the house of Priam, king by will of Zeus.

And so the Trojans buried Hector breaker of horses.

NOTES

THE GENEALOGY
OF THE ROYAL HOUSE
OF TROY

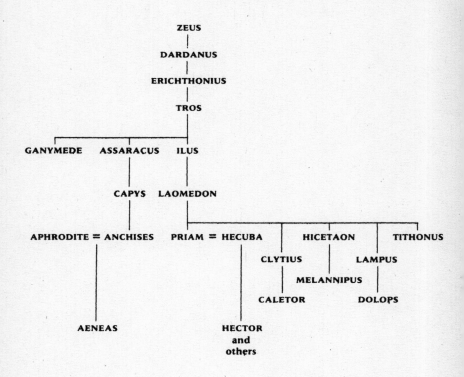

TEXTUAL VARIANTS FROM
THE OXFORD CLASSICAL TEXT

(Here and throughout the Pronouncing Glossary that follows, line numbers refer to the translation, where the line numbers of the Greek text will be found at the top of every page.)

1.1 *Goddess:* the Muse who personifies the inspiration for epic poetry.

1.1 *Peleus' son Achilles:* Achilles is the son of a mortal father and a divine mother, the sea goddess Thetis. Zeus was once in love with her but was warned that she would bear a son stronger than his father. So it was decided that she should wed a mortal. (See 18.97–101, 504–7, 24.72–76, 625–27, and note 24.35–36.) She later departed from Peleus, however, and went to live with her father, the Old Man of the Sea. According to one legend, she had attempted to make Achilles immortal by dipping him, as a child, in the water of the river Styx. But the heel by which she held him remained vulnerable, and it was there that later the arrow of Paris found its mark. See notes 19.494, 24.545.

1.45 *Smintheus:* ancient commentators disagreed about the meaning of this name of Apollo. Some derived it from Sminthe, a nearby town; others from the Mysian (non-Greek) word (*sminthos*) = mouse, and it is known that there was a festival in Rhodes called *Smintheia*, in honor of Apollo and Dionysus because they were thought to kill the mice that damaged the new vines.

1.53 *The arrows clanged at his back:* the arrows of Apollo are a metaphor for the onset of a plague.

1.273 *This scepter:* the scepter is passed by the heralds to anyone in the assembly who wishes to speak—while he holds it, he has the floor. It is a symbol of royal and divine authority, and also stands for the rule of law and due process in the community. It is not the same as Agamemnon's own royal scepter (2.118–26), which has come down to him from Zeus through several generations of Argive kings.

1.312 *Centaurs:* the Centaurs were a race of (literally) horse-men: half horse, half man. They were feared for their violence—all except one, Chiron, who was a healer and taught many heroes (see 4.251–52), including Achilles (see 11. 992–94), the arts of medicine.

1.470–83 *Your claims in father's halls:* this story of the near defeat of Zeus by Hera, Poseidon and Athena (incidentally, they are the three gods most passionately hostile to Troy in the *Iliad*) is unique in the rich variety of myths about the Olympian gods in that Zeus is almost defeated. It seems likely that Homer invented the story himself, to provide Thetis with a claim on Zeus's gratitude.

1.505 *Ocean River:* in the Homeric imagination, Ocean is a river that, rising from sources in the west, encircles the whole world. All the rivers of the world flow from it, connected often by subterranean channels. See Introduction, p. 63.

1.534–58 *The sacrifice for Apollo:* what happens in the following passage is a sacrifice to the gods which is also a feast for the human worshippers (this was the way meat was eaten in the ancient world). The cattle are arranged around the altar, and the sacrificers wash their hands to establish purity for the ritual. They scatter barley on the victims, then pull back their heads and cut their throats over the altar. The animal's skin is then taken off and a portion prepared for the gods. This is a choice portion, the meat of the thighbones: it is wrapped in a double fold of fat and the outside covered with small pieces of meat from different parts of the animal. This portion is then burned over the fire—the smoke and savor go up to the gods above. Wine is poured over it, a libation. The sacrificers then begin their meal—with the entrails, which they have roasted on forks over the fire. They then carve the carcass and roast portions of meat on spits and set them out for the feast.

1.596 *Crouching down at his feet:* Thetis assumes the position of the suppliant—kneeling, clasping the knees of the person supplicated, reaching up to his (or her) chin. It is a gesture that symbolizes the utter helplessness of the suppliant, his abject dependence, but at the same time applies a physical and moral constraint on the person so addressed. (See Introduction, p. 52.) The Greeks believed that Zeus was the protector and champion of suppliants.

1.712 *He seized my foot:* Hephaestus, the smith-god, is lame. This may be a reflection of the fact that in a community where agriculture and war are the predominant features in the life of its men, someone with weak legs and strong arms would probably become a blacksmith. He seems to have been lame from birth: at 18.461–64 he says that his mother, Hera, threw him out of Olympus because of this defect. The fall referred to here was probably a consequence of his attempt to help Hera when Zeus had hung her up from Mount Olympus with a pair of anvils tied to her feet. See 15.23–31 and note 18.462.

1.715 *The mortals there:* Homer identifies them as the Sintians. Lemnos was a center of the cult of Hephaestus; it was an island noted for its volcanic gas.

2.86 *Time-honored custom:* the Greek word used here, *themis*, describes conduct that is usual and proper. It seems unlikely that commanders normally made a discouraging, not to say despairing, speech to their troops when preparing to take the offensive, but that is what the word suggests.

2.121 *The giant-killing Guide:* in the Greek, two regular epithets of Hermes. He is called the guide or escort (the meaning of the word is disputed) because he is often sent by Zeus to act in that role, as in Book 24, when he escorts Priam to the tent of Achilles. The other epithet refers to the fact that, at the request of Zeus, he killed a monster of immense strength called Argos, who had eyes all over his body, so that he could keep some of them open when he slept. He was killed because Hera had sent him to guard Io, a woman Zeus was in love with, whom Hera had changed into a cow.

2.130 *Madness, blinding ruin:* the Greek word for this is *Atê*. The meanings of the word range from "delusion," "infatuation," "madness," to the "ruin," "disaster," "doom" that the mood can bring about. In 19.106–57 *Atê* is personified: Zeus, led astray by her, threw her out of Olympus, so that now she works among men. See Introduction, pp. 50, 54.

2.422–23 *Payment in full for the groans . . . / we have all borne for Helen:* the line could refer to vengeance for the struggles and groans *of* Helen—a vision of Helen as an unwilling victim of Paris, which is not found elsewhere in the poem. The ancient critic Aristarchus understood it to mean "the struggles and groans because of Helen," and we have followed his interpretation.

2.529 *Her awesome shield of storm:* this is the aegis (literally "goatskin"). It is sometimes displayed by Zeus himself, and by Apollo, as well as by Athena. Its shape is not easily determined from the text: at one point it seems to be a shield, for the figure of the Gorgon's head and other forms of terror appear on it. In any case, its effect seems to be to stiffen morale in the armies it is raised to protect and inspire terror in those who face it.

2.748 Heracles is the greatest of the Greek heroes; he eventually, after his death, became an immortal god. He was the son of Zeus and a mortal woman, Alcmena (14.387–88). Zeus intended that he should "lord it over all who dwell around him," but Zeus's jealous wife, Hera, contrived to have that destiny conferred on Eurystheus, king of Argos, to whom Heracles was to be subject (19.112–57). At Eurystheus' command, Heracles performed the famous twelve labors: among them was the capture of the three-headed dog, Cerberus, the guardian of the entrance to the underworld (8.419–21). For the story of his sack of Troy, many years before the Trojan War, see 14.300–8, 5.733–38 and note ad loc. Homer refers twice to his participation in battles at Pylos (5.446–62, 11.818–19): the passage in Book 5 has him wounding Hera and Hades, a story that does not appear elsewhere and that Homer may have invented (see note 5.434–62). Homer attributes Heracles' death to "Hera's savage anger" (18.141, see note 15.32–39), but in other poets' versions of his death Hera plays no part.

2.826 *The Argives would recall Philoctetes:* this refers to a well-known story about the final phase of the war. The Achaeans, unable to take Troy, learned of a prophecy that they would be able to do so only with the aid of Philoctetes and his bow, a famous weapon that he had inherited from Heracles. They had to send an embassy to Lemnos to persuade him to come and help them. This embassy is the subject of Sophocles' tragedy *Philoctetes*.

2.858 *Oath-stream of the gods:* the river Styx, the main river of the underworld, was the guarantor of oaths sworn by the gods. Any one of the gods, Hesiod tells us (*Theogony* 793–806), who pours a libation of the river's water and swears falsely is paralyzed for one year and for nine years after that is excluded from the feasts and assemblies of the gods.

3.77–81 *The lovely gifts / of golden Aphrodite:* see note 24.35–36 concerning the Judgment of Paris.

3.118 *Such limited vengeance:* we follow here the interpretation of *algos* ("hurt") and *phroneô* ("I intend") suggested by Kirk on 3.97–110 of the Greek (1985, pp. 276–77).

3.174 *The Scaean Gates:* not only the main gates of Troy but the scene of several lethal actions, including the death of Achilles beyond the compass of the poem but foreseen by Hector at 22.424.

3.247 *Once in the past:* in a last-minute attempt to avoid the war, Menelaus and Odysseus came to address the Trojan assembly, urging them to restore Helen to her husband. The Trojans refused; furthermore, as we learn later (11.161–64), one of them, Antimachus, even told the assembly that they should kill Menelaus then and there.

3.332 *You beneath the ground:* presumably the Furies. See 19.305–6.

3.386 *Greaves:* tin or leather armor that covered the leg below the knee, worn by fighters to protect them from arrows and salvos of rocks and also from being chafed by the lower edge of their shields. See 6.136–37.

4.8 *Boeotian Athena, guard of armies:* Athena here (and at 5.1052) is given an epithet that connects her with her cult at Alalcomenae in Boeotia.

4.24 *Plotting Troy's destruction:* for Hera's and Athena's hatred of Troy, see Introduction, p. 41, and note 24.35–36.

4.117 *Wolf-god: Lukêgenês* in Greek—its meaning is disputed. *Lukos* is the normal Greek word for "wolf," but some scholars would rather connect the title with the place name Lycia (*Lukia* in Greek).

4.345–56 Nestor's speech to his charioteers seems to envisage a charge against the enemy, something that never happens in the poem. The passage seems to preserve the memory of a time when massed chariot charges were the decisive element in land battles. See Introduction, p. 25, and note 12.61–64.

4.432 *Passageways of battle:* the Greek words are not fully understood. The word rendered "passageways" means "bridges" in later Greek: elsewhere in Homer it seems to mean something like "embankments" or "causeways." An ancient note explains it as "ways through the battle lines"—the clear spaces between the ranks or formations of troops.

4.433–66 *Tydeus:* the father of Diomedes was one of the Seven against Thebes and was killed in the unsuccessful assault on the city. Here we are given a story of a previous visit to Thebes, in which he came off victorious. The story is repeated, with some differences of detail, at 5.921–31 and referred to at 10.334–41. See notes 4.472, 5.926.

4.459–60 The Greek names translated as "Hunter," "Bloodlust," etc. are probably "significant names": i.e., names invented or selected by the poet for their obvious suggestiveness (e.g., "Bloodlust" in Greek is *Haimon* and the Greek word for blood is *haima*). See note 18.43–56.

4.472 We *are the ones:* after the failure of the assault by the Seven against Thebes, their sons, among them Diomedes and Sthenelus, attacked the city in their turn, this time successfully.

4.597 *Third-born of the gods:* this is a literal rendering of Athena's title *Tritogeneia*, but the meaning of the word is disputed. Some ancient sources connect it with Lake Tritonis in Libya, where Zeus sent Athena to be reared, or with the river Triton in Boeotia. A modern explanation compares the Athenian *Tritopateres*, i.e., genuine ancestors: this would give the meaning "genuine daughter of Zeus."

5.1ff. From time to time Homer inserts, in his account of the general melee, the preeminent deeds of one particular hero: such an excursus is known as an *aristeia* (from the Greek word *aristos*, "best"). Book 5 and the opening section of Book 6 constitute the *aristeia* of Diomedes: it is the longest and most murderous of all, except for that of Achilles in Books 20–22.

5.5 *The star that flames at harvest:* the Dog Star, Sirius; see note 22.35.

5.294 *Ganymede:* one of the three sons of Tros, the first king of Troy. He was "the handsomest mortal man on earth" (20.269), and Zeus carried him off to Olympus to be the cup-bearer and wine-pourer of the gods. For the genealogy of the Trojan royal line, see Aeneas' account in 20.248–79, note ad loc and the Genealogy, p. 617.

5.434–62 Dione comforts Aphrodite by pointing out that she is not the only god to be wounded by a mortal. Ares was imprisoned in a bronze cauldron by the young giants Ephialtes and Otus, and almost died before he was rescued by Hermes. Hera and Hades, the Death-god, were both wounded by Heracles, Hades apparently in the course of a battle at Pylos. None of these legends appears in other sources, and the ancient commentators were evidently puzzled by them. Homer may have invented them for the occasion. See note 2.748.

5.733–38 *What they say of mighty Heracles:* Heracles rescued the daughter of Laomedon, Hesione, from a sea monster sent by Poseidon. His reward was to be the famous horses of Laomedon, but the king refused to pay. Heracles took and sacked the city.

5.859–61 *The gates of heaven:* i.e., of Olympus, the house of the gods, consist, naturally enough, of clouds, and clouds are thought of as controlled by the Seasons of the year. So here they are, so to speak, the gate-keepers.

5.926 *The message into Thebes:* Adrastus, king of Argos, gave shelter to Polynices, son of Oedipus of Thebes, and organized an army (led by seven champions, the "Seven against Thebes") to restore him to the throne of Thebes, from which he had been expelled by his brother Eteocles. Tydeus, later one of the Seven, was sent with a demand that Eteocles give up his throne to Polynices.

5.976 *Helmet of Death:* this helmet, which made its wearer invisible, is attributed to the Death-god, Hades, because his name in Greek, *Aïdēs*, was thought to mean "the unseen one" (*a* = "not," and the root **id* = "see").

5.1017–18 *You gave her birth / from your own head:* according to legend, Zeus made love with Metis, a Titaness; she conceived a daughter, and Mother Earth prophesied that if Metis conceived again she would bear a son, who would dethrone his father. So Zeus swallowed her whole and then was seized with a raging headache; Hephaestus split his skull with an ax, and Athena sprang to light, full-blown, from Zeus's forehead.

6.153 *Maenads:* literally "madwomen." They are the female devotees of the god Dionysus, who range the hills in ecstasy, carrying the thyrsus (the "sacred stave"), a staff wreathed with ivy and topped by a pine cone.

6.157–60 *And Dionysus was terrified:* Homer's picture of a frightened Dionysus taking refuge with Thetis is very different from the terrifying figure of the god presented in Euripides' play *The Bacchae*.

6.385 *This anger:* commentators have wondered why Paris should be angry and proposed various solutions (for example, that the anger is that of the Trojans against Paris), but Paris' reply "from anger . . . at our people" (396–97) is clear enough. Hector thinks Paris is sulking because he senses the resentment of his fellow Trojans and is angry with them.

7.386–95 *A single great barrow . . . a landward wall:* see 7.503–11, 12.4–42, Introduction, p. 38, and notes 9.78, 14.35–44.

7.523–25 *Those ramparts I and Apollo / reared for Troy in the old days:* Apollo and Poseidon, as a punishment for their part in a revolt against Zeus, were sent to work for a year at the orders of Laomedon, king of Troy, Priam's father. While Apollo acted as a shepherd to the king's flocks, Poseidon built a wall around the city. At the end of the year, Laomedon cheated the two gods of the wages he had promised. Poseidon reminds Apollo of this in 21.505–22.

8.45 *Nothing I said was meant in earnest:* Zeus tones down the violence of his previous statement to the gods as he speaks to his favorite daughter, but of course he has not changed his mind.

8.82 *Fates of death:* the Greek word is *kêrês*. A *kêr* was a man's individual fate, especially his death. Sometimes the word is used impersonally to mean death or doom, and sometimes a *kêr* is a personified spirit of death, as on the shield of Achilles, 18.623.

8.149 *Irreversible chaos:* because Zeus's promise to Thetis would have been broken, the will of Zeus thwarted, if Diomedes' triumphant advance had continued.

8.331 *Tripod:* a large pot or cauldron standing on three legs so it can straddle a fire. Often highly ornamented for presentation as a gift or prize, its metal construction made it unusually valuable and rare.

8.399 *Or Ares':* we translate the reading of the ancient critic Zenodotus (*êe* = "or") rather than the reading of most manuscripts, and the Oxford Classical Text (*êde* = "and"), at line 349 in the Greek.

8.554 *Cronus and Iapetus:* the two most important of the Titans, the family of the gods that ruled before Zeus and the Olympians. (Cronus was the father of Zeus, Iapetus of Prometheus.) Zeus and his brothers and sisters overthrew Cronus and the Titans in a ten years' war: the Titans were all confined in Tartarus, the lowest depths of the world of the dead. See note 14.244.

9.73–75 These lines (63–64 in the Greek), obviously proverbial in expression, have been thought out of place here: what is their exact reference? And why the mention of civil war? But Nestor, though he must press Agamemnon to make a conciliatory move toward Achilles, must not go too far: Agamemnon is still a powerful king, a dangerous enemy. So his remarks are general—he could be attributing the danger of dissension, even fighting, among the Achaeans to Achilles, to Agamemnon, or to both of them.

9.78 *The trench we dug outside the rampart:* Homer's description of the wall and the ditch is unclear, even confusing at times. Here it seems that the Achaeans had left a level space between the rampart and the ditch: it is in this that the sentries are to take their posts.

9.176 *Bride-price:* expensive gifts offered by the suitor to the bride's father. This seems to have been the normal custom in heroic times (see, for example, 16.209, 16.225 and 22.555), but it is here combined with the later custom—a dowry offered by the bride's father.

9.505 *Death will not come on me quickly:* this line, which repeats in different wording the thought of the previous line, was condemned by two of the great Alexandrian editors of the *Iliad*, Zenodotus and Aristarchus, as an interpolation.

9.558–62 These lines (458–61 in the Greek) are not to be found in the manuscript tradition. Plutarch, writing in the first century A.D., quotes them and adds that Aristarchus, the most severe of the Alexandrian editors, expunged them, because he was shocked by them (if that is what Plutarch's word *phobētheis* means in this context).

9.646–729 The story of Meleager, as we know it from later sources, is very different from Homer's version. Elsewhere (in Aeschylus and Bacchylides, for example) Althaea was told by the fates that her newborn son Meleager would live as long as the log on the fire remained unconsumed. She took it off the fire, extinguished it and hid it in the chest. Later, when, in a quarrel over the spoils of the Calydonian hunt, Meleager killed Althaea's brother, she put the log back in the fire and he died. Homer's account makes Meleager's situation such a close parallel to that of Achilles that critics have suspected that he invented it. (See Introduction, pp. 50–52, and note 9.672.) This suspicion is reinforced by the fact that Cleopatra, who urged him to go back to the battle, as Patroclus does Achilles, has a name consisting of the same two elements as Patroclus' name (*patr-* and *cl-*), in reverse. And Homer goes out of his way to explain that Cleopatra was called by another name—Alcyone (Halcyon)—by her parents.

9.672 *Their own city walls:* the language is confusing here, and interpretation disputed. We have taken the lines to mean that the Aetolians beat the Curetes back to their own walls (as the Achaeans did the Trojans before Achilles withdrew from the battle): this fortifies Phoenix's parallel.

9.679–88 *Marpessa:* Idas and the god Apollo were both in love with Marpessa, and Apollo carried her off. Idas confronted him, and Zeus prevented a fight, asking Marpessa to choose between them. She chose Idas, and called her daughter Halcyon in commemoration of the time she wailed like the seabird on being parted from him.

9.741 *The great decree of Zeus:* we take the phrase *Dios aisēi* (608 in the Greek) in this sense, a reference to Zeus's promise to Thetis to make the Achaeans regret their treatment of Achilles. Other possible interpretations are: " 'by the dispensation of Zeus'; i.e., by [Achilles'] status and position in the world" (Willcock), "by the just measure [of Zeus]" (Leaf), "honored already in Zeus's ordinance" (Lattimore).

9.772 *Accept the blood-price:* see note 18.581–92.

10.325 *The lucky sign:* it was lucky because the heron was on their right hand. This idea that signs on the right are lucky and on the left unlucky is common in many cultures and languages: our word "sinister," for example, is the Latin word for "left." See 12.230–39, 24.377–81.

11.4 *Storm-shield:* Homer does not make it clear exactly what Strife holds in her fists: we suggest that it is the aegis of Zeus. See 5.846–50 and note 2.529.

11.892 *Their real father, Poseidon:* like Heracles and many another Greek hero, the twin Moliones had two fathers, one human and one divine. The Greek has no equivalent of the word "real," but it seemed called for by the situation—it is Poseidon who saves their lives.

12.61–64 There are more confused memories of war-chariots here: obviously a war-chariot pulled by horses could not leap over a wide ditch, though a man on a horse might.

12.205 *Blaze of war:* since fire is not much use against a rock wall, we have taken the Greek phrase as a metaphor.

13.6–8 *A world away:* all these peoples—Thracians, Mysians, Hippemolgi and the Abii—are located to the north of Troy.

13.14 *Samos facing Thrace:* the island usually known as Samothrace, not the large island of Samos off the south-central coast of Asia Minor, or the island off the western coast of Greece, part of Odysseus' kingdom, later known as Cephallenia. See note 24.97.

13.247 *[Poseidon's] own grandson:* i.e., Amphimachus (1), whose death is described in 221–23.

13.632 *The whole vein:* there is of course no such vein. Aristotle, who quotes the passage (*HA* 513b 26–29), identifies it with the *vena cava*, but this vein is not near enough to the surface to be "sheared . . . clear."

13.759–60 *No blood-price came his way . . . in battle:* see note 18.581–92.

13.918 *Fresh reserves just come from Ascania's fertile soil:* this passage does not square with the Catalogue in Book 2, where Ascanius and his contingent are already in place with the Achaean forces. "Once again, the normal accuracy of the poet causes us to notice a small inconsistency" (Willcock, vol. 2, p. 224).

14.35–44 The picture of the Achaean ships berthed on the beach is, at times, somewhat obscure. We have understood the lines to mean that the first ships to land (ten years before) were those of Diomedes, Odysseus and Agamemnon. They had been drawn up on the beach, "far away from the fighting"; a defensive wall was built ahead of their sterns (they were positioned ready for relaunching). This is not of course the same wall as that later built around the whole of the Greek encampment (see note 7.386–95). As the next contingents arrived, they could not be accommodated in the enclosure; their crews dragged them up in rows (presumably on either side of the first ships to land) and filled the whole stretch of the bay.

14.148 *One of Adrastus' daughters:* Tydeus married one of them, Polynices the other (Diomedes, son of Tydeus, married Aegialia, who was, according to some authorities, the daughter, according to others, the granddaughter, of Adrastus).

14.244 *Ocean, fountainhead of the gods, and Mother Tethys:* the word translated "fountainhead" suggests that Ocean and his wife Tethys were the parents of the Olympian gods. This is contrary to the standard version, Hesiod's *Theogony*, an account of the genealogy of the gods, which made Ocean and Tethys children of Uranus and Gaia, like all the Titans. There, Ocean is the father of all the rivers and the springs. During the war of the Olympians and the Titans, Rhea, wife of Cronus and mother of Zeus and Hera, had sent Hera to Ocean and Tethys for safekeeping. See note 8.554.

14.356 *All unknown to their parents:* Zeus and Hera are incestuous brother and sister, both born of Cronus and Rhea, as well as husband and wife, king and queen of the gods.

14.390–91 Demeter bore Zeus a daughter, Persephone, and his children by Leto were Apollo and Artemis.

15.32–39 *Grief for Heracles:* Hera, who hated Heracles and persecuted him throughout his life, since he was the son of Zeus by a mortal woman, Alcmena, had caused a storm to blow him off his course on his return from sacking Troy. See 14.300–16, 18.139–41, 19.112–46, Introduction, p. 42.

16.278–79 *The Selli / sleeping along the ground:* the priests of the oracle of Zeus at Dodona were an ascetic brotherhood, sleeping on the ground and going barefoot, probably to maintain contact with the chthonic deities.

16.715–16 These lines (614–15 in the Greek) are omitted by many of the manuscripts and excised as an interpolation by many editors.

17.623 *His mind had changed, at least for a moment:* i.e., Zeus now gives victory to the Achaeans. Some scholars think it means his mind had changed about allowing the gods to intervene, but that change of mind comes late, in Book 20. "At least for a moment" is not in the Greek but seems justified since in fact Zeus changes his mind again a few lines later (672–75).

18.43–56 *All the Nereids:* the translation attempts to render the Homeric names of the Nereids with reference to their root meanings in the Greek. The translator has followed the lead of William Arrowsmith's excellent version, the first in modern English to treat the passage in this way (*The Craft and Context of Translation*, ed. Arrowsmith and Shattuck [Austin, Tex., 1961], p. 19). In their translations of the *Odyssey*, W. H. D. Rouse (1937) and Robert Fitzgerald (1961) have done the same in rendering the Phaeacian princes' names (8.111–16 in the Greek), all of them fittingly nautical for a seafaring people.

18.462 *My great fall:* it is not clear whether this was the fall described in 1.712–16, or indeed whether Hephaestus' lameness was the result of that fall or a birth defect. The point of the story is simply to provide a reason for his willingness to help Thetis.

18.569–71 *The Wagon:* the constellation also known as the Big Dipper and the Great Bear. As seen from the northern hemisphere, it never disappears below the horizon or, as Homer puts it, "plunge[s] in the Ocean's baths." The Great Bear is referred to as "she" (570) because she was originally the nymph Callisto, who ranged the woods as one of the virgin companions of the goddess Artemis. Zeus made her pregnant, and when this could no longer be concealed, Artemis changed her into a bear and killed her. Zeus in turn changed her into the constellation.

18.581–92 *A quarrel had broken out:* as in many tribal societies, compensation for a killing might be offered to and accepted by the victim's relatives. (See 18.108, 21.32.) If it were not offered, the relatives would pursue the killer to exact blood for blood: his only recourse would be to go into exile, as so many of the Achaean heroes of the *Iliad* did (Patroclus, for example, 23.103–8, and Tlepolemus, 2.756–66). The language in this passage is ambiguous: it may mean that one side offered payment and the other refused (the interpretation we have followed) or that one man claims he has paid and the other disputes his statement.

18.595 *Or share the riches with its people:* i.e., they would cease hostilities if offered half the city's wealth.

18.666 *A dirge for the dying year:* the Greek word is *linos*. This was a dirge, a mourning song, appropriate for vintage time—the end of summer. The name may have come from the Greek expression of sorrow, corresponding to our "Alas!"—*ailinon*. But there was also a mythical figure, Linus, a great musician, who was killed and for whom there were ceremonies of mourning.

19.106 *Ruin, eldest daughter of Zeus:* see note 2.130.

19.145 *Born of your own stock:* Perseus was the son of Zeus and Danaë. See 14.383–84 and note 2.748.

19.494 *Cut down by a deathless god and mortal man:* eventually, beyond the compass of the *Iliad*, Achilles will fall at the hands of Paris. According to legend, Paris is either assisted by Apollo—who guides a fatal arrow to Achilles' right heel, the one vulnerable part of his body—or replaced by the god, who assumes his likeness and shoots Achilles down directly. See 22.422–24 and notes 1.1, 3.174.

20.65–89 The sides taken by the gods are consistent with the sympathies they display throughout the poem. Hera, Athena and Poseidon have aided the Achaeans from the start. (See note 24.35–36.) Hephaestus could be expected on the same side as his mother, Hera, and Hermes, born in a cave on Mount Cyllene in central Greece, naturally favored the Achaeans. Ares, Apollo and, of course, Aphrodite, to whom the Trojan Paris gave the prize in the beauty contest, have supported the Trojans all along. Leto and Artemis are the mother and sister of Apollo, and Xanthus is the principal Trojan river.

20.174 *Sea monster:* see note 5.733–38.

20.220–28 *The time I caught you:* Achilles refers to his capture of Lyrnessus, the town where he acquired Briseis as his share of the booty. See 2.784–88, 19.66–68 and 20.106–8.

20.248–79 Aeneas is to be the only survivor of the royal house of Troy, and here his lineage is established. (See the Genealogy, p. 617.) He will, as Poseidon says (355–56), "rule the men of Troy in power— / his sons' sons and the sons born in future years." But Troy will be destroyed, and not rebuilt: Aeneas' kingdom will be a new foundation. This was to be adopted by the Romans, the conquerors of Greece in the second century B.C., as their own foundation legend: Aeneas, with his son, Ascanius, and a band of Trojans who had escaped from the burning city, sailed west and landed in Italy, where Aeneas' descendants later settled on the site that became the imperial city of Rome. Virgil's great epic, the *Aeneid*, gave this legend its classic form.

20.286 *A ship with a hundred benches:* this would be an impossibly large ship.

21.378–79 *A worthy match:* since Hephaestus is a god whose element is fire, he is the obvious ally to call in against the waters of Scamander.

21.506 *Those troubles we suffered here alongside Troy:* see note 7.523–25.

21.551 *He lets you kill off mothers in their labor:* Artemis, as the goddess who presides over childbirth, causes deaths as well as safe deliveries.

22.35 *Orion's Dog:* the Dog Star, Sirius, is the brightest star in the heavens (the name "Dog" is now reserved for the constellation in which it is seen—*Canis Maior*). This constellation appears to be close to the side of Orion, named after a mythical great hunter. Sirius ushers in the "dog days" of late summer—harvest time and a period of intense heat in Mediterranean countries, and a sickly season for their inhabitants. See 5.5, 11.70.

22.438 *Stab his body:* on the conduct of the Achaeans here, an ancient commentator remarked: "The emotion [of triumph] is that of a low mob, and it magnifies the greatness of the dead man." (Cited from Griffin, p. 47.)

23.86 *The river:* the Styx. See note 2.858.

23.381 *Tight-strung car:* the front of the chariot (and some think the floor as well) consisted of a sort of mat of plaited leather straps.

23.492 *Take the oath:* see lines 646–50, where Menelaus challenges Antilochus to swear an oath that he did not commit a deliberate foul.

23.756 *When Oedipus fell:* the Greek word usually means "fell in battle"—a different fate from that of the hero of Sophocles' play.

24.35–36 *When they came to his shepherd's fold:* a reference to the legend of the Judgment of Paris. When the gods came to celebrate the marriage of Peleus and

Thetis, the goddess Strife threw a golden apple among the guests, announcing that it should be awarded as a prize to the most beautiful of the three goddesses Hera, Athena and Aphrodite. But no god was willing to take the responsibility of judging among them. Zeus finally appointed Paris, then minding his flocks on Mount Ida. All three of the goddesses offered him bribes. Hera promised to make him ruler of all Asia; Athena offered him wisdom and victory in all his battles; Aphrodite offered him the love of Helen, wife of Menelaus, the most beautiful woman in the world. He gave the apple to Aphrodite: the result was the Trojan War, and the undying hatred of Hera and Athena for Troy and the Trojans. (See Introduction, p. 41.) Poseidon hated Troy for a different reason: he had been cheated of his wages for building the walls of Troy by Laomedon, Priam's father. See 21.505–22 and note 7.523–25.

24.97 *Samos:* the island facing Thrace, later called Samothrace.

24.487 *This is the twelfth day:* we translate the reading *hêde* (line 413 in the Greek), not the *êôs* of the Oxford Classical Text.

24.545 *To host an immortal:* though Achilles and his divine mother Thetis do in fact meet face-to-face (1.422–510, 18.82–162), this is not true of most of the encounters of men and gods in the *Iliad*. Men meet the gods in disguise (in Book 13 Poseidon disguises himself as Calchas) or the god comes to men from behind, as Athena does to Achilles in Book 1 and Apollo to Patroclus in Book 16. In older, legendary times, however, men might entertain the gods in special circumstances; Hera, for example, reminds Apollo (at 24.74–76) that he and all the gods came to the wedding feast for the marriage of Peleus and Thetis.

24.613–22 The gods, presumably, are the only beings to receive unmixed portions from the jar of blessings.

24.708–27 *Niobe:* in the usual version of the Niobe legend, she turns into stone like the rock face on Mount Sipylus in Asia Minor, which "weeps"—i.e., water runs down it. Homer adds the detail that the people too are turned into stone to explain why they did not bury the slaughtered children who lay "nine days . . . in their blood." His most telling addition, however, is that Niobe, instead of being turned into stone immediately, dries her eyes, in effect, and turns her thoughts to food—"precisely because," as Willcock puts it, "that is what Achilles wants Priam to do" (vol. 2, p. 319).

24.866 *Hurl you headlong down from the ramparts:* the very fate that, after the fall of Troy, Astyanax would meet. See Introduction, p. 37.

24.899 *The twentieth year for me:* it does not seem likely that Helen and Paris would have taken ten years to get to Troy in the first place and then endured ten years of siege. The expression is probably just an emotional intensification, like our expression "If I've told you once, I've told you a thousand times . . ."

SUGGESTIONS FOR FURTHER READING

I. Texts and Commentaries

Homeri Opera. Ed. by D. B. Monro and T. W. Allen. Vols. I and II. Oxford Classical Texts. London, 1920.

The Iliad. Ed. with apparatus criticus, prolegomena, notes and appendixes by Walter Leaf. 2d ed., 2 vols. London, 1902.

The Iliad of Homer. Ed. with introduction and commentary by M. M. Willcock. 2 vols. London, 1978–84.

Iliad: Book XXIV. Ed. by C. W. MacLeod. Cambridge, England, 1982.

The Iliad: A Commentary. General Ed., G. S. Kirk. Vol. I: Books 1–4, Kirk. Cambridge, England, 1985. Vol. II: Books 5–8, Kirk, 1990. Vol. III: Books 9–12, J. B. Hainsworth, 1993; Vol. IV: Books 13–16, Richard Janko, 1992; Vol. V: Books 17–20, Mark W. Edwards, 1991; Vol. VI: Books 21–24, Nicholas Richardson, 1993.

Iliad: Book IX: Ed. by Jasper Griffin. Cambridge, England, 1995.

II. Critical Works

Atchity, Kenneth J. *Homer's Iliad: The Shield of Memory.* Carbondale, 1978.
——————————. *Critical Essays on Homer.* Boston, 1987.

Adkins, A. W. H. *Merit and Responsibility: A Study in Greek Values.* Oxford, 1960.

Arnold, Matthew. "On Translating Homer." In *On the Classical Tradition,* ed. R. H. Super. Ann Arbor and London, 1960.

Austin, Norman. *Archery at the Dark of the Moon: Poetic Problems in Homer's Odyssey.* Berkeley, Los Angeles and London, 1975.

Bakker, Egbert, and Ahuvia Kahane, eds. *Written Voices, Spoken Signs: Tradition, Performance, and the Epic Text.* Cambridge, Mass., 2000.

Bassett, S. E. *The Poetry of Homer.* Berkeley, 1938.

Beissinger, Margaret, Jane Tylus, and Susanne Wofford, eds. *Epic Traditions in the Contemporary World: The Poetics of Community.* Berkeley, 1999.

Bespaloff, Rachel. *On the Iliad.* Trans. Mary McCarthy. New York, 1947.

Beye, Charles R. *The Iliad, the Odyssey, and the Epic Tradition.* New York and London, 1966.

Bowra, Sir Maurice. *Tradition and Design in the Iliad.* London, 1930.

Bremer, J. M., I. J. F. de Jong, and J. Kalff, eds. *Homer: Beyond Oral Poetry: Recent Trends in Homeric Interpretation*. Amsterdam, 1987.

Camps, W. A. *An Introduction to Homer*. Oxford, 1980.

Carter, Jane B., and Sarah P. Morris, eds. *The Ages of Homer: A Tribute to Emily Townsend Vermeule*. Austin, 1995.

Chadwick, John. *The Mycenaean World*. London and New York, 1976.

Clarke, Howard. *Homer's Readers: A Historical Introduction to the Iliad and the Odyssey*. Newark, Delaware, 1981.

Crotty, Kevin. *The Poetics of Supplication: Homer's Iliad and Odyssey.* Ithaca and London, 1994.

Edwards, Mark W. *Homer: Poet of the Iliad*. Baltimore and London, 1987.

Fenik, Bernard. *Typical Battle Scenes in the Iliad: Studies in the Narrative Techniques of Homeric Battle Description*. Wiesbaden, 1968.

Ferrucci, Franco. *The Poetics of Disguise: The Autobiography of the Work in Homer, Dante, and Shakespeare*. Trans. A. Dunnigan. Ithaca, 1980.

Finley, Sir Moses. *The World of Odysseus*. 2d rev. ed. Harmondsworth, 1979.

Finnegan, Ruth. *Oral Poetry: Its Nature, Significance, and Social Context*. Cambridge, England, 1977.

Ford, Andrew. *Homer: The Poetry of the Past*. Ithaca and London, 1992.

Greene, Thomas M. *The Descent from Heaven: A Study in Epic Continuity*. Chapter 3, "The *Iliad*." New Haven, 1963.

Griffin, Jasper. *Homer*. Oxford, 1980.

——————————. *Homer on Life and Death*. Oxford, 1980.

Guthrie, W. K. C. *The Greeks and Their Gods*. London, 1949; repr. Boston, 1955.

Hainsworth, J. B. *The Flexibility of the Homeric Formula*. Oxford, 1968.

Hogan, James C. *A Guide to the Iliad: Based on the Translation by Robert Fitzgerald*. New York, 1979.

Jenkyns, Richard. *Classical Epic: Homer and Virgil*. Bristol Classical World series. London, 1992.

King, Katherine Callen. *Achilles: Paradigms of the War Hero from Homer to the Middle Ages*. Berkeley, Los Angeles and London, 1987.

Kirk, G. S. *The Songs of Homer*. Cambridge, England, 1962.

Lamberton, Robert. *Homer the Theologian: Neoplatonist Allegorical Reading and the Growth of the Epic Tradition*. Berkeley, Los Angeles and London, 1986.

——————————, and J. J. Keaney, eds. *Homer's Ancient Readers: The Hermeneutics of Greek Epic's Earliest Exegetes*. Princeton, 1992.

Lattimore, Deborah Nourse. *Achilles: Paradigms of the War Hero from Homer to the Middle Ages*. Berkeley, Los Angeles and London, 1987.

Lloyd-Jones, Sir Hugh. *The Justice of Zeus*. 2d ed. Sather Classical Lectures, Vol. 41. Berkeley, Los Angeles and London, 1983.

Lord, Albert. *The Singer of Tales*. Cambridge, Mass., 1960.

Martin, Richard. *The Language of Heroes: Speech and Performance in the Iliad*. Ithaca, 1989.

McAuslan, Ian, and Peter Walcot, eds. *Homer*. Oxford and New York, 1998.

Morris, Ian, and Barry Powell, eds. *A New Companion to Homer.* Leiden and New York, 1997.

Moulton, Carroll. *Similes in the Homeric Poems.* Göttingen, 1977.

Mueller, Martin. *The Iliad.* Unwin Critical Library, ed. Claude Rawson. London, 1984.

Myrsiades, Kostas, ed. *Approaches to Teaching Homer's Iliad and Odyssey.* New York, 1987.

Nagler, Michael. *Spontaneity and Tradition: A Study in the Oral Art of Homer.* Berkeley, Los Angeles and London, 1974.

Nagy, Gregory. *The Best of the Achaeans: Concepts of the Hero in Archaic Greek Poetry.* Baltimore and London, 1979.

Nilsson, M. P. *Homer and Mycenae.* London, 1933.

Otto, Walter F. *The Homeric Gods.* Trans. Moses Hadas. New York and London, 1954.

Page, Sir Denys. *History and the Homeric Iliad.* Sather Classical Lectures, Vol. 31. Berkeley, Los Angeles and London, 1959.

Parry, Adam M. *The Language of Achilles and Other Papers.* Foreword by Sir Hugh Lloyd-Jones. Oxford, 1989.

Parry, Milman. *The Making of Homeric Verse: The Collected Papers of Milman Parry.* Ed. Adam Parry. Oxford, 1971.

Rabel, Robert J. *Plot and Point of View in the Iliad.* Ann Arbor, 1997.

Redfield, J. M. *Nature and Culture in the Iliad: The Tragedy of Hector.* Chicago and London, 1975.

Rubino, Carl A., and Cynthia W. Shelmerdine, eds. *Approaches to Homer.* Austin, 1983.

Schein, Seth L. *The Mortal Hero: An Introduction to Homer's Iliad.* Berkeley, Los Angeles and London, 1984.

Scott, John A. *The Unity of Homer.* Berkeley, 1921.

Scully, Stephen, *Homer and the Sacred City.* Ithaca and London, 1990.

Segal, Charles. *The Theme of the Mutilation of the Corpse in the Iliad. Mnemosyne,* supp. vol. 17. Leiden, 1971.

Shay, Jonathan. *Achilles in Vietnam: Combat Trauma and the Undoing of Character.* New York, Toronto, 1994.

Shive, David M. *Naming Achilles.* New York, 1987.

Silk, M. S. *Homer: The Iliad.* Cambridge, England, 1987.

Slatkin, Laura M. *The Power of Thetis: Allusion and Interpretation in the Iliad.* Berkeley, Los Angeles and London, 1991.

Stanley, Keith. *The Shield of Homer: Narrative Structure in the Iliad.* Princeton, 1993.

Steiner, George, and Fagles, Robert, eds. *Homer: A Collection of Critical Essays.* Twentieth Century Views, ed. Maynard Mack. Englewood Cliffs, N.J., 1962.

—————————, ed., with Aminadov Dykman. *Homer in English.* Penguin Poets in Translation, ed. Christopher Ricks. Harmondsworth, 1996.

Suzuki, Mihoko. *Metamorphoses of Helen: Authority, Difference, and the Epic.* Chapter 1, *"The Iliad."* Ithaca and London, 1989.

Taplin, Oliver. *Homeric Soundings: The Shaping of the Iliad.* New York and London, 1992.

Thornton, Agathe. *Homer's Iliad, Its Composition and the Motif of Supplication.* Göttingen, 1984.

Vermeule, Emily T. *Greece in the Bronze Age.* Chicago and London, 1964.

——————————. *Aspects of Death in Early Greek Art and Poetry.* Sather Classical Lectures, Vol. 46. Berkeley, Los Angeles and London, 1979.

Vivante, Paolo. *Homer.* Hermes Books, ed. John Herington. New Haven and London, 1985.

——————————. *The Iliad: Action as Poetry.* Twayne's Masterwork Studies. Boston, 1990.

Wace, Alan J. B., and Stubbings, Frank. *A Companion to Homer.* London, 1962.

Wade-Gery, H. T. *The Poet of the Iliad.* Cambridge, England, 1952.

Weil, Simone. *The Iliad or The Poem of Force.* Trans. Mary McCarthy. Politics Pamphlet No. 1. New York, n.d.; rep. Wallingford, Pa., n.d.

Whitman, Cedric H. *Homer and the Heroic Tradition.* Cambridge, Mass., and London, 1958.

Willcock, Malcolm M. *A Companion to the Iliad: Based on the Translation by Richmond Lattimore.* Chicago and London, 1976.

Wofford, Susanne L. *The Choice of Achilles: The Ideology of Figure in the Epic.* Chapter 1, "The Politics of the Simile in the *Iliad.*" Stanford, Stanford University Press, 1992.

Wood, Robert. *An Essay on the Original Genius and Writings of Homer.* London, 1769; rep. Philadelphia, 1976.

Wright, John. *Essays on the Iliad: Selected Modern Criticism.* Bloomington and London, 1978.

PRONOUNCING GLOSSARY

The main purpose of this glossary is to indicate pronunciation. Identifications are brief, and only the first appearance of a name is listed.

Phonetic Equivalents:

a as in *cat*	*o* as in *pot*
ay as in *day*	*oh* as in *bone*
aw as in *raw*	*oo* as in *boot*
ai as in *air*	*or* as in *bore*
e as in *pet*	*s* as in *hiss*
ee as in *feet*	
	th as in *thin*
i as in *bit*	
eye as in *bite*	*u* as in *us*
	ur as in *burst*

Stress is indicated by an apostrophe *after* the stressed syllable (*af'-ter*).

ABANTES (*a-ban'-teez*): people of Euboea, 2.626.

ABARBAREA (*a-bar-ba-ree'-a*): nymph who bore two Trojans, Aesepus and Pedasus, to Bucolion, 6.25.

ABAS (*a'-bas*): son of the Trojan prophet Eurydamas, brother of Polyidus, killed by Diomedes, 5.165.

ABII (*a'-bi-eye*): northern tribe of Thrace, 13.8.

ABLERUS (*ab-lee'-rus*): Trojan killed by Antilochus, 6.37.

ABYDOS (*a-beye'-dos*): city on the southern shore of the Hellespont, northeast of Troy, 2.948.

ACAMAS (*a'-ka-mas*): (1) Trojan, son of Antenor, comrade of Aeneas, killed by Meriones, 2.934. (2) Trojan ally, son of Eussorus, commander of the Thracians, killed by Telamonian Ajax, 6.9.

ACESSAMENUS (*a-ke-sa'-men-us*): Thracian warlord, father of Periboea, 21.162.

ACHAEA (*a-kee'-a*): general, collective name for mainland Greece, 1.191.

ACHAEANS (*a-kee'-unz*): Greeks and their allies ranged against the Trojans, 1.2.

ACHELOUS (*a-ke-loh'-us*): (1) river in central and northwestern Greece, the largest river in Greece, 21.220. (2) River in Phrygia (Asia Minor), east of Troy, 24.725.

ACHILLES (*a-kil'-eez*): son of Peleus and Thetis, grandson of Aeacus, commander of the Myrmidons, Achaean allies, 1.1. See notes 1.1, 3.174, 19.494, 20.220–28.

ACRISIUS (*a-kri'-si-us*): king of Argos, father of Danaë, 14.383.

ACTOR (*ak'-tor*): (1) son of Azeus, father of Astyoche, 2.603. (2) Apparent forebear of Cteatus and Eurytus, the Moliones, 2.714. (3) Father of Menoetius, grandfather of Patroclus, 11.938. (4) Father of Echecles, 16.224.

ADAMAS (*a'-da-mas*): Trojan, son of Asius (1), killed by Meriones, 13.649.

ADMETUS (*ad-mee'-tus*): king of Thessaly, son of Pheres, husband of Alcestis, father of Eumelus, 2.814.

ADRASTUS (*a-dras'-tus*): king of Sicyon, father (or perhaps grandfather) of Aegialia, father-in-law of Diomedes, 2.663.

ADRESTIA (*a-dres-teye'-a*): city northeast of Troy, 2.939.

ADRESTUS (*a-drees'-tus*): (1) Trojan, son of Merops, brother of Amphius (1), commander of contingent from Adrestia, killed by Diomedes, 2.941. (2) Trojan killed by Menelaus and Agamemnon, 6.44. (3) Trojan killed by Patroclus, 16.812.

AEACIDES (*ee-a'-si-deez*): "grandson of Aeacus," patronymic of Achilles, 18.256.

AEACUS (*ee'-a-kus*): son of Zeus, father of Peleus, grandfather of Achilles, 9.230.

AEANTES (*ee-an'-teez*): the two Achaeans called Ajax when spoken of as a pair, 4.321.

AEGAE (*ee'-jee*): Achaean city in the northern Peloponnese and sacred to Poseidon, 8.230.

AEGAEON (*ee-jee'-on*): name used by mortals for the hundred-handed giant called Briareus by the gods, 1.479.

AEGEUS (*ee'-joos*): father of Theseus, 1.309.

AEGIALIA (*ee-ji-a-leye'-a*): daughter (or perhaps granddaughter) of Adrastus, wife of Diomedes, 5.471. See note 14.148.

AEGIALUS (*ee'-ji-a-lus*): city in Paphlagonia, 2.967.

AEGILIPS (*ee'-ji-lips*): city or vicinity in the kingdom of Odysseus, 2.727.

AEGINA (*ee-jeye'-na*): island in the Saronic Gulf, in the kingdom of Argos, 2.653.

AEGION (*ee'-ji-on*): city in the kingdom of Agamemnon, 2.665.

AENEAS (*ee-nee'-as*): Trojan, son of Anchises and Aphrodite, commander of the Dardanians and future king of the Trojans, 2.931. See note 20.248–79.

AENIUS (*ee'-ni-us*): Trojan ally, Paeonian killed by Achilles, 21.236.

AENUS (*ee'-nus*): city in Thrace, 4.603.

AEOLUS (*ee'-o-lus*): father of Sisyphus, 6.181.

AEPEA (*ee-pee'-a*): city in the realm of Pylos, in the southwestern Peloponnese, 9.182.

AEPY (*ee'-pee*): city near Pylos in Nestor's kingdom, 2.684.

AEPYTUS (*ee'-pi-tus*): a hero of Arcadia, his tomb a landmark near Mount Cyllene in that region, 2.697.

AESEPUS (*ee-see'-pus*): (1) river near Zelea, flowing seaward from the Idaean hills, 2.936. (2) Trojan, son of Bucolion, twin brother of Pedasus, killed by Euryalus, 6.24.

AESYETES (*ee-seye-ee'-teez*): (1) hero whose tomb is on the Trojan plain, 2.902. (2) Father of Trojan Alcathous, 13.495.

AESYME (*ee-seye'-mee*): city in Thrace, 8.347.

AESYMNUS (*ee-sim'-nus*): Achaean killed by Hector, 11.352.

AETHICES (*ee-theye'-seez*): tribe in Thessaly, 2.846.

AETHRA (*ee'-thra*): daughter of Pittheus and one of Helen's women, 3.173.

AETOLIANS (*ee-toh'-li-unz*): 2.738, people of **AETOLIA** (*ee-toh'-li-a*), a region in northwestern Greece, 2.732.

AGACLES (*a'-ga-kleez*): Trojan, father of the Achaean Epigeus, 16.668.

AGAMEDE (*a-ga-mee'-dee*): wife of Mulius, daughter of Augeas, king of the Epeans, 11.880.

AGAMEMNON (*a-ga-mem'-non*): Achaean, king of Mycenae, son of Atreus, husband of Clytemnestra, brother of Menelaus, supreme commander of all Achaea's armies and leader of the largest Achaean contingent, 1.8.

AGAPENOR (*a-ga-pee'-nor*): Achaean, son of Ancaeus, commander of the Arcadian contingent, 2.702.

AGASTHENES (*a-gas'-the-neez*): son of Augeas, father of the Achaean Polyxinus of Elis, 2.717.

AGASTROPHUS (*a-gas'-tro-fus*): Trojan, son of Paeon, killed by Diomedes, 11.394.

AGATHON (*a'-ga-thon*): Trojan, son of Priam, 24.295.

AGELAUS (*a-je-lay'-us*): (1) Trojan, son of Phradmon, killed by Diomedes, 8.295. (2) Achaean killed by Hector, 11.351.

AGENOR (*a-jee'-nor*): Trojan, son of Antenor, father of Echeclus, 4.540.

AGLAEA (*a-glee'-a*): mother of Achaean Nireus by King Charopus, 2.768.

AGRIUS (*a'-gri-us*): a prince of Calydon, son of Portheus, 14.143.

AJAX (*ay'-jax*): (1) Achaean, son of Telamon, Telamonian or Great Ajax, commander of the contingent from Salamis, 2.482. (2) Achaean, son of Oileus, Oilean or Little Ajax, commander of the contingent from Locris, 2.482.

ALASTOR (*a-las'-tor*): (1) Achaean, one of the Pylian captains, 4.338. (2) Trojan ally, Lycian killed by Odysseus, 5.777. (3) Achaean, comrade of Teucer, 8.380. (4) Trojan, father of Tros (2), 20.523.

ALCANDER (*al-kan'-der*): Trojan ally, Lycian killed by Odysseus, 5.778.

ALCATHOUS (*al-ka'-tho-us*): Trojan, son of Aesyetes (2), brother-in-law of Aeneas, killed by Idomeneus, 12.114.

ALCESTIS (*al-ses'-tis*): daughter of Pelias, wife of Admetus, mother of the Achaean Eumelus, 2.815.

ALCIMEDON (*al-sim'-e-don*): Achaean, son of Laerces, a Myrmidon commander, 16.232.

ALCIMUS (*al'-si-mus*): alternative name for Alcimedon, 19.464.

ALCMAON (*alk-may'-on*): Achaean, son of Thestor, killed by Sarpedon, 12.456.

ALCMENA (*alk-mee'-na*): queen of Thebes, wife of Amphitryon, mother of Heracles by Zeus, 14.387. See note 2.748.

ALEAN PLAIN (*a-lee'-an*): plain in Asia Minor where Bellerophon wandered, 6.238.

ALECTRYON (*a-lek'-tri-on*): father of the Achaean Leitus, 17.681.

ALEGENOR (*a-le-jee'-nor*): father of the Achaean Promachus, 14.589.

ALESION (*a-lee'-zi-on*): city of the Epeans, 2.710.

ALOEUS (*a-lee'-us*): father of the giants Ephialtes and Otus, 5.438.

ALOPE (*a'-lo-pee*): city in Pelasgian Argos, the kingdom of Achilles, 2.778.

ALPHEUS (*al-fee'-us*): river in the western Peloponnese, 2.684.

ALTES (*al'-teez*): king of the Leleges, father of Laothoë, one of Priam's wives, 21.97.

ALTHAEA (*al-thee'-a*): mother of Meleager, 9.676. See note 9.646–729.

ALUS (*a'-lus*): city in Pelasgian Argos, in the kingdom of Achilles, 2.778.

ALYBE (*a'-li-bee*): city of the Halizonians in Asia Minor, 2.968.

AMARYNCEUS (*a-ma-rins'-yoos*): hero of Elis, father of the Achaean Diores, 2.715.

AMAZONS (*am'-a-zonz*): a mythical nation of women warriors, vaguely located in the north, who are supposed to have invaded Phrygia in Asia Minor, 3.229.

AMISODARUS (*a-mi-soh'-da-rus*): Lycian warlord, father of Atymnius and Maris, Trojan allies, 16.387.

AMOPAON (*a-mo-pay'-on*): Trojan, son of Polyaemon, killed by Teucer, 8.316.

AMPHICLUS (*am'-fi-klus*): Trojan killed by Meges, 16.369.

AMPHIDAMAS (*am-fi'-da-mas*): (1) of Cythera, 10.314. (2) of Opois, whose son was killed by Patroclus, 23.105.

AMPHIGENIA (*am-fi-je-neye'-a*): city near Pylos, in Nestor's kingdom, 2.685.

AMPHIMACHUS (*am-fi'-ma-kus*): (1) Achaean, son of Cteatus, grandson of Poseidon, a commander of the Epeans, killed by Hector, 2.713. See note 13.247. (2) Trojan ally, son of Nomion and co-commander of the Carians, 2.982.

AMPHION (*am-feye'-on*): Achaean, a captain of the Epeans, 13.801.

AMPHITRYON (*am-fi'-tri-on*): husband of Alcmena and supposed father of her son, Heracles, actually sired by Zeus, 5.446.

AMPHIUS (*am-feye'-us*): (1) son of Merops, co-commander of Trojan allies from Adrestia, killed by Diomedes, 2.941. (2) Trojan ally, son of Selagus, killed by Great Ajax, 5.702.

AMPHOTERUS (*am-fo'-ter-us*): Trojan killed by Patroclus, 16.495.

AMYCLAE (*a-meye'-klee*): city near Sparta, in Lacedaemon, 2.676.

AMYDON (*a'-mi-don*): city of the Paeonians on the river Axius, 2.961.

AMYNTOR (*a-min'-tor*): son of Ormenus, father of Phoenix, 9.545.

ANCAEUS (*an-see'-us*): (1) father of the Achaean Agapenor, 2.702. (2) Of Pleuron, a wrestler defeated by Nestor, 23.708.

ANCHIALUS (*an-ki'-a-lus*): Achaean killed by Hector, 5.699.

ANCHISES (*an-keye'-seez*): (1) son of Capys, second cousin of Priam, father of Aeneas by Aphrodite, 2.930. (2) Achaean, father of Echepolus (2), 23.339.

ANDRAEMON (*an-dree'-mon*): father of the Achaean Thoas, 2.732.

ANDROMACHE (*an-dro'-ma-kee*): daughter of Eetion, wife of Hector, 6.441.

ANEMOREA (*a-ne-moh-ree'-a*): city in Phocis, 2.611.

ANTEA (*an-tee'-a*): wife of Proetus, king of Corinth, who tried to seduce Bellerophon, 6.189.

ANTENOR (*an-tee'-nor*): Trojan elder, counselor to King Priam, father of many sons who appear thorughout the *Iliad*, 3.178.

ANTHEA (*an-thee'-a*): city in vicinity of Pylos, 9.181.

ANTHEDON (*an-thee'-don*): city in Boeotia, 2.598.

ANTHEMION (*an-thee'-mi-on*): father of the Trojan Simoisius, 4.547.

ANTILOCHUS (*an-ti'-lo-kus*): son of Nestor, brother of Thrasymedes, a favorite of Achilles, 4.529.

ANTIMACHUS (*an-ti'-ma-kus*): father of the Trojans Pisander (1). Hippolochus (2) and Hippomachus, 11.154.

ANTIPHATES (*an-ti'-fa-teez*): Trojan killed by Leonteus, 12.220.

ANTIPHONUS (*an-ti'-fo-nus*): son of Priam, 24.296.

ANTIPHUS (*an'-ti-fus*): (1) Achaean, son of Thessalus, co-commander of the contingent from Cos, 2.774. (2) Trojan ally, son of Talaemenes, co-commander of the Maeonians, 2.976. (3) Trojan, son of Priam, killed by Agamemnon, 11.121.

ANTRON (*an'-tron*): city in Thessaly, in the kingdom of Protesilaus, 2.795.

APAESUS (*a-pee'-sus*): city in the Troad, northeast of Troy, 2.939.

APHARSUS (*a-far'-yoos*): son of Caletor, Achaean killed by Aeneas, 9.97.

APHRODITE (*a-fro-deye'-tee*): goddess of love, daugher of Zeus and Dione, mother of Aeneas, 2.931. See note 24.35–36.

APISAON (*a-pi-say'-on*): (1) Trojan, son of Phausias, killed by Euryplus, 11.682. (2) Trojan, son of Hippasus, killed by Lycomedes, 17.402.

APOLLO (*a-pol'-oh*): god, son of Zeus and Leto, twin brother of Artemis, a patron of the arts, especially music and poetry, 1.10. Also an archer—"lord of the silver bow"—and a prophet with a famous oracular shrine at Delphi, in central Greece. The principal divine champion of the Trojans. See notes, 1.45, 1.53, 4.117, 7.523–25, 9.679–88.

ARAETHYREA (*a-ree-thi-ree'-a*): city in Agamemnon's kingdom, 2.662.

ARCADIA (*ar-kay'-di-a*): region in the central Peloponnese, 2.696.

ARCESILAUS (*ar-se-si-lay'-us*): Achaean, leader of the Boeotians, killed by Hector, 2.585.

ARCHELOCHUS (*ar-ke'-lo-kus*): Trojan, son of Antenor, killed by Great Ajax, 2.934.

ARCHEPTOLEMUS (*ar-kep-to'-le-mus*): Trojan, son of Iphitus, charioteer of Hector, killed by Teucer, 8.147.

AREILYCUS (*a-ree-i'-li-kus*): (1) father of the Achaean Prothoënor, 14.530. (2) Trojan killed by Patroclus, 16.363.

AREITHOUS (*a-ree-i'-tho-us*): (1) father of the Achaean Menesthius (1), called the Great War-club, killed by Lycurgus (2), 7.10. (2) Trojan, charioteer of Rhigmus, killed by Achilles, 20.550.

ARENE (*a-ree'-nee*): city in Nestor's kingdom of Pylos, 2.683.

ARES (*ai'-reez*): god of war, son of Zeus and Hera, one of the Trojans' chief protectors, 2.129.

ARETAON (*a-re-tay'-on*): Trojan killed by Teucer, 6.37.

ARETUS (*a-ree'-tus*): Trojan killed by Automedon, 17.566.

ARGEAS (*ar'-jee-as*): father of Polymelus, 16.497.

ARGISSA (*ar-jis'-a*): city in Thessaly, in the kingdom of Polypoetes, 2.840.

ARGIVES (*ar'-geyevz*): alternate name for the Achaeans, 1.19.

ARGOS (*ar'-gos*): (1) city in the Argolid under the dominion of Diomedes, 2.650. (2) The entire Argolid, the kingdom of Agamemnon, 2.126. (3) The general region of the Achaeans, mainland Greece, 2.335. (4) Pelasgian Argos, in northeastern Greece, the kingdom of Achilles, 2.777.

ARIADNE (*a-ri-ad'-nee*): daughter of Minos, king of Crete, 18.692.

ARIMA (*a'-ri-ma*): region in Cilicia where the monster Typhoeus lies buried, 2.891.

ARION (*a-reye'-on*): renowned racehorse of Adrastus, 23.392.

ARISBAS (*a-riz'-bas*): father of the Achaean Leocritus, 17.399.

ARISBE (*a-riz'-bee*): city in the Troad, 2.948.

ARNE (*ar'-nee*): city in Boeotia, 2.597.

ARSINOUS (*ar-si'-no-us*): father of Hecamede, 11.737.

ARTEMIS (*ar'-te-mis*): goddess of the hunt, daughter of Zeus and Leto, sister of Apollo, 5.56. See note 21.551.

ASAEUS (*a-see'-us*): Achaean killed by Hector, 11.350.

ASCALAPHUS (*a-ska'-la-fus*): Achaean, son of Ares and Astyoche, co-commander of the Minyans from Orchomenos, killed by Deiphobus, 2.602.

ASCANIA (*a-ska'-ni-a*): city in Phrygia, 2.975.

ASCANIUS (*a-ska'-ni-us*): Trojan ally, son of Hippotion, co-commander of the Phrygians, 2.974. See note 13.918.

ASCLEPIUS (*a-sklee'-pi-us*): famous healer, father of the Achaeans Machaon and Podalirius, 2.833.

ASINE (*a'-si-nee*): city in the Argolid, at the head of the Argolic Gulf, 2.651.

ASIUS (*ay'-si-us*): (1) son of Hyrtacus, commander of Trojan allies from Percote and its environs, killed by Idomeneus, 2.949. (2) Son of Dymas, brother of Hecuba, uncle of Hector, 16.837.

ASOPUS (*a-soh'-pus*): river in Boeotia, 4.446.

ASPLEDON (*a-splee'-don*): city of the Minyans near Orchomenos, 2.601.

ASSARACUS (*a-sar'-a-kus*): son of Tros, brother of Ilus and Ganymede, father of Capys, great-grandfather of Aeneas, 20.268.

ASTERION (*a-ster'-i-on*): city in Thessaly, in the kingdom of Eurypylus, 2.837.

ASTEROPAEUS (*a-ste-ro-pee'-us*): Trojan ally, son of Pelegon, commander of the Paeonians, killed by Achilles, 12.123.

ASTYALUS (*a-steye'-a-lus*): Trojan killed by Polypoetes, 6.34.

ASTYANAX (*a-steye'-a-nax*): "Lord of the City," infant son of Hector and Andromache, 6.477. See note 24.866.

ASTYNOUS (*a-sti'-no-us*): (1) Trojan killed by Diomedes, 5.160. (2) Trojan charioteer, son of Protiaon, comrade of Polydamas, 15.531.

ASTYOCHE (*a-steye'-o-kee*): mother of Ascalaphus and Ialmenus by Ares, 2.603.

ASTYOCHEA (*a-sti-o-kee'-a*): mother of Tlepolemus by Heracles, 2.753.

ASTYPYLUS (*a-sti'-pi-lus*): Trojan ally, Paeonian killed by Achilles, 21.236.

ATHENA (*a-thee'-na*): or Pallas Athena, goddess, also called Tritogenia or Third-born of the Gods (see note 4.597), daughter of Zeus, defender of the Achaeans. A patron of human ingenuity and resourcefulness, whether exemplified by handicrafts, such as spinning, or by skill in human relations, such as that possessed by Odysseus, her favorite among the Greeks, 1.229. See notes 4.8, 5.1017–18.

ATHENIANS (*a-thee'-ni-unz*): 2.643, people of **ATHENS** (*a'-thenz*), the city of Erechtheus, in Attica, east central Greece, 2.637.

ATHOS (*ay'-thos*): mountain on a promontory in the northern Aegean Sea, 14.275.

ATREUS (*ay'-tryoos*): father of Agamemnon and Menelaus, 1.18.

ATRIDAE (*a-treye'-dee*): "sons of Atreus," collective patronymic for Agamemnon and Menelaus, 7.429.

ATRIDES (*a-treye'-deez*): "son of Atreus," patronymic of Agamemnon or Menelaus, 1.271.

ATYMNIUS (*a-tim'-ni-us*): (1) Trojan, father of Mydon, 5.668. (2) Trojan, son of Amisodarus, brother of Maris, killed by Antilochus, 16.375.

AUGEAE (*aw-jee'-ee*): (1) city in Locris, 2.622. (2) City in Lacedaemon, 2.675.

AUGEAS (*aw-jee'-as*): warlord of the Epeans from Elis, 2.717.

AULIS (*aw'-lis*): district in the narrow strait between Euboea and the Greek mainland, where the Greek fleet gathered before embarking for Troy, 2.356.

AUTOLYCUS (*aw-to'-li-kus*): maternal grandfather of Odysseus, 10.310.

AUTOMEDON (*aw-to'-me-don*): Achaean, son of Diores (2), Myrmidon comrade and charioteer of Achilles and Patroclus, 9.250.

AUTONOUS (*aw-to'-no-us*): (1) Achaean killed by Hector, 11.350. (2) Trojan killed by Patroclus, 16.812.

AXIUS (*ax'-i-us*): river and river god in Paeonia, father of Pelegon by Periboea, 2.961.

AXYLUS (*ax-eye'-lus*): Trojan ally from Arisbe, son of Teuthras, killed by Diomedes, 6.14.

AZEUS (*az'-yoos*): father of Actor (1), 2.603.

BATHYCLES (*bath'-i-kleez*): Achaean, son of Chalcon, killed by Glaucus, 16.693.

BELLEROPHON (*be-ler'-o-fon*): hero from Corinth, son of Glaucus (2), killer of the Chimaera, grandfather of Sarpedon and Glaucus, 6.182.

BESSA (*bee'-sa*): city in Locris, 2.622.

BIAS (*beye'-as*): (1) Achaean, Pylian captain under Nestor, 4.339. (2) Achaean, Athenian captain under Menestheus, 13.799. (3) Father of the Trojan Laogonus (2) and Dardanus (2), 20.520.

BIENOR (*bi-ee'-nor*): Trojan killed by Agamemnon, 11.107.

BOAGRIUS (*bo-a'-gri-us*): river in Locris, 2.623.

BOEBE (*bee'-bee*): Thessalian city in the kingdom of Eumelus, 2.813.

BOEBEIS, LAKE (*bee-bee'-is*): lake adjoining Boebe, 2.812.

BOEOTIANS (*bee-oh'-shunz*): 2.600, people of **BOEOTIA** (*bee-oh'-sha*), a region in central Greece, 2.584.

BOREAS (*bor'-e-as*): the North Wind, 23.224.

BORUS (*bor'-us*): (1) father of the Trojan Phaestus, 5.48. (2) Achaean, son of Perieres, husband of Polydora, nominal father of Menesthius (2), 16.208.

BRIAREUS (*bri-ar'-yoos*): name used by the gods for the hundred-handed giant called Aegaeon by mortals, 1.478.

BRISEIS (*breye-see'-is*): daughter of Briseus, captive of Achilles, 1.218.

BRISEUS (*breyes'-yoos*): father of Briseis, 1.466.

BRYSIAE (*breye-seye'-ee*): city in Lacedaemon, 2.675.

BUCOLION (*bew-kol'-i-on*): son of Laomedon, father of the Trojans Aesepus (2) and Pedasus (1), 6.25.

BUCOLUS (*bew'-ko-lus*): father of Sphelus, grandfather of Iasus, 15.398.

BUDION (*bew-deye'-on*): city in the domain of the Myrmidons, 16.669.

BUPRASION (*bew-pra'-si-on*): city and district of Elis, in the northwestern Peloponnese, 2.708.

CABESUS (*ka-bee'-sus*): city of unknown location, perhaps in the Troad, since it was allied with Troy, 13.422.

CAENEUS (*seen'-yoos*): Lapith hero of the generation of Nestor, father of Coronus, 1.308.

CALCHAS (*kal'-kas*): prophet of the Achaeans, son of Thestor (1), 1.79.

CALESIUS (*ka-lee'-si-us*): Trojan, charioteer of Axylus, killed by Diomedes, 6.21.

CALETOR (*ka-lee'-tor*): (1) father of the Achaean Aphareus, 13.627. (2) Trojan, son of Clytius, killed by Great Ajax. 15.490.

CALLIARUS (*ka-li'-a-rus*): city in Locris, 2.621.

CALYDNAE (*ka-lid'-nee*): islands in the southeastern Aegean, 2.773.

CALYDON (*ka'-li-don*): city in Aetolia, the site of a legendary struggle between Aetolians and Curetes, 2.734.

CAMIRUS (*ka-meye'-rus*): city in Rhodes, 2.751.

CAPANEUS (*ka'-pan-yoos*): father of the Achaean Sthenelus (1), 2.655.

CAPYS (*ka'-pis*): son of Assaracus, father of Anchises (1), grandfather of Aeneas, 20.276.

CARDAMYLE (*kar-da'-mi-lee*): city near Pylos, in the southwestern Peloponnese, 9.180.

CARESUS (*ka-ree'-sus*): river in the Troad, 12.23.

CARIANS (*kair'-i-unz*): Trojan allies, inhabitants of a region in southern Asia Minor who hold the city of Miletus, 2.979.

CARYSTUS (*ka-ris'-tus*): city of Euboea, 2.629.

CASSANDRA (*ka-san'-dra*): daughter of Priam, 13.424.

CASTIANIRA (*ca-sti-a-neye'-ra*): mother of the Trojan Gorgythion by Priam, 8.348.

CASTOR (*kas'-tor*): brother of Helen and Polydeuces, 3.283.

CASUS (*ka'-sus*): island near Crapathus in the southeastern Aegean, 2.772.

CAUCONIANS (*kaw-koh'-ni-unz*): Trojan allies, people of Asia Minor, 10.496.

CAYSTER (*kay-is'-ter*): river in Asia Minor, 2.546.

CEAS (*see'-as*): father of Troezenus, 2.959.

CEBRIONES (*se-breye'-o-neez*): Trojan, bastard son of Priam, brother of Hector, killed by Patroclus, 8.364.

CELADON (*se'-la-don*): river that may have bordered Arcadia and Pylos, 7.153.

CENTAURS (*sen'-tawrz*): wild creatures, part man and part horse, who live in the vicinity of Mount Pelion, 1.312.

CEPHALLENIANS (*se-fa-lee'-ni-unz*): 4.387, people of **CEPHALLENIA** (*se-fa-lee'-ni-a*), island off western Greece in the kingdom of Odysseus, 2.724. See Samos (1).

CEPHISUS (*se-feye'-sus*): river in Phocis and Boeotia, 2.612.

CEPHISUS, LAKE (*se-feye'-sus*): Lake Copais in Boeotia, 5.814.

CERINTHUS (*see-rin'-thus*): city in Euboea, 2.628.

CHALCIS (*kal'-sis*): (1) city in Euboea, 2.627. (2) City of Aetolia, 2.734.

CHALCODON (*kal-koh'-don*): father of the Achaean Elephenor, 2.631.

CHALCON (*kal'-kon*): father of the Achaean Bathycles, 16.694.

CHARIS (*ka'-ris*): goddess, one of the Graces, wife of Hephaestus, 18.446.

CHAROPS (*ka'-rops*): Trojan, son of Hippasus (1), brother of Socus, killed by Odysseus, 11.505.

CHAROPUS (*ka'-ro-pus*): father of the Achaean Nireus, 2.768.

CHERSIDAMAS (*kur-si'-da-mas*): Trojan killed by Odysseus, 11.500.

CHIMAERA (*keye-mee'-ra*): monster, "all lion in front, all snake behind, all goat between," reared by Amisodarus, killed by Bellerophon, 6.212.

CHIRON (*keye'-ron*): most humane of the Centaurs, healer and teacher of Asclepius, friend of Peleus and Achilles, 4.251.

CHROMIS (*kro'-mis*): Trojan ally, co-commander of the Mysians, killed by the Achilles, 2.970.

CHROMIUS (*kro'-mi-us*): (1) Achaean, Pylian captain under Nestor, 4.338. (2) Trojan, son of Priam, killed by Diomedes, 5.179. (3) Trojan ally, Lycian killed by Odysseus, 5.777. (4) Trojan killed by Teucer, 8.315. (5) Trojan captain, 17.250.

CHRYSE (*kreye'-see*): town in the Troad, home of Chryses, 1.44.

CHRYSEIS (*kreye-see'-is*): daughter of Chryses, captive of Agamemnon, 1.130.

CHRYSES (*kreye'-seez*): priest of Apollo, father of Chryseis, 1.13.

CHRYSOTHEMIS (*kreye-so'-the-mis*): one of Agamemnon's daughters, 9.174.

CICONES (*si-koh'-neez*): Trojan allies, living in Thrace, to the north of Troy, 2.958.

CILICIA (*si-li'-sha*): region surrounding Thebe, in the vicinity of Troy, its people ruled by Eetion (1), 6.469.

CILLA (*si'-la*): town in the Troad, 1.44.

CINYRAS (*sin'-i-ras*): lord of Cyprus who gave a breastplate to Agamemnon, 11.22.

CISSEUS (*sis'-yoos*): father of Theano, grandfather of the Trojan Iphidamas, 6.354.

CLEOBULUS (*kle-o-boo'-lus*): Trojan killed by Little Ajax, 16.389.

CLEONAE (*kle-oh'-nee*): city in the kingdom of Agamemnon, 2.661.

CLEOPATRA (*kle-o-pa'-tra*): daughter of Idas and Marpessa, called Halcyon by her parents, wife of Meleager, 9.678. See notes 9.646–729, 679–88.

CLITUS (*kleye'-tus*): Trojan, son of Pisenor, charioteer of Polydamas, killed by Teucer, 15.519.

CLONIUS (*klo'-ni-us*): Achaean, a captain of the Boeotians, killed by Agenor, 2.585.

CLYMENE (*kli'-me-nee*): one of Helen's attendant women, 3.173.

CLYTEMNESTRA (*kleye-tem-nes'-tra*): wife of Agamemnon, 1.133.

CLYTIUS (*kli'-ti-us*): (1) Trojan elder, son of Laomedon, brother of Priam, father of Caletor (2), 3.176. (2) Father of the Achaean Dolops (1), 11.351.

CLYTOMEDES (*kli-to-mee'-deez*): son of Enops (3), defeated by Nestor in boxing, 23.707.

COERANUS *(see'-ran-us):* (1) Trojan ally, Lycian killed by Odysseus, 5.777. (2) Achaean, charioteer of Meriones, killed by Hector, 17.689.

COON *(koh'-on):* Trojan, son of Antenor, killed by Agamemnon, 11.288.

COPAE *(koh'-pee):* city in Boeotia, 2.592.

COPREUS *(kop'-ryoos):* father of the Achaean Periphetes (2), herald of Eurystheus, 15.742.

CORINTH *(kor'-inth):* city in the kingdom of Agamemnon, 2.661.

CORONEA *(ko-roh-nee'-a):* city in Boeotia, 2.593.

CORONUS *(ko-roh'-nus):* son of Caeneus, father of the Achaean Leonteus, 2.848.

COS *(kohs):* island near the Calydnae in the southeastern Aegean, 2.773.

CRAPATHUS *(kra'-pa-thus):* island near Casus in the southeastern Aegean, 2.772.

CREON *(kree'-on):* father of the Achaean Lycomedes, 9.98.

CRETANS *(kree'-tunz):* 2.740, inhabitants of **CRETE** *(kreet),* the large island south of the Peloponnese in the Aegean, the kingdom of Idomeneus, 2.744.

CRETHON *(kree'-thon):* Achaean, son of Diocles, killed by Aeneas, 5.624.

CRISA *(kreye'-sa):* city in Phocis, 2.610.

CROCYLIA *(kro-si-leye'-a):* place in Ithaca, 2.727.

CROESMUS *(kreez'-mus):* Trojan killed by Meges, 15.605.

CROMNA *(krohm'-na):* city in Paphlagonia, 2.967.

CRONUS *(kro'-nus):* god, son of Uranus, father of Zeus, Hades, Poseidon, Hera, Demeter, 1.481. See notes 8.554, 14.244.

CTEATUS *(kte'-a-tus):* reputed son of Actor (2), whose real father was Poseidon, twin brother of Eurytus (2), father of the Achaean Amphimachus (1), 2.714.

CURETES *(koo-ree'-teez):* Aetolians living in Pleuron, who make war on Aetolians of Calydon, 9.646.

CYLLENE *(si-lee'-nee):* mountain in northern Arcadia, 2.696.

CYNUS *(seye'-nus):* city in Locris, 2.621.

CYPARISSEIS *(si-pa-ri-see'-is):* city near Pylos in Nestor's kingdom, 2.685.

CYPARISSUS *(si-pa-ri'-sus):* city in Phocis, 2.609.

CYPHUS *(seye'-fus):* city in northwestern Greece, 2.850.

CYPRUS *(seye'-prus):* large island in the eastern Mediterranean, 11.23.

CYTHERA (*si-thee'-ra*): island off the southern coast of the Peloponnese, 10.314.

CYTORUS (*si-toh'-rus*): city in Paphlagonia, 2.965.

DAEDALUS (*dee'-da-lus*): the "fabulous artificer" in the service of Minos, king of Crete, for whom he built the famous labyrinth, 18.690.

DAETOR (*dee'-tor*): Trojan killed by Teucer, 8.315.

DAMASTOR (*da-mas'-tor*): father of the Trojan Tlepolemus (2), 16.496.

DAMASUS (*da'-ma-sus*): Trojan killed by Polypoetes, 12.211.

DANAANS (*da'-nay-unz*): alternative name for the Achaeans, 1.49.

DANAË (*da'-nay-ee*): daughter of Acrisius; mother, by Zeus, of Perseus, 14.383.

DARDAN or **DARDANIAN GATES** (*dar'-dan, dar-day'-ni-an*): one of the main gates of Troy, 5.908.

DARDANIA (*dar-day'-ni-a*): kingdom of Dardanus (1), originally founded as a colony on the foothills of Mount Ida, and the predecessor of Troy, 20.252.

DARDANIANS (*dar-day'-ni-unz*): people descended from Dardanus (1), specifically those Trojans led by Aeneas, 2.930.

DARDANUS (*dar'-da-nus*): (1) son of Zeus, father of Erichthonius, forebear of Priam and the kings of Troy, 11.194. (2) Trojan, son of Bias, killed by Achilles, 20.520.

DARES (*dair'-eez*): priest of Hephaestus, father of the Trojans Phegeus and Idaeus (2), 5.9.

DAULIS (*daw'-lis*): city in Phocis, near Apollo's shrine in Pytho, 2.610.

DAWN: goddess of the morning, wife of Tithonus, 1.569.

DEATH: god, brother of Sleep, 1.3.

DEICOON (*dee-i'-koh-on*): Trojan, son of Pergasus, killed by Agamemnon, 5.616.

DEIOCHUS (*dee-i'-o-kus*): Achaean killed by Paris, 15.401.

DEIOPITES (*dee-i-o-peye'-teez*): Trojan killed by Odysseus, 11.497.

DEIPHOBUS (*dee-i'-fo-bus*): Trojan, son of Priam, 12.115.

DEIPYLUS (*dee-i'-pi-lus*): Achaean, comrade of Sthenelus, 5.363.

DEIPYRUS (*dee-i'-pi-rus*): Achaean killed by Helenus, 9.97.

DEMETER (*dee-mee'-tur*): goddess, sister of Zeus and mother of Persephone, she presides over the grain crops, 2.794.

DEMOCOON (*dee-mo'-koh-on*): Trojan, bastard son of Priam, killed by Odysseus, 4.576.

DEMOLEON (*dee-mo'-le-on*): Trojan, son of Antenor, killed by Achilles, 20.450.

DEMUCHUS (*dee-moo'-kus*): Trojan, son of Philetor, killed by Achilles, 20.517.

DEUCALION (*dew-kay'-li-on*): (1) Cretan hero, son of Minos, father of Idomeneus, 12.139. (2) Trojan killed by Achilles, 20.540.

DEXIUS (*dex'-i-us*): father of the Achaean Iphinous, 7.16.

DIOCLES (*deye'-o-kleez*): son of Ortilochus, father of the Achaeans Crethon and Orsilochus (1), 5.624.

DIOMEDE (*deye-o-mee'-dee*): daughter of Phorbas, mistress of Achilles, captured from Lesbos, 9.812.

DIOMEDES (*deye-o-mee'-deez*): Achaean, son of Tydeus, king of Argos, 2.482. See note 5.1ff.

DION (*deye'-on*): city in Euboea, 2.628.

DIONE (*deye-oh'-nee*): goddess, mother of Aphrodite, 5.417.

DIONYSUS (*deye-o-neye'-sus*): god, son of Zeus and Semele, a Theban princess; the god of ecstatic release, especially associated with wine, 6.153. See notes 6.153, 157–60.

DIORES (*deye-o'-reez*): (1) Achaean, son of Amarynceus, co-commander of the Epeans, killed by Pirous, 2.715. (2) Father of the Achaean Automedon, 17.544.

DISENOR (*deye-see'-nor*): Trojan captain, 17.250.

DIUS (*deye'-us*): Trojan, son of Priam, 24.297.

DODONA (*doh-doh'-na*): site in Epirus, in northwestern Greece, sanctuary of an oracle of Zeus, 2.852.

DOG STAR: 11.70, see **ORION'S DOG** and note 22.35.

DOLON (*doh'-lon*): Trojan scout, son of the herald Eumedes, killed by Diomedes and Odysseus, 10.366.

DOLOPES (*do'-lo-peez*): people in Phthia ruled by Phoenix. 9.586.

DOLOPION (*do-lo-peye'-on*): Trojan, priest of Scamander, father of Hypsenor (1), 5.85.

DOLOPS (*do'-lops*): (1) Achaean, son of Clytius (2), killed by Hector, 11.351. (2) Trojan, son of Lampus (1), killed by Menelaus, 15.608.

DORION (*doh'-ri-on*): city in the kingdom of Nestor, 2.686.

DORYCLUS (*do'-ri-clus*): Trojan, bastard son of Priam, killed by Great Ajax, 11.577.

DRACIUS (*dray'-shus*): Achaean, a captain of the Epeans, 13.801.

DRESUS (*dree'-sus*): Trojan killed by Euryalus, 6.23.

DRYAS (*dreye'-as*): (1) Lapith hero in Nestor's generation, 1.307. (2) Father of Lycurgus (1), 6.150.

DRYOPS (*dreye'-ops*): Trojan killed by Achilles, 20.515.

DULICHION (*dew-li'-ki-on*): island off western Greece in the kingdom of Meges, 2.718.

DYMAS (*deye'-mas*): father of Hecuba and Asius (2), 16.838.

ECHECLES (*e-kek'-leez*): Achaean, adoptive father of the Myrmidon captain Eudorus, son of Actor (4), husband of Polymela, 16.224.

ECHECLUS (*e-kek'-lus*): (1) Trojan killed by Patroclus, 16.812. (2) Trojan, son of Agenor, killed by Achilles, 20.536.

ECHEMMON (*e-kem'-on*): Trojan, son of Priam, killed by Diomedes, 5.179.

ECHEPOLUS (*e-ke-poh'-lus*): (1) Trojan, son of Thalysias, killed by Antilochus, 4.530. (2) Achaean, son of Anchises (2), 23.339.

ECHINADES (*e-keye'-na-deez*): islands off western Greece in the kingdom of Meges, 2.719.

ECHIUS (*ek'-i-us*): (1) father of the Achaean Mecisteus (2), 8.380. (2) Achaean killed by Polites, 15.399. (3) Trojan ally, Lycian killed by Patroclus, 16.496.

EETION (*ee-e'-ti-on*): (1) king of the Cilicians in Thebe, father of Andromache, killed by Achilles, 1.433. (2) Father of the Trojan Podes, 17.653. (3) A lord of Imbros and friend of Priam, 21.49.

EIONAE (*ee-i'-o-nee*): city in the Argolid, 2.652.

EIONEUS (*ee-i'-on-yoos*): (1) Achaean killed by Hector, 7.12. (2) Father of the Trojan ally Rhesus (1), 10.503.

ELASUS (*el'-a-sus*): Trojan killed by Patroclus, 16.814.

ELATUS (*el'-a-tus*): Trojan ally, killed by Agamemnon, 6.39.

ELEON (*el'-e-on*): city in Boeotia, 2.590.

ELEPHENOR (*e-le-fee'-nor*): Achaean, commander of the Abantes, killed by Agenor, 2.630.

ELIS (*ee'-lis*): realm of the Epeans, in the northwestern Peloponnese bordering Nestor's Pylos, 2.708.

ELONE (*ee-loh'-nee*): city in Thessaly, in the kingdom of Polypoetes, 2.841.

EMATHIA (*ee-ma'-thi-a*): region to the northeast of mainland Greece, later Macedonia, 14.272.

ENETIANS (*e-nee'-shunz*): people of Paphlagonia, Trojan allies, 2.964.

ENIENES (*e-ni-ee'-neez*): Achaean contingent from Thessaly, in northwestern Greece, 2.851.

ENIOPEUS (*ee-ni-op'-yoos*): Trojan, son of Thebaeus, charioteer of Hector, killed by Diomedes, 8.138.

ENISPE (*e-nis'-pee*): city in Arcadia, 2.699.

ENNOMUS (*en'-o-mus*): (1) Trojan augur and ally, co-commander of the Mysians, killed by Achilles, 2.970. (2) Trojan killed by Odysseus, 11.499.

ENOPE (*en'-o-pee*): city in Messenia near Pylos, 9.180.

ENOPS (*ee'-nops*): (1) father of the Trojan Satnius, 14.523. (2) Father of the Trojan Thestor, 16.477. (3) Father of Clytomedes, 23.707.

ENYEUS (*e-neye'-yoos*): king of Scyros, 9.816.

ENYO (*e-neye'-oh*): goddess of war, 5.373.

EPALTES (*e-pal'-teez*): Trojan ally, Lycian killed by Patroclus, 16.495.

EPEANS (*e-pee'-unz*): people of Elis and Buprasion, in the northwestern Peloponnese, 2.712.

EPEUS (*e-pee'-us*): Achaean, son of Panopeus (2), victor in the boxing match in the games for Patroclus, 23.741, and builder of the Trojan horse in the *Odyssey*.

EPHIALTES (*e-fi-al'-teez*): son of Aloeus, giant who with his brother Otus imprisoned Ares, 5.437.

EPHYRA (*e'-fi-ra*): city in Thesprotia, in northwestern Greece, on the Selleis River, 2.754.

EPHYRI (*e'-fi-reye*): a tribe in Thessaly attacked by Ares, 13.353.

EPICLES (*e'-pi-kleez*): Trojan ally, Lycian killed by Great Ajax, 12.436.

EPIDAURUS (*e-pi-daw'-rus*): city in the Argolid, in the kingdom of Diomedes, 2.652.

EPIGEUS (*e-peye'-joos*): Achaean ally, Myrmidon, son of Agacles, killed by Hector, 16.668.

EPISTOR (*e-pis'-tor*): Trojan killed by Patroclus, 16.813.

EPISTROPHUS (*e-pis'-tro-fus*): (1) Achaean, son of Iphitus (1), co-commander of the Phocians, 2.607. (2) Trojan, son of Euenus, lord of Lyrnessus, killed by Achilles, 2.789. (3) Trojan ally, co-commander of the Halizonians, 2.968.

ERECHTHEUS (*e-rek'-thyoos*): first king of Athens, reared by Athena, 2.638.

ERETRIA (*e-re'-tri-a*): city in Euboea, 2.627.

EREUTHALION (*er-yoo-thay'-li-on*): Arcadian champion killed by Nestor, 4.368.

ERIBOEA (*e-ri-bee'-a*): stepmother of Otus and Ephialtes, 5.442.

ERICHTHONIUS (*e-rik-thon'-i-us*): son of Dardanus (1), father of Tros (1), forebear of the kings of Troy, 20.255.

ERIOPIS (*e-ri-oh'-pis*): wife of Oileus (1) and stepmother of Medon (1), 13.806.

ERYLAUS (*e-ri-lay'-us*): Trojan killed by Patroclus, 16.490.

ERYMAS (*er'-i-mas*): (1) Trojan killed by Idomeneus, 16.407. (2) Trojan killed by Patroclus, 16.495.

ERYTHINI (*e-ri-theye'-neye*): city or vicinity in Paphlagonia, 2.967.

ERYTHRAE (*e-ri'-three*): city in Boeotia, 2.589.

ETEOCLES (*ee-tee'-o-kleez*): son of Oedipus, lord of the Thebans and their defender against the Argive Seven, 4.450. See note 5.926.

ETEONUS (*e-tee-oh'-nus*): city in Boeotia, 2.587.

EUAEMON (*yoo-ee'-mon*): father of Eurypylus (2), 2.838.

EUBOEA (*yoo-bee'-a*): large island lying off the coast of eastern Greece, 2.625.

EUCHENOR (*yoo-kee'-nor*): Achaean, son of Polyidus, killed by Paris, 13.764.

EUDORUS (*yoo-dor'-us*): Achaean, son of Hermes and Polymela, a Myrmidon captain, 16.211.

EUENUS (*yoo-ee'-nus*): (1) son of Selepius, father of the Trojans Mynes and Epistrophus (2), 2.790. (2) Father of Marpessa, 9.679.

EUIPPUS (*yoo-ip'-us*): Trojan ally, Lycian killed by Patroclus, 16.497.

EUMEDES (*yoo-mee'-deez*): Trojan herald, father of Dolon, 10.367.

EUMELUS (*yoo-mee'-lus*): Achaean, son of Admetus and Alcestis, commander of the Thessalians from Pherae, 2.815.

EUNEUS (*yoo-nee'-us*): king of Lemnos, son of Jason and Hypsipyle, 7.541.

EUPHEMUS (*yoo-fee'-mus*): Trojan ally, son of Troezenus, captain of the Cicones, 2.958.

EUPHETES (*yoo-fee'-teez*): lord of Ephyra, 15.616.

EUPHORBUS (*yoo-for'-bus*): Trojan, son of Panthous and Phrontis, who mortally wounds Patroclus, killed by Menelaus, 16.938.

EUROPA (*yoo-roh'-pa*): daughter of Phoenix (2), mother of Minos and Rhadamanthus, 14.385.

EURYALUS (*yoo-reye'-a-lus*): Achaean, son of Mecisteus (1), third in command, after Diomedes and Sthenelus, of the Argolid contingent, 2.656.

EURYBATES (*yoo-ri'-ba-teez*): (1) Achaean, herald of Agamemnon, 1.376. (2) Achaean, herald of Odysseus, 2.212.

EURYDAMAS (*yoo-ri'-da-mas*): interpreter of dreams, father of the Trojans Abas and Polyidus (1), 5.166.

EURYMEDON (*yoo-ri'-me-don*): (1) Achaean, son of Ptolemaeus, charioteer of Agamemnon, 4.261. (2) Achaean, charioteer of Nestor, 8.132.

EURYNOME (*yoo-ri'-no-mee*): goddess, daughter of Ocean, 18.466.

EURYPYLUS (*yoo-ri'-pi-lus*): (1) king of Cos, 2.773. (2) Achaean, son of Euaemon, commander of Thessalians from Ormenion, 2.838.

EURYSTHEUS (*yoo-ris'-thyoos*): king of Mycenae, son of Sthenelus (2), grandson of Perseus and taskmaster of Heracles, 8.419. See note 2.748.

EURYTUS (*yoo'-ri-tus*): (1) king of Oechalia, 2.688. (2) Son of Poseidon, supposed son of Actor (2), twin brother of Cteatus (together called the Moliones), father of the Achaean Thalpius, 2.714.

EUSSORUS (*yoo-sor'-us*): Trojan, father of Acamas (2), 6.9.

EUTRESIS (*yoo-tree'-sis*): city in Boeotia, 2.592.

EXADIUS (*ex-a'-di-us*): Lapith, hero of the generation of Nestor, 1.308.

FATE(S): shadowy but potent figures who ultimately control the destiny of mortals, 2.182.

FURIES: avenging spirits whose task it is to exact blood for blood when no human avenger is left alive, 9.554. They are particularly concerned with injuries done by one member of a family to another, and they have regulatory powers as well, as when they stop the voice of Achilles' stallion Xanthus, 19.495. See note 3.332.

GANYMEDE (*ga'-ni-meed*): son of Tros (1), made immortal as the cup-bearer to Zeus and the other gods, 5.294. See note ad loc.

GARGARON (*gar'-ga-ron*): the central peak of Mount Ida, and Zeus's favorite lookout point, 8.56.

GLAPHYRAE (*gla'-fi-ree*): city in Thessaly, in the kingdom of Eumelus, 2.813.

GLAUCUS (*glaw'-kus*): (1) Trojan ally, son of Hippolochus, one of the commanders of the Lycians, 2.988. (2) Son of Sisyphus, father of Bellerophon, great-grandfather of Glaucus (1), 6.181.

GLISAS (*gleye'-sas*): city in Boeotia, 2.594.

GONOËSSA (*go-no-es'-a*): Achaean city in the kingdom of Agamemnon, 2.664.

GORGON (*gor'-gon*): a fabulous female monster whose glance could turn a person into stone, the centerpiece of Zeus's aegis, 5.849.

GORGYTHION (*gor-ji'-thi-on*): Trojan, son of Priam and Castianira, killed by Teucer, 8.344.

GORTYN (*gor'-tin*): city in Crete, 2.741.

GRACES: attendant goddesses, daughters of Zeus who personify beauty and charm, often associated with the arts and the Muses, 5.379.

GRAEA (*gree'-a*): city in Boeotia, 2.588.

GREAT BEAR: constellation, also called the Wagon and the Big Dipper, 18.569. See note ad loc.

GRENICUS (*gree'-ni-kus*): river in the Troad, 12.24.

GUNEUS (*goon'-yoos*): Achaean, commander of the Enienes and Peraebians living near Dodona, 2.850.

GYGE, LAKE (*geye'-jee*): nymph of a lake in Maeonia, mother of the Trojan Mesthles and Antiphus (2) by Talaemenes, perhaps the mother of the Trojan Iphition by Otrynteus, 2.977.

GYRTIUS (*gur'-ti-us*): father of Hyrtius, 14.599.

GYRTONE (*jur-toh'-nee*): Thessalian city in the kingdom of Polypoetes, 2.840.

HADES (*hay'-deez*): ruler of the dead, son of Cronus and Rhea, brother of Zeus, Demeter and Poseidon, 15.225.

HAEMON (*hee'-mon*): (1) Achaean, one of the Pylian captains, 4.339. (2) Father of Laerces, 17.537.

HALCYON (*hal'-si-on*): a seabird, the name her parents gave Cleopatra, 9.684.

HALIARTUS (*ha-li-ar'-tus*): city in Boeotia, 2.593.

HALIUS (*ha'-li-us*): Trojan ally, Lycian killed by Odysseus, 5.778.

HALIZONIANS (*ha-li-zoh'-ni-unz*): Trojan allies, a tribe from south of the Black Sea, led by Odius (1) and Epistrophus (3), 2.968.

HARMA (*har'-ma*): city in Boeotia, 2.589.

HARMON (*har'-mon*): Trojan blacksmith, father of Tecton, 5.65.

HARPALION (*har-pay'-li-on*): Trojan ally from Paphlagonia, son of Pylaemenes, killed by Meriones, 13.742.

HEBE (*hee'-bee*): goddess of youth, daughter of Zeus and Hera, servant of the gods, 4.2.

HECAMEDE (*he-ka-mee'-dee*): daughter of Arsinous, Nestor's captive, 11.735.

HECTOR (*hek'-tor*): Trojan, son of Priam and Hecuba, supreme commander of the Trojans, 1.285.

HECUBA (*he'-kew-ba*): daughter of Dymas, Priam's queen, mother of Hector, 6.300.

HELEN (*he'-len*): daughter of Zeus, wife of Menelaus, consort of Paris, her abduction by him from Sparta the cause of the Trojan War, 2.189. See note 24.35–36.

HELENUS (*he'-le-nus*): (1) Achaean, son of Oenops, killed by Hector, 5.811. (2) Trojan, son of Priam, prophet and warrior, 6.88.

HELICAON (*he-li-kay'-on*): Trojan, son of Antenor, husband of Laodice, 3.148.

HELICE (*he'-li-see*): city or vicinity in the kingdom of Agamemnon, on the Corinthian Gulf, and sacred to Poseidon, 2.666.

HELIOS (*hee'-li-os*): the Sun, 3.331.

HELLENES (*hel'-eenz*): 2.780, people of **HELLAS** (*hel'-as*), a region in southern Thessaly, in the kingdom of Peleus and Achilles, 2.620.

HELLESPONT (*hel'-e-spont*): strait between the Troad and Thrace (the Dardanelles), 2.957.

HELOS (*hel'-os*): (1) city in Lacedaemon, 2.676. (2) City near Pylos in Nestor's kingdom, 2.686.

HEPHAESTUS (*he-fees'-tus*): god of fire, the great artificer, son of Hera, husband of Charis, 1.687. See notes 1.712, 18.462, 21.378–79.

HEPTAPORUS (*hep-ta'-po-rus*): river in the Troad, 12.23.

HERA (*heer'-a*): goddess, daughter of Cronus and Rhea, wife and sister of Zeus, defender of the Achaeans, 1.63. See notes 1.712, 2.748, 14.356.

HERACLES (*her'-a-kleez*): son of Zeus and Alcmena, father of Tlepolemus (1), 2.748. See notes 2.748, 5.434–62, 733–38, 15.32–39.

HERMES (*hur'-meez*): god, son of Zeus, guide and giant killer, 2.121. See note ad loc.

HERMIONE (*hur-meye'-o-nee*): city in the Argolid, in the kingdom of Diomedes, 2.651.

HERMUS (*hur'-mus*): river in Maeonia, 20.446.

HICETAON (*hi-ke-tay'-on*): son of Laomedon, Trojan elder, father of Melanippus (2), 3.177.

HIPPASUS (*hip'-a-sus*): (1) father of the Trojans Charops and Socus, 11.504. (2) Father of the Achaean Hypsenor (2), 13.477. (3) Father of the Trojan Apisaon (2), 17.402.

HIPPEMOLGI (*hi-pee-mol'-jeye*): people of the north, supposed nomads, "who drink the milk of mares," 13.7.

HIPPOCOON (*hi-po'-koh-on*): Trojan ally, cousin of Rhesus (1), 10.599.

HIPPODAMAS (*hi-po'-da-mas*): Trojan killed by Achilles, 20.455.

HIPPODAMIA (*hi-po-da-meye'-a*): (1) wife of Pirithous, mother of the Achaean Polypoetes, 2.844. (2) Daughter of Anchises (1), wife of the Trojan Alcathous, 13.497.

HIPPODAMUS (*hi-po'-da-mus*): Trojan killed by Odysseus, 11.390.

HIPPOLOCHUS (*hi-po'-lo-kus*): (1) father of the Trojan Glaucus (1), 6.138. (2) Trojan, son of Antimachus, killed by Agamemnon, 11.143.

HIPPOMACHUS (*hi-po'-ma-kus*): Trojan, son of Antimachus, killed by Leonteus, 12.217.

HIPPONOUS (*hi-po'-no-us*): Achaean killed by Hector, 11.352.

HIPPOTHOUS (*hi-po'-tho-us*): (1) Trojan ally, son of Lethus, co-commander of the Pelasgians, killed by Great Ajax, 2.952. (2) Trojan, son of Priam, 24.297.

HIPPOTION (*hi-po'-ti-on*): father of the Trojans Ascanius and Morys, killed by Meriones, 13.917.

HIRE (*heye'-ree*): city near Pylos, in the southwestern Peloponnese, 9.180.

HISTIAEA (*hi-sti-ee'-a*): city in Euboea, 2.627.

HYADES (*heye'-a-deez*): constellation, 18.568.

HYAMPOLIS (*heye-am'-po-lis*): city in Phocis, 2.611.

HYDE (*heye'-dee*): region of Maeonia, around Mount Tmolus, 20.439.

HYLE (*heye'-lee*): city in Boeotia, 2.590.

HYLLUS (*hil'-us*): river in Maeonia, 20.445.

HYPERENOR (*hi-pe-ree'-nor*): Trojan, son of Panthous, killed by Menelaus, 14.603.

HYPERESIA (*hi-pe-ree'-si-a*): Achaean city in the kingdom of Agamemnon, 2.664.

HYPERIAN SPRING (*hi-pe-reye'-an*): spring in Thessaly, in the kingdom of Euryplus, 2.836.

HYPIROCHUS (*hi-peye'-ro-kus*): (1) Trojan killed by Odysseus, 11.390. (2) Father of Itymoneus, 11.797.

HYPIRON (*hi-peye'-ron*): Trojan killed by Diomedes, 5.160.

HYPSENOR (*hip-see'-nor*): (1) Trojan, son of Dolopion, killed by Eurypylus, 5.84. (2) Achaean, son of Hippasus (2), killed by Deiphobus, 13.477.

HYPSIPYLE (*hip-si'-pi-lee*): mother of Euneus by Jason, 7.542.

HYRIA (*hi'-ri-a*): city in Boeotia, 2.586.

HYRMINE (*hur-meye'-nee*): city of the Epeans in Elis, 2.709.

HYRTACUS (*hur'-ta-kus*): father of the Trojan Asius (1), 2.949.

HYRTIUS (*hur'-ti-us*): Trojan, son of Gyrtius, commander of the Mysians, killed by Great Ajax, 14.598.

IALMENUS (*i-al'-me-nus*): Achaean, son of Ares and Astyoche, co-commander of the Minyans from Orchomenos, 2.602.

IALYSUS (*i-a'-li-sus*): city in Rhodes, 2.751.

IAMENUS (*eye-a'-me-nus*): Trojan killed by Leonteus, 12.223.

IAPETUS (*eye-a'-pe-tus*): one of the Titans, father of Prometheus. See note 8.554.

IARDANUS (*i-ar'-da-nus*): river in the western Peloponnese, on the frontier between Pylos and Arcadia, 7.155.

IASUS (*eye'-a-sus*): Achaean, son of Sphelus, a captain of the Athenians, killed by Aeneas, 15.392.

ICARIAN SEA (*eye-kair'-i-an*): sea off the coast of Asia Minor, 2.168.

IDA (*eye'-da*): central mountain and range of the Troad and favored seat of Zeus, 2.932.

IDAEUS (*eye-dee'-us*): (1) Trojan, herald of Priam, 3.296. (2) Trojan, son of Dares, 5.11.

IDAS (*eye'-das*): husband of Marpessa and father of Cleopatra, who contended against Apollo for Marpessa, 9.680. See note 9.679–88.

IDOMENEUS (*eye-do'-men-yoos*): Achaean, son of Deucalion, commander of the contingent from Crete, 1.171.

ILESION (*i-lee'-si-on*): city in Boeotia, 2.589.

ILIONEUS (*eye'-li-on-yoos*): Trojan, son of Phorbas, killed by Peneleos, 14.572.

ILIUM (*il'-i-um*): Troy, the city of Ilus, 2.133.

ILUS (*eye'-lus*): eldest son of Tros (1), father of Laomedon, grandfather of Priam, 10.481.

IMBRASUS (*im'-bra-sus*): Thracian, father of the Trojan Pirous, 4.602.

IMBRIUS (*im'-bri-us*): Trojan ally from Pedaeon, son of Mentor, son-in-law of Priam, killed by Teucer, 13.205.

IMBROS (*im'-bros*): island northwest of Troy, 13.41.

IOLCOS (*i-ol'-kos*): Thessalian city in the kingdom of Eumelus, 2.813.

IONIANS (*eye-oh'-ni-unz*): Athenians, 13.793.

IPHEUS (*eye'-fyoos*): Trojan ally, Lycian killed by Patroclus, 16.497.

IPHIANASSA (*eye-fi-a-nas'-a*): one of Agamemnon's daughters, 9.174.

IPHICLUS (*eye'-fi-klus*): son of Phylacus (1), father of the Achaeans Protesilaus and Podarces, runner defeated by Nestor, 2.806.

IPHIDAMAS (*eye-fi'-da-mas*): Trojan, son of Antenor, killed by Agamemnon, 11.256.

IPHINOUS (*eye-fi'-no-us*): Achaean, son of Dexius, killed by Glaucus, 7.16.

IPHIS (*eye'-fis*): mistress of Patroclus, captured from Scyros by Achilles, 9.814.

IPHITION (*eye-fi'-ti-on*): Trojan ally, son of Otrynteus and a water nymph, Gyge perhaps, killed by Achilles, 20.436.

IPHITUS (*eye'-fi-tus*): (1) son of Naubulus, father of the Achaeans Schedius (1) and Epistrophus (1), 2.608. (2) Father of the Trojan Archeptolemus, 8.146.

IRIS (*eye'-ris*): goddess, messenger of Zeus, 2.895.

ISANDER (*eye-san'-der*): son of Bellerophon, killed by Ares, 6.233.

ISUS (*eye'-sus*): Trojan, bastard son of Priam, killed by Agamemnon, 11.118.

ITHACA (*ith'-a-ka*): island off western Greece, the home of Odysseus, 2.725.

ITHAEMENES (*i-thee'-me-neez*): father of the Trojan Sthenelaus, 16.685.

ITHOME (*i-thoh'-mee*): Thessalian city in the kingdom of Podalirius and Machaon, 2.831.

ITON (*eye'-ton*): Thessalian city in the kingdom of Protesilaus, 2.794.

ITYMONEUS (*eye-ti'-mon-yoos*): Epean, son of Hypirochus (2), killed by Nestor, 11.796.

IXION (*ix-eye'-on*): reputed father of Pirithous, who was actually sired by Zeus with Ixión's wife, 14.381.

JASON (*jay'-son*): commander of the Argonauts, father of Euneus by Hypsipyle, 7.541.

LAAS (*lay'-as*): city in Lacedaemon, 2.677.

LACEDAEMON (*la-se-dee'-mon*): city and kingdom of Menelaus, in the southern Peloponnese, 2.673.

LAERCES (*lay-ur'-seez*): Myrmidon, son of Haemon (2), father of the Achaean Alcimedon, 16.232.

LAERTES (*lay-ur'-teez*): father of Odysseus, 2.201.

LAMPUS (*lam'-pus*): Trojan, son of Laomedon, father of Dolops (2), 3.176.

LAODAMAS (*lay-o'-da-mas*): Trojan, son of Antenor, killed by Great Ajax, 15.598.

LAODAMIA (*lay-o-da-meye'-a*): daughter of Bellerophon, mother of Sarpedon by Zeus, killed by Artemis, 6.233.

LAODICE (*lay-o'-di-see*): (1) Trojan, daughter of Priam, wife of Helicaon, 3.148. (2) One of Agamemnon's daughters, 9.174.

LAODOCUS (*lay-o'-do-kus*): (1) Trojan, son of Antenor, impersonated by Athena, 4.101. (2) Achaean, charioteer of Antilochus, 17.786.

LAOGONUS (*lay-o'-go-nus*): (1) Trojan, son of Onetor, killed by Meriones, 16.704. (2) Trojan, son of Bias (3), killed by Achilles, 20.520.

LAOMEDON (*lay-o'-me-don*): king of Troy, son of Ilus, father of Priam, Tithonus, Lampus, Clytius (1) and Hicetaon, 3.298. See note 5.733–38.

LAOTHOË (*lay-o'-thoh-ee*): daughter of Altes, mother of the Trojans Polydorus (1) and Lycaon (2) by Priam, 21.97.

LAPITHS (*la'-piths*): Thessalian tribe led by Polypoetes and Leonteus, 12.152.

LARISSA (*la-ris'-a*): city of the Pelasgians, Trojan allies, 2.953.

LECTOS (*lek'-tos*): cape and promontory southwest of Mount Ida in the Troad, 14.340.

LEITUS (*lee'-i-tus*): Achaean, son of Alectryon, co-commander with Peneleos of the Boeotians, 2.584.

LELEGES (*le'-le-jeez*): Trojan allies, people of northwestern Asia Minor, 10.496.

LEMNOS (*lem'-nos*): island in the northeastern Aegean, 1.714. See note 1.715.

LEOCRITUS (*lee-o'-kri-tus*): Achaean, son of Arisbas, killed by Aeneas, 17.398.

LEONTEUS (*le-on'-tyoos*): Achaean, son of Coronus, co-commander with Poly-poetes of the Lapiths from Argissa, 2.847.

LESBOS (*lez'-bos*): island and city off the coast of Asia Minor south of Troy, 9.154.

LETHUS (*lee'-thus*): son of Teutamus, father of the Trojan allies Hippothous (1) and Pylaeus, from Larissa, 2.955.

LETO (*lee'-toh*): goddess, mother of Apollo and Artemis by Zeus, 1.10.

LEUCUS (*lew'-kus*): Achaean, comrade of Odysseus, killed by Antiphus (3), 4.567.

LICYMNIUS (*li-sim'-ni-us*): uncle of Heracles, killed by his great-nephew Tlepolemus, 2.759.

LILAEA (*li-lee'-a*): city in Phocis, 2.613.

LINDOS (*lin'-dos*): city in Rhodes, 2.751.

LOCRIANS (*lo'-kri-unz*): 2.617, people of **LOCRIS** (*lo'-kris*), a region in north-eastern Greece, the kingdom of Little Ajax.

LYCAON (*leye-kay'-on*): (1) father of the Trojan Pandarus, 2.937. (2) Trojan, son of Priam and Laothoë, killed by Achilles, 3.389.

LYCASTUS (*li-kas'-tus*): city in Crete, 2.742.

LYCIANS (*li'-shunz*): Trojan allies, 2.988, people of **LYCIA** (*li'-sha*) (1), a region in southern Asia Minor allied to Troy, the kingdom of Sarpedon and Glaucus (1), 2.989. Not to be confused with **LYCIA** (2), the country around Zelea, close to Troy and the home of Pandarus, 5.115.

LYCOMEDES (*leye-ko-mee'-deez*): Achaean, son of Creon, killer of Apisaon (2), 9.98.

LYCON (*leye'-kon*): Trojan killed by Peneleos, 16.395.

LYCOPHONTES (*leye-ko-fon'-teez*): Trojan killed by Teucer, 8.315.

LYCOPHRON (*leye'-ko-fron*): Achaean, son of Mastor, comrade of Great Ajax, killed by Hector, 15.503.

LYCTOS (*lik'-tos*): city in Crete, 2.742.

LYCURGUS *(leye-kur'-gus)*: (1) son of Dryas, who attacked Dionysus and was blinded by Zeus in turn, 6.150. (2) Killer of Areithous (1), 7.163.

LYRNESSUS *(lur-nes'-us)*: city in the Troad below Mount Ida, the home of Briseis, 2.786.

LYSANDER *(leye-san'-der)*: Trojan killed by Great Ajax, 11.579.

MACAR *(ma'-kar)*: legendary founding king of Lesbos, 24.636.

MACHAON *(ma-kay'-on)*: Achaean, son of Asclepius, healer and co-commander with his brother Podalirius of the Thessalians from Tricca and Oechalia, 2.834.

MAEANDER *(mee-an'-der)*: river in Caria, in southern Asia Minor, near Miletus (2), 2.981.

MAEMALUS *(mee'-ma-lus)*: father of Pisander (3), 16.229.

MAEONIANS *(mee-oh'-ni-unz)*: Trojan allies, 2.978, people of **MAEONIA** *(mee-oh'-ni-a)*, a region around Lake Gyge in central Asia Minor, 2.976.

MAGNESIANS *(mag-nee'-shunz)*: people from a region on the northeastern coast of Thessaly, led by Prothous, 2.859.

MANTINEA *(man-ti-nee'-a)*: city in Arcadia, 2.700.

MARIS *(ma'-ris)*: Trojan ally, son of Amisodarus, Lycian killed by Thrasymedes, 16.377.

MARPESSA *(mar-pes'-a)*: daughter of Euenus (2), husband of Idas, mother of Cleopatra, 9.679. See note ad loc.

MASES *(may'-seez)*: city in the Argolid, the kingdom of Diomedes, 2.653.

MASTOR *(mas'-tor)*: father of the Achaean Lycophron, 15.502.

MECISTEUS *(mee-sis'-tyoos)*: (1) son of Talaus, father of the Achaean Euryalus, 2.657. (2) Achaean, son of Echius (1), killed by Polydamas, 8.380.

MEDEON *(me'-de-on)*: city in Boeotia, 2.591.

MEDESICASTE *(mee-de-si-kas'-tee)*: illegitimate daughter of Priam, wife of the Trojan Imbrius, 13.207.

MEDON *(me'-don)*: (1) Achaean, bastard son of Oileus (1), second in command of the Thessalians from Methone, killed by Aeneas, 2.829. (2) Trojan captain, 17.249.

MEGAS *(me'-gas)*: father of the Trojan Perimus, 16.813.

MEGES *(me'-jeez)*: Achaean, son of Phyleus, commander of the men from Dulichion and the Echinades, 2.720.

MELANIPPUS (*me-la-nip'-us*): (1) Trojan killed by Teucer, 8.316. (2) Trojan, son of Hicetaon, killed by Antilochus, 15.635. (3) Trojan killed by Patroclus, 16.813. (4) Achaean captain, 19.284.

MELANTHIUS (*me-lan'-thi-us*): Trojan killed by Eurypylus (2), 6.43.

MELAS (*me'-las*): son of Portheus, brother of Oeneus, 14.143.

MELEAGER (*me-le-ay'-ger*): son of Oeneus and Althaea, prince of the Aetolians in Calydon, 2.737. See note 9.646–729.

MELIBOEA (*me-li-bee'-a*): city in Thessaly, in the kingdom of Philoctetes, 2.818.

MENELAUS (*me-ne-lay'-us*): Achaean, son of Atreus, king of Lacedaemon, brother of Agamemnon, husband of Helen, 1.19. See note 3.247.

MENESTHES (*me-nes'-theez*): Achaean killed by Hector, 5.699.

MENESTHEUS (*me-nes'-thyoos*): Achaean, son of Peteos, commander of the Athenians, 2.643.

MENESTHIUS (*me-nes'-thi-us*): (1) Achaean, son of Areithous (1), killed by Paris, 7.9. (2) Achaean, son of Spercheus River, reputed son of Borus (2), a captain of the Myrmidons, 16.204.

MENOETIUS (*me-nee'-shus*): son of Actor (3), father of Patroclus, 9.243.

MENON (*me'-non*): Trojan killed by Leonteus, 12.223.

MENTES (*men'-teez*): Trojan, commander of the Cicones, impersonated by Apollo, 17.83.

MENTOR (*men'-tor*): father of the Trojan Imbrius, 13.204.

MERIONES (*me-reye'-o-neez*): Achaean, son of Molus, comrade of Idomeneus, second in command of the Cretans, 2.746.

MERMERUS (*mur'-me-rus*): Trojan killed by Antilochus, 14.600.

MEROPS (*me'-rops*): prophet from Percote, father of the Trojans Adrestus (1) and Amphius (1), 2.942.

MESSE (*mes'-ee*): city in Lacedaemon, 2.674.

MESSEIS (*me-see'-is*): spring in Greece, location unknown, 6.544.

MESTHLES (*mesth'-leez*): Trojan ally, son of Talaemenes, co-commander of the Maeonians, 2.976.

MESTOR (*mee'-stor*): Trojan, son of Priam, 24.305.

METHONE (*me-thoh'-nee*): Thessalian city in the kingdom of Philoctetes, 2.817.

MIDEA (*mi-dee'-a*): city in Boeotia, 2.598.

MILETUS (*meye-lee'-tus*): (1) city in Crete, 2.742. (2) City of the Carians, in southern Asia Minor, 2.980.

MINOS (*meye'-nos*): son of Zeus and Europa, father of Deucalion (1), king of Crete, 13.523.

MINYANS (*min'-yunz*): people of Orchomenos (1), commanded by Ascalaphus and Ialmenus, 2.601.

MINYEOS (*mi-ni-ee'-os*): river in the western Peloponnese on the border of Nestor's kingdom, 11.859.

MNESUS (*mnee'-sus*): Trojan ally, Paeonian killed by Achilles, 21.236.

MOLION (*mo-leye'-on*): Trojan, comrade of Thymbraeus, killed by Odysseus, 11.374.

MOLIONES (*mo-leye'-o-neez*): the twin brothers Cleatus and Eurytus (2), reputed sons of Actor (2) but actually sired by Poseidon, 11.843. See note 11.892.

MOLUS (*mo'-lus*): father of the Achaean Meriones, 10.315.

MORYS (*mo'-ris*): Trojan, son of Hippotion, killed by Meriones, 13.917.

MULIUS (*moo'-li-us*): (1) Epean hero, son-in-law of Augeas, killed by Nestor, 11.879. (2) Trojan killed by Patroclus, 16.814. (3) Trojan killed by Achilles, 20.533.

MUSES: goddesses, daughters of Zeus, nine in number, who preside over literature and the arts and are the sources of artistic inspiration, 1.726.

MYCALE (*mi-ka'-lee*): mountain in Caria, in southern Asia Minor, across from Miletus (2), 2.981.

MYCALESSUS (*mi-ka-les'-us*): city in Boeotia, 2.588.

MYCENAE (*mi-see'-nee*): city in the Argolid, Agamemnon's capital, just to the north of the city of Argos, 2.660.

MYDON (*meye'-don*): (1) Trojan, son of Atymnius, charioteer of Pylaemenes, killed by Antilochus, 3.667. (2) Trojan ally, Peonian killed by Achilles, 21.235.

MYGDON (*mig'-don*): commander of the Phyrgians, 3.226.

MYNES (*meye'-neez*): Trojan, king of Lyrnessus, son of Euenus (1), killed by Achilles, 2.789.

MYRINE (*mi-reye'-nee*): Amazon after whom the gods named a mound that rises before Troy, 2.925.

MYRMIDONS (*mur'-mi-donz*): the people of Phthia, in southern Thessaly, ruled by King Peleus and commanded at Troy by Achilles, 1.212.

MYRSINUS (*mur'-si-nus*): city of the Epeans in Elis, 2.709.

MYSIANS (*mi'-shunz*): (1) Trojan allies living to the east of Troy, 2.970. (2) Thracian tribe, 13.7.

NASTES (*nas'-teez*): Trojan ally, son of Nomion, co-commander of the Carians, killed by Achilles, 2.979.

NAUBOLUS (*naw'-bo-lus*): Phocian hero, father of Iphitus (1), 2.608.

NELEUS (*neel'-yoos*): father of Nestor, former king of Pylos, 2.23.

NEOPTOLEMUS (*ne-op-to'-le-mus*): son of Achilles, 19.394.

NEREIDS (*nee'-ree-idz*): sea-goddesses, daughters of Nereus, 18.43.

NEREUS (*nee'-ryoos*): sea-god, the Old Man of the Sea, father of Thetis and of all the Nereids, 18.60. See note 1.1.

NERITON (*nee'-ri-ton*): mountain on Ithaca, 2.726.

NESTOR (*nes'-tor*): Achaean, son of Neleus, king of the Pylians, father of Antilochus and Thrasymedes, the oldest of the Achaean chieftains, 1.290. See note 9.73–75.

NIGHT: goddess who wields power over gods and men; even Zeus responds to her with fear, 14.313.

NIOBE (*neye'-o-bee*): Phrygian woman whose six daughters and six sons were killed by Artemis and Apollo, 24.708. See note ad loc.

NIREUS (*neye'-ryoos*): Achaean, son of Charopus and Aglaea, captain of the men from Syme, 2.767.

NISA (*neye'-sa*): city in Boeotia, 2.598.

NISYRUS (*neye-seye'-rus*): island in the southeastern Aegean near Cos, 2.772.

NOËMON (*no-ee'-mon*): (1) Trojan ally, Lycian killed by Odysseus, 5.778. (2) Achaean, comrade of Antilochus, 23.681.

NOMION (*no-meye'-on*): father of the Trojans Amphimachus (2) and Nastes, 2.983.

NYSA (*neye'-sa*): mountain on the island of Euboea, sacred to Dionysus, 6.154.

OCALEA (*oh-ka-lee'-a*): city in Boeotia, 2.591.

OCEAN: the great river that surrounds the world and the god who rules its waters, 1.505. See note ad loc and note 14.244.

OCHESIUS (*o-kee'-si-us*): father of the Achaean Periphas (1), 5.974.

ODIUS (*od'-i-us*): (1) Trojan ally, co-commander of the Halizonians, killed by Agamemnon, 2.968. (2) Achaean herald, 9.204.

ODYSSEUS (*o-dis'-yoos*): Achaean, son of Laertes, father of Telemachus, warlord of Ithaca and the surrounding islands, 1.171.

OECHALIA (*ee-kay'-li-a*): Thessalian city of Eurytus (1), in the kingdom of Machaon and Podalirius, 2.688.

OEDIPUS (*ee'-di-pus*): son of Laius and Jocasta, king of Thebes (1), 23.756. See note ad loc.

OENEUS (*een'-yoos*): king of Calydon, son of Portheus, father of Tydeus and Meleager, 2.735.

OENOMAUS (*ee-no-may'-us*): (1) Achaean killed by Hector, 5.811. (2) Trojan killed by Idomeneus, 12.164.

OENOPS (*ee'-nops*): father of the Achaean Helenus (1), 5.812.

OETYLUS (*ee'-ti-lus*): city in Lacedaemon, 2.677.

OILEUS (*oh-eel'-yoos*): (1) Locrian king, father of Little Ajax, father of the Achaean Medon (1), 2.617. (2) Trojan killed by Agamemnon, 11.108.

OLENIAN ROCK (*oh-leen'-i-an*): landmark on the border of Elis, 2.710.

OLENUS (*oh'-le-nus*): city in Aetolia, 2.733.

OLIZON (*o-leye'-zon*): Thessalian city in the kingdom of Philoctetes, 2.818.

OLOOSSON (*o-loh-os'-on*): Thessalian city in the kingdom of Polypoetes, 2.841.

OLYMPUS (*o-lim'-pus*): mountain in northeastern Thessaly, the home of the gods, 1.51.

ONCHESTUS (*on-kees'-tus*): city in Boeotia, 2.596.

ONETOR (*o-nee'-tor*): father of the Trojan Laogonus (1) and priest of Zeus, 16.704.

OPHELESTES (*o-fe-les'-teez*): (1) Trojan killed by Teucer, 8.314. (2) Trojan ally, Paeonian killed by Achilles, 21.236.

OPHELTIUS (*o-fel'-ti-us*): (1) Trojan killed by Euryalus, 6.23. (2) Achaean killed by Hector, 11.351.

OPITES (*o-peye'-teez*): Achaean killed by Hector, 11.350.

OPOIS (*o'-poh-is*): city in Locris, Patroclus' birthplace, 2.621.

ORCHOMENOS (*or-ko'-me-nos*): (1) city of the Minyans, in eastern central Greece, bordering on Boeotia, 2.601. (2) City in Arcadia, 2.698.

ORESBIUS (*o-rez'-bi-us*): Achaean, Boeotian killed by Hector, 5.812.

ORESTES (*o-res'-teez*): (1) Achaean killed by Hector, 5.810. (2) Son of Agamemnon, 9.171. (3) Trojan killed by Leonteus, 12.223.

ORION (*o-reye'-on*): constellation, the Hunter, 18.568.

ORION'S DOG: the star Sirius, 22.35. See note ad loc.

ORMENION (*or-me'-ni-on*): Thessalian city in the kingdom of Eurypylus, 2.836.

ORMENUS (*or'-me-nus*): (1) Trojan killed by Teucer, 8.314. (2) Father of Amyntor, 9.546. (3) Trojan killed by Polypoetes, 12.216.

ORNIAE (*or-neye'-ee*): city in the kingdom of Agamemnon, 2.662.

ORSILOCHUS (*or-si'-lo-kus*): (1) Achaean, son of Diocles, killed by Aeneas, 5.624. (2) Trojan killed by Teucer, 8.314.

ORTHAEUS (*or-thee'-us*): Trojan captain, 13.916.

ORTHE (*or'-thee*): Thessalian city in the kingdom of Polypoetes, 2.841.

ORTILOCHUS (*or-ti'-lo-kus*): son of Alpheus, father of Diocles, 5.628.

ORUS (*oh'-rus*): Achaean killed by Hector, 11.352.

OTHRYONEUS (*o-thri-on'-yoos*): Trojan, affianced to Cassandra, killed by Idomeneus, 13.422.

OTREUS (*o'-tryoos*): a commander of the Phrygians, 3.226.

OTRYNTEUS (*o-trin'-tyoos*): father of the Trojan Iphition, 20.437.

OTUS (*oh'-tus*): (1) son of Aloeus, giant who, in league with his brother Ephialtes, imprisoned Ares, 5.437. (2) Achaean from Cyllene, a commander of the Epeans, killed by Polydamas, 15.600.

PAEON (*pee'-on*): father of the Trojan Agastrophus, 11.395.

PAEONIANS (*pee-oh'-ni-unz*): Trojan allies, 2.960, inhabitants of **PAEONIA** (*pee-oh'-ni-a*), a region to the northeast of Greece, later Macedonia, 17.404.

PAESUS (*pee'-sus*): city in the Troad, northeast of Troy, 5.703.

PALLAS (*pal'-as*): epithet of Athena, 1.232.

PALMYS (*pal'-mis*): Trojan captain, 13.917.

PAMMON (*pam'-on*): Trojan, son of Priam, 24.296.

PANDARUS (*pan'-da-rus*): son of Lycaon (1), commander of the Trojans from Zelea, killed by Diomedes, 2.938.

PANDION (*pan-deye'-on*): Achaean, comrade of Teucer, 12.428.

PANDOCUS (*pan'-do-kus*): Trojan killed by Great Ajax, 11.578.

PANOPEUS (*pan'-op-yoos*): (1) city in Phocis, 2.610. (2) Father of the Achaean Epeus, 23.742.

PANTHOUS (*pan'-tho-us*): Trojan elder, husband of Phrontis, father of Polydamas, Euphorbus, Hyperenor, 3.176.

PAPHLAGONIANS (*pa-fla-goh'-ni-unz*): 2.963, Trojan allies from **PAPHLAGONIA** (*pa-fla-goh'-ni-a*), a region on the southern shore of the Black Sea.

PARIS (*pa'-ris*): Trojan, son of Priam and Hecuba, who abducted Helen from Menelaus in Lacedaemon, 3.16.

PARRHASIA (*pa-ray'-zi-a*): region or district in Arcadia, 2.701.

PARTHENIUS (*par-the'-ni-us*): river in Paphlagonia, 2.966.

PASITHEA (*pa-si'-thee-a*): one of the Graces desired by Sleep, 14.331.

PATROCLUS (*pa-tro'-klus*): Achaean, son of Menoetius, brother-in-arms of Achilles, killed by Hector, 1.360. See note 18.581–92.

PEDAEON (*pee-dee'-on*): city in the Troad, 13.206.

PEDAEUS (*pee-dee'-us*): Trojan, bastard son of Antenor, killed by Meges, 5.76.

PEDASUS (*pee'-da-sus*): (1) Trojan, son of Bucolion, twin brother of Aesepus (2), killed by Euryalus, 6.24. (2) City in the Troad, on the Satniois River, 6.41. (3) City in the southwestern Peloponnese near Pylos, 9.182.

PELAGON (*pe'-la-gon*): (1) Achaean, one of the Pylian captains, 4.338. (2) Trojan ally, Lycian, comrade of Sarpedon, 5.797.

PELASGIANS (*pe-laz'-juns*): Trojan allies, a tribe located in Asia Minor, 2.952.

PELEGON (*pee'-le-gon*): son of Axius, father of the Trojan Asteropaeus, 21.161.

PELEUS (*peel'-yoos*): son of Aeacus, king of the Myrmidons, father of Achilles by Thetis, 1.1. See note ad loc.

PELIAN (*pee'-li-an*): of Achilles' spear, its timber hewn on Mount Pelion, 16.171.

PELIAS (*pe'-li-as*): king of Iolcus, father of Alcestis, 2.816.

PELIDES (*pe-leye'-deez*): "son of Peleus," patronymic of Achilles, 20.418.

PELION (*pee'-li-on*): mountain in Magnesia, home of the Centaurs, 2.846.

PELLENE (*pe-lee'-nee*): Achaean city in the kingdom of Agamemnon, 2.665.

PELOPS (*pel'-ops*): king of Argos, father of Atreus, grandfather of Agamemnon and Menelaus, 2.122.

PENELEOS (*pee-ne'-lee-ohs*): Achaean, co-commander with Leitus of the Boeotians, 2.584.

PENEUS (*pee-nee'-us*): river in Thessaly, 2.854.

PERAEBIANS (*pe-ree'-bi-unz*): people from Dodona, led by Guneus, 2.851.

PERCOTE (*pur-koh'-tee*): city in the Troad, to the northeast of Troy, 2.947.

PEREA (*pee-ree'-a*): locale in Thessaly where Apollo bred the mares of Eumelus, 2.871.

PERGAMUS (*pur'-ga-mus*): the citadel of Troy, 4.586.

PERGASUS (*pur'-ga-sus*): father of the Trojan Deicoon, 5.617.

PERIBOEA (*pe-ri-bee'-a*): daughter of Acessamenus, mother of Pelegon by the River Axius, 21.163.

PERIERES (*pe-ri-ee'-reez*): father of Borus (2), 16.208.

PERIMEDES (*pe-ri-mee'-deez*): father of the Achaean Schedius (2), 15.597.

PERIMUS (*per'-i-mus*): Trojan, son of Megas, killed by Patroclus, 16.813.

PERIPHAS (*per'-i-fas*): (1) Achaean, son of Ochesius, Aetolian killed by Ares, 5.973. (2) Trojan, son of the herald of Anchises, 17.375.

PERIPHETES (*pe-ri-fee'-teez*): (1) Trojan killed by Teucer, 14.602. (2) Achaean from Mycenae, son of Copreus, killed by Hector, 15.742.

PERSEPHONE (*pur-se'-fo-nee*): goddess of the underworld, daughter of Demeter, and wife of Hades, 9.557.

PERSEUS (*purs'-yoos*): son of Zeus by Danaë, grandfather of Eurystheus, father of Sthenelus (2), 14.384.

PETEON (*pet'-e-on*): city in Boeotia, 2.590.

PETEOS (*pet'-e-ohs*): father of the Achaean Menestheus, 2.643.

PHAENOPS (*fee'-nops*): (1) father of the Trojans Xanthus and Thoon, 5.169. (2) Father of the Trojan Phorcys, 17.360. (3) Trojan, son of Asius (1), impersonated by Apollo, 17.661.

PHAESTOS (*fees'-tos*): city in Crete, 2.743.

PHAESTUS (*fees'-tus*): Trojan ally, son of Borus (1), Maeonian killed by Idomeneus, 5.48.

PHALCES (*fal'-seez*): Trojan killed by Antilochus, 13.916.

PHARIS (*fay'-ris*): city in Lacedaemon, 2.674.

PHAUSIAS (*faw'-si-as*): father of the Trojan Apisaon (1), 11.682.

PHEGEUS (*fee'-joos*): Trojan, son of Dares, killed by Diomedes, 5.11.

PHENEOS (*fen'-ee-os*): city in Arcadia, 2.698.

PHERA (*fee'-ra*): city near Pylos, in the southwestern Peloponnese, 5.625.

PHERAE (*fee'-ree*): Thessalian city of Eumelus, 2.812.

PHERECLUS (*fe-rek'-lus*): Trojan, son of Tecton, shipwright who built Paris' ships, killed by Meriones, 5.64.

PHERES (*fee'-reez*): father of Admetus, grandfather of Eumelus, 2.867.

PHIA (*feye'-a*): city in the western Peloponnese, on the border between Arcadia and Pylos, 7.155.

PHIDAS (*feye'-das*): Achaean, a captain of the Athenians under Menestheus, 13.799.

PHIDIPPUS (*feye-dip'-us*): Achaean, son of Thessalus, co-commander of the contingent from Cos and adjacent islands, 2.774.

PHILETOR (*fi-lee'-tor*): father of the Trojan Demuchus, 20.517.

PHILOCTETES (*fi-lok-tee'-teez*): original commander of the Thessalians from Methone, marooned on Lemnos suffering from an infected snake bite, 2.819. See note 2.826.

PHLEGIANS (*fle'-junz*): tribe in Thessaly visited by Ares, 13.354.

PHOCIANS (*foh'-shunz*): 2.615, people of **PHOCIS** (*foh'-sis*), region in central Greece adjoining Boeotia, 2.607.

PHOEBUS (*fee'-bus*): epithet of Apollo, 1.50.

PHOENICIANS (*fee-ni'-shunz*): people living on the coast of Syria, 23.828.

PHOENIX (*fee'-nix*): (1) son of Amyntor, tutor and comrade of Achilles, 9.201. (2) Father of Europa, 14.385.

PHORBAS (*for'-bas*): (1) lord of Lesbos, father of Diomede, 9.811. (2) Father of the Trojan Ilioneus, 14.573.

PHORCYS (*for'-sis*): Trojan ally, son of Phaenops (2), co-commander of the Phrygians, killed by Great Ajax, 2.974.

PHRADMON (*frad'-mon*): father of the Trojan Agelaus (1), 8.295.

PHRONTIS (*fron'-tis*): wife of Panthous, 17.45.

PHRYGIANS (*fri'-junz*): Trojan allies, 2.974, inhabitants of **PHRYGIA** (*fri'-ja*), region in Asia Minor east of Troy, 3.224.

PHTHIANS (*ftheye'-unz*): 13.794, inhabitants of **PHTHIA** (*ftheye'-a*), a sector of southern Thessaly, kingdom of Peleus and home of Achilles, 1.182.

PHTHIRES (*ftheye'-reez*): mountain in Caria, in southern Asia Minor, 2.980.

PHYLACE (*fi'-la-see*): Thessalian city in the kingdom of Protesilaus, 2.793.

PHYLACUS (*fi'-la-kus*): (1) father of Iphiclus, 2.806. (2) Trojan killed by Leitus, 6.42.

PHYLAS (*feye'-las*): father of Polymela, 16.212.

PHYLEUS (*feye'-lyoos*): father of the Achaean Meges, defeated in the spear-throw by Nestor, 2.721.

PHYLOMEDUSA (*feye-lo-me-doo'-sa*): wife of Areithous (1), mother of the Achaean Menesthius (1), 7.11.

PIDYTES (*pi-deye'-teez*): Trojan ally from Percote, killed by Odysseus, 6.35.

PIERIA (*peye-ee'-ri-a*): area around Mount Olympus, in Thessaly, 14.272.

PIRAÏDES (*peye-ra'-i-deez*): patronymic of Ptolemaeus, 4.261.

PIRAS (*peye'-ras*): father of the Trojan Rhigmus, 20.547.

PIRITHOUS (*peye-ri'-tho-us*): son of Zeus, king of the Lapiths, father of the Achaean Polypoetes, 1.307.

PIROUS (*peye'-ro-us*): Trojan ally, son of Imbrasus, co-commander of the Thracians, killed by Thoas (1), 2.956.

PISANDER (*peye-san'-der*): (1) Trojan, son of Antimachus, killed by Agamemnon, 11.143. (2) Trojan killed by Menelaus, 13.693. (3) Achaean, son of Maemalus, a commander of the Myrmidons, 16.228.

PISENOR (*peye-see'-nor*): father of the Trojan Clitus, 15.519.

PITTHEUS (*pit'-thyoos*): father of Aethra, 3.173.

PITYEA (*pi-ti-ee'-a*): city on the Hellespont northeast of Troy, 2.940.

PLACOS (*pla'-kos*): mountain above Thebe, in Mysia, 6.468.

PLATAEA (*pla-tee'-a*): city in Boeotia, 2.594.

PLEIADES (*pleye'-a-deez*): constellation, 18.568.

PLEURON (*plyoo'-ron*): city in Aetolia, 2.733.

PODALIRIUS (*po-da-leye'-ri-us*): Achaean, son of Asclepius, healer and co-commander with his brother Machaon of the Thessalians from Tricca, 2.834.

PODARCES (*po-dar'-seez*): Achaean, son of Iphiclus, brother of Protesilaus, his successor as commander of the Thessalians from Phylace, 2.805.

PODES (*po'-deez*): Trojan, son of Eetion (2), killed by Menelaus, 17.653.

POLITES (*po-leye'-teez*): Trojan, son of Priam, 2.900.

POLYAEMON (*po-li-ee'-mon*): father of the Trojan Amopaon, 8.316.

POLYBUS (*pol'-i-bus*): Trojan, son of Antenor, 11.67.

POLYCTOR (*po-lik'-tor*): named as his father by Hermes when, in disguise, he meets Priam, 24.469.

POLYDAMAS (*po-li'-da-mas*): Trojan, son of Panthous, co-commander of the first Trojan contingent, 11.65.

POLYDEUCES (*po-li-dyoo'-seez*): brother of Helen and Castor, 3.283.

POLYDORA (*po-li-dor'-a*): daughter of Peleus, mother of the Achaean Menesthius (2) by the Spercheus River, 16.206.

POLYDORUS (*po-li-dor'-us*): (1) Trojan, son of Priam, killed by Achilles, 20.463. (2) Competitor defeated in the spear-throw by Nestor, 23.710.

POLYIDUS (*po-li-eye'-dus*): (1) Trojan, son of Eurydamas, killed by Diomedes, 5.165. (2) Prophet in Corinth, father of the Achaean Euchenor, 13.764.

POLYMELA (*po-li-mee'-la*): daughter of Phylas, mother of the Achaean Eudorus by Hermes, 16.213.

POLYMELUS (*po-li-mee'-lus*): Trojan ally from Lycia, son of Argeas, killed by Patroclus, 16.497.

POLYNICES (*po-li-neye'-seez*): son of Oedipus, commander of the Seven against Thebes, 4.439. See note 5.926.

POLYPHEMUS (*po-li-fee'-mus*): Lapith warrior of the generation of Nestor, 1.308.

POLYPHETES (*po-li-fee'-teez*): a Trojan captain, 13.916.

POLYPOETES (*po-li-pee'-teez*): Achaean, son of Pirithous, co-commander of the Lapiths from Argissa, 2.842.

POLYXINUS (*po-li-xeye'-nus*): Achaean, son of Agasthenes, co-commander of the Epeans, 2.716.

PORTHEUS (*por'-thyoos*): Aetolian hero, father of Agrius, Melas and Oeneus, grandfather of Tydeus, 14.141.

POSEIDON (*po-seye'-don*): god of the sea, son of Cronus and Rhea, younger brother of Zeus, 1.475. See notes 7.523–25, 11.892, 13.247.

PRACTIOS (*prak'-ti-os*): city on the Hellespont, 2.947.

PRAMNIAN WINE (*pram'-ni-an*): a wine often used medicinally, 11.755.

PRIAM (*preye'-am*): king of Troy, son of Laomedon of the line of Dardanus (1), father of Hector and Paris, 1.21.

PROETUS (*pree'-tus*): king of Argos (2), who plotted against the life of Bellerophon, 6.185.

PROMACHUS (*pro'-ma-kus*): Achaean, son of Alegenor, killed by Acamas (1), 14.559.

PRONOUS (*pro'-no-us*): Trojan killed by Patroclus, 16.474.

PROTESILAUS (*proh-te-si-lay'-us*): Achaean, son of Iphiclus, original commander of the men of Phylace, 2.796.

PROTHOËNOR (*pro-tho-ee'-nor*): Achaean, son of Areilycus, commander of the Boeotians, killed by Polydamas, 2.585.

PROTHOON (*pro-thoh'-on*): Trojan killed by Teucer, 14.602.

PROTHOUS (*pro'-thoh-us*): Achaean, son of Tenthredon, commander of the Thessalians from Magnesia, 2.859.

PROTIAON (*pro-ti-ay'-on*): father of the Trojan Astynous (2), 15.531.

PRYTANIS (*pri'-ta-nis*): Trojan ally, Lycian killed by Odysseus, 5.778.

PTELEOS (*pte'-le-ohs*): (1) city in the kingdom of Nestor, 2.686. (2) Thessalian city in the kingdom of Protesilaus, 2.795.

PTOLEMAEUS (*pto-le-mee'-us*): son of Piraeus, father of the Achaean Eurymedon (1), 4.261.

PYLAEMENES (*pi-lee'-me-neez*): Trojan ally, commander of the Paphlagonians, killed by Menelaus, 2.963.

PYLAEUS (*pi-lee'-us*): Trojan ally, son of Lethus, co-commander of the Pelasgians from Larissa, 2.954.

PYLARTES (*pi-lar'-teez*): (1) Trojan killed by Great Ajax, 11.579. (2) Trojan killed by Patroclus, 16.814.

PYLENE (*pi-lee'-nee*): city in Aetolia, 2.733.

PYLIANS (*peye'-li-unz*): 11.814, inhabitants of **PYLOS** (*peye'-los*), Nestor's capital city and also the region surrounding it in the southwestern Peloponnese, 1.291.

PYLON (*peye'-lon*): Trojan killed by Polypoetes, 12.216.

PYRAECHMES (*peye-reek'-meez*): Trojan ally, commander of the Paeonians, killed by Patroclus, 2.960.

PYRASUS (*peye'-ra-sus*): (1) Thessalian city in the kingdom of Protesilaus, 2.793. (2) Trojan killed by Great Ajax, 11.579.

PYRIS (*peye'-ris*): Trojan killed by Patroclus, 16.496.

PYTHO (*peye'-thoh*): place in Phocis sacred to Apollo, later called Delphi, 2.609.

RHADAMANTHYS (*ra-da-man'-this*): son of Zeus and Europa, brother of Minos, 14.386.

RHEA (*ree'-a*): goddess, wife of Cronus, mother of Zeus, Poseidon, Hades, Hera and Demeter, 14.246. See note 14.244.

RHENE (*ree'-nee*): mother of the Achaean Medon (1) by Oileus (1), 2.830.

RHESUS (*ree'-sus*): (1) Trojan ally, son of Eioneus (2), king of the Thracians, killed by Diomedes, 10.503. (2) River of the Troad, 12.23.

RHIGMUS (*rig'-mus*): Trojan ally from Thrace, son of Piras, killed by Achilles, 20.548.

RHIPE (*reye'-pee*): city in Arcadia, 2.699.

RHODIANS (*roh'-di-unz*): 2.749, people of **RHODES** (*rohdz*), an island in the southeastern Aegean, settled by Tlepolemus (1), 2.749.

RHODIUS (*roh'-di-us*): river of the Troad, 12.23.

RHYTION (*ri'-ti-on*): city in Crete, 2.743.

SALAMIS (*sa'-la-mis*): island off the coast of Athens in the Saronic Gulf, the home of Great Ajax, 2.648.

SAMOS (*sa'-mos*): (1) island off the western coast of Greece (later called Cephallenia), near Ithaca in the kingdom of Odysseus, 2.728. (2) Thracian island in the northeastern Aegean facing Thrace, later called Samothrace, 13.14. See notes 13.14, 24.97.

SANGARIUS (*san-ga'-ri-us*): river in Phrygia, 3.227.

SARPEDON (*sar-pee'-don*): Trojan ally, son of Zeus and Laodamia, co-commander of the Lycians, killed by Patroclus, 2.988.

SATNIOIS (*sat-ni'-oh-is*): river of the Troad, 6.40.

SATNIUS (*sat'-ni-us*): Trojan, son of Enops (1), killed by Little Ajax, 14.522.

SCAEAN GATES (*see'-an*): the main gates of Troy, 3.174. See note ad loc.

SCAMANDER (*ska-man'-der*): river-god and chief river of the Trojan plain, so called by mortals but called Xanthus by the gods, 2.550. See 20.88–89.

SCAMANDRIUS (*ska-man'-dri-us*): (1) Trojan, son of Strophius, killed by Menelaus, 5.54. (2) Alternative name for Astyanax, son of Hector and Andromache, 6.476.

SCANDIA (*skan-deye'-a*): city on Cythera, 10.315.

SCARPHE (*skar'-fee*): city in Locris, 2.622.

SCHEDIUS (*ske'-di-us*): (1) Achaean, son of Iphitus (1), commander of the Phocians, killed by Hector, 2.607. (2) Achaean, son of Perimedes, a Phocian captain killed by Hector, 15.597.

SCHOENUS (*skee'-nus*): city in Boeotia, 2.587.

SCOLUS (*skoh'-lus*): city in Boeotia, 2.587.

SCYROS (*skeye'-ros*): island in the central Aegean off the coast of Euboea, 9.816.

SEASONS: goddesses who keep the gates of Olympus, 5.859. See note ad loc.

SELAGUS (*sel'-a-gus*): father of the Trojan Amphius (2), 5.703.

SELEPIUS (*se-lee'-pi-us*): father of Euenus (1), 2.790.

SELLEIS (*se-lee'-is*): (1) river in northwestern Greece, 2.754. (2) River of the Troad, to the northeast of Troy, 2.951.

SELLI (*sel'-eye*): prophets in the service of Zeus at Dodona, 16.278. See note ad loc.

SEMELE (*sem'-e-lee*): a Theban princess, mother of Dionysus by Zeus, 14.387.

SESAMUS (*see'-sa-mus*): city of the Paphlagonians, 2.965.

SESTOS (*ses'-tos*): city on the northern or European shore of the Hellespont, allied with Troy, 2.948.

SICYON (*sis'-i-on*): city ruled by Adrastus in the kingdom of Agamemnon, 2.662.

SIDONIANS (*seye-do'-ni-unz*): 6.343, people of **SIDON** (*seye'-don*), city in Phoenicia, 6.344.

SIMOIS (*sim'-oh-is*): river of Troy, brother and tributary of Scamander, 4.549.

SIMOISIUS (*si-mo-ee'-si-us*): Trojan named after the Simois River, son of Anthemion, killed by Great Ajax, 4.548.

SIPYLUS (*sip'-i-lus*): mountain in Lydia, in Asia Minor, 24.724.

SISYPHUS (*sis'-i-fus*): hero of Corinth, son of Aeolus, grandfather of Bellerophon, 6.180.

SLEEP: god, brother of Death, 14.277.

SMINTHEUS (*smin'-thyoos*): epithet of Apollo that may identify him as the "mouse-god" and so perhaps the one who bears the plague, 1.45.

SOCUS (*soh'-kus*): Trojan, son of Hippasus (1), brother of Charops, killed by Odysseus, 11.505.

SOLYMI (*so'-li-meye*): tribe in Asia Minor, opposed by Bellerophon, 6.217.

SPARTA (*spar'-ta*): capital city of Lacedaemon, the home of Menelaus, 2.674.

SPERCHEUS (*spur-kee'-us*): river of Phthia, father of the Achaean Menesthius (2) by Polydora, 16.205.

SPHELUS (*sfee'-lus*): son of Bucolus, father of the Achaean Iasus, 15.398.

STENTOR (*sten'-tor*): Achaean famous for his enormous voice, impersonated by Hera, 5.903.

STHENELAUS (*sthe-ne-lay'-us*): Trojan, son of Ithaemenes, killed by Patroclus, 16.684.

STHENELUS (*sthen'-e-lus*): (1) Achaean, son of Capaneus, co-commander with Diomedes and Euryalus of the Argolid contingent, 2.655. (2) Son of Perseus, father of Eurystheus, 19.144.

STICHIUS (*sti'-ki-us*): Achaean, a captain of the Athenians, killed by Hector, 13.233.

STRATIA (*stra'-ti-a*): city in Arcadia, 2.699.

STROPHIUS (*stro'-fi-us*): father of the Trojan Scamandrius (1), 5.55.

STYMPHALUS (*stim-fay'-lus*): city in Arcadia, 2.701.

STYRA (*steye'-ra*): city in Euboea, 2.629.

STYX (*stix*): river of the underworld by which the gods swear their binding oaths, 2.857. See notes 1.1, 2.858, 23.86.

SYME (*seye'-mee*): island in the southeastern Aegean north of Rhodes, 2.767.

TALAEMENES (*ta-lee'-me-neez*): father of the Trojans Mesthles and Antiphus (2), 2.977.

TALAUS (*ta'-lay-us*): father of Mecisteus (1), 2.657.

TALTHYBIUS (*tal-thi'-bi-us*): Achaean, herald of Agamemnon, 1.376.

TARNE (*tar'-nee*): city of the Maeonians, 5.49.

TARPHE (*tar'-fee*): city in Locris, 2.623.

TARTARUS (*tar'-ta-rus*): the lowest, darkest depths of the house of Hades, the kingdom of the dead, where Zeus incarcerates his defeated enemies, 8.15. See note 8.554.

TECTON (*tek'-ton*): son of Harmon, father of the Trojan Phereclus, 5.64.

TEGEA (*te-jee'-a*): city in Arcadia, 2.700.

TELAMON (*tel'-a-mon*): father of Telamonian or Great Ajax and Teucer, 2.618.

TELEMACHUS (*te-le'-ma-kus*): son of Odysseus and Penelope, 2.304.

TENEDOS (*ten'-e-dos*): island in the northeastern Aegean off the coast of Troy, 1.45.

TENTHREDON (*ten-three'-don*): father of Prothous, 2.859.

TEREA (*tee-ree'-a*): mountain near the Hellespont to the northeast of Troy, 2.940.

TETHYS (*te'-this*): goddess, wife of Ocean, 14.244. See note ad loc.

TEUCER (*tyoo'-sur*): Achaean, bastard son of Telamon, half-brother of Great Ajax and a master-archer, 6.36.

TEUTAMUS (*tyoo'-ta-mus*): father of Lethus, 2.955.

TEUTHRAS (*tyoo'-thras*): (1) Achaean killed by Hector, 5.810. (2) Father of the Trojan Axylus, 6.15.

THALPIUS (*thal'-pi-us*): Achaean, son of Eurytus (2), a commander of the Epeans, 2.713.

THALYSIAS (*tha-li'-si-as*): father of the Trojan Echepolus (1), 4.530.

THAMYRIS (*tha'-mi-ris*): Thracian singer who rivaled the Muses and was punished by them, 2.687.

THAUMACIA (*thaw-may'-sha*): city in Thessaly, in the kingdom of Philoctetes, 2.817.

THEANO (*thee-ay'-no*): daughter of Cisseus, wife of Antenor and priestess of Athena, 5.77.

THEBAEUS (*thee-bee'-us*): father of the Trojan Eniopeus, 8.138.

THEBE (*thee'-bee*): city in the Troad, the home of Eetion and Andromache, sacked by Achilles, 1.433.

THEBES (*theebz*): (1) city of the Thebans in Boeotia, attacked by Polynices and the Seven, 4.441. (2) **LOWER THEBES**, city built below the ruins of Thebes (1) after its destruction by the sons of the Seven, 2.595. (3) City in Egypt, famous for its wealth and hundred gates, 9.466.

THEMIS (*the'-mis*): goddess whose province is established law and custom, 15.107. See note 2.86.

THERSILOCHUS (*thur-si'-lo-kus*): Trojan ally, Paeonian killed by Achilles, 17.249.

THERSITES (*thur-seye'-teez*): Achaean commoner who rails against the kings, put down by Odysseus, 2.246.

THESEUS (*thees'-yoos*): son of Aegeus, king of Athens, 1.309.

THESPIA (*thes-peye'-a*): city in Boeotia, 2.588.

THESSALUS (*thes'-a-lus*): son of Heracles, father of the Achaeans Phidippus and Antiphus (1), 2.775.

THESTOR (*thes'-tor*): (1) father of the Achaean prophet Calchas, 1.80. (2) Father of the Achaean Alcmaon, 12.456. (3) Trojan, son of Enops (2), killed by Patroclus, 16.477.

THETIS (*the'-tis*): sea-goddess, daughter of Nereus, married to Peleus and by him the mother of Achilles, 1.491. See note 1.1.

THISBE (*thiz'-bee*): city in Boeotia, 2.592.

THOAS (*thoh'-as*): (1) Achaean, son of Andraemon, commander of the Aetolians, 2.732. (2) King of Lemnos, 14.276. (3) Trojan killed by Menelaus, 16.367.

THOON (*thoh'-on*): (1) Trojan, son of Phaenops (1), killed by Diomedes, 5.170. (2) Trojan killed by Odysseus, 11.499. (3) Trojan killed by Antilochus, 13.631.

THRACIANS (*thray'-shunz*): Trojan allies, 2.956, the inhabitants of **THRACE** (*thrays*), country north of the Aegean and the Hellespont, 9.5.

THRASIUS (*thra'-si-us*): Trojan ally, Paeonian killed by Achilles, 21.236.

THRASYMEDES (*thra-si-mee'-deez*): Achaean, son of Nestor, co-commander with Antilochus of the Pylian contingent, 9.95.

THRASYMELUS (*thra-si-mee'-lus*): Trojan, charioteer of Sarpedon, killed by Patroclus, 16.550.

THRONION (*thro'-ni-on*): city in Locris, 2.623.

THRYON (*thri'-on*) or **THRYOËSSA** (*thri-oh-es'-a*): city in Nestor's kingdom of Pylos by the Alpheus River, 2.684, 11.845.

THYESTES (*theye-es'-teez*): son of Pelops, brother of Atreus, 2.124.

THYMBRA (*thim'-bra*): city near Troy, on the Scamander River, 10.497.

THYMBRAEUS (*thim-bree'-us*): Trojan killed by Diomedes, 11.372.

THYMOETES (*theye-mee'-teez*): Trojan elder, 3.176.

TIRYNS (*tir'-inz*): city in the Argolid, in the kingdom of Diomedes, 2.650.

TITANOS (*ti'-ta-nos*): place or district in Thessaly, in the kingdom of Eurypylus (2), 2.837.

TITANS (*teye'-tans*): the elder gods, children of Uranus confined by Zeus in Tartarus, 5.1040. See notes 8.554, 14.244.

TITARESSUS (*ti-tar-es'-us*): Thessalian river in northwestern Greece, tributary of the Peneus and a branch of the Styx, 2.853.

TITHONUS (*ti-thoh'-nus*): husband of the Dawn, son of Laomedon and brother of Priam, 11.1.

TLEPOLEMUS (*tle-po'-le-mus*): (1) Achaean, son of Heracles, commander of the Rhodian contingent, killed by Sarpedon, 2.748. See note 18.581–92. (2) Lycian ally of the Trojans, son of Damastor, killed by Patroclus, 16.496.

TMOLUS (*tmoh'-lus*): mountain in Maeonia, 2.978.

TRACHIS (*tray'-kis*): city in the Pelasgian Argos, near the Spercheus River in the kingdom of Peleus and Achilles, 2.778.

TRECHUS (*tree'-kus*): Achaean ally from Aetolia, killed by Hector, 5.811.

TRICCA (*trik'-a*): Thessalian city, in the kingdom of Machaon, 2.831.

TROEZEN (*tree'-zen*): city in the Argolid, in the kingdom of Diomedes, 2.652.

TROEZENUS (*tree-zee'-nus*): son of Ceas, father of the Trojan Euphemus, 2.959.

TROILUS (*troy'-lus*): Trojan, son of Priam, killed by unidentified Achaean, 24.305.

TROJANS (*troh'-junz*): people of the Troad and the allies of Troy arrayed against the Achaeans, 1.180.

TROS (*trohs*): (1) ancestral king of Troy, son of Erichthonius, father of Ilus, Assaracus and Ganymede, great-grandfather of Priam, 5.247. (2) Trojan, son of Alastor (4), killed by Achilles, 20.523.

TROY (*troy*): capital city of the Troad, city of Tros and the Trojans, alternatively called Ilium, 1.152.

TYCHIUS (*teye'-ki-us*): leather-smith from Hyle who made the battle-shield of Great Ajax, 7.253.

TYDEUS (*teye'-dyoos*): son of Oeneus, father of Diomedes, 2.482. See notes 4.433–66, 5.926.

TYDIDES (*ti-deye'-deez*): "son of Tydeus," patronymic of Diomedes, 4.429.

TYPHOEUS (*ti-fee'-us*): monster imprisoned beneath the earth by Zeus in the land of Arima, 2.891.

UCALEGON (*yoo-kal'-e-gon*): Trojan elder, 3.178.

WAGON: constellation, also called the Great Bear and the Big Dipper, 18.569. See note ad loc.

XANTHUS (*xan'-thus*): (1) River of Lycia, 2.989. (2) River of the Troad, so called by the gods but called Scamander by mortals, brother of the river Simois, 6.5. (3) Trojan, son of Phaenops (1), killed by Diomedes, 5.170.

ZACYNTHUS (*za-kin'-thus*): island off the western coast of Greece in the kingdom of Odysseus, 2.728.

ZELEA (*ze-lee'-a*): city in the northwestern Troad, 2.935.

ZEPHYR (*ze'-fur*): the West Wind, 23.224.

ZEUS (*zyoos*): king of the gods, son of Cronus and Rhea, brother and husband of Hera, father of the Olympians and many mortals too, 1.6. His spheres include the sky and the weather, hospitality and the rights of guests, the punishment of injustice, the sending of omens, and the governance of the universe, controlled to some extent by Fate as well. See notes passim.

FOR THE BEST IN PAPERBACKS, LOOK FOR THE 🐧

Garry Wills in *The New Yorker* calls Robert Fagles, winner of the PEN/Ralph Manheim Medal for Translation, "the best living translator of ancient Greek drama, lyric poetry, and epic into modern English."

☐ **THE ODYSSEY**
Homer
Introduction and Notes by Bernard Knox
Odysseus' perilous ten-year voyage from Troy to his home in Ithaca is recounted in a stunning new verse translation which "restores the original joys of the performing bard," (Paul Gray, *Time*).
deluxe Penguin paperback   ISBN 0-14-026886-3

THE ODYSSEY is also available on audiocassette from Penguin Audiobooks
(unabridged, read by Ian McKellen)   *ISBN 0-14-086430-X*

☐ **THE ILIAD**
Homer
Introduction and Notes by Bernard Knox
Fagles combines his talents as poet and scholar in this elegant translation of the stirring story of the Trojan War and the rage of Achilles.
"Astonishing . . . this should now become the standard translation for a new generation." —Peter Levi   *Penguin Classics   ISBN 0-14-044592-7*
deluxe Penguin paperback   ISBN 0-14-027536-3

THE ILIAD is also available on audiocassette from Penguin Highbridge Audio
(abridged, read by Derek Jacobi)   *ISBN 0-453-00774-0*

☐ **THE ORESTEIA**
(*Agamemnon, The Libation Bearers,* **and** *The Eumenides*)
Aeschylus
Introduction and Notes with W. B. Stanford
The only trilogy in Greek drama that survives from antiquity, the *Oresteia* takes on new depth and power in Fagles' acclaimed translation.
"Conveys more vividly and powerfully than any of the ten competitors I have consulted the eternal power of this masterpiece . . . a triumph."
—Bernard Levin   *Penguin Classics   ISBN 0-14-044333-9*

☐ **THE THREE THEBAN PLAYS**
(*Antigone, Oedipus the King,* **and** *Oedipus at Colonus*)
Sophocles
Introduction and Notes by Bernard Knox
Fagles' lucid translation captures the majesty of Sophocles' masterwork.
"I know of no better modern English version."
—Hugh Lloyd-Jones, Oxford University   *Penguin Classics   ISBN 0-14-044425-4*